THE ANNALS
OF
AMERICA

THE ANNALS OF AMERICA

Volume 6

1833 - 1840

The Challenge of a Continent

ENCYCLOPÆDIA BRITANNICA, INC.

Chicago London New Delhi Paris Sydney Taipei Tokyo Seoul

The editors wish to express their gratitude for permission to reprint
material from the following sources:

The Arthur H. Clark Company for Selections 4, 48,
49, 52, 53, 61, 80, from *A Documentary History of
American Industrial Society*, ed. by John R. Commons
et al.

Doubleday & Company, Inc. for Selection 92, from
Society, Manners and Politics in the United States, by
Michael Chevalier, tr. and ed. by John William Ward,
Copyright © 1961 by John William Ward.

Louisiana State University Press for Selection 45, from
*William Johnson's Natchez: The Ante-Bellum Diary of a
Free Negro*, ed. by William Hogan and Edwin Adams
Davis, Source Studies in Southern History, ed. by Ed-
win Adams Davis, No. I.

The Macmillan Company for Selection 63, from *The
Diary of George Templeton Strong*, ed. by Allan Nevins
and Milton Halsey Thomas, Vol. I, Copyright 1952
by The Macmillan Company.

The University of Minnesota Press for Selections 24,
91, from *Land of Their Choice: The Immigrants Write
Home*, ed. by Theodore C. Blegen, Minneapolis: The
University of Minnesota Press, © Copyright 1955 by
the University of Minnesota.

CODED SOURCES IN THIS VOLUME

Blegen

Land of Their Choice. Edited by Theodore C. Blegen. Minneapolis, 1955.

Colton

The Works of Henry Clay Comprising His Life, Correspondence and Speeches. Edited by Calvin Colton. In 10 vols. New York, 1904.

Commons

A Documentary History of American Industrial Society. Edited by John R. Commons *et al.* In 10 vols. Cleveland, 1910-1911.

Madison Letters

Letters and Other Writings of James Madison, Fourth President of the United States. Congress edition. In 4 vols. Philadelphia, 1865.

Nicolay-Hay

Complete Works of Abraham Lincoln. Edited by John G. Nicolay and John Hay. New and enlarged edition in 12 vols. New York, 1905.

11 Peters 419

Reports of Cases Argued and Adjudged in the Supreme Court of the United States. Edited by Richard Peters. Vol. 11, New York, 1884 (3rd edition), pp. 419ff.

Richardson

A Compilation of the Messages and Papers of the Presidents 1789-1897. Edited by James D. Richardson. In 10 vols. Washington, 1896-1899.

14 Wendell 2
14 Wendell 34
15 Wendell 397

Reports of Cases Argued and Determined in the Supreme Court of Judicature and in the Court for the Correction of Errors of the State of New-York. Edited by John L. Wendell. Vol. 14, Albany, 1837, pp. 2ff.; pp. 34ff. Vol. 15, Albany, 1842; pp. 397ff.

Contents

1835 - 1837

1836

| Index of Authors, 576

THE CHALLENGE OF A CONTINENT
In Pictures

As the principal cash crop in the plantation system, cotton
strengthened its grip on the Southern economy. Plantation
owners, comprising less than one percent of the population,
dominated politics, while the popular image of plantation
life ignored the diversity of the Southern population.

With Congress paralyzed by the slavery issue and Jackson locked in combat
over an array of fiscal and states' rights conflicts, the emerging
Abolitionist movement brought a strident activism to the political scene.

The romantic landscapes of the Hudson River School were
proclaimed by Thomas Cole as vital "American" art, even while
he questioned the depth and seriousness of his own work.

Probing the Far West 283-292

The Rocky Mountains and the "Great Basin" were explored and
trapped by the "mountain men" in the brief period of adventure
before the large fur companies took over the mountains and
the large westward migrations began. At the same time the
Santa Fe trail was opened between Missouri and the Southwest.

New York City 403-412

The largest city in the country and the hub of commerce, New York began
to suffer the problems of inadequate sanitation and public services,
congestion, crime, and poverty that precipitous growth and industrial
concentration would soon bring to many cities. At the same time industry
and commerce were affording a sizeable number of people a new prosperity.

The Midwest 445-454

In the states of the old Northwest the pioneer stage was ended
as settlers poured into the interior farmlands. River commerce
spurred the growth of numerous cities, and ambitious canal-building
projects taxed the states' financial resources.

Maritime New England 513-522

Putting out from a dozen New England ports, Yankee sailors dominated world
whaling markets and the China Trade. It was the last great era of sailing
vessels before oil killed the whaling industry and steam replaced the sail.

1833

1.

John Greenleaf Whittier: Man's Property in Man

The poetry of John Greenleaf Whittier was first published by William Lloyd Garrison, founder of the militant Abolitionist movement that got under way in the 1830s. Partly because of his association with Garrison, Whittier ardently espoused the Abolitionist cause. The cruelty of slavery, and the iniquity of a system that permitted one man to buy and sell another, became the ever-present subject of his poetry and prose. In May 1833, Whittier wrote and had printed at his own expense the pamphlet Justice and Expediency, *part of which is reproduced below. Five thousand copies of the pamphlet were later reissued by a wealthy merchant and humanitarian, Arthur Tappan.*

Source: *The Conflict with Slavery, etc., etc.,* London, 1889, pp. 9-57.

IT MAY BE INQUIRED of me why I seek to agitate the subject of slavery in New England, where we all acknowledge it to be an evil. Because such an acknowledgment is not enough on our part. It is doing no more than the slave master and the slave trader. "We have found," says James Monroe in his speech on the subject before the Virginia Convention, "that this evil has preyed upon the very vitals of the Union; and has been prejudicial to all the states in which it has existed." All the states in their several constitutions and declarations of rights have made a similar statement. And what has been the consequence of this general belief in the evil of human servitude? Has it sapped the foundations of the infamous system? No. Has it decreased the number of its victims? Quite the contrary. Unaccompanied by philanthropic action, it has been, in a moral point of view, worthless — a thing without vitality — sightless, soulless, dead.

But it may be said that the miserable victims of the system have our sympathies. Sympathy! the sympathy of the priest and the Levite, looking on and acknowledging, but holding itself aloof from mortal suffering. Can such hollow sympathy reach the broken of heart, and does the blessing of those who are ready to perish answer it? . . .

No! Let the truth on this subject, undisguised, naked, terrible as it is, stand out before us. Let us no longer seek to cover it; let us no longer strive to forget it; let us no more dare to palliate it. It is better to meet it here with repentance than at the bar of God. . . .

But it may be urged that New England has no participation in slavery and is not responsible for its wickedness.

Why are we thus willing to believe a lie? New England not responsible! Bound by the United States Constitution to protect the slaveholder in his sins, and yet not responsible! Joining hands with crime, covenanting with oppression, leaguing with pollution, and yet not responsible! Palliating the evil, hiding the evil, voting for the evil, do we not participate in it? Members of one confederacy, children of one family, the curse and the shame, the sin against our brother, and the sin against our God — all the iniquity of slavery which is revealed to man and all which crieth in the ear, or is manifested to the eye of Jehovah, will assuredly be visited upon all our people. . . .

Slavery is protected by the constitutional compact, by the standing army, by the militia of the free states. Let us not forget that should the slaves, goaded by wrongs unendurable, rise in desperation and pour the torrent of their brutal revenge over the beautiful Carolinas or the consecrated soil of Virginia, New England would be called upon to arrest the progress of rebellion, to tread out with the armed heel of her soldiery that spirit of freedom which knows no distinction of caste or color; which has been kindled in the heart of the black as well as in that of the white.

And what is this system which we are thus protecting and upholding? A system which holds 2 million of God's creatures in bondage; which leaves 1 million females without any protection, save their own feeble strength, and which makes even the exercise of that strength in resistance to outrage punishable with death; which considers rational, immortal beings as articles of traffic, vendible commodities, merchantable property; which recognizes no social obliga-

tions, no natural relations; which tears without scruple the infant from the mother, the wife from the husband, the parent from the child. In the strong but just language of another: "It is the full measure of pure, unmixed, unsophisticated wickedness; and scorning all competition or comparison, it stands without a rival in the secure, undisputed possession of its detestable preeminence."

So fearful an evil should have its remedies. The following are among the many which have been from time to time proposed:

1. Placing the slaves in the condition of the serfs of Poland and Russia, fixed to the soil, and without the right on the part of the master to sell or remove them. This was intended as a preliminary to complete emancipation at some remote period, but it is impossible to perceive either its justice or expediency.

2. Gradual abolition — an indefinite term, but which is understood to imply the draining away, drop by drop, of the great ocean of wrong; plucking off at long intervals some straggling branches of the moral Upas; holding out to unborn generations the shadow of a hope which the present may never feel; gradually ceasing to do evil; gradually refraining from robbery, lust, and murder: in brief, obeying a shortsighted and criminal policy rather than the commands of God.

3. Abstinence on the part of the people of the free states from the use of the known products of slave labor in order to render that labor profitless. Beyond a doubt, the example of conscientious individuals may have a salutary effect upon the minds of some of the slaveholders; but so long as our Confederacy exists, a commercial intercourse with slave states and a consumption of their products cannot be avoided.

4. Colonization.

The exclusive object of the American Colonization Society, according to the 2nd

Article of its constitution, is to colonize the free people of color residing among us in Africa or such other place as Congress may direct. Steadily adhering to this object, it has nothing to do with slavery; and I allude to it as a remedy only because some of its friends have in view an eventual abolition or an amelioration of the evil.

Let facts speak. The Colonization Society was organized in 1817. It has 218 auxiliary societies. The legislatures of fourteen states have recommended it. Contributions have poured into its treasury from every quarter of the United States. Addresses in its favor have been heard from all our pulpits. It has been in operation sixteen years. During this period nearly 1 million human beings have died in slavery; and the number of slaves has increased more than half a million, or in round numbers, 550,000.

The Colonization Society has been busily engaged all this while in conveying the slaves to Africa; in other words, abolishing slavery. In this very charitable occupation, it has carried away of manumitted slaves, 613 balance against the society, 549,387!

But enough of its abolition tendency. What has it done for amelioration? Witness the newly enacted laws of some of the slave states, laws bloody as the Code of Draco, violating the laws of God and the unalienable rights of His children. But why talk of amelioration? Amelioration of what? Of sin, of crime unutterable, of a system of wrong and outrage horrible in the eye of God! Why seek to mark the line of a selfish policy, a carnal expediency between the criminality of hell and that repentance and its fruits enjoined of heaven?

For the principles and views of the society we must look to its own statements and admissions; to its annual reports; to those of its auxiliaries; to the speeches and writings of its advocates; and to its organ, the *African Repository*.

1. It excuses slavery and apologizes for slaveholders. . . .

2. It pledges itself not to oppose the system of slavery. . . .

3. It regards God's rational creatures as property. . . .

4. It boasts that its measures are calculated to perpetuate the detested system of slavery, to remove the fears of the slaveholder, and increase the value of his stock of human beings. . . .

5. It denies the power of Christian love to overcome an unholy prejudice against a portion of our fellow creatures. . . .

6. It opposes strenuously the education of the blacks in this country as useless as well as dangerous. . . .

E. B. Caldwell, the first secretary of the American Colonization Society, in his speech at its formation, recommended them to be kept "in the lowest state of ignorance and degradation, for (says he) the nearer you bring them to the condition of brutes, the better chance do you give them of possessing their apathy." . . .

I seek to do the Colonization Society no injustice, but I wish the public generally to understand its character. The tendency of the society to abolish the slave trade by means of its African colony has been strenuously urged by its friends. But the fallacy of this is now admitted by all. . . .

I come now to the only practicable, the only just scheme of emancipation — immediate aboliton of slavery; an immediate acknowledgment of the great truth, that man cannot hold property in man; an immediate surrender of baneful prejudice to Christian love; an immediate practical obedience to the command of Jesus Christ: "Whatsoever ye would that men should do unto you, do ye even so to them."

A correct understanding of what is meant by immediate abolition must convince every candid mind that it is neither visionary nor dangerous; that it involves no disastrous consequences of bloodshed and desolation; but, on the contrary, that it is a safe, practicable, efficient remedy for the evils of the slave system.

The term "immediate" is used in contrast with that of "gradual." Earnestly as I wish it, I do not expect, no one expects, that the tremendous system of oppression can be instantaneously overthrown. The terrible and unrebukable indignation of a free people has not yet been sufficiently concentrated against it. The friends of abolition have not forgotten the peculiar organization of our Confederacy, the delicate division of power between the states and the general government. They see the many obstacles in their pathway; but they know that public opinion can overcome them all. They ask no aid of physical coercion. They seek to obtain their object not with the weapons of violence and blood but with those of reason and truth, prayer to God, and entreaty to man.

They seek to impress indelibly upon every human heart the true doctrines of the rights of man; to establish now and forever this great and fundamental truth of human liberty — that man cannot hold property in his brother — for they believe that the general admission of this truth will utterly destroy the system of slavery, based as that system is upon a denial or disregard of it. . . .

If our fathers intended that slavery should be perpetual, that our practice should forever give the lie to our professions, why is the great constitutional compact so guardedly silent on the subject of human servitude? If state necessity demanded this perpetual violation of the laws of God and the rights of man, this continual solecism in a government of freedom, why is it not met as a necessity, incurable and inevitable, and formally and distinctly recognized as a settled part of our social system? State necessity, that imperial tyrant, seeks no disguise. . . .

What, then, is our duty? To give effect to the spirit of our Constitution; to plant ourselves upon the great declaration and declare in the face of all the world that political, religious, and legal hypocrisy shall no longer cover as with loathsome leprosy the features of American freedom; to loose at once the bands of wickedness; to undo the heavy burdens and let the oppressed go free.

We have indeed been authoritatively told in Congress and elsewhere that our brethren of the South and West will brook no further agitation of the subject of slavery. What, then! Shall we heed the unrighteous prohibition? No; by our duty as Christians, as politicians, by our duty to ourselves, to our neighbor, and to God, we are called upon to agitate this subject; to give slavery no resting place under the hallowed aegis of a government of freedom; to tear it root and branch, with all its fruits of abomination, at least from the soil of the national domain. The slaveholder may mock us; the representatives of property, merchandise, vendible commodities, may threaten us; still our duty is imperative; the spirit of the Constitution should be maintained within the exclusive jurisdiction of the government. If we cannot "provide for the general welfare," if we cannot "guarantee to each of the states a republican form of government," let us at least no longer legislate for a free nation within view of the falling whip, and within hearing of the execrations of the taskmaster and the prayer of his slave! . . .

The slave will become conscious sooner or later of his brute strength, his physical superiority, and will exert it. His torch will be at the threshold and his knife at the throat of the planter. Horrible and indiscriminate will be his vengeance. Where, then, will be the pride, the beauty, and the chivalry of the South? . . .

Let the cause of insurrection be removed, then, as speedily as possible. Cease to oppress. "Let him that stole steal no more." Let the laborer have his hire. Bind him no longer by the cords of slavery, but with those of kindness and brotherly love. Watch over him for his good. Pray for him; instruct him; pour light into the darkness of his mind.

Let this be done and the horrible fears which now haunt the slumbers of the slaveholder will depart. Conscience will take down its racks and gibbets, and his soul will be at peace. His lands will no longer disappoint his hopes. Free labor will renovate them. . . .

The conflicting interests of free and slave labor furnish the only ground for fear in relation to the permanency of the Union. The line of separation between them is day by day growing broader and deeper; geographically and politically united, we are already, in a moral point of view, a divided people. But a few months ago we were on the very verge of civil war, a war of brothers, a war between the North and the South, between the slaveholder and the free laborer. The danger has been delayed for a time; this bolt has fallen without mortal injury to the Union, but the cloud from whence it came still hangs above us, reddening with the elements of destruction.

2.

LYDIA M. CHILD: Proposals for Equal Treatment of African Americans

William Lloyd Garrison and his fellow militant Abolitionists in the 1830s not only spoke out against the institution of slavery in the South, they also condemned all forms of prejudice against blacks, which existed then, as it does now, in both North and South. But their vision of social and political equality for all contravened the prevailing sentiment. Even in the North, they were attacked and condemned and often physically assaulted. Lydia M. Child was already a prominent novelist when she turned to writing on behalf of racial equality, and her early reform literature, a selection of which follows, was widely read. The excerpt is from her book, An Appeal in Favor of That Class of Americans Called Africans, *published in July 1833.*

Source: *An Appeal in Favor of That Class of Americans Called Africans,* Boston, 1833, Ch. 8.

WHILE WE BESTOW our earnest disapprobation on the system of slavery, let us not flatter ourselves that we are in reality any better than our brethren of the South. Thanks to our soil and climate and the early exertions of the Quakers, the *form* of slavery does not exist among us; but the very *spirit* of the hateful and mischievous thing is here in all its strength. The manner in which we use what power we have gives us ample reason to be grateful that the nature of our institutions does not entrust us with more. Our prejudices against colored people is even more inveterate than it is at the South. The planter is often attached to his Negroes, and lavishes caresses and kind words upon them, as he would on a favorite hound; but our coldhearted, ignoble prejudice admits of no exception — no intermission.

The Southerners have long continued habit, apparent interest and dreaded danger to palliate the wrong they do; but we stand without excuse. They tell us that Northern ships and Northern capital have been engaged in this wicked business; and the reproach is true. Several fortunes in this city have been made by the sale of Negro blood. If these criminal transactions are still carried on, they are done in silence and secrecy, because public opinion has made them disgraceful. But if the free states wished to cherish the system of slavery forever, they could not take a more direct course than they now do. Those who are kind and liberal on all other subjects unite with the selfish and the proud in their unrelenting efforts to keep the colored population in the lowest state of degradation; and the influence they unconsciously exert over children early infuses into their innocent minds the same strong feelings of contempt.

The intelligent and well-informed have the least share of this prejudice; and when their minds can be brought to reflect upon it, I have generally observed that they soon cease to have any at all. But such a general apathy prevails, and the subject is so seldom brought into view, that few are really aware how oppressively the influence of society is made to bear upon this injured class of the community. . . .

An unjust law exists in this commonwealth by which marriages between persons of different color is pronounced illegal. I am perfectly aware of the gross ridicule to which I may subject myself by alluding to this particular; but I have lived too long, and observed too much, to be disturbed by the world's mockery. In the first place, the government ought not to be invested with power to control the affections any more than the consciences of citizens. A man has at least as good a right to choose his wife as he has to choose his religion. His taste may not suit his neighbors; but so long as his deportment is correct, they have no right to interfere with his concerns. In the second place, this law is a *useless* disgrace to

Massachusetts. Under existing circumstances, none but those whose condition in life is too low to be much affected by public opinion will form such alliances; and they, when they choose to do so, *will* make such marriages, in spite of the law.

I know two or three instances where women of the laboring class have been united to reputable, industrious colored men. These husbands regularly bring home their wages and are kind to their families. If by some of the odd chances, which not unfrequently occur in the world, their wives should become heirs to any property, the children may be wronged out of it, because the law pronounces them illegitimate. And while this injustice exists with regard to *honest*, industrious individuals, who are merely guilty of differing from us in a matter of taste, neither the legislation nor customs of slaveholding states exert their influence against *immoral* connections.

In one portion of our country this fact is shown in a very peculiar and striking manner. There is a numerous class at New Orleans, called quateroons, or quadroons, because their colored blood has for several successive generations been intermingled with the white. The women are much distinguished for personal beauty and gracefulness of motion; and their parents frequently send them to France for the advantages of an elegant education. White gentlemen of the first rank are desirous of being invited to their parties, and often become seriously in love with these fascinating but unfortunate beings. Prejudice forbids matrimony, but universal custom sanctions temporary connections, to which a certain degree of respectability is allowed on account of the peculiar situation of the parties. These attachments often continue for years — sometimes for life — and instances are not unfrequent of exemplary constancy and great propriety of deportment. . . .

There is another Massachusetts law, which an enlightened community would not probably suffer to be carried into execution under any circumstances; but it still remains to disgrace the statutes of this commonwealth. It is as follows:

> No African or Negro, other than a subject of the emperor of Morocco, or a citizen of the United States (proved so by a certificate of the secretary of the state of which he is a citizen), shall tarry within this commonwealth longer than two months; and on complaint a justice shall order him to depart in ten days; and if he do not then, the justice may commit such African or Negro to the House of Correction, there to be kept at hard labor; and at the next term of the Court of C. P., he shall be tried, and if convicted of remaining as aforesaid, shall be whipped not exceeding ten lashes; and if he or she shall not *then* depart such process shall be repeated and punishment inflicted *tolies quoties.*

An honorable Haitian or Brazilian, who visited this country for business or information, might come under this law, unless public opinion rendered it a mere dead letter.

There is among the colored people an increasing desire for information and a laudable ambition to be respectable in manners and appearance. Are we not foolish as well as sinful in trying to repress a tendency so salutary to themselves and so beneficial to the community? Several individuals of this class are very desirous to have persons of their own color qualified to teach something more than mere reading and writing. But in the public schools, colored children are subject to many discouragements and difficulties; and into the private schools they cannot gain admission. A very sensible and well-informed colored woman in a neighboring town, whose family have been brought up in a manner that excited universal remark and approbation, has been extremely desirous to obtain for her eldest daughter the advantages of a private school; but she has been resolutely repulsed on account of her complexion. The girl is a very light mulatto, with great modesty and propriety of manners; perhaps no young person in the commonwealth was less likely to have a bad influence on her associates. The clergyman respected the family, and he remonstrated with the instructor; but while the latter admitted the injustice of the thing, he excused himself by saying such a step would occasion the loss of all his white scholars.

In a town adjoining Boston, a well-behaved colored boy was kept out of the public school more than a year, by vote of the trustees. His mother, having some information herself, knew the importance of knowledge, and was anxious to obtain it for her family. She wrote repeatedly and urgently; and the schoolmaster himself told me that the correctness of her spelling and the neatness of her handwriting formed a curious contrast with the notes he received from many white parents. At last, this spirited woman appeared before the committee and reminded them that her husband, having for many years paid taxes as a citizen, had a right to the privileges of a citizen; and if her claim were refused, or longer postponed, she declared her determination to seek justice from a higher source. The trustees were, of course, obliged to yield to the equality of the laws, with the best grace they could. The boy was admitted, and made good progress in his studies. Had his mother been too ignorant to know her rights, or too abject to demand them, the lad would have had a fair chance to get a living out of the state as the occupant of a workhouse or penitentiary.

The attempt to establish a school for African girls at Canterbury, Connecticut, has made too much noise to need a detailed account in this volume. I do not know the lady who first formed the project, but I am told that she is a benevolent and religious woman. It certainly is difficult to imagine any other motives than good ones for an undertaking so arduous and unpopular. Yet

Lydia M. Child at age 22

had the pope himself attempted to establish his supremacy over that commonwealth, he could hardly have been repelled with more determined and angry resistance. Town meetings were held, the records of which are not highly creditable to the parties concerned. Petitions were sent to the legislature, beseeching that no African school might be allowed to admit individuals not residing in the town where said school was established; and strange to relate, this law, which makes it impossible to collect a sufficient number of pupils, was sanctioned by the state. A colored girl who availed herself of this opportunity to gain instruction was warned out of town, and fined for not complying; and the instructress was imprisoned for persevering in her benevolent plan.

It is said, in excuse, that Canterbury will be inundated with vicious characters who will corrupt the morals of the young men; that such a school will break down the distinctions between black and white; and that marriages between people of different colors will be the probable result. Yet they seem

to assume the ground that colored people *must* always be an inferior and degraded class — that the prejudice against them *must* be eternal, being deeply founded in the laws of God and nature. Finally, they endeavored to represent the school as one of the *incendiary* proceedings of the Antislavery Society; and they appeal to the Colonization Society, as an aggrieved child is wont to appeal to its parent.

The objection with regard to the introduction of vicious characters into a village certainly has some force; but are such persons likely to leave cities for a quiet country town in search of moral and intellectual improvement? Is it not obvious that the *best* portion of the colored class are the very ones to prize such an opportunity for instruction? Grant that a large proportion of these unfortunate people *are* vicious, is it not our duty, and of course our wisest policy, to try to make them otherwise? And what will so effectually elevate their character and condition as knowledge? I beseech you, my countrymen, think of these things wisely and in season.

As for intermarriages, if there be such a repugnance between the two races, founded in the laws of *nature,* methinks there is small reason to dread their frequency.

The breaking down of distinctions in society, by means of extended information, is an objection which appropriately belongs to the emperor of Austria, or the sultan of Egypt.

I do not know how the affair at Canterbury is *generally* considered; but I have heard individuals of all parties and all opinions speak of it — and never without merriment or indignation. Fifty years hence, the *black* laws of Connecticut will be a greater source of amusement to the antiquarian than her famous *blue* laws.

A similar though less violent opposition arose in consequence of the attempt to establish a college for colored people at New Haven. A young colored man who tried to obtain education at the Wesleyan College in Middleton was obliged to relinquish the attempt on account of the persecution of his fellow students. Some collegians from the South objected to a colored associate in their recitations; and those from New England promptly and zealously joined in the hue and cry. A small but firm party were in favor of giving the colored man a chance to pursue his studies without insult or interruption; and I am told that this manly and disinterested band were all Southerners. As for those individuals who exerted their influence to exclude an unoffending fellow citizen from privileges which ought to be equally open to all, it is to be hoped that age will make them wiser; and that they will learn, before they die, to be ashamed of a step attended with more important results than usually belong to youthful follies. . . .

Let us seriously consider what injury a Negro college could possibly do us. It is certainly a fair presumption that the scholars would be from the better portion of the colored population; and it is an equally fair presumption that knowledge would improve their characters. There are already many hundreds of colored people in the city of Boston. In the street they generally appear neat and respectable; and in our houses they do not "come between the wind and our nobility." Would the addition of one or two hundred more even be perceived? As for giving offense to the Southerners by allowing such establishments — they have no right to interfere with our internal concerns any more than we have with theirs. Why should they not give up slavery to please us, by the same rule that we must refrain from educating the Negroes to please them? If they are at liberty to do wrong, we certainly ought to be at liberty to do right. They may talk and publish as much about us as they please; and we ask for no other influence over them.

It is a fact not generally known that the brave Kosciuszko left a fund for the establishment of a Negro college in the United States. Little did he think he had been fighting for a people who would not grant one rood of their vast territory for the benevolent purpose!

According to present appearances, a college for colored persons will be established in Canada; and thus, by means of our foolish and wicked pride, the credit of this philanthropic enterprise will be transferred to our mother country.

In Boston there is an infant school, three primary schools, and a grammar school. The two last are, I believe, supported by the public; and this fact is highly creditable. A building for the colored grammar school is not supplied by the city, though such provision is always made for similar institutions for white boys. The apartment is close and uncomfortable, and many pupils stay away who would gladly attend under more convenient circumstances. There ought likewise to be a colored teacher instead of a white one. Under the dominion of existing prejudices, it is difficult to find a white man, well qualified to teach such a school, who feels the interest he ought to feel in these Pariahs of our republic. The parents would repose more confidence in a colored instructor; and he, both from sympathy and pride, would be better fitted for his task.

It is peculiarly incumbent on the city authorities to supply a commodious building for the colored grammar school, because public prejudice excludes these oppressed people from all lucrative employments, and they cannot, therefore, be supposed to have ample funds of their own.

I was much pleased with the late resolution awarding Franklin medals to the colored pupils of the grammar school; and I was still more pleased with the laudable project, originated by Josiah Holbrook, Esq., for the establishment of a colored lyceum. Surely a better spirit *is* beginning to work in this cause; and when once begun, the good sense and good feeling of the community will bid it go on and prosper. . . .

In the theater, it is not possible for respectable colored people to obtain a decent seat. They must either be excluded, or herd with the vicious.

A fierce excitement prevailed, not long since, because a colored man had bought a pew in one of our churches. I heard a very kindhearted and zealous democrat declare his opinion that "the fellow ought to be turned out by constables, if he dared to occupy the pew he had purchased." Even at the communion table, the mockery of human pride is mingled with the worship of Jehovah. Again and again have I seen a solitary Negro come up to the altar, meekly and timidly, after all the white communicants had retired. One Episcopal clergyman of this city forms an honorable exception to this remark. When there is room at the altar, Mr. ——— often makes a signal to the colored members of his church to kneel beside their white brethren; and once, when two white infants and one colored one were to be baptized, and the parents of the latter bashfully lingered far behind the others, he silently rebuked the unchristian spirit of pride by first administering the Holy Ordinance to the little dark-skinned child of God. . . .

A well-known country representative, who makes a very loud noise about his democracy, once attended the Catholic Church. A pious Negro requested him to take off his hat while he stood in the presence of the Virgin Mary. The white man rudely shoved him aside, saying, "You son of an Ethiopian, do you dare to speak to me!" I more than once heard the hero repeat this story; and he seemed to take peculiar satisfaction in telling it. Had he been less ignorant, he would not have chosen "son of an *Ethiopian*" as an *ignoble* epithet; to have called the African his own equal would have been abundantly more sarcastic. The same republican dismissed a strong, industrious colored man who had been employed on the farm during his absence. "I am too great a democrat," quoth he, "to have anybody in my house who don't sit at my table; and I'll be hanged if I ever eat with the son of an Ethiopian."

Men whose education leaves them less excuse for such illiberality are yet vulgar enough to join in this ridiculous prejudice. The colored woman, whose daughter has been mentioned as excluded from a private school, was once smuggled into a stage, upon the supposition that she was a white woman with a sallow complexion. Her manners were modest and prepossessing, and the gentlemen were very polite to her. But when she stopped at her own door, and was handed out by her curly headed husband, they were at once surprised and angry to find they had been riding with a mulatto — and had, in their ignorance, been really civil to her! . . .

Mr. Garrison was the first person who dared to edit a newspaper in which slavery was spoken of as altogether wicked and inexcusable. For this crime the legislature of Georgia have offered $5,000 to anyone who will "arrest and prosecute him to conviction *under the laws of that state*." An association of gentlemen in South Carolina have likewise offered a large reward for the same object. It is, to say the least, a very remarkable step for one state in this Union to promulgate such a law concerning a citizen of another state, merely for publishing his opinions boldly. The disciples of Fanny Wright promulgate the most zealous and virulent attacks upon Christianity without any hindrance from the civil authorities; and this is done upon the truly rational ground that individual freedom of opinion ought to be respected — that what is false cannot stand, and what is true cannot be overthrown. We leave Christianity to take care of itself; but slavery is a "delicate subject," and whoever attacks that must be punished. Mr. Garrison is a disinterested, intelligent, and remarkably pure-minded man, whose only fault is that he cannot be moderate on a subject which it is exceedingly difficult for an honest mind to examine with calmness. Many who highly respect his character and motives regret his tendency to use wholesale and unqualified expressions; but it is something to have the truth told, even if it be not in the most judicious way.

Where an evil is powerfully supported by the self-interest and prejudice of the community, none but an ardent individual will venture to meddle with it. Luther was deemed indiscreet even by those who liked him best; yet a more prudent man would never have given an impetus sufficiently powerful to heave the great mass of corruption under which the church was buried. Mr. Garrison has certainly the merit of having first called public attention to a neglected and very important subject. I believe whoever fairly and dispassionately examines the question will be more than disposed to forgive the occasional faults of an ardent temperament, in consideration of the difficulty of the undertaking and the violence with which it has been opposed. . . .

We are told that the Southerners will of themselves do away slavery, and they alone understand how to do it. But it is an obvious fact that all their measures have tended to perpetuate the system; and even if we have the fullest faith that they mean to do their duty, the belief by no means absolves us from doing ours. The evil is gigantic; and its removal requires every heart and head in the community.

It is said that our sympathies ought to be given to the masters, who are abundantly more to be pitied than the slaves. If this be the case, the planters are singularly disinterested not to change places with their bondmen. Our sympathies *have* been given to the masters — and to those masters who seemed most desirous to remain forever in their pitiable condition. There are hearts at the South sincerely desirous of doing right in this cause; but their generous impulses are checked by the laws of their respective states and the strong disapprobation of their neighbors. I know a lady in Georgia who would, I believe, make any personal sacrifice to instruct her slaves and give them freedom; but if she were found guilty of teaching the alphabet or manumitting her slaves, fines and imprisonment would be the consequence; if she sold them, they would be likely to fall into hands less merciful than her own. Of such slave owners we cannot speak with too much respect and tenderness. They are comparatively few in number, and stand in a most perplexing situation; it is a duty to give all our sympathy to *them*. It is mere mockery to say what is so often said, that the Southerners, as a body, really wish to abolish slavery. If they wished it, they certainly would make the attempt. When the majority heartily desire a change, it is effected, be the difficulties what they may. The Americans are peculiarly responsible for the example they give; for in no other country does the unchecked voice of the people constitute the whole of government. . . .

The strongest and best reason that can be given for our supineness on the subject of slavery is the fear of dissolving the Union. The Constitution of the United States demands our highest reverence. Those who approve, and those who disapprove of particular portions, are equally bound to yield implicit obedience to its authority. But we must not forget that the Constitution provides for any change that may be required for the general good. The great machine is constructed with a safety valve by which any rapidly increasing evil may be expelled whenever the people desire it.

If the Southern politicians are determined to make a Siamese question of this also — if they insist that the Union shall not exist without slavery — it can only be said that they join two things which have no affinity with each other and which cannot permanently exist together. They chain the living and vigorous to the diseased and dying; and the former will assuredly perish in the infected neighborhood.

3.

Declaration of the American Anti-Slavery Society

Prior to the 1830s, American Abolition societies were typically small and timid, and most Abolitionists supported schemes to "colonize" African Americans, that is, to settle them in geographically isolated communities. William Lloyd Garrison injected a militant tone into the Abolitionist movement. He declared moral war on the slaveholders and demanded that they immediately and without compensation grant the slaves freedom and political and social equality within the white society. He had the effect of goading into action those already convinced of the injustice of slavery and provoking the violent response of those who opposed his views. The American Anti-Slavery Society, which convened for the first time in early December 1833, expressed the new Abolitionist sentiment. The Society was designed to give doctrinal and administrative coherence to the movement. Garrison drafted the following declaration for the Society; it was adopted with minor revisions on December 6. Within five years the Society had 1,350 local chapters.

Source: *First Annual Report of the American Anti-Slavery Society, etc., etc.,*
New York, 1834: "Declaration of the National Anti-Slavery Convention."

THE CONVENTION, assembled in the city of Philadelphia to organize a National Anti-slavery Society, promptly seize the opportunity to promulgate the following Declaration of Sentiments, as cherished by them in relation to the enslavement of one-sixth portion of the American people.

More than fifty-seven years have elapsed since a band of patriots convened in this place to devise measures for the deliverance of this country from a foreign yoke. The cornerstone upon which they founded the temple of freedom was broadly this: "That all men are created equal; and they are endowed by their Creator with certain inalienable rights; that among these are life, LIBERTY, and the pursuit of happiness." At the sound of their trumpet call 3 million people rose up as from the sleep of death and rushed to the strife of blood, deeming it more glorious to die instantly as freemen than desirable to live one hour as slaves.

They were few in number, poor in resources; but the honest conviction that TRUTH, JUSTICE, and RIGHT were on their side made them invincible.

We have met together for the achievement of an enterprise, without which that of our fathers is incomplete; and which, for its magnitude, solemnity, and probable results upon the destiny of the world as far transcends theirs as moral truth does physical force.

In purity of motive, in earnestness of zeal, in decision of purpose, in intrepidity of action, in steadfastness of faith, in sincerity of spirit, we would not be inferior to them.

Their principles led them to wage war against their oppressors and to spill human blood like water in order to be free. *Ours* forbid the doing of evil that good may come and lead us to reject, and to entreat the oppressed to reject the use of all carnal weapons for deliverance from bondage, relying solely upon those which are spiritual and mighty through God to the pulling down of strongholds.

Their measures were physical resistance — the marshaling in arms, the hostile array, the mortal encounter. *Ours* shall be such as only the opposition of moral purity to moral corruption — the destruction of error by the potency of truth, the overthrow of prejudice by the power of love, and the abolition of slavery by the spirit of repentance.

Their grievances, great as they were, were trifling in comparison with the wrongs and sufferings of those for whom we plead. Our fathers were never slaves; never bought and sold like cattle; never shut out from the light of knowledge and religion; never subjected to the lash of brutal taskmasters.

But those for whose emancipation we are striving, constituting at the present time at least one-sixth part of our countrymen, are recognized by the law and treated by their fellow beings as marketable commodities, as goods and chattels, as brute beasts; are plundered daily of the fruits of their toil without redress; really enjoying no constitutional nor legal protection from licentious and murderous outrages upon their persons; are ruthlessly torn asunder — the tender babe from the arms of its frantic mother, the heartbroken wife from her weeping husband — at the caprice or pleasure of irresponsible tyrants. For the crime of having a dark complexion, they suffer the pangs of hunger, the infliction of stripes, and the ignominy of brutal servitude. They are kept in heathenish darkness by laws expressly enacted to make their instruction a criminal offense.

These are the prominent circumstances in the condition of more than 2 million of our people, the proof of which may be found in thousands of indisputable facts and in the laws of the slaveholding states.

Hence we maintain that in view of the civil and religious privileges of this nation, the guilt of its oppression is unequaled by any other on the face of the earth; and,

therefore, that it is bound to repent instantly, to undo the heavy burden, to break every yoke, and to let the oppressed go free.

We further maintain that no man has a right to enslave or imbrute his brother; to hold or acknowledge him, for one moment, as a piece of merchandise; to keep back his hire by fraud; or to brutalize his mind by denying him the means of intellectual, social, and moral improvement.

The right to enjoy liberty is inalienable. To invade it is to usurp the prerogative of Jehovah. Every man has a right to his own body, to the products of his own labor, to the protection of law, and to the common advantages of society. It is piracy to buy or steal a native African and subject him to servitude. Surely the sin is as great to enslave an American as an African.

Therefore, we believe and affirm:

That there is no difference, *in principle*, between the African slave trade and American slavery.

That every American citizen who retains a human being in involuntary bondage as his property is (according to Scripture) a MAN STEALER.

That the slaves ought instantly to be set free and brought under the protection of law.

That if they had lived from the time of Pharaoh down to the present period, and had been entailed through successive generations, their right to be free could never have been alienated, but their claims would have constantly risen in solemnity.

That all those laws which are now in force, admitting the right of slavery, are, therefore, before God, utterly null and void, being an audacious usurpation of the Divine prerogative; a daring infringement on the law of nature; a base overthrow of the very foundations of the social compact; a complete extinction of all the relations, endearments, and obligations of mankind; and a presumptuous transgression of all the holy commandments; and that, therefore, they ought instantly to be abrogated.

We further believe and affirm that all persons of color who possess the qualifications which are demanded of others ought to be admitted forthwith to the enjoyment of the same privileges, and the exercise of the same prerogatives, as others; and that the paths of preferment, of wealth, and of intelligence should be opened as widely to them as to persons of a white complexion.

We maintain that no compensation should be given to the planters emancipating their slaves:

Because it would be a surrender of the great fundamental principle, that man cannot hold property in man;

Because SLAVERY IS A CRIME, AND THEREFORE IS NOT AN ARTICLE TO BE SOLD;

Because the holders of slaves are not the just proprietors of what they claim; freeing the slaves is not depriving them of property but restoring it to its rightful owner; it is not wronging the master, but righting the slave — restoring him to himself;

Because immediate and general emancipation would only destroy nominal, not real, property; it would not amputate a limb or break a bone of the slaves, but by infusing motives into their breasts would make them doubly valuable to the masters as free laborers; and

Because, if compensation is to be given at all, it should be given to the outraged and guiltless slaves and not to those who have plundered and abused them.

We regard as delusive, cruel, and dangerous any scheme of expatriation which pretends to aid, either directly or indirectly, in the emancipation of the slaves, or to be a substitute for the immediate and total abolition of slavery.

We fully and unanimously recognize the sovereignty of each state to legislate exclusively on the subject of the slavery which is tolerated within its limits; we concede that Congress, *under the present national compact,* has no right to interfere with any of the slave states, in relation to this momentous subject.

But we maintain that Congress has a right, and is solemnly bound, to suppress the domestic slave trade between the several states, and to abolish slavery in those portions of our territory which the Constitution has placed under its exclusive jurisdiction.

We also maintain that there are, at the present time, the highest obligations resting upon the people of the free states to remove slavery by moral and political action as prescribed in the Constitution of the United States. They are now living under a pledge of their tremendous physical force to fasten the galling fetters of tyranny upon the limbs of millions in the Southern states; they are liable to be called at any moment to suppress a general insurrection of the slaves; they authorize the slave owner to vote on three-fifths of his slaves as property, and thus enable him to perpetuate his oppression; they support a standing army at the South for its protection; and they seize the slave who has escaped into their territories and send him back to be tortured by an enraged master or a brutal driver. This relation to slavery is criminal and full of danger: IT MUST BE BROKEN UP.

These are our views and principles; these our designs and measures. With entire confidence in the overruling justice of God, we plant ourselves upon the declaration of our independence and the truths of Divine Revelation as upon the Everlasting Rock.

We shall organize antislavery societies, if possible, in every city, town, and village in our land.

We shall send forth agents to lift up the voice of remonstrance, of warning, of entreaty, and rebuke.

We shall circulate, unsparingly and extensively, antislavery tracts and periodicals.

We shall enlist the pulpit and the press in the cause of the suffering and the dumb.

We shall aim at a purification of the churches from all participation in the guilt of slavery.

We shall encourage the labor of freemen rather than that of slaves by giving a preference to their productions. . . .

We shall spare no exertions nor means to bring the whole nation to speedy repentance.

Our trust for victory is solely in God. We may be personally defeated, but our principles never. TRUTH, JUSTICE, REASON, HUMANITY must and will gloriously triumph. Already a host is coming up to the help of the Lord against the mighty, and the prospect before us is full of encouragement.

Submitting this declaration to the candid examination of the people of this country, and of the friends of liberty throughout the world, we hereby affix our signatures to it, pledging ourselves that, under the guidance and by the help of Almighty God, we will do all that in us lies, consistently with this declaration of our principles, to overthrow the most execrable system of slavery that has ever been witnessed upon earth; to deliver our land from its deadliest curse; to wipe out the foulest stain which rests upon our national escutcheon; and to secure to the colored population of the United States all the rights and privileges which belong to them as men and as Americans — come what may to our persons, our interests, or our reputations, whether we live to witness the triumph of LIBERTY, JUSTICE, and HUMANITY, or perish untimely as martyrs in this great, benevolent, and holy cause.

4.

New York Carpenters' Strike

In 1832 and 1833 the benevolent societies of individual trades — organized earlier in the century to underwrite the expenses of sickness and the like — were reorganized toward economic ends, and beginning in 1833 delegates from local trades combined to form general trades' unions. The General Trades' Union of New York, the first of its kind, had its roots in the journeyman carpenters' strike of 1833. When the carpenters struck for higher wages they were supported until their ends were achieved on funds voluntarily contributed by the other trades. After the strike the general union was formed. The following diatribe, directed against the journeymen in the New York *Journal of Commerce, is typical of the attacks on unions in their formative years.*

Source: *New York Journal of Commerce*, June 1, 1833 [Commons, V, pp. 209-211].

WE SEE BY NOTICES IN THE PAPERS that the journeymen of various other branches of business are rallying to sustain the carpenters. Well, their cause is as good and worthy of support as the combinations for the same purpose in any other occupation. Just as good as the combinations, where they exist, among lawyers, or doctors, or merchants, or manufacturers, or newspaper editors, or anybody else. Yet we apprehend that many will condemn the combination of journeymen, who think it very right for employers to combine to keep up the prices of their commodities, or even to keep down the price of labor. But according to our notions of the obligations of society, all combinations to compel others to give a higher price or take a lower one are not only inexpedient but at war with the order of things which the Creator has established for the general good, and therefore wicked. . . .

The means resorted to — to cement and sustain the combinations — whether they are simple individual pledges, or legislative enactments, or menaces and violence, are all wrong and in spirit equally so. The plans of each class have their distinctive evil features. The combinations of journeymen and others whose income is from labor are characterized with less craft and studied plot, but with more of direct appeals to force or fear. Disguise it as the associates may, no such combination is sustained but by threats, at least. There will always be a large number who are indisposed for the combination. These will keep up the operations of the trade, and unless forced into the ranks, render the combination abortive. It is surprising how such persons are deprived of their self-possession and drawn into the general league. The principal threat is that the combinants will never again permit those who do not join them to have employment. The expedient to accomplish this is the same to which the doctors and lawyers resort for the same purpose, viz., that the combinants will never consult — work with one who is not of their number. . . .

Combinations among journeymen are usually set on foot by the dissolute, improvident, and, therefore, restless; and in the outset chiefly sustained by the second- and third-rate class of hands. There is one thing about this infatuation at which we confess our astonishment. It is that prime hands so readily enter into combinations for a general average of price. It is a partnership in which some put in capital and others bankruptcy, yet all are to take out and share alike. Men whose wages would go up to the desired point, if they would but go upon their own merits, consent to stand in the attitude of lifting up the unworthy, though they sink themselves proportionally.

Turnouts are always miserably profitless jobs. If they are successful they cannot in the long run benefit the class whose wages are raised; for the diminution in the quantity of occupation and the increased number of laborers drawn to the spot will more than compensate for all the gains. If a day's work receives a higher reward, that advantage will be more than counterbalanced by days spent in idleness for want of occupation. The journeymen carpenters, now, in a harvest time, when all hands were employed, have turned out for an additional shilling. For this, they throw away the certainty of 11s. They have stood out some twenty days, so that their certain loss is already more than equal to the gain they demand, upon six months labor. And they are in no little danger of being displaced altogether by workmen who are coming in from surrounding places, and who, not being acquaintances of the turnouts, are effectually beyond the reach of their influence. To the master-carpenters we repeat what we said some days ago — that it is their duty, and the duty of all good citizens, to set their faces like a flint against all such combinations.

5.

ELY MOORE: Trade Unions and the "Mechanic" Arts

The short-lived labor movement that grew out of the Workingmen's Party flourished from 1834, when unions from six Eastern cities united in the National Trades' Union, until the Panic of 1837, when the ensuing depression wiped them out for a time. Ely Moore was an organizer and the first president of the General Trades' Union of New York City, which was formed in 1833, and of the National Trades' Union. The following speech, delivered before the General Trades' Union at the peak of Moore's career as a labor organizer, is an eloquent defense of the role that unions could play in achieving social justice. Moore argued that the accumulation of wealth in the hands of the few was unhealthy for everyone, and, what was more original, that the workingman was the necessary link between the invention and the enjoyment of those mechanical artifacts on which social progress depended. The address, a portion of which is reprinted here, was delivered on December 2, 1833.

Source: *Address Delivered Before the General Trades' Union of the City of New-York,* New York, 1833.

WE HAVE ASSEMBLED on the present occasion for the purpose of publicly proclaiming the motives which induced us to organize a general union of the various trades and arts in this city and its vicinity, as well as to defend the course and to vindicate the measures we deign to pursue. This is required of us by a due regard to the opinions of our fellowmen.

We conceive it, then, to be a *truth*, enforced and illustrated by the concurrent testimony of history and daily observation, that man is disposed to avail himself of the possessions and services of his fellowman, without rendering an equivalent, and to prefer claims to that which of right belongs to another. This may be considered a hard saying; but we have only to turn our eyes inward and examine ourselves in order to admit, to the full extent, the truth of the proposition that man by nature is selfish and aristocratic. . . .

In order to mitigate the evils that ever flow from inordinate desire and unrestricted selfishness; to restrain and chastise unlawful ambition; to protect the weak against the strong and to establish an equilibrium of power among nations and individuals, conventional compacts were formed. These confederative associations have never been fully able to stay the march of intolerance, of mercenary ambition, or of political despotism. Even in this fair land of freedom, where liberty and equality are guaranteed to all, and where our written constitutions have so wisely provided limitations to power and securities for rights, the twin fiends, *intolerance* and *aristocracy*, presume to rear their hateful crests!

But we have no cause to marvel at this. Wherever man exists, under whatever form of government or whatever be the structure or organization of society, this principle of his nature — selfishness — will appear, op-

Engraving of Ely Moore, 1837

erating either for evil or for good. To curb it sufficiently by legislative enactments is impossible. Much *can* be done, however, toward restraining it within proper limits by unity of purpose and concert of action on the part of the *producing classes.*

To contribute toward the achievement of this great end is one of the objects of the General Trades' Union. Wealth, we all know, constitutes the aristocracy of this country. Happily, no distinctions are known among us save what wealth and worth confer. No legal barriers are erected to protect exclusive privileges or unmerited rank. The law of primogeniture forms no part of American jurisprudence, and our Revolution has converted all feudal tenures into allodial rights.

The greatest danger, therefore, which threatens the stability of our government and the liberty of the people is an undue accumulation and distribution of wealth. And I do conceive that *real danger* is to be apprehended from this source, notwithstanding that tendency to distribution which

naturally grows out of the character of our statutes of conveyance, of inheritance, and descent of property; but by securing to the producing classes a fair, certain, and equitable compensation for their toil and skill, we insure a more just and equal distribution of wealth than can ever be effected by statutory law.

Unlike the septennial reversion of the Jews or the agrarian law of Rome, the principle for which we contend holds out to individuals proper motives for exertion and enterprise. We ask, then, what better means can be devised for promoting a more equal distribution of wealth than for the producing classes to *claim,* and, by virtue of union and concert, *secure their claims* to their respective portions? And why should not those who have the toil have the enjoyment also? Or why should the sweat that flows from the brow of the laborer be converted into a source of revenue for the support of the crafty or indolent?

It has been averred, with great truth, that all governments become cruel and aristocratical in their character and bearing in proportion as one part of the community is elevated and the other depressed, and that misery and degradation to the many is the inevitable result of such a state of society. And we regard it to be equally true that in proportion as the line of distinction between the employer and employed is *widened,* the condition of the latter inevitably verges toward a state of vassalage, while that of the former as certainly approximates toward supremacy; and that whatever system is calculated to make the many dependent upon or subject to the few not only tends to the subversion of the natural rights of man but is hostile to the best interests of the community as well as to the spirit and genius of our government.

Fully persuaded that the foregoing positions are incontrovertible, WE, in order to guard against the encroachments of aristocracy, to preserve our natural and political rights, to elevate our moral and intellectual condition, to promote our pecuniary interests, to narrow the line of distinction between the journeyman and employer, to establish the honor and safety of our respective vocations upon a more secure and permanent basis, and to alleviate the distresses of those suffering from want of employment, have deemed it expedient to form ourselves into a General Trades' Union.

It may be asked how these desirable objects are to be achieved by a general union of trades; how the encroachments of aristocracy, for example, are to be arrested by our plan. We answer — by enabling the producer to enjoy the full benefit of his productions, and thus diffuse the streams of wealth more generally and, consequently, more equally throughout all the ramifications of society. This point conceded, and conceded it must be, it is not requisite, we conceive, that the line of investigation should be dropped very deep in order to bring it up tinged with proof that the verity of our other positions necessarily follows. But for the particular means by which the several objects just enumerated are to be attained, we beg leave to refer to our constitution and to our general plan of organization.

There are, doubtless, many individuals who are resolved, right or wrong, to misrepresent our principles, impeach our measures, and impugn our motives. Be it so. They can' harm us not. Let them, if they please, draw the vengeful bow to the very double and let fly the barbed arrows; the temper and amplitude of the shield of the Union, we trust, will be found sufficient to ward off the stroke. . . .

We have the consolation of knowing that all good men, all who love their country and rejoice in the improvement of the condition of their fellowmen, will acknowledge the policy of our views and the purity of our motives. The residue, I trust, will not defame us with their approbation. Their censure we can endure, but their·praise we should regard as an eternal disgrace. And why, let me ask, should the character of our Union be obnoxious to censure? Wherefore is it wrong in principle? Which of its avowed objects reprehensible? What feature of it opposed to the public good? I defy the ingenuity of man to point to a single measure which it recognizes that is wrong in itself or in its tendency.

What! Is it wrong for men to unite for the purpose of resisting the encroachments of aristocracy? Wrong to restrict the principle of selfishness to its proper and legitimate bounds and objects? Wrong to oppose monopoly and mercenary ambition? Wrong to consult the interests and seek the welfare of the producing classes? Wrong to attempt the elevation of our moral and intellectual standing? Wrong to establish the honor and safety of our respective vocations upon a more secure and permanent basis? I ask — in the name of Heaven I ask — can it be wrong for men to attempt the melioration of their condition and the preservation of their natural and political rights?

I am aware that the charge of "illegal combination" is raised against us. The cry is as senseless as it is stale and unprofitable. Why, I would inquire, have not journeymen the same right to ask their own price for their own property or services that employers have, or that merchants, physicians, and lawyers have? Is that equal justice which makes it an offense for journeymen to combine for the purpose of maintaining their present prices or raising their wages, while employers may combine with impunity for the purpose of lowering them? I admit that such is the common law. All will agree, however, that it is neither wise, just, nor politic, and that it is directly opposed to the spirit and genius of our free institutions and ought, therefore, to be abrogated.

It is further alleged that the General Trades' Union is calculated to encourage strikes and turnouts. Now, the truth lies in the converse. Our constitution sets forth that "Each trade or art may represent to the Convention, through their delegates, their grievances, who shall take cognizance thereof and decide upon the same." And, further, that "No trade or art shall strike for higher wages than they at present receive without the sanction of the Convention." True, if the Convention shall, after due deliberation, decide that the members of any trade or art there represented are aggrieved and that their demands are warrantable, then the Convention is pledged to sustain the members of such trade or art to the uttermost.

Hence, employers will discover that it is idle, altogether idle, to prolong a contest with journeymen when they are backed by the Convention. And journeymen will perceive that in order to obtain assistance from the Convention, in the event of a strike or turnout, that their claims must be founded in justice, and all their measures be so taken as not to invade the rights or sacrifice the welfare of employers. So far, then, from the Union encouraging strikes or turnouts, it is destined, we conceive, to allay the jealousies and abate the asperities which now unhappily exist between employers and the employed.

We all know that whenever journeymen stand out for higher wages that the public are sufferers, as well as the parties more immediately concerned. The Trades' Union, we conceive, will have a tendency to correct this evil.

Again, it is alleged that it is setting a dangerous precedent for journeymen to combine for the purpose of coercing a compliance with their terms. It may, indeed, be dangerous to aristocracy, dangerous to monopoly, dangerous to oppression, but not to the general good or the public tranquillity. Internal danger to a state is not to be apprehended from a general effort on the part of the people to improve and exalt their condition, but from an alliance of the crafty, designing, and intriguing few. What! Tell us, in this enlightened age, that the welfare of the people will be endangered by a voluntary act of the people themselves; that the people will wantonly seek their own destruction; that the safety of the state will be plotted against by three-fourths of the members comprising the state! O, how worthless, how poor and pitiful are all such arguments and objections!

Members of the General Trades' Union, permit me at this time, and before I leave this part of my subject, to caution you against the wiles and perfidy of those individuals who will approach you as friends but who, in reality and in truth, are your secret enemies. You will know them by this sign: an attempt to excite your jealousy against certain individuals who, peradventure, may stand somewhat conspicuous among you; by insinuations that these men have ulterior designs to accomplish; that political ambition lies at the root of the whole matter, and all that. This will be done, recollect, not so much to injure the individuals against whom the insinuations are ostensibly directed as to abuse you by impairing your confidence in the Union.

It is the heart of the Union at which these assassins aim the stroke! 'Tis the Union, your political safeguard, that they would prostrate! 'Tis the Union, the citadel of your hopes, that they would sack and destroy! I entreat you, therefore, to shun such counselors as you would the pestilence. Remember the tragedy in the Garden of Eden and hold no communion with the adversary. But why caution you thus when your own good sense would so readily teach you that the very attempt to deceive you was an insult to your understandings? Because, did they not presume upon your ignorance and credulity, they would never attempt to alienate your affections from the Union.

Remember, then, fellow mechanics, that the man who attempts to seduce you from your duty to yourselves, to your families, and your brother mechanics by misrepresenting the objects of the Union offers you not only an insult but an *injury!* Remember that those defamers would exult at your misfortunes, would "laugh at your calamity, and mock when your fear cometh." Aye, would trample down your liberties and rejoice at beholding

The seal of bondage on your brows —
Its badge upon your breasts! . . .

Once more, then, permit me to ask why it is that artists and mechanics have so far lost sight of the importance of their callings? Why is it that those who produce, prepare, and distribute the comforts, the pleasures, and conveniences of life should not consider themselves (what they really are) the benefactors of mankind, and assume that station in society to which their callings and their worth so justly entitle them? Do you marvel at it? Do you think it strange and mysterious? You need not. A reason can be readily assigned why other classes of society regard you as their inferiors.

Know, then, that you have, by your servility, by your want of self-respect, by your lack of confidence in yourselves and in each other courted your present standing. You alone have been instrumental in assigning yourselves the subordinate and humiliating station in society of which you now complain. You have long had the power to better your general condition, but you have either been too indolent or too careless to exercise it.

I congratulate you — most sincerely do I congratulate you — upon your present prospects. Never did your affairs wear so cheering an aspect as at present. You have, at length, wisely concluded to throw yourselves upon your rights — to gather up your energies and consolidate your strength. Only be true to yourselves and faithful to each other and the issue cannot be doubtful. All the circumstances that surround you are auspicious — the general diffusion of knowledge; the rapid march of improvement; and especially the excellent plan of organization which you have recently adopted — all augur well for your future prosperity. But should you neglect to avail yourselves of the advantages that are now presented, you would not only *merit* but *receive* opprobrium and oppression. Beware, therefore, that you do not sacrifice your present advantages and prospects by folly or indolence, lest slavery and infamy be your portion, and your offspring, at some future day, drag their *inherited* chains across your graves and load your memories with reproaches and imprecations!

I am aware we shall be told that republican governments are unpropitious to the cultivation and encouragement of the arts, especially the fine arts. This has long been a fashionable doctrine; but it is as false as fashionable. It is a libel on popular governments. . . . The history of our own country, and within the last half century, has furnished ample testimony that not only mechanical genius but the intellectual powers generally are more universally developed in *free* than in despotic governments. Where is the nation that can point to such illustrious names in war — in eloquence — in philosophy — in astronomy — in mechanics — and in painting as those of Washington, and Henry, and Franklin, and Rittenhouse, and Fulton, and West?

The greatest efforts of the human mind have ever been made under the auspices of free governments. . . . The fact is, a nation's freedom and its genius *rise* and *fall together*. And so with regard to the arts. They are fostered and cultivated in proportion as the government is free, and the people enlightened and happy. But when liberty declines, the arts decline with her, and they inevitably sink into one common grave!

So far from the government under which we live being unfavorable to our interests as artists and mechanics, it is, in every respect, *most propitious!* There never was a land under heaven where the intellectual powers of man had so fine a field and such fair play as they have in our own country and in our own times. If our march, therefore, is not *onward* to honor, competency, and fame, the fault is all our own.

Will you meet me with the excuse that your early opportunities in life were limited; that you have no time for improvement; that it is too late to enter the lists for distinction; and that you must, therefore, be content to live and die in obscurity? Such are the common apologies of the indolent, the spiritless, and the dissolute. Let no such pretexts, therefore, be made by members of the Trades' Union.

Would you have your ambition fired, your hopes elevated, or your resolution strengthened by glorious example? Then contemplate for a moment the history of those illustrious men whose names stand as "landmarks on the cliffs of fame," who were the artificers of their own fortunes, and who, like yourselves, were mechanics and artists. FRANKLIN, who astonished and confounded the schoolmen of Europe and with impunity dallied with the lightnings of heaven, was once an obscure journeyman printer! His elevation was the result of his own efforts. ROGER SHERMAN, one of the most extraordinary men in the extraordinary age in which he lived, and WILLIAM GIFFORD, the immortal author of the *Baviad* and *Maeviad*, were both shoemakers. GEORGE WALTON, the distinguished patriot and jurist of Georgia, acquired his education by torchlight during the term of his apprenticeship to a carpenter! General KNOX was a bookbinder, and General GREENE (the second Washington), a blacksmith. But we are not limited to the past for examples. Our distinguished townsman FRAZEE was a common stonemason. As a sculptor, he now stands unequaled in this country, and as a self-taught artist, unsurpassed by any in the world.

Would you enjoy the fame of those illustrious men? Then follow their example and imitate their virtues. Like them, be diligent, be honest, be firm, be indefatigable. Pursue knowledge with a diligence that never tires and with a perseverance that never falters; and honor and glory and happiness will be your reward! You have no longer an excuse why you should not prosper and flourish, both as a body and as individuals. You know your rights and, consequently, feel your strength. If mortification and defeat should attend you, blame not your fellowmen; the cause will be found within yourselves. Neither blame your country; the fault will not be hers!

No, Land of Genius, Land of Refuge, Land of the Brave and Free! Thy sons have no cause to reproach thee! All thy deserving children find favor in thine eyes, support on thy arm, and protection in thy bosom!

Nature will not have us fret and fume. She does not like our benevolence or our learning much better than she likes our frauds and wars. When we come out of the caucus, or the bank, or the Abolitionist convention, or the Temperance meeting, or the Transcendental club into the fields and woods, she says to us, "So hot? my little Sir."

RALPH WALDO EMERSON, *Essays: First Series*

6.

Mathew Carey: The Poor in a Land of Milk and Honey

The economic expansion of the 1820s was accompanied by the creation of an urban working class. From Europe, and from the farms and rural communities, men crowded into the cities to work, but the steady influx of job seekers, especially from abroad, swelled the labor market and kept wages low. To many working men and women "the land of milk and honey" seemed more like a land of unremitting toil. The underpaid workers were for the most part ignored by those who still adhered to the view that poverty was the fault of the individual. In 1833 Mathew Carey, a prosperous publisher and an influential economist, pointed out the plight of the very poor, but for a solution to their problems he could only appeal to the conscience of the rich.

Source: *Appeal to the Wealthy of the Land,* Philadelphia, 1833, pp. 5-7.

I PROPOSE . . . to consider and attempt to refute certain pernicious errors which too generally prevail respecting the situation, the conduct, the characters, and the prospects of those whose sole dependence is on the labor of their hands; who comprise, throughout the world, two-thirds, perhaps three-fourths, of the human race; and on whose services the other third or fourth depend for their necessaries, their comforts, their enjoyments, and their luxuries.

According to these calculations, the number of persons in the United States depending on wages for their support must be 8 or 9 million. This is a deeply interesting view of the subject, and fully proves its immense importance; and how solicitous we should be to guard against errors in discussing it — errors which may perniciously affect the interests and happiness of so large a portion of the human family. Whatever concerns their comfort or happiness; whatever tends to increase or decrease their comforts; to improve or deteriorate their morals, demands the most serious attention of the friends of humanity, of all whose views extend beyond their own narrow, selfish concerns, and who, without the services of this class, would be forlorn and helpless.

The class in question is susceptible of two great subdivisions — those who are so well remunerated for their labors as to be able, not merely to provide, when employed, for seasons of stagnation and sickness, but by industry, prudence, and economy, to save enough in the course of a few years to commence business on a small scale on their own account. With this fortunate description, which is numerous and respectable, I have no concern at present.

My object is to consider the case of those whose services are so inadequately remunerated, owing to the excess of labor beyond the demand for it, that they can barely support themselves while in good health and fully employed; and, of course, when sick or unemployed, must perish unless relieved by charitable individuals, benevolent societies, or the guardians of the poor. I use the word "perish" with due deliberation and a full conviction of its appropriate application to the case, however revolting it may seem to the reader; for as these people depend for daily support on their daily or weekly wages, they are, when those wages are stopped by whatever means, utterly destitute of wherewith to support their existence, and actually become paupers, and, therefore, without the aid above stated, would, I repeat, "perish" of want.

The crisis of suffering through which this class about three years since passed here and elsewhere, and the occurrence of similar suffering in all hard winters (and, in other seasons, from sickness and destitution of employment), often without receiving that extra aid which such a state of things loudly demands, appears to require a sober and serious investigation in order to probe to the bottom so deplorable a state of things whereby the comfort and happiness of such a large portion of human beings are so cruelly shipwrecked, and to ascertain what are the causes of the evil and whether it be susceptible of any remedy.

The erroneous opinions to which I have alluded are:

1. That every man, woman, and grown child, able and willing to work, may find employment.

2. That the poor, by industry, prudence, and economy, may at all times support themselves comfortably, without depending on eleemosynary aid. And, as a corollary from these positions,

3. That their sufferings and distresses chiefly, if not wholly, arise from their idleness, their dissipation, and their extravagance.

4. That taxes for the support of the poor, and aid afforded them by charitable individuals, or benevolent societies, are pernicious as, by encouraging the poor to depend on them, they foster their idleness and improvi-

dence, and thus produce, or at least increase, the poverty and distress they are intended to relieve.

These opinions, so far as they have operated — and, through the mischievous zeal and industry of the school of political economists by which they have been promulgated, they have spread widely — have been pernicious to the rich and the poor. They tend to harden the hearts of the former against the sufferings and distresses of the latter, and of course prolong those sufferings and distresses.

> Posterity will scarcely credit the extent to which the popular feeling has been worked upon and warped by the ravings of some of our modern economists. They, truly, have done all that in them lay TO EXTINGUISH IN THE BOSOMS OF THE MORE OPULENT CLASSES EVERY SPARK OF GENEROUS AND BENEVOLENT FEELING TOWARD THE DESTITUTE AND NEEDY PAUPER. In their eyes, pauperism is a crime, for which nothing short of absolute starvation can form an adequate punishment.
> — *London Quarterly Review*, July 1828.

Many wealthy individuals, benevolent and liberal, apprehensive lest by charitable aid to persons in distress they might produce evil to society, are, by these pernicious and cold-blooded doctrines, prevented from indulging the feelings of their hearts, and employing a portion of their superfluous wealth for the best purpose to which it can be appropriated — that purpose which, at the hour of death, will afford the most solid comfort on retrospection — that is, "to feed the hungry; to give drink to the thirsty; to clothe the naked; to comfort the comfortless."[1]

The economists in question, when they

1. How transcendently superior are those who, like Mr. Perkins and Mr. Philips of Boston, Mr. Brown of Rhode Island, Mr. Oliver of Baltimore, Mr. Rutgers of New York, Mr. Ralston, Mr. Henry, and Mrs. Stott of Philadelphia, etc., *bestow* thousands and tens of thousands on public charities or other benevolent objects, to those who retain their millions to the last moment of their existence! Ten thousand dollars *bestowed* during life have more real merit than a million *bequeathed* at the last gasp, when it can be no longer grasped.

are implored by the starving poor for "bread," tender them "a stone." To the unfeeling and uncharitable of the rich (and such unhappily there are), these doctrines afford a plausible pretext, of which they are not slow to avail themselves, for withholding their aid from the poor. They have, moreover, tended to attach a sort of disrepute to those admirable associations of ladies and gentlemen, for the relief of the poor, on which Heaven looks down with complacence, and which form a delightful oasis in the midst of the arid deserts of sordid selfishness which on all sides present themselves to the afflicted view of the contemplative observer. . . .

There is scarcely any propensity more universal among mankind than the tendency to generalize from inadequate particulars. From the good or the bad qualities of half a dozen persons or things, most people are disposed to draw general conclusions affecting the whole species or genus to which the half dozen belong. It is not, therefore, wonderful, although greatly to be regretted, that on beholding a number of worthless poor, so many superficial persons feel disposed to set down the mass as worthless. A little reflection will prove the folly and injustice of this procedure. The estimable part of the poor, who struggle with their poverty, who resist the temptations to fraud and transgressions of every kind, are generally in the background — they escape notice. Hundreds of them may be within a few squares of us and never attract our attention.

Let us suppose a case. A man has, in the course of a year, dealings with 500 of those persons who depend on their labor for support; among this large number, he discovers ten or a dozen tricky and worthless who are on the watch to cheat and deceive him. Will he not, in his conversation about his affairs (and how many are there who have no other subject of conversation?) dwell more on the frauds and tricks of these than on the correct conduct of the 480 or 490? And will not superficial persons be disposed

Mathew Carey; from a painting by John Neagle

to generalize and stigmatize the whole from his statements?

Far from being surprised that among the poor there are to be found many worthless persons, it appears that the surprise, all things considered, ought to be that there are so few. In the first place, it is well known that we are the creatures of education and example; and how lamentably deficient the mass of the poor are in point of education and example we all know. No small proportion have had no education; others, only a mere smattering; and the examples which they are to copy, are, alas, too generally ill qualified to form them as useful or estimable members of society.

The higher orders of society have generally enjoyed the advantages of a good education and good examples; the censorial eye of the public is on them and serves as a curb to restrain them from guilt; regard to character has a powerful operation. Nevertheless, do we not unfortunately see considerable numbers of them who lapse from the paths of rectitude? How powerfully do such lapses tend to extenuate those of the poor, who are under no such controlling or restraining circumstances, and have so much stronger incentives to abberation!

The population of Philadelphia is about 160,000 souls, of whom about 100,000 depend on the labor of their hands; 40,000 are probably laborers, hodmen, seamstresses, families of workmen on the canals and railroads. The utmost industry and economy they can employ will scarcely suffice to sustain them if not unremittingly employed; and few of them are so fortunate as to be employed through the year.

7.

Edward Everett: A Plea for Support of an Ohio College

The following address was delivered by Edward Everett at a public meeting held at St. Paul's Church in Boston on May 21, 1833, on behalf of Kenyon College, in Ohio. Representing the college was the Right Reverend Charles McIlvaine, bishop of Ohio's Episcopal Church. Everett, a distinguished statesman and educator (he was to become secretary of state and president of Harvard), looked forward to a time when the cultured, "reasonable" East would no longer have the balance of power in the country. He appealed to his audience to expand the role of reason in government and, specifically, to extend the refined intelligence of New England to the untamed West, by supporting Western education.

Source: *Orations and Speeches on Various Occasions*, Boston, 1836, pp. 323-331.

I UNDERSTAND THE OBJECT of the meeting to be to aid the funds of a rising seminary of learning in the interior of the state of Ohio, particularly with a view to the training up of a well-educated ministry of the gospel in that part of the United States; and to consider the claims of such an object on this community.

As to the general question of the establishment and support of places of education, there are principally two courses which have been pursued in the practice of nations. One is to leave them, so to say, as an afterthought, the last thing provided for; to let the community grow up, become populous, rich, powerful; an immense body of unenlightened peasants, artisans, traders, soldiers, subjected to a small privileged class; and then let learning creep in with luxury; be itself esteemed a luxury, endowed out of the surplus of vast private fortunes or endowed by the state; and instead of diffusing a wholesome general influence, of which all partake, and by which the entire character of the people is softened and elevated, forming itself but another of those circumstances of disparity and jealous contrast of condition, of which too many were in existence before; adding the aristocracy of learning, acquired at expensive seats of science, to that of rank and wealth. This is, in general, the course which has been pursued with respect to the establishment of places of education in some countries of Europe. The other method is that introduced by our forefathers, namely, to lay the foundations of the commonwealth on the cornerstone of religion and education; to make the means of enlightening the community go hand in hand with the means for protecting it against its enemies, extending its commerce, and increasing its numbers; to make the care of the mind, from the outset, a part of its public economy; the growth of knowledge, a portion of its public wealth.

This, sir, is the New England system. It is the system on which the colony of Massachusetts was led, in 1647, to order that a school should be supported in every town; and which, eleven years earlier, caused the foundations of Harvard College to be laid by an appropriation out of the scanty means of the country, and at a period of great public distress, of a sum equal to the whole amount raised during the year for all other public charges. I do not know in what words I can so well describe this system as in those used by our fathers themselves. Quoted as they have been, times innumerable, they will bear quoting again, and seem to me peculiarly apposite to this occasion:

> After God had carried us safe to New England, and we had builded our houses, provided necessaries for our livelihood, reared convenient places for God's worship, and settled the civil government, one of the next things we longed for and looked after was to advance learning, and perpetuate it to posterity; dreading to leave an illiterate ministry to the churches, when the present ministers shall be in the dust.

Now, sir, it is proposed to assist our brethren in Ohio to lay the foundations of their commonwealth on this good old New England basis; and if ever there was a region where it was peculiarly expedient that this should be done, most assuredly the western part of America — and the state of Ohio as much as any other portion of it — is that region. It is two centuries since New England was founded, and its population by the last census fell short of 2 million. Forty years ago, Ohio was a wilderness, and, by the same enumeration, its population was little less than 1 million. At this moment, the population of Ohio (the settlement of which was commenced in 1788 by a small

party from our counties of Essex and Middlesex) is almost twice as large as that of our ancient and venerable Massachusetts.

I have seen this wonderful state with my own eyes. The terraqueous globe does not contain a spot more favorably situated. Linked to New Orleans on one side by its own beautiful river and the father of waters, and united to New York on the other side by the lake and the Erie Canal, she has, by a stupendous exertion of her own youthful resources, completed the vast circuit of communication between them. The face of the country is unusually favorable to settlement. There is little waste or broken land. The soil is fertile, the climate salubrious; it is settled by as truehearted and substantial a race as ever founded a republic; and there they now stand, 1 million souls gathered into a political community in a single generation!

Now, it is plain that this extraordinary rapidity of increase requires extraordinary means to keep the moral and intellectual growth of the people on an equality with their advancement in numbers and prosperity. These last take care of themselves. They require nothing but protection from foreign countries and security of property, under the ordinary administration of justice. But a system of institutions for education — schools and colleges — requires extra effort and means. The individual settler can fell the forest, build his log house, reap his crops, and raise up his family in the round of occupations pursued by himself; but he cannot, of himself, found or support a school, far less a college; nor can he do as much toward it as a single individual in older states, where ampler resources and a denser population afford means, cooperation, and encouragement at every turn. The very fact, therefore, that the growth of the country in numbers has been unexampled, instead of suggesting reasons why efforts in the cause of education are superfluous, furnishes an increased and increasing claim on the sympathy and good offices of all the friends of learning and education.

What, then, are the reasonable grounds of the claim as made on us? I think I perceive several.

We live in a community comparatively ancient, possessed of an abundance of accumulated capital, the result of the smiles of Providence on the industry of the people. We profess to place a high value on intellectual improvement, on education, on religion, and on the institutions for its support. We habitually take credit that we do so. To whom should the infant community, destitute of these institutions, desirous of enjoying their benefits, and as yet not abounding in disposable means, to whom should they look? Whither shall they go but to their brethren who are able to appreciate the want, and competent to relieve it? Someone must do it. These institutions, struggling into existence, must be nurtured, or they sink. To what quarter can they address themselves, with any prospect of success, if they fail here? Where will they find a community more likely to take an interest in the object, to feel a livelier sympathy in the want, more liberal, more able to give, more accustomed to give?

It is not merely in the necessity of things that young and rising communities, if assisted at all, should derive that assistance from the older and richer; but the period is so short since we ourselves stood in that relation to the mother country, and derived from her bounty benefactions to our institutions, that the obligation to requite these favors, in the only practicable way, is fresh and strong, and like that which requires a man to pay his debts. Dr. Franklin was accustomed, sometimes, to bestow a pecuniary favor on a young man, and, instead of requiring payment, to enjoin the object of his bounty, when advanced in life and in prosperous circumstances, to give the same sum of money, with a like injunction, to some other meritorious and needy young person.

The early annals of our country contain many instances of liberality from beyond the ocean. Our own university and that of New Haven were largely indebted, particularly ours, to pious and benevolent individuals in England. I know no mode of requiting these favors (which we cannot repay to the country from which we received them; she wants nothing we can give) more natural and more simple than by imitating the liberality of which we have profited, and supplying the wants of others, at that stage of their social progress at which our own were supplied.

The inducements to such an exercise of liberality, on our part, toward our brethren in the West are certainly stronger than those which could have influenced England to assist the rising institutions of America. The settlers of the Western country are not the aggrieved and persecuted children of the older states. We have not driven them out from among us by cruel Star Chamber edicts; nor have they, in leaving us, shaken off from their feet the dust of an unfriendly soil. They have moved away from the paternal roof to seek a new but not a foreign home. They have parted from their native land, neither in anger nor despair, but full of buoyant hope and tender regret. They have gone to add to the American family, not to dismember it. They are our brethren, not only after the flesh but after the spirit also, in character and in feeling.

We, in our place, regard them neither with indifference, jealousy, nor enmity, but with fraternal affection and true goodwill. Whom, in the name of Heaven, should we assist, if we refuse to assist them? . . .

On a theme like this, I am unwilling to appeal to anything like interest; nor will I appeal to an interest of a low and narrow character; but I cannot shut my eyes on those great considerations of an enlarged policy, which demand of us a reasonable liberality toward the improvement of these Western communities. In the year 1800, the state of Ohio sent one member to Congress; and Massachusetts, not then separated from Maine, sent twenty-one. Now, Ohio sends nineteen; and Massachusetts, recently, and I am constrained to add, in my judgment, unfairly, deprived of one of her members, sends but twelve. Nor will it stop here. "They must increase," and we, in comparison, "must decrease." At the next periodical enumeration Ohio will probably be entitled to nearly thirty representatives, and Massachusetts to little more than a third of this number.

Now, sir, I will not, on this occasion, and in this house of prayer, unnecessarily introduce topics and illustrations better befitting other resorts. I will not descant on interests and questions which, in the divided state of the public councils, will be decided, one way or the other, by a small majority of voices. I really wish to elevate my own mind, and, as far as lies in me, the minds of those I have the honor to address, to higher views. I would ask you, not in reference to this or that question, but in reference to the whole complexion of the destinies of the country, as depending on the action of the general government; I would ask you as to that momentous future which lies before us and our children. By whom, by what influence, from what quarter is our common country, with all the rich treasure of its character, its hopes, its fortunes, to be controlled, to be sustained, and guided in the paths of wisdom, honor, and prosperity, or sunk into the depth of degeneracy and humiliation?

Sir, the response is in every man's mind, on every man's lips. The balance of the country's fortunes is in the West. There lie, wrapped up in the folds of an eventful futurity, the influences which will most powerfully affect our national weal and woe. We have, in the order of Providence, allied ourselves to a family of sister communities, springing into existence and increasing with unexampled rapidity. We have called them into a full partnership in the government; the course of events has put crowns on their

Detroit Institute of Arts

Edward Everett; painting by Samuel F. B. Morse

heads and scepters in their hands; and we must abide the result.

But has the power indeed departed from us — the efficient, ultimate power? That, sir, is in a great measure as we will. The real government, in this country, is that of opinion. Toward the formation of the public opinion of the country, New England, while she continues true to herself, will, as in times past, contribute vastly beyond the proportion of her numerical strength. But besides the general ascendency which she will maintain through the influence of public opinion, we can do two things to secure a strong and abiding interest in the West, operating, I do not say in our favor, but in favor of principles and measures which we think sound and salutary. The first is promptly to extend toward the West, on every fitting occasion which presents itself, consistently with public and private duty, either in the course of legislation or the current of affairs, those good offices which of right pertain to the relative condition of the two parts of the country; to let the West know by experience, both in the halls of Congress and the channels of commercial and social intercourse, that the East is truly, cordially, and effectively her friend, not her rival nor enemy.

The kindly influence thus produced will prove of great power and value, and will go far to secure a return of fraternal feeling and political sympathy; but it will not, of itself, on great and trying occasions of a supposed diversity of sectional interest, always prove strong enough to maintain a harmony of councils. But we can do another thing of vastly greater moment. We can put in motion a principle of influence of a much higher and more generous character. We can furnish the means of building up institutions of education. We can, from our surplus, contribute toward the establishment and endowment of those seminaries where the mind of the West shall be trained and enlightened.

Yes, sir, we can do this; and it is so far optional with us, whether the power to which we have subjected ourselves shall be a power of intelligence or of ignorance; a reign of reflection and reason or of reckless strength; a reign of darkness or of light. This, sir, is true statesmanship; this is policy of which Washington would not be ashamed. While the partisan of the day plumes himself upon a little worthless popularity, gained by bribing the interest of one quarter, and falling in with the prejudices of another; it is truly worthy of a patriot, by contributing toward the means of steadily, diffusively, and permanently enlightening the public mind, as far as opportunity exists, in every part of the country, to secure it in a wise and liberal course of public policy. . . .

When, then, the right reverend bishop and the friends of the West ask you, on this occasion, to help them, they ask you, in ef-

fect, to spare a part of your surplus means for an object in which, to say the least, you have a common interest with them. They ask you to contribute to give security to your own property by diffusing the means of light and truth throughout the region where so much of the power to preserve or shake it resides. They ask you to contribute to perpetuate the Union by training up a well-educated population in the quarter which may hereafter be exposed to strong centrifugal influences. They ask you to recruit your waning strength in the national councils by enlisting on your side their swelling numbers, reared in the discipline of sound learning and sober wisdom; so that, when your voice in the government shall become comparatively weak, instead of being drowned by a strange and unfriendly clamor, from this mighty region it may be reechoed, with increased strength and a sympathetic response, from the rising millions of the Northwestern states.

Yes, sir, they do more. They ask you to make yourselves rich, in their respect, goodwill, and gratitude; to make your name dear and venerable in their distant shades. They ask you to give their young men cause to love you, now, in the springtime of life, before the heart is chilled and hardened; to make their old men who, in the morning of their days, went out from your borders, lift up their hands for a blessing on you, and say, "Ah, this is the good oldfashioned liberality of the land where we were born!" Yes, sir, we shall raise an altar in the remote wilderness. Our eyes will not behold the smoke of its incense as it curls up to heaven. But there the altar will stand; there the pure sacrifice of the spirit will be offered up; and the worshiper who comes, in all future time, to pay his devotions before it, will turn his face to the eastward and think of the land of his benefactors.

8.

Play-Party Songs

Play-party songs were danced to or sung without instrumental accompaniment. They grew up under the influence of a strong Protestant prejudice against the fiddle and against the wilder figures of the square dance. Among the most popular of the play-party songs were those, such as "Jennie Jenkins," "Bowling Green," and "Cindy," in which whole verses or verse lines were improvised. Frequently, however, more complex songs that had already been popularized in minstrel shows or by banjoists were sung at play-party gatherings. "Old Dan Tucker," written by Daniel Decatur Emmett, the composer of "Dixie," is an example of the latter type.

Source: *Old Dan Emmit's Original Banjo Melodies*, Boston, 1843.

⅋ JENNIE JENKINS

Will you wear red, oh my dear, oh my dear,
Will you wear red, Jennie Jenkins?
No, I won't wear red,
It's the color of my head —

Chorus:
But I'll buy me a foldy-roldy
Use a double, cause a double,
Roll and roll away to find me —
Roll, Jennie Jenkins, roll.

Will you wear green, oh my dear, oh my dear,
Will you wear green, Jennie Jenkins?
No, I won't wear green,
I'm ashamed to be seen —

Will you wear blue, oh my dear, oh my dear,
Will you wear blue, Jennie Jenkins?
No, I won't wear blue,
The color is too true —

Will you wear yeller, oh my dear, oh my dear,
Will you wear yeller, Jennie Jenkins?
No, I won't wear yeller,
'Cause I'd never get a feller —

Will you wear purple, oh my dear, oh my dear,
Will you wear purple, Jennie Jenkins?
No, I won't wear purple,
It's the color of a turtle —

What will you wear, oh my dear, oh my dear,
What will you wear, Jennie Jenkins?
Oh what do you care
If I just go bare? —

🕮 BOWLING GREEN

I wish I was in Bowling Green,
  Sitting in a chair;
One arm round my liquor keg,
  Other round my dear,
  Other round my dear.
    Bowling Green,
Hey, good old Bowling Green.

If you see that man of mine,
  Tell him once for me,
If he loves another girl,
  Yes, I'll set him free,
  Yes, I'll set him free.
    Bowling Green,
Hey, good old Bowling Green.

Wish I was a bumblebee
  Sailing through the air,
Sail right down to my feller's side,
  Touch him if you dare,
  Touch him if you dare.
    Bowling Green,
Hey, good old Bowling Green.

Going through this whole wide world,
  Going through alone;
Going through this whole wide world,
  I ain't got no home,
  I ain't got no home.
    Bowling Green,
Hey, good old Bowling Green.

🕮 CINDY

You ought to see my Cindy,
  She lives way down south;
She's so sweet the honey bees
  Swarm around her mouth.

Chorus:
Get-a-long home, Cindy, Cindy,
Get-a-long home, Cindy, Cindy,
Get-a-long home, Cindy, Cindy,
  I'll marry you some day.

The first time I saw Cindy
  She was standing in the door,
Her shoes and stockings in her hand,
  Her feet all over the floor.

She took me to her parlor,
  She cooled me with her fan;
She said I was the prettiest thing
  In the shape of mortal man.

She kissed me and she hugged me,
  She called me sugar plum;
She throwed her arms around me,
  I thought my time had come.

Oh, Cindy is a pretty girl,
  Cindy is a peach;
She throwed her arms around my neck,
  And hung on like a leech.

And if I was a sugar tree
  Standing in the town,
Every time my Cindy passed
  I'd shake some sugar down.

And if I had a needle and thread
  Fine as I could sew,
I'd sew that girl to my coat tails
  And down the road I'd go.

OLD DAN TUCKER

Now old Dan Tucker's a fine old man,
Washed his face in a frying pan,
Combed his hair with a wagon wheel
And died with a toothache in his heel.

  Chorus:
  Get out of the way, old Dan Tucker,
  You're too late to get your supper.
  Get out of the way, old Dan Tucker,
  You're too late to get your supper.

Now old Dan Tucker he came to town,
Riding a billy goat, leading a hound;
Hound dog bark and billy goat jump,
Land Dan Tucker on top of a stump.

Now old Dan Tucker he got drunk,
Fell in the fire and kicked up a chunk;
Red hot coal got in his shoe
And oh my Lord how the ashes flew.

Now old Dan Tucker he came to town,
Swinging the ladies round and round;
First to the right and then to the left,
Then to the girl that he loves the best.

                    DANIEL DECATUR EMMETT

9.

WILLIAM M. GOUGE: Paper Money and Banking

William Gouge formulated the economic principles of Jacksonian Democracy in his book, A Short History of Paper Money and Banking, *from which the excerpts below are taken. First printed in 1833, the book went through several editions, was serialized in two Democratic Party newspapers — the* New York Evening Post *and the* Washington Globe — *and was reprinted in London as* The Curse of Paper-Money and Banking. *Although contemporary advocates of hard money looked to him as an authority, Gouge has been attacked as a shabby economist whose simplistic theories were inapplicable to a growing industrial society. In any event, Gouge's book is the best formulation of the hard money position that underlay Jackson's veto of the Bank Bill of 1832.*

Source: *A Short History of Paper Money and Banking in the United States, etc., etc.,* Philadelphia, 1833, pp. 41-44, 84-90, 123-140.

AGAINST CORPORATIONS of every kind, the objection may be brought that whatever power is given to them is so much taken from either the government or the people. As the object of charters is to give to members of companies powers which they would not possess in their individual capacity, the very existence of monied corporations is incompatible with equality of rights.

Corporations are unfavorable to the progress of national wealth. As the Argus eyes of private interest do not watch over their concerns, their affairs are much more carelessly and much more expensively conducted than those of individuals. What would be the condition of the merchant who should trust everything to his clerks, or of the farmer who should trust everything to his laborers? Corporations are obliged to trust everything to stipendiaries, who are oftentimes less trustworthy than the clerks of the merchant or the laborers of the farmer.

Such are the inherent defects of corporations that they never can succeed, except when the laws or circumstances give them a monopoly or advantages partaking of the nature of a monopoly. Sometimes they are protected by direct inhibitions to individuals to engage in the same business. Sometimes they are protected by an exemption from liabilities to which individuals are subjected. Sometimes the extent of their capital or of their credit gives them a control of the market. They cannot, even then, work as cheap as the individual trader, but they can afford to throw away enough money in the contest to *ruin* the individual trader, and then they have the market to themselves.

If a poor man suffers aggression from a rich man, the disproportion of power is such that it may be difficult for him to obtain redress; but if a man is aggrieved by a corporation, he may have all its stockholders, all its clerks, and all its protégés for parties against him. Corporations are so powerful as frequently to bid defiance to government.

If a man is unjust or an extortioner, society is, sooner or later, relieved from the burden by his death. But corporations never die. What is worst of all (if worse than what has already been stated be possible) is that want of moral feeling and responsibility which characterizes corporations. A celebrated English writer expressed the truth, with some roughness but with great force, when he declared that "corporations have neither bodies to be kicked, nor souls to be damned."

All these objections apply to our American banks. They are protected, in most of the states, by directed inhibitions on individuals engaging in the same business. They are exempted from liabilities to which individuals are subjected. If a poor man cannot pay his debts, his bed is, in some of the states, taken from under him. If that will not satisfy his creditors, his body is imprisoned. The shareholders in a bank are entitled to all the gain they can make by banking operations; but if the undertaking chances to be unsuccessful, the loss falls on those who have trusted them. They are responsible only for the amount of stock they may have subscribed.

For the old standard of value, they substitute the new standard of bank credit. Would government be willing to trust to corporations the fixing of our standards and measures of length, weight, and capacity? Or are our standards and measures of value of less importance than our standards and measures of other things?

They coin money out of paper. What has always been considered one of the most important prerogatives of government has been surrendered to the banks.

In addition to their own funds, they have the whole of the spare cash of the community to work upon. The credit of every businessman depends on their nod. They have it in their power to ruin any merchant to whom they may become inimical.

We have laws against usury; but if it was the intention of the legislature to encourage usurious dealings, what more efficient means could be devised than that of establishing incorporated paper money banks? Government extends the credit of these institutions by receiving their paper as an equivalent for specie, and exerts its whole power to protect and cherish them. Whoever infringes any of the chartered privileges of the banks is visited with the severest penalties.

Supposing banking to be a thing good in itself, why should bankers be exempted from liabilities to which farmers, manufacturers, and merchants are subjected? It will not surely be contended that banking is more conducive than agriculture, manufactures, and commerce to the progress of national wealth.

Supposing the subscribers to banks to be substantial capitalists, why should artificial power be conferred on them by granting them a charter? Does not wealth of itself confer sufficient advantages on the rich man? Why should the competition among capitalists be diminished by forming them into companies and uniting their wealth in one mass?

Supposing the subscribers to banks to be speculators without capital, what is there so praiseworthy in their design of growing rich without labor that government should exert all its powers to favor the undertaking?

Why should corporations have greater privileges than simple copartnerships? On what principle is it that, in a professedly republican government, immunities are conferred on individuals in a collective capacity that are refused to individuals in their separate capacity? . . .

If two individuals should trade with one another, on the same principle that the banks trade with the community, it would soon be seen on which side the advantage lay. If A should pay interest on all the notes he gave and finally pay the notes themselves with his own wealth, and if B should receive interest on all the notes he issued and finally pay the notes themselves with *A*'s wealth, *A*'s loss and *B*'s gain would be in proportion to the amount of transactions between them.

This is the exact principle of American banking operations; but, owing to the multitude of persons concerned, the nature of the transaction is not discovered by the public. Regard the whole banking interest as one body corporate and the whole of the rest of the community as one body politic, and it will be seen that the body politic pays interest to the body corporate for the whole amount of notes received, while the body corporate finally satisfies the demands of the body politic by transferring the body politic's own property to its credit.

In private credit, there is a reciprocity of burdens and of benefits. Substantial wealth is given when goods are sold, and substantial wealth is received when payment is made, and an equivalent is allowed for the time during which payment is deferred. If *A* took a note from *B*, endorsed by the richest man in the country, he would require interest for the time for which payment was postponed. But the banking system reverses this natural order. The interest which is due to the productive classes that receive the bank notes is paid to the banks that issue them.

If the superior credit the banks enjoy grew out of the natural order of things, it would not be a subject of complaint. But the banks owe their credit to their charters — to special acts of legislation in their favor, and to their notes being made receivable in payment of dues to government. The kind of credit which is created for them by law, being equipollent with cash in the market, enables them to transfer an equal amount of substantial wealth from the productive classes to themselves, giving the productive classes only representatives of credit or evidences of debt in return for the substantial wealth which they part with. . . .

To infer that because a system produces great evil it must soon give way would be to argue in opposition to all experience. If mere suffering could produce reformation, there would be little misery in the world. Too many individuals have an interest in incorporated paper money banks to suffer the truth in relation to such institutions to have free progress. Too many prejudices remain in the minds of a multitude who have no such interest to permit the truth to have its proper effect.

It is, therefore, rational to conclude that the present system may, at least with modifications, continue to be the system of the country — not forever, as some seem to think, but for a period which cannot be definitely calculated. It is also rational to conclude that the effect it will have on society in time to come will be similar to the effect it has had in time past. We have, then, in the present state of the country, the means of judging of its future condition.

No system of policy that can be devised can prevent the United States from advancing in wealth and population. Our national prosperity has its seat in natural causes which cannot be effectually counteracted by any human measures, excepting such as would convert the government into a despotism like that of Turkey, or reduce the nation to a state of anarchy resembling that of some countries of South America.

Our wealth and population will increase till they become equal for each square mile to the wealth and population of the continent of Europe. We are now very far from this limit. Under a good system, we cannot reach it in less than 100 or 200 years. Under a bad system, in not less, perhaps, than 300 or 400. . . .

The progress of opulence in the United States in the next forty or fifty years will probably be very great. Many of the natural sources of wealth are as yet unappropriated. In no part of the country has their productiveness been fully developed. The people have now sufficient capital to turn their land and labor to more profit than was possible in any previous period of our country's history.

The daily improvements in productive machinery, and especially in the application of steam power, the discoveries in science, the introduction of new composts and new courses of crops in agriculture, the extension of roads and canals have all a tendency to increase the wealth of the country till the aggregate shall be enormous.

But this increase of wealth will be principally for the benefit of those to whom an increase of riches will bring no increase of happiness, for they have already wealth enough or more than enough. Their originally small capitals have, in the course of a few years, been doubled, trebled, and, in some instances, quadrupled. They have now large capitals, which will go on increasing in nearly the same ratio.

As no kind of property is prevented from being the prize of speculation by laws of entail, it is not easy to set bounds to the riches which some of our citizens may acquire. Their incomes may be equal to those of the most wealthy of the European nobility. Think, for a moment, of the immense accession of wealth certain families in the neighborhood of large cities and other improving towns must receive from the conversion of tracts of many acres into building lots. For ground which cost them but $100 an acre, they may get $10,000, $20,000, or $25,000. This will be without any labor or expenditure of capital on their part. The land will be increased in value by the improvements made around it at the expense of other men. . . .

To place the subject fairly before the reader, we shall bring together the principal propositions that have been supported in this essay, and leave the decision to his candid judgment.

We have maintained:

1. That real money is that valuable by reference to which the value of other articles is estimated, and by the instrumentality of which they are circulated. It is a *commodity*, done up in a particular form to serve a particular use, and does not differ *essentially* from other items of wealth.

2. That silver, owing to its different physical properties, the universal and incessant demand for it, and the small proportion the annual supply bears to the stock on hand, is as good a practical standard of value as can reasonably be desired. It has no variations except such as *necessarily* arise from the nature of value.

3. That real money diffuses itself through different countries and through different parts of a country in proportion to the demands of commerce. No prohibitions can prevent its departing from countries where wealth and trade are declining; and no obstacle, except spurious money, can prevent its flowing into countries where wealth and trade are increasing.

4. That money is the tool of all trades, and is, as such, one of the most useful of productive instruments, and one of the most valuable of laborsaving machines.

5. That bills of exchange and promissory notes are a *mere commercial medium*, and are, as *auxiliaries* of gold silver money, very useful; but they differ from metallic money in having no inherent value and in being evidences of debt. The expressions of value in bills of exchange and promissory notes are according to the article which law or custom has made the standard; and the failure to pay bills of exchange and promissory notes does not affect the value of the currency or the standard by which all contracts are regulated.

6. That bank notes are *mere evidences of debt* due by the banks; and in this respect differ not from the promissory notes of the merchants; but, being received in full of all demands, they become to all intents and purposes the money of the country.

7. That banks owe their credit to their charters; for, if these were taken away, not

even their own stockholders would trust them.

8. That the circulating quality of bank notes is in part owing to their being receivable in payment of dues to government; in part to the interest which the debtors to banks and bank stockholders have in keeping them in circulation; and in part to the difficulty, when the system is firmly established, of obtaining metallic money.

9. That so long as specie payments are maintained, there is a limit on bank issues; but this is not sufficient to prevent successive "expansions" and "contractions," which produce ruinous fluctuations of prices; while the means by which bank medium is kept "convertible" inflict great evils on the community.

10. That no restriction which can be imposed on banks, and no discretion on the part of the directors, can prevent these fluctuations; for bank credit, as a branch of commercial credit, is affected by all the causes, natural and political, that affect trade or that affect the confidence man has in man.

11. That the "flexibility" or "elasticity" of bank medium is not an excellence but a defect, and that "expansions" and "contractions" are not made to suit the wants of the community, but from a simple regard to the profits and safety of the banks.

12. That the uncertainty of trade produced by these successive "expansions" and "contractions" is but *one* of the evils of the present system. That the banks cause credit dealings to be carried to an extent that is highly pernicious — that they cause credit to be given to men who are not entitled to it and deprive others of credit to whom it would be useful.

13. That the granting of exclusive privileges to companies, or the exempting of companies from liabilities to which individuals are subject, is repugnant to the fundamental principles of American government; and that the banks, inasmuch as they have exclusive privileges and exemptions, and have the entire control of credit and currency, are the most pernicious of money corporations.

14. That a *nominal* responsibility may be imposed on such corporations, but that it is impossible to impose on them an effective responsibility. They respect the laws and public opinion so far only as is necessary to promote their own interest.

15. That on the supposition most favorable to the friends of the banking system, the whole amount gained by the substitution of bank medium for gold and silver coin is equal only to about 40 cents per annum for each individual in the country; but that it will be found that nothing is in reality gained *by the nation* if due allowance be made for the expense of supporting 300 or 400 banks, and for the fact that bank medium is a machine which performs its work badly.

16. That some hundreds of thousands of dollars are annually extracted from the people of Pennsylvania, and some millions from the people of the United States, for the support of the banks, insomuch as through banking the natural order of things is reversed, and interest paid to the banks on evidences of debt due by them, instead of interest being paid to those who part with commodities in exchange for bank notes.

17. That into the formation of the bank capital of the country very little substantial wealth has ever entered, that capital having been formed principally out of the promissory notes of the original subscribers, or by other means which the operations of the banks themselves have facilitated. They who have bought the script of the banks at second hand may have honestly paid cent per cent for it; but what they have paid has gone to those from whom they bought the script and does not form any part of the capital of the banks.

18. That if it was the wish of the legisla-

ture to promote usurious dealings, it could not well devise more efficient means than incorporating paper money banks. That these banks, moreover, give rise to many kinds of stockjobbing, by which the simple-minded are injured and the crafty benefited.

19. That many legislators have, in voting for banks, supposed that they were promoting the welfare of their constituents; but the prevalence of false views in legislative bodies in respect to money corporations and paper money is to be attributed chiefly to the desire certain members have to make money for themselves, or to afford their political partisans and personal friends opportunities for speculation.

20. That the banking interest has a pernicious influence on the periodical press, on public elections, and the general course of legislation. This interest is so powerful that the establishment of a system of sound currency and sound credit is impracticable, except one or other of the political parties into which the nation is divided makes such an object its primary principle of action.

21. That through the various advantages which the system of incorporated paper money banking has given to some men over others, the foundation has been laid of an *artificial* inequality of wealth, which kind of inequality is, when once laid, increased by all the subsequent operations of society.

22. That this artificial inequality of wealth adds nothing to the substantial happiness of the rich, and detracts much from the happiness of the rest of the community; that its tendency is to corrupt one portion of society and debase another.

23. That the sudden dissolution of the banking system, without suitable preparation, would put an end to the collection of debts, destroying private credit, break up many productive establishments, throw most of the property of the industrious into the hands of speculators, and deprive laboring people of employment.

24. That the system can be got rid of without difficulty by prohibiting, after a certain day, the issue of small notes and proceeding gradually to those of the highest denomination.

25. That the feasibility of getting rid of the system is further proved by the fact that the whole amount of bank notes and bank credits, is, according to Mr. Gallatin's calculation, only about $109 million. By paying $10 or $11 million a year, the whole can be liquidated in the term of ten years. If, however, twenty or thirty years should be required for the operation, the longest of these is but a short period in the lifetime of a nation.

26. That it has not been through the undervaluation of gold at the Mint, that eagles and half-eagles have disappeared, but from the free use of bank notes. Nevertheless, a new coinage of pieces containing $4 and $8, or $5 and $10, worth of gold is desirable to save the trouble of calculating fractions. The dollar being the money of contract and account, no possible confusion or injustice can be produced by an adjustment of the gold coinage to the silver standard.

27. That incorporating a paper money bank is not the "necessary and proper" or "natural and appropriate" way of managing the fiscal concerns of the Union; but that the "necessary and proper" or "natural and appropriate" way, is by subtreasury offices.

28. That incorporating a paper money bank is not "the necessary and proper" or "natural and appropriate" way of correcting the evils occasioned by the state banks, inasmuch as a national bank, resting on the same principles as the state banks, must produce similar evils.

29. That "convertible" paper prevents the accumulation of such a stock of the precious metals as will enable the country to bear transitions from peace to war and insure the punctual payment of war taxes; and that the "necessary and proper" or "natural and appropriate" way of providing for all public exigencies is by making the

government *a solid-money government,* as was intended by the framers of the Constitution.

30. That if Congress should, from excessive caution or some less commendable motive, decline passing the acts necessary to insure the gradual withdrawal of bank notes, they may greatly diminish the evils of the system by declaring that nothing but gold and silver shall be received in payment of duties, and by making the operations of the government entirely distinct from those of the banks.

31. That, on the abolition of incorporated paper money banks, private bankers will rise up, who will receive money on deposit and allow interest on the same, discount promissory notes, and buy and sell bills of exchange. Operating on sufficient funds and being responsible for their engagements in the whole amount of their estates, these private bankers will not by sudden and great "expansions" and "curtailments" derange the whole train of mercantile operations. In each large city, an office of deposit and transfer . . . will be established, and we shall thus secure all the good of the present banking system and avoid all its evils.

32. That, if the present system of banking and paper money shall continue, the wealth and population of the country will increase from natural causes, till they shall be equal for each square mile to the wealth and population of Europe. But, with every year, the state of society in the United States will more nearly approximate to the state of society in Great Britain. Crime and pauperism will increase. A few men will be inordinately rich, some comfortable, and a multitude in poverty. This condition of things will naturally lead to the adoption of that policy which proceeds on the principle that a legal remedy is to be found for each social evil, and nothing left for the operations of nature. This kind of legislation will increase the evils it is intended to cure.

33. That there is reason to *hope* that, on the downfall of monied corporations and the substitution of gold and silver for bank medium, sound credit will take the place of unsound, and legitimate enterprise the place of wild speculation. That the moral and intellectual character of the people will be sensibly though gradually raised, and the causes laid open of a variety of evils under which society is now suffering. That the sources of legislation will, to a certain extent, be purified by taking from members of legislative bodies inducements to pass laws for the special benefit of themselves, their personal friends, and political partisans. That the operation of the natural and just causes of wealth and poverty will no longer be inverted, but that each cause will operate in its natural and just order, and produce its natural and just effect — wealth becoming the reward of industry, frugality, skill, prudence, and enterprise, and poverty the punishment of few, except the indolent and prodigal.

10.

CHARLES A. DAVIS: A Humorist's View of the Bank Controversy

"Major Jack Downing" was created by Seba Smith in 1830 and adopted by Charles A. Davis in 1833. Davis was a friend of Nicholas Biddle and a director of the New York Branch of the United States Bank. Davis' Major associated casually with the chief persons in the government and commented irreverently on Jackson's fiscal policies. Davis' Major Downing letters were published originally in the New York Daily Advertiser. *The Major was greatly appreciated at the time; a collection of the* Letters *went through ten editions in two years.*

Source: *Letters of J. Downing, Major, etc., etc.,* New York, 1834, pp. 121-153.

I.

MAJOR J. DOWNING to MR. DWIGHT, November 12

I HAVE ALWAYS BEEN TELLIN THE GINERAL, as you know, that of all troubles there was none so tuff to git round as money troubles, and when such matters git in a snarl it was worse than tryin to straiten a melitia line arter dinner. I was always afraid that we was gittin too many folks to handle the money, and to be figerin at the 'counts. Ever since I was a boy I always had a notion that the fewer hands in countin the better, and the less you handle money the better, for the more you handle it, somehow, the less it grows. And then agin I tell'd the Gineral, over and over agin, 'Don't meddle with the Bank,' says I; 'the money is safe enuff there, and one pocket,' says I, 'Gineral, is better than twenty.' But you know when I was in New-York with Zekel Bigelow tryin to find out the cause of money bein scarce, and when Zekel broke his watch showin me how the United States Bank worked among other banks,

and folks somehow got round the Gineral, and the deposits was removed.

I have been lookin out for trouble ever since, though I was bound to stick to the Gineral, right or wrong, as I told him I would.

Tother day, when we came to that part of the message where we have to speak of mony matters, we sent for Mr. Taney, our new Secretary of the Treasury, to bring in his accounts. He warn't quite ready, for he ain't as quick at siferin yet as he will be to rights; so we waited for him a spell, and left a place here and there in the message, jest big enuff to put in figers: and so last night the Gineral sent agin, and said he must have the 'counts, 'ready or not ready,' and up they came, sure enuff, and not more than half-cooked; but the Gineral won't wait for nothin when he's in a hurry.

'Now,' says he, 'Major, turn to and see how they stand with last year.' And so at it I went, comparin all the amounts of out lays, the Gineral all the while smokin and thinkin pretty hard, with his feet up on the mantle. I figered up the sums pretty quick, considerin there was a good many on 'em called *estimates;* and when I got to the eend on't, 'Now,' says I, 'Gineral, you know I tell'd you that we could git up and put down nullification in no time — we could turn out a cabinet and appint other folks — we could send ministers abroad, and let 'em come home as soon as they pleased, and send other folks in their places, and give all full pay too — we could nock the United States Bank and Squire Biddle all into splinters — we could let our folks go on the Ingin lands in one place and drive them off in other places, and git up an Ingin War — and appint new officers here and there — and have new auditers to settle 'counts — and let things go on in the Post Office and Land Office pretty much to suit the folks there — and instead of havin one Bank for our money, scatter it about among the banks of our friends. All this we could do, and have done, and have taken the responsibility too, and the folks like us the better for it; but,' says I, 'when they come to see what it all costs there'll be trouble, now I tell you,' says I.

'Why, Major,' says the Gineral, 'what's the matter? ain't 'the Government' economical?' says he: 'do you expect to make reforms without costin somethin? Can you clear up swamps, and cut ditches, and remove old stumps without expense?' 'Yes,' says I, 'Gineral, that's all true. But, plague on't,' says I, 'it's ben goin on so now nigh upon 5 years; and,' says I, 'it keeps costin more and more, and we are nearer bein swamp'd and stump'd than ever — here,' says I, 'now jest look and see what 'the Government' costs now, and what it cost when Mr. Adams was President; and that ain't the worst on't,' says I, 'our money is here, there, and everywhere; and I don't see how we shall find it when we want it.'

As soon as I mention'd the amount of the sums I had figered up, the Gineral jumps up, and he did stomp about a spell, I tell you — he smash'd down his pipe, and it flew into more than forty pieces — says

he, 'Major, ain't you mistaken?' 'No,' says I, 'thare's no mistake about me, Gineral.' 'Let me see them accounts,' says he; and he begun to feel for his spectacles, first in one pocket, and then in another — for he had no less than 7 pockets besides his watch fob — and he couldn't find his spectacles — says he, 'Major, have you seen my spectacles?' 'No,' says I, 'Gineral, I hain't — where do you keep 'em?' says I — 'Why,' says he, 'I used always to keep 'em in this side breast-pocket, but I have been so pester'd lately, I must have chang'd pockets' — 'That's bad,' says I, 'Gineral, especially,' says I, 'when one wants any thing in a hurry. Now,' says I, 'I only keep one pocket; and I got that notion,' says I, 'from Squire Biddle, for he keeps eny most every thing in one pocket, and he can tell in a minit pretty much all about eny thing.'

The Gineral kept all the while feelin and turnin his pockets inside out, but no spectacles. Says he, 'Major, I reckon them 'ere spectacles are somewhere in one of these pockets, and I'll find 'em,' says he, 'if I have to take my shirt off'; and at it he went, and he off coat and jacket, and I don't know what all, and I all the while shakin 'em to find the spectacles — by-and-by I see a hole in his pantaloons-pocket; 'I'm on track now,' says I, 'Gineral; here's a hole:' and, sure enuff, when he came to take off his boots, there was his best gold-rim specs, and all broke to flinders — and if we hadn't been lookin for 'em, and if I hadn't seen that 'ere hole, you never would say they ever had been specs, for they were all jam'd to nothin.

There was a curious notion then jest come into my head, and I stood stock still, holdin the Gineral's pantaloons in one hand and his right boot upside down in tother, and there lay the specs on the floor (or what there was left on 'em); and the Gineral stood lookin at me with eny most nothin on him, and the Message and the Treasury 'counts and my slate lay on the table —

there warn't a word said for more than 10 minits — an awful time to stand so.

So to rights the Gineral he spoke, and says he, 'Major, what are you thinkin on?' 'Why,' says I, 'Gineral, I was thinkin,' says I, 'if you had kept your spectacles in your side breast-pocket, they would be on your nose now; but,' says I, 'that ain't the worst on't, I'm afeard,' says I, 'Gineral, we've got too many pockets for our money, and when we want it we shall all have to come to our shirts and boots before we find it.'

The Gineral got as hornety as all nature at this; and says he, 'Major, I wish now you was only Calhoun, or Biddle, or Clay, or M'Duffy, or Don Pedro, or Black Hawk, or any one but Major Downing — for I feel as if I should like to give some one a thrashing.' 'Why,' says I, 'Gineral, you ain't mad nor nothin, be you? for I am too,' says I; 'and ev'ry time I look at the 'counts,' says I, 'I feel as if I would like to git hold of some one, and thrash 'em too,' — and so we stomped about a spell, cussin and discussin most things, till we got cool agin — but it was a considerable of a storm, I tell you.

II.

DOWNING to DWIGHT, December 14

WE HAVE GOT BUSINESS ENUF now on our hands, I tell you; and nigh upon every day we have a squall that brings all hands to the helm. We have had fair wind so long, that few on us know exactly how to steer now-a-days, when every wind comes right in our teeth. I hain't had my coat off since Congress met; and the Gineral says we must watch them fellows closely. 'Keep a sharp look out, Major' says he, 'on Clay — he is a *bold*, *independent* fellow, and will speak out his notions if the devil stands at the door; and if he had the people with him,' says the Gineral, 'as I have, there is no tel-lin what trouble he would give us. He would make as good a Gineral as ever was. But it will never do *to trust that man with power.*'

'Very well,' says I, 'Gineral — but, plague on't,' says I, 'the crittur somehow keeps law on his side all the while.' 'That's true enuf,' says the Gineral, 'and therefore we must keep a sharper eye on him, and the time is come now, Major, when we must all on us try our popularity — for when the law is agin us, we shan't have nothin else to stand on. — There is nothin,' says the Gineral, 'like war-times, Major — for then, when these troublesome fellows talk about law I'd give 'em martial law, and that makes short work.'

Jest after breakfast yesterday, I and the Gineral had a high time together. I had ben expecting every day to see the Bank come out with a *reply*; and I tell'd the Gineral, says I, 'Gineral, I'm afraid we'll git a stumper from Philadelphy one of these days, that will nock us all into kindlin-wood.' But he kept sayin there was no fear of that. 'Why,' says he, 'Major, you forgit that we first give the Bank a most mortal weltin 3 years ago and left 'em no other defence than to print reports and speeches; and that show'd they hadn't much spunk; and we have been criplin on 'em ever since. And when I see they began to stagger, I give 'em our hull battery, and opened upon 'em in flank, front, and rear, our sharp shooters, headed by that amazin cute little District Attorney, open'd first on 'em. Then come my Proclamation — and then my Message — and then Mr. Tany's report — and the Globe all the while throwin shells and rockets.

'Why,' says the Gineral, gittin up and takin his Hickory, and givin it a whack on the floor — 'if the Bank stands all that racket, Major, it's tuffer than a pepperage log. No, no, Major,' says the Gineral, 'don't you fear that the Bank will ever say a word in reply — it's as dead now,' says the Gineral, 'as a skin'd racoon.' And the words warn't out of his mouth afore in came a hull bundle of letters and newspapers, and the first thing I see among 'em was the 'Bank reply.' 'Now,' says I, 'Gineral, here's trouble! — here's the very thing,' says I, 'I've been afraid on all the while.'

The Gineral laft a spell; and says he, 'Major, suppose you and I now jest take a bout, and you'll see how easy I can nock that reply into nothin.' 'Well,' says I, 'Gineral, its a bargain. — Now,' says I, 'let us sit down, and you may take,' says I, 'the Globe, or our District Attorney's report, or your Proclamation, or your Message, or Mr. Tany's report — ary one on 'em, — or,' says I, 'come to think on't, you may take 'em all together, — for they are pretty much *all one* — and I'll take this 'Bank reply,' and then let's see what kind of a fight it will turn out.' 'Well,' says the Gineral, 'you are a man of spunk, Major, and I like you for it: and if I make a prisoner on you, I'll treat you like a brave soldier.' 'And so will I you, Gineral,' says I, 'and if you fall in the fight,' says I, 'Gineral, I'll bury you,' says I, 'with the honors of war'; and then we shook hands.

'Now, Major,' says the Gineral, 'as I am to begin the fight, don't you fire till I fire, and then we'll go threw, shot by shot.' 'Well,' says I, 'I want to know first, if I have a right to fire back *your shot*, if they miss me, and I can pick 'em up?' 'O yes,' says the Gineral, 'that's fair in war.' 'Use the enemies shot and shells, and guns too, if you can, Major, — *that's the true art of war.*' The Gineral all the while kept fixing his papers all in a string on one side the table. He put his own Messages and Proclamation in the middle, and flank'd off with our District Attorney and Mr. Tany's reports; and then he sifted the Globe about, and call'd them *scouts* and *foragers* — 'There,' says he, 'Major, I am now nearly ready;' and he took off his specs, and gin 'em a good rubbin and put 'em on agin.

'Now, Major,' says he, 'take your station.' And I went round tother side, and sat down. 'Are you ready?' says the Gineral. — 'All ready,' says I — and at it we went.

The Gineral, he open'd his fire first, as agreed; and he fir'd away from his first Message — And then his second — then he took the Globe, and then the reports, — and he blaz'd away like all wrath, for an hour; and as soon as he stop'd to take breath — 'Now,' says I, 'its my time,' — and I read the reply a spell, and answered all he said in three minits. And I gin him a look! The Gineral twisted his face most shockin, and scratched his head too. But he went at it agin as spunky as ever; for he is an amazin tuff crittur in a fight, and hangs on like a snappin turtle when he gits hold. He banged away a spell agin like all natur; and jest as he took his specs off to give 'em a rub, I gin him the reply agin. The Gineral gin his face another plagy hard rumple; and I sot waitin for him to fire agin. Says he, 'Major, that's a sharp piece you are firin with there.' 'It's a peeler,' says I, 'Gineral, I tell you — but you hain't got the best on't yet — it's jest gettin warm,' says I.

'Major,' says the Gineral, 'suppose we change batteries — let me take that reply, and you take all these documents. I like to fight,' says the Gineral, 'when there is ten to one agin me.' 'So do I,' says I, 'Gineral, and so we'd better fight it out as we sit.'

The Gineral looked a spell at his paper agin; and, says he, 'Major, I reckon we had better have a truce.' 'Not now,' says I, 'I've got my hand in now, and want to see the fight out.' 'Well,' says the Gineral, 'you see, Major, what comes when any one attempts to drive the executive;' and with that he got up, and took off his specs, and put 'em in his pocket, and put on his hat and took his Hickory, and fetched a whack on the table, — 'Veto,' says he — 'That's enuff,' says I, 'Gineral.'

'And now,' says the Gineral, 'let's go and take a walk' — and so we went. The Gineral didn't say nothin for more than a mile, and I nother. So, to rights, says he, 'Major, everybody says money is very scarce.' 'That's true enuf,' says I, 'and it's not got as scarce as it will be afore winter is over;' and then I tell'd the Gineral the cause on't. 'Well,' says the Gineral, 'I believe you are right; and if the worst comes to the worst,' says he, 'we'll have a new Bank, and that will make money plenty agin, wont it?' 'Yes,' says I, 'I suppose so; but we can't git a new Bank, Gineral, afore this one's time is out, and that's nigh three years yet; and long afore that time,' says I, 'there will be trouble enuf, as this one must all the while be collectin in its own money; and folks will fail, and be bankrupt; and then twenty new Banks will do them no good.' 'I don't see that,' says the Gineral. 'If we could make a new Bank now,' says I, 'right off, and let it take up the business of the old one, it wouldn't make much odds. But the law won't allow that, you know, Gineral.'

And jest then the Gineral got in a way he has of twitchin with his suspender buttons behind; and to rights he broke one off. 'There,' says he, 'Major, here is this confounded button off agin.' 'Well,' says I, 'that's a small matter — here is a tailor's shop, — let's go in and make him put it on' — and so in we went. The tailor happened to be one of our party, and was tickled to death to see the President, and thought he was goin to git an office right off, and was plagily cut down when he come to find it was ony a button off; and so he jumped back on his board, and sat down on his heels agin, and said if the Gineral would take off his pantaloons, he'd put it on in a few minutes. —

I looked at the Gineral and he looked at me — and we both looked at the tailor. 'Why,' says the Gineral, 'this is the worst thing, Major, I ever met — I'm stump'd completely! It will never do to risk walking home with this button off; for if 'tother one comes off, it's all over with me; and if I sit

here without my pantaloons till that fellow puts on a button, I'll kitch my death of cold! Look here, Major,' says the Gineral, 'that other button is taken all the strain, and it will come off in less than five minutes — what is to be done? It seems to me, Major,' said the Gineral, 'that no man is placed so often in such real trouble as I am.' — 'Yes,' says I, 'Gineral, but it's fortunate for you, you always have me with you.' 'I know it, Major,' says he, 'and I hope you will be as true a friend now as ever you have been.'

And with that, says I to the tailor, 'Can't you fix things now, so as to git over all this trouble?' 'There is only one way,' says the tailor, 'and that I've stated, and another thing,' says he, 'the Gineral wants a new pair.' 'You rascal,' says the Gineral, 'you can't make a better pair, and one that fits me better, if you try a month — these pantaloons,' said the Gineral, 'are better than a new pair; and if they only had new buttons here they would last me to my dying day. — It takes me weeks and months to git a pair to sit easy. I won't have a new pair,' says the Gineral, 'that I'm determined on. I see,' says the Gineral, 'what you are after — you want a new job.'

'Well,' says I, 'Gineral, let me try' — and with that I wax'd a thread, and got a new button; and whilst the Gineral stood up, I sot down behind him, and stitched on the button in three minits — the Gineral all the while shakin his hickory at the tailor, and tellin him that he had no more brains in his head than he had in his thimble. — 'You are a pretty fellow to belong to my party,' says he; 'I should have been soon in a pritty condition, if I had taken your advice,' says the Gineral. 'Let me ever ketch you at the White House agin.'

So to rights, the tailor got mad too, and said he didn't belong to the Gineral's party — he was a Tany-Kindle-Van-Buren-Jackson-man; he knew which side his bread was butter'd; and he looked plagey knowin too — it was jest as much as I could do to keep the Gineral from smashin him — so says I, 'Come, Gineral, let's be movin;' and we went home — the Gineral all the while talkin about his escape from an awful state that tailor was about getting him in. — 'Well,' says I, 'Gineral, little things sometimes give us a kink and a notion of bigger ones; and now,' says I, 'do you know, Gineral, we are in a scrape now, pretty much like that one we jest got out on.' 'How so?' says the Gineral. 'Why,' says I, 'the Bank, there it is,' says I, 'jest like your pantaloons, *better than new*; and only wants a new button; and some of these ere political tailors about us here want us to sit shiverin and shakin, and runnin the risk of gettin a rheu-matiz that will last us our lives, jest for them to get the job of makin a new one.'

'And now,' says I, 'I guess you and I had better disappoint 'em, as we did the tailor jest now — stitch on a new button, and things will go smooth agin.' The Gineral didn't say a word; but he got thinkin plagey hard, till we got home agin, and he got his pipe, and I got mine, and jest as were lighten 'em, says he, 'Major, there are some fellows about us here that pester me most desperately — we must all go as a 'Unit,' or I must blow 'em all up, and git a new set. We'll think of it,' said the Gineral, and with that we cock'd our feet on the mantle-tree, and in less than five minutes you couldn't see no more on us than our toes.

11.

Henry Clay: The Bank and the Power of the Executive

After vetoing the bill to recharter the Bank of the United States, President Jackson prepared to break the bank by withdrawing the federal deposits. The secretary of the treasury, William J. Duane, refused to execute the President's policy and on September 23, 1833, he was replaced as secretary by Roger B. Taney. Three days after his appointment Taney ordered that the federal funds be removed to the Girard Bank of Philadelphia. On December 26, 1833, Henry Clay, the leader of the Whig Party, proposed to the Senate a series of resolutions censuring the President for overstepping his authority. On March 28, 1834, the substance of the resolutions was adopted in the Senate by a vote of 26 to 20. Portions of Clay's speech in support of the resolutions are reprinted here.

Source; Colton, II, pp. 115-118.

Sir, I am surprised and alarmed at the new source of executive power which is found in the result of a presidential election. I had supposed that the Constitution and the laws were the sole source of executive authority; that the Constitution could only be amended in the mode which it has itself prescribed; that the issue of a presidential election was merely to place the chief magistrate in the post assigned to him; and that he had neither more nor less power, in consequence of the election, than the Constitution defines and delegates. But it seems that if, prior to an election, certain opinions, no matter how ambiguously put forth by a candidate, are known to the people, these loose opinions, in virtue of the election, incorporate themselves with the Constitution, and afterward are to be regarded and expounded as parts of the instrument! . . .

I have rarely seen any state paper characterized by so little gravity, dignity, and circumspection as the report displays. The secretary is perfectly reckless in his assertions of matters of fact, and culpably loose in his reasoning. . . .

He [the secretary] represents the bank as endeavoring to operate on the public by alternate bribery and oppression, with the same object in both cases, of influencing the election or the administration of the President. Why this perpetual reference of all the operations of the institution to the executive? Why does the executive think of nothing but itself? It is I! It is I! It is I, that is meant! appears to be the constant exclamation. . . .

We have, Mr. President, a most wonderful financier at the head of our Treasury Department. He sits quietly by in the cabinet and witnesses the contest between his colleague and the President; sees the conflict in the mind of that colleague between his personal attachment to the President on the one hand, and his solemn duty to the public on the other; beholds the triumph of conscientious obligation; contemplates the noble spectacle of an honest man, preferring to surrender an exalted office with all its honors and emoluments rather than betray the interests of the people; witnesses the contemptuous and insulting expulsion of that colleague from office; and then coolly enters the vacated place, without the slightest sympathy or the smallest emotion! He was installed on the 23rd of September,

and by the 26th, the brief period of three days, he discovers that the government of the United States had been wrong from its origin; that every one of his predecessors from Hamilton down, including Gallatin (who, whatever I said of him on a former occasion, and that I do not mean to retract, possessed more practical knowledge of currency, banks, and finance than any man I have ever met in the public councils), Dallas, and Crawford, had been mistaken about both the expediency and constitutionality of the bank; that every chief magistrate, prior to him whose patronage he enjoyed, had been wrong; that the Supreme Court of the United States and the people of the United States, during the thirty-seven years that they had acquiesced in or recognized the great utility of a bank, were all wrong. And, opposing his single opinion to their united judgments, he dismisses the bank, scatters the public money, and undertakes to regulate and purify the public morals, the public press, and popular elections!

If we examine the operations of this modern Turgot, in their financial bearing, merely, we shall find still less for approbation.

First, he withdraws the public moneys, where, by his own deliberate admission, they were perfectly safe, with a bank of $35 million of capital, and $10 million of specie, and places them at great hazard with banks of comparatively small capital and but little specie, of which the Metropolis Bank is an example.

Second, he withdraws them from a bank created by, and over which, the federal government had ample control, and puts them in other banks, created by different governments, and over which it has no control.

Third, he withdraws them from a bank in which the American people, as a stockholder, were drawing their fair proportion of interest accruing on loans, of which those deposits formed the basis, and puts them where the people of the United States draw no interest.

Fourth, from a bank which has paid a bonus of $1,500,000, which the people of the United States may now be liable to refund, and puts them in banks which have paid to the American people no bonus.

Fifth, depreciates the value of stock in a bank where the general government holds $7 million, and advances that of banks in whose stock it does not hold a dollar, and whose aggregate capital does not probably much exceed that very $7 million. And finally,

Sixth, he dismisses a bank whose paper circulates in the greatest credit throughout the Union, and in foreign countries, and engages in the public service banks, whose paper has but a limited and local circulation in their "immediate vicinities."

These are immediate and inevitable results. How much that large and long-standing item of *unavailable funds*, annually reported to Congress, will be swelled and extended remains to be developed by time.

And now, Mr. President, what, under all these circumstances, is it our duty to do? Is there a senator who can hesitate to affirm, in the language of the resolution, that the President has assumed a dangerous power over the Treasury of the United States, not granted to him by the Constitution and the laws; and that the reasons assigned for the act, by the secretary of the treasury, are insufficient and unsatisfactory?

The eyes and the hopes of the American people are anxiously turned to Congress. They feel that they have been deceived and insulted; their confidence abused; their interests betrayed; and their liberties in danger. They see a rapid and alarming concentration of all power in one man's hands. They see that, by the exercise of the positive authority of the executive, and his negative power exerted over Congress, the will of one man alone prevails and governs the republic. The question is no longer what laws will Congress pass, but what will the executive not veto? The President, and not Congress, is addressed for legislative action.

We have seen a corporation, charged with the execution of a great national work, dismiss an experienced, faithful, and zealous president, afterward testify to his ability by a voluntary resolution, and reward his extraordinary services by a large gratuity, and appoint in his place an executive favorite, totally inexperienced and incompetent, to propitiate the President. We behold the usual incidents of approaching tyranny. The land is filled with spies and informers, and detraction and denunciation are the orders of the day. People, especially official incumbents in this place, no longer dare speak in the fearless tones of manly freedom but in the cautious whispers of trembling slaves.

The premonitory symptoms of despotism are upon us; and if Congress do not apply an instantaneous and effective remedy, the fatal collapse will soon come on, and we shall die — ignobly die! base, mean, and abject slaves — the scorn and contempt of mankind — unpitied, unwept, unmourned!

The advice nearest my heart and deepest in my convictions is, that the Union of the states be cherished and perpetuated. Let the open enemy of it be regarded as a Pandora with her box opened, and the disguised one as the serpent creeping with his deadly wiles into paradise.

JAMES MADISON, "Advice to My Country, Conclusion," found among his papers after his death

Planter's house and sugar plantation on the Mississippi River

THE SOUTH

Although the plantation system completely dominated the Southern economy, the plantation owners were far outnumbered by small farmers — in many instances, merely subsistence farmers or those to whom a small cash crop of cotton or tobacco was incidental. As late as 1850, when cotton was complete and undisputed king, less than one percent of the Southern citizens owned more than twenty slaves. The average Mississippi farm was smaller than 200 acres in extent.

While many small farmers owned a few slaves, the weight of slavery as an institution depended on the large plantation. In the Black Belt of Alabama, more than 40 percent of the farmers owned no slaves at all. But in any typical county of the South, the handful of plantation owners controlled the public offices and all forms of credit. The tenant sharecropper and the independent small farmer could not survive without credit, and the will of the planter became virtual law.

Every small farmer had, in theory, the potential to become a planter. But neither planter nor small farmer was inclined to adopt the revolutionary agricultural techniques so effective in other parts of the nation. Wasteful depletion of the soil, which had already destroyed uncounted thousands of acres of tobacco land, was now allowed to play havoc with fertile cotton land too. The small farmer had a vested interest in preserving the fertility of the soil, but no rationalization could ever convince the slave that he had any such vested interest in his master's well-being.

The poorer the land became, the more intensively cultivation had to be practised. And this meant that the overseer had to drive the slaves to ever higher levels of productivity. In such an environment, increased abuse of the slave became inevitable. For a time, the opening of new lands, notably in Texas, preserved the whole system, but the South was already falling so far behind the North economically that the plantation system, retrospectively at any rate, appeared to be doomed to extinction in fairly short order. A few voices called for scientific farming methods, diversified crops, and establishment of local industry — but too few.

Mississippi River Plantation Scene; by John Banvard

Plantations

Just as manufacturing was the great investment for Northern venture capital, plantations were the Southern investment. To pay the interest and principal on loans meant somehow showing a profit. Costs had to be minimized, and even then a fluctuation in market prices could turn a profit into a loss. Since railroads were more costly than water transportation, every plantation was alongside a river down which the cotton could be shipped. By the 1840s the average plantation comprised 1,500 acres.

Houses on a tobacco plantation in Virginia; from a watercolor by George Harvey

View of the original mansion at Andrew Jackson's home, The Hermitage

Loading cotton on a steamboat in Mississippi

(Left) Patent drawing for cotton drying process

View of the New Orleans waterfront in 1839

The Other South

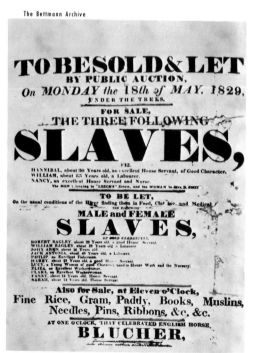

Despite the uniformity imposed by the undisputed sway of cotton, there were other factors operating in the South. Although immigration hardly touched the area, Louisiana had its old French culture, its Creole aristocracy, and its Catholicism to set it apart. New Orleans was the nation's most cosmopolitan city and most active slave market. Moreover, sugar cane was close to cotton in local importance. And Louisiana law, based on the Code Napoleon, had little in common with English law.

Rice was an important crop in lowland Georgia and the Carolinas. Tobacco was a major crop in North Carolina, Virginia, and other border states. And the urban centers, though nowhere as important economically as in the North, had their own lives, with a moderate number of skilled workers, although relatively few engaged in manufacturing. If a cotton gin broke down, parts had to be shipped from the North. Only border cities like Baltimore had substantial manufactures.

"Sale of Estates, Pictures and Slaves in the Rotunda, New Orleans," 1842
Library of Congress

Custom House in Charleston, South Carolina

The Charlestown Female Seminary

Rice fields in South Carolina

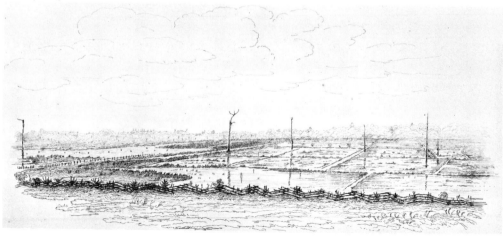

Southeast view of Greenville, S. C.; painting by Joshua Tucker

City Hall, Augusta, Ga.

Branch of the U.S. Bank, Savannah, Ga.

View of Baltimore, Md., from Federal Hill; aquatint by W. T. Bennet, 1831

(Left) "Safety coaches" on the Phoenix Line which ran between Washington and Baltimore in five hours

(Below) "Election Scene, Catonsville, Baltimore County" by Alfred J. Miller

Troops stationed at Tampa Bay on the Gulf of Mexico; Florida, 1837

The Seminoles in Florida

Florida had been acquired from Spain in 1819, but white settlement was fiercely resisted by the native Seminoles. The peninsula was garrisoned by Army troops throughout the 1830s, and clashes between Indians and whites in border areas of the South occurred regularly. The Second Seminole War broke out in 1835 and government troops undertook an active campaign to subdue the Indians. Osceola, a principal chief, was captured in 1837, but the war dragged on until 1842, when the Seminoles were transferred to Oklahoma.

(Right) "Osceola of Florida" by George Catlin, 1838; (below) Camp Volusia or Fort Barnwell on the St. John River, Florida, 1837

1834

12.

ANDREW JACKSON: The Autonomy of the Executive

On March 28, 1834, the Senate, by a vote of 26 to 20, passed a resolution censuring the President for assuming too much authority in the proceedings relating to the public revenue. On April 15, Jackson sent the following protest to the Senate. Jackson argued against the Whig contention that Congress, not the executive, had the final authority to prescribe the tenure, terms, and conditions of such offices as the secretary of the treasury. The Senate refused to enter the President's protest into the record; however, on January 16, 1837, the resolution of censure was rescinded.

Source: Richardson, III, pp. 69-93.

THE CUSTODY OF THE PUBLIC PROPERTY, under such regulations as may be prescribed by legislative authority, has always been considered an appropriate function of the Executive Department in this and all other governments. In accordance with this principle, every species of property belonging to the United States (excepting that which is in the use of the several coordinate departments of the government as means to aid them in performing their appropriate functions) is in charge of officers appointed by the President, whether it be lands, or buildings, or merchandise, or provisions, or clothing, or arms and munitions of war. The superintendents and keepers of the whole are appointed by the President, responsible to him, and removable at his will.

Public money is but a species of public property. It cannot be raised by taxation or customs, nor brought into the Treasury in any other way except by law; but whenever or howsoever obtained, its custody always has been and always must be, unless the Constitution be changed, entrusted to the Executive Department. No officer can be created by Congress for the purpose of taking charge of it whose appointment would not by the Constitution at once devolve on the President and who would not be responsible to him for the faithful performance of his duties. The legislative power may undoubtedly bind him and the President by any laws they may think proper to enact; they may prescribe in what place particular portions of the public property shall be kept and for what reason it shall be removed, as they may direct that supplies for the Army or Navy shall be kept in particular stores, and it will be the duty of the President to see that the law is faithfully executed; yet will the custody remain in the Executive Department of the government.

Were the Congress to assume, with or without a legislative act, the power of appointing officers, independently of the President, to take the charge and custody of the public property contained in the military and naval arsenals, magazines, and storehouses, it is believed that such an act would be regarded by all as a palpable usurpation of executive power, subversive of the form as well as the fundamental principles of our government. But where is the difference in principle whether the public property be in the form of arms, munitions of war, and supplies, or in gold and silver or banknotes? None can be perceived; none is believed to exist. Congress cannot, therefore, take out of the hands of the Executive Department the custody of the public property or money without an assumption of executive power and a subversion of the first principles of the Constitution.

The Congress of the United States have never passed an act imperatively directing that the public moneys shall be kept in any particular place or places. From the origin of the government to the year 1816, the statute book was wholly silent on the subject. In 1789, a treasurer was created, subordinate to the secretary of the treasury, and through him to the President. He was required to give bond safely to keep and faithfully to disburse the public moneys, without any direction as to the manner or places in which they should be kept. By reference to the practice of the government, it is found that from its first organization the secretary of the treasury, acting under the supervision of the President, designated the places in which the public moneys should

be kept, and especially directed all transfers from place to place.

This practice was continued, with the silent acquiescence of Congress, from 1789 down to 1816; and although many banks were selected and discharged, and although a portion of the moneys were first placed in the state banks, and then in the former Bank of the United States, and upon the dissolution of that were again transferred to the state banks, no legislation was thought necessary by Congress, and all the operations were originated and perfected by executive authority. The secretary of the treasury, responsible to the President, and with his approbation, made contracts and arrangements in relation to the whole subject matter, which was thus entirely committed to the direction of the President under his responsiblities to the American people and to those who were authorized to impeach and punish him for any breach of this important trust.

The act of 1816 establishing the Bank of the United States directed the deposits of public money to be made in that bank and its branches in places in which the said bank and branches thereof may be established, "unless the secretary of the treasury should otherwise order and direct," in which event he was required to give his reasons to Congress. This was but a continuation of his preexisting power as the head of an Executive Department to direct where the deposits should be made, with the superadded obligation of giving his reasons to Congress for making them elsewhere than in the Bank of the United States and its branches. It is not to be considered that this provision in any degree altered the relation between the secretary of the treasury and the President, as the responsible head of the Executive Department, or released the latter from his constitutional obligation to "take care that the laws be faithfully executed." On the contrary, it increased his responsibilities by adding another to the long list of laws which it was his duty to carry into effect.

It would be an extraordinary result if, because the person charged by law with a public duty is one of his secretaries, it were less the duty of the President to see that law faithfully executed than other laws enjoining duties upon subordinate officers or private citizens. If there be any difference, it would seem that the obligation is the stronger in relation to the former, because the neglect, is in his presence and the remedy at hand.

It cannot be doubted that it was the legal duty of the secretary of the treasury to order and direct the deposits of the public money to be made elsewhere than in the Bank of the United States *whenever sufficient reasons existed for making the change.* If in such a case he neglected or refused to act, he would neglect or refuse to execute the law. What would be the sworn duty of the President? Could he say that the Constitution did not bind him to see the law faithfully executed because it was one of his secretaries and not himself upon whom the service was specially imposed? Might he not be asked whether there was any such limitation to his obligations prescribed in the Constitution; whether he is not equally bound to take care that the laws be faithfully executed, whether they impose duties on the highest officer of state or the lowest subordinate in any of the departments?

Might he not be told that it was for the sole purpose of causing all executive officers, from the highest to the lowest, faithfully to perform the services required of them by law that the people of the United States have made him their chief magistrate and the Constitution has clothed him with the entire executive power of this government? The principles implied in these questions appear too plain to need elucidation.

But here also we have a contemporaneous construction of the act which shows that it was not understood as in any way changing the relations between the President and secretary of the treasury, or as placing the latter out of executive control even in relation to the deposits of the public money. Nor on that point are we left to any equivocal testimony. The documents of the Treasury Department show that the secretary of the treasury did apply to the President and obtained his approbation and sanction to the original transfer of the public deposits to the present Bank of the United States, and did carry the measure into effect in obedience to his decision.

They also show that transfers of the public deposits from the branches of the Bank of the United States to state banks at Chillicothe, Cincinnati, and Louisville, in 1819, were made with the approbation of the President and by his authority. They show that upon all important questions appertaining to his department, whether they related to the public deposits or other matters, it was the constant practice of the secretary of the treasury to obtain for his acts the approval and sanction of the President. These acts and the principles on which they were founded were known to all the departments of the government, to Congress and the country, and until very recently appear never to have been called in question.

Thus was it settled by the Constitution, the laws, and the whole practice of the government that the entire executive power is vested in the President of the United States; that as incident to that power the right of appointing and removing those officers who are to aid him in the execution of the laws, with such restrictions only as the Constitution prescribes, is vested in the President; that the secretary of the treasury is one of those officers; that the custody of the public property and money is an executive function which, in relation to the money, has always been exercised through the secretary of the treasury and his subordinates; that in the performance of these duties he is subject to the supervision and control of the President, and in all important measures having relation to them consults the chief magistrate and obtains his approval and sanction; that the law establishing the bank did not, as it could not, change the relation between the President and the secretary — did not release the former from his obligation to see the law faithfully executed nor the latter from the President's supervision and control; that afterward and before the secretary did in fact consult and obtain the sanction of the President to transfers and removals of the public deposits, and that all departments of the government, and the nation itself, approved or acquiesced in these acts and principles as in strict conformity with our Constitution and laws.

During the last year the approaching termination, according to the provisions of its charter and the solemn decision of the American people, of the Bank of the United States made it expedient, and its exposed abuses and corruptions made it, in my opinion, the duty of the secretary of the treasury to place the moneys of the United States in other depositories. The secretary did not concur in that opinion, and declined giving the necessary order and direction. So glaring were the abuses and corruptions of the bank, so evident its fixed purpose to persevere in them, and so palpable its design by its money and power to control the government and change its character, that I deemed it the imperative duty of the executive authority, by the exertion of every power confided to it by the Constitution and laws, to check its career and lessen its ability to do mischief, even in the painful alternative of dismissing the head of one of the departments. At the time the removal was made, other causes sufficient to justify it existed, but if they had not, the secretary would have been dismissed for this cause only.

His place I supplied by one whose opinions were well known to me, and whose frank expression of them in another situation and generous sacrifices of interest and feeling when unexpectedly called to the station he now occupies ought forever to have shielded his motives from suspicion and his character from reproach. In accordance with the views long before expressed by him, he proceeded, with my sanction, to make arrangements for depositing the moneys of the United States in other safe institutions.

The resolution of the Senate as originally framed and as passed, if it refers to these acts, presupposes a right in that body to interfere with this exercise of executive power. If the principle be once admitted, it is not difficult to perceive where it may end. If by a mere denunciation like this resolution the President should ever be induced to act in a matter of official duty contrary to the honest convictions of his own mind in compliance with the wishes of the Senate, the constitutional independence of the Executive Department would be as effectually destroyed and its power as effectually transferred to the Senate as if that end had been accomplished by an amendment of the Constitution. But if the Senate have a right to interfere with the executive powers, they have also the right to make that interference effective; and if the assertion of the power implied in the resolution be silently acquiesced in, we may reasonably apprehend that it will be followed at some future day by an attempt at actual enforcement. The Senate may refuse, except on the condition that he will surrender his opinions to theirs and obey their will, to perform their own constitutional functions, to pass the necessary laws, to sanction appropriations proposed by the House of Representatives, and to confirm proper nominations made by the President.

It has already been maintained (and it is not conceivable that the resolution of the Senate can be based on any other principle) that the secretary of the treasury is the officer of Congress and independent of the President; that the President has no right to control him, and consequently none to remove him. With the same propriety and on similar grounds may the secretary of state, the secretaries of war and the navy, and the postmaster general, each in succession, be declared independent of the President, the subordinates of Congress, and removable only with the concurrence of the Senate. Followed to its consequences, this principle will be found effectually to destroy one coordinate department of the government, to concentrate in the hands of the Senate the whole executive power, and to leave the President as powerless as he would be useless — the shadow of authority after the substance had departed.

The time and the occasion which have called forth the resolution of the Senate seem to impose upon me an additional obligation not to pass it over in silence. Nearly forty-five years had the President exercised, without a question as to his rightful authority, those powers for the recent assumption of which he is now denounced. The vicissitudes of peace and war had attended our government; violent parties, watchful to take advantage of any seeming usurpation on the part of the executive, had distracted our councils; frequent removals, or forced resignations in every sense tantamount to removals, had been made of the secretary and other officers of the treasury; and yet in no one instance is it known that any man, whether patriot or partisan, had raised his voice against it as a violation of the Constitution. The expediency and justice of such changes in reference to public officers of all grades have frequently been the topic of discussion, but the constitutional right of the President to appoint, control, and remove the head of the Treasury as well as all other departments seems to have been universally conceded.

And what is the occasion upon which other principles have been first officially asserted? The Bank of the United States, a great moneyed monopoly, had attempted to obtain a renewal of its charter by controlling the elections of the people and the action of the government. The use of its corporate funds and power in that attempt was fully disclosed, and it was made known to the President that the corporation was putting in train the same course of measures, with the view of making another vigorous effort, through an interference in the elections of the people, to control public opinion and force the government to yield to its demands. This, with its corruption of the press, its violation of its charter, its exclusion of the government directors from its proceedings, its neglect of duty and arrogant pretensions, made it, in the opinion of the President, incompatible with the public interest and the safety of our institutions that it should be longer employed as the fiscal agent of the Treasury.

A secretary of the treasury appointed in the recess of the Senate, who had not been confirmed by that body, and whom the President might or might not at his pleasure nominate to them, refused to do what his superior in the Executive Department considered the most imperative of his duties, and became, in fact, however innocent his motives, the protector of the bank. And on this occasion it is discovered for the first time that those who framed the Constitution misunderstood it; that the First Congress and all its successors have been under a delusion; that the practice of near forty-five years is but a continued usurpation; that the secretary of the treasury is not responsible to the President, and that to remove him is a violation of the Constitution and laws for which the President deserves to stand forever dishonored on the journals of the Senate.

13.

JAMES MADISON: On Presidential Appointments and the Balance of Powers

Many of the political conflicts of the Jacksonian Era involved opposed interpretations of the constitutional doctrine of the balance of governmental power. Some issues — for example, that of the propriety of the Bank of the United States, that of the executive veto power, and that of the power of the executive to remove appointees from office and to control diplomatic and consular personnel — produced struggles between the Executive and Legislative branches of government. On other issues — for example, the right of a state to nullify a congressional act, and the right to legislate a tariff — the federal and state governments clashed. The following dispassionate analysis of these conflicts was addressed by James Madison to Edward Coles on October 15, 1834. Madison, a principal architect of the Constitution and now eighty-three, still favored a strong executive despite his dislike of Jackson.

Source: *Madison Letters*, IV, pp. 366-371.

I HAVE RECEIVED, MY DEAR SIR, your letter of the 15th ultimo. I did not anticipate a complaint that mine was not full enough, being an effort which, in my present condition, I had rarely made. It was not my object to offer either a *plenary* or a *public* review of the agitated topics, but to satisfy a friend that I ought not, in my eighty-fourth year, and with a constitution crippled by disease, to put myself forward on the implied ground that my opinions were to have an effect which I ought not to presume, and which I was well persuaded they would not have. If I did not extend my remarks to every obnoxious doctrine or measure of the executive, I was under no apprehension of an inference from my silence that I approved them; and there was the less occasion to guard against the inference, as I had, with respect to the omitted cases, freely expressed my views of them in our private conversations.

Notwithstanding your cogent observations on the comparative dangers from the popularity and example of General Jackson, and from the doctrines and example of South Carolina, I must adhere to the opinion that the former are daily losing, and the latter gaining ground; for the proof of which, I renew my appeal to the facts of daily occurrence. And if the declension of his popular influence be such during his official life, and with the *peculiar* hold he has on party feelings, there is little reason to suppose that any succeeding President will attempt a like career. That a series of them should do so with the support of the people is a *possibility* opposed to a moral *certainty*.

May I not appeal, also, to facts which will satisfy yourself of the error which supposes that a respect for my opinion, even naked opinion, would control the adverse opinions of others? On the subject of the bank, on that of the tariff, and on that of nullification, three great constitutional questions of the day, my opinions, with the grounds of them, are well known, being in print with my name to them. Yet the bank was, perhaps, never more warmly opposed than at present; the tariff seems to have lost none of its unpopularity; while nullification has been for some time, and is at present, notoriously advancing, with some of my best personal, and heretofore political, friends among its advocates.

It must not be thought that I am displeased or disappointed at this result. On the contrary, I honor the independent judgment that decides for itself; and I know well that a spirit of party is not less unyielding.

You observe that the absorbing question of executive misrule has diverted attention from nullification. This may be true, and it is a reason for not mitigating the danger from it; for it is equally observable, that while nullification is, on one hand, taking advantage of the diverted attention, it is, on the other, propagating itself under the name of state rights, by diminishing the importance of questions between the executive and other departments of the federal government, compared with questions between the federal and state governments, and by inculcating the necessity of nullification as the only safeguard to the latter against the former. In a late speech of the reputed author of the heresy, which has been lauded as worthy of letters of gold, this view of the subject is presented in the form most likely to make converts of the state rights opponents of the tariff and other unpopular measures of the federal policy.

Your reasoning, ingenious as it is, has not disproved the fairness of the distinction between a claim to the custody of the public money and a claim to the absolute use or appropriation of it. In inferring abuses of power from particular instances, it is always proper to keep within the range of a certain degree of probability. The distinction in this case is so palpable, and so important that the inference from a claim to the custody, however unsound, to a claim of appropriation, is not only disavowed by the partisans of the former, who are, probably, not numerous, but the distinction is triumphantly urged against their adversaries, who disregard it, as a proof of their disingenuous and fallacious purposes.

You are at a loss for the innovating doctrines of the Senate to which I alluded. Permit me to specify the following:

The claim, on *constitutional* ground, to a share in the removal as well as appointment of officers, is in direct opposition to the uniform practice of the government from its commencement. It is clear that the innovation would not only vary, essentially, the existing balance of power, but expose the executive, occasionally, to a total inaction, and at all times to delays fatal to the due execution of the laws.

Another innovation brought forward in the Senate claims for the legislature a discretionary regulation of the tenure of offices. This, also, would vary the relation of the departments to each other, and leave a wide field for legislative abuses. The power of removal, like that of appointment, ought to be *fixed* by the Constitution, and both, like the right of suffrage and apportionment of representatives, to be not dependent on the legislative will. In republican governments the organization of the Executive Department will always be found the most difficult and delicate, particularly in regard to the appointment and, most of all, to the removal of officers. It may well deserve consideration how far the present modification of these powers can be *constitutionally* improved.

But apart from the distracting and dilatory operation of a veto in the Senate on the removal from office, it is pretty certain that the large states would not invest with that additional prerogative a body constructed like the Senate, and endowed, as it already is, with a share in all the departments of power, Legislative, Executive, and Judiciary. It is well known that the large states, in both the federal and state conventions, regarded the aggregate powers of the Senate as the most objectionable feature in the Constitution.

Another novelty of great practical importance is the alleged limitation of the qualified veto of the President to constitutional objections. That it extends to cases of inexpediency also, and was so understood and so vindicated (see *The Federalist*) cannot be doubted. My veto to the bank was *expressly* to the *inexpediency* of its plan, and the validity of the veto was never questioned. As a shield to the Executive Department against legislative encroachments, and a general barrier to the Constitution against them, it was doubtless expected to be a valuable provision.

But a primary object of the prerogative most assuredly was that of a check to the instability in legislation, which had been found the besetting infirmity of popular governments, and been sufficiently exemplified among ourselves in the legislatures of the states; and I leave yourself to decide how far, in a reversal of the case, an application of the veto to a defense of the bank against a legislative hostility to it would have been welcomed by those who now denounce it as a usurpation. It should be kept in mind that each of the departments has been alternately in and out of favor, and that changes in the organization of them hastily made, particularly in accordance with the vicissitudes of party ascendancy, would produce a constitutional instability worse than a legislative one.

Another innovation of great practical importance espoused by the Senate relates to the power of the executive to make diplomatic and consular appointments in the recess of the Senate. Hitherto it has been the practice to make such appointments to places calling for them, whether the places had or had not before received them. Under no administration was the distinction more disregarded than under that of Mr. Jefferson, particularly in consular appointments, which rest on the same text of the Constitution with that of public ministers. It is now assumed that the appointments can only be made for occurring vacancies; that is, places which had been previously filled.

The error lies in confounding foreign missions under the law of nations with municipal officers under the local law. If they were officers in the *constitutional* sense, a legislative creation of them being expressly required, they could not be created by the President and Senate. If, indeed, it could be admitted that as offices they would *ipso facto* be created by the appointment from the President and Senate, the office would expire with the appointment, and the next appointment would create a new office, not fill a vacant one. By regarding those missions, not as offices but as stations or agencies, always existing under the law of nations for governments agreeing, the one to send the other to receive the proper functionaries, the case, though not perhaps altogether free from difficulty, is better provided for than by any other construction. The doctrine of the Senate would be as injurious in practice as it is unfounded in authority.

It might and probably would be of infinitely greater importance to send a public minister where one had never been sent than where there had been a previous mission. If regarded as offices, it follows, moreover, that the President would be bound, as in case of other offices, to keep them always filled, whether the occasion required it or not; the opposite extreme of not being permitted to provide for the occasion, however urgent.

The new doctrine involves a difficulty also in providing for treaties, even treaties of peace, on favorable emergencies, the functionaries not being officers in a constitutional sense, nor perhaps ministers to any foreign government. An attempt was, I believe, made by a distinguished individual to derive a power in the President to provide for the case of terminating a war, from his military power to establish a truce. This would have opened a wider door for construction than has yet been contended for.

I might add the claim for the Senate of a right to be consulted by the President, and to give their advice previous to his foreign negotiations; a course of proceeding which I believe was condemned by the result of a direct or analogous experiment, and which it was presumed would not again be revived. That the secrecy generally essential in such negotiations would be safe in a numerous body, however individually worthy of the usual confidence, would be little short of a miracle.

If you call for proofs of the reality of these claims, by or in behalf of the Senate, I may refer to their equal notoriety with facts on which you rely, and to a greater authenticity than those which you state on hearsay only.

I have thrown together these remarks, as suggested by the one-sided view you have taken of subjects which ought to be viewed on both sides, whatever be the decision on them. It is not improbable that a free and full conversation would bring us much nearer together on the most important points than might be inferred from our correspondence on paper. When or whether at all such a conversation can take place will depend on the movements on your part and contingencies on mine.

In the meantime I beg you to regard the present desultory communication in the same confidential light with the former, and to be assured of my constant affection, and my best wishes for the happy life of which you have so flattering a prospect.

14.

A Petition Against Usury Laws

The desire to take advantage of the demand for financing in a vigorous economy suffering from a shortage of capital prompted more than 200 citizens of Boston to sign the following petition urging revision of the laws restricting interest rates to 6 percent. It was submitted to the Massachusetts state senate on March 4, 1834. Although the committee reviewing the petition was reluctant to make a drastic change, it did recommend repeal of the laws regulating promissory notes and bills of exchange scheduled to be paid within specific dates. The recommendation was enacted into law before the year was up.

Source: *Documents Printed by Order of the Senate of the Commonwealth of Massachusetts, During the Session of the General Court, A.D. 1834,* Boston, 1834, Senate Document No. 66.

THE UNDERSIGNED CITIZENS OF BOSTON, having long experienced the inconveniences arising from the existing usury laws of Massachusetts and being persuaded that the honorable legislature will, whenever the subject is properly brought before them, provide an adequate remedy for the evils complained of, have deemed it suitable and proper to appear as petitioners before that honorable body, setting forth in their petition the inconveniences to which the present laws give rise and praying such a modification of those laws as will in their opinion remove the evil.

We, your petitioners, would therefore respectfully represent that, in our judgment, the existing usury laws, so far as they limit the rate of interest, are founded on erroneous principles and are at variance with the commercial spirit of the age. We think that every article of human traffic, whether money or any other thing, is alike subject to fluctuations of value, and that consequently the market price of them all is constantly liable to change. We think that the price of money, or more properly speaking, the price of its use, not less than the price of lumber, corn, tobacco, cotton, or any other great commercial staple, is and must be regulated by the extent of the demand in the market, and that every attempt to fix the value and render the price of either of these articles invariable is not only vain but wholly unjust; and that it is, in the case of all these commodities, an equal infringement of private rights.

We are of opinion that 6 percent per annum is not the highest value to which money rises in the course of business, any more than it is the limit of profits made by traffic in any other commodity. But, on the contrary, that whenever the use of money, in the regular course of business, produces a large amount of profit, the value of that use is proportionately increased; and that, at such times and at all others when money is scarce and the demand for it great, as well as in cases where the risk of lending is very much increased, the real value of monied capital is, and the market price ought to be, vastly more than 6 percent, being always in the exact compound proportion of the demand and risk.

We think that the law is wrong in imposing any restraint upon the absolute freedom of commercial transactions, which, in order to be successful, must be left unfettered. In the case of money, which represents every other commodity, the evil is far greater than it could be in the case of any other article of traffic. We know that in former ages, when the laws, by a mistaken policy, forbade the receiving of any interest, condemning it as morally wrong, commerce and the arts were almost completely destroyed; and

that as the opinion of mankind changed on this subject, and the laws became more liberal, commerce revived and extended its transactions, and scattered wider and wider its blessings. And we are firmly persuaded that neither this nor any other department of human industry will attain its perfection until men of business are as unrestrained in buying and selling the media of exchange as in buying and selling any other merchandise whatsoever.

We are also of opinion that while the present restrictions were intended to favor the interests of borrowers, they are even more injurious to borrowers than to lenders. But before demonstrating this proposition we beg leave respectfully to express our convictions that any attempt of the law to favor one particular class of citizens to the injury of any other class is unjust, unconstitutional, and contrary to the spirit of freedom and equal rights; and although in this case the attempt is wholly unsuccessful, yet we cannot regard it, on that account, as less contrary to sound principles; and, both as borrowers and as lenders, we are equally hostile to the laws which sustain the attempt.

We will now endeavor to show that, in their practical effect, these laws are injurious to borrowers of money. Whenever the demand for money is such in the market as to render it worth more than the established rate of interest, the borrower, however pressing his want, however strong his necessity, cannot raise the requisite loan; for the money owner is not compelled to part with his money at less than its worth; and he will not be so foolish as to lend when he can find more profitable modes of investment. And the borrower, although willing to pay any premium for relief, must suffer all the pressure of his emergency without the possibility of obtaining assistance. Cases of this sort we have all experienced and observed very frequently; and we know them to form the most serious obstructions to successful enterprise.

So also we are aware that many instances occur in which the personal character of the borrower is such as to render the owner of money reluctant to venture on his credit at the usual rate; while, did the law allow, the applicant would be glad to pay a premium proportioned to the risk. In this manner, borrowers experience a compound evil, being unable to pay for the desired article according to its market value or their own necessities; and many a man is ruined who, if he could have been allowed to offer 7 or 8 or more percent, would have realized a fortune. Can any reason be assigned why the privilege of charging interest proportioned to the risk, allowed on bottomry loans, should not be extended to every other species of loan?

The inconvenience experienced by money lenders under the laws, though great, is yet less than that felt by borrowers, although these laws were intended for the borrowers' advantage; for, if the holders of money cannot lend at an interest equivalent to the value of the capital, they can invest that capital in those more profitable modes of traffic which create the money demand. Thus, to them, only one avenue of business is closed, while, to the borrower, every resource is cut off. But it is certainly worthy of legislative attention that, even in a single particular, the process of business is impeded; and legislators, as such, in our opinion, are to be held responsible for the losses that the community may suffer in the person of its citizens from this impediment.

The law is manifestly wrong in supposing that, if left unrestricted, moneylenders would acquire an overgrown influence and exercise an oppressive power. Nothing of this sort can be reasonably feared while we have such a host of banks and other monied corporations in addition to individual lenders, all in the market, and all engaged in active competition. No inconvenience of this kind is ever complained of in the case of bottomry loans, where the lenders are not restricted by any statute. No evil is found to exist in the matter of insurance premiums, where the risk is uniformly the measure of the rate. Competition, as much in the pecuniary facilities required by businessmen, as in the facilities of travel by land and sea, determines the price of those facilities. And is there not as much probability that the public will be burdened with exorbitant stage and steamboat fares, as with extortionous charges for the use of money?

We are firm in the opinion that all money transactions should be regulated, like those in other articles of trade, only by this spirit of competition; and that no greater evils would or could, in the present age, arise from the traffic in money being thus unrestricted than are now felt from the perfect freedom allowed to traffic in other commodities. And it passes our understanding to see why that, whether money or goods, which is made the instrument of profit to him who uses it, should not in all cases be sold at its real value.

The evils that grow out of our laws are enhanced by the fact that the rate of interest in a neighboring state is 1 percent per annum higher than in Massachusetts. In consequence of this difference, by which a constant drain is produced from our market, a vast amount of capital which, if they were fettered by no law, would remain in circulation among our fellow citizens, is drawn into the New York market and totally lost to our borrowers, whose embarrassments are thereby increased. This evil is constantly and severely felt. But at particular times, as in the present pressure on the money market, its burden is especially heavy and causes the greatest distress, particularly to those who are least able to sustain it, viz., young businessmen whose capital is small and of whom credit is the support. Were the present laws repealed, our own capital would remain in our own use, and the capital of the neighboring states would flow in upon us in such a manner that our business would be greatly extended and increased.

We would respectfully direct the attention of the legislature to the numerous modes that have been devised for evading the laws; modes of transacting business which, besides being circuitous and inconvenient, and besides taking away the sanction and protection of the law from those who engage in them, leaving no security but what is termed honor, thus increasing the risk, and of course the premium paid — besides these evils, which are loss of time, money, comfort, and security — produce a fearful disregard of the laws, and establish a precedent of the utmost danger, while they tend to throw pecuniary negotiations in the hands of unprincipled and dangerous men. We need not specify the various methods by which the law is now evaded, and by which interest above 6 percent is taken, in defiance of law, under the various names of "premium," "exchange," and "commission"; for these are matters of notoriety and need only be alluded to in order to secure the attention of the legislature. So long as our laws remain unchanged, it is vain to hope for a better state of things.

Such being the opinion of your petitioners, they respectfully pray that the usury laws may be so modified as to leave the rate of interest, like the rate of premiums on insurances, perfectly open to contract; providing, however, that in all cases where interest accrues, and the particular rate has not been expressly agreed upon between the parties, the present shall remain the legal rate.

15.

FREDERICK ROBINSON: Labor as the Source of Reform

The members of the Boston Trades' Union who gathered to listen to Frederick Robinson on July 4, 1834, knew that as of that day imprisonment for debt was abolished in Massachusetts and that the important reform was owing largely to the efforts of their speaker. With the support of the union, Robinson had been elected to the Massachusetts state legislature and was later to lead the state's Democratic Party. Like other Jacksonians, Robinson was concerned about the ever-widening economic gap between the "producing" and the "nonproducing" classes, and in the address which appears here, discoursed on the role of unions in reversing the trend.

Source: *An Oration Delivered Before the Trades Union of Boston, etc., etc.,* Boston, 1834.

EQUALITY COMPRISES EVERYTHING that is good; inequality everything that is evil. Equality is liberty. Liberty without equality is dead. It is a word without meaning, mere "sounding brass, and a tinkling cymbal." Equality is democracy. Everyone who truly loves the human race will favor such governments, constitutions, laws, and administrations as he believes to be productive of equality. Equality will be the test, the measure of every question, on which he is to act. In all his intercourse with his fellowmen, in all his dealings, it will be his governing principle — to do unto others as he would that others should do unto him.

This is the rock on which democracy is

founded. The man that indulges himself in ostentation; that feels the pride of wealth or of birth; that plumes himself on his talents, learning, or professional skill, and looks down with contempt on what he calls the ignorant and the vulgar; that feels himself better than the laborer, the mechanic, or the fisherman, and is not free to take him by the hand and treat him as a brother — whatever he may call himself, he is not a democrat. For the spirit of democracy, which is equality, teaches us that the laborer, the producer, and not the talented, the rich, and the learned, are the benefactors of mankind. It is the laborer that provides us with food and clothing, that builds our houses, ships, and factories, digs the canals, levels the railroads, and procures for us all the necessaries, conveniences, and luxuries of life. . . .

In the savage state, each individual produces for himself whatever he consumes, and of course no union with others is required to protect his labor. But in a state of society where no one labors for his own consumption alone, but each receives the labor of others in exchange for his own, the price of labor in each division of labor, to prevent fraud, ought to be fixed by agreement among the laborers themselves. The right of the producer to fix the price of his own labor is unquestionable, for its denial admits the right of slavery.

But every effort which the producing classes have ever made for the enjoyment of this most obvious right has always met with the most determined opposition of the aristocracy. Wherever they have held all political power, laws have been enacted inflicting fines, imprisonment, and transportation on those that attempt by unions among themselves to fix the price of their labor. Where they have not all political power, they have recourse to everything within their reach, to every argument, to every quibble, every sophistry in order to flatter the people to relinquish or drive them to renounce this right. Those that have not the unblushing

confidence to deny this right altogether contend that it is an individual and not a social right; for although each individual may fix the price of his own labor, yet no two or more individuals have a right to agree among themselves to fix the price. But when men enter into a state of society, all those rights which it is impossible to enjoy without the aid of others, become social rights, and must be enjoyed if at all, by concert with others.

It is unreasonable to suppose that we are possessed of rights which we have not the power to enjoy. But if we have not the social right to fix the price of our own labor, it is perfectly useless to allow us the right at all; for how can an unaided individual without wealth, without education, ignorant of the world, and even of the value of his own labor, who must command immediate employment or starve, enjoy this right as an individual right? If he enjoy it at all, the interests of others engaged in the same or other employments must secure it to him. No law has ever been enacted in this country in relation to this subject; but the aristocracy have notwithstanding attempted to frighten the people with the semblance of law.

The judiciary in this state, and in every state where judges hold their office during life, is the headquarters of the aristocracy; and every plan to humble and subdue the people originates there. One of the most enormous usurpations of the judiciary is the claim and possession of common law jurisdiction. Common law, although contained in 10,000 different books, is said to be unwritten law, deposited only in the head of the judge, so that whatever he says is common law, *must be* common law, and it is impossible to know, before the judge decides, what the law is. But still, in order to justify the judge in all iniquitous decisions, they have recourse to precedents or previous decisions. And however unjust and wicked any decision may be, if a previous decision of the same kind can be found, either in ancient or modern times, in Great Britain or in any of the states in this Union, the judge justifies himself before the public and escapes with impunity. . . .

One of the judges in this city, not long since, charged the grand jury to indict the workingmen who attempt, by unions, to fix the price or regulate the hours of labor; although this judge, and indeed all the judges, are members of a secret trades union of lawyers, called the bar, that has always regulated the price of their own labor, and by the strictest concert contrived to limit competition by denying to everyone the right of working in their trade who will not in every respect comply with the rules of the bar.

All prices fixed by bar rules are in the *minimum*, allowing no one to take less than a fixed sum for each service; but everyone may take as much more as he can. What, then, ought we to think of the man who, being a member of the secret trades union of the bar, calls upon the jury to indict the members of the open trades union of the people, who join not for the purpose of injuring others but for the enjoyment of their most inestimable right; to be deprived of which, must always keep them in want, ignorance, and slavery? Does it not become us, fellow citizens, when we see the enemies of the equal rights of man everywhere combined to maintain their ascendency, to unite and employ our power of numbers against the power of their wealth and learning for the recovery and protection of our rights?

Who are they who complain of trades unions? Are they not those whose combinations cover the land, and who have even contrived to invest some of their combinations with the sanctity of law? Are they not those who are the owners of all kinds of monopolies, who pass their lives in perpetual caucuses, on [the] Exchange, in halls connected with banks, composing insurance companies, manufacturing companies, turnpike, bridge, canal, railroad, and all other legalized combinations? Do not each of the learned professions constitute unions among themselves to control their own business? And have they not fortified their unions by alliance with each other and with the rich, and thus established a proud, haughty, overbearing, fourfold aristocracy in our country?

Well may the capitalists, monopolists, judges, lawyers, doctors, and priests complain of trades unions. They know that the secret of their own power and wealth consists in the strictest concert of action — and they know that when the great mass of the people become equally wise with themselves, and unite their power of numbers for the possession and enjoyment of equal rights, they will be shorn of their consequence, be jumbled of their pride, and brought to personal labor for their own subsistence. They know from experience that unions among themselves have always enabled the few to rule and ride the people; and that, when the people shall discover the secret of their power, and learn to use it for their own good, the scepter will fall from their hands, and they themselves will become merged in the great "vulgar" mass of the people. . . .

It is for the interest of this trades union of lawyers to have the laws as unintelligible as possible, since no one would pay them for advice concerning laws which he himself could understand. . . .

But the evil of the secret trades union of the bar does not stop here. When the legislature assembles, every senator and every representative of the bar is prepared. They are all acquainted with each other; they feel that it is for their interest to act in concert. United efforts are always made by this fraternity to choose the president of the Senate and the speaker of the House of Representatives from the bar. This effected, the whole business of legislation is completely in their hands. The president of the Senate and the speaker of the House have the appointing of all committees, and, being lawyers, they are always careful to put a majority of their brethren on every committee which has anything to do with the laws; and in this way laws are drafted, introduced, and *talked through* the legislature by members of the bar. While the people submit to these abuses, it is easy to account for the continued existence of the dark and intricate labyrinth of our laws.

Of all the reforms which we have pledged ourselves to accomplish, the reform of the judiciary, and of the laws, is the most important. Let us then go about the work, with never ceasing efforts, until the great mass of our fellow laborers, who always constitute an overwhelming majority, shall see the necessity of a thorough law reform. In the first place, judges should be made responsible to the people by periodical elections. The boast of an independent judiciary is always made to deceive you. We want no part of our government independent of the people. Those, who are responsible to nobody, ought to be entrusted by nobody.

But to whom are the judges responsible? The aristocracy always center around power placed beyond the reach of the people; and until we can fill the bench with men of learning, good sense, and sound judgment, who do not belong to the secret fraternity of the bar, all attempts to simplify the laws, and the practice of the law, will be in vain. For why need we attempt to legislate, while the judges hold legislative power and can nullify our laws at their pleasure?

Of all the contrivances of the aristocracy, next to the usurpation of the judiciary, and thus turning the most potent engine of the people's government against themselves, their unions in the shape of incorporate monopolies are the most subtile and the best calculated to promote the ends of the few, the ignorance, degradation, and slavery of the many. This Hydra of the adversary has, within a few years, grown up around us, until the monster covers the whole land, branching out annually into new heads of different shape, each devouring the substance and destroying the rights of the people. But the most potent and deadly is the bank — a monopoly which takes everything from the people and gives them nothing in return.

The whole value of paper money consists in the consent of the people to give it currency, and all the advantages of such a currency of right should accrue to the people. A bank monopoly consists in the exclusive power of issuing notes of hand without interest and receiving the notes of hand of others bearing interest with good security. And whatever notes of hand the banks may issue, more than the gold and silver which they have to redeem them, is an absolute cheat upon society, as much so as it would be to forge the same notes. . . .

No people . . . can ever be safe in confiding legislative power to those whose interests are different from their own; for the motives of duty are inferior to those of interest. There may be exceptions to this rule, but they are only exceptions. When duty and interest agree in our public servants, we can rest assured of their fidelity; but when the performance of their duty to us runs counter to their own interests, we ought not to be astonished to find ourselves betrayed. . . .

Wherever anything is produced in greater abundance than is wanted for immediate consumption, its value will depreciate below the costs of its production. The least surplus injures the producer, and excessive abundance is his destruction. But when the market is but scantily supplied, the producer receives a more adequate return for his labor, and the nonproducer is obliged to part with a larger portion of his funds to command the necessaries, conveniences, and luxuries of life.

In such times, things tend to equality; but in times of great abundance, the competition of laborers reduces their produce often below the means of supporting life; and the nonproducing part of society speculate upon it, hoard the surplus in storehouses, and thus control the market and become rich at the expense of the laborer. While the one is rolling in wealth and living in luxury and splendor, the real producer of his wealth is reduced to the most deplorable poverty, wretchedness, and want. It becomes us, then, to learn the law that governs our productions, and to live in such accordance therewith as to secure our own happiness, and avoid the evils which the violation of this law has inflicted upon the great majority of the human race, in all nations, and in every age; for, while the productive classes remain ignorant of this principle, the law of individual competition will prevail; and everyone, supposing that the more he produces the more he will receive in return for his produce, is stimulated on, until the market is full.

Prices now begin to fall; he is obliged to labor harder in order to supply his accustomed enjoyments; and thus the market is still farther overstocked, and the prices still more reduced, until his greatest exertions fail to supply him with the necessaries of life. What misery now stares him in the face. He sees his wife and little ones famishing for bread, which again stimulates him to still greater exertion. But like the man in the morass, every effort to extricate himself sinks him deeper and deeper into the mire, until his continued and excessive productions have entirely glutted the market, and he has completely worked himself out of employment, like Tantalus up to his chin in water, perishing with thirst — in the midst of excessive abundance, he is dying with hunger. He sees his children, one after another, sicken and die around him for want of nourishment, his body is worn with labor and weakened by abstinence, and his mind distracted with his numerous troubles, until at last he sinks under the weight of his accumulated misery. In this way alone the market relieves itself, by working the destruction of the producer. . . .

How important then are trades unions, not for the purpose of controlling the price of labor while the market is glutted, for this is impossible. The nonproducer laughs at your every effort, while his storehouses are bursting with the fruit of your labor; but how important for the purpose of seeing that no more is produced, than barely enough to supply the demand. It should be the first object of the members of every productive employment to ascertain the actual daily and yearly consumption of the articles of their produce, and to regulate their hours of labor in such accordance therewith as nearly as possible to supply the demand. When the market is not oversupplied, the producer has the power of setting any reasonable price on his own labor. But it is impossible for trades unions, or any other power, to keep up prices when the market is glutted; for, in such case, the producer loses his natural and rightful control over the price of his own labor, and the nonproducer fixes the price. . . .

It would be easy, fellow citizens, to suggest to you improvements for the relief of the wretched, the instruction of the ignorant, the reform of the vicious, the exaltation of the humble, and the humiliation of the proud, until the shades of night envelop the hemisphere. For what have we yet done in these respects since our fathers wrought out for us political independence and equality of privileges, and put into our hands the power of perfecting our government and securing our happiness? The millions have been lulled into a fatal security, while the thousands have been active in promoting their own interests. Yet we have still reason to rejoice that, while we have been sleeping on our post, the enemy have not yet completely subdued us; that, although we have been inactive, while they have been busy in dividing our ranks, bribing our officers, and filling their army with the venal and profligate; that, while we have been at ease within the walls of the citadels erected for our safety by the toil of our fathers, they have been silently sapping the foundations, preparing their engines, building their arsenals, rearing their fortifications, digesting their plans, and providing their great financial institutions for the payment of their troops and the corrupting of our sentinels.

Yet, we have reason to rejoice that our weapons are still in our hands; that the ballot box, the wooden scepter of the sovereignty of the people, has not yet been wrested from our possession; that our citadels are yet in our own keeping, although the enemy have found means to send in their ass loads of gold. And, if we gird on our armor, heal the divisions in our own ranks, expel the corrupt and the disaffected, we can easily regain the vantage ground; and, on the day of battle, sally forth, destroying their engines, leveling their fortifications, breaking up their strongholds, scattering their forces, demolishing their monopolies, and triumphantly restore the liberties of the people into their own hands.

16.

William Leggett: The Struggle for Power Between the Many and the Few

William Leggett became an assistant to William Cullen Bryant, the publisher and editor of the New York Evening Post, *in 1829, and over the years wrote a series of editorials on the general principles of government. Leggett, like many Jacksonians, believed that in America the struggle between the laboring masses and the privileged few was more or less perpetual, and that to secure their interests, the privileged few would try to monopolize the advantages of the central government and expand the realm of its activity. To restrain the privileged few, the activity of the central government must be restrained — as the Constitution intended it should be. The following editorial against the National Bank, which appeared in the* Post *for November 4, 1834, is an example of his view.*

Source: *A Collection of the Political Writings of William Leggett,* Theodore Sedgwick, Jr., ed., New York, 1840, Vol. I, pp. 64-68.

Since the organization of the government of the United States, the people of this country have been divided into two great parties. One of these parties has undergone various changes of name; the other has continued steadfast, alike to its appellation and to its principles, and is now, as it was at first, the *democracy.* Both parties have ever contended for the same opposite ends which originally caused the division — whatever may have been, at different times, the particular means which furnished the immediate subject of dispute. The great object of the struggles of the democracy has been to confine the action of the general government within the limits marked out in the Constitution; the great object of the party opposed to the democracy has ever been to overleap those boundaries and give to the general government greater powers and a wider field for their exercise. The doctrine of the one party is that all power not expressly and clearly delegated to the general government remains with the states and with the people; the doctrine of the other party is that the vigor and efficacy of the general government should be strengthened by a free construction of its powers. The one party sees danger from the encroachments of the general government; the other affects to see danger from the encroachments of the states.

This original line of separation between the two great political parties of the republic, though it existed under the old Confederation, and was distinctly marked in the controversy which preceded the formation and adoption of the present Constitution, was greatly widened and strengthened by the project of a national bank, brought forward in 1791. This was the first great question which occurred under the new Constitution to test whether the provisions of that instrument were to be interpreted according to their strict and literal meaning; or whether they might be stretched to include objects and powers which had never been delegated to the general government, and which, consequently, still resided with the states as separate sovereignties.

The proposition of the bank was recommended by the secretary of the treasury on the ground that such an institution would be "of primary importance to the prosperous administration of the finances, and of the greatest utility in the operations connected with the support of public credit." This scheme, then as now, was opposed on various grounds; but the constitutional objection constituted then, as it does at the present day, the main reason of the uncompromising and invincible hostility of the democracy to the measure. They considered it as the exercise of a very important power which had never been given by the states or the people to the general government, and which the general government could not therefore exercise without being guilty of usurpation.

Those who contended that the government possessed the power, effected their immediate object; but the controversy still exists. And it is of no consequence to tell the democracy that it is now established by various precedents, and by decisions of the Supreme Court, that this power is fairly incidental to certain other powers expressly granted, for this is only telling them that the advocates of free construction have, at times, had the ascendancy in the Executive and Legislative, and, at all times, in the Judiciary Department of the government.

The bank question stands now on precisely the same footing that it originally did; it is now, as it was at first, a matter of controversy between the two great parties of this country — between parties as opposite as day and night — between parties which contend, one for the consolidation and enlargement of the powers of the general government, and the other for strictly limiting that government to the objects for which it was instituted, and to the exercise of the means with which it was entrusted. The one party is for a popular government; the other for an aristocracy. The one party is composed, in a great measure, of the farmers, mechanics, laborers, and other producers of the middling and lower classes (according to the common gradation by the scale of wealth), and the other of the consumers — the rich, the proud, the privileged — of those who, if our government were converted into an aristocracy, would become our dukes, lords, marquises, and baronets. The question is still disputed between these two parties — it is ever a new question — and whether the democracy or the aristocracy shall succeed in the present struggle, the fight will be renewed whenever the defeated party shall be again able to muster strength enough to take the field.

The privilege of self-government is one which the people will never be permitted to enjoy unmolested. Power and wealth are continually stealing from the many to the few. There is a class continually gaining ground in the community, who desire to monopolize the advantages of the government, to hedge themselves round with exclusive privileges, and elevate themselves at the expense of the great body of the people.

These, in our society, are emphatically the aristocracy; and these, with all such as their means of persuasion, or corruption, or intimidation, can move to act with them, constitute the party which are now struggling against the democracy, for the perpetuation of an odious and dangerous moneyed institution.

Putting out of view, for the present, all other objections to the United States Bank — that it is a monopoly, that it possesses enormous and overshadowing power, that it has been most corruptly managed, and that it is identified with political leaders to whom the people of the United States must ever be strongly opposed — the constitutional objection alone is an insurmountable objection to it.

The government of the United States is a limited sovereignty. The powers which it may exercise are expressly enumerated in the Constitution. None not thus stated, or that are not "necessary and proper" to carry those which are stated into effect can be allowed to be exercised by it. The power to establish a bank is not expressly given; neither is incidental, since it cannot be shown to be "necessary" to carry the powers which are given, or any of them, into effect. That power cannot, therefore, be exercised without transcending the constitutional limits.

This is the democratic argument stated in its briefest form. The aristocratic argument in favor of the power is founded on the dangerous heresy that the Constitution says one thing and means another; that *necessary* does not mean *necessary*, but simply *convenient*. By a mode of reasoning not looser than this, it would be easy to prove that our government ought to be changed into a monarchy, Henry Clay crowned king, and the opposition members of the Senate made peers of the realm; and power, place, and perquisites given to them and their heirs forever.

17.

Theodore Dwight: The Arts in America

Travel books like Theodore Dwight's Things As They Are *(1834) were especially popular in America during the late eighteenth and early nineteenth centuries. Such books were usually didactic and discursive, and often advocated the search for and use of native American themes and art forms. The portion of Dwight's book reprinted below is typical both of the style of writing and of the preoccupation with this theme. It was republished in 1847 under the title* Summer Tours.

Source: *Things As They Are: or, Notes of a Traveller Through Some of the Middle and Northern States,* New York, 1834, pp. 46-53, 76-85, 113-117, 177-179.

It is strange to see how much better the public taste is often understood by booksellers than authors; and with what certainty they can sometimes foretell the fate of a book after hearing only a brief description of it, or after glancing at the table of contents or the title page, than the man who studied and labored over the pages for months or years, and lay awake whole nights to cut and piece it in conformity with the state of society. This fact, which no one can doubt after proper inquiry, is so much in opposition to common rules applying to other subjects that I sought light on it while in New York.

We always should expect to find a tailor better acquainted with the size of his customers' shoulders than anybody else, and more likely to discover whether a coat be too narrow to fit, too long in the sleeves, or too tight under the arms. But it is not so with your author and his work. He deliberates for weeks or months upon his subject, then upon his plan, then on the size of his book, the mode and time for its appearance; and, after having fixed all these and changed his intention over and over again, and at length completed his work as he finally determines, he is the most anxious man in the nation till he ascertains whether he has succeeded or failed. This he now feels utterly unable to judge of until he has facts to form an opinion upon, and actually sees whether or not his book has sold.

But not so with the bookseller. He has rules, or instinct, or some other guide by which he often can judge of the fate of a work before it has been grasped after or rejected by a single customer; and, as if by some secret electricity, a uniform presentiment concerning a book sometimes pervades the whole trade from the moment of its appearance, or even from a very early period after its announcement.

There are cases in which they have experience to refer to, and then they may prejudge as we might the shoemaker who had pinched us in the toes and was about to shoe a neighbor with still larger feet than our own. But, in the great majority of cases, the bulk of the booksellers do not know the author, or are not well acquainted with the subject on which he writes, or both, and therefore cannot judge of what is to come from what has happened.

To show what kind of satisfaction I got from some conversation on books during my stay in New York, I will give a brief recapitulation of what I heard in some of the printing offices and bookstores. Some of these are exceedingly large and rich; and the grand review of the whole typographic park and batteries of the capital is worthy of the attention of an intelligent traveler. The most magnificent presses in the world are racking and groaning in a hundred different streets, from Messrs. Harper's mammoth power press downward, like so many mills for grinding the wheat, bran, and shorts with which even the almost insatiable literary appetite of the American public is surfeited. The four or five principal stereotype foundries are also very large establishments, some of which are connected with typefoundries and printing offices of twenty and thirty presses.

"My friend," said a most intelligent and virtuous South American just from Europe, on entering a spacious room where two rows of men were casting types in the old way, one at a time, "my friend, despotism will never prevail against us." On being introduced, however, into a place where twenty boys, with machines, were doing the work of forty men, he was lost in surprise and pleasure, and declared that he almost pitied the poor despots who had to contest against such weapons so rapidly forged and so irresistible. The truth is, we ought to exhibit the press to our children as a machine little understood and consequently much abused. It would be an improving lesson to every child to be led to the village printing office once a year and hear comments on the nature, history, and uses of this great implement of civilization, morality, and religion.

But to return to bookstore conversation. "Have you seen the new number of this magazine? It is astonishingly popular. The publisher had but one course to pursue, and he took the right one. He had not capital enough to spend a large sum at once to pay an editor of known talents, and therefore could not expect his support from the learned. So he got it up as handsomely as he knew how, and has taken measures to have it well puffed in the newspapers. The consequence is that he has had great success."

I saw this publisher; and remarked to him that his merits, as I had understood, were generally acknowledged. Yes, he replied, he had taken good care about that. It would be in vain, he said, if any man should expect his works to be esteemed, if the newspapers did not commend them over and over again; and, to secure this end, means must be used. "If I should lie down under my counter and expect the public to give me credit for my merits, they would never know or care whether I had any or not. They would not know whether it was a man or a dog there in the dark. So I have given my numbers as good an appearance and as great a variety as possible, and now shall be able to do what I please with such patronage as I enjoy."

I expressed a hope that his periodical would soon aim to exceed the best of its class in other countries. Yes, he hoped it would be an honor to our own by having no superior in the world. He had taken great pains to get such paper as is used in England, and was to put a cover on the next number of the same color and devices as the London ———, which was extremely elegant and universally admired. Literature, thought I, has abundant reason to smile at her prospects in America, or rather to laugh at them! Lucky that none of the foreign tourists were present to tell this story abroad! "You may blame us as much as you please," said another publisher; "I have no more public spirit, perhaps, than the rest of my craft, but I have at least no objection to my books having real merit or to their being written by Americans. At any rate, I have made some exertions to secure both, and paid a good deal of money. But all the blame does not rest with us. We must sell our books or we must stop printing; that is very clear. If, then, there is nobody to inform the public of the merits of different works, how will they ever know them?

"You literary gentlemen do not establish reviews in which the public place much confidence, and, what is worse, you do not read one-half the books which appear while they are fresh, as you say, for want of time. You must settle that with your consciences; I do not pretend to judge you. You will not attempt to improve or even to direct public taste, and have left it to itself and to us. Now judge whether we have done our duty better than yourselves or not. We had to begin with a low taste, and have had to raise it, if it has been raised.

"Well, we did it in what we believe to be the only way in our power. We have always endeavored to print as good books as the public could be brought to read, and have more than once overshot our mark, perhaps, without ever falling below it. The result thus far has been a perceptible and general improvement in certain classes of books; and as we are encouraged in pursuing our course, we intend to persist in it, and hope to see still more important results.

"But to give you an idea . . . of the form and circumstances under which public taste appears to our craft, a publisher, perhaps, pays a young man who has a profession and leisure $100 to make a volume of newspaper scraps, and put some odd name to it; or he'll meet with a manuscript of the *Adventures of Timothy Terrible*, or some other well-known individual, and will bargain with the author for it. By the time it has been out a fortnight, we have orders for the whole edition, and half another. A correspondent writes from the South — The fifty *Timothy T.* received, and please send us seventy-five more. From the North we get — Please send, on receipt of this, one hundred copies of *Tim. Terrible.* — P.S. By first boat.

"Well, we think we'll try a little more American literature, as that appears to be rising. Come, we'll give 'em something a little solid. So we come out, we will suppose, with a learned work on the *History, Character, and Condition of the Crim Tartars*, past, present, and to come; and almost simultaneously with the *Life and Writings of General Somebody*, one of the greatest men in our republican history, the property of the nation. For each of these we'll suppose we pay $800 — cash, you understand. Well, our customers, in about ten days, begin to write — Send us no more *Generals* or *Crim Tartars*. They don't go down. — N.B. Too dry and too true. Gentlemen, we send you back forty-nine *Crim Tartars* and all the *Generals*. They don't suit our market.

"Now mind, here's two octavo volumes: investment on each about $3,000 yes, $3,500, including copyright. Well, they are good books, that is, so people say; and they sell easy along, one here and one there. But here comes in old Squire Jones, or Colonel West, or some such gentleman, and takes one of these books. "Well," he says, "here's a work I'm glad to see. I know the author, sir, and he's a man of sterling merit. Why I knew him when your father was so high. Yes, sir, that book ought to sell — it will sell — don't you find it so?" "Why, yes, Colonel, I suppose it would if everybody had your penetration. How many shall I send you?" "Oh, oh, why, I don't know, I have no time to read just now; but perhaps I'll call in some time when I have. I suppose I can get it any day this month, can't I?" "Yes, I'm afraid so, or next year either."

"Well, Dr. Studious expresses his pleasure at the appearance of a book so profound on the Crim Tartars. "Come here, sir, I'll sit down and tell you what I know about the author and his faithful investigations into his subject." "Why, doctor," says I, "I think you had better read the book and give me a short, pithy recommendation of it for the information of the public. My own opinion is already made up." "Why, sir," says the doctor, "I have a share in a library where I expect to find it; and if I should want it, perhaps you'll have a cheaper edition by and by."

"Now so it goes; and while I'm talking with one of the learned gentlemen, two or three men come in, and want eight or ten *Timothy Terribles* apiece; and the amount of it is that, while we must wait two or perhaps three years to get a profit of $600 or $700 on an investment of $3,500, in six months we run off two editions of a work that we've got up for $600 each, and have cleared, perhaps, $1,000, besides the stereotype plates ready for more. Encouraging solid literature and American authors is a good thing to talk about; it sounds very well; and I should like much to practise it more and more. It is easy to say — O, it's all the publisher's fault; you've no business to print such trash, and you should not go out of the country so much for books. But here you see are the facts. Now what are you going to do in such a case?

"Go and ask the learned and the good, the intelligent and the influential, why they can't take the trouble to examine works as they appear, or before, and let their countrymen know which are good and which bad. A few just commendations would seal the success of good works and good writers now overlooked and unknown; and a few good deathblows against bad books would kill, along with the works, their authors, and perhaps the taste which sustains them. . . ."

It is difficult for me to express all the gratification the traveler experiences on entering the Franklin Institute, which is connected with one of the principal inns in New Haven. Whoever heard, in any other city or country, of such a union? In a spacious wing of the hotel, over the dining room, the lodger may cross a passage and enter a fine lecture room, furnished with seats for 200 or 300 people, with a desk for a lecturer, having a neat laboratory and apparatus in view, a niche for receivers, with a flue to take off offensive gases, a study adjoining, and a private passage to a fine mineralogical cabinet, occupying the third story, to which you are next introduced. This institution is due entirely to the intelligence and liberality of Mr. Abel Brewster, a wealthy mechanic of this city, who planned and founded it at his own expense for the benefit of the citizens.

A course of scientific lectures is delivered every winter, principally by the professors of Yale College, to which tickets are obtained for $2. The professors and other literary gentlemen of the place afford it their countenance and labors; and the influence upon the inhabitants has been very beneficial, especially those who have not many other sources of instruction. Such an example, from an intelligent and highly philanthropic individual, should provoke to imitation some of those in other places who possess the power of promoting the great interests of the public in a similar manner.

New Haven has been greatly enriched within a few months by the acquisition of some of the invaluable paintings of Colonel John Trumbull, which are now deposited in a building erected by subscription in the rear of the College Lyceum. This edifice is itself worthy of particular attention on account of its neat and correct architecture, and its appropriate plan for the objects designed.

It is notorious that in all the picture galleries of Europe there is not one in which the proper arrangements have been made for the favorable disposition of paintings and admission of light. Numerous windows, generally large and opening nearly from the ceiling to the floor, give a multitude of cross lights; or else a portion of the apartment is thrown into deep obscurity. You may walk through the whole gallery of the Louvre, about one-third of a mile in length, and not see a painting in the best light; while in Italy the pictures in private collections are often hung upon hinges; and those of the Vatican, among others, suffer from the evils above mentioned. Some of the exhibition rooms in Philadelphia, New York, and perhaps some of our other cities, are now more judiciously lighted from above. The rotunda of the Capitol is a noble specimen of the same kind, reminding one of the Pantheon of Rome; and, although constructed primarily for a different purpose, affords one of the finest galleries for paintings in the world.

After visiting the well-known mineralogical cabinet of Yale College, I entered the gallery where, under the advantage of a light admitted from above, are seen the pictures of Colonel Trumbull; and it is doubly gratifying to find so many of them deposited in a permanent situation, in his native state, which he has done so much to honor, and to know that this arrangement has been made by the liberality of some of his fellow citizens.

Of the full value of the national paintings of this artist, it will be impossible to judge, until time shall have enabled the public more justly to appreciate it. But how happy it is that an officer of Washington's family should have been able, as well as disposed, to record the principal events of our Revolution in this most interesting and instructive manner, and to preserve the portraits of the most distinguished actors. While on the spot, I could not but wish that a suggestion I heard made some months since might ere long be carried into effect, viz., that lectures should be delivered, to the students and others, on these pictures, embracing those instructive historical and biographical details in which our Revolutionary period so greatly abounded, and in which our youth ought to be frequently and familiarly schooled.

I was exceedingly mortified, however, to find in the statehouse a copy of Trumbull's Declaration of Independence, furtively made by a raw young artist, which has been purchased by the legislature and hung up in the hall. This appeared to me as discreditable a reflection upon the want of taste and the abundance of parsimony as that body could have cast upon itself.

The statehouse is a beautiful edifice, built on the model of a fine Grecian temple, in pure taste, and is handsomely stuccoed in imitation of granite. These perishable materials appear ill when betrayed under the thin disguise of mock stone. The Gothic church nearby already shows the white pine under the glazing of brown paint and sand. Apropos, speaking of the Gothic style — Why should it be introduced into America? There is not a feature in society here which bears the slightest affinity with it; and so utterly opposed is it to the principles of pure and refined taste that nothing makes it at all tolerable in Europe, except its known connection with the days of semi-barbarism in which it flourished.

But it is more agreeable to approve than to condemn. Let us take this favorable opportunity to reflect a moment on a national taste in the fine arts appropriate to our country. In architecture it is much easier to say what does not than what does suit our circumstances. I will leave that to others for the present, hoping they may apply to it those principles of common sense which I wish to suggest in respect to a sister art. In painting, we ought to fix our principles distinctly. We ought not in this or anything else, servilely to follow the example of any, even the masters of the art. We are to imitate the style of the best ancient orators, poets, and historians, when we speak and write; but how? By using exactly their words? No; but by saying what they would have said if they had been like us and in our places. So, when we come to painting or to sculpture, we should not merely copy Jupiters, or Apollos, or Laocoons. Apelles and Praxiteles would not have produced

such personages if they had flourished in our days in the Western continent.

Long were the arts smothered in Europe under the weight of ancient example; and when [Benjamin] West roused up from the revery enough to throw off the drapery of antiquity, they breathed more freely. But West went not into the proper American domain. He was, indeed, unfavorably situated to do so, for he was in Europe. We find him, therefore, when out of Scripture and poetical subjects, commemorating the death of Wolfe at Quebec, and making his hero with his last breath applaud a victory in which no principle was involved, and from which flowed no result of interest to mankind. The tale to be told on his canvass was the old, bald tale of military adventure: directed by a ministry 3,000 miles distant, with money which they seem to have expended chiefly for their own credit. Military glory is the highest motive you can attribute to any of the personages of whom the groups must be formed; and the whole work is but the old song of false praise to war and bloody victory.

But how different from all this are the paintings of Trumbull! How much more appropriate to the principles we profess! Each of the personages presents an instructive lesson in his history. Here is no son whose name was inscribed on the army list merely to secure him a profession. The simple insignia of these soldiers were not purchased with money, and no accident or fatality brought them together. The war in which they engaged had not been waged for the exaltation of an ambitious general, or to slake the thirst of any tyrant for blood; and the actors were not the blind servants of one whose commands might not be questioned.

Each man had independently acted in obedience to his own judgment and in accordance with his own feelings. His education had been such as to strengthen his mind and to cultivate pure motives; and the great proof of the patriotism of our Army was shown by their quietly disbanding and returning to their homes when the war had been terminated. Other troops, after obtaining victory, would have considered their own great object yet unaccomplished while their pay was withheld; and would have been ready to ravage their country to reward or revenge themselves. But the men whom our great artist has preserved on his canvass maintained the attachment of children to their country, and voluntarily resigned that power by which alone they might have compelled the satisfaction of their claims, although they were just and undisputed. Posterity will have the discrimination which we want and appreciate such works according to their merits. . . .

I have been visiting some of the artists and exhibition rooms; and, having already indulged in a few remarks on paintings and painters, I might apply some of the same views to sculpture; but shall not stop here to be very particular. I would briefly remark that taste or genius, as it is called in sculpture, need not be of so gradual growth in our country as many persons think. Many of our travelers abroad will tell you that an hour spent in the museum of Florence, or in the select society of Apollo and Co., in the palace of the Vatican, would be sufficient to convert the most rude taste to something very refined and intelligent. And as for genius, did not Canova grow up in a few years; and was not his life more than long enough to revolutionize the world of artists? Even in the most refined countries, every new generation must be educated to refinement. We have, therefore, only to use the proper means, and in a very short time might have taste and genius, and the results of both combined.

It is a slavish doctrine, too, that no artist can be worthy of respect who has not worked in Rome. Let not our youth be discouraged. Take a chisel, look at a man, and make the rock look as much like him as you can. But the rock is hard. Then take plaster or common red clay from a brickyard. It will wash off from the hands of genius — Canova used it often. Set about gravely to do what you have attempted when a boy with the snow. Try to make a man — it is not so puerile a business, neither is it so very difficult. You are not to be perplexed with colors, lights, and shades, or in any way required to make a flat surface look like what it is not. You may measure every part, turn it this way and that by moving the block on which it stands, and alter, remold, and begin again.

Nothing is spent but a little leisure time, a little attention and ingenuity, for which you will be more attentive and ingenious hereafter, and a better judge of other people's work. The clay is as good as it was before, and you are not obliged to show your work or to try again. You are already like an artist in one respect; you have failed in your first attempt to do as well as you wished. Even if you had tried to chisel a stone and broken it, your tool, or your skin, I dare say Canova and Thorwaldson themselves have done worse.

There have been fewer good sculptors than good painters; but sculpture is a much more natural and simple art than painting. It has its peculiar principles, and in certain details there are more niceties; but in general this is not the case. For example, there must be caution used to guard against any unmeaning, incorrect, or ridiculous effect in every point of view from which a statue or group is to be seen, while a picture has but one side. But how natural is the attempt to mold a material mass into the form of humanity; and how much better do even children succeed in making images of snow than in drawing men with coal or chalk! And how much more readily do the uninstructed express their opinions of statues than of paintings, because they feel better competent to judge!

I need but remark, in addition, how Mr.

Augur has astonished us all with his "Jephtha and His Daughter," because he had independence enough to act on these principles, and with extraordinary taste and perseverance. (How strangely I forgot to speak of Augur with praise while at New Haven!) And how has the Scotch stonecutter Thom, with the coarsest stone and in spite of his degraded subject, viz., a low alehouse group, imitated nature almost to perfection, without the benefit of instruction or a single model.

I have said a good deal about taste, perhaps to very little purpose, yet I must express my displeasure for that shown by many of my countrymen in several recent instances. While works of real merit, recommended by patriotic, or at least respectable historical associations are offered for exhibition almost in vain; while artists of extraordinary talent, pure character, and commendable intentions are shut up in humble corners by public neglect, we can rush in crowds to see a poor and meager composition, whose merits are merely of an inferior order and whose tendency is of a decidedly corrupting character.

I speak of the "great *immoral* painting" of "Adam and Eve in Paradise". This picture has indeed a Scripture subject, but that is its only merit, except the mere mechanical execution of the figures. The composition has not the essential quality of a just conception of the scene portrayed. There is no Eden, unless a few flowers on a green

bank may express it; and no one could ever judge of the artist's intention or his subject if the serpent and apple were withdrawn. On the contrary, everything else, except the nudity of the personages, would lead to a very opposite idea. And as to the intellectual character of the piece, how mean, as well as how detestable, appears the character of the mind expressed in this painting!

Such an artist would make the Eden of purity a mere Mohammedan paradise. Nature is represented as destitute of beauty; and man, in his state of perfection, as devoid of every exalted and ennobling sentiment. From woman, every intellectual trait seems to be removed; and how insufferable is this, in such a scene, where the acquisition of knowledge was the great instrument of temptation — the object to which she had yielded and which she used as the ground of her argument with Adam!

For my own part, this miserable failure of a foreign artist will ever be doubly displeasing to me because it has been so extensively rendered popular by the notice of men who, in my opinion, ought to have possessed more taste and discernment.

Because it was a Scripture painting, fathers and mothers, laymen and clergymen crowded to see it, indifferent or unsuspicious with regard to the impression which their example would have on virtuous and blushing youth, and on immoral and debased members of society, who rejoice when evil sentiments are allowed to walk in the sunshine.

By beauty I mean the promise of function, by action I mean the presence of function, by character I mean the record of function.
HORATIO GREENOUGH, *Artist's Creed*

18.

Francis Lieber: Space and Time in America

Francis Lieber came from his native Germany to the United States in 1827 and thereafter made America his home. Among the many enterprises which earned him preeminence among statesmen and scholars, he founded the Encyclopedia Americana *and published voluminously on political science and law. Shortly after arriving in this country, he wrote a travel book in the discursive style in vogue at the time. But while most of the travel books written by foreigners degraded America, Lieber extolled it; and American literary critics delighted in his praise. The book, a portion of which appears below, was entitled* Letters to a Gentleman in Germany Being Written After a Trip from Philadelphia to Niagara *and was published in 1834. In the English edition the title was changed, without Lieber's permission, to* The Stranger in America.

Source: *The Stranger in America; or, Letters to a Gentleman in Germany, etc., etc.,* Philadelphia, 1835, pp. 283-288.

Buffalo, the western point of termination of the grand canal, is an interesting place, both for its situation on Lake Erie and its rapid growth, which it bids fair to continue for a long time. It is astonishing to see wide streets (a little too wide, indeed, like those of Washington) of handsome and high houses of the best appearance, where but a few years ago an inconsiderable village was all that was to be seen.

What is to be done, my dear friend, if the plan of a place is at once to be laid out? Wherever I have seen towns built according to a regular plan, they seemed to be failures, contrivances which look very well on paper, or sound well if you hear them described, but are very different in reality. From the concentric circles of Carlsruhe to the compound plan of Washington, all these places have a thousand inconveniences in practice, and as to the rectangular plan, on which Philadelphia, Mannheim, and many places here and in Europe are laid out — taste, in matters of this kind, is no subject of discussion, but I dislike the eternal sameness of this plan, if the place be of any considerable magnitude, particularly if to the rectangular prose be joined the abstract numbers in the appellation of the streets.

Man is a systematizing being; systematizing is, in part, thinking itself; hence his fondness for seeing principles carried through; but very often principles only sound well, because they appear simple, while applied, they offer little for approbation. Such is to me the rule after which the Philadelphia streets are called. I have a peculiarly good sense of locality, and never lost my way in a foreign place, with the only exception of Philadelphia, where to this day I am continually obliged to ask, "What street is this; Seventh, Eighth, Ninth?" while directions given to me, escape my mind much easier than those in other places, owing to the character of generality attached to all these numbered streets. And as to the numbers combined with the letters of the alphabet, as in Washington, they require a man born for a mathematician, to remember these *viatic* formulas. . . .

Before I entered the city of Buffalo, close to it, I found an instance which very strikingly exemplified the immense power which custom exercises. I saw a farmer's house built of stone, and having the appearance of being owned by a man of substantial wealth, yet, though of brick and spacious, it was built on the Westphalian plan — the cattle and horses standing with their heads turned into the barn, at the end of which are the hearth and sitting room of the family. Here the farmer had the examples of much more convenient farmhouses around him, he had all the means of imitating them, yet he followed a plan which originated in times when neither cleanliness, health, safety, nor even interest was made a subject of unprejudiced reasoning, and improvements were but rarely made. Thus the migrating nations, in the beginning of the Middle Ages, carried a thousand customs with them into countries for which they were not calculated. . . .

What distances and cheapness! . . . Distances are not considered in this country as in Europe. . . . And what is the reason that 1,000 miles in the United States are not as much as 1,000 miles in Europe? There are several reasons for it, in my opinion. First, the early settlers had to think of many thousand miles off, whenever they thought of their beloved home. Thus, a far different unit by which to estimate other distances was laid down in their minds. It is clear that a person settling 100 miles from them could not appear far away to those who had their original home some 1,000 miles off. And, although a generation born on this continent soon grew up, their rela-

tions to Europe still continued to be of such a character that all considered themselves intimately connected with her; and even to this day, we feel that, as to everything in science and civilization, we are closely connected with Europe; and a lady in New York thinks no more of going to Havre or Liverpool than a lady in London of going to Paris.

This feeling, together with the vast, unsettled continent before them, induced people to push on and settle at great distances, especially as the life of the early colonists was such as to develop a daring spirit of enterprise, which gradually has settled down into a fixed trait of American character. General Moreau, when residing in this country — so said a French gentleman, an acquaintance of mine — believed that no soldier would be equal to an American if well and thoroughly disciplined; (to be sure, the present militia would require some "rubbings") because, said he, "An American doubts of nothing." It was true what Moreau observed, that an American doubts of nothing; sometimes owing to enterprising boldness, sometimes to want of knowledge or to self-confidence, always, in a measure, to the fact that want of success in an enterprise is not followed in the United States by obloquy or ridicule, even though the undertaking may have been injudicious. This, though often calculated to mislead, is, on the whole, an excellent thing; and, even supposing a man to have miscalculated his strength in one attempt, he may take better care the next time.

This spirit of enterprise and adventure pushed new settlers far into all directions, a consequence of which is that we now dwell in a vast country, inhabited by people of the same language, and living under the same laws — another reason why distances appear shorter to us. The comparatively small number of mountain chains is a third cause of the same singular fact. As we require objects by which to judge distances —

thus, for instance, objects seen over a wide expanse of water appear nearer to us than when the view lies across an equally extensive tract of land — so a distance by land, if we have to pass through many different languages and governments, and over mountains, appears to us greater than if no such intervening objects existed.

In the Atlantic states, people are, besides, so familiar with voyages to Canton, the Pacific, Buenos Aires, etc., that I have seen in Europe more bustle in a family, a member of which was going to a university, perhaps some sixty miles off, than I have here when the son or brother was embarking for China or the Manilas [Philippines]. The steamboats, which greatly facilitate traveling — the population being scattered over so vast a country — and the migratory disposition of the American in general, originally caused by the above given reasons, contribute, in turn, their full part to the production of the same effect. The next nation after the Americans, in this respect, are the English, whose possessions in all quarters of the globe would make them consider distances as still less than the Americans were their own country not itself so very confined. Every mile has there its full value.

Not distances alone are measured here by a standard different from that of other countries; time, too, receives a different value, but it is measured by a smaller standard than in Europe. An American wants to perform within a year what others do within a much longer period. Ten years in America are like a century in Spain. The United States really change in some respects more within ten years than a country like Spain

has within a hundred. England moves, in all practical affairs, quicker than the continent; the United States move quicker still, in some respects, than England. There are many reasons for this more rapid movement, which I will not oblige you to read; let me only observe that it influences all relations of life.

According to recent statements, a female servant in London remains, on average, 462 days in the same situation. I have no doubt that, if similar accounts could be obtained from Germany, we would find that they remain much longer there in the same place, and the corresponding period in New York would average much less. Sometimes individuals long for a stationary country, where things remain in their place for some time, and where one does not feel all the time as if tied to the wing of a windmill. This desire is very natural; whether they would be pleased by a change for a long time or not, is quite a different question. For the rest — the choice is not with the nations.

There are, at present, two classes of nations, which, in all your inquiries, you must strictly distinguish from each other; namely, moving nations and stationary nations. The former would be utterly ruined were they to counteract their own impetus. I speak here chiefly of industry, and diffusion and application of knowledge. This movement has become with them one of the "historical tasks" which they have to perform. They *must* have steamboats, though a sailing boat may grace the landscape a thousand times more; they *must* have railroads, though traveling on them be a dull thing.

19.

Davy Crockett: Frontier Politics

Davy (David) Crockett was a backwoodsman from Tennessee. His skill as an Indian fighter, hunter, and storyteller, and — it is said — the generosity of his backers in dispensing liquor got him elected to two terms in the Tennessee legislature and to three terms in Congress. He died a hero's death at the Alamo in 1836. Davy Crockett enjoyed a semi-mythical reputation, even in his own lifetime. Stories of his uncouth ways appealed to Eastern readers, and his activities were widely publicized by the Whigs in their bid for frontier votes after Crockett switched to their party in the early 1830s. The many narratives attributed to his pen were probably written by others. The following selection, describing how Crockett was elected to the state legislature, first appeared in an 1834 publication. Although the election took place in 1821, this account was intended for Whig voters of 1834.

Source: *A Narrative of the Life of David Crockett, of the State of Tennessee,* New York, 1845, pp. 137-145.

I . . . SET OUT ELECTIONEERING, which was a bran-fire new business to me. It now became necessary that I should tell the people something about the government and an eternal sight of other things that I knowed nothing more about than I did about Latin, and law, and such things as that. . . . In those days none of us called General Jackson the government, nor did he seem in as fair a way to become so as I do now; but I knowed so little about it, that if any one had told me he was "the government," I should have believed it, for I had never read even a newspaper in my life, or anything else, on the subject. But over all my difficulties, it seems to me I was born for luck, though it would be hard for anyone to guess what sort. I will, however, explain that hereafter.

I went first into Heckman County to see what I could do among the people as a candidate. Here they told me that they wanted to move their town nearer to the center of the county, and I must come out in favor of it. There's no devil if I knowed what this meant, or how the town was to

be moved; and so I kept dark, going on the identical same plan that I now find is called "noncommittal."

About this time there was a great squirrel hunt on Duck River, which was among my people. They were to hunt two days; then to meet and count the scalps, and have a big barbecue, and what might be called a tip-top country frolic. The dinner and a general treat was all to be paid for by the party having taken the fewest scalps. I joined one side, taking the place of one of the hunters, and got a gun ready for the hunt. I killed a great many squirrels, and when we counted scalps, my party was victorious.

The company had everything to eat and drink that could be furnished in so new a country, and much fun and good humor prevailed. But before the regular frolic commenced, I mean the dancing, I was called on to make a speech as a candidate; which was a business I was as ignorant of as an outlandish Negro.

A public document I had never seen, nor did I know there were such things; and how to begin I couldn't tell. I made many apologies, and tried to get off, for I know'd I had a man to run against who could speak prime, and I know'd, too, that I wa'n't able to shuffle and cut with him. He was there, and knowing my ignorance as well as I did myself, he also urged me to make a speech. The truth is, he thought my being a candidate was a mere matter of sport; and didn't think, for a moment, that he was in any danger from an ignorant backwoods bear hunter. But I found I couldn't get off, and so I determined just to go ahead, and leave it to chance what I should say.

I got up and told the people, I reckoned they know'd what I come for, but if not, I could tell them. I had come for their votes, and if they didn't watch mighty close, I'd get them too. But the worst of all was, that I couldn't tell them anything about government. I tried to speak about something, and I cared very little what, until I choked up as bad as if my mouth had been jam'd and cram'd chock full of dry mush. There the people stood, listening all the while, with their eyes, mouths, and ears all open, to catch every word I would speak.

At last I told them I was like a fellow I had heard of not long before. He was beating on the head of an empty barrel near the roadside, when a traveler, who was passing along, asked him what he was doing that for. The fellow replied that there was some cider in that barrel a few days before, and he was trying to see if there was any then, but if there was he couldn't get at it. I told them that there had been a little bit of a speech in me a while ago, but I believed I couldn't get it out. They all roared out in a mighty laugh, and I told some other anecdotes, equally amusing to them, and believing I had them in a first-rate way, I quit and got down, thanking the people for their attention. But I took care to remark that I was as dry as a powder horn, and that I thought it was time for us all to wet our whistles a little; and so I put off to the liquor stand, and was followed by the greater part of the crowd.

I felt certain this was necessary, for I knowed my competitor could open government matters to them as easy as he pleased. He had, however, mighty few left to hear him, as I continued with the crowd, now and then taking a horn, and telling good-humored stories, till he was done speaking. I found I was good for the votes at the hunt, and when we broke up, I went on to the town of Vernon, which was the same they wanted me to move. . . .

Their court commenced on the next Monday, as the barbecue was on a Saturday, and the candidates for governor and for Congress, as well as my competitor and myself, all attended.

The thought of having to make a speech made my knees feel mighty weak, and set my heart to fluttering almost as bad as my first love scrape with the Quaker's niece. But as good luck would have it, these big candidates spoke nearly all day, and when they quit, the people were worn out with fatigue, which afforded me a good apology for not discussing the government. But I listened mighty close to them, and was learning pretty fast about political matters. When they were all done, I got up and told some laughable story, and quit. I found I was safe in those parts, and so I went home, and didn't go back again till after the election was over. But to cut this matter short, I was elected, doubling my competitor, and nine votes over.

A short time after this, I was in Pulaski, where I met with Colonel Polk, now a member of Congress from Tennessee. He was at that time a member elected to the legislature, as well as myself; and in a large company he said to me, "Well, Colonel, I suppose we shall have a radical change of the judiciary at the next session of the legislature." "Very likely, sir," says I, and I put out quicker, for I was afraid someone would ask me what the judiciary was; and if I knowed, I wish I may be shot. I don't indeed believe I had ever before heard that there was any such thing in all nature; but still I was not willing that the people there should know how ignorant I was about it.

When the time for meeting of the legislature arrived, I went on, and before I had been there long, I could have told what the judiciary was, and what the government was too; and many other things that I had known nothing about before.

20.

"Zip Coon"

The minstrel show dominated the theater through much of the nineteenth century. Tradition assigns its origins to white actor Thomas Rice, who, the story goes, was struck one day in 1828 by a song of an African American longshoreman. In performance, Rice blackened his face and adopted the longshoreman's style of dress. Its use of caricature may distract modern readers, and even seem offensive, but those who can penetrate these layers of anachronism will find some political commentary within. "Zip Coon," also known as "Turkey in the Straw," is one of the many songs that was popularized by the traveling minstrel shows and that then acquired its own folk tradition. It is supposed to have been first performed at the Bowery Theater on August 11, 1834, by Bob Farrell, who was possibly its author. The song attracted numerous topical verses, of which two are reprinted here.

Source: *Minstrel Songs, Old and New,* Boston, 1882.

✺ ZIP COON

That tarnal critter Crockett, he never say his prayers,
He kill all the wild cats, the coons, and the bears;
And then he go to Washington to help to make the laws,
And there he find the Congressmen sucking of their paws.

Chorus:
Old Zip Coon is a very learned scholar,
Old Zip Coon is a very learned scholar,
Old Zip Coon is a very learned scholar,
He plays on the banjo — cooney in the hollar.

Oh glory be to Jackson, for he blew up the banks,
And glory be to Jackson for his many funny pranks,
And glory be to Jackson for the battle of Orleans,
For there he gave the enemy the hot butter beans.

1835

21.

Davy Crockett: A Tour of the Lowell Mills

Disenchanted with Jackson's policies on finance, land, and Native Americans, Davy Crockett, the backwoods congressman from Tennessee, turned Whig in the early 1830s. To augment the appeal of their party, the Whigs publicly displayed their new catch. As part of their display, the Whigs sponsored Crockett in a tour of the Northeast that brought him to Lowell, Massachusetts, in 1834. The Lowell cotton mills were the showcase of American business. The mills were operated by single women recruited from the surrounding areas. In addition to receiving comparatively good wages, the women were well housed and fed and strictly supervised. Although Crockett probably did not write the following narrative, Lowell is accurately described. The Account *was published in 1835.*

Source: *An Account of Col. Crockett's Tour to the North and Down East, etc., etc.,* Philadelphia, 1835, pp. 91-99.

NEXT MORNING I rose early and started for Lowell in a fine carriage with three gentlemen who had agreed to accompany me. I had heard so much of this place that I longed to see it; not because I had heard of the "mile of gals"; no, I left that for the gallantry of the President who is admitted, on that score, to be abler than myself; but I wanted to see the power of machinery, wielded by the keenest calculations of human skill; I wanted to see how it was that these Northerners could buy cotton, and carry it home, manufacture it, bring it back, and sell it for half nothing; and in the meantime, be well to live, and make money besides.

We stopped at the large stone house at the head of the falls of the Merrimac River, and having taken a little refreshment, went down among the factories. The dinner bells were ringing, and the folks pouring out of the houses like bees out of a gum. I looked at them as they passed, all well dressed, lively, and genteel in their appearance; indeed, the girls looked as if they were coming from a quilting frolic. We took a turn round, and after dining on a fine salmon, again returned, and entered the factories.

The outdoor appearance was fully sustained by the whole of the persons employed in the different rooms. I went in among the young girls, and talked with many of them. Not one expressed herself as tired of her employment, or oppressed with work; all talked well, and looked healthy. Some of them were very handsome; and I could not help observing that they kept the prettiest inside, and put the homely ones on the outside rows.

I could not help reflecting on the difference of conditions between these females, thus employed, and those of other populous countries, where the female character is degraded to abject slavery. Here were thousands, useful to others, and enjoying all the blessings of freedom, with the prospect before them of future comfort and respectability; and however we, who only hear of them, may call their houses workshops and prisons, I assure my neighbors there is every enjoyment of life realized by these persons, and there can be but few who are not happy. It cannot be otherwise; respectability depends upon being neighborlike; here everybody works, and therefore no one is degraded by it; on the contrary, those who don't work are not estimated.

There are more than 5,000 females employed in Lowell; and when you come to see the amount of labor performed by them, in superintending the different machinery, you will be astonished.

Twelve years ago, the place where Lowell now rises in all its pride was a sheep pasture. It took its name from Francis C. Lowell, the projector of its manufactories, and was incorporated in 1826 — then a mere village. The fall, obtained by a canal from the Merrimac River, is thirty-two feet, affording two levels for mills, of thirteen and seventeen feet; and the whole water of the river can be used.

There are about 14,000 inhabitants. It contains nine meetinghouses; appropriates $7,500 for free schools; provides instruction for 1,200 scholars, daily; and about 3,000 annually partake of its benefits. It communicates with Boston by the Middlesex Canal (the first ever made in the United States); and in a short time the railroad to Boston will be completed, affording every facility of intercourse to the seaboard.

This place has grown by, and must depend on, its manufactures. Its location ren-

Davy Crockett; lithograph from painting by S. S. Osgood

ders it important, not only to the owners but to the nation. Its consumption not only employs the thousands of its own population but many thousands far away from them. It is calculated not only to give individual happiness and prosperity but to add to our national wealth and independence; and instead of depending on foreign countries, to have our own materials worked up in our own country.

Some of the girls attended three looms; and they make from $1.75 to $3 per week, after paying their board. These looms weave 55 yards per day; so that one person makes 165 yards per day. Everything moves on like clockwork, in all the variety of employments; and the whole manufacture appears to be of the very best.

The owner of one of these mills, Mr. Lawrence, presented me with a suit of broadcloth, made out of wool bought from Mark Cockral, of Mississippi, who sold them about 4,000 pounds, and it was as good cloth as the best I ever bought for best imported.

The calico made here is beautiful, and of every variety of figure and color. To attempt to give a description of the manner in which it is stamped and colored is far beyond my abilities. One thing I must state, that after the web is wove, and before they go further, it is actually passed over *a red-*

hot cylinder, to scorch off the furze. The number of different operations is truly astonishing; and if one of my country women had the whole of the persons in her train that helped to make her gown, she would be like a captain on a field muster; and yet, when you come to look at the cost, it would take a trunk full of them to find these same people in living for one day.

I never witnessed such a combination of industry, and perhaps never will again. I saw the whole process, from the time they put in the raw material until it came out completely finished. In fact, it almost came up to the old story of a fellow walking into a patent machine with a bundle of wool under his arm, and coming out at the other end with a new coat on.

Nothing can be more agreeable than the attention that is paid by everyone connected with these establishments. Nothing appears to be kept secret; every process is shown, and with great cheerfulness. I regret that more of our Southern and Western men do not go there, as it would help much to do away with their prejudices against these manufactories. . . .

I met the young gentlemen of Lowell, by their particular request, at supper. About one hundred sat down. Everything was in grand order and went off well. They toasted *me,* and I enlightened *them* by a speech as good as I could make; and, indeed, I considered them a good set of fellows, and as well worth speaking to as any ones I had met with. The old saying, "them that don't work should not eat," don't apply to them, for they are the "rale workies," and know how to act genteel, too; for, I assure you, I was not more kindly, and hospitably, and liberally treated anywhere than just by these same people.

22.

John James Audubon: Frontier Law and Mississippi Squatters

John James Audubon spent many years of his life on the American Frontier, sketching, painting, and studying American wild life. Between 1826 and 1839 he published, in England, the work that brought him immediate and enduring fame: a series of giant folio plates collectively entitled The Birds of America, *and five separate volumes of explanatory text called* Ornithological Biography. *To make the explanatory text entertaining, Audubon interspersed it with what he termed "Episodes" or "Delineations of American Scenery and Character," two of which are reprinted below. They were published at various times between 1831 and 1839, and refer to the Frontier as it had been ten or fifteen years before.*

Source: Maria R. Audubon, *Audubon and His Journals,* New York, 1897, Vol. II, pp. 231-234, 443-449.

THE REGULATORS

THE POPULATION of many parts of America is derived from the refuse of every other country. I hope I shall elsewhere prove to you, kind reader, that even in this we have reason to feel a certain degree of pride, as we often see our worst denizens becoming gradually freed from error and at length changing to useful and respectable citizens. The most depraved of these emigrants are forced to retreat farther and farther from the society of the virtuous, the restraints imposed by which they find incompatible with their habits and the gratification of their unbridled passions. On the extreme verge of civilization, however, their evil propensities find more free scope, and the dread of punishments for their deeds, or the infliction of that punishment, are the only means that prove effectual in reforming them.

In those remote parts, no sooner is it discovered that an individual has conducted himself in a notoriously vicious manner, or has committed some outrage upon society, than a conclave of the honest citizens takes place for the purpose of investigating the case with a rigor without which no good result could be expected. These honest citizens, selected from among the most respectable persons in the district, and vested with powers suited to the necessity of preserving order on the frontiers, are named Regulators. The accused person is arrested, his conduct laid open, and if he is found guilty of a first crime, he is warned to leave the country and go farther from society, within an appointed time.

Should the individual prove so callous as to disregard the sentence and remain in the same neighborhood to commit new crimes, then woe be to him; for the Regulators, after proving him guilty a second time, pass and execute a sentence, which, if not enough to make him perish under the infliction, is at least forever impressed upon his memory. The punishment inflicted is usually a severe castigation, and the destruction, by fire, of his cabin. Sometimes, in cases of reiterated theft or murder, death is considered necessary; and, in some instances, delinquents of the worst species have been shot, after which their heads have been stuck on poles, to deter others from following their example. I will give you an account of one of these desperadoes as I received it from a person who had been instrumental in bringing him to punishment.

The name of Mason is still familiar to many of the navigators of the Lower Ohio and Mississippi. By dint of industry in bad deeds he became a notorious horse stealer, formed a line of worthless associates from the eastern parts of Virginia (a state greatly celebrated for its fine breed of horses) to New Orleans, and had a settlement on Wolf Island, not far from the confluence of the Ohio and Mississippi, from which he issued to stop the flatboats and rifle them of such provisions and other articles as he and his party needed. His depredations became the talk of the whole Western country; and to pass Wolf Island was not less to be dreaded than to anchor under the walls of Algiers. The horses, the Negroes, and the cargoes his gang carried off and sold. At last, a body of Regulators undertook, at great peril and for the sake of the country, to bring the villain to punishment.

Mason was as cunning and watchful as he was active and daring. Many of his haunts were successively found out and searched, but the numerous spies in his employ enabled him to escape in time. One day, however, as he was riding a beautiful horse in the woods, he was met by one of the Regulators, who immediately recognized him, but passed him as if an utter stranger. Mason, not dreaming of danger, pursued his way leisurely, as if he had met no one. But he was dogged by the Regulator, and in such a manner as proved fatal to him. At dusk, Mason, having reached the lowest part of a ravine no doubt well known to him, hobbled (tied together the forelegs of) his stolen horse to enable it to feed during the night without chance of straying far, and concealed himself in a hollow log to spend the night. The plan was good, but proved his ruin.

The Regulator, who knew every hill and hollow of the woods, marked the place and the log with the eye of an experienced hunter, and as he remarked that Mason was most efficiently armed, he galloped off to the nearest house, where he knew he should find assistance. This was easily procured, and the party proceeded to the spot. Mason, on being attacked, defended himself with desperate valor; and as it proved impossible to secure him alive, he was brought to the ground with a rifle ball. His head was cut off and stuck on the end of a broken branch of a tree, by the nearest road to the place where the affray happened. The gang soon dispersed in consequence of the loss of their leader, and this infliction of merited punishment proved beneficial in deterring others from following a similar predatory life.

The punishment by castigation is performed in the following manner. The individual convicted of an offense is led to some remote part of the woods under the escort of sometimes forty or fifty Regulators. When arrived at the chosen spot, the criminal is made fast to a tree, and a few of the Regulators remain with him, while the rest scour the forest to assure themselves that no strangers are within reach, after which they form an extensive ring, arranging themselves on their horses, well armed with rifles and pistols, at equal distances and in each other's sight. At a given signal that "all's ready," those about the culprit, having provided themselves with young twigs of hickory, administer the number of lashes prescribed by the sentence, untie the sufferer, and order him to leave the country immediately.

One of these castigations which took place more within my personal knowledge was performed on a fellow who was neither a thief nor a murderer, but who had misbehaved otherwise sufficiently to bring himself under the sentence with mitigation. He was taken to a place where nettles were known to grow in great luxuriance, completely stripped, and so lashed with them that, although not materially hurt, he took it as a hint not to be neglected, left the country, and was never again heard of by any of the party concerned.

Probably at the moment when I am copying these notes respecting the early laws of our frontier people, few or no Regulating Parties exist, the terrible examples that were made having impressed upon the new settlers a salutary dread which restrains them from the commission of flagrant crimes.

THE SQUATTERS OF THE MISSISSIPPI

ALTHOUGH EVERY EUROPEAN TRAVELER who has glided down the Mississippi at the rate of ten miles an hour has told his tale of the Squatters, yet none has given any other account of them than that they are "a sallow, sickly looking sort of miserable beings," living in swamps, and subsisting on pignuts, Indian corn, and bear's flesh. It is obvious, however, that none but a person acquainted with their history, manners, and condition can give any real information respecting them.

The individuals who become squatters choose that sort of life of their own free will. They mostly remove from other parts of the United States after finding that land has become too high in price; and they are persons who, having a family of strong and hardy children, are anxious to enable them to provide for themselves. They have heard from good authorities that the country extending along the great streams of the West is of all parts of the Union the richest in its soil, the growth of its timber, and the abundance of its game; that, besides, the Mississippi is the great road to and from all the markets in the world; and that every vessel borne by its waters affords to settlers some chance of selling their commodities or of exchanging them for others. To these recommendations is added another, of ever greater weight with persons of the above denomination, namely, the prospect of being able to settle on land, and perhaps to hold it for a number of years, without purchase, rent, or tax of any kind. How many thousands of individuals in all parts of the globe would gladly try their fortune with such prospects, I leave to you, reader, to determine.

As I am not disposed too highly to color the picture which I am about to submit to your inspection, instead of pitching on individuals who have removed from our eastern boundaries, and of whom certainly there are a good number, I shall introduce to you the members of a family from Virginia, first giving you an idea of their condition in that country, previous to their migration to the West. The land which they and their ancestors have possessed for a hundred years, having been constantly forced to produce crops of one kind or another, is now completely worn out. It exhibits only a superficial layer of red clay, cut up by deep ravines, through which much of the soil has been conveyed to some more fortunate neighbor, residing in a yet rich and beautiful valley. Their strenuous efforts to render it productive have failed. They dispose of everything too cumbrous or expensive for them to remove, retaining only a few horses, a servant or two, and such implements of husbandry and other articles as may be necessary on their journey or useful when they arrive at the spot of their choice.

I think I see them at this moment harnessing their horses and attaching them to their wagons, which are already filled with bedding, provisions, and the younger children; while on their outside are fastened spinning wheels and looms; and a bucket filled with tar and tallow swings between the hind wheels. Several axes are secured to the bolster, and the feeding trough of the horses contains pots, kettles, and pans. The servant, now become a driver, rides the near saddled horse, the wife is mounted on another, the worthy husband shoulders his gun, and his sons, clad in plain, substantial homespun, drive the cattle ahead and lead the procession, followed by the hounds and other dogs.

Their day's journey is short and not agreeable: the cattle, stubborn or wild, frequently leave the road for the woods, giving the travelers much trouble; the harness of the horses here and there gives way and needs immediate repair; a basket which has accidentally dropped must be gone after, for nothing that they have can be spared; the roads are bad, and now and then all hands are called to push on the wagon or prevent it from upsetting. Yet, by sunset, they have proceeded perhaps twenty miles. Rather fatigued, all assemble round the fire which has been lighted, supper is prepared, and a camp being erected, there they pass the night.

Days and weeks, nay, months, of unremitting toil pass before they gain the end of their journey. They have crossed both the Carolinas, Georgia, and Alabama. They have been traveling from the beginning of May to that of September, and with heavy hearts they traverse the state of Mississippi. But now, arrived on the banks of the broad stream, they gaze in amazement on the dark, deep woods around them. Boats of various kinds they see gliding downward with the current, while others slowly ascend against it. A few inquiries are made at the nearest dwelling, and, assisted by the inhabitants with their boats and canoes, they at once cross the Mississippi and select their place of habitation.

The exhalations arising from the swamps and morasses around them have a powerful effect on these new settlers, but all are intent on preparing for the winter. A small patch of ground is cleared by the axe and the fire, a temporary cabin is erected, to each of the cattle is attached a jingling bell before it is let loose into the neighboring canebrake, and the horses remain about the house, where they find sufficient food at that season. The first trading boat that stops at their landing enables them to provide themselves with some flour, fishhooks, and ammunition, as well as other commodities.

The looms are mounted, the spinning wheels soon furnish some yarn, and in a few weeks the family throw off their ragged clothes and array themselves in suits adapted to the climate. The father and sons, meanwhile, have sown turnips and other vegetables; and from some Kentucky flatboat a supply of live poultry has been procured.

October tinges the leaves of the forest, the morning dews are heavy, the days hot, the nights chill, and the unacclimated family in a few days are attacked with ague. The lingering disease almost prostrates their whole faculties, and one seeing them at such a period might well call them sallow and sickly. Fortunately, the unhealthy season soon passes over, and the hoarfrosts make their appearance. Gradually each individual recovers strength. The largest ash trees are felled; their trunks are cut, split, and corded in front of the building; a large fire is lighted at night on the edge of the water; and soon a steamer calls to purchase the wood and thus add to their comforts during the winter.

This first fruit of their industry imparts new courage to them; their exertions multiply, and when spring returns the place has a cheerful look. Venison, bear's flesh, wild turkeys, ducks, and geese, with now and then some fish, have served to keep up their strength, and now their enlarged field is planted with corn, potatoes, and pumpkins. Their stock of cattle, too, has augmented; the steamer, which now stops there as if by preference, buys a calf or a pig, together with the whole of their wood. Their store of provisions is renewed, and brighter rays of hope enliven their spirits.

Who is he of the settlers on the Mississippi that cannot realize some profit? Truly, none who is industrious. When the autumnal months return, all are better prepared to encounter the ague which then prevails. Substantial food, suitable clothing, and abundant firing repel its attacks; and before another twelvemonth has elapsed, the family is naturalized.

The sons by this time have discovered a swamp covered with excellent timber, and as they have seen many great rafts of saw logs bound for the mills of New Orleans floating past their dwelling, they resolve to try the success of a little enterprise. Their industry and prudence have already enhanced their credit. A few cross-saws are purchased, and some broad-wheeled "carry-logs" are made by themselves. Log after log is hauled to the bank of the river, and in a short time, their first raft is made on the shore and loaded with cordwood. When the next freshet sets it afloat, it is secured by long grapevines or cables, until the proper time being arrived, the husband and sons embark on it and float down the mighty stream.

After encountering my difficulties, they arrive in safety at New Orleans, where they dispose of their stock, the money obtained for which may be said to be all profit; supply themselves with such articles as may add to their convenience or comfort, and with light hearts, procure a passage on the upper deck of a steamer, at a very cheap rate, on account of the benefit of their labor in taking in wood or otherwise.

And now the vessel approaches their home. See the joyous mother and daughters as they stand on the bank! A store of vegetables lies around them, a large tub of fresh milk is at their feet, and in their hands are plates filled with rolls of butter. As the steamer stops, three broad straw hats are waved from its upper deck; and soon, husband and wife, brothers and sisters are in each other's embrace. The boat carries off the provisions for which value has been left, and, as the captain issues his orders for putting on the steam, the happy family enter their humble dwelling. The husband gives his bag of dollars to the wife, while the sons present some token of affection to their sisters. Surely, at such a moment, the

Squatters are richly repaid for all their labors.

Every successive year has increased their savings. They now possess a large stock of horses, cows, and hogs, with abundance of provisions and domestic comfort of every kind. The daughters have been married to the sons of neighboring Squatters and have gained sisters to themselves by the marriage of their brothers. The government secures to the family the lands on which, twenty years before, they settled in poverty and sickness. Larger buildings are erected on piles, secure from the inundations; where a single cabin once stood, a neat village is now to be seen; warehouses, stores, and workshops increase the importance of the place. The Squatters live respected and in due time die, regretted by all who knew them.

Thus are the vast frontiers of our country peopled, and thus does cultivation, year after year, extend over the Western wilds. Time will no doubt be when the great valley of the Mississippi, still covered with primeval forests interspersed with swamps, will smile with cornfields and orchards, while crowded cities will rise at intervals along its banks, and enlightened nations will rejoice in the bounties of Providence.

23.

Joseph H. Ingraham: The Plantations of Mississippi

The writings of Joseph Ingraham are rarely consulted today, except by historians. However, in the late 1830s and 1840s, his novels (many published in newspapers) were enormously popular. "A young, dark man, with soft voice," Longfellow noted in 1846. "He says he has written eighty novels, and of these twenty during the last year." While a young man, Ingraham, a New Englander, toured southwestern Mississippi, and his first book, and probably his best, The South-West, *records what he observed there. It was published anonymously (signed "By a Yankee") in 1835. Sections from it appear below.*

Source: *The South-West,* New York, 1835, Vol. II, pp. 84-93, 204-209, 247-255.

THERE ARE MANY CAUSES, both moral and physical, which concur to render the inhabitants of the South dissimilar to those of the North. Some of these may be traced to climate, more to education and local relations, and yet more to that peculiar state of things which necessarily prevails in a planting country and all newly organized states. The difference is clearly distinguishable through all its grades and ramifications, and so strongly marked as to stamp the Southern character with traits sufficiently distinctive to be dignified with the term "national."

A plantation, well stocked with hands, is the *ne plus ultra* of every man's ambition who resides at the South. Young men who come to this country "to make money" soon catch the mania, and nothing less than a broad plantation, waving with the snow-white cotton bolls, can fill their mental vision as they anticipate by a few years in their dreams of the future the result of their plans and labors. Hence, the great number of planters and the few professional men of long or eminent standing in their several professions. In such a state of things, no men grow old or gray in their profession if at all successful. As soon as the young lawyer acquires sufficient to purchase a few hundred acres of the rich alluvial lands and a few slaves, he quits his profession at once, though perhaps just rising into eminence, and turns cotton planter. The bar at Natchez is composed, with but few exceptions, entirely of young men. Ten years hence, probably not four out of five of these, if living, will remain in their profession.

To the prevalence of this custom of retiring so early from the bar, and not to want of talent, is to be attributed its deficiency of distinguished names. There is much talent now concentrated at this bar and throughout the state. But its possessors are young men; and this mania for planting will soon deprive the state of any benefit from it in a professional point of view. As the lawyers are young, the judges cannot, of course, be much stricken in years. The Northerner, naturally associates with the title of "Judge" a venerable, dignified personage, with locks of snow, a suit of sober black, and powdered queue, shoe buckles, and black silk stockings. Judge my surprise at hearing at the public table a few days since a young gentleman, apparently not more than four or five and twenty, addressed as "Judge"! I at first thought it applied as a mere "soubriquet," till subsequently assured that he was really on the bench.

Physicians make money much more rapidly than lawyers, and sooner retire from practice and assume the planter. They, however, retain their titles, so that medico-planters are now numerous, far outnumbering the regular practitioners, who have not

yet climbed high enough up the wall to leap down into a cotton field on the other side.

Ministers, who constitute the third item of the diploma'd triad, are not free from the universal mania, and as writing sermons is not coining money, the plantations are like the vocative in Latin pronouns. They, however, by observing the command in Gen. 9:1, contrive ultimately to reach the same goal. The merchant moves onward, floundering through invoices, ledgers, packages, and boxes. The ginwright and overseer also have an eye upon this Ultima Thule, while the more wealthy mechanics begin to form visions of cotton fields and talk knowingly upon the "staple." Even editors have an eye that way! . . .

Among Northerners, Southern planters are reputed wealthy. This idea is not far from correct — as a class they are so, perhaps more so than any other body of men in America. Like our Yankee farmers, they are tillers of the soil. "But why" you may ask, "do they who are engaged in the same pursuits as the New England farmer so infinitely surpass him in the reward of his labors?" The Northern farmer cannot at the most make more than 3 percent on his farm. He labors himself, or pays for labor. He *must* do the first or he cannot live. If he does the latter, he can make nothing. If by hard labor and frugal economy the common, independent Yankee farmer, such as the traveler meets with anywhere in New England, lays up annually from $400 to $700, he is a thriving man and "getting rich." His daughters are attractive, and his sons will have something "handsome" to begin the world with.

But the Southern farmer can make from 15 to 30 percent by his farm. He works on his plantation a certain number of slaves, say thirty, which are to him what the sinewy arms of the Yankee farmer are to himself. Each slave ought to average from seven to eight bales of cotton during the season, especially on the new lands. An acre will generally average from one to two bales. Each bale averages 400 pounds, at from twelve to fifteen cents a pound. This may not be an exact estimate, but it is not far from the true one. Deducting $2,500 for the expenses of the plantation, there will remain the net income of $11,000.

Now suppose this plantation and slaves to have been purchased on a credit, paying at the rate of $600 apiece for his Negroes, the planter would be able to pay for nearly two-thirds of them the first year. The second year, he would pay for the remainder, and purchase ten or twelve more; and the third year, if he had obtained his plantation on a credit of that length of time, he would pay for that also, and commence his fourth year with a valuable plantation, and thirty-five or forty slaves, all his own property, with an increased income for the ensuing year of some thousands of dollars. Henceforward, if prudent, he will rank as an opulent planter. Success is not, however, always in proportion to the outlay or expectations of the aspirant for wealth. It is modified and varied by the wear and tear, sickness and death, fluctuations of the market, and many other ills to which all who adventure in the great lottery of life are heirs.

In the way above alluded to, numerous plantations in this state have been commenced, and thus the wealth of a great number of the opulent planters of this region has originated. Incomes of $20,000 are common here. Several individuals possess incomes of from $40,000 to $50,000 and live in a style commensurate with their wealth. The amount is generally expressed by the number of their Negroes and the number of "bales" they make at a crop. To know the number of either is to know accurately their incomes. And as this is easily ascertained, it is not difficult to form a prompt estimate of individual wealth.

To sell cotton in order to buy Negoes — to make more cotton to buy more Negroes,

ad infinitum, is the aim and direct tendency of all the operations of the thoroughgoing cotton planter; his whole soul is wrapped up in the pursuit. It is, apparently, the principle by which he "lives, moves, and has his being." There are some who "work" 300 and 400 Negroes, though the average number is from 30 to 100. "This is all very fine," you say, "but the slaves! — there's the rub." True; but without slaves there could be no planters, for whites will not and cannot work cotton plantations beneath a broiling Southern sun. Without planters there could be no cotton; without cotton no wealth. Without them, Mississippi would be a wilderness and revert to the aboriginal possessors. Annihilate them tomorrow and this state and every Southern state might be bought for a song. . . .

Many of the planters are Northerners. When they have conquered their prejudices, they become thorough, driving planters, generally giving themselves up to the pursuit more devotedly than the regular-bred planter. Their treatment of their slaves is also far more rigid. Northerners are entirely unaccustomed to their habits, which are perfectly understood and appreciated by Southerners, who have been familiar with Africans from childhood; whom they have had for their nurses, playfellows, and "bearers," and between whom and themselves a reciprocal and very natural attachment exists, which, on the gentleman's part, involuntarily extends to the whole dingy race, exhibited in a kindly feeling and condescending familiarity, for which he receives gratitude in return. On the part of the slave, this attachment is manifested by an affection and faithfulness which only cease with life.

Of this state of feeling, which a Southern life and education can only give, the Northerner knows nothing. Inexperience leads him to hold the reins of government over his novel subjects with an unsparing severity, which the native ruler of these domestic colonies finds wholly unnecessary. The slave always prefers a Southern master, because he knows that he will be understood by him. His kindly feelings toward, and sympathies with, slaves, as such, are as honorable to his heart as gratifying to the subjects of them. He treats with suitable allowance those peculiarities of their race which the unpractised Northerner will construe into idleness, obstinacy, laziness, revenge, or hatred. There is another cause for their difference of treatment to their slaves. The Southerner, habituated to their presence, never fears them, and laughs at the idea. It is the reverse with the Northerner: he fears them and hopes to intimidate them by severity. . . .

THE TOWNS AND VILLAGES of Mississippi, as in European states, are located perfectly independent of each other, isolated among its forests, and often many leagues apart, leaving in the intervals large tracts of country covered with plantations and claiming no minuter subdivision than that of "county." Natchez, for instance, is a corporation one mile square, but from the boundaries of the city to Woodville, the next incorporated town south, there is an interval of thirty-eight miles. It is necessary for the planters who reside between towns so far asunder to have some more particular address than the indefinite one arising from their vicinity to one or another of these towns. Hence has originated the pleasing custom of naming estates, as in England; and names so given are always regarded by the planters themselves, and by the community, as an inseparable part of their address. These names are generally selected with taste, such as "Monmouth," "Laurel-Hill," "Grange," "Magnolia Grove," "The Forest," "Cottage," "Briars," "Fatherland," and "Anchorage" — the last given by a retired Navy officer to his plantation. The name is sometimes adopted with reference to some characteristic of the domain, as "The Oaks," "China Grove," "New Forest," etc., but more frequently it is a mere matter of fancy.

Towns in this state have usually originated from the location of a county seat, after the formation of a new county. Here the courthouse is placed, and forms the center of an area which is soon filled with edifices and inhabitants. If the county lies on the river, another town may arise, for a shipping port, but here the accumulation of towns usually ceases. A county seat and a cotton mart are all that an agricultural country requires. The towns in this state are thus dispersed two or three to each county, nor so long as this is a planting country will there be any great increase to their number, although in wealth and importance they may rival, particularly the shipping ports, the most populous places in the valley of the West. In these towns are the banks, the merchants, the post offices, and the several places of resort for business or pleasure that draw the planter and his family from his estate.

Each town is the center of a circle which extends many miles around it into the country and daily attracts all within its influence. The ladies come in their carriages "to shop," the gentlemen, on horseback, to do business with their commission merchants, visit the banks, hear the news, dine together at the hotels, and ride back in the evening. The Southern town is properly the "Exchange" for the neighboring planters, and the "Broadway" for their wives and daughters. And as no plantation is without a private carriage, the number of these gay vehicles, filling the streets of the larger towns on pleasant mornings in the winter, is surprising. I have counted between thirty and forty private carriages in the streets of Natchez in one morning. In a small country village, I once numbered seventeen, standing around a Methodist chapel. Showy carriages and saddle horses are the peculiar characteristics of the "moving spectacle" in the streets of Southwestern towns.

Every village is a nucleus of Southern society, to which the least portion is generally contributed by itself. When a public ball is given by the bachelors in one of these towns — for private parties are scarcely known — the tickets of invitation fly into the retirement of the plantations, within the prescribed circle, often to the distance of thirty miles. Thus families who reside several leagues apart, on opposite sides of the town, and who might otherwise never associate, unless on "change" or in "shopping," meet together, like the inhabitants of one city. This state of things unites, in a social bond, the intelligent inhabitants of a large extent of country, who are nearly equally wealthy, and creates a state of society in the highest degree favorable to hospitality and social feeling. These social "circles" often revolve within one another, and sometimes enlarge, until they embrace several towns.

The Mississippians are remarkable for their "locomotivity"; an organ which they have plainly developed, if we reason, as phrenologists sometimes do, from effect to cause — and whose existence is manifest from their propensity annually to depopulate their state by taking Northern tours during the summer months. During the season of gayety, in the winter months, the public assemblies and private coteries of Natchez are unsurpassed by those of any other city, in the elegance, refinement, or loveliness of the individuals who compose them. If you will bear in mind that the Southern females of wealth are usually educated in the most finished style, at the first female seminaries in the North, and, until recently, not seldom in Europe; and recollect the personal beauty, sprightliness, and extreme refinement of the Southern lady, you will not be surprised that elegant women grace the private circles and shine in the gay assemblies of Southern cities. . . .

Less attention is paid to the mental or personal cultivation of the male youth of this state than to that of the females. Many of them are partially educated at home; and, by the time they attain the age at which Northern boys enter college, become assistants on the plantation, which they expect one day to inherit; or, at the age of nineteen or twenty, receive from their parents land and Negroes, and commence planting for themselves. At the age of twenty-one or two they frequently marry. Many planters are opposed to giving their sons, whom they destine to succeed them as farmers, a classical education. A common practical education they consider sufficient for young gentlemen who are to bury themselves for life in the retirement of a plantation.

But Mississippi, in this age and at this juncture, from the peculiar construction of her political and social laws, demands an educated youth. The majority of the planters are able to educate their children in a superior manner; and if they do this, they will elevate the rising generation high in the scale of society, and give Mississippi an honorable rank among the republics of America. Although education is not indigenous, and is too frequently a secondary consideration in the minds of many, children in the towns are probably as well educated as they would be at the North, under similar circumstances, for no village is without private schools.

But the education of young children on plantations is much neglected. Many boys and girls, whose parents reside five or ten miles from any town or academy, and do not employ tutors, grow up to the age of eight or ten unable either to read or write. Some planters, who have but one or two children, and do not think it worth while to employ a tutor for so small a number, thoughtless of the injury their children may sustain, suffer them to grow up at home, almost ignorant even of the alphabet, till of an age to be sent away to a boarding school or an academy, where they first learn to read. In such a state of things, it is not uncommon to meet with very interesting and intelligent children wholly ignorant of those childish studies and that storybook information which throw such a charm over their little society, invigorating the intellectual faculties, and laying a foundation for a superstructure of mind. Often several families will unite and employ a tutor, constructing, for the purpose, a schoolhouse, in a central position among their plantations. But those who look forward to a high rank in American and European society for their children employ private tutors in their own houses, even if they have but one child. Some gentlemen send their children, when quite young, to the North and visit them every summer. Two-thirds of the planters' children of this state are educated out of it. . . .

THERE ARE PROPERLY THREE distinct classes of slaves in the South. The first, and most intelligent, class is composed of the domestic slaves, or "servants," as they are properly termed, of the planters. Some of these both read and write, and possess a great degree of intelligence; and as the Negro, of all the varieties of the human species, is the most imitative, they soon learn the language and readily adopt the manners of the family to which they are attached. It is true they frequently burlesque the latter and select the high-sounding words of the former for practice; for the Negro has an ear for euphony, which they usually misapply or mispronounce.

"Ben, how did you like the sermon today?" I once inquired of one, who, for pompous language and high-sounding epithets, was the Johnson of Negroes. "Mighty obligated wid it, master, de 'clusive 'flections werry distructive to de ignorum."

In the more fashionable families, Negroes feel it their duty — to show their aristocratic breeding — to ape manners and to use language to which the common herd cannot aspire. An aristocratic Negro, full of his master's wealth and importance which he feels to be reflected upon himself, is the most aristocratic personage in existence. He supports his own dignity and that of his own master, or "family," as he phrases it, which he deems inseparable, by a course of conduct befitting colored gentlemen. Always about the persons of their masters or mistresses, the domestic slaves obtain a better knowledge of the modes of civilized life than they could do in the field, where Negroes can rise but little above their original African state.

So identified are they with the families in which they have been "raised," and so accurate, but rough, are the copies which they individually present of their masters that were all the domestic slaves of several planters' families transferred to Liberia or Haiti, they would there constitute a by no means inferior state of African society, whose model would be found in Mississippi. Each family would be a faithful copy of that with which it was once connected; and should their former owners visit them in their new home, they would smile at its resemblance to the original. It is from this class that the friends of wisely regulated emancipation are to seek material for carrying their plans into effect.

The second class is composed of town slaves, which not only includes domestic slaves, in the families of the citizens, but also all Negro mechanics, draymen, hostlers, laborers, hucksters, and washwomen, and the heterogeneous multitude of every other occupation who fill the streets of a busy city — for slaves are trained to every kind of manual labor. The blacksmith, cabinet maker, carpenter, builder, wheelwright — all have one or more slaves laboring at their trades. The Negro is a third arm to every workingman who can possibly save money enough to purchase one. He is emphatically the "right-hand man" of every man. Even free Negroes cannot do without them; some of them own several, to whom they are the severest masters.

"To whom do you belong?" I once inquired of a Negro whom I had employed. "There's my master," he replied, pointing to a steady old Negro who had purchased himself, then his wife, and subsequently his three children, by his own manual exertions and persevering industry. He was now the owner of a comfortable house, a piece of land, and two or three slaves, to whom he could add one every three years. It is worthy of remark, and serves to illustrate one of the many singularities characteristic of the race, that the free Negro who "buys his wife's freedom," as they term it, from her master by paying him her full value ever afterward considers her in the light of property.

"Thomas, you are a free man," I remarked to one who had purchased himself and wife from his master by the profits of a poultry yard and vegetable garden, industriously attended to for many years in his leisure hours and on Sundays. "You are a free man; I suppose you will soon have Negroes of your own."

"Hi! Hab one now, master." "Who, Tom?" "Ol' Sarah, master." "Old Sarah! She is your wife." "She my nigger too; I pay master five hun'red dollar for her."

Many of the Negroes who swarm in the cities are what are called "hired servants." They belong to planters or others, who, finding them qualified for some occupation in which they cannot afford to employ them, hire them to citizens as mechanics, cooks, waiters, nurses, etc., and receive the monthly wages for their services. Some steady slaves are permitted to "hire their own time"; that is, to go into town and earn what they can as porters, laborers, gardeners, or in other ways, and pay a stipulated sum weekly to their owners, which will be regulated according to the supposed value of the slave's labor. Masters, however, who are sufficiently indulgent to allow them to "hire their time" are seldom rigorous in rating their labor very high. But whether the slave earns less or more than the specified sum, he must always pay that

and neither more nor less than that to his master at the close of each week as the condition of this privilege.

Few fail in making up the sum and generally they earn more, if industrious, which is expended in little luxuries, or laid by in an old rag among the rafters of their houses, till a sufficient sum is thus accumulated to purchase their freedom. This they are seldom refused, and if a small amount is wanting to reach their value, the master makes it up out of his own purse, or rather, takes no notice of the deficiency. I have never known a planter refuse to aid, by peculiar indulgences, any of his steady and well-disposed slaves who desired to purchase their freedom. On the contrary, they often endeavor to excite emulation in them to the attainment of this end. This custom of allowing slaves to "hire their time," ensuring the master a certain sum weekly and the slave a small surplus, is mutually advantageous to both.

The majority of town servants are those who are hired to families by planters, or by those living in town who own more than they have employment for, or who can make more by hiring them out than by keeping them at home. Some families, who possess not an acre of land but own many slaves, hire them out to different individuals; the wages constituting their only income, which is often very large. There are indeed few families, however wealthy, whose incomes are not increased by the wages of hired slaves, and there are many poor people, who own one or two slaves, whose hire enables them to live comfortably. From three to five dollars a week is the hire of a female, and seventy-five cents or a dollar a day for a male. Thus, contrary to the opinion at the North, families may have good servants and yet not own one, if they are unable to buy, or are conscientious upon that ground, though there is not a shade of difference between hiring a slave, where prejudices are concerned, and owning one. Those who think otherwise, and thus compound with conscience, are only making a distinction without a difference.

Northern people, when they come to this country, who dislike either to hire or purchase, often bring free colored or white servants (helps) with them. The first soon marry with the free blacks, or become too lofty in their conceptions of things, in contrasting the situation of their fellows around them with their own, to be retained. The latter, if they are young and pretty, or even old and ugly, assume the fine lady at once, disdaining to be servants among slaves, and Hymen, in the person of some spruce overseer, soon fulfills their expectations. I have seen but one white servant, or domestic, of either sex in this country, and this was the body servant of an Englishman who remained a few days in Natchez, during which time John sturdily refused to perform a single duty of his station. . . .

The third and lowest class consists of those slaves who are termed "field hands."[1] Many of them rank but little higher than the brutes that perish in the scale of intellect, and they are, in general, as a class, the last and lowest link in the chain of the human species. Secluded in the solitude of an extensive plantation, which is their world, beyond whose horizon they know nothing; their walks limited by the "quarters" and the field; their knowledge and information derived from the rude gossip of their fellows, straggling runaways, or house servants; and without seeing a white person except their master or overseer as they ride over the estate, with whom they seldom hold any conversation, they present the singular feature of African savages, disciplined to subordination and placed in the heart of a civilized community.

Mere change of place will not change the savage. Moral and intellectual culture alone will elevate him to an equality with his civilized brethren. The African transplanted from the arid soil of Ebo, Sene-Gambia, or Guinea, to the green fields of America, without mental culture, will remain still the wild African, though he may wield his ox-whip, whistle after his plough, and lift his hat when addressed, like his more civilized fellows. His children, born on the plantation to which he is attached, and suffered to grow up as ignorant as himself, will not be one degree higher in the scale of civilization than they would have been had they been born in Africa. The next generation will be no higher advanced; and though they may have thrown away the idols of their country and been taught some vague notions of God and the Christian religion, they are, in almost every sense of the word, Africans, as rude and barbarous but not so artless as their untamed brethren beyond the Atlantic.

This has been, till within a few years, the general condition of "field hands" in this country, though there have been exceptions on some plantations, highly honorable to their proprietors. Within a few years, gentlemen of intelligence, humanity, and wealth, themselves the owners of great numbers of slaves, have exerted themselves and used their influence in mitigating the condition of this class. They commenced a reformation of the old system, whose chief foundation was unyielding rigor, first upon their own plantations. The influence of their example was manifest by the general change which gradually took place on other estates. This reformation is still in progress, and the condition of the plantation slave is now meliorated, so far as policy will admit, while they remain in their present relation.

---

1. "Field hands," "Force," "Hands," "People," and "Niggers" are terms applied to the purchased laborers of a plantation; but "Slaves" — never. "Boys" is the general term for the men, and "women," for females. It is common to address a Negro forty years of age as "boy." If much older, he is called "daddy" or "uncle"; but "mister" or "man" — never. The females, in old age, become "aunty," "granny," or "old lady."

THE PRO-SLAVERY RIOT OF NOVEMBER 7, 1837, ALTON, ILL.   DEATH OF
REV. E. P. LOVEJOY. FROM WOODCUT MADE IN 1838.

"I WILL BE HEARD!"

During Jackson's second term, new political alignments were developing around the issues of financial policy and the national bank, states' rights, and the "spoils system." Anti-Jackson politicians coalesced in 1834 into the Whig Party, which joined supporters of Clay's "American System" and Calhoun's states' rights position on nullification with former Democrats alienated by Jackson's bank policy and some Northern industrialists.

In the midst of these developments the gathering vehemence of the Abolition movement brought organized radical agitation onto the political scene for the first time since the Sons of Liberty. Antislavery societies had functioned for some time. The American Colonization Society had been trying to "eliminate" slavery gradually since 1816 by sending slaves back to Africa, but these efforts were manifestly not ending slavery. There were 750,000 slaves in 1790; the number had grown to over 2,000,000 by 1830. The slave trade had been outlawed in 1808, but enforcement was slack

and smuggling general. The new antislavery voices, the Abolitionists, were fired with moral righteousness and admitted no compromise short of the radical extirpation of slavery. William Lloyd Garrison's "Liberator" proclaimed, "I will be heard!" in its first issue, in spite of admonitions that Abolitionism threatened the Union.

White agitation was not an imposition on passive, satisfied slave populations. Desperate revolts dotted the history of slavery, among them Gabriel Prosser's plot (1800), Denmark Vesey's conspiracy (1822), and, most famous of all, Nat Turner's revolt in 1831. Fear of black insurrection was at the root of Southern restrictions on education and freeing of slaves.

In Congress, mention of slavery inevitably raised fears for the Union. Abolitionist petitions demanding Congressional action threatened the uneasy balance between Southern and Northern interests. But fear of disunion negated Abolitionist arguments and a "gag rule" in the House prevented discussion of the issue for 10 years.

"Set to Between Old Hickory and Bully Nick"; caricature in "The Globe," 1834, depicts the clash between Biddle and Jackson over the latter's attacks on the national bank

Engraving of Andrew Jackson

The Bank

Bitterness over Jackson's bank policy continued during his second term. The renewal of the United States Bank charter had been vetoed by Jackson before the 1832 election. However, instead of letting the old charter run out in 1836, Jackson removed government assets in 1833 and deposited them in state banks. A congressional motion to censure the President for this drew together opposition forces led by Clay, Webster, and Calhoun to form the Whig Party. An element of the new party's position was Clay's "American System" calling for high protective tariffs and a national program of internal improvements.

Attempted assassination of Jackson in January 1835 by Richard Lawrence, both of whose guns misfired

Oil by John Neagle, 1843, depicting Henry Clay with symbols of his "American system"

"Symptoms of a Locked Jaw"; caricature dealing with the controversy between Clay and Jackson

This cartoon, not entirely sympathetic to either side, shows Jackson roasted by "Public Opinion" over the removal of deposits, while Clay, Webster, Calhoun and others enjoy the show

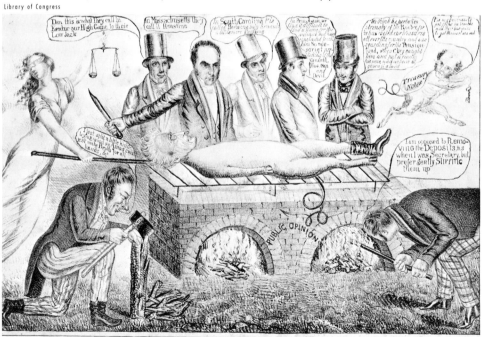

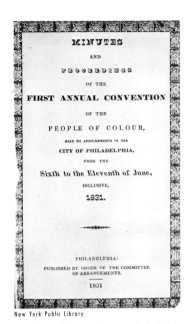

(Right) William Whipper, Philadelphian active in early Abolitionist activities

African Americans Take Action

Blacks, slave or free, did not wait for whites to solve their problems. As early as 1739 the Cato conspiracy in South Carolina showed the readiness of slaves to break their shackles. By 1831, free blacks were holding a national convention. In 1839 captives seized the "Amistad," a Spanish slave-ship. Two years later the Supreme Court declared the mutineers free.

Toussaint L'Ouverture, black Haitian liberator, symbolized Southern fears. The violence of Nat Turner's insurrection and the even greater violence of retaliation shook the country. Most of the slave states changed their constitutions to make the freeing of even one's own slaves illegal. Even the teaching of Christianity to slaves was forbidden.

(Left) Joseph Cinque, chief of "Amistad" captives; (right) Toussaint L'Ouverture

(Top) "Nat Turner and his Confederates"; steel engraving, 1863, after Felix Darley; (left) the capture of Nat Turner; illustration from "Scribner's Popular History"; (below) wood engraving from "An Authentic Narrative of the Seminole War," 1836

Massacre of the Whites by the Indians and Blacks in Florida.

The above is intended to represent the horrid Massacre of the Whites in Florida, in December 1835, and January, February, March and April 1836, when near Four Hundred (including women and children) fell victims to the barbarity of the Negroes and Indians.

THE LIBERATOR.

VOL. I.]   WILLIAM LLOYD GARRISON AND ISAAC KNAPP, PUBLISHERS.   [NO. 22.

BOSTON, MASSACHUSETTS.]   OUR COUNTRY IS THE WORLD—OUR COUNTRYMEN ARE MANKIND.   [SATURDAY, MAY 28, 1831.

The Granger Collection

Metropolitan Museum of Art

Garrison's "Liberator" was the most prominent Abolitionist journal. Started in 1831, it adopted a "no compromise" position calling for immediate abolition of slavery. Garrison was nearly lynched in the streets of Boston in 1835, but was undeterred by the incident. Acts of violence against Abolitionists were common — arson in Philadelphia, and numerous lynchings — but the militants continued to pour books, pamphlets, and vitriolic speeches against the monster slavery. While the incidents they depicted were true, they were often exceptional rather than common. All was fair in war.

(Top) Masthead from "The Liberator," 1831; (left) daguerreotype of William Lloyd Garrison; (bottom) cartoon showing Garrison and English Abolitionist George Thompson mobbed in Boston, 1835

New York Historical Society

Fire destroying Pennsylvania Hall, home of the Abolition Society in Philadelphia

(Left) Engraving from a broadside, "Slave Market of America," 1836, showing a free citizen being sold in Washington to pay his jail fees; (below) two engravings from "Picture of Slavery" by G. Bourne, 1834; (left) selling females by the pound; (right) auction at Richmond

In 1836, Harrison, backed by Clay and Webster, ran against Van Buren, backed by Jackson and Benton

(Above) Van Buren and his attorney general, Felix Grundy; cartoon below attacks both Democratic fiscal policy and the spoils system. Van Buren, drawn by spoilsmen, crushes the people. Officeholders get gold, while others get only currencies "good for a shave"

Joshua Giddings (left) and John Quincy Adams led the anti-gag rule minority in the House

Van Buren

Martin Van Buren won the 1836 election handily, in part because the Whigs could not agree on a candidate. Webster was nominated by a Massachusetts caucus. Hugh White was nominated by Tennessee anti-Jackson Democrats, while the anti-Masons, still operating independently, nominated William Henry Harrison. In New York, radical Democrats, called Loco-Focos, took up the mantle of the defunct Workingman's Party and accused Tammany of catering to special financial interests. The Loco-Focos advocated hard money, free trade, and an end to monopolies and special privilege, but were not a factor in the election, even though the 1837 crash verified their financial fears. The term Loco-Foco came to be the opposition name for all Democrats.

The opposition saw a probe into a Tammany man's theft of $1,000,000 as a "whitewash"

Every inch of this cartoon contains bitter references to the causes and effects of the Panic of 1837

It was Van Buren's misfortune to be elected only months before the country plunged into financial panic. A major cause was reckless speculation. Too much of the country's capital and credit were tied up in unrealized investments: stock companies, canal projects, uncultivated land, railroads operating at a loss. Anti-inflation measures, such as the Specie Circular barring paper money in public land sales, curbed land speculation, but also devalued state bank notes. Credit collapsed as foreign creditors and, in turn, Eastern banks, called in loans.

Foxy Van Buren deviates from Jackson-Benton policies

British lampoon of the kinds of unwise investment that helped cause the Panic

24.

GJERT HOVLAND: Opportunities for Land and for Work

For immigrants who elected to be farmers America was indeed a land of opportunity, provided they could afford to pay $1.25 for an acre of public land. Like other Norwegians who emigrated to the United States before the mid-1830s, Gjert Hovland settled first in northwestern New York and then moved to Illinois. Had Hovland arrived later, he would probably have moved to a Norwegian community in Wisconsin or Minnesota instead of Illinois. The following encouraging letter from Kendall settlement in New York was addressed to one Torjuls Maeland on April 22, 1835.

Source: Blegen, pp. 21-25.

I MUST TAKE THIS OPPORTUNITY to let you know that we are in the best of health, and that both my wife and I are exceedingly well satisfied. Our son attends the English school and talks English as well as the native-born. Nothing has made me more happy and contented than that we left Norway and came to this country. We have gained more since our arrival here than I did during all the time I lived in Norway, and I have every prospect of earning a living here for myself and my family, even if my family becomes larger, so long as God gives me good health.

Such excellent plans have been developed here that, even though one be infirm, no one need go hungry. Competent men are elected to see that no needy persons, either in the cities or in the country, shall have to beg. If a man dies and leaves a widow and children who are unable to support themselves, as often happens, they have the privilege of petitioning these officials. Each one will then receive every year as much clothing and food as he needs, and no discrimination is shown between the native-born and those from foreign countries. These things I have learned through daily observation, and I do not believe there can be better laws and arrangements for the benefit and happiness of the common man in the whole world. I have talked with a sensible person who has traveled in many countries, who has lived here twenty-six years, and has full knowledge of the matter; I asked both him and other reliable persons, for I wish to let everyone know the truth.

When assemblies are held to elect officials to serve the country, the vote of the common man carries just as much authority and influence as that of the rich and powerful man. Neither in the matter of clothes nor in manners are distinctions noticeable, whether one be a farmer or a clerk. The one enjoys just as much freedom as the other. So long as he comports himself honestly he meets no interference. Everybody is free to travel about in the country, wherever he wishes, without passports or papers. Everyone is permitted to engage in whatever business he finds most desirable, in trade or commerce, by land or by water. But if anyone is found guilty of crime, he is prosecuted and severely punished.

No duties are levied upon goods that are produced in the country and brought to the city by water or by land. In case of death, no registration is required; the survivor, after paying the debts, is free to dispose of the property for himself and his family just as he pleases. There is no one here who snatches it away, like a beast of prey, wanting only to live by the sweat of others and to make himself heir to the money of others. No, everyone must work for his living here, whether he be of low or high estate. It would greatly please me to learn that all of you who are in need and have little chance of supporting yourselves and your families have decided to leave Norway and come to America; for, even if many more come, there will still be room here for all. Those who are willing to work will not lack employment or business here. It is possible for all to live in comfort and without want.

I do not believe that any who suffer oppression and who must rear their children in poverty could do better than to come to America. But alas, many who want to come lack the means, and many others are so stupid as to believe that it is best to live in the country where they have grown up even if they have nothing but hard bread to satisfy their hunger. It is as if they thought that those who move to a better land, a land of plenty, do wrong. But I cannot find that our Creator has forbidden us to seek our food in an honorable way. I should like to talk to many persons in Norway for a little while, but we do not wish to live in Norway. We lived there altogether too long. Nor have I talked with any immigrant in this country who wished to return.

We left our home in Norway on June 24, 1831. Sailing from Gothenburg on July 30, we landed in America September 18, and by October 4 we had reached this place in the interior where we now live. The day after my arrival I began to work for an American. In December I bought myself fif-

ty acres of land. I put up a house which we moved into in the month of March 1832. I then set to work with the greatest will and pleasure, for the land was covered with trees. In the fall I planted about one barrel of wheat, and in the spring of 1833 we planted about half a bushel of Indian corn and three bushels of potatoes (the latter in May). The next fall we harvested fifteen barrels of wheat, six barrels of Indian corn, and fourteen barrels of potatoes. Wheat, which is grown almost everywhere, is used for daily food. It costs from $3 to $4 a barrel, corn costs from $1.50 to $2 a barrel, and potatoes 50 cents a barrel. Oats are $1 a barrel, being used not for human food, but for the cattle and horses. We purchased a cow in April of the first year we were here for $18, from which we milked six cans a day and sometimes more. A pound of butter costs, in the towns, from 8 to 12 skillings, salt pork from 4 to 8 skillings a pound, and meat 4 skillings a pound.

Land is measured off here with a pole eight ells and six inches long, this being called a rod. An acre measures sixteen rods in length by ten in breadth. One hundred acres, here called a lot, is a piece of land of considerable size. I am certain that from fifty acres here, we harvest many times more than from a *gaard* in Norway. I believe that an acre is something more than a *tφnde saed* in Norway; it takes two bushels of wheat to sow an acre.

Six families of the Norwegians who had settled in this place sold their farms last summer and moved farther west in the country to a place called Illinois. We and another Norwegian family have also sold our farms and intend to journey, this May, to that state, where land can be bought at a better price, and where it is easier to get started. There are only enough trees there to meet actual needs. Cattle can be fed there at little cost, for one can cut plenty of hay. The United States owns an untold amount of land which is reserved by law at a set price for the one who first buys it from the government. It is called public land and is sold for $1.25 per acre. Land thus bought and paid for is held in allodial possession for the purchaser and his heirs. Whether native-born or foreign, a man is free to do with it whatever he pleases.

This is a beautiful and fertile country. Prosperity and contentment are almost everywhere. Practically everything needed can be sown or planted here and grows splendidly, producing a yield of manyfold without the use of manure.

Law and order exist here, and the country is governed by wise authorities.

I sold my land last summer, in July 1834, and by the transaction got $500 in cash. I have now decided to buy 160 acres, which can be had for $200. The eight Norwegian families still in this neighborhood want to sell their land as soon as they can and move west, for they prefer to live near each other, although many of the natives are people just as good.

In America you associate with good and kindly people. Everyone has the freedom to practise the teaching and religion he prefers. The only tax a man pays here is on the land he owns, and even that tax is not large. Nor are there other useless expenditures for the support of persons — as in many places in Europe — who are of more harm than benefit to the country. For the fifty acres I sold I paid $1 a year in taxes. On the piece of land we sold there were more trees than I could count of the kind that produces sugar, and these trees were common everywhere. We took no more than we needed for our own use each year. Usually we did this work in March, when the sap begins to rise in the trees. With a small iron we chopped an opening in the bark of the tree, placing under it a piece of hollowed-out wood as a trough. A tree yields from two to three pails of sweet sap a day, and this sap makes sugar, syrup, ale, and vinegar.

There is much more I could write to you about, but I will close for this time, with hearty greetings from me and my wife and son to you, my relatives, and acquaintances. Let us be happy in heart and consecrated in spirit so that when the race has been run, when the pilgrim's staff has been laid down, we may be worthy of hearing the glorious words: "Blessed of my Father, come ye and inherit the kingdom and the righteousness prepared for you." Wherever we may wander in this earthly sphere, let us seek Him who is the true light and life, and follow His voice which calls to our hearts, no matter where we go or stand. Live well in the sight of God: that is my wish as your friend. Greetings to Knud Oppedal and Johannes Hovland and to all who inquire about me.

25.

Theophilus Fisk: The War of Capital Against Labor

Theophilus Fisk delivered the address, "Capital Against Labor," to the mechanics of Boston in May 1835. At the time he was editor of the Boston Reformer, *the organ of the Radical Democrats. Fisk had abandoned a career as a Universalist minister to edit a violently anti-clerical newspaper, and later his passion was expended against the capitalist. He concurred in the Jacksonian view that the main division of society was between the few and the many, but he went further in holding that the conflict between the two was potentially explosive. A portion of his address is reprinted here.*

Source: *New York Evening Post*, August 6, 1835.

THE HISTORY OF THE PRODUCERS of wealth, of the industrious classes, is that of a continued warfare of HONESTY against FRAUD, WEAKNESS against POWER, JUSTICE against OPPRESSION. The purchasers of labor have in all ages had the advantage of the sellers and they have rarely failed to use their power to the furtherance of their own interest. Until within a comparatively short period of time, the laboring classes even in England and Scotland were slaves, serfs, bondmen. Colliers in the latter country even down to as late a period as 1776 were slaves in fact as well as in name.

Gradually, however, the rust of time weakened their chains of bondage; the period at length arrived when the grievous burdens upon their shoulders were too galling longer to be borne; the collar was slipped from the galled neck; and their aristocratic masters, finding it impossible longer to ride in safety, consented with an ill grace to forgo a privilege they were no longer able to preserve. But in losing the NAME of slaves, we are not to suppose that the sellers of labor were allowed to assume the place in society that God and nature designed for them.

That the laborer had natural, inalienable rights, that they were free and independent members of society and possessed the right, if they sold their labor, to fix their own price upon it would have been scouted at as of all things the most leveling, disorganizing, and dangerous. Hence the government, those who purchased labor, were continually passing partial, unequal, unjust laws and paying for it according to the ideas of its value by those who wanted to use it. Then commenced the struggle between the two great dealers in the market of the world, viz., Capital and Labor; and as Capital had always the government with its legion of bayonets to support its claims, the result may easily be imagined.

During the existence of the ancient monopolies, called guilds or fraternities, Capital and Labor were identified. These fraternities were composed both of masters and workmen whose interests were one and the same; at length, however, the privileges of these bodies, which had originally been conferred upon them for their protection against the violence of the feudal nobility, became so odious and oppressive that it became indispensable that they should be abridged. The parties then became opponents; the one endeavoring to raise, the other to depress the prices of labor.

Combinations were then formed. As early as 1548, we find a notice in a preamble of an act of Parliament, in these words:

> Artificers, handicraftsmen, and laborers have made confederacies and promises and have sworn mutual oaths, not only that they should not meddle with one another's work and perform and finish that another hath begun, but also to constitute and appoint how much work they shall do in a day and what hours and times they shall work, contrary to the laws and statutes of this Realm, to the great injury and impoverishment of His Majesty's subjects.

Parliament also passed sundry acts expressly prohibiting combinations for the purpose of raising the prices of labor. In 1824, after long experience had tested the folly and inutility of laws of that nature; that they were partial and unjust; that they raised one class and depressed another; that they were impolitic, unwise, and inexpedient, the system was abandoned and the laws repealed.

By this brief and imperfect outline, it may be seen that those who live without labor are and have been the enemies of the producing classes. Their interests, although naturally, where justice prevails, one and the same, have almost always clashed with each other. We find by glancing at the past that the laboring classes have been struggling for centuries under the iron yoke of despotism, against fraud, tyranny, and injustice. "Upward and onward" has been their watchword, until now they are enabled, from the proud eminence to which they have attained, to look forward and behold the promised land. If they are true to themselves they must inevitably enter in and possess it. Although the Jebusites and Gershashites and Parasites, all the various classes, castes, and tribes of the Canaanites who live by prey and plunder may look fierce and "talk big," the inheritance is ours.

The history of the amelioration, improvement, and elevation of the working classes is but the history of the progress of wealth, civilization, and all that ennobles, dignifies, and exalts humanity. It is the history of all the wonderful improvements in the arts and sciences, in manufactures and commerce.

The record of the past affords the highest encouragement for the present and the future. If the laboring classes have been able, with all the stupendous obstacles that have been thrown in their way, to fight an uphill battle against the omnipotent power of Capital and to possess themselves of many of the privileges that belong to free citizenship, we can easily determine the question of their ultimate emancipation and triumph. The controversy will never cease, the warfare will never end until all are placed upon the broad tableland of perfect political equality. The sellers of labor will yet wrest from the unholy grasp of the apostles of Mammon the right to govern themselves, to make their own laws, and to select their own agents to execute them.

Though the power of wealth in the hands of the FEW may for a time keep down the industrious MANY, yet the hazard of experimenting too far with those who have suffered so much and so long had better be taken into the calculation before a system of continued, permanent robbery be determined upon; before they determined to treat the unmanacled workingman as they would a convict in the state prison, they would do well to pause. Beneath their feet an earthquake slumbers. There is a period in the affairs of men when forbearance ceases to be a virtue, when patient endurance becomes criminal. Let the interested beware how they accelerate the sands in Time's hourglass and thereby hasten a season when resistance and not resignation and passive obedience will be the rallying watchword.

The laws by which we are governed were not made by us, although said to be — had they been, they would have been equal, equitable, and impartial — for the benefit and protection of the masses, the great whole of which society is composed. It is quite impossible for the laboring classes to make laws to rob one another; they cannot steal from themselves by partial legislation. What is for the interest of one is for the interest of all. But let the privileged few make the laws and what is the result? What has been the natural consequence in all past time? Why, that the many have been ground up to feed the nabobs. What has been, will be. Like causes produce like effects under similar circumstances.

Pore over the musty folios of the past and the startling truth meets you at every page — that all laws made by rich men have been in favor of Capital, never in favor of Labor. And yet our blood-proud and purse-proud nobility talk of PROTECTING THE LABORER! "Such protection as the vulture gives to lambs, covering and devouring them!" Their misnamed laws of PROTECTION always have made them rich at our expense, have ever added to their already overflowing coffers by filching the products of industry from the pockets of the poor.

The laborer asks no protection; their offers, therefore, are entirely gratuitous; the laborer can and does both protect himself and the nonproducer into the bargain. In case of invasion or insurrection, who talks of protecting them? When the appalling cry of "Fire!" falls upon the ear, who protects the scanty property of the laborer, the "palaces of the poor"? Not the men who make the laws. They do not even protect their own gorgeous mansions from the devouring element. No. We ask no protection; we simply desire TO BE LET ALONE.

A great deal of affectionate regard is, and has been, manifested by the aristocracy for the interests of the "dear people." They have clung to them like the poisonous ivy to the monarch of the wood, palsying the faculties, throwing fetters of bondage upon

the intellect, until at last they perish in the entwining folds of hollow-hearted dissimulation. All the friendly embraces of those who fatten upon the toil of others are, like the hug of the bear, certain death. Let our motto be, "Take your delicate fingers from our throats; 'white paws,' if you please, gentlemen."

But the monopolists, the professional men, the men of wealth, THEY labor, it is said, as well as the farmer and the mechanic. They do labor to be sure, but IT IS LABORING TO COLLECT THAT WHICH OTHERS HAVE EARNED. The lawyer's "may it please your honor" never made the pot boil. The presidents' and cashiers' printed paper rags, covered with false promises to pay, never crowned the hill with ripening sheaf, nor made the valley smile. The lazy drone, by sticking a quill behind his ear, never yet felled the boundless forest and reared the castle's dome, breaking the repose of ages with the busy tones of hardy enterprise.

If our houses could spring up spontaneously, like mushrooms; if we could sit in our seats like dried mummies and by single scratch of a pen could construct canals, bridges, and railroads, we might then talk about equality of rights and privileges with some degree of propriety. But, no. If houses are to be erected, it is to be done by the hard hand of labor, in sweat, and toil, and fatigue. The legislature grants no charters for the workingmen to build houses without labor and to grow rich without being industrious.

We hear at almost every corner of the streets the stereotyped billingsgate about the "lower classes." "Lower classes" indeed! The time has been when they were as low as the sordid spirit of avarice and the iron heel of bloodsucking ambition could tread them down; thousands living and dying, mere cogs in the social machine; dragging out a miserable existence in the squalor of toil, want, and degradation. They have stood still as stocks, quiet as the charnel house, while "lisping infancy" has been foredoomed, by the unholy lust of gold, to labor twelve, fourteen, sixteen hours per day, withering and blasting the bud of youth ere its petals were unfolded to the sun. If they dared to remonstrate, to utter a word of expostulation, the dry, hard, cold lip of unfeeling selfishness would contract with scorn and malignity, and the stony eye of unpitying brutality would "look daggers," while the hand used them. This has been borne; their taskmasters were rich and could talk Latin.

The natural consequences of laziness, the penalty of idleness, has fallen upon the industrious classes instead of the rich capitalist, who lives without labor; those who earn and save have been compelled to toil early and late for a pittance barely sufficient to keep their families from starving, that the indolent drones might be clothed in purple and fine linen and fare sumptuously every day. The natural reward of honest industry has been wrested from the laborer by unjust laws and given to those who were never guilty of earning a dollar in their lives — who are too lazy to work and too proud to beg — but the days of oppression are numbered; God grant they may soon be finished.

The subject which has called us from our homes this evening is vitally important inasmuch as it seems the dawning light of a coming day. It will have this good effect if nothing more: it will teach those who live by plunder that a part of mankind were never born to be hewers of wood and drawers of water to those no better than themselves. It will call upon the public for their strong reasons why the producers of wealth should be kept in ignorance, servility, and bondage; why they must longer be debarred the blessings they have purchased with tears and blood, and lazy men riot upon the miseries of the poor! It calls upon the philanthropist and Christian to advocate and demand the immediate emancipation of the "white slaves of the North," and to declare to the world that the workers are, and of right ought to be, free and independent citizens of these United States.

The recent movements among our industrious fellow citizens speak a language that can neither be perverted nor misunderstood. The world is told by acts that speak more plainly than volumes of words that "he who will shun the exertions and sacrifices necessary to qualify him to know his rights, and also to maintain them, deserves to be duped, to groan in perpetual slavery, to wear the inextricable chains the FEW are forging for the MANY."

Knowledge and virtue being the only sure foundation of American liberty, you have taken the proper steps toward a resumption of your sacred rights. By reducing the number of hours of labor, you give yourselves opportunity to obtain that knowledge which is power. They whose god is gain have long feared that if the laborer should be allowed to take his nose from the grindstone five minutes at a time, he would be learning how to govern and provide for himself, so he must be compelled to toil on like a galley slave at the oar. . . .

Eight hours for work, eight hours for sleep, and eight hours for amusement and instruction is the equitable allotment for the twenty-four. But to a great majority of the buyers of labor even the granting of your present just demand that ten hours shall constitute a day's work seems preposterous in the extreme. They think that mankind were not only born to trouble as the sparks fly upward, but according to their creed we were born to labor as the sweat drops downward.

Says *Blackwood's Magazine*, "Are not the poor the 'working classes?' Then let them work — work — work. If they are to have resting hours on weekdays, pray, what is the use of the Sabbath? Work is the chief end and whole duty of man." Nobody thinks of asking what rest do the laws of nature require? We are governed by the laws of avarice, which, like bigotry, "has no head and cannot think, no heart and cannot feel." We even seem to forget there ever were laws of nature, we are groping in such an unnatural state of society. We might almost as well talk of the empire of chaos as of the empire of mind while it is fettered with chains of midnight. . . .

But it is objected that if the "ten-hour system" succeeds, the young men, the apprentices will become wild and unruly. The objection is a base and unfounded libel, both upon masters and men. They have one whole day in seven to themselves under the present system; the same moral or physical restraints that operate on that day would upon other days in the week. The master or the guardian would hardly become relaxed in their rules of duty even if the apprentices did not labor more than four hours in the day.

But they will get less wages because they will produce less. We must have other proof than mere assertion for this before it can be deemed worthy of credence. If a man works better when he is fresh than when he is fatigued, then, we could hardly suppose he would do less in a twelvemonth upon the system you are contending for than upon the barbarous "all day" bondage. Suppose he does less and receives less — how much less? Why, only one-twelfth part at most; and what is one-twelfth part of a week's wages compared with the amount of happiness that would be thus increased at the family hearthstone?

If he works less, he will suffer less, and it will cost him less to live. The fees to the doctor, the apothecary, and the nurse will be sensibly diminished. It will also be an immense saving to the nation. The health and strength of the operatives being no longer broken by excessive toil, the workhouse will no longer be thronged. They would not only perform as much labor as at present but would become healthy and wise, if not wealthy.

The efforts you are now making to relieve yourselves of the odious oppressions which for ages have disgraced humanity are deserving the warmest approbation of every friend to the right of man throughout the world. . . .

A mighty spirit is abroad in the earth, overthrowing the pillars of despotism and the fetters of bondage. With the friends of freedom throughout the world let us be co-workers. Let the present effort be but the glimmering twilight of a day of unclouded glory. Remember that this is but the lopping off of but one single head of the political monster that feeds on human gore; the other ninety-nine are hissing and sputtering fiercely as ever. So long as you allow Capital to make laws for Labor, standing out for higher wages or reducing the hours of toil will only be doing the work by halves. There must be a radical reform and this can only be accomplished at the ballot boxes.

Allow the Capitalists to make a compromise with you, allow them to play the lawgiver, and they will not care a brass farthing how few hours you work or what prices you receive. They will take good care how to strike the balance when they come to pay you for your labor. For every hour you abstract from toil, they will levy an indirect tax upon you that shall treble its value. No. There is not a nabob in Boston that would raise a finger to prevent the "ten-hour system" if he thought the great work of reform would stop there; for all that could be remedied in a hundred ways by partial legislation next winter.

But the great fear of those who grow rich upon your industry is that if you get time to improve your minds, you will get your eyes open to the monstrous frauds that have been perpetrated upon you by the heathen idolaters, the worshipers of Mammon. Let their worst fears be realized. Shoulder to shoulder, man to man, our fathers fought and triumphed; let their sons profit by their illustrious example. Shrink not, disband not, and fear nothing.

Teach the lawgivers a salutary lesson at the polls; vote for no man who is not pledged to maintain your cause at all risks and at every hazard. If you are united, your strength is well-nigh omnipotent. Throw away all party names; all parties are, and ever have been, opposed to your interests. Form a party of your own that shall be all-controlling and uncontrollable. Take any name you please, I care not. Call yourselves Whigs, Tories, Democrats, Federalists — it is all one to me, so that you are united.

Your opposers will seek to divide you by some party jealousy because they know that divide and ruin is the only policy that will overthrow you. Bind yourselves together by the strongest of all bonds — that of self-interest. You have all one common cause, one common name, one common interest: the interest of Labor, the interest of honest industry. Keep this one single object in view — no longer at elections throw the rope over the roof of the house and pull at each end, but all one way; give one steady "yo yeave yoo" the long, strong, and the pull altogether, and the mass of human wrong, inequality, and oppression will be scattered to the four winds of heaven.

26.

GEORGE S. WHITE: The Moral Influence of Manufacturing

In the 1830s the merits of industrialism were vigorously debated. The affirmative argument given below is taken from a book by George S. White about Samuel Slater, the ingenious Englishman who founded the American cotton industry. In 1835, when the book was published, the use of complicated and expensive machinery was restricted to a few industries, notably cotton textiles, but the factory system was becoming widespread. The craftsman, instead of working for profit at home or in a small shop with his own tools, now worked as one of many wage earners for a merchant who owned both the "manufacturing establishment" and the tools, and who also bought the raw materials and sold the finished goods. It was this transformation of the economic enterprise that gave rise to the permanent labor union.

Source: *Memoir of Samuel Slater . . . Connected with a History of the Rise and Progress of the Cotton Manufacture in England and America*, 2nd edition, Philadelphia, 1836, pp. 113-120.

WE HAVE ALREADY SEEN that manufacturing establishments exert a powerful and permanent influence in their immediate neighborhoods, and time, if not already, will teach the lesson that they will stamp indelible traits upon our moral and national character. Evidences abound, wherever man exists, that his character is modified by localities, by a diversity of pursuits, by a facility of acquiring a living, by the quality and fashion of the living itself, by a restrained or free exercise of his rational powers, and by restraint on the enjoyment of liberty. Different climates and different countries produce indelible peculiarities. In the same climate and in the same country similar changes appear from the effects of immoral habits, and from what may be termed artificial or mechanical causes. The effects of immoral habits are well known to all observers of human nature.

Those pursuing different occupations are aware that these exert an influence upon character, producing moral, no less than physical, varieties. For example, butchers become hard-hearted and cruel, and in England are excluded from the jury box; those who are confined to a particular routine against their will, peevish and discontented; those who are always ordered or driven,' and expect to be so, exercise little control or discernment for themselves.

Manufacturing establishments become a blessing or a curse according to the facilities which they create for acquiring a living, to the necessary articles which they provide, and the general character which they produce. To set up and encourage the manufacturing of such articles, the use and demand of which produces no immoral tendency, is one of the best and most moral uses which can be made of capital. The moral manufacturer, without the power or disposition to overreach, is in reality a benefactor. The acquisition of wealth in this way is the most laudable. In point of benevolence and real worth of character it claims a decided advantage over the cent-per-cent process of accumulation. Some have not the requisite ability to carry on manufacturing establishments; capital, then, with great propriety is loaned to those who have. The moral influence of a community is not promoted by creating or submitting to a manufacturing, or any other aristocracy solely in the pursuit of interest, in which selfishness is wont to predominate.

The manufacturing interest in a flourishing state naturally creates power and wealth. The value of labor and the value of money are then at his disposal; but, in this free country, there is a sufficient counteracting influence to keep up the price of labor and to equalize the prices of their commodities with the value of the products of the earth. Without such a resisting power, a few would abound in wealth and influence, while the multitude would be in poverty and reduced to servitude. But there always exists a counteracting influence in the rival establishments and the general spirit of enterprise. On the supposition that the manufacturing interest was strictly benevolent and moral, dispensing its favors according to merit and precisely as they are needed, the community might not be losers by such a state of things. This must be always the case where a people are left free to use and purchase according to their free choice.

With the common experience of mankind it could not be expected so. Only a few look beyond their own interest; when that is provided for, the employed who have assisted in the provision are left to shift for themselves. Benevolence is not so general among mankind as to expect it uniformly. But in the progress of manufactures among us, every department becomes interested in its prosperity, the operatives receive a greater emolument for their services than in any other part of the world, while capital receives but a small interest compared with other branches of industry.

With such a power established merely by selfishness, morality is promoted so far and no further than interest; but the promotion of morals becomes their interest. And if religion appears something in name or in sectarianism more than in reality, still its promotion is for the interest of the whole community. It is said, on the presumption that the capitalists are aiming at their personal wealth, the facility for acquiring a fair compensation becomes less and less at every pressure. A rise of wages is then adapted to convenience or pleasure. But it must be remembered that the pressure bears as heavy on the employer as the employed, and renders him liable to lose all the earnings of many years of labor and the savings of much self-denial, and renders him poor and dependent.

There are two sides to this question, and the operatives in good times ought to lay up for time of need. Then they would not be obliged to bring their labor into market the best way they can to obtain their daily bread. To take advantage of such a position is one of the greatest immoralities. The liabilities of its consequences are as bad in creating discord and producing civil commotions. But the owners of factories are not known to stop their mills till obliged by dire necessity; they generally run them till they become bankrupt. The real power belongs to the laboring class; no one ought to expect to employ this without paying for it and no one does expect it. It is power when rightly used and most often ceases to be so when abused.

Those who are so thoughtless, negligent, or squandering, as to trust wholly to the present occasion for a bare subsistence, can hardly be thought powerful compared with what they would be did not necessity compel them to take what they can get for the present occasion. It is a mistaken notion to suppose the manufacturing interest promoted by creating poverty or, in the end, by heavy reduction of wages. The articles manufactured very soon sink in like proportion, and the profits are swallowed up in the payment of the operative. Besides these consequences, the ability to purchase does not exist, a consideration which more or less affects the value of every article brought into market.

Our day has witnessed the surprising effects of the ingenuity of man, in calling into existence and putting in operation labor-saving machinery. If it would be, in reality, promoting human existence and human happiness in our present character and condition, that our food should come to us ready made, our habitations ready built, our conveyances already in motion, and our understandings already improved, the nearer we approach such a state of things the better.

But if not, if the desires and pursuits of objects be no less blessings than their possessions, if human nature be bettered, and the grand object of existence benefited by employment, there must be a point beyond which to obtain food and clothing and other things without application would be objectionable. To be moral and desirable, labor-saving machinery must bring along with it some particular benefit to the community as well as to individuals. . . .

It is well known that vice grows worse by contact with its kind. If it can be proved that manufacturing establishments tend to accumulate, consolidate, and perpetuate vicious propensities, and their consequences on the community, this will serve as no inconsiderable drawback upon the apparent prosperity which is indicated in their immediate vicinity. If found so, the condition must be charged directly to the establishments or to their consequences and abuses. It is evidently an abuse to collect a mass of vicious population and keep them in a state of ignorance and irreligion. When this is done, the whole community has a right to complain. If it can be shown that such things are frequently done, it is contended that they are not necessary consequences of manufacturing establishments. The owners of such establishments have it in their power to change the current of vice from its filthy and offensive channel, and make peace, order and comfort among those they employ. . . .

Industry, directed by honest and intelligent views in moral pursuits and honorably rewarded, holds a very high rank among moral causes. To maintain good order and sound government it is more efficient than the sword or bayonet. At the anniversary dinner of the public schools in Boston, the following toast was given by Edward Everett: "Education: a better safeguard for liberty than a standing army. If we retrench the wages of the schoolmaster, we must raise the wages of the recruiting sergeant." So far as manufacturing establishments have promoted industry, and furnished means for an honest livelihood, thus far they have exerted a salutary influence on the character of those who have been employed. Multitudes of women and children have been kept out of vice simply by being employed, and instead of being destitute, provided with an abundance for a comfortable subsistence. . . .

On the score of employment, manufacturing establishments have done much to support the best interests of society. It appears also, at the present time, that they have done so by their improvements. On the supposition that one or a few individuals, by the invention of labor-saving machinery, succeed, so as to furnish any particular article much cheaper than it could be done in the ordinary way, in this country where it deprives no one of a living and goes to forward and hasten the general improvement, it cannot fail to be a benefit to the community. The diminution of price in the articles has been such that the people have been doubly paid for all the protection granted; and commerce has been benefited by the opening of a foreign market. The failures and fluctuations in the manufacturing establishments have arisen from their weak and incipient state and the competition of European fabrics. This cause appears greater than want of management and calculation, for the same men have alternately succeeded and failed on the same ground.

Fluctuations, whatever may be the cause, and whether they relate to business, morality, or religion, exert a wide influence on individual and national character. Those to which we are here attending give currency to monstrous species of swindling and form a most suitable juncture for unprincipled and unfeeling knavery to grasp with an unsparing hand, while industry and honesty are thrown into the background or kicked out-of-doors. When such occurrences happen, and the intriguer goes off rewarded and applauded, while the honest man is stripped, despised and neglected, they give a turn to the whole character of the community. The flooding of our cities with foreign importations has had this kind of tendency and produced those evil effects.

Shrewdness and overreaching are common events. Morality, however much respected in principle, is extremely liable to be set aside in practice. These are some of the bad tendencies of seeking out many useless inventions, and too eager a grasp after traffic and exchange of property, or what is technically called *speculation*. The acquisition and possession of property are made the main objects of existence, whether it be needed or not. On the other hand, it will be granted that every objection vanishes when mechanical inventions acquire permanency, and can be subjected to the regularity of calculations. It may dignify and exalt man to triumph over the known laws of nature, and bring out the hidden treasures of air, earth, and water, in tame submission to his use. For aught we can discern, it would have no injurious effect upon his character, could he extend his journeys and researches further than this globe. One thing is certain: the more he studies and understands the works of nature and Providence, the greater will be his admiration of the display and application of wisdom and goodness. If applied as intended, the more of the resources which have been provided he brings into action, the more he adds to his true dignity and happiness.

Contrivances to favor selfish views and selfish ends are common to the animal creation. The human family are distinguished from the infinity of being, only by a greater possession and cultivation of moral and intellectual faculties. Unlike the most of the animal creation, man is left to provide for himself. Strength and powers are given him, objects are placed before him, and the strongest conceivable motives presented to use this world as not abusing it.

There must be a limit beyond which refinement will be objectionable. When excessive it is a precursor of a relapse in civilization.

When wealth and its appearance abound, children are most often brought up in idleness and indulged in extravagance. Supposing labor a burden and retrenchment the ruin of happiness, they are made liable to be overtaken by poverty, and with their last energies and ruined characters to be plunged in real misery. Individual calamities of this description, as they accumulate, become national calamities and foment domestic dissensions. Suffering pride is all the while meditating revenge. It has nothing to lose and will endure anything to regain what it has lost. Appearances and extravagances are prominent causes of dissension, when a part are rioting, and a part are suffering. Distinctions of rank are introduced. Individuals and nations who have run into excesses in making and maintaining such distinctions sooner or later are wont to be caught in their own snares. Poverty feels the burden of degradation when the power is lost to remove it.

In the present happy condition of the manufacturing districts there are no advantages enjoyed by the rich that are not reciprocated with the poor. Labor was never better paid and the laborer more respected, at any period or in any part of the world, than it is at present among us. And that man is not a friend to the poor who endeavors to make those dissatisfied with their present condition, who cannot hope, by any possibility of circumstances, to be bettered by a change. This is emphatically *the poor man's country.*

27.

ANONYMOUS: Land Speculation as a Cause of Strikes

The editorial printed below is taken from a May 1835 issue of a workingmen's paper The Man. *Its editor, George H. Evans, led the movement to inform the workingman about his stake in the westward movement. To Evans, the solution of all social problems would attend the break-up of the monopoly in land, for a "free land" policy in the West would function as an effective drain on the Eastern labor market, thereby lessening unemployment and raising wages. The editorial was probably written by Evans but, in any event, expresses his ideas.*

Source: *The Man,* May 21, 1835.

THE SHOEMAKERS OF NEWARK have been some time "on the strike" for an advance of about 12 percent in their wages, which were before miserably inadequate to their comfortable subsistence. The Ladies' Branch of the trade in this city have also turned out from the same cause the present week, and the Journeymen Boot Makers of Newark have turned out "for a redress of grievances." We wish all these useful mechanics success in their object, knowing as we do that they deserve it, but we tell them again, as we have often told them before, that they must look to something more radical than *turnouts* to give them a just remuneration for their labor. They must look to a removal of the cause which creates a surplus of laborers in each mechanical branch: *the monopoly of the land by speculators.*

We do not propose that the system which enables a single individual to hold immense tracts of land in barrenness till he can get his *price* for it should be at once reversed, however unjust and contrary to natural right we consider that system to be; nor, perhaps, had our predecessors made the air or the water private property, should we advocate that everyone might breathe such a portion of the one or drink such a portion of the other as he might find unappropriated to the use of any other person. But we have proposed, and do propose, that the PUBLIC lands should no longer be sold, but

that any man, unpossessed of land, should be allowed to take possession of a certain portion of the unappropriated domain for the purpose of cultivation, and, to prevent speculation, that no one should be allowed to hold *more* than a certain portion.

If this proposal were adopted, it would, to be sure, prevent a few individuals from becoming immensely rich, in a day, without labor (the only just foundation of riches) by "land speculations"; but, as a set off for this, it would prevent a *surplus of laborers* in any mechanical branch and, consequently, the necessity of *turnouts.*

28.

George Bancroft: The Common Man in Art, Politics, and Religion

George Bancroft is best known as the author of a ten-volume History of the United States *(to 1782), the writing of which occupied him intermittently for most of his life. He was also active in public affairs, especially in the days of Andrew Jackson, of whom he was an outspoken admirer. His party services led to his appointment as secretary of the navy (1845-1846), minister to England (1846-1849), and minister to Prussia [later Germany] (1867-1874). The first volume of the* History *(1834), which revealed his conviction that "universal decision is the nearest criterion of truth," was considered as laying the philosophical foundations of the Jacksonian cult of the common man. The same theme is apparent in an oration delivered at Williamstown College in August 1835, portions of which appear below. In identifying "the common judgment in taste, politics, and religion" with "the highest authority on earth" Bancroft gave a theoretical justification not only for democratic government but also for the broadened suffrage that had prevailed since the 1820s.*

Source: *Literary and Historical Miscellanies,* New York, 1855, pp. 408-435: "The Office of the People in Art, Government, and Religion."

THE MATERIAL WORLD does not change in its masses or in its powers. The stars shine with no more luster than when they first sang together in the glory of their birth. The flowers that gemmed the fields and the

forests, before America was discovered, now bloom around us in their season. The sun that shone on Homer shines on us in unchanging luster. The bow that beamed on the patriarch still glitters in the clouds. Nature is the same. For her no new forces are generated; no new capacities are discovered. The earth turns on its axis, and perfects its revolutions, and renews its seasons, without increase or advancement.

But a like passive destiny does not attach to the inhabitants of the earth. For them the expectations of social improvement are no delusion; the hopes of philanthropy are more than a dream. The five senses do not constitute the whole inventory of our sources of knowledge. They are the organs by which thought connects itself with the external universe; but the power of thought is not merged in the exercise of its instruments. We have functions which connect us with heaven, as well as organs which set us in relation with earth. We have not merely the senses opening to us the external world, but an internal sense, which places us in connection with the world of intelligence and the decrees of God.

There is a *spirit in man*: not in the privileged few; not in those of us only who by the favor of Providence have been nursed in public schools. IT IS IN MAN. It is the attribute of the race. The spirit, which is the guide to truth, is the gracious gift to each member of the human family.

Reason exists within every breast. I mean not that faculty which deduces inferences from the experience of the senses but that higher faculty which from the infinite treasures of its own consciousness originates truth, and assents to it by the force of intuitive evidence; that faculty which raises us beyond the control of time and space, and gives us faith in things eternal and invisible. There is not the difference between one mind and another which the pride of philosophers might conceive. To them no faculty is conceded which does not belong to the meanest of their countrymen. In them there cannot spring up a truth which does not equally have its germ in every mind. They have not the power of creation; they can but reveal what God has implanted in every breast.

The intellectual functions by which relations are perceived are the common endowments of the race. The differences are apparent, not real. The eye in one person may be dull, in another quick, in one distorted, and in another tranquil and clear; yet the relation of the eye to light is in all men the same. Just so judgment may be liable in individual minds to the bias of passion, and yet its relation to truth is immutable and is universal.

In questions of practical duty conscience is God's umpire, whose light illumines every heart. There is nothing in books which had not first and has not still its life within us. Religion itself is a dead letter wherever its truths are not renewed in the soul. Individual conscience may be corrupted by interest or debauched by pride, yet the rule of morality is distinctly marked; its harmonies are to the mind like music to the ear; and the moral judgment, when carefully analyzed and referred to its principles, is always founded in right.

The Eastern superstition, which bids its victims prostrate themselves before the advancing car of their idols, springs from a noble root, and is but a melancholy perversion of that self-devotion which enables the Christian to bear the cross and subject his personal passions to the will of God. Immorality of itself never won to its support the inward voice; conscience, if questioned, never forgets to curse the guilty with the memory of sin, to cheer the upright with the meek tranquillity of approval. And this admirable power, which is the instinct of Deity, is the attribute of every man; it knocks at the palace gate, it dwells in the meanest hovel. Duty, like death, enters every abode, and delivers its message. Conscience, like reason and judgment, is universal.

That the moral affections are planted everywhere needs only to be asserted to be received. The savage mother loves her offspring with all the fondness that a mother can know. Beneath the odorous shade of the boundless forests of Chile, the native youth repeats the story of love as sincerely as it was ever chanted in the valley of Vaucluse. The affections of family are not the growth of civilization. The charities of life are scattered everywhere, enameling the vales of human being, as the flowers paint the meadows. They are not the fruit of study, nor the privilege of refinement, but a natural instinct.

Our age has seen a revolution in works of imagination. The poet has sought his theme in common life. Never is the genius of Scott more pathetic than when, as in *The Antiquary*, he delineates the sorrows of a poor fisherman, or as in *The Heart of Midlothian*, he takes his heroine from a cottage. And even Wordsworth, the purest and most original poet of the day, in spite of the inveterate character of his political predilections, has thrown the light of genius on the walks of commonest life. He finds a lesson in every grave of the village churchyard; he discloses the boundless treasures of feeling in the peasant, the laborer and the artisan; the strolling peddler becomes, through his genius, a teacher of the sublimest morality; and the solitary wagoner, the lonely shepherd, even the feeble mother of an idiot boy, furnishes lessons in the reverence for humanity.

If from things relating to truth, justice, and affection, we turn to those relating to the beautiful, we may here still further assert that the sentiment for the beautiful resides in every breast. The lovely forms of the external world delight us from their adaptation to our powers.

> Yea, what were mighty Nature's self?
>   Her features could they win us,
> Unhelped by the poetic voice
>   That hourly speaks within us?

The Indian mother, on the borders of Hudson's Bay, decorates her manufactures with ingenious devices and lovely colors, prompted by the same instinct which guided the pencil and mixed the colors of Raphael. The inhabitant of Nootka Sound tattoos his body with the method of harmonious arabesques. Every form, to which the hands of the artist have ever given birth, sprung first into being as a conception of his mind, from a natural faculty, which belongs not to the artist exclusively but to man. Beauty, like truth and justice, lives within us; like virtue and like moral law, it is a companion of the soul. The power which leads to the production of beautiful forms, or to the perception of them in the works which God has made, is an attribute of humanity.

But I am asked if I despise learning? Shall one who has spent much of his life in schools and universities plead the equality of uneducated nature? Is there no difference between the man of refinement and the savage?

"I am a man," said Black Hawk nobly to the chief of the first republic in the world; "I am a man," said the barbarous chieftain, "and you are another."

I speak for the universal diffusion of human powers, not of human attainments; for the capacity for progress, not for the perfection of undisciplined instincts. The fellowship which we should cherish with the race receives the Comanche warrior and the Kaffir within the pale of equality. Their functions may not have been exercised, but they exist. Immure a person in a dungeon; as he comes to the light of day, his vision seems incapable of performing its office. Does that destroy your conviction in the relation between the eye and light? The rioter over his cups resolves to eat and drink and be merry; he forgets his spiritual nature in his obedience to the senses; but does that destroy the relation between conscience and eternity?

"What ransom shall we give?" exclaimed the senators of Rome to the savage Attila. "Give," said the barbarian, "all your gold and jewels, your costly furniture and treasures, and set free every slave." "Ah," replied the degenerate Romans, "what then will be left to us?" "I leave you your souls," replied the unlettered invader from the steppes of Asia, who had learned in the wilderness to value the immortal mind and to despise the servile herd that esteemed only their fortunes and had no true respect for themselves. You cannot discover a tribe of men but you also find the charities of life and the proofs of spiritual existence. Behold the ignorant Algonquin deposit a bow and quiver by the side of the departed warrior; and recognize his faith in immortality. See the Comanche chieftain, in the heart of our continent, inflict on himself severest penance; and reverence his confession of the needed atonement for sin. The barbarian who roams our Western prairies has like passions and like endowments with ourselves. He bears within him the instinct of Deity, the consciousness of a spiritual nature, the love of beauty, the rule of morality.

And shall we reverence the dark-skinned Kaffir? Shall we respect the brutal Hottentot? You may read the right answer written on every heart. It bids me not despise the sable hunter that gathers a livelihood in the forests of southern Africa. All are men. When we know the Hottentot better, we shall despise him less.

IF IT BE TRUE THAT THE GIFTS of mind and heart are universally diffused, if the sentiment of truth, justice, love, and beauty exists in everyone, then it follows, as a necessary consequence, that the common judgment in taste, politics, and religion is the highest authority on earth and the nearest possible approach to an infallible decision. From the consideration of individual powers I turn to the action of the human mind in masses.

If reason is a universal faculty, the universal decision is the nearest criterion of truth. The common mind winnows opinions; it is the sieve which separates error from certainty. The exercise by many of the same faculty on the same subject would naturally lead to the same conclusions. But if not, the very differences of opinion that arise prove the supreme judgment of the general mind. Truth is one. It never contradicts itself. One truth cannot contradict another truth. Hence truth is a bond of union. But error not only contradicts truth but may contradict itself; so that there may be many errors, and each at variance with the rest. Truth is therefore of necessity an element of harmony; error is necessarily an element of discord. Thus there can be no continuing universal judgment but a right one. Men cannot agree in an absurdity; neither can they agree in a falsehood.

If wrong opinions have often been cherished by the masses, the cause always lies in the complexity of the ideas presented. Error finds its way into the soul of a nation only through the channel of truth. It is to a truth that men listen; and if they accept error also, it is only because the error is for the time so closely interwoven with the truth that the one cannot readily be separated from the other.

Unmixed error can have no existence in the public mind. Wherever you see men clustering together to form a party, you may be sure that however much error may be there, truth is there also. Apply this principle boldly; for it contains a lesson of candor and a voice of encouragement. There never was a school of philosophy, nor a clan in the realm of opinion, but carried along with it some important truth. And therefore every sect that has ever flourished has benefited humanity; for the errors of a sect pass away and are forgotten; its truths are received into the common inheritance. To know the seminal thought of every prophet and leader of a sect is to gather all the wisdom of mankind.

IN LIKE MANNER the best government rests on the people and not on the few, on persons and not on property, on the free development of public opinion and not on authority, because the munificent Author of our being has conferred the gifts of mind upon every member of the human race without distinction of outward circumstances. Whatever of other possessions may be engrossed, mind asserts its own independence. Lands, estates, the produce of mines, the prolific abundance of the seas, may be usurped by a privileged class. Avarice, assuming the form of ambitious power, may grasp realm after realm, subdue continents, compass the earth in its schemes of aggrandizement, and sigh after other worlds; but mind eludes the power of appropriation: it exists only in its own individuality; it is a property which cannot be confiscated and cannot be torn away; it laughs at chains; it bursts from imprisonment; it defies monopoly.

A government of equal rights must, therefore, rest upon mind, not wealth, not brute force; the sum of the moral intelligence of the community should rule the state. Prescription can no more assume to be a valid plea for political injustice; society studies to eradicate established abuses, and to bring social institutions and laws into harmony with moral right; not dismayed by the natural and necessary imperfections of all human effort, and not giving way to despair because every hope does not at once ripen into fruit.

The public happiness is the true object of legislation, and can be secured only by the masses of mankind themselves awakening to the knowledge and the care of their own interests. Our free institutions have reversed the false and ignoble distinctions between men; and refusing to gratify the pride of caste, have acknowledged the common mind to be the true material for a commonwealth. Everything has hitherto been done for the happy few. It is not possible to endow an aristocracy with greater benefits than they have already enjoyed; there is no room to hope that individuals will be more highly gifted or more fully developed than the greatest sages of past times. The world can advance only through the culture of the

moral and intellectual powers of the people. To accomplish this end by means of the people themselves is the highest purpose of government. If it be the duty of the individual to strive after a perfection like the perfection of God, how much more ought a nation to be the image of Deity. The common mind is the true Parian marble, fit to be wrought into likeness to a God. The duty of America is to secure the culture and the happiness of the masses by their reliance on themselves.

The absence of the prejudices of the Old World leaves us here the opportunity of consulting independent truth; and man is left to apply the instinct of freedom to every social relation and public interest. We have approached so near to nature that we can hear her gentlest whispers; we have made humanity our lawgiver and our oracle; and, therefore, the nation receives, vivifies and applies principles, which in Europe the wisest accept with distrust. Freedom of mind and of conscience, freedom of the seas, freedom of industry, equality of franchises, each great truth is firmly grasped, comprehended and enforced; for the multitude is neither rash nor fickle. In truth, it is less fickle than those who profess to be its guides. Its natural dialectics surpass the logic of the schools.

Political action has never been so consistent and so unwavering as when it results from a feeling or a principle, diffused through society. The people are firm and tranquil in their movements, and necessarily act with moderation, because they become but slowly impregnated with new ideas; and effect no changes, except in harmony with the knowledge which they have acquired. Besides, where they are permanently possessed of power, there exists neither the occasion nor the desire for frequent change. They are not the parent of tumult; sedition is bred in the lap of luxury, and its chosen emissaries are the beggared spendthrift and the impoverished libertine. The government by the people is in very truth the strongest government in the world. Discarding the implements of terror, it dares to rule by moral force, and has its citadel in the heart.

Such is the political system which rests on reason, reflection, and the free expression of deliberate choice. There may be those who scoff at the suggestion that the decision of the whole is to be preferred to the judgment of the enlightened few. They say in their hearts that the masses are ignorant; that farmers know nothing of legislation; that mechanics should not quit their workshops to join in forming public opinion. But true political science does indeed venerate the masses. It maintains not as has been perversely asserted that "the people can make right" but that the people can DISCERN right. Individuals are but shadows, too often engrossed by the pursuit of shadows; the race is immortal. Individuals are of limited sagacity; the common mind is infinite in its experience. Individuals are languid and blind; the many are ever wakeful. Individuals are corrupt; the race has been redeemed. Individuals are time-serving; the masses are fearless. Individuals may be false; the masses are ingenuous and sincere. Individuals claim the Divine sanction of truth for the deceitful conceptions of their own fancies; the Spirit of God breathes through the combined intelligence of the people.

Truth is not to be ascertained by the impulses of an individual: it emerges from the contradictions of personal opinions; it raises itself in majestic serenity above the strifes of parties and the conflict of sects; it acknowledges neither the solitary mind nor the separate faction as its oracle but owns as its only faithful interpreter the dictates of pure reason itself, proclaimed by the general voice of mankind. The decrees of the universal conscience are the nearest approach to the presence of God in the soul of man.

Thus the opinion which we respect is, indeed, not the opinion of one or of a few but the sagacity of the many. It is hard for the pride of cultivated philosophy to put its ear to the ground and listen reverently to the voice of lowly humanity; yet the people collectively are wiser than the most gifted individual, for all his wisdom constitutes but a part of theirs. When the great sculptor of Greece was endeavoring to fashion the perfect model of beauty he did not passively imitate the form of the loveliest woman of his age; but he gleaned the several lineaments of his faultless work from the many.

And so it is that a perfect judgment is the result of comparison, when error eliminates error and truth is established by concurring witnesses. The organ of truth is the invisible decision of the unbiased world: she pleads before no tribunal but public opinion; she owns no safe interpreter but the common mind; she knows no court of appeals but the soul of humanity. It is when the multitude give counsel that right purposes find safety; theirs is the fixedness that cannot be shaken; theirs is the understanding which exceeds in wisdom; theirs is the heart of which the largeness is as the sand on the seashore.

It is not by vast armies, by immense natural resources, by accumulations of treasure, that the greatest results in modern civilization have been accomplished. The traces of the career of conquest pass away hardly leaving a scar on the national intelligence. The famous battlegrounds of victory are, most of them, comparatively indifferent to the human race: barren fields of blood, the scourges of their times, but affecting the social condition as little as the raging of a pestilence. Not one benevolent institution, not one ameliorating principle in the Roman state, was a voluntary concession of the aristocracy; each useful element was borrowed from the democracies of Greece, or was a reluctant concession to the demands of the people. The same is true in modern political life. It is the confession of an enemy to democracy that "ALL THE GREAT AND NOBLE INSTITUTIONS OF THE WORLD HAVE COME FROM POPULAR EFFORTS."

It is the uniform tendency of the popular

element to elevate and bless humanity. The exact measure of the progress of civilization is the degree in which the intelligence of the common mind has prevailed over wealth and brute force; in other words, the measure of the progress of civilization is the progress of the people. Every great object, connected with the benevolent exertions of the day, has reference to the culture of those powers which are alone the common inheritance. For this the envoys of religion cross seas and visit remotest isles; for this the press in its freedom teems with the productions of maturest thought; for this the philanthropist plans new schemes of education; for this halls in every city and village are open to the public instructor.

Not that we view with indifference the glorious efforts of material industry, the increase in the facility of internal intercourse, the accumulations of thrifty labor, the varied results of concentrated action. But even there it is mind that achieves the triumph. It is the genius of the architect that gives beauty to the work of human hands and makes the temple, the dwelling, or the public edifice, an outward representation of the spirit of propriety and order. It is science that guides the blind zeal of cupidity to the construction of the vast channels of communication which are fast binding the world into one family. And it is as a method of moral improvement that these swifter means of intercourse derive their greatest value. Mind becomes universal property; the poem that is published on the soil of England finds its response on the shores of Lake Erie and the banks of the Missouri, and is admired near the sources of the Ganges. The defense of public liberty in our own halls of legislation penetrates the plains of Poland, is echoed along the mountains of Greece, and pierces the darkest night of Eastern despotism.

The universality of the intellectual and moral powers, and the necessity of their development for the progress of the race, proclaim the great doctrine of the natural right of every human being to moral and intellectual culture. It is the glory of our fathers to have established in their laws the equal claims of every child to the public care of its morals and its mind. From this principle we may deduce the universal right to leisure; that is, to time not appropriated to material purposes but reserved for the culture of the moral affections and the mind. It does not tolerate the exclusive enjoyment of leisure by a privileged class; but defending the rights of labor, would suffer none to sacrifice the higher purposes of existence in unceasing toil for that which is not life.

Such is the voice of nature; such the conscious claim of the human mind. The universe opens its pages to every eye; the music of creation resounds in every ear; the glorious lessons of immortal truth that are written in the sky and on the earth address themselves to every mind and claim attention from every human being. God has made man upright that he might look before and after; and he calls upon everyone not merely to labor but to reflect; not merely to practise the revelations of Divine Will but to contemplate the displays of Divine Power. Nature claims for every man leisure, for she claims every man as a witness to the Divine Glory manifested in the created world.

Yet evermore, through years renewed
In undisturbed vicissitude
Of seasons balancing their flight
On the swift wings of day and night,
Kind nature keeps a heavenly door
Wide open for the scattered poor,
Where flower-breathed incense to
    the skies
Is wafted in mute harmonies;
And ground fresh cloven by the plough
Is fragrant with an humbler vow;
Where birds and brooks from leafy dells
Chime forth unwearied canticles,
And vapors magnify and spread
The glory of the sun's bright head;

Still constant in her worship, still
Conforming to the Almighty Will,
Whether men sow or reap the fields,
Her admonitions nature yields;
That not by bread alone we live,
Or what a hand of flesh can give;
That every day should leave some part
Free for a sabbath of the heart;
So shall the seventh be truly blest,
From morn to eve, with hallowed rest.

The right to universal education being thus acknowledged by our conscience, not less than by our laws, it follows that the people is the true recipient of truth. Do not seek to conciliate individuals; do not dread the frowns of a sect; do not yield to the proscriptions of a party; but pour out truth into the common mind. Let the waters of intelligence, like the rains of heaven, descend on the whole earth. And be not discouraged by the dread of encountering ignorance. *The prejudices of ignorance are more easily removed than the prejudices of interest; the first are blindly adopted; the second willfully preferred.*

Intelligence must be diffused among the whole people; truth must be scattered among those who have no interest to suppress its growth. The seeds that fall on the exchange, or in the hum of business, may be choked by the thorns that spring up in the hotbed of avarice; the seeds that are let fall in the saloon may be like those dropped by the wayside which take no root. Let the young aspirant after glory scatter the seeds of truth broadcast on the wide bosom of humanity in the deep, fertile soil of the public mind. There it will strike deep root and spring up, and bear a hundredfold, and bloom for ages, and ripen fruit through remote generations.

It is alone by infusing great principles into the common mind that revolutions in human society are brought about. They never have been, they never can be, effected by superior individual excellence. The age of the Antonines is the age of the greatest glory of the Roman Empire. Men distinguished by every accomplishment of culture and science, for a century in succession, possessed undisputed sway over more than a hundred millions of men; till at last, in the person of Marcus Aurelius, philosophy herself seemed to mount the throne. And did she stay the downward tendencies of the Roman Empire? Did she infuse new elements of life into the decaying constitution? Did she commence one great, beneficent reform? Not one permanent amelioration was effected; philosophy was clothed with absolute power, and yet absolute power accomplished nothing for humanity. It could accomplish nothing. Had it been possible, Aurelius would have wrought a change. Society can be regenerated, the human race can be advanced, only by moral principles diffused through the multitude. . . .

Yes, reforms in society are only effected through the masses of the people, and through them have continually taken place. New truths have been successively developed and, becoming the common property of the human family, have improved its condition. This progress is advanced by every sect precisely because each sect, to obtain vitality, does of necessity embody a truth; by every political party, for the conflicts of party are the war of ideas; by every nationality, for a nation cannot exist as such, till humanity makes it a special trustee of some part of its wealth for the ultimate benefit of all. The irresistible tendency of the human race is therefore to advancement, for absolute power has never succeeded, and can never succeed, in suppressing a single truth.

An idea once revealed may find its admission into every living breast and live there. Like God it becomes immortal and omnipresent. The movement of the species is upward, irresistibly upward. The individual is often lost; Providence never disowns the race. No principle once promulgated has ever been forgotten. No "timely tramp" of a despot's foot ever trod out one idea. The world cannot retrograde; the dark ages cannot return. Dynasties perish; cities are buried; nations have been victims to error, or martyrs for right; humanity has always been on the advance, gaining maturity, universality, and power.

Yes, truth is immortal, it cannot be destroyed; it is invincible, it cannot long be resisted. Not every great principle has yet been generated; but when once proclaimed and diffused it lives without end in the safe custody of the race. States may pass away; every just principle of legislation which has been once established will endure. Philosophy has sometimes forgotten God; a great people never did. The skepticism of the last century could not uproot Christianity because it lived in the hearts of the millions.

Do you think that infidelity is spreading? Christianity never lived in the hearts of so many millions as at this moment. The forms under which it is professed may decay, for they, like all that is the work of man's hands, are subject to the changes and chances of mortal being. But the spirit of truth is incorruptible: it may be developed, illustrated, and applied; it never can die; it never can decline.

No truth can perish; no truth can pass away. The flame is undying, though generations disappear. Wherever moral truth has started into being, humanity claims and guards the bequest. Each generation gathers together the imperishable children of the past, and increases them by new sons of light alike radiant with immortality.

29.

Thaddeus Stevens: Education as a Public Duty

Attempts to establish an elementary public school system in Pennsylvania were blocked on the one hand by the well-to-do, who educated their children in private schools, and on the other hand by the German community, which wanted to preserve its national identity. In 1834, a bill was finally passed that gave each district the option of contributing to a state fund earmarked for free schools, or paying local taxes for the establishment of free schools outside the state system. When, in 1835, the tax increases necessary to finance the schools were calculated, the law came up for repeal. In April 1835, Thaddeus Stevens, who had been elected to the state legislature in 1833 on the Anti-Masonic (or common man's) ticket, delivered a spirited speech, a portion of which is reprinted here, that saved the law and elevated him to national fame.

Source: *Report of the Commissioner of Education for the Year 1898-99,* Washington, 1900, Vol. I, pp. 518-524.

I will briefly give you the reasons why I shall oppose the repeal of the school law.

This law was passed at the last session of the legislature with unexampled unanimity, but one member of this house voting against it. It has not yet come into operation, and none of its effects have been tested by experience in Pennsylvania. The passage of such a law is enjoined by the constitution; and has been recommended by every governor since its adoption. Much to his credit, it has been warmly urged by the present executive in his annual messages delivered at the opening of the legislature. To repeal it now, before its practical effects have been discovered, would argue that it contained some glaring and pernicious defect, and that the last legislature acted under some strong and fatal delusion which blinded every man of them to the interests of the commonwealth.

I will attempt to show that the law is salutary, useful, and important, and that consequently the last legislature acted wisely in passing and the present would act unwisely in repealing it. That, instead of being oppressive to the people, it will lighten their burdens while it elevates them in the scale of human intellect.

It would seem to be humiliating to be under the necessity, in the nineteenth century, of entering into a formal argument to prove the utility and, to free governments, the absolute necessity of education. More than 2,000 years ago the deity who presided over intellectual endowments, ranked highest for dignity, chastity, and virtue among the goddesses worshiped by cultivated pagans. And I will not insult this house or our constituents by supposing any course of reasoning necessary to convince them of its high importance. Such necessity would be degrading to a Christian age, a free republic.

If, then, education be of admitted importance to the people, under all forms of government, and of unquestioned necessity when they govern themselves, it follows, of course, that its cultivation and diffusion is a matter of public concern and a duty which every government owes to its people. In accordance with this principle, the ancient republics, who were most renowned for their wisdom and success, considered every child born subject to their control, as the property of the state, so far as its education was concerned: and during the proper period of instruction they were withdrawn from the control of their parents and placed under the guardianship of the commonwealth.

There, all were instructed at the same school; all were placed on perfect equality, the rich and the poor man's sons; for all were deemed children of the same common parent of the commonwealth. . . .

If an elective republic is to endure for any great length of time, every elector must have sufficient information, not only to accumulate wealth and take care of his pecuniary concerns but to direct wisely the legislature, the ambassadors, and the executive of the nation — for some part of all these things, some agency in approving or disapproving of them, falls to every freeman. If, then, the permanency of our government depends upon such knowledge, it is the duty of government to see that the means of information be diffused to every citizen. This is a sufficient answer to those who deem education a private and not a public duty — who argue that they are willing to educate their own children but not their neighbors' children.

But while but few are found ignorant and shameless enough to deny the advantages of general education, many are alarmed at its supposed burdensome operation. A little judicious reflection, or a single year's experience, would show that education, under the free-school system, will cost more than one-half less, and afford better and more permanent instruction than the present disgraceful plan pursued by Pennsylvania. . . .

The amendment which is now proposed as a substitute for the School Law of last session, is, in my opinion, of a most hateful and degrading character. It is a reenactment of the Pauper Law of 1809. It proposes that the assessors shall take a census and make a record of the poor. This shall be revised and a new record made by the county commissioners, so that the names of those who have the misfortune to be poor men's children shall be forever preserved, as a distinct class, in the archives of the county! The teacher, too, is to keep in his school a pauper book, and register the names and attendance of poor scholars; thus pointing out and recording their poverty in the midst of their companions. Sir, hereditary distinctions of rank are sufficiently odious; but that which is founded on poverty is infinitely more so. Such a law should be entitled "An act for branding and marking the poor, so that they may be known from the rich and proud."

Many complain of this tax, not so much on account of its amount as because it is for the benefit of others and not themselves. This is a mistake; it is for their own benefit, inasmuch as it perpetuates the government and insures the due administration of the laws under which they live, and by which their lives and property are protected. Why do they not urge the same objection against all other taxes? The industrious, thrifty, rich farmer pays a heavy county tax to support criminal courts, build jails, and pay sheriffs and jail keepers; and yet, probably, he never has, and never will have, any direct personal use of either. He never gets the worth of his money by being tried for a crime before the court, by being allowed the privilege of the jail on conviction, or receiving an equivalent from the sheriff or his hangman officers! He cheerfully pays the tax which is necessary to support and punish convicts, but loudly complains of that which goes to prevent his fellow being from becoming a criminal, and to obviate the necessity of those humiliating institutions.

This law is often objected to because its benefits are shared by the children of the profligate spendthrift equally with those of the most industrious and economical habits. It ought to be remembered that the benefit is bestowed, not upon the erring parents but the innocent children. Carry out this objection and you punish children for the crimes or misfortunes of their parents. You virtually establish cases and grades founded on no merit of the particular generation, but on the demerits of their ancestors; an aristocracy of the most odious and insolent kind — the aristocracy of wealth and pride.

It is said that its advantages will be un-justly and unequally enjoyed because the industrious, moneymaking man keeps his whole family constantly employed, and has but little time for them to spend at school; while the idle man has but little employment for his family and they will constantly attend school. I know, sir, that there are some men whose whole souls are so completely absorbed in the accumulation of wealth and whose avarice so increases with success that they look upon their very children in no other light than as instruments of gain — that they, as well as the ox and the ass within their gates, are valuable only in proportion to their annual earnings. And, according to the present system, the children of such men are reduced almost to an intellectual level with their co-laborers of the brute creation.

This law will be of vast advantage to the offspring of such misers. If they are compelled to pay their taxes to support schools, their very meanness will induce them to send their children to them to get the worth of their money. Thus it will extract good out of the very penuriousness of the miser. Surely a system which will work such wonders ought to be as greedily sought for, and more highly prized than that coveted alchemy which was to produce gold and silver out of the blood and entrails of vipers, lizards, and other filthy vermin.

Why, sir, are the colleges and literary institutions of Pennsylvania now, and ever have been, in a languishing and sickly condition? Why, with a fertile soil and genial climate, has she, in proportion to her population, scarcely one-third as many collegiate students as cold, barren New England? The answer is obvious; she has no free schools. Until she shall have, you may in vain endow college after college; they will never be filled, or filled only by students from other states. In New England, free schools plant the seeds and the desire of knowledge in every mind, without regard to the wealth of the parent or the texture of the pupil's garments. When the seed, thus universally sown, happens to fall on fertile soil, it springs up and is fostered by a generous public until it produces its glorious fruit.

Those who have but scanty means and are pursuing a collegiate education find it necessary to spend a portion of the year in teaching common schools. Thus imparting the knowledge which they acquire, they raise the dignity of the employment to a rank which it should always hold, honorable in proportion to the high qualifications necessary for its discharge. Thus devoting a portion of their time to acquiring the means of subsistence, industrious habits are forced upon them and their minds and bodies become disciplined to a regularity and energy which is seldom the lot of the rich. It is no uncommon occurrence to see the poor man's son, thus encouraged by wise legislation, far outstrip and bear off the laurels from the less industrious heirs of wealth. Some of the ablest men of the present and past days never could have been educated except for that benevolent system. . . .

When I reflect how apt hereditary wealth, hereditary influence, and perhaps, as a consequence, hereditary pride are to close the avenues and steel the heart against the wants and the rights of the poor, I am induced to thank my Creator for having from early life bestowed upon me the blessings of poverty. Sir, it is a blessing, for if there be any human sensation more ethereal and divine than all others, it is that which feelingly sympathizes with misfortune. . . .

I would not foster nor flatter ignorance to gain political victories which, however they might profit individuals, must prove disastrous to our country. Let it not be supposed from these remarks that because I deem this a paramount object that I think less highly than heretofore of those great, important, cardinal principles which for years past have controlled my political action. They are, and ever shall be, deeply cherished in my inmost heart. But I must be allowed to exercise my own judgment as to the best means of effecting that and every other object which I think beneficial to the community. And, according to that judgment, the light of general information will as surely counteract the pernicious influence of secret, oath-bound, murderous institutions as the sun in heaven dispels the darkness and damp vapors of the night. . . .

Gentlemen will hardly contend for the doctrine of cherishing and obeying the prejudices and errors of their constituents. Instead of prophesying smooth things and flattering the people with the belief of their present perfection, and thus retarding the mind in its onward progress, it is the duty of faithful legislators to create and sustain such laws and institutions as shall teach us our wants, foster our cravings after knowledge, and urge us forward in the march of intellect. The barbarous and disgraceful cry which we hear abroad in some parts of our land, "that learning makes us worse — that education makes men rogues," should find no echo within these walls. Those who hold such doctrines anywhere would be the objects of bitter detestation if they were not rather the pitiable objects of commiseration, for even voluntary fools require our compassion as well as natural idiots. . . .

In giving this law to posterity you act the part of the philanthropist, by bestowing upon the poor as well as the rich the greatest earthly boon which they are capable of receiving; you act the part of the philosopher by pointing if you do not lead them up the hill of science; you act the part of the hero if it be true as you say that popular vengeance follows close upon your footsteps. Here, then, if you wish true popularity, is a theater in which you may acquire it. What renders the name of Socrates immortal but his love of the human family, exhibited under all circumstances and in contempt of every danger? But courage, even with but little benevolence may confer lasting renown. It is this which makes us bow with involuntary respect at the name of Napoleon, of Caesar, and of Richard of the Lion Heart.

But what earthly glory is there equal in luster and duration to that conferred by education? What else could have bestowed such renown upon the philosophers, the poets, the statesmen, and orators of antiquity? What else could have conferred such undisputed applause upon Aristotle, Demosthenes, and Homer; on Virgil, Horace, and Cicero? And is learning less interesting and important now than it was in centuries past, when those statesmen and orators charmed and ruled empires with their eloquence? . . .

Let all, therefore, who would sustain the character of the philosopher or philanthropist sustain this law. Those who would add thereto the glory of the hero can acquire it here; for in the present state of feeling in Pennsylvania, I am willing to admit that but little less dangerous to the public man is the war club and battle ax of savage ignorance than to the Lion-hearted Richard was the keen scimitar of the Saracen. He who would oppose it, either through inability to comprehend the advantages of general education, or from unwillingness to bestow them on all his fellow citizens, even to the lowest and the poorest, or from dread of popular vengeance, seems to me to want either the head of the philosopher, the heart of the philanthropist, or the nerve of the hero.

30.

William H. Seward: Prosperity and Education

William H. Seward became prominent in New York state politics with the rise of the Anti-Masonic movement under whose banner he served two terms as state senator (1830-1834); later, as a Whig (they had supplanted the Anti-Masons), he served two terms as governor (1838-1842). Although Seward embraced Whig economic policies, he nevertheless shared the Democrats' concern for the common man. In the following speech delivered on October 14, 1835, at the laying of the cornerstone of the works erected for the improvement of the Owasco River at Auburn, New York, Seward demonstrated his usual sympathies by advocating both the expansion of the internal transportation system and universal education. (Later, in 1840, Seward was instrumental in establishing a state public school system.) The Erie Canal, to which he refers, had been financed by New York state bonds that were bought largely by foreign investors. The cost of construction had been paid back in tolls less than ten years after the canal's completion in 1825.

Source: *The Works of William H. Seward*, George E. Baker, ed., New edition, Vol. III, Boston, 1887, pp. 128-134.

Whether we shall secure the advantages which are within our reach depends in no inconsiderable degree upon ourselves. To do so requires enlarged and liberal principles in the transaction of business. It requires that we reprobate the cent-per-cent investment of money in usurious loans, most frequently productive of ruin to the borrower, and of perplexity and dishonor to the lender. Liberal confidence must be reposed in the abundant resources of the country, and in the advantages of our location. That malicious and envious spirit must be discountenanced which delights in the destruction of individual credit. That contracted spirit must be put down which is jealous when foreign capital seeks investment among us.

That bigoted spirit must be kept far from us which would churlishly exclude from among us those whose religious or political faith does not accord with its own and which tolerates no diverging creed, as if the narrow way that leads to life was a line of faith and not of practice, and the seekers of that path were amenable to human tribunals and not to their final Judge; and as if, in a government which rests upon free discussion of every principle of moral, social, or religious action, individual opinion must or ought to be subjected to arbitrary and despotic intolerance. Thus acting, the enterprise of our citizens will be called into vigorous exercise; and it is morally certain that foreign capital, if liberally invited, will seek investment in those places where domestic capital is most liberally and profitably employed.

It is, moreover, necessary to cherish a liberal spirit in regard to public improvements in other parts of the state and of the country. And such a spirit is no less enlightened and just than it is expedient for us to indulge it. I regret to say that on this subject there has been, in my judgment, much error prevailing among us and throughout the state. The eastern counties, while the value of their lands has been enhanced nearly twofold and their towns have increased in nearly the same proportion by means of the great increase of commerce effected by the construction of the Erie Canal, have not yet altogether surmounted the jealousy with which they regarded the prosecution of that great work. Finding they are not, as they at first anticipated they would be, oppressed with taxation to defray the cost of its construction, many of their citizens now deem it just to impose upon the canal the expense

of the support of the government at the hazard of driving into other channels that very trade which makes it productive and so excites their cupidity.

The denial of the applications, at the last session of the legislature, for charters for constructing railroads from Utica to Syracuse and from Auburn to Rochester was a part of the same policy and proceeded upon the ground that railroads parallel to the Erie Canal would have the effect, by diminishing the canal tolls, to reduce the revenue of the state; as if it were wise, or magnanimous, or just, for the state, because it had made thoroughfares, to refuse permission to its citizens, with their private funds, to make other thoroughfares to compete with it in accommodating the public. So, also, a portion of our citizens have opposed the construction of the New York and Erie Railroad through the southern counties under an apprehension that it would depreciate property in the northern counties; and in retaliation, "the sequestered counties," as those are called which are on the route of the southern railroad, unite with the eastern counties to prevent the improvements required by ourselves. Plausible pretexts are never wanted to cover the real odiousness of these sectional jealousies; and these may generally be resolved into a great and anxious concern for the safety of the state treasury.

Now, in my humble opinion, a state can no more wisely conduct its affairs than by contributing to the internal improvement of the territory within its limits a large proportion of its revenues and credits. Every such improvement develops new resources, adds to the capital and commerce of the country, and increases the mass of taxable property on which the government, in order to secure full accountability to the people, ought always to rely for its support. Where individual enterprise and capital are sufficient to accomplish a desirable work, they ought to be at once called into exercise. Where they are incompetent, the state ought, in justice and sound policy, to contribute. And yet the very opposite of this is the doctrine maintained by many of our statesmen, who hold that the state ought to embark only in those improvements which will be immediately productive. But, as such works will be made by citizens with private funds, it follows, according to this principle, that the state ought never to make any improvements. With such men, there is an everlasting apprehension of irredeemable public debt and eternal taxation. And yet, if all the internal improvements required to cross this state in every direction with roads, at such intervals as to leave not a single sequestered county or town within its limits, were to be made at once, the debt which would be created would not impair the public credit in the least degree, or retard the public prosperity a single year. The expenses of a single year of war would exceed the whole sum of such cost. Every year after their construction would show the resources of the state to be so much increased that a nominal tax would be sufficient to establish a sinking fund, ample for the redemption of the debt within one generation; if, indeed, it were just that one generation should bear the entire expense of improvements destined to become more and more productive, while the government should endure.

To compare such appropriations to the heavy expenses incurred by monarchical governments in desolating and exterminating wars is as unsound in politics as to assimilate in agriculture the effects of invigorating rains to the sterility produced by the burning sun. The popular error on this subject unquestionably arises from an inability to understand the extent of the resources of this great country. It is forgotten that besides the lands we cultivate, there is a territory of almost inconceivable dimensions lying on our borders, with an annual increase of strong and willing hands to reclaim and bring it into a productive condition. It is forgotten that every five or six years brings a new state into this confederacy with its fresh and fertile soil yielding most luxuriant gifts, while the older states are all the time increasing in wealth and prosperity. It is forgotten that this is a government made for the reign of peace and humanity; that we have no wars, nor rumors of wars, to render necessary standing armies and navies, and thereby to exhaust the productions of the soil. It is forgotten that we have not, and that, with the favor of God, we never will have, any aristocracy, pensioners, and placemen in church or state, to consume the substance of the people. It is forgotten that we are daily demonstrating, by our experience, the new and gratifying theory that national poverty, as well as individual destitution, are not decreed by a harsh and offended Deity, but happen through the fault of men and are therefore avoidable.

All this is forgotten, and false terrors of bankruptcy are derived from the history of nations, whose wealth was in the keeping of an inert, profligate aristocracy, and whose peasantry were ground to the earth with the burdens of centuries of wars carried on to gratify the avarice, ambition, and revenge of despots. It is time, fellow citizens, that we should explode these prejudices and should rise to the sublime conviction that Providence has spread around us an immense territory to improve, to cultivate, and to make the abode of peace, of science, and of liberty. When we shall have embraced this truth, and shall have become imbued with its influence, we shall rejoice in every work which will improve the condition of any portion of the people and which will add to the prosperity of any part of the country.

I am sure, fellow citizens, that I should have discharged the responsibility imposed upon me, as unsatisfactorily to the enlightened board by whose invitation I address you, as it would have been unworthily, were I to close this address without having adverted to one other consideration of a character different from any which has been presented.

Splendid as will be the results of the work we this day commence, and bright as are the visions of national prosperity dawning upon us, it ought to be borne in mind that those results and those prospects are not, and ought not to be, the chief end of our exertions. While it is true that individual wealth and national prosperity tend to increase and multiply domestic enjoyments, and elevate and refine the social condition, it is equally true that the perpetuity of this Union, under its existing form of government is, and ought to be, the object of the most persevering and watchful solicitude on the part of every American citizen. And it is as certainly true that neither the happiness of our people, nor the stability of our government depends on the length or number of our canals and railroads, or the individual or collective wealth of our citizens. On the other hand, wealth and prosperity have always served as the guides which introduced vice, luxury, and corruption into republics. And luxury, vice, and corruption have subverted every republic which has preceded us that had force enough in its uncorrupted state to resist foreign invasion. So closely are moral good and moral evil, political good and political evil associated in this world.

But, in addition to the other eminent blessings by which we are distinguished, our lot has been cast in an age and situation when we can change this tendency of wealth and prosperity and convert them into agents for the preservation and maintenance of the liberty we enjoy. We are under a fearful responsibility to posterity and to the friends of free government throughout the world, that the institutions established here, dearer to them than all the wealth of the ancient East and the modern West, shall not be subverted through our fault.

That responsibility can be discharged faithfully, successfully, triumphantly by the education of the people. This great work it is practicable for us to accomplish; and herein is that great distinction of our lot over that of all preceding republics and all other states. The improvements in the art of teaching and in the books of instruction favor this end; the cheapness of printing favors this end; the interest every citizen feels that himself and his children have in the government favors this end; and, above all, the comparatively equal distribution of wealth, and the absolute equality of civil and political rights existing among us, enable us to bring all within the scope of a general system of education. There is one only obstacle to the work: and that is the prevailing belief that it is already accomplished. Our orators, and some of our statesmen, point boastingly to statistics which show that almost every citizen can read and write, and thereupon unhesitatingly pronounce us the wisest and most enlightened of all the nations of the earth. We "lay this flattering unction to our souls," and rest content. But it is a dangerous, it is a universal (God grant it do not prove a fatal) delusion.

That the mass of the American people have been instructed to read and write and that they make profitable use of those precious acquirements, I am as proud to declare as any citizen. But are the acquirements of reading and writing, knowledge? No, fellow citizens, they are only the means of acquiring it; and without some higher cultivation of the mind, the ability to read and write may be perverted to the perpetuation of error, as well as applied to the acquisition of truth. It prepares us to become the sport of demagogues, and the slaves of popular passion, caprice, and excitement. Something more is wanting. It is necessary, if we would be qualified to discharge the duties of electors, that we should understand some of the principles of political economy, of the philosophy of the human mind, and, above all, of moral and religious science. When the minds of all the people shall be thus instructed, it will be eminently and practically true that "error of opinion may safely be tolerated, where reason is left free to combat it." Then it will be true that "the voice of the people is the voice of God."

For this purpose, let me earnestly press upon the attention of my fellow citizens the importance of carrying into effect a law of the last legislature, providing for the establishment of small libraries in connection with the district schools. Those libraries may be the germ from which, after much cultivation, the fruits I have described as so important may be gathered; for, although the acquisition of knowledge is the labor, or the partial pursuit, of a whole life, yet the desire, without which the acquisition is never made, must be developed in early years. Considered in this view, it is impossible to estimate the influence of these libraries, properly established, upon the future character of the people of this state. And let it be always remembered that to elevate the standard of general education, and to extend its benefits, is the most important duty of the age in which we live.

Better would it be for our successors that the waters of the Erie and Hudson had pursued their ancient passages to the ocean, strangers to each other, as they were before the towering intellect of Clinton compelled them to mingle and flow together. Better for them would it be that the Atlantic cities were a forest and the valley of the Mississippi had remained an inhospitable prairie, than that we should transmit to them, with the mighty improvements of this age, a subtle poison which should undermine their social condition. We must make our improvements of the minds of the people keep progress with those of our territory if we would preserve those institutions without which all the wealth and prosperity we can secure will only invite more avaricious and rigorous oppression, will only serve, by showing the height of our present elevation, to make more manifest the deplorable depth of our fall.

Perhaps, at some distant day, the curious searcher of antiquities may find, in the ruins which sooner or later must cover this work like all other human inventions, the cornerstone we are now to deposit in the earth, and studiously decipher the inscription it bears, as a memorial of a people whose career will have terminated and over whose memory Oblivion will have begun to draw her dark mantle. Then, when all the notoriety given to the proceedings of this day by an ephemeral press, and the scarcely less ephemeral memory of these thousand witnesses shall have passed away, we shall not be judged by the improvements we shall have made in our lakes or our rivers, upon our mountains or in our valleys, nor yet by the wealth we shall have accumulated, or the monuments we shall have reared; but we shall be judged by the indelible impression we shall have left upon the moral condition of our country.

So far, my fellow citizens, as our influence may go in forming the character of the age in which we live, let not the discovery of these relics recall the memory of a people who acquired wealth without wisdom and enjoyed the luxury that it brought, reckless of their responsibility to posterity and mankind; but let it rather call forth a tribute of gratitude to our memories, the most valuable of all posthumous fame, as men who employed the unparalleled prosperity that God had given them, in enlarging the base and adding numerous and more splendid columns to the temple of civil and religious liberty.

31.

CHARLES G. FINNEY: The Work of Man and the Work of God

Jacksonian Democracy had its religious complement in evangelical revivalism. Of the revivalists who traveled the country in search of souls, Charles Finney was the most renowned. He was not only eminently successful as a preacher but he also developed systematic revivalist techniques that were widely imitated. His philosophy of religion was grounded in transcendentalist thought. He held man to be perfectible and endorsed many religious and secular reform movements. In 1835 he joined the faculty of America's first non-segregated, coeducational institution of higher learning, Oberlin College in Ohio, and in 1851 he became Oberlin's second president. The lecture, part of which appears here, was published in the New York Evangelist *in December 1834, and then, in a somewhat expanded version, in 1835.*

Source: *Lectures on Revivals of Religion*, New York, 1838: "What a Revival of Religion Is."

RELIGION IS THE WORK OF MAN. It is something for man to do. It consists in obeying God with and from the heart. It is man's duty. It is true; God induces him to do it. He influences him by His Spirit, because of his great wickedness and reluctance to obey. If it were not necessary for God to influence men, if men were disposed to obey God, there would be no occasion to pray, "O Lord, revive thy work." The ground of necessity for such a prayer is that men are wholly indisposed to obey; and unless God interpose the influence of His Spirit, not a man on earth will ever obey the commands of God.

A *revival of religion* presupposes a declension. Almost all the religion in the world has been produced by revivals. God has found it necessary to take advantage of the excitability there is in mankind, to produce powerful excitements among them, before he can lead them to obey. Men are so sluggish, there are so many things to lead their minds off from religion and to oppose the influence of the gospel, that it is necessary to raise an excitement among them, till the tide rises so high as to sweep away the opposing obstacles. They must be so excited that they will break over these counteracting influences before they will obey God. . . .

There is so little principle in the church, so little firmness and stability of purpose, that unless the religious feelings are awakened and kept excited, counter worldly feeling and excitement will prevail, and men will not obey God. They have so little knowledge and their principles are so weak, that unless they are excited they will go back from the path of duty and do nothing to promote the glory of God. The state of the world is still such, and probably will be till the millennium is fully come, that religion must be mainly promoted by means of revivals. How long and how often has the experiment been tried, to bring the church to act steadily for God without these periodical excitements! Many good men have supposed, and still suppose, that the best way to promote religion is to go along uniformly and gather in the ungodly gradually and without excitement. But however such reasoning may appear in the abstract, facts demonstrate its futility. If the church were far enough advanced in knowledge, and had stability of principle enough to keep awake, such a course would do; but the church is so little enlightened, and there are so many counteracting causes, that she will not go steadily to work without a special interest being awakened. As the millennium advances, it is probable that these periodical excitements will be unknown. Then the church will be enlightened, and the counteracting causes removed, and the entire church will be in a state of habitual and steady obedience to God. The entire church will stand and take the infant mind and cultivate it for God. Children will be trained up in the way they should go and there will be no such torrents of worldliness, and fashion, and covetousness, to bear away the piety of the church as soon as the excitement of a revival is withdrawn.

It is very desirable it should be so. It is very desirable that the church should go on steadily in a course of obedience without these excitements. Such excitements are liable to injure the health. Our nervous system is so strung that any powerful excitement, if long continued, injures our health and unfits us for duty. If religion is ever to have a pervading influence in the world, it cannot be so; this spasmodic religion must be done away. Then it will be uncalled for. Christians will not sleep the greater part of the time, and once in a while wake up, and rub their eyes, and bluster about, and vociferate a little while, and then go to sleep again. Then there will be no need that ministers should wear themselves out and kill themselves, by their efforts to roll back the flood of worldly influence that sets in upon the church. But as yet the state of the Christian world is such that to expect to promote religion without excitements is unphilosophical and absurd. The great political and other worldly excitements that agitate Christendom are all unfriendly to religion and divert the mind from the interests of the soul. Now these excitements can only be counteracted by religious excitements. And until there is religious principle in the world to put down irreligious excitements, it is vain to try to promote religion, except by counteracting excitements. This is true in philosophy and it is a historical fact. . . .

These remarks are designed only as an introduction to the discourse. I shall now proceed with the main design, to show:

I. What a revival of religion is not;
II. What it is; and,
III. The agencies employed in promoting it.

I. A REVIVAL OF RELIGION IS NOT A MIRACLE

1. A miracle has been generally defined to be a Divine interference, setting aside or suspending the laws of nature. It is not a miracle in this sense. All the laws of matter and mind remain in force. They are neither suspended nor set aside in a revival.

2. It is not a miracle according to another definition of the term miracle: something above the powers of nature. There is nothing in religion beyond the ordinary powers of nature. It consists entirely in the right exercise of the powers of nature. It is just that, and nothing else. When mankind become religious, they are not enabled to put forth exertions which they were unable before to put forth. They only exert the powers they had before in a different way and use them for the glory of God.

3. It is not a miracle, or dependent on a miracle, in any sense. It is a purely philosophical result of the right use of the constituted means, as much so as any other effect produced by the application of means. There may be a miracle among its antecedent causes, or there may not. The apostles employed miracles, simply as a means by which they arrested attention to their message, and established its Divine authority.

Rev. Charles G. Finney, 1835 engraving

But the miracle was not the revival. The miracle was one thing; the revival that followed it was quite another thing. The revivals in the apostles' days were connected with miracles, but they were not miracles.

I said that a revival is the result of the right use of the appropriate means. The means which God has enjoyed for the production of a revival doubtless have a natural tendency to produce a revival. Otherwise God would not have enjoined them. But means will not produce a revival, we all know, without the blessing of God. No more will grain, when it is sowed, produce a crop without the blessing of God. It is impossible for us to say that there is not as direct an influence or agency from God, to produce a crop of grain, as there is to produce a revival. What are the laws of nature, according to which, it is supposed, that grain yields a crop? They are nothing but the constituted manner of the operations of God. In the Bible, the Word of God is compared to grain, and preaching is compared to sowing seed, and the results to the springing up and growth of the crop. And

the result is just as philosophical in the one case as in the other, and is as naturally connected with the cause; or, more correctly, a revival is as naturally a result of the use of the appropriate means as a crop is of the use of its appropriate means. It is true that religion does not properly belong to the category of cause and effect; but although it is not caused by means, yet it has its occasion, and may as naturally and certainly result from its occasion as a crop does from its cause. . . .

There is one fact under the government of God worthy of universal notice and of everlasting remembrance; which is, that the most useful and important things are most easily and certainly obtained by the use of the appropriate means. This is evidently a principle in the Divine administration. Hence, all the necessaries of life are obtained with great certainty by the use of the simplest means. The luxuries are more difficult to obtain; the means to procure them are more intricate and less certain in their results; while things absolutely hurtful and poisonous, such as alcohol and the like, are often obtained only by torturing nature and making use of a kind of infernal sorcery to procure the death-dealing abomination. This principle holds true in moral government, and as spiritual blessings are of surpassing importance, we should expect their attainment to be connected with great certainty with the use of the appropriate means; and such we find to be the fact. And I fully believe that could facts be known, it would be found that when the appointed means have been rightly used, spiritual blessings have been obtained with greater uniformity than temporal ones.

II. I AM TO SHOW WHAT A REVIVAL IS

It is the renewal of the first love of Christians, resulting in the awakening and conversion of sinners to God. In the popular sense, a revival of religion in a community is the arousing, quickening, and reclaiming of the more or less backslidden church and the more or less general awakening of all classes and insuring attention to the claims of God.

It presupposes that the church is sunk down in a backslidden state, and a revival consists in the return of the church from her backslidings and in the conversion of sinners.

1. A revival always includes conviction of sin on the part of the church. Backslidden professors cannot wake up and begin right away in the service of God without deep searchings of heart. The fountains of sin need to be broken up. In a true revival, Christians are always brought under such convictions; they see their sins in such a light that often they find it impossible to maintain a hope of their acceptance with God. It does not always go to that extent; but there are always, in a genuine revival, deep convictions of sin and often cases of abandoning all hope.

2. Backslidden Christians will be brought to repentance. A revival is nothing else than a new beginning of obedience to God. Just as in the case of a converted sinner, the first step is a deep repentance, a breaking down of heart, a getting down into the dust before God, with deep humility and forsaking of sin.

3. Christians will have their faith renewed. While they are in their backslidden state they are blind to the state of sinners. Their hearts are as hard as marble. The truths of the Bible only appear like a dream. They admit it to be all true; their conscience and their judgment assent to it; but their faith does not see it standing out in bold relief in all the burning realities of eternity. But when they enter into a revival, they no longer see men as trees walking, but they see things in that strong light which will renew the love of God in their hearts. This will lead them to labor zealously to bring others to Him. They will feel grieved that others do not love God when they love Him so much. And they will set themselves feelingly to persuade their neighbors to give Him their hearts. So their love to men will be renewed. They will be filled with a tender and burning love for souls. They will have a longing desire for the salvation of the whole world. They will be in agony for individuals whom they want to have saved: their friends, relations, enemies. They will not only be urging them to give their hearts to God but they will carry them to God in the arms of faith, and with strong crying and tears beseech God to have mercy on them and save their souls from endless burnings.

4. A revival breaks the power of the world and of sin over Christians. It brings them to such vantage ground that they get a fresh impulse toward heaven. They have a new foretaste of heaven and new desires after union to God; and the charm of the world is broken and the power of sin overcome.

5. When the churches are thus awakened and reformed, the reformation and salvation of sinners will follow, going through the same stages of conviction, repentance, and reformation. Their hearts will be broken down and changed. Very often the most abandoned profligates are among the subjects. Harlots, and drunkards, and infidels, and all sorts of abandoned characters, are awakened and converted. The worst part of human society is softened and reclaimed, and made to appear as a lovely specimen of the beauty of holiness.

III. I AM TO CONSIDER THE AGENCIES EMPLOYED IN CARRYING FORWARD A REVIVAL OF RELIGION

ORDINARILY, there are three agents employed in the work of conversion and one instrument. The agents are God, some person who brings the truth to bear on the mind, and the sinner himself. The instrument is the truth. There are always two agents, God and the sinner, employed and active in every case of genuine conversion.

1. The agency of God is twofold: by His Providence and by His Spirit.

(a) By His providential government, He so arranges events as to bring the sinner's mind and the truth in contact. He brings the sinner where the truth reaches his ears or his eyes. It is often interesting to trace the manner in which God arranges events so as to bring this about, and how He sometimes makes everything seem to favor a revival. The state of the weather and of the public health, and other circumstances concur to make everything just right to favor the application of truth with the greatest possible efficacy. How He sometimes sends a minister along, just at the time he is wanted! How He brings out a particular truth, just at the particular time when the individual it is fitted to reach is in the way to hear!

(b) God's special agency by His Holy Spirit. Having direct access to the mind, and knowing infinitely well the whole history and state of each individual sinner, He employs that truth which is best adapted to his particular case, and then sets it home with Divine power. He gives it such vividness, strength, and power that the sinner quails, and throws down his weapons of rebellion, and turns to the Lord. Under His influence, the truth burns and cuts its way like fire. He makes the truth stand out in such aspects that it crushes the proudest man down with the weight of a mountain. If men were disposed to obey God, the truth is given with sufficient clearness in the Bible; and from preaching they could learn all that is necessary for them to know. But because they are wholly disinclined to obey it, God clears it up before their minds, and pours in a blaze of convincing light upon their souls which they cannot withstand, and they yield to it and obey God and are saved.

2. The agency of men is commonly employed. Men are not mere instruments in the hands of God. Truth is the instrument. The preacher is a moral agent in the work; he acts; he is not a mere passive instrument; he is voluntary in promoting the conversion of sinners.

3. The agency of the sinner himself. The conversion of a sinner consists in his obeying the truth. It is therefore impossible it should take place without his agency, for it consists in his acting right. He is influenced to this by the agency of God and by the agency of men. Men act on their fellowmen, not only by language, but by their looks, their tears, their daily deportment. See that impenitent man there who has a pious wife. Her very looks, her tenderness, her solemn, compassionate dignity, softened and molded into the image of Christ, are a sermon to him all the time. He has to turn his mind away, because it is such a reproach to him. He feels a sermon ringing in his ears all day long.

Mankind are accustomed to read the countenances of their neighbors. Sinners often read the state of a Christian's mind in his eyes. If his eyes are full of levity, or worldly anxiety and contrivance, sinners read it. If they are full of the Spirit of God, sinners read it; and they are often led to conviction by barely seeing the countenance of Christians. . . .

If Christians have deep feeling on the subject of religion themselves, they will produce deep feeling wherever they go. And if they are cold, or light and trifling, they inevitably destroy all deep feeling, even in awakened sinners.

I knew a case, once, of an individual who was very anxious, but one day I was grieved to find that her convictions seemed to be all gone. I asked her what she had been doing. She told me she had been spending the afternoon at such a place, among some professors of religion, not thinking that it would dissipate her convictions to spend an afternoon with professors of religion. But they were trifling and vain, and thus her convictions were lost. And no doubt those professors of religion, by their folly, destroyed a soul, for her convictions did not return.

The church is required to use the means for the conversion of sinners. Sinners cannot properly be said to use the means for their own conversion. The church uses the means. What sinners do is to submit to the truth or to resist it. It is a mistake of sinners to think they are using means for their own conversion. The whole drift of a revival, and everything about it, is designed to present the truth to your mind for your obedience or resistance.

32.

Gustave de Beaumont: Religious Sects and Religious Freedom in America

From May 1831 to February 1832, Alexis de Tocqueville, who later achieved fame with Democracy in America, *and Gustave de Beaumont, his good friend and traveling companion, toured the United States with a commission from the French government to study American prisons. Their main purpose in coming, however, was to make a study of a working democracy. By prearrangement, each concentrated on different aspects of American society. Beaumont covered race relations and religion and his observations are recorded in a novel about the courtship and marriage of a Frenchman and a mulatto woman entitled* Marie; or, Slavery in the United States. *To the novel were appended three essays, excerpts from one of which, on "Religious Movements in the United States," appear below. The work was published in France in 1835, but it received relatively little notice.*

Source: *Marie ou l'Esclavage aux États-Unis,* Paris, 1835, Vol. II, pp. 183-225.

THE PRINCIPAL established religious sects in North America are the Methodists, Anabaptists, Catholics, Presbyterians, Episcopalians, Quakers or Friends, Universalists, Congregationalists, Unitarians, Dutch Reformed, German Reformed, Moravians, Evangelical Lutherans, etc. The Anabaptists are divided into Calvinists or related groups, Mennonites, Free-Church, Dunkers, etc. The most populous Protestant congregation is that of the Methodists; it numbered 550,000 members at the beginning of the year 1834. There are no exact figures for the other communions.

I shall first examine the relations of different religious persuasions with each other and secondly, the relations of all of the sects with the state.

RELATION OF THE DENOMINATIONS WITH EACH OTHER

IN THIS REGARD, it is first of all necessary to distinguish between members of the congregation and their ministers within the religious sects.

In general, perfect harmony is seen to prevail among members of different communions; the mutual goodwill that Americans bear toward each other is not at all altered by the divergence of religious beliefs. The prosperity of a congregation, the eloquence of a preacher, may well inspire in other communities less fortunate, or whose orators are less brilliant, some feelings of jealousy; but these sentiments are ephemeral and leave behind no real bitterness; the rivalry certainly does not go so far as to become hatred.

With regard to ministers of opposing faiths, it would be too much to say that they are hostile to each other; but one might at least venture to say that little goodwill exists between them. The principal reason for this is that the greater or lesser success of their churches is for them not only a matter of self-respect but also a question of self-interest. In general, the emoluments of the minister are more or less considerable according to the affluence of the group under his guidance. I am speaking here only of the Protestant sects, which, in America, comprise the faith with the largest membership. Protestant ministers do not in any way constitute a clergy subject to hierarchical rules and to surveillance by a higher power; the only authority to which they are subordinated is that of the congregation which has elected them; but nothing limits [the choice of] a congregation which is looking for a minister. It may select whomever it pleases.

The candidate has no need to take any degree in theology nor to undergo any examination, nor to pursue any special course of studies to be fitted for ecclesiastical functions: such is the accepted practice. Actually, almost all who seek to exercise the holy office are put to a kind of test. In all of the large cities, there is a group of enlightened persons whose mission is to examine the aspirants. The candidate delivers a sermon and the assembly grants him a certificate commensurate with his success; in general, he receives this certificate couched in the most favorable wording possible. Armed with this paper, he presents himself to a congregation that, needing a minister, accepts him at once in this role. Sometimes not even any proof is required; he proclaims a great piety and an ardent zeal for religion, raises his eyes to heaven and beats his breast, and on this evidence, which is not always sincere, the committee of individuals who want a preacher declare him *minister*.

This ease of arrival at the sacred office among the Americans gives the Protestant minister a peculiar stamp. The result is that anyone can, with no preparation or previous study, become a churchman. The religious ministry thus becomes a career into which one can enter at any age, in any posture, according to the circumstances. This one whom you see at the head of a respectable congregation began his career as a merchant; his business having fallen off, he became a minister; this other one began his career as a priest, but as soon as he had a certain amount of money at his command, he left the pulpit for business. In the eyes of many, the religious ministry is truly a business career.

The Protestant minister presents no characteristic resemblance to the Catholic priest. In general, the latter espouses his parish; his whole life is spent among the same people, on whom he exercises not only the influence of his sacred role but also the moral effect of his virtues; in no sense is he practising a trade; he is fulfilling a duty. The life of a Protestant minister, to the contrary, is essentially mobile; nothing binds him to one congregation when his personal interest calls him to another; he belongs rightfully to the community which pays him best. When I was traveling through Canada, where the Catholic religion is dominant, someone told me of the instance of a priest who, not wishing to be separated from his parishioners, had just refused a bishopric. More than one Methodist or Anabaptist minister would promptly abandon his church if there were $100 more to be gained in another. Nothing is more unusual than to see a Protestant minister with white hair. The major goal that the American in the ministry pursues is his own welfare and that of his wife and children. When he has materially improved his condition, his end is achieved; he retires. In his old age, he takes his ease.

It is easy to deduce the outcome of this situation. The relationships that ministers of different Protestant sects have with one another are comparable to the relations of other people of similar profession. They do not seek to harm one another, because it is a useful principle for everyone that each should practise his trade freely; but they maintain a real competition, from which result clashes of private interest, necessarily arousing in those who experience them feelings hardly Christian. The reader will easily comprehend that I do not in any sense mean to apply to all American Protestant ministers the business-minded character that I have just painted here. I have encountered several whose sincere faith and ardent zeal could only be compared to their charity and to their disinterestedness in temporal matters; but here I am presenting those characteristics applicable to the large majority.

I have said that a great goodwill appears to prevail among members of different religious sects and that the petty passions born from the success of one and the decline of another resolve themselves into feelings of self-satisfaction or discontent without reaching the pitch of hatred. However, there are two exceptions to this general fact. The first is the feeling of the Protestants, notably the Presbyterians, toward the Catholics.

Among the innumerable sects which exist in the United States, Catholicism is the only confession whose principles are contrary to those of the others. It takes authority as its point of departure. The others proceed from reason. Catholicism in America is the same as it is everywhere; it recognizes absolutely the authority of the see of Rome, not only in matters of dogma but also in everything concerning church administration. The United States is divided into eleven dioceses, for each of which there is a bishop. When a bishopric is vacant, the clergy gathers, chooses candidates, and sends their names to the pope, who has complete freedom of choice. He could name the last person on the list; usually, he chooses the one who is presented first, but it is not without precedent that he may do otherwise. It is the bishops who appoint the priests; and the company of the faithful takes no part in these elections. The state not being involved at all in religious matters, members of the Catholic group contribute to the support of the clergy and needs of the church according to their means. The method generally employed to provide for these expenses is to levy a considerable contribution on all those who occupy pews in the church.

Since only the rich can bear such expenses, the poor are admitted to the church free, where they occupy the places reserved for them. When funds from pew rents are not adequate, recourse is made to extraordinary taxes, which the Catholic community never fails to impose upon itself. The unity of Catholicism, the principle of authority from which it proceeds, the fixity of its doctrines in the midst of the divided Protestant sects with their mutually contradictory theories — although they start from a common principle (which is the right of discussion and examination) — all tend to arouse among the Protestants some feelings that are hostile to the Catholics.

The Catholic religion has still another characteristic which is peculiar to it and which has aggravated inimical attitudes. I mean proselytism.

In Maryland, the principal educational institutions are in the hands of priests or Catholic nuns, and the greater part of the students are Protestants. The directors of these institutions no doubt use great discretion in their opportunities to influence the students; but this influence is inevitable. It is surely exercised more fully in the institutions for young girls.

The Catholic clergy never sets itself against the marriage of Catholics with Protestants. It has been noted in America that the former never give up their religion to assume that of their Protestant wives, and it is not at all unusual for Protestants married to Catholic wives to adopt their religion. In any event, when the wife is Catholic, the children are, too, because it is the wife who rears the children. Everywhere in the United States, the Catholic faith makes the same efforts to propagate itself. It thus finds itself in direct opposition to the principles of certain sects that consider proselytism as affecting freedom of conscience (for example, the Quakers), and it is the adversary of all.

Catholicism draws partisans to itself, not only because of the zeal of its ministers but also by the very nature of its doctrine. It suits both superior spirits who wish to rest from their doubts in the bosom of authority and mediocre spirits incapable of choosing beliefs for themselves, and who would never have any principles if no one gave them a fully-developed religion. Catholicism seems, for this one reason alone, the best confession for the greatest number. Distinct from the Protestant congregations, which form something like select societies in which the members are generally of the same rank and social position, the Catholic churches receive indifferently people of all classes and conditions. In their embrace, the poor is the equal of the rich, the slave of the master, the Negro of the white; it is the religion of the masses.

One could add to all of these causes a fact which must necessarily influence the destiny of Catholicism in the United States: the morality of the Catholic clergy in that country. I cannot refrain from repeating on this subject the exact words of an English writer whom I have already had occasion to quote. Here is the language in which Colonel Hamilton, a Protestant, speaks of the Catholic clergy in the United States:

> All that I have learned . . . of the zeal of the Catholic priests in this country is truly exemplary. These holy ministers never forget that a being in its most hideous form contains a soul which ennobles it, as precious in their eyes as that of the sovereign Pontiff whom they obey. . . . Divesting themselves of all pride of caste, they mingle with slaves and understand their obligation toward the unfortunate better than all other Christian ministers.
>
> I am not a Catholic, but no prejudice will keep me from doing justice to the priests whose zeal is not excited by any temporal interest, who pass their lives in humility, without any other concern than to spread the truths of religion and to console all miseries of humanity.

It seems quite well established that Catholicism is gaining in the United States and that its ranks are continually growing, while other communions tend to split off from one another. Also, it is truthful to observe that although the Protestant sects are jealous of one another, all of them hate their common enemy, Catholicism. The Presbyterians are the ones whose enmity is deepest; they have stronger feelings than all of the other Protestants because they have a livelier faith; and furthermore, Catholic proselytizing annoys them, not because they find fault with it in principle, as the Quakers do, but because they practise it themselves. . . .

I have said that there are two exceptions to the principle of mutual goodwill which tend to unite the members of different sects in the United States. I have just discussed the first, which is the hostility of the Protestants to the Catholics. The second is the hostility of all of the Christian sects to the Unitarians.

The Unitarians are the philosophers of the United States. Everyone in America is forced by public opinion to adhere to a confession of faith; Unitarianism is usually the religion of those who have none. In France, the philosophy of the 18th century attacked religion and its ministers openly. In America, philosophy works away at the same purpose; but it is obliged to conceal its intent behind a religious veil. Unitarian doctrine is its cloak. Here are the major points of this doctrine in the United States.

The Unitarians believe:

1. in a God, in one person and not in three;
2. that the Bible is not a direct emanation from God, but the work of a man describing the revelation;
3. that Jesus Christ is not in any way a God, but the agent of a God;
4. that there is no Holy Ghost;
5. that Jesus came to earth, not to expiate the sins of men by his death, but to give them the example of virtue;
6. that man has no *original sin;* that he is a being who was born good, having nothing else to do but to perfect himself;
7. that the wicked will not be eternally unhappy;
8. that, to achieve an eternally happy life, men should not base any hope upon Jesus Christ, but only count upon their good works;
9. that the observance of Sunday is not necessary, etc., etc.

This doctrine, which reverses Christianity from top to bottom, is nothing other than a consequence of that Protestantism which, rejecting the principle of authority, wishes that each belief be subjected to the scrutiny of reason. The Presbyterians, therefore, are scarcely logical when they reproach the Unitarians for not believing certain things, while they allow themselves the right to reject certain beliefs. The Presbyterians would like to prop up the edifice that they have shaken; the Unitarians think that it is more sensible that collapse follow the commotion.

All of the dissident sects, who disagree with some portions of any other dogmas, are in accord with the greater portion of them; but the Unitarian Church recognizes none of them. Truly, Unitarianism is no religious belief, it is a philosophy; it forms the connecting link between Protestantism and natural religion. It is the last halting place of human reason which, having escaped Catholicism, placed at the foundation of the Christian religion, ascends, through all of the degrees of Protestantism, to the summits of philosophy, where having arrived, it launches itself into space at the risk of being lost.

The Unitarian sect, known in Europe as the Socinians, has been introduced into the United States only within the last twenty or twenty-five years. Boston was its cradle and it is expanding today in that city under the influence of the Reverend Doctor Channing, the most eloquent preacher and one of the most remarkable authors in the United States. The Unitarian doctrine makes progress every day in the large cities, where the philosophical spirit first gains acceptance. But up to the present time it has spread very little in the country regions, whose inhabitants, in general, show a great amount of religious zeal. . . .

The Catholics are perhaps the least concerned of all of the Christians in the United States about the gains of Socinianism. They believe that, in the end, there will be only two religions in America: Catholicism, that is, Christianity based upon authority; and Deism, or natural religion, based upon reason. They believe, moreover, that since a form of public worship is necessary, and natural religion has none, all of those who have forsaken Christianity for philosophy will return to the Christian religion by way of Catholicism.

It can be seen that the enmity of the Protestant sects toward the Unitarians, and their hatred for the Catholics, have two diametrically opposed foundations: they reproach the latter for blind faith and the former for none; one, for prohibiting the right of free inquiry, the other, for abusing [the right].

Between these two extreme positions, Catholicism and Unitarianism, there is a vast area occupied by a multitude of other sects: a thousand intermediate degrees between authority and reason, between faith and doubt, show themselves; a thousand efforts of thought projected into the unknown; a thousand expressions of intellectual pride that will not be gainsaid. The human spirit ranges through all of these degrees, often impelled by the noblest passions, now plunged into error by the love of truth, now into folly by the counsels of reason.

The tableau of all of the wanderings and weaknesses of that human intelligence which tortures itself endlessly in a circle where it never finds the resting place that it seeks should be a spectacle full of philosophical lessons. One should never regard without pity and astonishment the unwinding of the long chain which binds one to the other among all these aberrations. . . .

I shall not continue the examination of the divergencies of the Protestant sects. Let it suffice to observe on this subject that all of these sects, whose doctrines vary beyond infinity, from the community of the Quakers, whose theory would let a man die without defense, to the congregation of the Shakers, whose principles would bring about the end of civilization, all have one point in common, where they are in perfect agreement. That point is the moral purity that each professes.

Presbyterianism, whose passions of hatred I have already mentioned, is probably, of all the Protestant communities, the most prolific in its good works. The same fanaticism that gives rise to crimes also engenders virtues.

The itinerant preachers of the Methodist congregation, which is often ridiculed, make the American forests resound with their enthusiastic cries and their inspired exhortations; but their zeal, more ardent than enlightened, is always sincere. Do they not, at risk of their lives, range the most savage countries to carry the word of the gospel there? Without these pious pilgrims, what would become of the inhabitants of the Western states, where the dwellings scattered here and there are far from any church? The Methodists who travel about the desert are also the best messengers of civilization, and the surest source of consolation in times of misfortune.

All of these confessions are founded on a pure morality, because all are Christian; they are divided by opposing doctrines, but they have a strong bond with each other: that of virtue.

RELATION OF THE CHURCHES
WITH THE STATE

Nowhere is the separation of church and state better established than in North America. The state never interferes in the church nor the church in the state.

All of the American constitutions proclaim freedom of conscience and the liberty and equality of all of the confessions. . . .

Hence, in the United States, there exists neither a state religion nor a religion considered to be that of the majority — nor any preeminence of one church body above another. The state is a stranger to all of the churches. Each religious congregation governs itself as it chooses, appoints its ministers, levies taxes among its members, and pays its debts, without being accountable to political authority, which asks no questions.

In a large number of states, ministers of the churches, to whatever sect they belong, are declared ineligible by law to fulfill any civil or military function. "Whereas," the constitution of New York says, "ministers of the gospel are, by nature of their status, devoted to the service of God and to the cure of souls, nothing should divert them from the important duties of their ministry."

Political life, therefore, is completely forbidden to ministers of the church. One can deduce from this that no power can be exerted upon the ministers of a sect other than that of another congregation.

I have already discussed the general principles; I must now indicate some exceptions.

The constitution of Massachusetts proclaims the freedom of the various faiths in the sense that it does not wish to persecute any of them; but it recognizes within the state only Christians and protects only the Protestants.

In the terms of this constitution, the communions that do not provide for the expenses and the maintenance of their Protestant worship in a suitable manner may be constrained to do so by an injunction of the legislature. The assessment collected as a result of this measure can be applied by each person to the maintenance of the sect to which he belongs; but none can free himself from the obligation to pay it on the pretext that he practises no faith.

Maryland's constitution also declares that all of the faiths are free, and that no one is forced to contribute to the maintenance of a particular church. However, it gives the legislature the right to establish a general tax, according to the circumstances, for the support of the Christian religion.

The constitution of Vermont recognizes only the Christian faiths, and says specifically that every congregation of Christians should celebrate the Sabbath or the Lord's Day, and observe the religious worship which seems to it most pleasing to the will of God, manifested by revelation.

Sometimes the American constitutions offer religious bodies some indirect assistance: thus, Maryland law declares that, to be admitted to public office, it is necessary to be a Christian. In New Jersey, one must be a Protestant. The Pennsylvania constitution requires that one believe in the existence of God and in a future life of punishments or rewards.

The provisions which I have pointed out are the only legal protection given to a religious body in the United States. Aside from these exceptions, there is no contact between state and church other than that each religious congregation, at its founding, receives the sanction of the legislature, which is called in English "incorporation." This is not exactly a legal authorization, for the power to authorize the existence of religious associations and congregations would involve the right to prohibit them, and the legislatures of the American states do not possess this right.

Accurately speaking, incorporation is not established for the benefit of the state but only on behalf of the association which is being formed. The effect is to vest the congregation with the right to act at law, to own property, to give and to receive, etc. It confers civil life upon a society which can then act as an individual, one which previously had no power of action except through each of its members.

Whatever may be the lesser or greater favor accorded to this or that religious sect by the laws of various states, one may at least say, in the most sweeping and positive terms, that in North America there is no clergy forming a politically organized body and recognized as such by the state or by the force of custom.

But if ministers of the faith are entirely strangers to the government of the state, such is not the case with religion. Religion in America is not only a moral institution but also a political institution. All of the American constitutions exhort the citizens to practise religious worship as a safeguard both to good morals and to public liberties. In the United States, the law is never atheistic. . . .

There is no political ceremony in America that does not begin with a pious invocation. I have seen a meeting of the Senate in Washington open with a prayer, and the anniversary festival of the Declaration of Independence consists, in the United States, of an entirely religious ceremony.

I have just indicated how the law, which recognizes neither the authority nor even the existence of a clergy, confirms the power of religion.

I shall add that the religious sects, which remain strangers to party activity, are far from showing themselves indifferent to political interests and to the government of the country. They all take a lively interest in the maintenance of American institutions; they protect these institutions through the voice of their ministers in the sacred pulpit and even in political assemblies. In America, Christian religion is always at the service of freedom.

It is a principle of the United States legislature that, to be a good citizen, it is necessary to be religious; and it is a no less well-established rule that, to fulfill one's duty toward God, it is necessary to be a good citizen. In this respect, the sects compete in zeal and devotion. Catholicism, like the Protestant communions, lives in very close harmony with American institutions; it grows and flourishes under this regime of equality. In this country, it has the good fortune to be neither the protector of the government nor the protégé of the state.

There is only one congregation in America which is hostile to the laws of the land, the Quakers. The same principle that forbids them individually from resisting the violence of an aggressor leads them to believe that society has no right to repel the attacks of an enemy by force; never before came such an unsocial theory from a sect so moral and so pure! Be that as it may, the Quakers refuse to be part of the Army or even of the American militia. . . .

Here, nevertheless, I must remark that the Quakers are not hostile to American institutions or to the republican government of the United States; on the contrary, no sect is more democratic. But they are hostile to all society because the first law of all beings, individuals or social bodies, is self-preservation beginning with self-defense.

I have reviewed the relations between organized religions and the state with respect to American laws. . . . But in this matter laws are far less powerful than custom.

Although not all American state constitutions impose religious beliefs and the practice of faith as a condition of political privileges, there is not a single state where public opinion and the customs of the inhabitants do not forcefully constrain an obligation to these beliefs. In general, anyone who adheres to one of the religious sects, whose number is immense in the United States, enjoys all of his social and political rights in peace.

But the man who would claim to have neither a church nor religious beliefs would not only be excluded from all civil employment and from all political offices, voluntary or salaried, but, furthermore, would be an object of moral persecution of all kinds. No one would care to have any social relations with him, even less to contract family ties; no one would buy from him or sell to him. No one in the United States believes that a man without religion could be an honest man.

I have just pointed out the infringements upon religious freedom by the laws of several states. I should add, in conclusion, that these violations are disappearing daily from American laws and customs. It must not be forgotten that New England, the home of Puritanism, was for a long time religious to the point of fanaticism, and if one recalls that the political law of that land formerly punished miscreants by death (that is, those who were not Presbyterians), one will recognize what progress Massachusetts and the other states of the North have made in tolerance and freedom.

33.

Samuel F. B. Morse: The Dangers of Foreign Immigration

Mounting Irish-Catholic immigration to the United States in the 1830s provoked an outburst of nativist sentiment. Nativist societies organized and attempted to overcome the influence of the growing Roman Catholic Church and to restrict the role of the immigrant in politics and labor. Pamphlets and newspaper articles were published, contending that Roman Catholicism and democracy were incompatible. Samuel F. B. Morse, painter and inventor of the telegraph, was a prolific writer on the subject. He wrote a series of eleven articles for the New York Journal of Commerce, *which were collected in a short book in 1835. Numbers Six and Eleven appear below.*

Source: *Imminent Dangers to the Free Institutions of the United States Through Foreign Immigration, and the Present State of the Naturalization Laws,* by An American, New York, 1835, Nos. 6, 11.

I HAVE SET FORTH in a very brief and imperfect manner the evil the great and increasing evil that threatens our free institutions from *foreign interference.* Have I not shown that there is real cause for alarm? Let me recapitulate the facts in the case, and see if any one of them can be denied; and if not, I submit it to the calm decision of every American whether he can still sleep in fancied security while incendiaries are at work; and whether he is ready quietly to surrender his liberty, civil and religious, into the hands of foreign powers.

1. It is a fact that in this age the subject of civil and religious liberty agitates in the most intense manner the various European governments.

2. It is a fact that the influence of American free institutions in subverting European despotic institutions is greater now than it has ever been, from the fact of the greater maturity and long-tried character of the American form of government.

3. It is a fact that popery is opposed in its very nature to democratic republicanism; and it is, therefore, as a political system, as well as religious, opposed to civil and religious liberty, and consequently to our form of government.

4. It is a fact that this truth, respecting the intrinsic character of popery, has lately been clearly and demonstratively proved in public lectures by one of the Austrian cabinet, a devoted Roman Catholic, and with the evident design (as subsequent events show) of exciting the Austrian government to a great enterprise in support of absolute power.

5. It is a fact that this member of the Austrian cabinet, in his lectures, designated and proscribed this country by name, as the "great nursery of destructive principles; as the revolutionary school for France and the rest of Europe," whose contagious example of democratic liberty had given, and would still give, trouble to the rest of the world, unless the evil were abated.

6. It is a fact that very shortly after the delivery of these lectures, a society was organized in the Austrian capital, called the St. Leopold Foundation, for the purpose "of promoting the greater activity of Catholic missions in America."

7. It is a fact that this society is under

the patronage of the emperor of Austria; has its central direction at Vienna; is under the supervision of Prince Metternich; that it is an extensive combination, embodying the civil as well as the ecclesiastical *officers,* not only of the whole Austrian Empire, but of the neighboring despotic states; that it is actively at work collecting moneys and sending agents to this country to carry out into effect its designs.

8. It is a fact that the agents of these foreign despots are, for the most part, Jesuits.

9. It is a fact that the effects of this society are already apparent in the otherwise unaccountable increase of Roman Catholic cathedrals, churches, colleges, convents, nunneries, etc., in every part of the country; in the sudden increase of Catholic emigration; in the increased clannishness of the Roman Catholics, and the boldness with which their leaders are experimenting on the character of the American people.

10. It is a fact that an unaccountable disposition to riotous conduct has manifested itself within a few years, when exciting topics are publicly discussed wholly at variance with the former peaceful, deliberative character of our people.

11. It is a fact that a species of police, unknown to our laws, has repeatedly been put in requisition to keep the peace among a certain class of foreigners who are Roman Catholics, viz., priest-police.

12. It is a fact that Roman Catholic priests have interfered to influence our elections.

13. It is a fact that politicians on both sides have propitiated these priests to obtain the votes of their people.

14. It is a fact that numerous societies of Roman Catholics, particularly among the Irish foreigners, are organized in various parts of the country, under various names and ostensibly for certain benevolent objects; that these societies are united together by correspondence, all which may be innocent and praiseworthy, but viewed in con-

nection with the recent aspect of affairs are at least suspicious.

15. It is a fact that an attempt has been made to organize a military corps of Irishmen in New York, to be called the O'Connel Guards; thus commencing a military organization of foreigners.

16. It is a fact that the greater part of the foreigners in our population is composed of Roman Catholics.

Facts like these I have enumerated might be multiplied, but these are the most important, and quite sufficient to make every American settle the question with himself whether there is or is not danger to the country from the present state of our naturalization laws. I have stated what I believe to be facts. If they are *not* facts they will easily be disproved, and I most sincerely hope they will be disproved. If they are facts and my inferences from them are wrong, I can be shown where I have erred, and an inference more rational and more probable, involving less, or perhaps no danger to the country can be deduced from them; which deduction, when I see it, I will most cheerfully accept as a full explanation of these most suspicious doings of foreign powers.

I have spoken in these numbers freely of a particular religious sect, the Roman Catholics, because from the nature of the case it was unavoidable; because the foreign political conspiracy is identified with that creed. With the *religious tenets,* properly so called, of the Roman Catholic, I have not meddled. If foreign powers hostile to the principles of this government have combined to spread any religious creed, no matter of what denomination, that creed does by that very act become a subject of political interest to all citizens, and must and will be thoroughly scrutinized. We are compelled to examine it. We have no choice about it. If, instead of combining to spread with the greatest activity the Catholic religion throughout our country, the monarchs of Europe had united to spread Presbyterianism or Methodism, I presume there are few who would not see at once the propriety and the necessity of looking most narrowly at the political bearings of the peculiar principles of these sects, or of any other Protestant sects; and members of any Protestant sects, too, would be the last to complain of the examination. I know not why the Roman Catholics in this land of scrutiny are to plead exclusive exemption from the same trial. . . .

THE PROPRIETY, nay, the imperious necessity of a change in the naturalization laws is the point to which it is indispensable to the safety of the country that the attention of Americans, as a whole people, should at this moment be concentrated. It is a national question, not only separate from but *superior* to all others. All other questions which divide the nation are peculiarly of a domestic character; they relate to matters between American and American. Whether the bank system is or is not adverse to our democratic institutions; whether internal improvement is constitutionally entrusted to the management of the general government or reserved to the states respectively; whether monopolies of any kind are just or unjust; whether the right of instructing representatives is to be allowed or resisted; whether the high offices of the nation are safest administered by these or by those citizens; all these and many kindred questions are entirely of a domestic character, to be settled between ourselves, in the just democratic mode, by majority, by the prevailing voice of the American people declared through the *ballot box.*

But the question of *naturalization,* the question whether *foreigners, not yet arrived,* shall or shall not be admitted to the American right of balloting is a matter in which the American people are in a certain sense, on one side as the original and exclusive possessors of the privilege and foreigners on the other, as petitioners for a participation in that privilege; for the privilege of ex-

pressing their opinion upon and assisting to decide all the other questions I have enumerated. It is, therefore, a question separate and *superior* to all these. It is a fundamental question; it affects the very foundation of our institutions, it bears directly and vitally on the *principle of the ballot* itself, that principle which decides the gravest questions of policy among Americans, nay, which can decide the very existence of the government or can change its form at any moment. And surely this vital principle is amply protected from injury. To secure this point, every means which a people jealous of their liberties could devise was doubtless gathered about it for its preservation.

It is not guarded. Be astonished, Americans, at the oversight. The mere statement of the provisions of the naturalization law, is sufficient, one would think, to startle any American who reflects at all. FIVE YEARS' RESIDENCE GIVES THE FOREIGNER, WHATEVER BE HIS CONDITION OR CHARACTER, THIS MOST SACRED PRIVILEGE OF ASSISTING TO CONTROL, AND ACTUALLY OF CONTROLLING (*there is not a guard to prevent*), ALL THE DOMESTIC INTERESTS OF AMERICA. A simple *five years' residence* allows any foreigner (no matter what his character, whether friend or enemy of freedom, whether an exile from proscription or a pensioned Jesuit, commissioned to serve the interests of imperial despots) to handle this "lock of our strength."

How came it to pass? How is it possible that so vital a point as the ballot box was not constitutionally surrounded with double, ay, with treble guards? How is it that this *heart* of democracy was left so exposed; yes; this very *heart* of the body politic, in which, in periodical pulsations, the opinions of the people meet, to go forth again as law to the extremities of the nation; this *heart* left so absolutely without protection, that the murderous eye of imperial despots across the deep cannot only watch it in all its movements but they are invited from its very nakedness to reach out their hands to stab it. The figure is not too strong; their blow is aimed, now, while I write, at this very heart of our institutions.

How is it that none of our sagacious statesmen foresaw this danger to the republic through the unprotected ballot box? It was foreseen. It did not escape the prophetic eye of Jefferson. He foresaw, and from the beginning foretold the evil, and uttered his warning voice. *Mr. Jefferson denounced the encouragement of emigration.* And, oh! consistency, where is thy blush? He who is now urging Jefferson's own recommendation on this vital point is condemned by some who call themselves Jeffersonian Democrats; by some journalists who in one column profess Jeffersonian principles, while in the next they denounce both the principles and the policy of Jefferson, and (with what semblance of consistency let them show if they can) defend a great political evil against which Jefferson left his written protest.

It may be convenient, for purposes best known to themselves, for such journalists to desert their democratic principles while loudly professing still to hold them; but the people, who are neither blind nor deaf, will soon perceive whose course is most consistent with that great apostle of democratic liberty. Do they ask, would you defend Mr. Jefferson's opinions when they are wrong? I answer, prove them to be wrong and I will desert them. Truth and justice are superior to all men. I advocate Jefferson's opinions, not because they are Jefferson's, but because his opinions are in accordance with truth and sound policy. Let me show that Mr. Jefferson's opinions in relation to emigration are proved by experience to be sound.

What were the circumstances of the country when laws so favorable to the foreigner were passed to induce him to emigrate and settle in this country? The answer is obvious. Our early history explains it. In our national infancy we needed the strength of *numbers*. Powerful nations, to whom we were accessible by fleets, and consequently also by armies, threatened us. Our land had

Addison Gallery of American Art

Self-portrait by Samuel F. B. Morse

been the theater of contests between French, and English, and Spanish armies for more than a century. Our numbers were so few and so scattered that as a people we could not unite to repel aggression. The War of Independence, too, had wasted us. We wanted *numerical strength;* we felt our weakness in numbers. *Safety,* then, national *safety,* was the motive which urged us to use every effort to increase our population, and to induce a foreign emigration. Then foreigners seemed all-important, and the policy of alluring them hither too palpable to be opposed successfully even by the remonstrances of Jefferson.

We could be benefited by the emigrants, and we in return could bestow on them a gift beyond price by simply making them citizens. Manifest as this advantage seemed in the increase of our numerical strength, Mr. Jefferson looked beyond the advantage of the moment, and saw the distant evil. His reasoning, already quoted in a former number, will bear to be repeated. "I beg leave," says Mr. Jefferson, to propose a doubt. The present desire of America is to produce rapid population by as great importations of foreigners as possible. But is this founded in good policy? The advantage proposed is the multiplication of numbers. But are there no inconveniences to be thrown into the scale against the advantage expected from a multiplication of numbers by the importation of foreigners? It is for the happiness of those united in society to harmonize as much as possible in matters which they must of necessity transact together.

Civil government being the sole object of forming societies, its administration must be conducted by common consent. Every species of government has its specific principles. Ours, perhaps, are more peculiar than those of any other in the universe. It is a composition of the freest principles of the English constitution with others derived from the natural right and natural reason. To these, nothing can be more opposed than the maxims of absolute monarchies. Yet, from such, we are to expect the greatest number of emigrants.

They will bring with them the principles of the governments they leave imbibed in their early youth; or, if able to throw them off, it will be in exchange for an unbounded licentiousness, passing, as is usual, from one extreme to another. It would be a miracle were they to stop precisely at the point of temperate liberty. These principles, with their language, they will transmit to their children. In proportion to their numbers, they will share with us the legislation. They will infuse into it their spirit, warp, and bias its directions, and render it a heterogeneous, incoherent, distracted mass.

I may appeal to experience for a verification of these conjectures. But if they be not certain in event, are they not possible, are they not probable? Is it not safer to wait with patience for the attainment of any degree of population desired or expected? May not our government be more homogeneous, more peaceable, more durable?

He asks, what would be the condition of France if 20 million Americans were suddenly imported into that kingdom? and adds:

> If it would be more turbulent, less happy, less strong, we may believe that the addition of half a million of foreigners would produce a similar effect here. If they come of themselves, they are entitled to all the rights of citizenship; but I doubt the expediency of inviting them by extraordinary encouragements.

Now, if under the most favorable circumstances for the country, when it could most be benefited, when numbers were most urgently needed, Mr. Jefferson could discover the evil afar off and protest against encouraging foreign immigration, how much more is the measure now to be deprecated, when circumstances have so entirely changed that instead of *adding strength* to the country, immigration *adds weakness,* weakness physical and moral! And what overwhelming force does Mr. Jefferson's reasoning acquire, by the vast change of circumstances which has taken place both in Europe and in this country, in our earlier and in our later condition.

Then we were few, feeble, and scattered. *Now* we are numerous, strong, and concentrated. *Then* our accessions by immigration were real accessions of strength from the ranks of the learned and the good, from the enlightened mechanic and artisan and intelligent husbandman. *Now* immigration is the accession of weakness, from the ignorant and the vicious, or the priest-ridden slaves of Ireland and Germany, or the outcast tenants of the poorhouses and prisons of Europe. And again. *Then* our beautiful system of government had not been unfolded to the world to the terror of tyrants; the rising brightness of American democracy was not yet so far above the horizon as to wake their slumbering anxieties, or more than to gleam faintly, in hope, upon their enslaved subjects. *Then* emigration was natural, it was an attraction of affinities, it was an attraction of liberty to liberty. Emigrants were the proscribed for conscience' sake, and for opinion's sake, the real lovers of liberty, Europe's loss and our gain.

Now American democracy is denounced by name by foreign despots, waked with its increasing brilliancy. Its splendor dazzles them. It alarms them, for it shows their slaves their chains. And it must be extinguished. *Now* emigration is changed; naturalization has become the door of entrance, not alone to the ever welcome lovers of liberty but also for the priest-ridden troops of the Holy Alliance, with their Jesuit officers well-skilled in all the arts of darkness. Now emigrants are selected for a service to their tyrants and by their tyrants, not for their affinity to liberty but for their mental servitude and their docility in obeying the orders of their priests. They are transported in thousands, nay, in *hundreds of thousands,* to our shores, to our loss and Europe's gain.

It may be, Americans, that you still doubt the *existence* of a conspiracy, and the reality of danger from foreign combination; or, if the attempt is made, you yet doubt the *power* of any such secret intrigue in your society. Do you wish to test its existence and its power? It is easy to apply the test. *Test it by attempting a change in the naturalization law.* Take the ground that such a change must be made, that no *foreigner who comes into the country after the law is passed shall ever be allowed the right of suffrage.* Stand firmly to this single point and you will soon discover where the enemy is and the tactics he employs. This is the spear of Ithuriel. Apply its point. You will find your enemy, though now squat like a toad fast by the ear of our confidence, suddenly roused to show his infernal origin.

Look a moment at the proposition. You will perceive that in its very nature there is nothing to excite the opposition of a single citizen, native or naturalized, in the whole country, provided, be it distinctly borne in mind, that *he is not implicated in the conspiracy.* This prohibition, in the proposed change of the law, it is evident, touches not in any way the native American, neither does it touch in the slightest degree the already granted privileges of the naturalized citizen, nor the foreigner now in the country who is waiting to be naturalized, nor even the foreigner on his way hither; no, not an individual in the whole country is unfavorably affected by the provisions of such a law, not an individual *except alone the foreign Jesuit, the Austrian stipendiary with his intriguing myrmidons.*

And how is he affected by it? He is deprived of his passive obedience forces; he can no longer use his power over his slaves, to interfere in our political concerns; he can no longer use them in his Austrian master's service; and he, therefore, be assured, will resist with all the desperation of a detected brigand. He will raise an outcry. He will fill the public ear with cries of *intolerance.* He will call the measure religious bigotry, and illiberality, and religious persecution, and other popular catchwords to deceive the unreflecting ear. But, be not deceived; when you hear him, set your mark upon him. That is the man. Try then this test. Again, I say, let the proposition be that the law of the land be so changed, that NO FOREIGNER WHO COMES INTO THE COUNTRY AFTER THE LAW IS PASSED SHALL EVER BE ENTITLED TO THE RIGHT OF SUFFRAGE. This is just ground; it is practicable ground; it is defensible ground, and it is safe and prudent ground; and I cannot better close than in the words of Mr. Jefferson: "The time to guard against corruption and tyranny is *before* they shall have gotten hold on us; IT IS BETTER TO KEEP THE WOLF OUT OF THE FOLD THAN TO TRUST TO DRAWING HIS TEETH AND TALONS AFTER HE HAS ENTERED."

34.

ANDREW JACKSON: A Permanent Habitation for the American Indians

As army officer and as an Indian agent for the War Department, Andrew Jackson had helped to implement the policy of removing Native Americans living east of the Mississippi River from their tribal lands. As President he was determined to see the process completed. In his first annual message to Congress, Jackson put forth a proposal to reestablish the remaining Creeks, Cherokees, and other Southern tribes, in territories west of the Mississippi. In 1830 Congress granted him the power to remove the tribes and in 1834 it designated a special territory in the West for their settlement. The following extract from Jackson's seventh annual message to Congress on December 7, 1835, reflects his belief that this segregation of Native Americans, secured from further white settlement, would be the final solution to the "Indian problem."

Source: Richardson, III, pp. 147-177.

THE PLAN OF REMOVING the aboriginal people who yet remain within the settled portions of the United States to the country west of the Mississippi River approaches its consummation. It was adopted on the most mature consideration of the condition of this race, and ought to be persisted in till the object is accomplished, and prosecuted with as much vigor as a just regard to their circumstances will permit, and as fast as their consent can be obtained. All preceding experiments for the improvement of the Indians have failed. It seems now to be an established fact that they can not live in contact with a civilized community and prosper. Ages of fruitless endeavors have at length brought us to a knowledge of this principle of intercommunication with them. The past we can not recall, but the future we can provide for.

Independently of the treaty stipulations into which we have entered with the various tribes for the usufructuary rights they have ceded to us, no one can doubt the moral duty of the government of the United States to protect and if possible to preserve and perpetuate the scattered remnants of this race which are left within our borders. In the discharge of this duty an extensive region in the West has been assigned for their permanent residence. It has been divided into districts and allotted among them. Many have already removed and others are preparing to go, and with the exception of two small bands living in Ohio and Indiana not exceeding 1,500 persons, and of the Cherokees, all the tribes on the east side of the Mississippi, and extending from Lake Michigan to Florida, have entered into engagements which will lead to their transplantation.

The plan for their removal and reestablishment is founded upon the knowledge we have gained of their character and habits, and has been dictated by a spirit of enlarged liberality. A territory exceeding in extent that relinquished has been granted to each tribe. Of its climate, fertility, and capacity to support an Indian population the representations are highly favorable. To these districts the Indians are removed at the expense of the United States, and with certain supplies of clothing, arms, ammunition, and other indispensable articles; they are also furnished gratuitously with provisions for the period of a year after their arrival at their new homes. In that time, from the nature of the country and of the products raised by them, they can subsist themselves by agricultural labor, if they choose to resort to that mode of life; if they do not they are upon the skirts of the great prairies, where countless herds of buffalo roam, and a short time suffices to adapt their own habits to the changes which a change of the animals destined for their food may require.

Ample arrangements have also been made for the support of schools; in some instances council houses and churches are to be erected, dwellings constructed for the chiefs, and mills for common use. Funds have been set apart for the maintenance of the poor; the most necessary mechanical arts have been introduced, and blacksmiths, gunsmiths, wheelwrights, millwrights, etc., are supported among them. Steel and iron, and sometimes salt, are purchased for them, and plows and other farming utensils, domestic animals, looms, spinning wheels, cards, etc., are presented to them. And besides these beneficial arrangements, annuities are in all cases paid, amounting in some instances to more than thirty dollars for each individual of the tribe, and in all cases sufficiently great, if justly divided and prudently expended, to enable them, in addition to their own exertions, to live comfortably. And as a stimulus for exertion, it is now provided by law that "in all cases of the appointment of interpreters or other persons employed for the benefit of the Indians a preference shall be given to persons of Indian descent, if such can be found who are properly qualified for the discharge of the duties."

Such are the arrangements for the physical comfort and for the moral improvement of the Indians. The necessary measures for their political advancement and for their separation from our citizens have not been neglected. The pledge of the United States has been given by Congress that the country destined for the residence of this people shall be forever "secured and guaranteed to them." A country west of Missouri and Arkansas has been assigned to them, into which the white settlements are not to be pushed. No political communities can be formed in that extensive region, except those which are established by the Indians themselves or by the United States for them and with their concurrence. A barrier has thus been raised for their protection against the encroachment of our citizens, and guarding the Indians as far as possible from those evils which have brought them to their present condition.

Summary authority has been given by law to destroy all ardent spirits found in their country, without waiting the doubtful result and slow process of a legal seizure. I consider the absolute and unconditional interdiction of this article among these people as the first and great step in their melioration. Halfway measures will answer no purpose. These can not successfully contend against the cupidity of the seller and the overpowering appetite of the buyer. And the destructive effects of the traffic are marked in every page of the history of our Indian intercourse.

Some general legislation seems necessary for the regulation of the relations which will exist in this new state of things between the government and people of the United States and these transplanted Indian tribes, and for the establishment among the latter, and with their own consent, of some principles of intercommunication which their juxtaposition will call for; that moral may be substituted for physical force, the authority of a few and simple laws for the tomahawk, and that an end may be put to those bloody wars whose prosecution seems to have made part of their social system.

After the further details of this arrangement are completed, with a very general su-pervision over them, they ought to be left to the progress of events. These, I indulge the hope, will secure their prosperity and improvement, and a large portion of the moral debt we owe them will then be paid.

35.

James Kirke Paulding: Uncle Sam

The nickname "Uncle Sam" seems to have originated during the War of 1812, and probably derived from the initials "U.S." stamped on the uniforms and provisions of the United States Army. In any event James Kirke Paulding used the nickname in a fable, The Diverting History of John Bull and Brother Jonathan. *John Bull (the common nickname for Englishmen or England) had a son, Brother Jonathan (colonial America), who when grown and independent became known as Uncle Sam (the United States). In a new edition of* The Diverting History *published in 1835, Paulding brought the life of Uncle Sam and his quarreling children (the states) up to date. The following selection, taken from a supplement to the new edition, is concerned with the sectional conflicts that arose over internal improvements and the tariff in the 1830s.*

Source: *The Diverting History of John Bull and Brother Jonathan,* New edition, New York, 1835, pp. 177-193: "The History of Uncle Sam and His Boys."

ONCE UPON A TIME there lived, and lives still, in a country lying far to the west, a famous squire, rich in lands and paper money. Report made him out to be the son of John Bull, who everyone knows has children in all parts of the world. But, if the truth were known, I believe he had a great many fathers, though his mother was a very honest woman, for he looked like as many people as there were hairs on his chin. But old Squire Bull had the credit of being his father, and truly there was a great likeness between them. Like Bull, he was somewhat given to boasting, tippling, fighting, and sailing boats; and was apt to hold his neighbors in contempt, dubbing them a pack of sniveling, pitiful rascals that did not dare to call their souls their own, or look their king in the face, as every cat had a right to do. He took after his father in another respect; that is to say, nobody could tell which he was most fond of, making money like a horse or spending it like an ass. But for all this he did not so much favor John Bull but that you could now and then catch an expression in his face that put you in mind of everybody you had ever seen in the world.

John Bull had christened this son of his by the name of Jonathan; but by and by, when he became a man grown, being a good, hearty fellow, about half horse, half alligator, his friends and neighbors gave him the nickname of Uncle Sam; a sure sign that they liked him, for I never knew a respectable nickname given to a scurvy fellow in my life. Be this as it may, his family and all his neighbors at last came to call him nothing else but Uncle Sam; and all his beef, pork, and flour, in fact everything that belonged to him, was marked with a huge U.S., six inches long. . . .

You may suppose Uncle Sam had but little to begin with; but he was a stirring blade who did not mind trouble at first, if he could only see his way clear to something better in the end. He set himself to the business of clearing and selling new lands. As fast as he became pretty comfortable in one farm, he sold out at a profit and set off for another; so that he was seldom or ever more than two or three years in the same place. But for all this he never lost sight of the main chance; for there was nothing on the face of the earth he loved so dearly as a bargain or a profitable speculation. By good management and good luck he at last got to have a vast property in lands, which he was everyday adding to by buying out the Indians, or taking farms for debts that were owing him. In short, he prospered in all his undertakings, and became, in process of time, a great man among his neighbors.

But to my mind he was not above half as clever a fellow as when he was poor. Then he was a jolly, careless, high-minded dog — generous as a prince and hospitable as a Turk. He would swear a little at times, but he never meant any harm by it. But as he got rich, he set himself to be mighty genteel; aped the manners of all the would-be fashionable stragglers that came that way; never invited anybody to his house except to show off his new finery; and left off all his honest old habits by little and little.

The fact is, and I don't care who knows it, he took to canting, and turned the embroidered side of his jacket outward, as a Turk does when he goes to court. Many people doubted whether he was anything the better for this; and, if I must speak my mind, I think he lost more than he gained; for, as respects myself, I had rather a man should swear and drink punch a little than pick my pocket while he is canting about

brotherly love and goodwill to all men. If Uncle Sam is angry at this, let him scratch his back and get pleased again.

As Uncle Sam got rich, and withal stout and hearty as a young giant, the neighboring gentry, who called him an upstart and looked askance at his prosperity, would shake their heads very wisely and cry out, "Ah! poor man, to be sure he looks well and hearty; but anybody can see with half an eye he is not long for this world." And then they would sigh and take a pinch of snuff to the success of their prognostications. But it happened somehow or other that every attack he had and every rub he met with only served to show the strength of his constitution, and make it still stronger, until at last these false prophets began to say to themselves, "The rogue will certainly last forever."

Now I don't pretend to say this would have been the case, seeing there is an end of all things; but I verily believe he would have lived to a happy and green old age had it not been for the undutiful behavior of his children, which made his latter days one scene of trouble and turmoil.

You must know that as soon as Uncle Sam thought himself able to maintain a family comfortably he got him a wife, who proved an excellent housekeeper; and in the course of twice as many years his children amounted to four-and-twenty — all jolly, strapping, roistering blades, with the exception of two or three that were rather stunted in the growth, or, as Uncle Sam used to say in joke, "shrunk in the boiling." These last were rather conceited and jealous, as most little people I believe are.

As fast as these lads grew up, Uncle Sam portioned them off on his farms, which they were to pay for when they were able, at very low prices. They all turned out pretty clever, industrious fellows, with the exception of here and there one who was rather lazy, and got all his work done by Negroes. They all differed in some respects; but there was a family likeness among them — all took after the mother, who was a pretty considerable particular talker. One was a famous fellow for cod fishing; another a great hand at splitting shingles; a third was an amateur of roadmaking and ditching; a fourth was mighty fond of barbecues, taking after his father in that particular; a fifth dealt largely in wooden bowls and onions; a sixth was a great cultivator of rice and cotton; a seventh was a pretty high-handed fellow, fond of a good horse, and of an independent, openhearted spirit; and so on. They all lived together like loving brothers, having a rich father who could do what he pleased with his money — that is to say, they were as jealous of each other as two cocks running in the same yard.

If Uncle Sam made a Christmas present to one, or conferred a particular kindness on another, there was the deuce to pay among the rest. They accused the old man of being more partial to one than the other, and never gave him any rest till he put them all on a level; which he had no sooner done then they, one and all, began to grumble and find fault, saying the poor man was in his dotage only because he had not given each one a preference over his brother. Uncle Sam sometimes said to himself, "Happy is the man who has nothing to give away, for his children won't quarrel about his estate."

But this was not the worst of it. The old Harry got into them about improving their farms, which they all swore was Uncle Sam's business; he was devouring all the money they could rake and scrape together to pay for the lands he had sold them. They said it was a sin and a shame for him to make them pay everything, seeing they were his natural-born children, entitled to bed, board, education, and an outfit. Besides, the old man was now become so rich he did not know what to do with his money, and it was actually a kindness to rid him of its management in his old age.

Thus these cunning varlets agreed in the propriety of sharing Uncle Sam's money,

but they fell out about the manner of dividing it, like a parcel of undutiful rogues as they were. The big fellows argued that they ought to share according to weight, and insisted they should all go down to the mill and be weighed. But the little fellows who had been "shrunk in the boiling" demurred to this, and swore it was all in my eye, Betty Martin. They were as much the lawful sons of Uncle Sam as the best and biggest of them, and were determined to have their share at the point of the bayonet.

There was one little fellow particularly, who lived on an island about as big as my thumbnail, who talked like a giant and threatened to dissolve the family union and set up for himself if they did not treat him like a full-grown man. They had a great many hard bouts at words, and some of the neighbors feared they would come together by the ears. But though they quarreled like so many old women, like old women they seldom came to blows. They had a sort of sneaking kindness for one another at the bottom, which always prevented their proceeding to extremities.

But for all this they were forever falling out about nothing, or some trifle next to nothing, and never gave each other a good word except when they all put their heads together, as they often did, to diddle Uncle Sam out of a few thousands for the improvement of their farms. Fortunately, however, for the old man's pocket, it was seldom they could agree about the division of the spoils, or it would not have been long before he was as poor as a rat.

Be this as it may, the good man had no peace of his life, and was several times on the point of making over all his property to build meetinghouses and educate the children of other people. Certain it is he had good reason to do so, for these undutiful boys left him no rest day or night on account of his money. Not being able to agree to the plan of dividing Uncle Sam's surplus income according to weight, it was proposed to do it by measure; but here again the little fellows that were "shrunk in the boiling" made a most infernal rout, and opposed it tooth and nail. They swore they were as good as the big fellows any day in the week and as much the sons of Uncle Sam as the others; and they insisted that the apportionment should be made according to merit, not weight or size.

They all agreed to this, and the matter was just on the point of being amicably settled had it not been for a trifling difficulty which occurred in adjusting the scale of merit. The roistering barbecue fellow swore he was equal to any man you could throw a stick at; the splitter of shingles maintained the superiority of his art; the young squire, who was fond of riding a fine horse and doing nothing, declared he considered himself the most of a gentleman; the raisers of rice and cotton claimed precedence on the score of administering both to the back and stomach; and the little fellow that lived on his island put in his claim on the score of morality. This would not do, and so the old man escaped being plundered this time.

But these fine boys had another iron in the fire, which they heated till it was red hot. Quoth one of the cunning varlets, I believe it was the barbecue chap, "Let us set about improving our farms, and make the old boy pay the piper"; upon which they all agreed, and set up a hurrah about internal improvement, which used in old times to be considered improvement of mind and morals, but now means digging ditches, pulling up snags, and making roads through the desert.

Upon this, one of them went and set up a loom in his back building, as he said, for the encouragement of domestic industry, and hired other people to come and tend it. When he had done this, he went to Uncle Sam and insisted he should give him a handful or two of money to encourage him in such patriotic and praiseworthy undertakings.

"Stop, there, my little fellow," cried the

Library of Congress
Engraving of James Kirke Paulding

biggest brother of all, who had a fist like a sledge hammer, "stop, if you please. I have set up my looms at my own expense; and I'll be switch'd if the old man is going to pay you for doing what I have done for myself."

Then another chap of the family set up a blacksmith shop for making hobnails, and made the same claim to touch a few thousands of the old gentleman's money for the encouragement of domestic industry, which about this time began to be very low-spirited, and wanted a little patting.

"Avast, there, you landlubber," exclaimed one of the brothers, a bold, hearty Jack tar who had sailed round and round the world and was a mighty navigator. "Avast, there, none of your freshwater gabble. I should like to know the reason why you should be paid for making hobnails any more than I am for building ships. Avast, there, I say, you lubber, or I'll be foul of your deadlights."

Next came another brother, who was a great hand at raising sheep, which he called being a wool grower, to demand that as people could not exist without clothes, Uncle Sam should shell out a few dollars to reward him for being a great public benefactor.

"Fudge!" exclaimed the cotton growing brother, "where one man is clothed in wool, a thousand wear cotton. Why not encourage me, then, instead of this wooly fellow? Away with your bleating, or I'll be into your mutton before you can say Jack Robinson."

Next came a sober, sedate, economical brother, who had set up a shoe shop and wanted Uncle Sam's protection — that is to say, some of his money.

"Rot your sole," cried the high-handed gentleman, who despised hard work and had rather ride a blood horse than make his own shoes a thousand times. "What are you talking about there? It's mighty natural, to be sure, that you should be asking encouragement for making shoes. If it were horseshoes now, I'd talk to you." So saying, he mounted his horse and challenged Uncle Sam to run a race for a thousand dollars.

After this, for there was no end of their persecution of the poor old man. After this came another brother, a great mechanical genius who had invented a machine for peeling apples, and wanted encouragement of Uncle Sam for the great saving of time and labor in making apple pies.

"Whoo! whoo! whoop!" cried the wild, harem-scarem, barbecue boy, one of Uncle Sam's youngest sons, who had just settled a town away off West and had not yet thrown off his moccasins; "Whoop! mister, mind which way you point your rifle there — I can turn a flip-flap somerset, grease your head with bear's meat, and swallow you whole without a pang. You'd better take 'keer how you steer your steamboat, or you'll run foul of a snag."

By and by came another of this hopeful family, with a long story of the great advantage Uncle Sam would derive from clearing out a ditch, at his own expense, for the benefit of other people.

Here, the great big fellow mentioned before, who was the richest of the brothers, put in his oar and cried out: "None of that fun, Brother Johathan; I've done all my own ditching myself, and I'll be tetotally ramswisled if I am going to let daddy pay you for what I did all myself. Dig your own ditches, my boy, as I have done."

Then came a fine fellow, one of the young fry, who wanted to persuade Uncle Sam to pony up for a lane he was about making from his barn to his bog meadow, which he assured the old man would be a vast public improvement; for that, whereas his carts stuck in the mud now, they would be able to get along like a streak of lightning as soon as the improvement was made.

"Thunder and blarney!" exclaimed three or four of the elder brothers all at once, "haven't we made our own roads at our own cost and without asking daddy for a cent; and do you think, you sniveling blockhead, we'll stand by and see the old man cheated out of what belongs to us?"

"Goody gracious!" at length cried Uncle Sam, throwing up his eyes, "goody gracious! What can be the matter with these boys? I believe they mean to eat me up alive! I wish — I wish I was as poor as Job's turkey."

Now all that was required for Uncle Sam to be just as he wished was to let the boys have all his money as they wanted to do. But what is very remarkable, he never thought of this, and continued wishing himself poor, without once hitting on the best possible way of becoming so.

Things went on, getting worse and worse, for some time afterward. Uncle Sam was almost everyday pestered for money to pay for some improvement or other in the boys' farms. He kept an account of these and the amount they would cost, and found that it would take all he was worth in the world, and more besides, to get through with half of them. So one day he put his hands in his breeches pockets and swore roundly they were a brood of ungrateful rogues that wanted to get him on the parish, and not another penny would he pony up for man or beast.

This raised a terrible hue and cry among the boys, who threatened to disinherit the old man and set up for themselves. But he was a pretty stiff old fellow when his pluck was up, and he thought himself in the right. You might as well try to move a mountain as Uncle Sam when he put his foot down and toed the mark. He told the boys he had honest debts to pay, and meant to pay every penny he owed in the world before he began to talk about laying out money in improvements.

These graceless young rogues were a little stumped at the stand Uncle Sam had taken, and began to plot together to turn the old man out of house and home, and take possession of all his estate as soon as they could bring matters to bear. Accordingly, they went about among their neighbors and people, insinuating that the old man was in his dotage and could not manage his affairs any longer. It was high time, they said, that he should give up his estates into their hands and set about preparing for a better world. They raised all sorts of stories against him, as how he did not care any more about the law or the gospel than a pagan; how he tucked up people just for the pleasure of seeing them kick their heels in the air; and how he threatened to cut off the ears of a member of Congress only because he told stories about him.

In this way these roistering boys raised a great clamor against Uncle Sam, which emboldened them at last to hatch a diabolical plan for taking away all his lands at one blow. . . .

Not finding any law for this, they determined to get one passed for the purpose; accordingly they went among the people and told them a hundred cock-and-bull stories about this, that, and the other thing. They swore the land of right belonged to

them when they came of age according to an old settlement which declared that Uncle Sam's children should all share his estates equally after his death. But they kept the last part to themselves, as you may suppose, and pretended that they had a right to take the old man's property while he was alive. Besides, they would say, the poor old gentleman don't know what to do with so much land; half of it lies waste for want of proper attention, and if we only had it, we would make it ten times more valuable and pay the taxes, which he is exempted from by virtue of an old charter.

The notion of getting money by taxation is a bait which generally takes with people whose business is lawmaking, not tax paying, as I have always heard. So the legislature which governed where Uncle Sam's property lay, rubbed their hands and were mightily tickled with the notion of being able to squeeze a little money from Uncle Sam's new lands. Perceiving this argument told, the boys hatched another notion about Uncle Sam receiving all the money for the lands he sold, and then forcing those who bought them to work their fingers to the bone to make themselves whole again, as if this were not the way all over the world.

Uncle Sam defended his bacon to the last, like a stout old hero as he was; but by degrees the influence of these ungrateful rogues prevailed, and a law was passed taking away all his property, dividing it equally among the boys, so that those who were "shrunk in the boiling" got the same portion as the big, roistering blades, who, rather than not come in for a slice, consented at last to share and share equally. They were all specially enjoined to take care of Uncle Sam, and see that he wanted for nothing; but the poor old man fared pretty much as people generally do who make over all their property to their children in their lifetime.

At first they treated him pretty well, for decency's sake; but by degrees they began to deprive him of all his usual comforts. First they took away his pipe, because the young madams the sons had married could not bear tobacco smoke. Then the eldest boy took possession of his armchair and his seat in the chimney corner. Next they took the blankets from his bed, because, they said, it would injure his health to lie too warm; and next they all but starved him to death for fear he should die of apoplexy. Finally, losing all respect for the ties of blood, and all recollection of the early benefits they had derived from the good old man, they fairly turned him out-of-doors. The last I heard of Uncle Sam he was in the poorhouse.

36.

John Savage: *People* v. *Fisher*

The labor movement, which was gaining momentum in the 1830s, was repeatedly checked by the courts. People v. Fisher *established a precedent that endured for a decade, of interpreting combinations to raise wages as criminal conspiracies injurious to trade. The journeymen boot and shoemakers of Geneva, New York, had agreed not to work for any master shoemaker who refused to abide by the union rules. A certain Pennock agreed to work for wages below those established by the union, and when the union fined him he refused to pay the fine. The union struck against the employer until Pennock was discharged, whereupon the employers obtained an indictment of the journeymen for combining to prevent others from working for lower wages, to the injury of trade. The case came before the state Supreme Court in 1835 on a writ of error. Chief Justice Savage wrote the court's opinion, a portion of which is reprinted here, upholding the employer's position.*

Source: 14 Wendell 2.

THE LEGISLATURE HAVE GIVEN US their definition of conspiracies and abrogated the common law on the subject. We must therefore see whether this case comes within the statute. The legislature have said, "If two or more persons shall conspire either (1) to commit any offense; or (2) falsely and maliciously to indict another for any offense, or to procure another to be charged or arrested for any such offense; or (3) falsely to move or maintain any suit; or (4) to cheat and defraud any person of any property by any means which are in themselves criminal; or (5) to cheat and defraud any person of any property, by any means which if executed would amount to a cheat, or to obtaining money or property by false pretenses; or (6) *to commit any act injurious to the public health, to public morals, or to trade or commerce;* or for the perversion or obstruction of justice or the due administration of the laws — they shall be deemed guilty of a misdemeanor." . . . In Section 9, it is declared that "no conspiracies, other than such as are enumerated in the last section, are punishable criminally." If the conspiracy charged in the indictment is an offense under this statute, it must be embraced under the sixth subdivision, and *is an act injurious to trade or commerce.*

The conspiracy in this case was *not to commit an offense* within the meaning of the statute; the raising of wages is no offense — *the conspiracy is the offense*, if any has been committed. Nor was the object to indict anyone; to move or maintain a suit; to cheat anyone by criminal means or by any means which, if executed, would amount to a cheat; nor to obstruct the course of justice or the administration of the laws.

The question, therefore, is — is a conspiracy to raise the wages of journeymen shoemakers an act injurious to trade or commerce. . . .

Coarse boots and shoes are made in many parts of our country; not for particular persons who are to wear them but as an article of trade and commerce. Probably such is the case in Geneva, where this offense was committed. If journeymen bootmakers, by extravagant demands for wages, so enhance the price of boots made in Geneva, for instance, that boots made elsewhere, in Auburn, for example, can be sold cheaper, is not such an act injurious to trade? It is surely so to the trade of Geneva in that particular article, and that, I apprehend, is all that is necessary to bring the offense within the statute.

It is important to the best interests of society that the price of labor be left to regulate itself, or rather be limited by the demand for it. Combinations and confederacies to *enhance* or *reduce* the prices of labor, or of any articles of trade or commerce, are injurious. They may be oppressive by compelling the public to give more for an article of necessity or of convenience than it is worth; or, on the other hand, of compelling the labor of the mechanic for less than its value. Without any officious and improper interference on the subject, the price of labor or the wages of mechanics will be regulated by the demand for the manufactured article and the value of that which is paid for it; but the right does not exist either to enhance the price of the article or the wages of the mechanic by any forced and artificial means.

The man who owns an article of trade or commerce is not obliged to sell it for any particular price, nor is the mechanic obliged by law to labor for any particular price. He may say that he will not make coarse boots for less than one dollar per pair, but *he has no right to say that no other mechanic shall make them for less.* The cloth merchant may say that he will not sell his goods for less than so much per yard, but has no right to say that any other merchant shall not sell for a less price. If one individual does not possess such a right over the conduct of another, no number of individuals can possess such a right. All combinations, therefore, to effect such an object are injurious, not only to the individual particularly oppressed but to the public at large.

In the present case, an industrious man was driven out of employment by the unlawful measures pursued by the defendants, and an injury done to the community by diminishing the quantity of productive labor and of internal trade. Insofar as the individual sustains an injury, the remedy by indictment is taken away by our revised statutes, and the sufferer is left to his action on the case; but insofar as the public are concerned, in the embarrassment to trade by the discouragement of industry, the defendants are liable to punishment by indictment.

If combinations of this description are lawful in Geneva, they are so in every other place. If the bootmakers may say that boots shall not be made for less than one dollar per pair, it is optional with them to say that ten or even fifty dollars shall be paid, and no man can wear a pair of boots without giving such price as the journeymen bootmakers may choose to require. This, I apprehend, would be a monopoly of the most odious kind. The journeymen mechanics might, by fixing their own wages, regulate the price of all manufactured articles, and the community be enormously taxed. Should the journeymen bakers refuse to work, unless for enormous wages which the master bakers could not afford to pay, and should they compel all the journeymen in a city to stop work, the whole population must be without bread; so of journeymen tailors, or mechanics of any description.

Such combinations would be productive of derangement and confusion, which certainly must be considered "injurious to trade." Such consequences would follow were such combinations universal. It is true that no great danger is to be apprehended on account of the impracticability of such universal combinations. But if universally or even generally entered into, they would be prejudicial to trade and to the public; they are wrong in each particular case.

The truth is that industry requires no such means to support it. Competition is the life of trade. If the defendants cannot make coarse boots for less than one dollar per pair, let them refuse to do so; but let them not directly or indirectly undertake to say that others shall not do the work for a less price.

It may be that Pennock, from greater industry or greater skill, made more profit by making boots at seventy-five cents per pair than the defendants at a dollar. He had a right to work for what he pleased. His employer had a right to employ him for such price as they could agree upon. The interference of the defendants was unlawful; its tendency is not only to individual oppression but to public inconvenience and embarrassment.

I am of opinion that the offense is indictable and that the judgment of the general sessions of Ontario County should be reversed.

37.

THEODORE SEDGWICK: Corporations and Currency

Theodore Sedgwick's thoughts on corporations and currency were first published in late 1834 as a series of articles for the New York Evening Post. *In 1835 the articles were collected and expanded in a pamphlet,* What Is A Monopoly?, *part of which is reprinted below. William Leggett, then the* Post's *acting editor, wrote several editorials strongly advocating Sedgwick's ideas and in this form they became widely known. Like other Jacksonians, Sedgwick deplored corporations, banks, and paper money — i.e., credit extended by banks — because they benefited only the privileged few. But instead of abolishing the corporations and outlawing paper money, Sedgwick wanted to extend the right to incorporate and to issue paper money to everyone, trusting that free competition would curtail the evils of inflation.*

Source: *What Is A Monopoly?*, New York, 1835, pp. 9-37.

PUBLIC CORPORATIONS, as they exist among us, are of two classes: banks, whether of circulation, as the safety fund banks, or of deposit, as the safety banks; and internal communication or internal improvement corporations, including those chartered for the purpose of making canals, railroads, turnpike roads, bridges, etc. . . . .

The trading community is divided into borrowers and lenders. The lenders have a surplus capital beyond their wants, while the borrowers have not enough money to meet their necessities. The former, therefore, loan to the latter. But the lenders having capital have also credit, and derive the same advantage from their character as capitalists that men of truth do from their character for veracity. The assertions of the one will be believed without collateral evidence, and the other can lend though he has no money in his possession. He can give his promise to lend at a future day. This is lending credit.

A bank of circulation is an institution for the loan of money and the loan of credit. It is plain that this is the whole direct operation of such an institution. Its capital consists, we will say, of $1 million in money or specie. This is at once loaned out to the borrowers; so far it is a loan of money — now comes the credit. A merchant wishes to discount his note, that is to say, he wishes to obtain ready money in exchange for his promise to pay an equal sum at a future day. His own credit is not a matter of general notoriety, or, in other words, he is not generally known to pay all his just debts when due; and he has recourse to the bank, a public institution of large property, and the reputation of which is known to every one.

The bank has, however, loaned all its own specie — what does it do? It investigates the business character of the applicant, and, if satisfied, gives him the money in a roundabout but sure mode. It takes the merchant's promissory note for the sum he wants, payable at a future day, and gives him its own promissory notes (deducting the discount or interest upon the sum, for the use of the money, up to the time when the merchant's note is due), payable at sight, and which, owing to the good standing of the bank, everybody will take as cash.

This, then, is all that a bank can do. It lends its money and it lends its credit; but credit is nothing more than the expectation or certainty of money at some future period; and, therefore, a loan of credit is a promise to lend money when it shall be called for. A bank can consequently lend nothing but money. Its whole business is to make loans, either in cash, which is a loan of money in hand, or in paper notes, which are promises to lend money at some future day. *Its whole business is to lend money — such is the direct agency of a bank.* Is not loaning money a private business?

We have next to consider the indirect results of these issues of promissory notes. The promissory note of a private individual is presented at its maturity, paid and goes out of circulation. Not so with a bank promissory note. Contrary to the expectation or design of their first devisers, it has been found that the creation of banks of circulation effects a complete revolution in circulating medium.

The reason is apparent. A certain quantity in value, it has been said, is necessary for the exchanges of the country, and before the institution of banks, gold and silver was used for the purpose. But money is like everything else — any cheaper mode of making it drives the dearer fabric from the market. So long as the bank is in good credit, its notes answer all the purposes of gold and silver coin, and, consequently, as paper is cheaper than specie, it is adopted in its place. The specie, not being wanted, falls in price, as compared with other countries where paper is not used, and is exported where it is more in demand.

It may be set down as certain, then, that where there is a papermaking institution in good credit, specie will not exist; that is to say, the paper drives out the gold and silver to the extent that it is in good credit. If its credit was absolutely beyond a question, not an ounce of gold or silver would be seen. But there is always uncertainty, more or less, from time to time, in regard to every bank, and specie is kept in circulation to the extent of this suspicion. Indeed, if one could devise a bank that would be without the possibility of breaking, and if this state of things could be made to last, specie would not be wanted, and a paper currency would then be the most economical invention in the world; but unfortunately this cannot be realized.

During the summer season, a people might be satisfied with a paper promise to give each man a woolen suit when the first frost should come; but when the frost comes, the paper clothing will not answer; so it is with paper money. The frost is sure to come: overtrading, internal commotion, foreign aggression, any of those disturbances to which societies are liable, and which compel everyone to suspect the solvency of his neighbor, forces upon the holders of the bank promises the question whether they are as good as specie. What, then, is the condition of that country whose legislation is devised to favor paper money and to give it an advantage over specie, and where the inevitable consequences of the introduction of the former medium are not counterbalanced by the operation of free and unlimited competition? In such a country, bank paper has been well called "suspicion asleep." The moment it wakes up, woe to the bank, and, unfortunately, woe to the holders also.

What, then, is the first and only answer to the staggering question? Why, "If the bank is sound, I am safe," and you have the whole currency resting on an *if*. Away then to the bank, bad luck to the hindmost! And what can the bank do? It presses its debtors, they can afford no help, the specie has left the country, the notes cannot be paid; then comes a suspension of payments, a depreciation of the notes, a confusion of all the exchanges of the country, panic, failures, distress, and finally an importation of specie, that specie which never should have been exported. Confidence then begins to reappear, the banks to resume payment, and things are gradually restored to their original state. This is no fancy sketch. This same disorder and suffering has taken place in England, in France, and in this country; it will take place everywhere where paper money has a legal advantage given it over specie. . . .

That banks, privileged as at present, cause a fluctuation in the value of money, cannot be a matter of doubt. It is made their interest so to do. We have already said that a certain amount in value of paper is necessary to effect the exchanges of a country; consequently, the moment this amount is increased, the currency must begin to depreciate, for the plain reason that the surplus is not wanted. But the more paper issued by the banks, the greater their profits are. Their interest is to make a glut of paper money, which is in direct opposition to the interest of the community. Nor are we to lose sight of the fact that all fluctuations of the currency fall chiefly upon those who live by wages — the hardworking poor. It is well settled that wages are the first to be affected by a depreciated medium and the last to adapt themselves to it. The poor are therefore the first victims of overissues.

By the present system, then, three distinct objects are effected, and it is a pity they were not introduced into every bank charter, as thus: "Whereas the rate of interest being but 7 percent, it is considered expedient to give the persons hereinafter named the privilege of making 12 or 15; whereas it is considered expedient to export the specie from the country; and whereas it is deemed desirable to cause fluctuations in the value of money, therefore be it enacted ——." This would be a very popular preamble, and yet would only express the real end of every bank charter.

It is said that banks have made the country prosper. It is pure assertion without a shadow of proof. What does it mean? That institutions created to lend money have made money. That they have caused a rapid circulation and have stimulated enterprise is true, and so would free private banking to an infinitely greater extent. But they have, in fact, caused great public and private injury to the community. It is not by means of them, but in spite of them, that the country has prospered. It has prospered, as did England before the reform bill; as did America under the tariff. Yet not for that are rotten boroughs, manufacturing bounties, and monopoly corporations great national blessings.

The bank commissioners, in their report of January 1835, say, "Banks have justly been esteemed as among the most powerful agents in developing the resources and stimulating the industry of the country. Actual capital could not have spread half the canvass which now whitens the ocean, or given motion to half the spindles which are now in operation. Credit, as a substitute for capital," has done it. All this comes from an ignorance of the true character of banks and the real meaning of credit. Every accumulation and addition to the mass of property is effected by the means of capital and labor. There is no such thing as credit distinct from capital. The only peculiarity of this country is that the idle capital has been freely invested in the hands of needy and industrious borrowers. This is the effect of credit, or credit itself.

Does any one suppose that we wanted *chartered* banks for this object? Will it be said that money would not have been loaned if the legislature had not granted any exclusive privilege of doing it to a certain small number of individuals? No! *As compared with what would have been effected under a free trade system*, the banks have been a clog upon the industry of this country; they have embarrassed the transfers of money; and any assertion to the contrary is unsupported by facts and flies in the face of first principles.

To the evils already enumerated are to be added the pernicious political and moral effects of the system; the lobbying and intriguing at Albany; the bonuses thus placed in the hands of the legislature (of 10 or 15 percent upon every bank capital granted, for that is the amount which they almost invariably rise above par, immediately upon distribution) to be parceled out among political adherents; the bribes of stock to the members; the commissionerships given to partisan friends, that the stock may be allotted to those well-known for party devotion.

Look at the manner in which the time of the legislature is spent. During the session of 1832, 333 acts were passed, of which 150 were acts of incorporation and 9 bank charters. In 1833, out of 323 acts, 126 were corporate grants and 8 bank charters. In 1834, where 320 acts were made, 133 were charters, 11 creating banks. Thus nearly one-half of the time of the legislature, chosen for public objects, is consumed in satisfying the demands of private interest. . . .

And, now, what can be done to remedy these evils? The measure of last winter was a positive and decided improvement. By abolishing the bills under $5, and carrying up the prohibition to bills of $10 if not $20, we shall add much to the specie, and drive a quantity of worthless paper from circulation. A restriction of bank issues to the amount of their respective capitals would be another valuable measure, for we find all those with capitals of less than $200,000, issuing from 150 to 200 percent on them.

These are, however, but temporary and partial expedients. They render further reform more easy but not less indispensable. These remedies partake too of the narrow and restrictive character of the system. The whole system itself must be done away. Let the same axe which strikes at corporate grants be laid deep into the root of privileged banking; let this lucrative business be thrown open to universal competition. What would be the necessary consequence if these two reforms went hand in hand, and banking were placed under the provisions of the general law of *corporate* partnerships, already suggested?

In the first place, the business of lending money, discounting paper, and issuing notes would be immediately taken up and carried on by private individuals, and more particularly by corporate partnerships, in which persons of the most moderate means might make investments.

Second, the banks would have a more local character and credit, and their issues a more restricted circulation than they have now. Large institutions would immediately spring up (such as Messrs. Prime, Ward, and King might establish tomorrow, which would have a national reputation; but we should not see bills, like the Chatauqua notes, issued by companies insignificant in point of wealth, traveling hundreds of miles from where those who issue them are known, and owing their currency solely to two cabalistic words, "safety fund," inscribed on them by the state).

Third, the profits on this business would be reduced to an equality with those on every other branch of trade by the universal competition.

Fourth, a sufficient amount of specie would be kept in the country. Each bank or banking partnership would be pressing on its neighbors; driving back its notes, and, from the impossibility of any concert between them, they would be compelled to keep on hand specie enough to prevent all danger of panic. It has been thought that the effect of this reform would be to banish absolutely all paper currency; but with much respect for those who entertain this idea, I apprehend that though the amount will be exceedingly diminished, it would not be completely done away by the free-trade system. Paper is cheaper than specie, to the amount that gold and silver are economized by its use, and they may be economized to a considerable extent, compatible with the soundness of a paper medium.

Fifth, for the very same reasons, the fluctuations of the currency would be done away with to the greatest possible extent.

Sixth, the temptation of participating in unequal profits would be taken away from the members of the legislature and the means of corruption placed beyond their reach.

In conclusion, it is scarcely necessary to say that I look upon banking as belonging, absolutely, to the class of private dealings, and that, as such, it should be left under the provisions of a general partnership law, such as I have already suggested. It has been doubted whether, under such a law, small notes should not be prohibited and landed security required. Neither provision is necessary. Leave the matter to be regulated by competition, and you would have such notes issued by such persons as the public convenience required and the public confidence allowed. There can be no reason why the lenders of money should be obliged to give real security any more than the importers of woolens. The paper of a large commercial house is often afloat to a greater amount than the issues of many a bank. If we could but imbue ourselves with the idea that banking is only the lending of money, and that lending money is a matter between man and man, government would be saved a world of trouble. . . .

I COME NOW TO THE LAST CLASS of corporations, comprising those created for purposes of internal communication, or as we have styled it in this country, "internal improvement." They are companies chartered to make canals, railroads, turnpike roads, bridges. This class of corporate grants is the only one which presents any difficulties under the free-trade system, and is the only one creating any difference of opinion among the opponents of monopoly. It will be seen that institutions of this kind differ from the others which we have been considering in one important respect. In those cases, all that the individual asks is to employ his own property in the manner and for the objects which seem good to him.

But in these he wishes to appropriate the property of others. No railroad or canal can be made without an invasion or deprivation of the rights of property, unless you suppose all the owners of land, on the line of the work, to consent to it — a supposition not frequently to be realized. . . . Now this right of property is one which society is bound most religiously to guard and respect, and which nothing but the highest expediency can authorize it to violate. But that there may be cases of such expediency, I apprehend no man will deny; for surely that body which can take away our lives and restrain our liberties must have equal power over our possessions. But while society, or the government, can safely divest this right for the good of the whole body, it cannot be done otherwise; and if this be so, it will seem difficult, if not impossible, to devise any more equal or impartial means than those at present used to construct these great works.

There is a species of monopolies which may be mentioned in speaking of this class, though they do not necessarily spring from corporate grants. Steamboat and ferry privileges are often given to companies or individuals to the exclusion of all others. In these cases, only a right of property or of passage at the termini or point of embarkation and debarkation is necessary; the waters traversed being highways free to everyone, and any exclusive right is wholly uncalled for. There is no reason why as many ferry boats should not run from New York to Brooklyn as commerce demands, just as freely as the steamboats now run from New York to Albany; and where simply the right of wharfage is necessary, no grant of special license should be made.

The waters of our rivers, lakes, and estuaries may be as safely declared free for the purpose of carrying passengers as for that of pleasure boating; no one could establish a ferry unless he had a right of wharfage at either terminus of the voyage; and this business might thus be safely left to the provisions of the general law, which we have suggested for private corporations, throwing the business completely open.

Those institutions more properly belonging to the class of internal improvement corporations and which I have already enumerated, viz.: where it is necessary to enter upon the property of others, as railroads, turnpikes, canals, etc., are environed by more difficulty. It has been suggested, on one hand, for the purpose of avoiding the evil of monopoly grants, that the state should take into its own hands the construction of all these works; but I believe such an idea will be generally rejected. All the arguments which have been adduced against a general system of internal improvement by the federal government apply, although on a smaller scale, to this proposition. The absurdity of a government purveying for the wants of a people, which are so much more rapidly suggested and supplied by private interest — the well-known extravagance of government contracts, the abuses of government patronage — form conclusive objections to this scheme.

It has, on the other hand, been urged that a general law might be passed providing a mode for the uniform and equitable assessment of property desired for these objects, and that they might then be thrown open to individual enterprise. There are objections equally fatal, I fear, to this proposition. It sanctions, in the first place, a direct invasion of the right of property, which is guaranteed by the whole body of society, and which should be divested only, as it now is, by the decree of that whole body. The doctrines of free trade dictate that every man should have an absolute control over his own property, but, by no means, over that of others. This system would, besides, place in the hands of the rich an absolute power over the property of their poorer neighbors, and they might harass and dispossess them at their pleasure under the pretext of making roads and cutting canals through their lands.

A third proposition has been made, to pass no law on the subject, and to leave the matter entirely to consent and contract. Acccording to this plan, no road could be made until all the owners on the line of the work should agree with the planners of it as to the price and terms on which they might go over their lands. This would prove an effectual barrier to the creation of all those great works which are developing, with so wonderful a rapidity, the resources of the country. The cupidity of some of the owners — the stupidity and ignorance of a single one — would create a necessity of such endless discussions as to weary out the patience of the contractors; and if, after the road was begun, a single owner were to recede from his bargain, the work must necessarily stop until the courts should decide upon the binding force of the contract. I do not believe this will ever be thought wise; nor do I believe that it is expedient for the body politic to renounce that right over private property which may be exercised in so many beneficial ways.

If these three schemes fall to the ground, we must revert to that system which is now established among us, and which, with certain trifling modifications, would be almost, if not wholly, unexceptionable. It seems, indeed, absolutely necessary to combine the interest of the public, or body politic, with private interest, and to render charters of incorporation from the legislature requisite for the creation of those works of internal improvement which are left to individual enterprise. If the clause be inserted uniformly, in all corporations, for these objects, reserving to the legislature the right to dissolve them or resume the grant at their pleasure, one great danger is guarded against and no perpetuity is created. We should not then see any repetition of the enormous mistake New Jersey has committed in actually selling away so large a portion of her territory.

Such corporations might also be compelled to make an annual statement of their profits and to pay into the state treasury everything over an equitable (not a monopoly) percentage; and, finally, the state might, as it does now in the case of turnpike roads, reserve an absolute right of preemption, at any time, upon the payment of the capital and an interest which should cover the risk of investment. There is still, in this, some little monopoly, but of a very modified and guarded nature, and the monopolists could only receive a very moderate interest on their venture. It is still, however, an evil — every monopoly is an evil, every barrier in the path of natural right is an impediment to freedom.

The remarks here made apply equally to turnpike roads and to bridges, which are rarely made but as a portion of some road.

I have thus completed my examination of the different kinds of corporations, and it may be well to make a brief summary of the principles which have, I believe, been established.

Corporations are legitimate, for political objects, in the case of towns and counties, under the provisions of a general law in which villages and cities should also be included.

Corporate powers may be safely granted by a general law to all persons desiring to form those associations which I have classed under the head of private corporations.

Banking or lending money, being strictly a private traffic, ought to be left to the provisions of the same general law, and should be thrown open to the competition of private partnerships and individuals.

Exclusive corporations for transportation by water are unreasonable monopolies; and corporations, as they are now created by legislative grant, are only legitimate for the purpose of internal communications by land.

38.

John Young: Property Under the Common Law

After a long fight against conservative opposition revised statutes of law went into effect in the state of New York on January 1, 1830. But, in practice, the New York courts were very slow in adopting the revised code. In Coster *v.* Lorillard *(1835), in which some of the provisions of Lorillard's will were contested, Senator John Young argued that the principles that underlay the disposition of property under the common law were incompatible with the principles of American society. His speech before the court, reprinted in part below, is a good example of the revisionist position.*

Source: 14 Wendell 34.

THE PROVISIONS contained in the will of George Lorillard which have given rise to this appeal, are sufficiently detailed by the vice-chancellor of the first circuit, and also by the chancellor, in their respective decrees, and in the opinions appended to the same, respectively; and without a recapitulation of those provisions, I shall content myself with a reference to these decrees and opinions. . . .

The main question to be decided is, whether the trusts created, or attempted to be created, by the testator are valid in the whole, or in part; or rather, whether the decree of the chancellor, which establishes the validity of these trusts to a certain extent, is correct and ought to be sustained. . . . In the examination which I have given to this cause, I have come to the conclusion that its decision must be wholly controlled by the Revised Statutes; that the common law, in reference to real property, to its tenure and transmission, with all their incidents, is wholly abolished. . . .

Modern science has clearly developed the important and fundamental truth that the welfare and happiness of states and nations is materially dependent on the increase and proper distribution of wealth. Every rule or law, therefore, which impedes or discourages the acquisition or alienation of property is a subtraction from the elements of public prosperity. The desire to accumulate, which is both the cause and the effect of civilization, should be unfettered and permitted to exercise its influence freely upon all; for it is only when the incentives to amass by industry and frugality are equally operative upon all that the greatest and most beneficial results will be attained.

If a portion of those who are to occupy the theater of life fifty or one hundred years hence were to be born and educated with the knowledge that, on attaining the age of twenty-one, they were to come into possession of great wealth, that they were freed from the necessity of labor and industry, that they were a privileged class, *nati con-*

sumere fruges, and exempted from the ordinary wants and contingencies of human life — what more effectual means could be adopted to paralyze their industry and poison their morals — and the contagious example of idleness, extravagance and dissipation upon the rest of the community would tend to the most pernicious consequences. To appreciate the result of such a state of things, we have only to turn our eyes to the land of the common law, where property, power, and pride are transmissible to the eldest born, from generation to generation, and where those who are thus shielded from the common wants and necessities of mankind are also exempt from those virtues and sympathies which are the ordinary concomitants of man's nature. . . .

Every branch of the common law (and there are many) which has been molded to the form and structure of the British government is at war with the simplicity of our republican institutions. The aggregation of wealth in the hands of an aristocracy, its exclusion from alienation in perpetuity or for long periods of years, by remainders, trusts, uses and powers, to gratify the vanity of the possessor and the pride of the recipient, are regulations diametrically opposed to those principles of equality upon which our government is founded. At common law, when a man dies intestate, his real property descends to his eldest son in entire exclusion of all his other children. . . .

The Revised Statutes, when carefully examined, will be found to have remedied these mischiefs, and to have provided every requisite rule and regulation with respect to the acquisition, the enjoyment, and the transmission of property, real and personal; and to simplify this important subject, so that it might be understood by the community, every common law rule and regulation is abrogated. . . . All the uses and trusts of the common law are thus abrogated; and none whatever can be tolerated in this state, except those which are specially authorized, defined, and modified by the statute.

The language of the statute in relation to powers is equally explicit. Section 73 . . . is as follows: "Powers, as they now exist by law, are abolished; and from the time this chapter shall be in force, the creation, construction, and execution of powers shall be governed by the provisions of this article." The language of these several sections tends to one simple object — the entire abrogation, the utter repeal of all common law tenures, with all their complicated incidents and appurtenances; and the substitution in their stead of a new tenure, and new trusts, uses, and powers adapted to the simplicity of our institutions. The constitution of this state authorizes the abrogation of the common law; and unless this ancient, complicated, and barbarous system exercises a power and a thralldom over us, superior to the constitution and laws, it is entirely abrogated in relation to the tenure, the acquisition, the enjoyment, and the transmission of property, both real and personal. . . .

One of the leading objects of the revision was to disenthrall the community from the common law in relation to every rule respecting the tenure and transmission of property. These rules favored trusts and uses, which were incompatible with our institutions. They authorized testamentary accumulations of property, without any other obvious design than to gratify human vanity; they sanctioned trusts for long periods of years, so that the rich man could throw over posterity the dark shadow of his accumulated wealth. They permitted any amount of the great capital of the community (which is composed of the aggregate wealth of all) to be diverted from the business purposes of life — to be dragged from the prolific stream of alienation, and lashed to sterile rocks upon the shore. These were the evils of the old system, which it was the object of the legislature to remedy; and if the obvious intent of the statute is not perverted, the remedy will be found to be complete.

To understand the statute, it is only necessary to know the meaning of the words which are used; and definitions are often given in the statute. All uses and trusts, of every description, which might have been created previous to the revision, are wholly abolished. . . . The language of these sections is so strong against the creation of any trusts whatever that the legislature deemed it necessary to introduce a qualification into the 50th Section, which provides that "the preceding sections shall not be construed to prevent or affect the creation of such express trusts as are hereafter authorized and defined." No trust, therefore, of any description, can be created for any purpose whatever, except such as are expressly "authorized," and not only authorized but "defined" by subsequent parts of the statute.

The only authority to create express trusts is found in the 55th Section. This section defines the only purposes for which any trust can be created. It is as follows: "Express trusts may be created, for any or either of the following purposes: 1. To sell lands for the benefit of creditors. 2. To sell, mortgage, or lease lands for the benefit of legatees, or for the purpose of satisfying any charge thereon. 3. To receive the rents and profits of lands, and apply them to the education and support, or either, of any person, during the life of such person, or for any shorter term, subject to the rules prescribed in the first article of this title. 4. To receive the rents and profits of lands, and to accumulate the same, for the purposes and within the limits prescribed in the first article of this title." It will be perceived, on examination, that the four purposes specified in this section, and to subserve which alone trusts can be created, are purposes of utility and not of pride or vanity; and if it were necessary to defend the legislature from the charge of having authorized or permitted any portion of the capital of the community to be abstracted from circulation in order to sustain idle or ostentatious trusts, or any trusts which are not required by the wants

of mankind, the materials for such defense are amply afforded by the Revised Statutes.

The interests of society are best promoted when all property, both real and personal, is wholly unfettered and freely transmissible from man to man; nor should any departure from this principle be tolerated, except where individual benefit is paramount to the public injury. This is the spirit of the Revised Statutes. The utility of the first class of trusts, "for the benefit of creditors," is sufficiently obvious. The object of the second, to sell, mortgage, or lease lands in order to pay legacies or debts, is equally apparent and useful. Under this class, some of the trust powers authorized by the statute can be exercised. The third and fourth classes of trusts, as defined and illustrated by other parts of the statute, are as simple and salutary as the first and second. The fourth authorizes a trust to receive and accumulate the rents and profits of lands for an infant during the period of minority, and no longer. The third purpose for which trusts are authorized is the only one under which the trusts in the will of the testator can be sustained, if indeed they are in any respect sustainable, and it is therefore important to bestow upon the third purpose, to effect which trusts are permitted, a more careful examination.

The power given by the Revised Statutes to accomplish the third purpose is to appoint trustees "to receive the rents and profits of lands, and apply them to the education and support, or either, of any person, during the life of such person, or for any shorter term, subject to the rules prescribed in the first article of this title." This is the language of the Revised Statutes. But after they were printed, and their several provisions more minutely and carefully examined, it was perceived that this clause would authorize rents and profits to be applied for the education of a person, during the life of such person; and as education is usually bestowed only during the period of minority, and as infants were amply provided for in other parts of the statute, an amendment was made by which the words "education and support, or either," were stricken out, and the word "use" substituted in their stead. . . .

If these principles are applied to the will in question, it will be perceived that the trusts attempted to be created by the testator are wholly invalid. He appoints his twelve nephews and nieces trustees, together with Jacob Lorillard; and afterward constitutes the same twelve nephews and nieces the beneficiaries of the trust. This junction in the same individuals of the character of trustee and beneficiary is wholly incompatible with the provisions of the statute. Beside this, the testator, in direct contravention of the statute, authorizes the beneficiaries to assign and sell their right to the rents and profits, provided a majority of them, not to be less than three, shall give their written consent to such assignment or sale. These facts speak a language which cannot be misunderstood. They are tantamount to a declaration in the will that the trusts which the testator designs to create are not such as the laws of this state authorize.

The trustees in the will are directed to "pay over" the rents and profits to themselves (excepting Jacob Lorillard), while the trust authorized by the statute is "to apply to the use." The difference is important and material. "To apply to the use" in the meaning of the statute is to deal out with circumspection; and this circumspection, either original or delegated, will always be manifest in every genuine and valid trust under the 3rd subdivision of the 55th Section; for it is hardly possible to conceive a case in which the benefactor, who was about to create a trust for life or for a shorter period for the support of those who were incompetent or unable to hold and manage property, would not particularly specify in the instrument the times and manner of the application of his bounty, or

specially confide this office to the judgment and discretion of the trustee.

The testator, after the payment of legacies and annuities, gives the whole income of his estate, which now amounts to between $80,000 and $90,000 annually, to his twelve nephews and nieces, and he directs that this income shall be divided between them "during their natural lives, and to the survivors and survivor of them, equally to be divided between them, or such of them as shall from time to time be living, share and share alike." By this provision, as the number is diminished by death, the survivors take the whole income. The estate is mostly in the city of New York, and what is not, is by the will to be converted into real estate in that city, so that with the increase of property, it is probable that the income to be received by the last of the twelve would amount to nearly or quite $200,000 annually.

It may possibly be presumed, when there is nothing to repel the presumption, that all the nephews and nieces of a testator, amounting to twelve in number, are of that description of individuals for whose benefit alone this species of trust is authorized — that they are all incompetent to be trusted with the management and disposition of property; but it requires an extravagant effort of the imagination to presume that a testator can foresee that this incompetency will be cumulative, that it will constantly increase as the numbers diminish, so that the last will require for support the application of rents and profits to the amount of $100,000 or $200,000 annually. Can such a trust be sustained without an entire perversion of the obvious intent and meaning of the statute? And if such a disposition of property should receive a judicial sanction, is there not danger that the precedent may be pernicious, that the rich hereafter, under the benevolent guise of providing a permanent support for imbecile and unfortunate connections, may erect whole families into aristocracies?

39.

JOHN VETHAKE: Banks, Monopolies, and the Good of the Greatest Number

Democratic Party candidates in New York City pledged that they would oppose all further issuance of bank charters in exchange for labor's endorsement in the state elections in 1834. After their landslide victory, however, the Democrats broke their pledge and awarded charters to deserving party members and supporters. When, in the fall of 1835, the Democrats refused to pledge opposition to monopolies, the Anti-Monopolists broke with the party. Soon after, the Anti-Monopoly Democrats organized the short-lived but engagingly named Equal Rights or "Locofoco" Party. The article reprinted below was an appeal to all Democrats to support the Anti-Monopolists. It was unsigned, but scholars assign it to John Vethake, a physician and journalist.

Source: *New York Evening Post*, October 21, 1835.

TO PREVENT MISUNDERSTANDING and possible misrepresentations, the Anti-Monopoly Democrats of the city of New York tender to their brethren of the Democratic family the following address:

The equal rights of mankind and free competition in all departments of social industry were held by our political fathers to be the primitive elements of republican government. Accordingly, these, with all the subprinciples which distinctly flow from them, as, for example, universal suffrage; a liberal code of naturalization laws; liberty of conscience, of speech, and of the press; purity of elections; right of instruction; limited term of official tenures; and careful avoidance of legal favoritism in any possible form, constitute with us, as they did with our ancestors, the essential ingredients of democratic institutions. By these, as by the beaconlights to social happiness, or monumental signals directing to the *greatest good of the greatest number,* do we propose to be always exclusively guided, in full confidence of the inherent justice of the Democratic cause and the ultimately permanent success of our united exertions.

But, however proud of our victorious party and confident of our principles, there are in vogue some grievous perversions thereof, which it is our leading object to remedy.

It will not be questioned that the sovereignty of the people is, in theory, an indisputable truth; but in its practical bearing, in its direct operation upon systems of law and public policy, it is not in the power even of universal suffrage, unless exercised with a severe and jealous vigilance, to preserve it from gradually sinking into an empty sound. It has been well said that it is the natural tendency of power "to steal from the many to the few." The selfishness of individual character, augmented by the confiding indulgence of the many, is continually encouraging the forwardness of some *spoiled children* in the republican family.

It has, therefore, happened that during a just-now terminated period of deep repose, when, for a long series of years, all the cardinal interests of society were utterly forgotten in a mere moneymaking mania, the tacit and thoughtless assent of the people to some one exclusive privilege or to the establishment of a monopoly having a specious outside was greedily seized upon by the aforesaid *forward ones* as a pretext for other and much larger favors, until special grants and charters upon charters have come to constitute nearly the whole mass of legislative enactments; while, by a coordinate procedure, the pert few for whose benefit these things are have usurped all the powers and claim even the name itself of "the party" or "the people."

The monopoly principle has thus been artfully and corruptly engrafted upon democratic institutions, and its weedy spread has so entirely covered up the Jeffersonian basis of the Constitution that all distinction has vanished between practical democracy and practical Toryism. The common good, the interests of the many have long been entirely neglected in a confused scramble for personal favors; and instead of leaving one businessman to cope with another, on the fair and equitable principles which nature and the Constitution sanction, the legislature, the *democratic* legislature of the state of New York, by means of chartered privileges, has been all along engaged in *siding* with some to the injury of others and in doing all that is possible to make the *unchartered* multitude "poor indeed."

Special charters for particular objects are rarely applied for unless they will contribute to special and particular gain. This is emphatically true of *moneyed* incorporations, which are always sought for with a zeal commensurate with the unfair advantages expressed to be derived from them. Under the flimsy disguise of some secondary measure of public utility, which but too often is itself a deception, or even of a winning and popular title such as the name of some revered patriot or mechanic occupation, personal and evidently exorbitant profit is in every case the real object of the application and the real substance of the grant.

The price, or "bonus," as it is insidiously termed, which is sometimes paid for such privileges; the open and the half-developed bribery to which such legislation is eminently subject; the indefatigable labor bestowed by *lobbying* agents in furthering the acquisition of these abominations; and the ravenous grasp very generally made for a portion of them when granted by law are glaring and resistless proofs of their wholly artificial character, their injustice, and their evil nature.

If the public good, as is often and falsely alleged, were the actual motive for the creation of moneyed incorporations, if mercantile or any other convenience really called for such things, they would come into being, as do all *impartial* enactments, by the spontaneous, unbought, and ordinary action of the legislature. It is, therefore, but too plainly evident that gross selfishness, the most mercenary spirit, and mere private considerations are at the basis of this species of legislation.

But it has been repeatedly said, and with effect upon the thoughtless, that banks, insurance companies, ferry grants, etc., however accompanied with objectionable qualities, are indispensable to "the business wants of the community." That there is gross deception in this claim will be briefly shown by the following remarks and accompanying illustrations.

The wealthy of the land are the strong of the *legal* world, as the athletic are of the *natural*; in haughtiness and in oppressive disposition the analogy is perfect between them. Relatively considered, it is now precisely as if all things were in a state of nature; the *strong* tyrannize over the weak; live, as it were, in a continual victory, and glut themselves on incessant plunder. It is as humiliating now to be poor as in the state of nature to be feeble of body; and although the ordinary difference between the rich and the poor, as between the athletic and feeble, is clearly unavoidable and doubtless right, just, proper, and expedient;

yet that such difference should be enhanced by legal enactments, that the rich or the strong should be artificially legislated into still greater riches or still greater strength, is not only unnecessary but decidedly improper and even *cruel.* True it is, civilization, in substituting an artificial mode of relative strength for that which is natural, has brought within control an ungovernable quality of varying man; a control, however, which we think has of late been exercised more for general woe than weal.

But let us for an instant suppose that human muscularity, as is human wealth, were manageable by law and that it was proposed to INCORPORATE — that is, to give *individuality* and, in some cases, *immortality* to a considerable number of ordinary men, say one hundred, and thus to constitute a giant being, or some fifty of them, for the city of New York — we are confident that the public voice would exclaim against such a project with extraordinary unanimity. It might be said in vain, and uselessly repeated again and again, that such creatures are well calculated to aid in the erection of massive buildings and the extinction of fires, and *might be* extremely useful in case of a sudden insurrection or invasion. Such reasoning would be futile indeed.

The huge arms of the proposed monsters, wielded by a multiplied selfishness and without fear of immediate death, would be anticipated in fancy as but too likely to be used for other purposes than the public good; and a general conviction would possess the whole community that the aggregate of evils to be reasonably apprehended from such incorporations would render all their positive advantage to society an inconsiderable mite. Nay, we risk nothing in saying that if enacted into being all civil power and social influence would soon come into their exclusive possession and their oppressions know no other bounds than is remotely fixed by their own peculiar and mutual interests.

The above picture, fellow Democrats, is but an allegory of the real state of things. There are now in the midst of us many of the peculiar giants of civilized society. All honor be to the energy of democratic freemen and to the firmness and skill of their venerable chief; the Goliath is slain, but there remain vast numbers of his dangerous kind among the Philistines of wealth. Habit, long endurance, and the bias of early education have indeed rendered these beings familiar to us all and blunted our perception of their more abhorrent characteristics.

But it needs not demonstration to show that if *moneyed* incorporations, say fifty of them for the city of New York, were to be now for the first time suggested, the proposition would be quite as revolting to an unsophisticated community as the supposed case of incorporated athletes. It would be grievous folly to recommend their creation by asserting that a poor man, if rich in friends, might occasionally borrow a small sum of money from them; it would at once be seen that if they did not exist, did not absorb, so to speak, the *loanable* means of society, aided by a friend, he could borrow of individuals.

It would be alike useless to argue that they might work wonders on great public emergencies; it would be distinctly perceived that like, as by a monster's touch, wholly destitute of gentleness, their benefits — if benefits they can be called — and injuries would be always at unhealthy extremes: at one time effecting mushroom prosperity; at another, unreasonable distress; and it would then be most clearly absurd to attribute to such artificial creations, as is now too often done, the multiplication of valuable capital and the production of indispensable facilities for mercantile business. Such qualities belong not to their nature but are simply impressed upon them by the neglect of other commercial means.

If incorporated banks were at once suppressed, an event by no means desirable but contemplated only for the argument's sake, not a cent of money would be lost to the business community. The evolutions of capital and of credit, in all abundance, would be conducted by active and intelligent individuals under a measure of competition and a degree of personal responsibility to society, which, when compared with incorporated institutions, would be vastly great and vastly advantageous to the humbler circles of businessmen. The "indispensable utility" of moneyed incorporations is at best but a common and empty prejudice. . . .

Let but this sort of employment be left free to general competition and paper money be forbidden, private bankers will stand in a very different and much safer relation to the community than they, or even chartered banks, have ever stood. Banking institutions will lose much of that spurious character upon which their undue credit is based, and the public be effectually protected against the most dangerous, because the most insidious, of impositions.

For the reasons here assigned, we, as constituent members of an ascendant political party, call for the repeal of the Restraining Law which forbids private banking, and require that no more moneyed incorporations be henceforth created. We are satisfied that the repeal of the law alluded to will, by opening a wide, unlimited field for competition, sufficiently disarm the incorporated institutions now in being and, in all probability, cause even their premature death in the ordinary progress of business. So far from relatively increasing the money monopolies now existing by refusing to create more, the repeal of the Restraining Law will at once destroy much that belongs to them of the monopoly character; and even without such repeal, it may be justly said that the profits and influence of incorporated banks are always at the full, in proportion to their capitals, and therefore cannot be enhanced by diminution of numbers.

And instead of our plan promoting the social and political power of the few individuals who possess actual capital, we are confident that their power would be greatly abbreviated, inasmuch as, under the present system, it is their private *influence at bank,* much more than the loan of their money, that renders them the objects of servile homage and productive of degrading adulation! The high grandeur of giant incorporations forbids the near approach of but a select few, and through that few all moneyed operations must now be transacted; these are thereby constituted a virtual nobility, not by their own power or wealth but by the sovereign pleasure of the magisterial monopolies.

Again, we desire the repeal of the famous Restraining Law on the principle of even-handed justice. There is no such protection in existence for the mechanic or producing classes. If solicited, for example, by an association of carpenters, if these were to ask for a restraining law to prevent persons from following their craft unless specially chartered so to do by law, they would be hooted at as presumptuous fools, and thus tacitly informed that *they* are not entitled to so very exclusive a privilege; that such legislative favors belong only to the wealthy and *respectable* among our citizens; and that if such matters were to become general, in accordance with *mechanics'* ideas of justice, they would cease to be advantageous. The partiality of the obnoxious law constitutes at once its whole value and its gross unfairness. . . .

A general law by which any two or more individuals may declare themselves in business partnership, as well for wood sawing, if they choose, as for manufacturing or banking, and regulated by such provisions as careful inquiry and practical experience may point out, would possess nothing of an exclusive or monopoly character. Without some such law, the suspension of special charters would totally prevent the prosecution of every business which requires a heavy capital, inasmuch as ordinary partnerships are constantly liable to be suddenly dissolved by the death or self-will of a member. A limited form of permanent succession and a circumscribed right to transfer an interest in such partnerships seems to us to be perfectly reasonable and requisite.

We are confident that a wholesome system of general business on this scheme would grow up gradually amongst us, infinitely more favorable than the present to the small capitalist, on account of the plenitude of semi-incorporated partnerships to which it would give rise and its evident tendency to divide, and not, as the present system, to concentrate patronage. We are sure an unprecedented activity on equitable principles would thereby come to pervade all occupations, and, instead of as now, a few becoming rich at the expense of the many, the advances of society would be comparatively uniform and in mass; and, instead of observing as now nought but rapid and destructive fluctuations of prosperity and adversity, with continual commercial alarm, the money market would be relatively stable and the public mind settled and serene.

40.

Songs of the Sea

Sailors in the age of sail sang almost all the time when they weren't asleep — at work, at rest (infrequent), ashore. The first of the songs, "Leave Her, Johnny," reprinted below was a capstan chantey, traditionally the last one sung when the voyage was over and the bilge was being pumped out for the last time, or even when the crew was actually leaving the ship and joyfully walking, or running, down the pier. This version makes reference to the popular New York-Liverpool run, but there was a version for practically every voyage and port. The second song, "Blow Ye Winds," derives from the whaling fisheries, centered during this period at New Bedford, Massachusetts, and on the offshore islands of Martha's Vineyard and Nantucket. The industry was important in the 1830s and 1840s, since whale oil was the main source of illumination. When "coal oil" was discovered in Pennsylvania in 1859, whaling quickly decreased, and is no longer carried on by Americans. Nor do sailors sing much anymore.

⚜ LEAVE HER, JOHNNY!

I thought I heard the Old Man say,
  Leave her, Johnny, leave her!
You can go ashore and draw your pay,
  It's time for us to leave her.

The winds were foul, the work was hard,
  Leave her, Johnny, leave her!
From Liverpool docks to the Brooklyn yard,
  It's time for us to leave her.

The winds were foul, the ship was slow,
  Leave her, Johnny, leave her!
The grub was bad and the wages low,
  It's time for us to leave her.

She shipped it green and she made us curse —
  Leave her, Johnny, leave her!
The mate is a devil and the old man worse,
  It's time for us to leave her.

The rats have gone, and we the crew,
Leave her, Johnny, leave her!
It's time, by God, that we went too,
It's time for us to leave her.

❦ BLOW YE WINDS

'Tis advertised in Boston, New York, and Buffalo,
Five hundred brave Americans a-whaling for to go.

Chorus:
Singing blow ye winds in the morning, blow ye winds, high-o!
Clear away your running gear and blow, boys, blow!

They send you to New Bedford, that famous whaling port,
And give you to some land-sharks to board and fit you out.

They tell you of the clipper-ships a-going in and out,
And say you'll take five hundred sperm before you're six months out.

It's now we're out to sea, my boys, the wind comes on to blow;
One half the watch is sick on deck, the other half below.

But as for the provisions, we don't get half enough;
A little piece of stinking beef and a blamed small bag of duff.

Next comes the running rigging, which you're all supposed to know;
'Tis "Lay aloft, you son-of-a-gun, or overboard you go!"

The skipper's on the quarter-deck a-squinting at the sails
When up aloft the lookout sights a school of spouting whales.

"Now clear away the boats, my boys, and after him we'll travel,
But if you get too near his fluke, he'll kick you to the devil!"

Now we have got him turned up, we tow him alongside;
We over with our blubber-hooks and rob him of his hide.

Next comes the stowing down, my boys; 'twill take both night and day,
And you'll all have fifty cents apiece on the hundred and ninetieth lay.

When we get home, our ship made fast, and we get through our sailing,
A winding glass around we'll pass and damn this blubber whaling!

41.

George McDuffie: The Natural Slavery of Blacks

At the end of the eighteenth century, informed Northerners and Southerners alike looked forward to the natural demise of slavery. But the invention of the cotton gin made cotton the basis of the Southern economy after 1800, and slaves seemed to become more and more necessary as the wealth of the region grew. A message delivered to the South Carolina legislature by Governor George McDuffie in 1835 (excerpts appear below) marked the beginning of the South's counterattack against Northern Abolitionist propaganda. The speech reflected the transition in Southern thought from the notion of slavery as a necessary evil to the notion of slavery as a positive good, for white and black alike. McDuffie's main thesis, that blacks were "destined by providence to occupy this condition of servile dependence," was thereafter central in all defenses of slavery.

Source: *American History Leaflets, Colonial and Constitutional,* Albert B. Hart and Edward Channing, eds., No. 10, July 1893.

SINCE YOUR LAST ADJOURNMENT, the public mind throughout the slaveholding states has been intensely, indignantly, and justly excited by the wanton, officious, and incendiary proceedings of certain societies and persons in some of the nonslaveholding states, who have been actively employed in attempting to circulate among us pamphlets, papers, and pictorial representations of the most offensive and inflammatory character, and eminently calculated to seduce our slaves from their fidelity and excite them to insurrection and massacre. These wicked monsters and deluded fanatics, overlooking the numerous objects in their own vicinity, who have a moral if not a legal claim upon their charitable regard, run abroad in the expansion of their hypocritical benevolence, muffled up in the saintly mantle of Christian meekness, to fulfill the fiendlike errand of mingling the blood of the master and the slave, to whose fate they are equally indifferent, with the smoldering ruins of our peaceful dwellings.

No principle of human action so utterly baffles all human calculation as that species of fanatical enthusiasm which is made of envy and ambition, assuming the guise of religious zeal and acting upon the known prejudices, religious or political, of an ignorant multitude. Under the influence of this species of voluntary madness, nothing is sacred that stands in the way of its purposes. Like all other religious impostures, it has power to consecrate every act, however atrocious, and every person, however covered with "multiplying villainies," that may promote its diabolical ends or worship at its infernal altars. By its unholy creed, murder itself becomes a labor of love and charity, and the felon renegade, who flies from the justice of his country, finds not only a refuge but becomes a sainted minister in the sanctuary of its temple. . . .

The crime which these foreign incendiaries have committed against the peace of the state is one of the very highest grade known to human laws. It not only strikes at the very existence of society but seeks to accomplish the catastrophe, by the most horrible means, celebrating the obsequies of the state in a saturnalian carnival of blood and murder, and while brutally violating all the charities of life and desecrating the very altars of religion, impiously calling upon Heaven to sanction these abominations. It is my deliberate opinion that the laws of every community should punish this species of interference by death without benefit of clergy, regarding the authors of it as "enemies of the human race." Nothing could be more appropriate than for South Carolina to set this example in the present crisis, and I trust the legislature will not adjourn till it discharges this high duty of patriotism.

It cannot be disguised, however, that any laws which may be enacted by the authority of this state, however adequate to punish and repress offenses committed within its limits, will be wholly insufficient to meet the exigencies of the present conjuncture. If we go no further than this, we had as well do nothing. . . .

It will, therefore, become our imperious duty, recurring to those great principles of international law which still exist in all their primitive force among the sovereign states of this confederacy, to demand of our sovereign associates the condign punishment of those enemies of our peace who avail themselves of the sanctuaries of their respective jurisdictions, to carry on schemes of incendiary hostility against the institutions, the safety, and the existence of the state. In performing this high duty to which we are constrained by the great law of self-preservation, let us approach to our co-states with all the fraternal mildness which becomes us as members of the same family of confederate republics and, at the same time, with that firmness and decision which becomes a sovereign state, while maintaining her dearest interests and most sacred rights.

For the institution of domestic slavery we hold ourselves responsible only to God, and it is utterly incompatible with the dignity and the safety of the state to permit any foreign authority to question our right to maintain it. It may nevertheless be appropriate, as a voluntary token of our respect for the opinions of our confederate brethren, to present some views to their consideration on this subject, calculated to disabuse their minds of false opinions and pernicious prejudices.

No human institution, in my opinion, is more manifestly consistent with the will of God than domestic slavery, and no one of His ordinances is written in more legible characters than that which consigns the African race to this condition, as more conducive to their own happiness, than any other of which they are susceptible. Whether we consult the sacred Scriptures or the lights of nature and reason, we shall find these truths as abundantly apparent as if written with a sunbeam in the heavens. Under both the Jewish and Christian dispensations of our religion, domestic slavery existed with the unequivocal sanction of its prophets, its apostles, and finally its great Author. The patriarchs themselves, those chosen instruments of God, were slaveholders. In fact, the divine sanction of this institution is so plainly written that "he who runs may read" it, and those overrighteous pretenders and Pharisees who affect to be scandalized by its existence among us would do well to inquire how much more nearly they walk in the ways of godliness than did Abraham, Isaac, and Jacob.

That the African Negro is destined by Providence to occupy this condition of servile dependence is not less manifest. It is marked on the face, stamped on the skin, and evinced by the intellectual inferiority and natural improvidence of this race. They have all the qualities that fit them for slaves, and not one of those that would fit them to be freemen. They are utterly unqualified, not only for rational freedom but for self-government of any kind. They are, in all respects, physical, moral, and political, inferior to millions of the human race who have for consecutive ages dragged out a wretched existence under a grinding political despotism, and who are doomed to this hopeless condition by the very qualities which unfit them for a better. It is utterly astonishing that any enlightened American, after contemplating all the manifold forms in which even the white race of mankind is doomed to slavery and oppression, should suppose it possible to reclaim the African race from their destiny.

The capacity to enjoy freedom is an attribute not to be communicated by human power. It is an endowment of God, and one of the rarest which it has pleased His inscrutable wisdom to bestow upon the nations of the earth. It is conferred as the reward of merit, and only upon those who are qualified to enjoy it. Until the "Ethiopian can change his skin," it will be in vain to attempt, by any human power, to make freemen of those whom God has doomed to be slaves by all their attributes.

Let not, therefore, the misguided and designing intermeddlers who seek to destroy our peace imagine that they are serving the cause of God by practically arraigning the decrees of His providence. Indeed, it would scarcely excite surprise if, with the impious audacity of those who projected the Tower of Babel, they should attempt to scale the battlements of heaven and remonstrate with the God of wisdom for having put the mark of Cain and the curse of Ham upon the African race instead of the European.

If the benevolent friends of the black race would compare the condition of that portion of them which we hold in servitude with that which still remains in Africa, totally unblessed by the lights of civilization or Christianity and groaning under a savage despotism, as utterly destitute of hope as of happiness, they would be able to form some tolerable estimate of what our blacks have lost by slavery in America and what they have gained by freedom in Africa. Greatly as their condition has been improved by their subjection to an enlightened and Christian people — the only mode under

heaven by which it could have been accomplished — they are yet wholly unprepared for anything like a rational system of self-government. Emancipation would be a positive curse, depriving them of a guardianship essential to their happiness, and they may well say in the language of the Spanish proverb, "Save us from our friends and we will take care of our enemies."

If emancipated, where would they live and what would be their condition? The idea of their remaining among us is utterly visionary. Amalgamation is abhorrent to every sentiment of nature; and if they remain as a separate caste, whether endowed with equal privileges or not, they will become our masters, or we must resume the mastery over them. This state of political amalgamation and conflict, which the Abolitionists evidently aim to produce, would be the most horrible condition imaginable and would furnish Dante or Milton with the type for another chapter illustrating the horrors of the infernal regions. The only disposition, therefore, that could be made of our emancipated slaves would be their transportation to Africa, to exterminate the natives or be exterminated by them; contingencies either of which may well serve to illustrate the wisdom, if not the philanthropy, of these superserviceable madmen who in the name of humanity would desolate the fairest region of the earth and destroy the most perfect system of social and political happiness that ever has existed.

It is perfectly evident that the destiny of the Negro race is either the worst possible form of political slavery or else domestic servitude as it exists in the slaveholding states. The advantage of domestic slavery over the most favorable condition of political slavery does not admit of a question. . . .

In all respects, the comforts of our slaves are greatly superior to those of the English operatives, or the Irish and continental peasantry, to say nothing of the millions of paupers crowded together in those loathsome receptacles of starving humanity, the public poorhouses. Besides the hardships of incessant toil, too much almost for human nature to endure, and the sufferings of actual want, driving them almost to despair, these miserable creatures are perpetually annoyed by the most distressing cares for the future condition of themselves and their children.

From this excess of labor, this actual want, and these distressing cares, our slaves are entirely exempted. They habitually labor from two to four hours a day less than the operatives in other countries; and it has been truly remarked, by some writer, that a Negro cannot be made to injure himself by excessive labor. It may be safely affirmed that they usually eat as much wholesome and substantial food in one day as English operatives or Irish peasants eat in two. And as it regards concern for the future, their condition may well be envied even by their masters. There is not upon the face of the earth any class of people, high or low, so perfectly free from care and anxiety. They know that their masters will provide for them, under all circumstances, and that in the extremity of old age, instead of being driven to beggary or to seek public charity in a poorhouse, they will be comfortably accommodated and kindly treated among their relatives and associates. . . .

In a word, our slaves are cheerful, contented, and happy, much beyond the general condition of the human race, except where those foreign intruders and fatal ministers of mischief, the emancipationists, like their arch-prototype in the Garden of Eden and actuated by no less envy, have tempted them to aspire above the condition to which they have been assigned in the order of Providence. . . .

Reason and philosophy can easily explain what experience so clearly testifies. If we look into the elements of which all political communities are composed, it will be found that servitude, in some form, is one of the essential constituents. No community ever has existed without it, and we may confidently assert none ever will. In the very nature of things there must be classes of persons to discharge all the different offices of society, from the highest to the lowest. Some of those offices are regarded as degrading, though they must and will be performed; hence those manifold forms of dependent servitude which produce a sense of superiority in the masters or employers and of inferiority on the part of the servants. Where these offices are performed by members of the political community, a dangerous element is introduced into the body politic; hence the alarming tendency to violate the rights of property by agrarian legislation, which is beginning to be manifest in the older states, where universal suffrage prevails without domestic slavery, a tendency that will increase in the progress of society with the increasing inequality of wealth.

No government is worthy of the name that does not protect the rights of property, and no enlightened people will long submit to such a mockery. Hence it is that, in older countries, different political orders are established to effect this indispensable object; and it will be fortunate for the nonslaveholding states if they are not, in less than a quarter of a century, driven to the adoption of a similar institution, or to take refuge from robbery and anarchy under a military despotism.

But where the menial offices and dependent employments of society are performed by domestic slaves, a class well defined by their color and entirely separated from the political body, the rights of property are perfectly secure without the establishment of artificial barriers. In a word, the institution of domestic slavery supersedes the necessity of an order of nobility and all the other appendages of a hereditary system of government. If our slaves were emancipated and admitted, bleached or unbleached, to an equal participation in our political privileges, what a commentary should we furnish upon the doctrines of the emancipationists, and what a revolting spectacle of republican equality should we exhibit to the mockery of the world! No rational man would consent to live in such a state of society if he could find a refuge in any other.

Domestic slavery, therefore, instead of being a political evil, is the cornerstone of our republican edifice. No patriot who justly estimates our privileges will tolerate the idea of emancipation, at any period, however remote, or on any conditions of pecuniary advantage, however favorable. I would as soon open a negotiation for selling the liberty of the state at once as for making any stipulations for the ultimate emancipation of our slaves. So deep is my conviction on this subject that, if I were doomed to die immediately after recording these sentiments, I could say in all sincerity and under all the sanctions of Christianity and patriotism, "God forbid that my descendants, in the remotest generations, should live in any other than a community having the institution of domestic slavery as it existed among the patriarchs of the primitive church and in all the free states of antiquity."

If the legislature should concur in these general views of this important element of our political and social system, our confederates should be distinctly informed, in any communications we may have occasion to make to them, that in claiming to be exempted from all foreign interference, we can recognize no distinction between ultimate and immediate emancipation.

It becomes necessary, in order to ascertain the extent of our danger, and the measures of precaution necessary to guard against it, that we examine into the real motives and ultimate purposes of the Abolition societies and their prominent agents. To justify their officious and gratuitous interference in our domestic affairs — the most insulting and insolent outrage which can be offered to a community — they profess to hold themselves responsible for the pretended sin of our domestic slavery, because, forsooth *they* tolerate its existence among *us*. If they are at all responsible for the sin of slavery, whatever that may be, it is not because they tolerate it now but because their ancestors were the agents and authors of its original introduction. These ancestors sold ours the slaves and warranted the title, and it would be a much more becoming labor of filial piety for their descendants to pray for their souls, if they are Protestants, and buy masses to redeem them from purgatory, if they are Catholics, than to assail their warranty and slander their memory by denouncing them as "man-stealers and murderers."

But this voluntary and gratuitous assumption of responsibility, in imitation of a recent and high example in our history, but imperfectly conceals a lurking principle of danger, which deserves to be examined and exposed. What is there to make the people of New York or Massachusetts responsible for slavery in South Carolina any more than the people of Great Britain? To assume that the people of those states are responsible for the continuance of this institution is distinctly to assume that they have a right to abolish it. And whatever enforced disclaimers they may make, their efforts would be worse than unprofitable on any other hypothesis. The folly of attempting to convert the slaveholders to voluntary emancipation, by a course of slander and denunciation, is too great to be ascribed even to fanaticism itself. They do not, indeed, disguise the fact that their principal object is to operate on public opinion in the nonslaveholding states. And to what purpose? They cannot suppose that the opinion of those states, however unanimous, can break the chains of slavery by some moral magic. The whole tenor of their conduct and temper of their discussions clearly demonstrate that their object is to bring the slaveholding states into universal odium, and the public opinion of the nonslaveholding to the point of emancipating our slaves by federal legislation, without the consent of their owners.

Disguise it as they may, "to this complexion it must come at last."

It is in this aspect of the subject that it challenges our grave and solemn consideration. It behooves us, then, in my opinion, to demand, respectfully, of each and every one of the nonslaveholding states:

1. A formal and solemn disclaimer, by its legislature, of the existence of any rightful power, either in such state or the United States, in Congress assembled, to interfere in any manner whatever with the institution of domestic slavery in South Carolina.

2. The immediate passage of penal laws by such legislature, denouncing against the incendiaries of whom we complain, such punishments as will speedily and forever suppress their machinations against our peace and safety. Though the right to emancipate our slaves by coercive legislation has been very generally disclaimed by popular assemblages in the nonslaveholding states, it is nevertheless important that each of those states should give this disclaimer and the authentic and authoritative form of a legislative declaration, to be preserved as a permanent record for our future security. Our right to demand of those states the enactment of laws for the punishment of those enemies of our peace, who avail themselves of the sanctuary of their sovereign jurisdiction to wage a war of extermination against us, is founded on one of the most salutary and conservative principles of international law. Every state is under the most sacred obligations, not only to abstain from all such interference with the institutions of another as is calculated to disturb its tranquility or endanger its safety but to prevent its citizens or subjects from such interference, either by inflicting condign punishment itself, or by delivering them up to the justice of the offending community. As between separate and independent nations, the refusal of a state to punish these offensive proceedings against another, by its citizens or subjects makes the state so refusing an accomplice in the outrage and furnishes a just cause of war.

These principles of international law are universally admitted, and none have been more sacredly observed by just and enlightened nations. The obligations of the nonslaveholding states to punish and repress the proceedings of their citizens against our domestic institutions and tranquillity are greatly increased, both by the nature of those proceedings and the fraternal relation which subsists between the states of this confederacy. For no outrage against any community can be greater than to stir up the elements of servile insurrection, and no obligation to repress it can be more sacred than that which adds to the sanctions of international law the solemn guarantee of a constitutional compact, which is at once the bond and the condition of our Union. The liberal, enlightened, and magnanimous conduct of the people in many portions of the nonslaveholding states forbids us to anticipate a refusal on the part of those states to fulfill these high obligations of national faith and duty.

And we have the less reason to look forward to this inauspicious result from considering the necessary consequences which would follow to the people of those states and of the whole commercial world from the general emancipation of our slaves. These consequences may be presented, as an irresistible appeal, to every rational philanthropist in Europe or America. It is clearly demonstrable that the production of cotton depends, not so much on soil and climate as on the existence of domestic slavery. In the relaxing latitudes where it grows, not one-half the quantity would be produced but for the existence of this institution; and every practical planter will concur in the opinion that if all the slaves in these states were now emancipated, the American crop would be reduced the very next year from 1,200,000 to 600,000 bales.

No great skill in political economy will

be required to estimate how enormously the price of cotton would be increased by this change, and no one who will consider how largely this staple contributes to the wealth of manufacturing nations, and to the necessaries and comforts of the poorer classes all over the world, can fail to perceive the disastrous effects of so great a reduction in the quantity and so great an enhancement in the price of it. In Great Britain, France, and the United States, the catastrophe would be overwhelming, and it is not extravagant to say that for little more than 2 million Negro slaves, cut loose from their tranquil moorings and set adrift upon the untried ocean of at least a doubtful experiment, 10 million poor white people would be reduced to destitution, pauperism, and starvation.

An anxious desire to avoid the last sad alternative of an injured community prompts this final appeal to the interests and enlightened philanthropy of our confederate states. And we cannot permit ourselves to believe that our just demands, thus supported by every consideration of humanity and duty, will be rejected by states who are united to us by so many social and political ties, and who have so deep an interest in the preservation of that Union.

42.

Resolutions on Abolitionist Propaganda

Riled by Abolitionist literature that was flooding the mails, the South Carolina legislature passed the following resolutions in December 1835. It then petitioned the various Northern legislatures to prohibit Abolitionist activity in their states, and also asked the postmaster general to ban the literature from the mails. Other Southern states acted similarly. Abolitionists were not popular, and the petitions were extensively debated. President Jackson himself, no slavery enthusiast, recommended legislation to prohibit the circulation of incendiary material. Congress came to the conclusion in 1836 that to do so would be unconstitutional, but the practice of Southern postmasters in refusing to deliver Abolitionist propaganda was not interfered with by the federal government.

Source: *Acts and Resolutions of the General Assembly of the State of South Carolina Passed in December, 1835*, Columbia, 1836, pp. 26-28.

YOUR COMMITTEE, desirous of making a matter of record, both of our rights and the assertion of the just expectation that they will be respected by those who are united with us in the bonds of a common Union, beg leave to offer the following resolutions for the adoption of both branches of the legislature.

1. *Resolved,* that the formation of the abolition societies, and the acts and doings of certain fanatics calling themselves Abolitionists, in the nonslaveholding states of this Confederacy, are in direct violation of the obligations of the compact of the Union, dissocial and incendiary in the extreme.

2. *Resolved,* that no state having a just regard for her own peace and security can acquiesce in a state of things by which such

conspiracies are engendered within the limits of a friendly state, united to her by the bonds of a common league of political association, without either surrendering or compromising her most essential rights.

3. *Resolved,* that the legislature of South Carolina, having every confidence in the justice and friendship of the nonslaveholding states, announces to her co-states her confident expectation, and she earnestly requests that the governments of these states will promptly and effectually suppress all those associations within their respective limits purporting to be abolition societies; and that they will make it highly penal to print, publish, and distribute newspapers, pamphlets, tracts, and pictorial representations calculated and having an obvious tendency to excite the slaves of the Southern states to insurrection and revolt.

4. *Resolved,* that, regarding the domestic slavery of the Southern states as a subject exclusively within the control of each of the said states, we shall consider every interference by any other state or the general government as a direct and unlawful interference, to be resisted at once and under every possible circumstance.

5. *Resolved,* in order that a salutary negative may be put on the mischievous and unfounded assumption of some of the Abolitionists, the nonslaveholding states are requested to disclaim by legislative declaration all right, either on the part of themselves or the government of the United States, to interfere in any manner with domestic slavery, either in the states or in the territories where it exists.

6. *Resolved,* that we should consider the abolition of slavery in the District of Columbia as a violation of the rights of the citizens of that District, derived from the implied conditions on which that territory was ceded to the general government, and as a usurpation to be at once resisted as nothing more than the commencement of a scheme of much more extensive and flagrant injustice.

7. *Resolved,* that the legislature of South Carolina regards with decided approbation the measures of security adopted by the Post Office Department of the United States in relation to the transmission of incendiary tracts. But if this highly essential and protective policy be counteracted by Congress, and the United States mail becomes a vehicle for the transmission of the mischievous documents with which it was recently freighted, we, in this contingency, expect that the chief magistrate of our state will forthwith call the legislature together that timely measures may be taken to prevent its traversing our territory.

8. *Resolved,* that the governor be requested to transmit a copy of this report and resolutions to the executives of the several states that they may be laid before their respective legislatures.

If you put a chain around the neck of a slave, the other end fastens itself around your own.

RALPH WALDO EMERSON, *Essays: First Series*

43.

Abolitionist Protest Against the President

In July 1835 a group of South Carolinians stormed the post office in Charleston and burned packages of Abolitionist literature awaiting distribution. The incident raised the issue of state interference with the delivery of the U.S. mails. In December 1835 President Jackson presented his views to Congress. He condemned what he called "wicked attempts" to "instigate the slaves to insurrection" and recommended legislation to prohibit the circulation of incendiary mail in Southern states. The Abolitionists protested the President's speech in the letter reproduced below. It was issued on December 26, 1835, and featured in the Abolitionist press. The President's bill did not become law, mainly because Congress refused to give any state or the federal government the right to censor the mail.

Source: William Jay, *A View of the Action of the Federal Government in Behalf of Slavery,* New York, 1839, pp. 229-240.

To the President of the United States:

Sir:

In your message to Congress of the 7th instant are the following passages:

"I must also invite your attention to the painful excitement produced in the South, by attempts to circulate through the mails, inflammatory appeals, *addressed to the passions of the slaves,* in prints and in various sorts of publications, *calculated to stimulate them to insurrection and produce all the horrors of a servile war.* There is, doubtless, no respectable portion of our countrymen who can be so far misled as to feel any other sentiment than that of indignant regret at conduct so destructive of the harmony and peace of the country and *so repugnant to the principles of our national compact and to the dictates of humanity and religion.*"

You remark that it is fortunate that the people of the North have "given so strong and impressive a tone to the sentiments entertained against the proceedings of the misguided persons who have engaged in these *unconstitutional and wicked attempts."* And you proceed to suggest to Congress "the propriety of passing such a law as will prohibit, under severe penalties, the circulation in the Southern states, through the mails, of incendiary publications, *intended to instigate the slaves to insurrection."*

A servile insurrection, as experience has shown, involves the slaughter of the whites, without respect to sex or age. Hence, sir, the purport of the information you have communicated to Congress and to the world is that there are American citizens who, in violation of the dictates of humanity and religion, have engaged in unconstitutional and wicked attempts to circulate, through the mails, inflammatory appeals addressed to the passions of the slaves, and which appeals, as is implied in the object of your proposed law, are *intended* to stimulate the slaves to indiscriminate massacre. Recent events irresistibly confine the application of your remarks to the officers and members of the American Antislavery Society and its auxiliaries.

On the 28th of March, 1834, the Senate of the United States passed the following resolution:

Resolved, that the President, in relation to the public revenue, has assumed upon himself authority and power not conferred by the Constitution and laws, but in derogation of both.

On the 5th of the ensuing month, you transmitted to that body your "solemn protest" against their decision. Instructed by your example, we now, sir, in behalf of the Society of which we are the constituted organs and in behalf of all who are associated with it, present to you this, our "solemn protest," against your grievous and unfounded accusations.

Should it be supposed, that in thus addressing you, we are wanting in the respect due to your exalted station, we offer, in our vindication, your own acknowledgement to the Senate: "Subject only to the restraints of truth and justice, the free people of the United States have the undoubted right as individuals or collectively, orally or in writing, at such times and in such language and form as they may think proper, to discuss his (the President's) official conduct and to express and promulgate their opinions concerning it."

In the exercise of this "undoubted right," we protest against the judgment you have pronounced against the Abolitionists.

First, because, in rendering that judgment officially, you assumed a power not belonging to your office.

You complained that the resolution censuring your conduct, "though adopted by the Senate in its legislative capacity, is, in its effects and in its characteristics, essentially *judicial.*" And thus, sir, although the charges of which we complain were made by you in your executive capacity, they are, equally with the resolution, essentially *judicial.* The Senate adjudged that your conduct was unconstitutional. You pass the same judgment on our efforts. Nay, sir, you go farther than the Senate. That body forbore

to impeach your motives; but you have assumed the prerogatives, not only of a court of law but of conscience, and pronounce our efforts to be *wicked* as well as unconstitutional.

Second, we protest against the *publicity* you have given to your accusations.

You felt it to be a grievance that the charge against you was "spread upon the *Journal* of the Senate, published to the nation and to the world — made part of our enduring archives and incorporated in the history of the age. The punishment of removal from office and future disqualification does not follow the decision; but the *moral influence* of a solemn declaration by a majority of the Senate, that the accused is guilty of the offense charged upon him, has been as effectually secured as if the like declaration had been made upon an impeachment expressed in the same terms."

And is it nothing, sir, that we are officially charged by the President of the United States with wicked and unconstitutional efforts and with harboring the most execrable intentions; and, this, too, in a document spread upon the *Journals* of both houses of Congress, published to the nation and to the world, made part of our enduring archives, and incorporated in the history of the age? It is true that, although you have given judgment against us, you cannot award execution? We are not, indeed, subjected to the penalty of murder; but need we ask you, sir, what must be the *moral influence* of your declaration, that we have intended its perpetration?

Third, we protest against your condemnation of us *unheard.*

What, sir, was your complaint against the Senate? "Without notice, *unheard* and untried, I find myself charged, on the records of the Senate and in a form unknown in our country, with the high crime of violating the laws and Constitution of my country. No notice of the charge was given to the accused, and no opportunity afforded him to respond to the accusation — to meet his accusers face to face — to cross-examine the witnesses — to procure counteracting testimony or to be heard in his defense."

Had you, sir, done to others as it thus seems you would that others should do to you, no occasion would have been given for this protest. You most truly assert, in relation to the conduct of the Senate, "It is the policy of our benign system of jurisprudence to secure in all criminal proceedings, and even in the most trivial litigations, a fair, unprejudiced, and impartial trial." And by what authority, sir, do you except such of your fellow citizens as are known as Abolitionists from the benefit of this benign system? When has a fair, unprejudiced, and impartial trial been accorded to those who dare to maintain that all men are equally entitled to life, liberty, and the pursuit of happiness? What was the trial, sir, which preceded the judgment you have rendered against them?

Fourth, we protest against the *vagueness* of your charges.

We cannot more forcibly describe the injustice you have done us than by adopting your own indignant remonstrance against what you deemed similar injustice on the part of the Senate: Some of the first principles of natural right and enlightened jurisprudence have been violated in the very form of the resolution. It carefully abstains from averring in *which* of the late proceedings of the President has assumed upon himself authority and power not conferred by the Constitution and laws. Why was not the certainty of the offense, the nature and cause of the accusation, set out in the manner required in the Constitution, before even the humblest individual, for the smallest crime, can be exposed to condemnation? Such a specification was due to the accused that he might direct his defense to the real points of attack. A more striking illustration of the soundness and necessity of the rules which forbid *vague and indefinite generalities* and require a reasonable certainty in all judicial allegations, and a more glaring instance of the violation of these rules has seldom been exhibited.

It has been reserved for you, sir, to exhibit a still more striking illustration of the importance of these rules and a still more glaring instance of their violation. You have accused an indefinite number of your fellow citizens, without designation of name or residence, of making unconstitutional and wicked efforts and of harboring intentions which could be entertained only by the most depraved and abandoned of mankind; and yet you carefully abstain from averring *which* article of the Constitution they have transgressed; you omit stating when, where, and by whom these wicked attempts were made; you give no specification of the inflammatory appeals which you assert have been addressed to the passions of the slaves. You well know that the *"moral influence"* of your charges will affect thousands of your countrymen, many of them your political friends — some of them heretofore honored with your confidence — most, if not all of them, of irreproachable characters; and yet, by the very vagueness of your charges, you incapacitate each one of this multitude from proving his innocence.

Fifth, we protest against your charges, because they are *untrue*. Surely, sir, the burden of proof rests upon you. If you possess evidence against us, we are, by your own showing, entitled to "an opportunity to cross-examine witnesses, to procure counteracting testimony, and to be heard in [*our*] defense." You complained that you had been denied such an opportunity. It was not to have been expected, then, that you would make the conduct of the Senate the model of your own. Conscious of the wrong done to you and protesting against it, you found yourself compelled to enter on your defense. You have placed us in similar circumstances, and we proceed to follow your example:

The substance of your various allegations may be embodied in the charge, that we have attempted to circulate, through the mails, appeals addressed to the passions of the slaves, calculated to stimulate them to insurrection, and with the intention of producing a servile war.

It is deserving of notice that the *attempt* to circulate our papers is alone charged upon us. It is not pretended that we have put our appeals into the hands of a single slave, or that, in any instance, our endeavors to excite a servile war have been crowned with success. And in what way was our most execrable attempts made? By secret agents, traversing the slave country in disguise, stealing by night into the hut of the slave, and there reading to him our inflammatory appeals? You, sir, answer this question by declaring that we attempted the mighty mischief by circulating our appeals "THROUGH THE MAILS!" And are the Southern slaves, sir, accustomed to receive periodicals by mail? Of the thousands of publications mailed from the Antislavery office for the South, did you ever hear, sir, of one solitary paper being addressed to a slave? Would you know to whom they were directed, consult the Southern newspapers, and you will find them complaining that they were sent to public officers, clergymen, and other influential citizens.

Thus it seems we are incendiaries who place the torch in the hands of him whose dwellings we would fire! We are conspiring to excite a servile war, and announce our design to the masters, and commit to their care and disposal the very instruments by which we expect to effect our purpose! It has been said that thirty or forty of our papers were received at the South, directed to free people of color. We cannot deny the assertion because these papers may have been mailed by others for the sinister purpose of charging the act upon us. We are, however, ready to make our several affidavits that not one paper, with our knowledge or by our authority, has ever been sent to any such person in a slave state. The free people of color at the South can exert no

influence in behalf of the enslaved; and we have no disposition to excite odium against them by making them the recipients of our publications.

Your proposal that a law should be passed punishing the circulation, through the mails, of papers *intended to excite the slaves to insurrection* necessarily implies that such papers are now circulated; and you expressly and positively assert that we have attempted to circulate appeals addressed to the passions of the slaves and *calculated to produce all the horrors of a servile war.* We trust, sir, your proposed law, so portentous to the freedom of the press, will not be enacted till you have furnished Congress with stronger evidence of its necessity than unsupported assertions. We hope you will lay before that body, for its information, the papers to which you refer. This is the more necessary as the various public journals and meetings which have denounced us for entertaining insurrectionary and murderous designs have in no instance been able to quote from our publications a single exhortation to the slaves to break their fetters or the expression of a solitary wish for a servile war.

How far our writings are "calculated" to produce insurrection is a question which will be variously decided according to the latitude in which it is discussed. When we recollect that the humble schoolbook, the tale of fiction, and the costly annual have been placed under the ban of Southern editors for trivial allusions to slavery — and that a Southern divine has warned his fellow citizens of the danger of permitting slaves to be present at the celebration of our national festival, where they might listen to the Declaration of Independence and to eulogiums on liberty — we have little hope that our disquisitions on human rights will be generally deemed safe and innocent where those rights are habitually violated. Certain writings of one of your predecessors, President Jefferson, would undoubtedly be regarded, in some places, so insurrectionary as to expose to popular violence whoever should presume to circulate them.

As, therefore, sir, there is no common standard by which the criminality of opinions respecting slavery can be tested, we acknowledge the foresight which prompted you to recommend that the "severe penalties" of your proposed law should be awarded, not according to the character of the publication but the *intention* of the writer. Still, sir, we apprehend that no trivial difficulties will be experienced in the application of your law. The writer may be anonymous or beyond the reach of prosecution, while the porter who deposits the papers in the post office and the mail carrier who transports them, having no evil intentions, cannot be visited with the "severe penalties"; and thus will your law fail in securing to the South that entire exemption from all discussion on the subject of slavery, which it so vehemently desires. The success of the attempt already made to establish a censorship of the press is not such as to invite further encroachment on the rights of the people to publish their sentiments.

In your protest, you remarked to the Senate: "The whole executive power being vested in the President, who is *responsible* for its exercise, it is a necessary consequence that he should have a right to employ agents of his *own choice*, to aid him in the performance of his duties, and to *discharge* them when he is no longer *willing* to be RESPONSIBLE for their acts. He is equally bound to take care that the laws be faithfully executed, whether they impose duties on the highest officer of state or the *lowest subordinates* in any of the departments."

It may not be uninteresting to you, sir, to be informed in what manner your "subordinate" in New York, who, on your "responsibility," is exercising the functions of Censor of the American press, discharges the arduous duties of this untried and, until now, unheard of office. We beg leave to assure you, that his task is executed with a simplicity of principle and celerity of dispatch

unknown to any Censor of the press in France or Austria. Your subordinate decides upon the incendiary character of the publications committed to the post office by a glance at the wrappers or bags in which they are contained. No packages sent to be mailed from our office and directed to a slave state can escape the vigilance of this inspector of canvass and brown paper. Even your own protest, sir, if in an anti-slavery envelope, would be arrested on its progress to the South as "inflammatory, incendiary and insurrectionary in the highest degree."

No veto, however, is *as yet* imposed on the circulation of publications from any printing office but our own. Hence, when we desire to send "appeals" to the South, all that is necessary is to insert them in some newspaper that espouses our principles, pay for as many thousand copies as we think proper, and order them to be mailed according to our instructions.

Such, sir, is the worthless protection purchased for the South, by the most unblushing and dangerous usurpation of which any public officer has been guilty since the organization of our federal government. . . .

And now, sir, permit us respectfully to suggest to you the propriety of ascertaining the *real* designs of Abolitionists before your apprehensions of them lead you to sanction any more trifling with the LIBERTY OF THE PRESS. You assume it as a fact that Abolitionists are miscreants who are laboring to effect the massacre of their Southern brethren. Are you aware of the extent of the reproach which such an assumption casts upon the character of your countrymen? In August last, the number of Antislavery societies known to us was 263; we have *now* the names of more than 350 societies, and accessions are daily made to the multitude who embrace our principles. And can you think it possible, sir, that these citizens are deliberately plotting murder and furnishing us with funds to send publications to the South "intended to instigate the slaves to insurrection"? Is there anything in the character and manners of the free states to warrant the imputation on their citizens of such enormous wickedness? Have you ever heard, sir, of whole communities in these states subjecting obnoxious individuals to a mock trial, and, then, in contempt of law, humanity, and religion, deliberately murdering them? You have seen in the public journals great rewards offered for the perpetration of horrible crimes. We appeal to your candor and ask, were these rewards offered by Abolitionists or by men whose charges against Abolitionists you have condescended to sanction and disseminate?

And what, sir, is the character of those whom you have in your message held up to the execration of the civilized world? Their enemies being judges, they are *religious* fanatics. And what are the haunts of these plotters of murder? The pulpit, the bench, the bar, the professor's chair, the hall of legislation, the meeting for prayer, the temple of the Most High. But strange and monstrous as is this conspiracy, still you believe in its existence and call on Congress to counteract it. Be persuaded, sir, the moral sense of the community is abundantly sufficient to render this conspiracy utterly impotent the moment its machinations are exposed. Only PROVE the assertions and insinuations in your message, and you dissolve in an instant every Antislavery society in our land. Think not, sir, that we shall interpose any obstacle to an inquiry into our conduct. We invite, nay, sir, we entreat the appointment by Congress of a committee of investigation to visit the Antislavery office in New York. They shall be put in possession of copies of all the publications that have been issued from our press. Our whole correspondence shall be submitted to their inspection; our accounts of receipts and expenditures shall be spread before them, and we ourselves will cheerfully answer under oath whatever interrogatories they may put

to us relating to the charges you have advanced.

Should such a committee be denied and should the law you propose, stigmatizing us as felons, be passed without inquiry into the truth of your accusation and without allowing us a hearing, then shall we make the language of your protest our own, and declare that, "If such proceedings shall be approved and sustained by an intelligent people, then will the great contest with arbitrary power which had established in statutes, in bills of rights, in sacred charters, and in constitutions of government, the right of every citizen to a notice before trial, to a hearing before condemnation, and to an impartial tribunal for deciding on the charge, have been made in VAIN."

Before we conclude, permit us, sir, to offer you the following assurances.

Our principles, our objects, and our measures are wholly uncontaminated by considerations of party policy. Whatever may be our respective opinions as citizens of men and measures, as Abolitionists we have expressed no political preferences and are pursuing no party ends. From neither of the gentlemen nominated to succeed you have we anything to hope or fear; and to neither of them do we intend, as Abolitionists, to afford any aid or influence. This declaration will, it is hoped, satisfy the partisans of the rival candidates that it is not necessary for them to assail our rights by way of convincing the South that they do not possess our favor.

We have addressed you, sir, on this occasion, with republican plainness and Christian sincerity, but with no desire to derogate from the respect that is due to you or wantonly to give you pain. . . .

When convinced that our endeavors are wrong, we shall abandon them; but such conviction must be produced by other arguments than vituperation, popular violence, or penal enactments.

44.

ALEXIS DE TOCQUEVILLE: About *Democracy in America*

Part One of Alexis de Tocqueville's Democracy in America *was published in
1835, and Part Two in 1840. English translations appeared in the same years, and
the book won immediate and universal recognition. While the accuracy of its insights
was debated in America, reviewers agreed that, unlike the books of other visitors,
Tocqueville's work was sincerely undertaken and brilliantly and unbiasedly executed.
Material for the book was collected during a nine-month tour of the United States that
began in May 1831. Tocqueville and Gustave de Beaumont ostensibly came as French
delegates to study American penal institutions, but in fact they were determined to
study and to write about democracy in action. Tocqueville stated his reasons for
writing the book in its introduction, and also in a letter to his boyhood friend
Eugene Stoffels, dated February 21, 1835, both of which are reprinted here.*

Source: *Memoir, Letters, and Remains of Alexis de Tocqueville*, Boston, 1862, Vol. I, pp. 376-378.
        *The Republic of the United States of America, and its Political Institutions,
        Reviewed and Examined* [*Democracy in America*], translated by Henry Reeve[s],
        New York, 1856, pp. 1-15.

I.

Letter to EUGENE STOFFELS

I MAY SAY, DEAR FRIEND, that the impression
produced on you by my book, though in
one respect stronger than I intended, is not
of a kind that alarms or surprises me. This
is the political object of the work.

I wished to show what in our days a
democratic people really was; and by a rigorously accurate picture, to produce a double effect on the men of my day. To those
who have fancied an ideal democracy, a
brilliant and easily realized dream, I endeavored to show that they had clothed the picture in false colors; that the republican government which they extol, even though it
may bestow substantial benefits on a people
that can bear it, has none of the elevated
features with which their imagination

would endow it, and moreover, that such a
government cannot be maintained without
certain conditions of intelligence, of private
morality, and of religious belief, that we, as
a nation, have not reached, and that we
must labor to attain before grasping their
political results.

To those for whom the word "democracy" is synonymous with destruction, anarchy, spoliation, and murder, I have tried to
show that under a democratic government
the fortunes and the rights of society may
be respected, liberty preserved, and religion
honored; that though a republic may develop less than other governments some of the
noblest powers of the human mind, it yet
has a nobility of its own; and that after all
it may be God's will to spread a moderate
amount of happiness over all men, instead
of heaping a large sum upon a few by allowing only a small minority to approach

perfection. I attempted to prove to them that whatever their opinions might be, deliberation was no longer in their power; that society was tending everyday more and more toward equality, and dragging them and everyone else along with it; that the only choice lay between two inevitable evils; that the question had ceased to be whether they would have an aristocracy or a democracy, and now lay between a democracy without poetry or elevation indeed, but with order and morality; and an undisciplined and depraved democracy, subject to sudden frenzies, or to a yoke heavier than any that has galled mankind since the fall of the Roman Empire.

I wished to diminish the ardor of the Republican Party, and, without disheartening them, to point out their only wise course.

I have endeavored to abate the claims of the aristocrats, and to make them bend to an irresistible future; so that the impulse in one quarter and resistance in the other being less violent, society may march on peaceably toward the fulfillment of its destiny. This is the dominant idea in the book — an idea which embraces all the others, and that you ought to have made out more clearly. Hitherto, however, few have discovered it. I please many persons of opposite opinions, not because they penetrate my meaning but because, looking at only one side of my work, they think that they find in it arguments in favor of their own convictions. But I have faith in the future, and I hope that the day will come when all will see clearly what now only a few suspect.

II.

Author's Introduction

AMONG THE NOVEL OBJECTS that attracted my attention during my stay in the United States, nothing struck me more forcibly than the general equality of conditions. I readily discovered the prodigious influence which this primary fact exercises on the whole course of society, by giving a certain direction to public opinion, and a certain tenor to the laws; by imparting new maxims to the governing powers, and peculiar habits to the governed.

I speedily perceived that the influence of this fact extends far beyond the political character and the laws of the country, and that it has no less empire over civil society than over the government; it creates opinions, engenders sentiments, suggests the ordinary practices of life, and modifies whatever it does not produce.

The more I advanced in the study of American society, the more I perceived that the equality of conditions is the fundamental fact from which all others seem to be derived, and the central point at which all my observations constantly terminated.

I then turned my thoughts to our own hemisphere, where I imagined that I discerned something analogous to the spectacle which the New World presented to me. I observed that the equality of conditions is daily advancing toward those extreme limits which it seems to have reached in the United States; and that the democracy which governs the American communities appears to be rapidly rising into power in Europe.

I hence conceived the idea of the book which is now before the reader.

It is evident to all alike that a great democratic revolution is going on among us; but there are two opinions as to its nature and consequences. To some it appears to be a novel accident, which as such may still be checked; to others it seems irresistible, because it is the most uniform, the most ancient, and the most permanent tendency which is to be found in history.

Let us recollect the situation of France 700 years ago, when the territory was divided among a small number of families, who were the owners of the soil and the rulers of the inhabitants; the right of governing descended with the family inheritance from generation to generation; force was the only means by which man could act on man; and landed property was the sole source of power.

Soon, however, the political power of the clergy was founded, and began to exert itself; the clergy opened its ranks to all classes, to the poor and the rich, the villain and the lord; equality penetrated into the government through the church, and the being who, as a serf, must have vegetated in perpetual bondage, took his place as a priest in the midst of nobles, and not unfrequently above the heads of kings.

The different relations of men became more complicated and more numerous, as society gradually became more stable and more civilized. Thence the want of civil laws was felt; and the order of legal functionaries soon rose from the obscurity of the tribunals and their dusty chambers to appear at the court of the monarch, by the side of the feudal barons in their ermine and their mail.

While the kings were ruining themselves by their great enterprises, and the nobles exhausting their resources by private wars, the lower orders were enriching themselves by commerce. The influence of money began to be perceptible in state affairs. The transactions of business opened a new road to power, and the financier rose to a station of political influence in which he was at once flattered and despised.

Gradually the spread of mental acquirements, and the increasing taste for literature and art, opened chances of success to talent; science became the means of government, intelligence led to social power, and the man of letters took a part in the affairs of the state.

The value attached to the privileges of birth decreased in the exact proportion in which new paths were struck out to advancement. In the eleventh century nobility was beyond all price; in the thirteenth it might be purchased; it was conferred for the first time in 1270; and equality was thus introduced into the government by the aristocracy itself.

In the course of these 700 years, it sometimes happened that, in order to resist the authority of the Crown or to diminish the power of their rivals, the nobles granted a certain share of political rights to the people. Or, more frequently, the king permitted the lower orders to enjoy a degree of power, with the intention of repressing the aristocracy.

In France the kings have always been the most active and the most constant of levelers. When they were strong and ambitious, they spared no pains to raise the people to the level of the nobles; when they were temperate or weak, they allowed the people to rise above themselves. Some assisted the democracy by their talents, others by their vices. Louis XI and Louis XIV reduced every rank beneath the throne to the same subjection; Louis XV descended, himself and all his court, into the dust.

As soon as land was held on any other than a feudal tenure, and personal property began in its turn to confer influence and power, every improvement which was introduced in commerce or manufacture was a fresh element of the equality of conditions. Henceforward every new discovery, every new want which it engendered, and every new desire which craved satisfaction was a step toward the universal level. The taste for luxury, the love of war, the sway of fashion, the most superficial as well as the deepest passions of the human heart cooperated to enrich the poor and to impoverish the rich.

From the time when the exercise of the intellect became the source of strength and of wealth, it is impossible not to consider every addition to science, every fresh truth, and every new idea, as a germ of power placed within the reach of the people. Poetry, eloquence, and memory, the grace of wit, the glow of imagination, the depth of thought, and all the gifts which are bestowed by Providence with an equal hand, turned to the advantage of the democracy; and even when they were in the possession of its adversaries, they still served its cause by throwing into relief the natural greatness of man; its conquests spread, therefore, with those of civilization and knowledge; and literature became an arsenal, where the poorest and weakest could always find weapons to their hand.

In perusing the pages of our history, we shall scarcely meet with a single great event, in the lapse of 700 years, which has not turned to the advantage of equality.

The Crusades and the wars of the English decimated the nobles and divided their possessions; the erection of communes introduced an element of democratic liberty into the bosom of feudal monarchy; the invention of firearms equalized the villain and the noble on the field of battle; printing opened the same resources to the minds of all classes; the post was organized so as to bring the same information to the door of the poor man's cottage and to the gate of the palace; and Protestantism proclaimed that all men are alike able to find the road to Heaven. The discovery of America offered a thousand new paths to fortune, and placed riches and power within the reach of the adventurous and the obscure.

If we examine what has happened in France at intervals of fifty years, beginning with the eleventh century, we shall invariably perceive that a twofold revolution has taken place in the state of society. The noble has gone down on the social ladder, and the *roturier* has gone up; the one descends as the other rises. Every half century brings them nearer to each other, and they will very shortly meet.

Nor is this phenomenon at all peculiar to France. Whithersoever we turn our eyes, we shall discover the same continual revolution throughout the whole of Christendom.

The various occurrences of national existence have everywhere turned to the advantage of democracy; all men have aided it by their exertions; those who have intentionally labored in its cause, and those who have served it unwittingly — those who have fought for it, and those who have declared themselves its opponents — have all been driven along in the same track, have all labored to one end, some ignorantly, and some unwillingly; all have been blind instruments in the hands of God.

The gradual development of the equality of conditions is, therefore, a providential fact, and it possesses all the characteristics of a divine decree; it is universal, it is durable, it constantly eludes all human interference, and all events as well as all men contribute to its progress.

Would it, then, be wise to imagine that a social impulse which dates from so far back can be checked by the efforts of a generation? Is it credible that the democracy which has annihilated the feudal system, and vanquished kings, will respect the citizen and the capitalist? Will it stop now that it has grown so strong and its adversaries so weak?

None can say which way we are going, for all terms of comparison are wanting; the equality of conditions is more complete in the Christian countries of the present-day than it has been at any time, or in any part of the world; so that the extent of what already exists prevents us from foreseeing what may be yet to come.

The whole book which is here offered to the public has been written under the impression of a kind of religious dread, produced in the author's mind by the contemplation of so irresistible a revolution, which has advanced for centuries in spite of such amazing obstacles, and which is still proceeding in the midst of the ruins it has made.

It is not necessary that God Himself should speak in order to disclose to us the unquestionable signs of His will; we can discern them in the habitual course of nature, and in the invariable tendency of events; I know, without a special revelation, that the planets move in the orbits traced by the Creator's finger.

If the men of our time were led by attentive observation and by sincere reflection to acknowledge that the gradual and progressive development of social equality is at once the past and future of their history, this solitary truth would confer the sacred character of a divine decree upon the change. To attempt to check democracy would be in that case to resist the will of God; and the nations would then be constrained to make the best of the social lot awarded to them by Providence.

The Christian nations of our age seem to me to present a most alarming spectacle; the impulse which is bearing them along is so strong that it cannot be stopped, but it is not yet so rapid that it cannot be guided. Their fate is in their hands; yet a little while and it may be so no longer.

The first duty which is at this time imposed upon those who direct our affairs is to educate the democracy; to warm its faith, if that be possible; to purify its morals; to direct its energies; to substitute a knowledge of business for its inexperience, and an acquaintance with its true interests for its blind propensities; to adapt its government to time and place, and to modify it in compliance with the occurrences and the actors of the age.

A new science of politics is indispensable to a new world.

This, however, is what we think of least; launched in the middle of a rapid stream, we obstinately fix our eyes on the ruins which may still be descried upon the shore we have left, while the current sweeps us along, and drives us backward toward the gulf.

In no country in Europe has the great social revolution which I have been describing made such rapid progress as in France; but it has always been borne on by chance. The heads of the state have never had any forethought for its exigences, and its victories have been obtained without their consent or without their knowledge. The most powerful, the most intelligent, and the most moral classes of the nation have never attempted to connect themselves with it in order to guide it. The people have consequently been abandoned to its wild propensities, and it has grown up like those outcasts who receive their education in the public streets, and who are unacquainted with aught but the vices and wretchedness of society. The existence of a democracy was seemingly unknown, when, on a sudden, it took possession of the supreme power. Everything was then submitted to its caprices; it was worshiped as the idol of strength; until, when it was enfeebled by its own excesses, the legislator conceived the rash project of annihilating its power, instead of instructing it and correcting its vices; no attempt was made to fit it to govern, but all were bent on excluding it from the government.

The consequence of this has been that the democratic revolution has been effected only in the material parts of society, without that concomitant change in laws, ideas, customs, and manners which was necessary to render such a revolution beneficial. We have gotten a democracy, but without the conditions which lessen its vices, and render its natural advantages more prominent; and although we already perceive the evils it brings, we are ignorant of the benefits it may confer.

While the power of the Crown, supported by the aristocracy, peaceably governed the nations of Europe, society possessed, in the midst of its wretchedness, several different advantages which can now scarcely be appreciated or conceived.

The power of a part of his subjects was an insurmountable barrier to the tyranny of the prince; and the monarch who felt the almost divine character which he enjoyed in the eyes of the multitude, derived a motive for the just use of his power from the respect which he inspired.

High as they were placed above the people, the nobles could not but take that calm and benevolent interest in its fate which the shepherd feels toward his flock; and without acknowledging the poor as their equals, they watched over the destiny of those whose welfare Providence had entrusted to their care.

The people, never having conceived the idea of a social condition different from its own, and entertaining no expectation of ever ranking with its chiefs, received benefits from them without discussing their rights. It grew attached to them when they were clement and just, but it submitted without resistance or servility to their exactions, as to the inevitable visitations of the arm of God. Custom, and the manners of the time, had moreover created a species of law in the midst of violence, and established certain limits to oppression.

As the noble never suspected that anyone would attempt to deprive him of the privileges which he believed to be legitimate, and as the serf looked upon his own inferiority as a consequence of the immutable order of nature, it is easy to imagine that a mutual exchange of goodwill took place between two classes so differently gifted by fate. Inequality and wretchedness were then to be found in society; but the souls of neither rank of men were degraded.

Men are not corrupted by the exercise of power or debased by the habit of obedience, but by the exercise of power which they believe to be illegal, and by obedience to a rule which they consider to be usurped and oppressive.

On one side were wealth, strength, and leisure, accompanied by the refinement of luxury, the elegance of taste, the pleasures of wit, and the religion of art. On the other were labor, and a rude ignorance; but in the midst of this coarse and ignorant multitude, it was not uncommon to meet with energetic passions, generous sentiments, profound religious convictions, and independent virtues.

The body of a state thus organized might boast of its stability, its power, and above all, of its glory.

But the scene is now changed, and gradually the two ranks mingle; the divisions which once severed mankind are lowered; property is divided, power is held in common, the light of intelligence spreads, and the capacities of all classes are equally cultivated; the state becomes democratic, and the empire of democracy is slowly and peaceably introduced into the institutions and manners of the nation.

I can conceive a society in which all men would profess an equal attachment and respect for the laws of which they are the common authors; in which the authority of the state would be respected as necessary, though not as divine; and the loyalty of the subject to the chief magistrate would not be a passion but a quiet and rational persuasion. Every individual being in the possession of rights which he is sure to retain, a kind of manly reliance and reciprocal courtesy would arise between all classes, alike removed from pride and meanness.

The people, well acquainted with its true interests, would allow, that in order to profit by the advantages of society, it is necessary to satisfy its demands. In this state of things, the voluntary association of the citizens might supply the individual exertions of the nobles, and the community would be alike protected from anarchy and from oppression.

I admit that in a democratic state thus constituted, society will not be stationary; but the impulses of the social body may be regulated and directed forward; if there be less splendor than in the halls of an aristocracy, the contrast of misery will be less frequent also; the pleasures of enjoyment may be less excessive, but those of comfort will be more general; the sciences may be less perfectly cultivated, but ignorance will be less common; the impetuosity of the feelings will be repressed, and the habits of the nation softened; there will be more vices and fewer crimes.

In the absence of enthusiasm and of an ardent faith, great sacrifices may be obtained from the members of a commonwealth by an appeal to their understandings and their experience; each individual will feel the same necessity for uniting with his fellow citizens to protect his own weakness; and as he knows that if they are to assist he must cooperate, he will readily perceive that his personal interest is identified with the interest of the community.

The nation, taken as a whole, will be less brilliant, less glorious, and perhaps less strong; but the majority of the citizens will enjoy a greater degree of prosperity, and the people will remain quiet, not because it despairs of melioration but because it is conscious of the advantages of its condition.

If all the consequences of this state of things were not good or useful, society would at least have appropriated all such as were useful and good; and having once and forever renounced the social advantages of aristocracy, mankind would enter into possession of all the benefits which democracy can afford.

But here it may be asked what we have adopted in the place of these institutions, those ideas, and those customs of our forefathers which we have abandoned.

The spell of royalty is broken, but it has not been succeeded by the majesty of the laws; the people have learned to despise all authority. But fear now extorts a larger tribute of obedience than that which was formerly paid by reverence and by love.

I perceive that we have destroyed those independent beings which were able to cope with tyranny singlehanded; but it is the government that has inherited the privileges of which families, corporations, and individuals have been deprived, the weakness of the whole community has, therefore, succeeded to that influence of a small body of citizens, which, if it was sometimes oppressive, was often conservative.

The division of property has lessened the distance which separated the rich from the poor; but it would seem that the nearer they draw to each other, the greater is their mutual hatred, and the more vehement the envy and the dread with which they resist each other's claims to power; the notion of right is alike insensible to both classes, and force affords to both the only argument for the present, and the only guarantee for the future.

The poor man retains the prejudices of his forefathers without their faith, and their ignorance without their virtues; he has adopted the doctrine of self-interest as the rule of his actions, without understanding the science which controls it, and his egotism is no less blind than his devotedness was formerly.

If society is tranquil, it is not because it relies upon its strength and its well-being, but because it knows its weakness and its infirmities: a single effort may cost it its life; everybody feels the evil, but no one has courage or energy enough to seek the cure; the desires, the regret, the sorrows, and the joys of the time produce nothing that is visible or permanent, like the passions of old men which terminate in impotence.

We have, then, abandoned whatever advantages the old state of things afforded, without receiving any compensation from our present condition; having destroyed an aristocracy, we seem inclined to survey its ruins with complacency, and to fix our abode in the midst of them.

The phenomena which the intellectual world presents are not less deplorable. The democracy of France, checked in its course or abandoned to its lawless passions, has overthrown whatever crossed its path, and has shaken all that it has not destroyed. Its control over society has not been gradually introduced, or peaceably established, but it has constantly advanced in the midst of disorder and the agitation of a conflict. In the heat of the struggle each partisan is hurried beyond the limits of his opinions by the opinions and the excesses of his opponents, until he loses sight of the end of his exertions, and holds a language which disguises his real sentiments or secret instincts. Hence arises the strange confusion which we are beholding.

I cannot recall to my mind a passage in history more worthy of sorrow and of pity than the scenes which are happening under our eyes; it is as if the natural bond which unites the opinions of man to his tastes, and his actions to his principles, was now broken; the sympathy which has always been acknowledged between the feelings and the ideas of mankind appears to be dissolved, and all the laws of moral analogy to be abolished.

Zealous Christians may be found among us, whose minds are nurtured in the love and knowledge of a future life, and who readily espouse the cause of human liberty as the source of all moral greatness. Christianity, which has declared that all men are equal in the sight of God, will not refuse to acknowledge that all citizens are equal in the eye of the law. But by a singular concourse of events, religion is entangled in those institutions which democracy assails, and it is not unfrequently brought to reject the equality it loves, and to curse that cause of liberty as a foe, which it might hallow by its alliance.

By the side of these religious men I discern others whose looks are turned to the earth more than to Heaven; they are the partisans of liberty, not only as the source of the noblest virtues but more especially as the root of all solid advantages; and they sincerely desire to extend its sway, and to impart its blessings to mankind. It is natural that they should hasten to invoke the assis-

tance of religion, for they must know that liberty cannot be established without morality, nor morality without faith; but they have seen religion in the ranks of their adversaries, and they inquire no farther; some of them attack it openly, and the remainder are afraid to defend it.

In former ages, slavery has been advocated by the venal and slavish-minded, while the independent and the warmhearted were struggling without hope to save the liberties of mankind. But men of high and generous characters are now to be met with, whose opinions are at variance with their inclinations, and who praise that servility which they have themselves never known. Others, on the contrary, speak in the name of liberty as if they were able to feel its sanctity and its majesty, and loudly claim for humanity those rights which they have always disowned.

There are virtuous and peaceful individuals whose pure morality, quiet habits, affluence, and talents fit them to be the leaders of the surrounding population; their love of their country is sincere, and they are prepared to make the greatest sacrifices to its welfare, but they confound the abuses of civilization with its benefits, and the idea of evil is inseparable in their minds from that of novelty.

Not far from this class is another party, whose object is to materialize mankind, to hit upon what is expedient without heeding what is just; to acquire knowledge without faith, and prosperity apart from virtue; assuming the title of the champions of modern civilization, and placing themselves in a station which they usurp with insolence, and from which they are driven by their own unworthiness.

Where are we then?

The religionists are the enemies of liberty, and the friends of liberty attack religion; the high-minded and the noble advocate subjection, and the meanest and most servile minds preach independence; honest and enlightened citizens are opposed to all progress, while men without patriotism and without principles are the apostles of civilization and of intelligence.

Has such been the fate of the centuries which have preceded our own? and has man always inhabited a world, like the present, where nothing is linked together, where virtue is without genius, and genius without honor; where the love of order is confounded with a taste for oppression, and the holy rites of freedom with a contempt of law; where the light thrown by conscience on human actions is dim and where nothing seems to be any longer forbidden or allowed, honorable or shameful, false or true?

I cannot, however, believe that the Creator made man to leave him in an endless struggle with the intellectual miseries which surround us. God destines a calmer and a more certain future to the communities of Europe; I am unacquainted with His designs, but I shall not cease to believe in them because I cannot fathom them, and I had rather mistrust my own capacity than His justice.

There is a country in the world where the great revolution which I am speaking of seems nearly to have reached its natural limits; it has been effected with ease and simplicity, say rather that this country has attained the consequences of the democratic revolution which we are undergoing, without having experienced the revolution itself.

The emigrants who fixed themselves on the shores of America in the beginning of the seventeenth century severed the democratic principle from all the principles which repressed it in the old communities of Europe, and transplanted it unalloyed to the New World. It has there been allowed to spread in perfect freedom, and to put forth its consequences in the laws by influencing the manners of the country.

It appears to me beyond a doubt that sooner or later we shall arrive, like the Americans, at an almost complete equality of conditions. But I do not conclude from this that we shall ever be necessarily led to draw the same political consequences which the Americans have derived from a similar social organization. I am far from supposing that they have chosen the only form of government which a democracy may adopt; but the identity of the efficient cause of laws and manners in the two countries is sufficient to account for the immense interest we have in becoming acquainted with its effects in each of them.

It is not, then, merely to satisfy a legitimate curiosity that I have examined America; my wish has been to find instruction by which we may ourselves profit. Whoever should imagine that I have intended to write a panegyric would be strangely mistaken, and on reading this book, he will perceive that such was not my design; nor has it been my object to advocate any form of government in particular, for I am of opinion that absolute excellence is rarely to be found in any legislation; I have not even affected to discuss whether the social revolution, which I believe to be irresistible, is advantageous or prejudicial to mankind; I have acknowledged this revolution as a fact already accomplished or on the eve of its accomplishment; and I have selected the nation, from among those which have undergone it, in which its development has been the most peaceful and the most complete, in order to discern its natural consequences, and, if it be possible, to distinguish the means by which it may be rendered profitable. I confess that in America I saw more than America; I sought the image of democracy itself, with its inclinations, its character, its prejudices, and its passions, in order to learn what we have to fear or to hope from its progress.

In the first part of this work [*Democracy in America*] I have attempted to show the tendency given to the laws by the democracy of America, which is abandoned almost without restraint to its instinctive propensities; and to exhibit the course it prescribes to the government, and the influence it exercises on affairs. I have sought to discover the evils and the advantages which it produces. I have examined the precautions used by the Americans to direct it, as well as those which they have not adopted, and I have undertaken to point out the causes which enable it to govern society.

It was my intention to depict, in a second part, the influence which the equality of conditions and the rule of democracy exercise on the civil society, the habits, the ideas, and the manners of the Americans; I begin, however, to feel less ardor for the accomplishment of this project, since the excellent work of my friend and traveling companion, M. de Beaumont, has been given to the world. I do not know whether I have succeeded in making known what I saw in America, but I am certain that such has been my sincere desire, and I have never, knowingly, molded facts to ideas, instead of ideas to facts.

Whenever a point could be established by the aid of written documents, I have had recourse to the original text, and to the most authentic and approved works. I have cited my authorities in the notes, and anyone may refer to them. Whenever an opinion, a political custom, or a remark on the manners of the country was concerned, I endeavored to consult the most enlightened men I met with. If the point in question was important or doubtful, I was not satisfied with one testimony, but I formed my opinion on the evidence of several witnesses. Here the reader must necessarily believe me upon my word. I could frequently have quoted names which are either known to him, or which deserve to be so, in proof of what I advance; but I have carefully abstained from this practice. A stranger frequently hears important truths at the fireside of his host, which the latter would perhaps conceal even from the ear of friendship; he consoles himself with his guest, for the silence to which he is restricted, and the shortness of the traveler's stay takes away

all fear of his indiscretion. I carefully noted every conversation of this nature as soon as it occurred, but these notes will never leave my writing case; I had rather injure the success of my statements than add my name to the list of those strangers who repay the generous hospitality they have received by subsequent chagrin and annoyance.

I am aware that, notwithstanding my care, nothing will be easier than to criticize this book, if anyone ever chooses to criticize it.

Those readers who may examine it closely will discover the fundamental idea which connects the several parts together. But the diversity of the subjects I have had to treat is exceedingly great, and it will not be difficult to oppose an isolated fact to the body of facts which I quote, or an isolated idea to the body of ideas I put forth. I hope to be read in the spirit which has guided my labors, and that my book may be judged by the general impression it leaves, as I have formed my own judgment not on any single reason, but upon the mass of evidence.

It must not be forgotten that the author who wishes to be understood is obliged to push all his ideas to their utmost theoretical consequences, and often to the verge of what is false or impracticable; for if it be necessary sometimes to quit the rules of logic in active life, such is not the case in discourse, and a man finds that almost as many difficulties spring from inconsistency of language, as usually arise from consistency of conduct.

I conclude by pointing out myself what many readers will consider the principal defect of the work. This book is written to favor no particular views, and in composing it I have entertained no design of serving or attacking any party. I have undertaken not to see differently, but to look farther than parties, and while they are busied for the morrow, I have turned my thoughts to the future.

1835 - 1837

45.

WILLIAM JOHNSON: Diary of a Free African American

Before the Civil War the activities of free African Americans were severely curtailed by various laws in the Southern states. Such persons often had to carry a certificate of freedom, secure a license to sell merchandise, and observe a curfew. Throughout the South no African American, slave or free, could vote or receive instruction. In view of these restrictions, the life of William Johnson, a free African American, was remarkable. Johnson was wealthy; he owned at least three barber shops, and kept a few slaves. White men traded with him, borrowed money from him, and sought his advice. The diary that he kept for sixteen years was passed on through his family. In 1938 it was entrusted to two historians, and in 1951 it was published as William Johnson's Natchez. *The portion reprinted here deals with events of the years 1835–1837.*

Source: *William Johnson's Natchez: The Anti-Bellum Diary of a Free Negro,* William R. Hogan and Edwin A. Davis, eds., Baton Rouge, 1951, pp. 71-167.

Oct. 30, 1835. Race between Fanny Kemble & Redd Mariah — 2 Miles and Repeate — $2000 aside — Redd Mariah made 4 or five very bad starts — When they did start F. K. was held up No start Mariah ran two miles Out The 2d start they had Mariah Jumped the fence and threw the Boy — she did not Run for it. The money was given up to Fanny Kemble — My opinion was that Red Mariah would have won the Money — Rouland & a Mr. Lupton fights Luton Bruised him very much and had him Down for a ½ minute. Rouland Resiled with him & threw him & the fall Broke his Leg in someway or other.

31 I Loaned Dr. Benbrook $3.00 I went to the Race track First Race between Mr. Rich. Harrisons Little Black Rachel Jackson & a grey mare of Mr Hocket Woods. Bets were all in favor of Rachel Jackson — Single Dash of a mile. The grey or Mary won the Race with perfect Ease beating the other about 60 or 80 feet — Second Race Mr. H. Woods bay Colt & Big Indian, 2 miles Out Won by big Indian about 40 or fifty yards — I did bet one Dollar on Rachel Jackson with a Stranger & I bet one on the bay Colt against Indian — also with the Stranger, & ten Dollars with Mr. Saml. Gosien — Lost all — A Mr Simington

Died at the Forks of the Road. He was a Negro trader. I paid Mr Barlow $3.75 for the Hyre 3 days of Ben. . . .

Nov. 3 Mr. Hough Leaves this place for New Orleans on S. B. Chester, I sent a Dayly paper & a Letter to Jas Miller — He Directs me to Collect the money that he Owes me from his partner Mr Skeggs — Mr Bledsoe Orders a wig to be made very Light Hair — Finds William at Mr Parkers Kitchen with his Girls Struck him with the whip 1st and then with the stick He ran home and I followed him there and whiped him well for it, having often told him about going Down there — He then Comes Out on Bill Nix and Seys that he Bought five finger Rings &c.

4 I took Bill Nix and gave him a whiping. He then Confessed that he had taken the Key of Side Bourd which unlocked Mothers trunk and that he had got money frequently to the amount of Eight or ten Dollars He had bought a finger Ring of Cockarill & Surie, cost $3.00, a whip from Mr Spielmans Zack, cost 1.00, a pair of Boots from Middleton, cost $2.50 He paid John for a pair of Pantaloons His Mother was greatly Hurt at the Conduct of Her Degraded Son — Mr Bledsoe teling Mr. Bradley that Capt Myres after having Settled with the owners of the Boat and given them a Receipt in full for the money that they Owed him he went to New Orleans and Collected money to the amount of a thousand Dollars and kept it by saying the Boat owed Him

5 The Dayly Paper anoncees the Result of the Election Col Bingaman & Mr McMurran, Representatives, Mr Chambers, Shreriff. Miss Sarai Newman gets married to a Mr Foster of Woodville, a merchant — I paid Phill $3.00 for water Out of the pond for seven Days — Mr Duolon paid me for two months shaving $2.00 I paid Mr Mellen five Dollars for One years Subscription to the Weekly Courier & Journal for Mr Jas Miller — Mr Smith paid me for

One months Shaving 1.50 I paid Mr Bledsoes Boy $11 for 2 Gunea pigs

6 I paid $2.50 for a Bundle of Shingles. The Citizens went Out to the Race track in search of the Gamblers; the Brought in Elick Piper from Mr Mardice's place — Had a meeting at the Court House for the purpose of trying him — Gridley took him from them and put him to Jail — Twas their Intention to have whipd him — Mr Bray puts up his new sign. His men all got Drunk Made a great noise.

7 Col Bingaman & Mr Chambers gives a Dinner at Mr Parkers. Underwood & John Mason fights. Underwood whiped him very Easy — I paid Mr S. Cotten $27.00 the amount Due to Dr Hunt, Deceased. I Loaned Mr Whiting $8.00 pd Mr Harrison Black mare runs a mile against Sorril mare Called the Sumpter Filly — Black M. won the Race very Easy, by 30 yards — Cryzers horse ran against the one Eyed Sorrel mare The mare won the race by Eleven feet. They ran 750 yards

8 The Fencibles [Natchez, Miss., volunteer militia] Left Here for Vicksburg on Bourd of the Steam Boat Ponchartrain. They Left here about 1 Oclock in the Evening — 31 in Number — Gave William $2.00 Stephen pd me $12.00

9 I Commenced to pull Down the part of the Stable to Rebuild it up again — Paid $10.00 for 2000 Shingles — The Jone Left here at Night taking 4 or 5 more of the Fencibles to Vicksburg Mr Massy Came to buy my Land for Mr Flecheo — Mr Newman pays me $5.00 that he Borrowed Tuesday 27th day of October I Loaned Dr Benbrook $2.00

10 Mrs. Merricks House on Main street Sold at Auction and was Bought by Abby for five thousand & Eighty Dollars — Hyred ——— To Drive for me — 1.50 per Day — Receid a Letter by Greenburg Wade for [from] Orleans. Mrs Miller wishes me to purchase a house & Lot Down there at $3500. Mr F. Rowland pays me $50.00 the ballance of the money Due me from Mr Robert for house Rent. I stoped Stephen in to work for Mr Rowes from 9 Oclock untill Night, tho he did not work any.

11 Maj. Miller Came to Natchez. Mr Harden took my Letter to Mrs Miller I sent $15 to get a wig for Mr Bledsoe — My mule ranaway I sent John & Stephen down to Ragleys place for him. They Could not find him Mr Rowes has my old Roan Horse all Day — I gave Mr Jackson Five Dollars. He commenced work after Dinner, worked untill night — Mr Whiting paid me $8.00 that he Borrowed on Saturday November 7th

12 Mc & myself went out to Parson Connelly Sale to Look at his Cows. They were all Dry — Stephen & John went to Rayley place for my mule Came home with him at 11 A. M. Oclock Mr M. Williams sends his sick Boy to Bourd until he returns from Red River I made Maj Dunbar a present of 2 guinea pigs

13 Bought a Sorrel Horse — Rob. Roy — at Auction for $106 cash — I thought Mc would take him when I Bought him and when he came up I asked him if wanted to buy a Horse and he told no, that food was too high — I then told him to take him to his stable and keep him to ride for his feed — He then said as above stated that corn was too high — I then proposed for him ride him on Sunday — He said no that he was agoing to ride Mr Browns Horse to try him — Mr Gilbert auditer &c. came down from Jackson — Fencibles Returned from Vicksburg They Looked very well. Higly pleased with the citizens of that place would not suffer them to pay for anything what every — Mr Barber Returned from the North — Mother Buys Mary and her Child from Mr Murcherson for $800.00. . . .

22 I gave old French $2.00 I did not see old Mc the whole day. Two Irishman commenced boxing in fun and then began to fight. The one kicked the other in such a seviere maner that he broke his gaul. His Head was bruised also — He Died in 8 or ten hours after the fight His name was Russell He was Killed by,———. He was put in Jail on Monday 23d inst

23 Mr Bledsoe gets the wig that I sent to Orleans for He pays me $15.00 for it. Tis what it cost me — I Loaned Mr. Whiting $10 I told Mr Flecheo that he could take my Land at 8 dollars per acre. I Loaned Mr Gilbert my Horse to wride out to Col Bingamans — Northern mail arrived. Brings News to Gilbert that Linch was Elected by small majority — Old Fletcheo Gets Drunk and came in the shop Play, Tour de Nesle or the Chamber of Death Margariett of Bergundy, Mrs Lyons Farce, dead Shot.

24 I Loaned Dr Hubbard One hundred and 75 dollars — Mr Baynton arrives here. The Little Dwarf arrives here. The play is Hunch Back. Master Walter by Mr Parsons — A Bear belonging [to] Mr Phiffs Killed a Little Yellow Child Down at Mr Parkers Hotel They had to shoot him Dead to Loose him — Mc takes his horse home to his own stable — Mr Pulling and Milne has a sort of a fight about the moving of some coal. Mr P. threw a Hatchet at Mr M. and it mist him Mr M attempted to get a gun Down to shoot. . . .

May 19, 1836. The Volunteers from Madison County Left here for Texas. To Day it was that I Found Old Pagg. in possession of a Black man belonging Mr Barber. The Boys name was Patrick, I Brought him Out of his yard with the Saddle, Bridle, Martingale and all on the Horse. I got on him and rode home on him, After having showed the Horse to his master he promised me that he would pay any Damage that I seen proper to Charge him for the Horse

20 Mr Barber sells the Black man Patrick that stoled my Horse, he Sold him on that account alone. To Day the Old Gentleman that Lost his Wife by her Runing away with a Big whiskered man by the name of Clayton, the old man swears that he will kill Clayton on the first site Mr Patterson paid me $10 that was due me from the Vicksburgh Volunteers — To day I Bot at Sorias Auction 12 pair of Pantaloons at 94 cents per pair. I gave John 1 pair, Charles 1 pair, Bill Nix 1 pair, Steven 1 pair, Louis 1 pair. . . .

June 3 I Bot Moses from a man by the name of William Good, at Least I Bot him at auction under the Hammer for four Hundred Dollars cash — I Bot also 2 Boxes of wine at 2.87½ per Box and 5 small Boxes of shaving soap, 43 cents per Box Mr Samuel Davis sells his Family Residence to Mr Gildart for twenty thousand Dollars. No Sail I Bot of Mr Chew all the Birds that Mr Grayson Left here and their Cages also for ten Dollars Cash. . . .

22 Buisness only Tolerably Brisk, Mr McGetrick makes a Bet with Mr Cobler to day of $25 that his Brown Horse would beat Mr Mardices Little Bay mare a ½ mile Race They gave me the $50 to hold as there stakes The winner was to have the fifty Dollars — I Loaned Dr Hubbard $400 to be paid on Monday; Some Talk about town of Lynching—————— the Painter for taking off Dr ———s Daughter.

23 Dr Hubbard pd me $100, that being a part of Four Hundred that I Loaned him yesterday — He prescribed for John 20 grs of Calamal & 5 grs of James Powders News to day that fifteen thousand Mexicans were Marching towards Texas and that six hundred thousand Dollars were subscribed by the Mexicans in One Single Day

24 Roberson and Dr Hogg has a kind of a fight, old Dr Hogg made him Travell pretty fast. Particulars are those, Roberson Owed the Dr 12 dollars for Medical Services. The Dr gave his account to Whiting to Collect for him so he presented the Acct. to Roberson & R. said that he was not the man, so Dr suied on it, & Robs. Came to

his office to abuse him about it, and the old Dr told him to Leave his office. The Dr and him came to Blowes, and the Dr struck him with a chair & R. ran in the Street and struck him in the Breast with a Brick, then ran up Street as Hard as he could split and the old Dr after him So Roberson run throuh Thistles Stable and came out at the Back side of the Stable and went Home The Dr & Maj Miller went around to Robs House Dr went in & struck him with his cane and R. caught the stick and the sword came out, and the Dr would have killed him if his arm had not been caught by Mr Ross — Roberson then Broke and run as hard as he could split to the Jail, and went in for Safe Keeping — In time of the fight Robs Brother Struck Maj Miller on the head with a Brick Bat and then Run and the old Maj after him as hard as he could split The Maj stumbled and fell and as he fell he made a cut at Robison and Cut him in the Butt Mr. ————— gave Dr ——— the plain Talk about His Daughter &c.

26 Mc and myself wrode Out as far as the Race track. Good many young men from town were Out there Drunk Mr Debins, Mr Abona, Mr ———, Mr S Davis, Mr Hyram Hanchet and a good many Others

July 2 Tarlton Brings my mule

4 Big marching about town The Huzars turned Out for the first time in the streets on parade — the Fencibles and the Mechanicks also — Big Dinner at Mr West tavern — Mr Calmes Died this morning Early after having been to Market, He Broke a Blood vessell and Died before Dr Hogg could get to see him

5 Mr Calmes, the Jailer, was Buried to Day by the Masons, Large procession — I sent my mule up to Spraigue & Howell to be sold but they did not sell her There were no purchasers Little William Winston came to stay with me to Lern the Barbers trade. . . .

Aug. 29 I herd to day that Last Saturday

when the Bunker Hill Left here that there was on Bourd of her 100 men Bound for Texas Comanded by a Capt Williams — The Boat Landed at Peter Littles place to wood & those men went on shore and Robbed his Hen Roos and then whiped his Negro Boy — The old man his self then Came Out and they partly knocked him Down and then pouned him pretty severely — they then Left and went on Bourd of the Steam Boat taking with them all the old Fellows Chickens & Turkeys — To Day a Boy belonging to Mr S. Davis was hung on the other side of the River His name was Nim Rod — He was Hung for Killing the overseer by the name of Levels I believe, Early this Evening Mr Vannerson gets married to old Mrs Purnell. . . .

Nov. 27 I got up this morning before Day and took my gun Out to Scotts old Field and put her under a Log and Came home I got back to town at Day Break — I Rode Out in the afternoon, took my gun from under the Log and commenced Shooting Crows. I Killed 2 crows at One Shot and I Killed four at four other Single Shots, making in all Six and I Shot 1 Rice Bird, 1 gold Finch & 1 Tom Tit — Bill Nix & Simpson was with me, I then when in the old Field, made the Boys Take a Race Charles wrode my Little mare & Bill Nix wrde my Sorrill Horse Rob Roy — the Horse could Out Run her very Easy — I did not get in untill night

28 To Day we had Bloody work for a while in the streets up at Throckmortons Corner. Last night up at Mrs Rowans Bourding House several gentlemen were in conversation about a Duel that was fought in South Carolina. When Mr Charles Stewart stated that those Gentlement that fought actually fought with Bullits, Mr Dalhgreen Said that they must fought with paper Bullits — Mr C. Stewart then Said if any man would say that they fought with paper Bullits that he is a Damed Lyar and a Dd Scoundrel & a Dmd Coward — this was at the Supper Table Mr Dalhgreen Jumped

up and Slaped Mr C. Stewarts Cheek one very hard slapp

They were then parted so young Stewart told him that they would settle it in the morning — So this morning young Stewart took a Stand up at Carpenters Drug Store for the purpose of making the attackt upon Dalhgreen as he would be going to the Bank — Dr Hubbard at the Request of his Brother went up to Carpenters with young Stewart to see him Out in the affair Elick Stewart said that he would not take any part in the affair and he took a stand over on Sorias Corner — and as Dalhgreen past the Door Stewart steped up to him and told him that now was to Settle therr Dispute and at the Same time Struck Mr Dalhgreen with his stick, Mr D then Struck him Back with an umberralla — Stewart Struck him with the Stick again —

Mr D. then steped Back and Drew a Pistol and Fired at Mr S. and missed Him — Mr S. then Drew and Fired and the Ball Lodged under the arm in the Left Side of Mr Dalhgreen, Mr D. then steped in at Throckmortons Store S steped in at the Door but finding that D. had another Pistol he steped Back and stood in the caseing of the Door D. then advanced on him, shot Him on Left Side of the face on the Temple or uper hinge of the Jaw Bone and the instant the Ball took Effect he Droped on his Knees and Fell over on the pavement as Dead, so Dead that he Barely Breathed. At the instant he fell Mr Elick Stewart ran up and struck D. with his fist D then advanced on him with an Empty Pistol and in doing so Dr Hubbard shoved Him Back, E. S. Drew a Bouye Knife and commenced cuting at him — Mr D. had no weapon at this time and was fighting with his naked hands and Mr E. S. with the Knife —

It was one of the gamest fights that we have Ever had in Our City before — E. S cut him twice over the Head and cut his Little finger nearly off and split his hand pretty Bad Mr R. Bledsoe and Mr Hewit has a small fist fight. After a Blow or two past, Mr Bledsoe went and got his Pistols. I am told as Soon as Mr Hewit saw the pistol he Said whoorer and ran Down the street and got in a Store and Mr Bledsoe made him retract what he had Said in writing before he would Let him go — this he did from fear

29 To Day I went up to the Agricultural Bank and Received in cash Seventeen Hundred and Fifty Dollars being the amount of a note that I Received from Flecheaux given him by Mr R. Bledsoe for Land that I sold to Flecheaux which Said Flecheaux Sold to Mr R. Bledsoe — I went to day around to Dr Hubbards office to shave young Mr Stewarts head, he was quite ill — I then went on up to Mrs Rowans to Shave Dr Dalhgreens Beard off — he was very Comfortably Situated and in a thriving condition I made a mistake in this. Col. Bingaman Sent Steven in town to me to day and instead of Coming in he went under the Hill and got Drunk I Supose; I found him on a Dray and I sent Dr Hogg to see what was the matter with him and the Dr pronounced him Drunk at first site. . . .

Dec. 8 To Day about Dinner they had had a Learg quantity of Gentlemen were on the Bluff to See the car Start, They had put Down about 40 feet of Rails and had put on a Car, and they were a Runing it Backwards and fowards on the Small Road that they had constructed, There were present Gov. Quitman, Mr Vanison, W. P. Mellon, R. Fields, T. Jones, W Chambers, Rice, Holton, Capt Cotten and a greate many more To Day I Bot the improve-ments that Flecho put on my House, that is the window and Several other things and the Counter also — He is to Leave the House on the 16th of this month without Fail — Wheathers Bot the House that he Lives in at auction to Day, It Sold for 17 hundred Dollars I had to whip Bill Winston and Bix Nix for fighting in the shop to night when gentleman was in the Shop. I had to give it to them Both.

9 I received of Mr Proctor to Day thirty Barrels of coal, price 1 Dollar per Barrell Mc He got 20 Barrells of the same man, I gave the Carpenters to day $2 to Buy Liquor with, The[y] commenced puting on the weather Bourding to day for the first. I had to give William a few cracks this Evening for insolent Language whilst Cutting a gentlemans Hair, it was at dinner time. . . .

March 6, 1837. Col A L. Bingaman Received a challenge from Col Osburn Claibourne To fight. The Col. Came in very Early this morning and got shaved He seemed to be wraped up in thought, he had nothing to say — The Roumer Says that they are to fight with Riffles — I am very Sorry to heare that they are agoing to fight — I only wish that they may be preventd from fighting for I Like them Both — Col. Clabourne has 40 of his Slaves put up to be Sold at auction, Report Seys they are sold for debt Lawyer Baker has old Armstead in Jail and gave him to day One Hundred & fifty Lashes He Seys that he stoled four Hundred Dollars from him — Mr Duffield was put in Jail Last night for debt.

"Daniel Boone on the Banks of Great Osage Lake"; oil by Thomas Cole

AN UNCERTAIN VISION

American painting began to find itself in the late 1820s and '30s. Starting with Thomas Cole, a fully articulated native school developed with its philosophical base in the Romantic's passionate love of nature. Cole proclaimed that "all nature here is new to art" and found the appropriate subject for that art in the Catskill Mountains and the Hudson River Valley. In style, the Hudson River School, as it came to be called, combined painstaking detail with a poetic infusion of light and warmth. But even Cole was restless in this new-found vision. He worried about being merely a "leaf painter" and turned often to the allegorical paintings that he regarded as his best work. And, while few of the Hudson River painters confined themselves to romantic landscapes, the confidence and clear vision of these paintings inspired the final break from portraiture and began to awaken a public taste for imaginative painting. Painters still went to Europe to learn their craft and patrons of the arts were still few in number, but after Cole American painters were less insecure about their art.

"The Course of Empire"

In turning to ambitious classical and Biblical allegories even while he was claiming nature as central to American experience, Cole was expressing the ambivalence so general in American art. To him, landscapes lacked scope and depth. An allegorical series such as "The Course of Empire" seemed more profound than simple landscapes. In the "Empire" series, the opulence of civilization is pictured as an intrusion on nature that soon passes. Perhaps Cole was commenting also on the American empire, which, in 1836, was just entering a period of violent expansion.

Paintings in the series "Course of Empire" by Thomas Cole. (Above) "Savage State" or "Commencement of Empire"; (below) "Arcadian" or "Pastoral State"

(Top) "The Consummation of Empire"; (center) "Destruction"; (bottom) "Desolation"

(Above) "Expulsion from Garden of Eden" by Thomas Cole; (left) Thomas Cole; portrait by Thomas Cummings

"Montevideo, Summer Home of Daniel Wadsworth," by Thomas Cole

"Dismissal of School on an October Afternoon" by Henry Inman

Henry Inman

(Below) Self-portrait by Henry Inman; (bottom right) "Mumble the Peg" by Inman

Henry Inman (1801-1846) began as an apprentice to John Wesley Jarvis and made his main reputation as a portraitist. As a founder of the National Academy of Design, however, his career touched several aspects of American painting, without being central to any of them. He painted numerous landscapes but also produced genre scenes in the mode that later became widely popular. He died while working on a series of historical paintings commissioned for the U.S. Capitol.

(Above) "In the Catskills" by Asher B. Durand; (below) Portrait of Durand by an anonymous artist

A. B. Durand

Asher B. Durand (1796-1886), after an early career as an engraver, became one of the most successful painters of the Hudson River School. His landscapes, which often look out into brilliant summer sunlight from cool mountain glens, show the school in its most idyllic mood. In addition, Durand remained the most skilled engraver of his time and his engraved copies of landscapes by Cole and other artists were widely reproduced.

"The Capture of Major Andre" (above) and "Kindred Spirits" by Asher B. Durand. The latter painting, a memorial to Thomas Cole, shows Cole with William Cullen Bryant in a Catskill ravine

"Audubon the Naturalist"; painting by his son, John

Audubon

John James Audubon (1785-1851) was born in Santo Domingo, went with his father to France in 1789, and came to America in 1803. The only continuous thread in his unsteady, wandering life was ornithology. Until publication began of his "Birds of America," he was constantly in debt and had failed in several business ventures and in repeated efforts to have his bird pictures published. Despite criticism of his work both as art and as science, the scope and pictorial interest of "Birds of America" insure Audubon's place as a leading naturalist.

(Above) "Snowshoe Hare"; (below) "Osprey and Otter," both by Audubon

(Above left) "Bald Eagle"; (above right) "Passenger Pigeon"; (below left) "Cardinal"; (below right) "Whooping Crane". Watercolors by Audubon painted during the 1820s for his work "The Birds of America"

"The Peaceable Kingdom" by Edward Hicks

Edward Hicks' Kingdom

Edward Hicks (1780-1849) was a sign painter and Quaker preacher in Pennsylvania whose individualistic style has given him a special place among primitive painters. His Biblical scenes and the painting "Peaceable Kingdom," which he recreated over 100 times, embody the popular image of Quaker life in the early 19th century. However, Hicks and his cousin Elias were prominent in a separatist movement within the church that somewhat belies the tranquility of his paintings.

"Noah's Ark" by Hicks, 1846

1836

46.

THOMAS COLE: American Scenery

Thomas Cole was born in England and came to America in 1819, at the age of eighteen, and learned to paint from an itinerant portraitist in Ohio. Cole imitated his teacher's style of life, but without much success until he reached New York and displayed some of his landscapes in the window of a restaurant. They caught the eye of some of the cognoscenti of the day, and Cole's career was made. His romantic conception of the American landscape had an influence on his time and his fellows that was considerable, and he was a founder of the famous Hudson River School of painting. His "Essay on American Scenery," reprinted below, expressed the attitude of the group.

Source: *American Monthly Magazine*, January 1836.

THE ESSAY, WHICH IS HERE OFFERED, is a mere sketch of an almost illimitable subject — American scenery; and in selecting the theme the writer placed more confidence in its overflowing richness than in his own capacity for treating it in a manner worthy of its vastness and importance.

It is a subject that to every American ought to be of surpassing interest; for, whether he beholds the Hudson mingling waters with the Atlantic, explores the central wilds of this vast continent, or stands on the margin of the distant Oregon, he is still in the midst of American scenery — it is his own land; its beauty, its magnificence, its sublimity, all are his; and how undeserving of such a birthright if he can turn toward it an unobserving eye, an unaffected heart!

Before entering into the proposed subject in which I shall treat more particularly of the scenery of the Northern and Eastern states, I shall be excused for saying a few words on the advantages of cultivating a taste for scenery, and for exclaiming against the apathy with which the beauties of external nature are regarded by the great mass, even of our refined community.

It is generally admitted that the liberal arts tend to soften our manners; but they do more: they carry with them the power to mend our hearts.

Poetry and painting sublime and purify thought by grasping the past, the present, and the future; they give the mind a foretaste of its immortality, and thus prepare it for performing an exalted part amid the realities of life. And rural nature is full of the same quickening spirit; it is, in fact, the exhaustless mine from which the poet and the painter have brought such wondrous treasures — an unfailing fountain of intellectual enjoyment, where all may drink and be awakened to a deeper feeling of the works of genius and a keener perception of the beauty of our existence. For those whose days are all consumed in the low pursuits of avarice, or the gaudy frivolities of fashion, unobservant of nature's loveliness, are unconscious of the harmony of creation:

Heaven's roof to them
Is but a painted ceiling hung with
    lamps;
No more — that lights them to their
    purposes —
They wander 'loose about'; they nothing
    see,
Themselves except, and creatures like
    themselves,
Short lived, short sighted.

What to them is the page of the poet where he describes or personifies the skies, the mountains, or the streams, if those objects themselves have never awakened observation or excited pleasure? What to them is the wild Salvator Rosa or the aerial Claude Lorrain?

There is in the human mind an almost inseparable connection between the beautiful and the good, so that if we contemplate the one, the other seems present; and an excellent author has said, "It is difficult to look at any objects with pleasure — unless where it arises from brutal and tumultuous emotions — without feeling that disposition of mind which tends toward kindness and benevolence; and surely, whatever creates such a disposition, by increasing our pleasures and enjoyments, cannot be too much cultivated."

It would seem unnecessary to those who can see and feel for me to expatiate on the loveliness of verdant fields, the sublimity of lofty mountains, or the varied magnificence of the sky; but that the number of those who *seek* enjoyment in such sources is comparatively small. From the indifference with which the multitude regard the beauties of

nature, it might be inferred that she had been unnecessarily lavish in adorning this world for beings who take no pleasure in its adornment, who, in groveling pursuits, forget their glorious heritage. Why was the earth made so beautiful, or the sun so clad in glory at his rising and setting, when *all* might be unrobed of beauty without affecting the insensate multitude so they can be "lighted to their purposes"?

It *has not* been in vain — the good, the enlightened of all ages and nations have found pleasure and consolation in the beauty of the rural earth. Prophets of old retired into the solitudes of nature to wait the inspiration of heaven. It was on Mount Horeb that Elijah witnessed the mighty wind, the earthquake, and the fire; and heard the "still small voice." That voice is YET heard among the mountains! St. John preached in the desert; the wilderness is YET a fitting place to speak of God. The solitary Anchorites of Syria and Egypt, though ignorant that the busy world is man's noblest sphere of usefulness, well knew how congenial to religious musings are the pathless solitudes.

He who looks on nature with a "loving eye" cannot move from his dwelling without the salutation of beauty; even in the city the deep blue sky and the drifting clouds appeal to him. And if to escape its turmoil — if only to obtain a free horizon, land and water in the play of light and shadow yields delight — let him be transported to those favored regions where the features of the earth are more varied, or yet add the sunset, that wreath of glory daily bound around the world, and he, indeed, drinks from pleasure's purest cup. The delight such a man experiences is not merely sensual, or selfish, that passes with the occasion leaving no trace behind; but in gazing on the pure creations of the Almighty, he feels a calm, religious tone steal through his mind; and when he has turned to mingle with his fellowmen, the chords which have been struck in that sweet communion cease not to vibrate.

In what has been said I have alluded to wild and uncultivated scenery; but the cultivated must not be forgotten, for it is still more important to man in his social capacity, necessarily bringing him in contact with the cultured. It encompasses our homes and, though devoid of the stern sublimity of the wild, its quieter spirit steals tenderly into our bosoms, mingled with a thousand domestic affections and heart-touching associations — human hands have wrought, and human deeds hallowed all around.

And it is here that taste, which is the perception of the beautiful, and the knowledge of the principles on which nature works can be applied, and our dwelling places made fitting for refined and intellectual beings.

If, then, it is indeed true that the contemplation of scenery can be so abundant a source of delight and improvement, a taste for it is certainly worthy of particular cultivation; for the capacity for enjoyment increases with the knowledge of the true means of obtaining it.

In this age, when a meager utilitarianism seems ready to absorb every feeling and sentiment, and what is sometimes called improvement in its march makes us fear that the bright and tender flowers of the imagination shall all be crushed beneath its iron tramp, it would be well to cultivate the oasis that yet remains to us, and thus preserve the germs of a future and a purer system. And now, when the sway of fashion is extending widely over society, poisoning the healthful streams of true refinement and turning men from the love of simplicity and beauty to a senseless idolatry of their own follies, to lead them gently into the pleasant paths of taste would be an object worthy of the highest efforts of genius and benevolence.

The spirit of our society is to contrive but not to enjoy, toiling to produce more toil, accumulating in order to aggrandize. The pleasures of the imagination, among which the love of scenery holds a conspicuous place, will alone temper the harshness of such a state; and, like the atmosphere that softens the most rugged forms of the landscape, cast a veil of tender beauty over the asperities of life.

Did our limits permit I would endeavor more fully to show how necessary to the complete appreciation of the fine arts is the study of scenery, and how conducive to our happiness and well-being is that study and those arts; but I must now proceed to the proposed subject of this essay — American scenery!

There are those who through ignorance or prejudice strive to maintain that American scenery possesses little that is interesting or truly beautiful; that it is rude without picturesqueness and monotonous without sublimity; that being destitute of those vestiges of antiquity, whose associations so strongly affect the mind, it may not be compared with European scenery. But from whom do these opinions come? From those who have read of European scenery, of Grecian mountains, and Italian skies, and never troubled themselves to look at their own; and from those traveled ones whose eyes were never opened to the beauties of nature until they beheld foreign lands, and when those lands faded from the sight were again closed and forever, disdaining to destroy their transatlantic impressions by the observation of the less fashionable and unfamed American scenery. Let such persons shut themselves up in their narrow shell of prejudice — I hope they are few — and the community, increasing in intelligence, will know better how to appreciate the treasures of their own country.

I am by no means desirous of lessening in your estimation the glorious scenes of the Old World — that ground which has been the great theater of human events; those mountains, woods, and streams made sacred in our minds by heroic deeds and immortal song, over which time and genius have suspended an imperishable halo. No! But I would have it remembered that nature has shed over *this* land beauty and magnificence, and although the character of its scenery may differ from the Old World's, yet inferiority must not therefore be inferred; for though American scenery is destitute of many of those circumstances that give value to the European, still it has features, and glorious ones, unknown to Europe.

A very few generations have passed away since this vast tract of the American continent, now the United States, rested in the shadow of primeval forests, whose gloom was peopled by savage beasts and scarcely less savage men, or lay in those wide grassy plains called prairies:

> The Gardens of the Desert, these
> The unshorn fields, boundless and
> beautiful.

And, although an enlightened and increasing people have broken in upon the solitude, and with activity and power wrought changes that seem magical, yet the most distinctive, and perhaps the most impressive, characteristic of American scenery is its wildness.

It is the most distinctive because in civilized Europe the primitive features of scenery have long since been destroyed or modified — the extensive forests that once overshadowed a great part of it have been felled; rugged mountains have been smoothed and impetuous rivers turned from their courses to accommodate the tastes and necessities of a dense population; the once tangled wood is now a grassy lawn; the turbulent brook, a navigable stream; crags that could not be removed have been crowned with towers; and the rudest valleys tamed by the plow.

And to this cultivated state our Western world is fast approaching; but nature is still predominant, and there are those who regret that with the improvements of cultivation the sublimity of the wilderness should pass away. For those scenes of solitude from which the hand of nature has never been lifted affect the mind with a more deep-toned emotion than aught which the hand of man has touched. Amid them the consequent associations are of God the Creator; they are His undefiled works, and the mind is cast into the contemplation of eternal things.

As mountains are the most conspicuous objects in landscape, they will take the precedence in what I may say on the elements of American scenery.

It is true that in the eastern part of this continent there are no mountains that vie in altitude with the snow-crowned Alps, that the Alleghenies and the Catskills are in no point higher than 5,000 feet; but this is no inconsiderable height. Snowdon in Wales and Ben Nevis in Scotland are not more lofty; and in New Hampshire, which has been called the Switzerland of the United States, the White Mountains almost pierce the region of perpetual snow. The Alleghenies are, in general, heavy in form; but the Catskills, although not broken into abrupt angles like the most picturesque mountains of Italy, have varied, undulating, and exceedingly beautiful outlines. They heave from the valley of the Hudson like the subsiding billows of the ocean after a storm.

American mountains are generally clothed to the summit by dense forests, while those of Europe are mostly bare, or merely tinted by grass or heath. It may be that the mountains of Europe are on this account more picturesque in form, and there is a grandeur in their nakedness; but in the gorgeous garb of the American mountains there is more than an equivalent. And when the woods "have put their glory on," as an American poet has beautifully said, the purple heath and yellow furze of Europe's mountains are in comparison but as the faint secondary rainbow to the primal one.

But in the mountains of New Hampshire there is a union of the picturesque, the sublime, and the magnificent. There the bare peaks of granite, broken and desolate, cradle the clouds, while the valleys and broad bases of the mountains rest under the shadow of noble and varied forests; and the traveler who passes the Sandwich Range on his way to the White Mountains, of which it is a spur, cannot but acknowledge that, although in some regions of the globe nature has wrought on a more stupendous scale, yet she has nowhere so completely married together grandeur and loveliness. There he sees the sublime melting into the beautiful, the savage tempered by the magnificent.

I will now speak of another component of scenery without which every landscape is defective — it is water. Like the eye in the human countenance, it is a most expressive feature. In the unrippled lake, which mirrors all surrounding objects, we have the expression of tranquillity and peace; in the rapid stream, the headlong cataract, that of turbulence and impetuosity.

In this great element of scenery, what land is so rich? I would not speak of the Great Lakes, which are in fact inland seas, possessing some of the attributes of the ocean, though destitute of its sublimity; but of those smaller lakes, such as Lake George, Champlain, Winnipisiogee, Otsego, Seneca, and a hundred others, that stud like gems the bosom of this country. There is one delightful quality in nearly all these lakes — the purity and transparency of the water. In speaking of scenery it might seem unnecessary to mention this; but independent of the pleasure that we all have in beholding pure water, it is a circumstance which contributes greatly to the beauty of landscape; for the reflections of surrounding objects, trees, mountains, sky, are most perfect in the clearest water; and the most perfect is the most beautiful.

I would rather persuade you to visit the "Holy Lake," the beautiful "Horican" [Lake George], than attempt to describe its scenery; to behold you rambling on its storied shores, where its southern expanse is spread, begemmed with isles of emerald and curtained by green, receding hills; or to see you gliding over its bosom, where the steep and rugged mountains approach from either side, shadowing with black precipices the innumerable islets, some of which bearing a solitary tree, others a group of two or three or a "goodly company," seem to have been sprinkled over the smiling deep in nature's frolic hour. These scenes are classic; history and genius have hallowed them. War's shrill clarion once waked the echoes from these now silent hills; the pen of a living master has portrayed them in the pages of romance; and they are worthy of the admiration of the enlightened and the graphic hand of genius.

Though differing from Lake George, Winnipisiogee resembles it in multitudinous and uncounted islands. Its mountains do not stoop to the water's edge, but through varied screens of forest may be seen ascending the sky softened by the blue haze of distance; on the one hand rise the Gunstock Mountains; on the other, the dark Ossipees, while above and far beyond, rear the "cloud capt" peaks of the Sandwich and White Mountains.

I will not fatigue [you] with a vain attempt to describe the lakes that I have named, but would turn your attention to those exquisitely beautiful lakes that are so numerous in the Northern states, and particularly in New Hampshire. In character they are truly and peculiarly American. I know nothing in Europe which they resemble. The famous lakes of Albano and Nemi and the small and exceedingly picturesque lakes of Great Britain may be compared in size but are dissimilar in almost every other respect. Embosomed in the primitive forest and sometimes overshadowed by huge mountains, they are the chosen places of tranquillity; and when the deer issues from the surrounding woods to drink the cool waters, he beholds his own image as in a polished mirror; the flight of the eagle can be seen in the lower sky; and if a leaf falls, the circling undulations chase each other to the shores unvexed by contending tides.

There are two lakes of this description situated in a wild mountain gorge called the

Franconia Notch in New Hampshire. They lie within a few hundred feet of each other, but are remarkable as having no communication — one being the source of the wild Amonoosuck, the other of the Pemigiwasset. Shut in by stupendous mountains which rest on crags that tower more than 1,000 feet above the water, whose rugged brows and shadowy breaks are clothed by dark and tangled woods, they have such an aspect of deep seclusion, of utter and unbroken solitude, that, when standing on their brink, a lonely traveler, I was overwhelmed with an emotion of the sublime such as I have rarely felt. It was not that the jagged precipices were lofty, that the encircling woods were of the dimmest shade, or that the waters were profoundly deep, but that over all — rocks, wood, and water — brooded the spirit of repose and the silent energy of nature stirred the soul to its inmost depths.

I would not be understood that these lakes are always tranquil; but that tranquillity is their great characteristic. There are times when they take a far different expression; but in scenes like these the richest chords are those struck by the gentler hand of nature.

And now I must turn to another of the beautifiers of the earth, the waterfall, which in the same object at once presents to the mind the beautiful but apparently incongruous idea of fixedness and motion — a single existence in which we perceive unceasing change and everlasting duration. The waterfall may be called the voice of the landscape; for, unlike the rocks and woods which utter sounds as the passive instruments played on by the elements, the waterfall strikes its own chords, and rocks and mountains re-echo in rich unison. And this is a land abounding in cataracts; in these Northern states where shall we turn and not find them? Have we not Kaaterskill, Trenton, the Flume, the Genesee, stupendous Niagara, and a hundred others, named and nameless ones, whose exceeding beauty must be acknowledged when the hand of taste shall point them out?

In the Kaaterskill we have a stream, diminutive indeed, but throwing itself headlong over a fearful precipice, into a deep gorge of the densely wooded mountains, and possessing a singular feature in the vast arched cave that extends beneath and behind the cataract. At Trenton there is a chain of waterfalls of remarkable beauty, where the foaming waters, shadowed by steep cliffs, break over rocks of architectural formation, and tangled and picturesque trees mantle abrupt precipices, which it would be easy to imagine crumbling and "time disparting towers."

And Niagara! that wonder of the world! — where the sublime and beautiful are bound together in an indissoluble chain. In gazing on it we feel as though a great void had been filled in our minds; our conceptions expand, we become a part of what we behold! At our feet the floods of a thousand rivers are poured out, the contents of vast inland seas. In its volume we conceive immensity; in its course, everlasting duration; in its impetuosity, uncontrollable power. These are the elements of its sublimity. Its beauty is garlanded around in the varied hues of the water, in the spray that ascends the sky, and in that unrivaled bow which forms a complete cincture round the unresting floods.

The river scenery of the United States is a rich and boundless theme. The Hudson, for natural magnificence, is unsurpassed. What can be more beautiful than the lakelike expanses of Tapaan and Haverstraw as seen from the rich orchards of the surrounding hills — hills that have a legend which has been so sweetly and admirably told that it shall not perish but with the language of the land? What can be more imposing than the precipitous Highlands, whose dark foundations have been rent to make a passage for the deep-flowing river? And, ascending still, where can be found scenes more enchanting? The lofty Catskills stand afar off, the green hills gently rising from the flood recede like steps by which we may ascend to a great temple whose pillars are those everlasting hills and whose dome is the blue, boundless vault of heaven.

The Rhine has its castled crags, its vine-clad hills, and ancient villages; the Hudson has its wooded mountains, its rugged precipices, its green, undulating shores — a natural majesty and an unbounded capacity for improvement by art. Its shores are not besprinkled with venerated ruins or the palaces of princes; but there are flourishing towns and neat villas, and the hand of taste has already been at work. Without any great stretch of the imagination we may anticipate the time when the ample waters shall reflect temple, and tower, and dome, in every variety of picturesqueness and magnificence.

In the Connecticut we behold a river that differs widely from the Hudson. Its sources are amid the wild mountains of New Hampshire; but it soon breaks into a luxuriant valley and flows for more than a hundred miles, sometimes beneath the shadow of wooded hills, and sometimes glancing through the green expanse of elm-besprinkled meadows. Whether we see it at Haverhill, Northampton, or Hartford, it still possesses that gentle aspect; and the imagination can scarcely conceive Arcadian vales more lovely or more peaceful than the valley of the Connecticut. Its villages are rural places where trees overspread every dwelling and the fields upon its margin have the richest verdure.

Nor ought the Ohio, the Susquehanna, the Potomac, with their tributaries, and a thousand others, be omitted in the rich list of the American rivers; they are a glorious brotherhood; but volumes would be insufficient for their description.

In the forest scenery of the United States, we have that which occupies the greatest space and is not the least remarkable; being primitive, it differs widely from the European. In the American forest we find trees in every stage of vegetable life and decay; the slender sapling rises in the shadow of the lofty tree, and the giant in his prime stands by the hoary patriarch of the wood. On the ground lie prostrate, decaying ranks that once waved their verdant heads in the sun and wind. These are circumstances productive of great variety and picturesqueness — green umbrageous masses, lofty and scathed trunks, contorted branches thrust athwart the sky, the moldering dead below, shrouded in moss of every hue and texture, from richer combinations than can be found in the trimmed and planted grove.

It is true that the thinned and cultivated wood offers less obstruction to the feet, and the trees throw out their branches more horizontally and are consequently more umbrageous when taken singly; but the true lover of the picturesque is seldom fatigued, and trees that grow widely apart are often heavy in form and resemble each other too much for picturesqueness. Trees are like men, differing widely in character; in sheltered spots, or under the influence of culture, they show few contrasting points; peculiarities are pruned and trained away, until there is a general resemblance. But in exposed situations, wild and uncultivated, battling with the elements and with one another for the possession of a morsel of soil, or a favoring rock to which they may cling, they exhibit striking peculiarities and sometimes grand originality.

For variety, the American forest is unrivaled; in some districts are found oaks, elms, birches, beeches, planes, pines, hemlocks, and many other kinds of trees commingled, clothing the hills with every tint of green and every variety of light and shade.

There is a peculiarity observable in some mountainous regions, where trees of a genus band together; there often may be seen a mountain whose foot is clothed with deciduous trees, while on its brow is a sable crown of pines; and sometimes belts of dark green encircle a mountain horizontally, or are stretched in well-defined lines from the summit to the base. The nature of the soil or the courses of rivulets are the causes of this variety, and it is a beautiful instance of the exhaustlessness of nature. Often where we should expect unvarying monotony, we behold a charming diversity. Time will not permit me to speak of the American forest trees individually; but I must notice the elm, that paragon of beauty and shade; the maple, with its rainbow hues; and the hemlock, the sublime of trees, which rises from the gloom of the forest like a dark and ivy-mantled tower.

There is one season when the American forest surpasses all the world in gorgeousness; that is the autumnal. Then every hill and dale is riant [pleasing] in the luxury of color; every hue is there, from the liveliest green to deepest purple, from the most golden yellow to the intensest crimson. The artist looks despairingly upon the glowing landscape, and in the Old World his truest imitations of the American forest, at this season, are called falsely bright and scenes in Fairyland.

The sky will next demand our attention. The soul of all scenery, in it are the fountains of light, and shade, and color. Whatever expression the sky takes, the features of the landscape are affected in unison, whether it be the serenity of the summer's blue or the dark tumult of the storm. It is the sky that makes the earth so lovely at sunrise and so splendid at sunset. In the one, it breathes over the earth the crystal-like ether; in the other, the liquid gold.

The climate of a great part of the United States is subject to great vicissitudes, and we complain; but nature offers a compensation. These very vicissitudes are the abundant sources of beauty. As we have the temperature of every clime, so have we the skies; we have the blue unsearchable depths of the northern sky; we have the upheaped thunderclouds of the Torrid Zone, fraught with gorgeousness and sublimity; we have the silver haze of England and the golden

atmosphere of Italy. And if he who has traveled and observed the skies of other climes will spend a few months on the banks of the Hudson, he must be constrained to acknowledge that for variety and magnificence American skies are unsurpassed. Italian skies have been lauded by every tongue and sung by every poet, and who will deny their wonderful beauty? At sunset the serene arch is filled with alchemy that transmutes mountains, and streams, and temples into living gold.

But the American summer never passes without many sunsets that might vie with the Italian, and many still more gorgeous, that seem peculiar to this clime.

Look at the heavens when the thundershower has passed, and the sun stoops behind the western mountains. There the low purple clouds hang in festoons around the steeps; in the higher heaven are crimson bands interwoven with feathers of gold, fit for the wings of angels; and still above is spread that interminable field of ether, whose color is too beautiful to have a name.

It is not in the summer only that American skies are beautiful; for the winter evening often comes robed in purple and gold, and in the westering sun the iced groves glitter as beneath a shower of diamonds; and through the twilight heaven innumerable stars shine with a purer light than summer ever knows.

I will now venture a few remarks on what has been considered a grand defect in American scenery: the want of associations, such as arise amid the scenes of the Old World.

We have many a spot as umbrageous as Vallombrosa and as picturesque as the solitudes of Vaucluse; but Milton and Petrarch have not hallowed them by their footsteps and immortal verse. He who stands on Mont Albano and looks down on ancient Rome has his mind peopled with the gigantic associations of the storied past; but he who stands on the mounds of the West, the most venerable remains of American antiquity, *may* experience the emotion of the sublime, but it is the sublimity of a shoreless ocean unislanded by the recorded deeds of man.

Yet American scenes are not destitute of historical and legendary associations. The great struggle for freedom has sanctified many a spot, and many a mountain, stream, and rock has its legend, worthy of poet's pen or the painter's pencil. But American associations are not so much of the past as of the present and the future. Seated on a pleasant knoll, look down into the bosom of that secluded valley, begirt with wooded hills. Through those enameled meadows and wide, waving fields of grain a silver stream winds lingeringly along; here, seeking the green shade of trees, there, glancing in the sunshine. On its banks are rural dwellings shaded by elms and garlanded by flowers; from yonder dark mass of foliage the village spire beams like a star. You see no ruined tower to tell of outrage, no gorgeous temple to speak of ostentation; but freedom's offspring — peace, security, and happiness — dwell there, the spirits of the scene.

On the margin of that gentle river the village girls may ramble unmolested, and the glad schoolboy, with hook and line, pass his bright holiday. Those neat dwellings, unpretending to magnificence, are the abodes of plenty, virtue, and refinement. And in looking over the yet uncultivated scene, the mind's eye may see far into futurity; where the wolf roams, the plough shall glisten; on the gray crag shall rise temple and tower. Mighty deeds shall be done in the now pathless wilderness, and poets yet unborn shall sanctify the soil.

It was my intention to attempt a description of several districts remarkable for their picturesqueness and truly American charac-

ter; but I fear to trespass longer on your time and patience. Yet I cannot but express my sorrow that the beauty of such landscapes is quickly passing away; the ravages of the axe are daily increasing; the most noble scenes are made desolate, and oftentimes with a wantonness and barbarism scarcely credible in a civilized nation. The wayside is becoming shadeless, and another generation will behold spots, now rife with beauty, desecrated by what is called improvement; which, as yet, generally destroys nature's beauty without substituting that of art. This is a regret rather than a complaint; such is the road society has to travel. It may lead to refinement in the end; but the traveler who sees the place of rest close at hand dislikes the road that has so many unnecessary windings.

I will now conclude in the hope that, though feebly urged, the importance of cultivating a taste for scenery will not be forgotten. Nature has spread for us a rich and delightful banquet. Shall we turn from it? We are still in Eden; the wall that shuts us out of the garden is our own ignorance and folly. We should not allow the poet's words to be applicable to us:

Deep in rich pasture do thy flocks
    complain?
Not so; but to their master is denied
To share the sweet serene.

May we at times turn from the ordinary pursuits of life to the pure enjoyment of rural nature; which is in the soul like a fountain of cool waters to the wayworn traveler; and let us

Learn
The laws by which the Eternal doth
    sublime
And sanctify his works, that we may see
The hidden glory veiled from vulgar eyes.

47.

Charles P. McIlvaine: The Scourge of Intemperance

The crusade to temper the consumption of alcoholic beverages was one of the many reform movements undertaken by the religious benevolent societies of the 1820s and 1830s. Like many of these, the American Society for the Promotion of Temperance, organized in 1826, was interdenominational and used the methods of revivalism to achieve its end. The following "Address to the Young Men of the United States on Temperance" was prepared by the Bishop of the Protestant Episcopal Church in Ohio, the Right Reverend Charles P. McIlvaine. In it he advocated the total abstinence that was demanded by the later teetotalers. The address, probably circulated in the middle 1830s by the American Tract Society, is typical of the literally thousands of such tracts that appeared during this period.

Source: *Tracts of the American Tract Society,* General series, New York, n.d., Vol. VII, No. 244, pp. 1-23.

In addressing the young men of the United States in regard to the great enterprise of promoting the universal prevalence of temperance, we are not aware that any time need be occupied in apology. Our motives cannot be mistaken. The magnitude of the cause and the importance of that cooperation in its behalf which this address is designed to promote will vindicate the propriety of its respectful call upon the attention of those by whom it shall ever be received.

It is presumed that every reader is already aware of the extensive and energetic movements at present advancing in our country in behalf of temperance. That an unprecedented interest in this work has been recently excited and is still rapidly strengthening in thousands of districts; that talent, wisdom, experience, learning, and influence are now enlisted in its service, with a measure of zeal and harmony far surpassing what was ever witnessed before in such a cause; that great things have already been accomplished; that much greater are near at hand; and that the whole victory will be eventually won if the temperate portion of society are not wanting to their solemn duty, must have been seen already by those living along the main channels of public thought and feeling. Elevated, as we now are, upon a high tide of general interest and zeal — a tide which may either go on increasing its flood till it has washed clean the very mountain tops and drowned intemperance in its last den, or else subside and leave the land infected with a plague, the more malignant and incurable from the dead remains of a partial inundation — it has become a question of universal application, which those who are now at the outset of their influence in society should especially consider: "What can *we* do, and what *ought* we to do in this cause?" For the settlement of this question we invite you to a brief view of the whole ground on which temperance measures are now proceeding.

It cannot be denied that our country is most horribly scourged by intemperance. In the strong language of Scripture: "it groaneth and travaileth in pain, to be delivered from the bondage of this corruption." Our country is free; *with a great price obtained we this freedom.* We feel as if all the force of Europe could not get it from our embrace. Our shores would shake into the depth of the sea the invader who should presume to seek it. One solitary citizen led away into captivity, scourged, chained by a foreign enemy, would rouse the oldest nerve in the land to indignant complaint and league the whole nation in loud demand for redress. And yet it cannot be denied that our country is enslaved. Yes, we are groaning under a most desolating bondage. The land is trodden down under its polluting foot. Our families are continually dishonored, ravaged, and bereaved; thousands annually slain and hundreds of thousands carried away into a loathsome slavery, to be ground to powder under its burdens or broken upon the wheel of its tortures.

What are the statistics of this traffic? Ask the records of madhouses and they will answer that one-third of all their wretched inmates were sent there by intemperance. Ask the keepers of our prisons and they will testify that, with scarcely an exception, their horrible population is from the schools of intemperance. Ask the history of the 200,000 paupers now burdening the hands of public charity and you will find that two-thirds of them have been the victims, directly or indirectly, of intemperance. Inquire at the gates of death and you will learn that no less than 30,000 souls are annually passed for the judgment bar of God, driven there by intemperance.

How many slaves are at present among us? We ask not of slaves to man but to intemperance, in comparison with whose bondage the yoke of the tyrant is freedom. They are estimated at 480,000! And what does the nation pay for the honor and happiness of this whole system of ruin? *Five times as much every year as for the annual support of its whole system of government.* These are truths, so often published, so widely sanctioned, so generally received, and so little doubted, that we need not detail the particulars by which they are made out. What, then, is the whole amount of guilt and of woe which they exhibit? Ask Him "unto whom all hearts are open, all desires known, and from whom no secrets are hid." Ask *eternity! . . .*

Another assertion is equally unquestionable. *The time has come when a great effort must be made to exterminate this unequaled destroyer.* It was high time this was done when the first drunkard entered eternity to receive the award of Him who has declared that no drunkard shall enter the kingdom of God. The demand for this effort has been growing in the peremptory tone of its call, as "the overflowing scourge" has passed with constantly extending sweep through the land. But a strange apathy has prevailed among us. As if the whole nation had been drinking the cup of delusion, we saw the enemy coming in like a flood and we lifted up scarcely a straw against him.

As if the magicians of Egypt had prevailed over us by their enchantments, we beheld our waters of refreshment turned into blood, and a destroying sword passing through till "there was a great cry" in the land, for there was scarcely "a house where there was not one dead"; and still our hearts were hardened, and we would not let go the great sin for which these plagues were brought upon us. It seems as if some foul demon had taken his seat upon the breast of the nation, and was holding us down with the dead weight of a horrid nightmare, while he laughed at our calamity and mocked at our fear — when our fear came as desolation and our destruction as a whirlwind.

Shall this state continue? Is not the desolation advancing? Have not facilities of intemperance, temptations to intemperance, examples to sanction intemperance been fast increasing ever since this plague began? Without some effectual effort, is it not certain they will continue to increase till intemperate men and their abettors will form the public opinion and consequently the public conscience and the public law of this land — till intemperance shall become, like Leviathan of old, "king over all the children of pride," whose breath kindleth coals, and a "flame goeth out of his mouth?" Then what will effort of man avail? "Canst thou draw out Leviathan with a hook? His heart is as firm as a stone; yea, as hard as a piece of the nether millstone. He drinketh up a river, and hasteth not. When he raiseth up himself, the mighty are afraid."

It is too late to put off any longer the effort for deliverance. It is granted by the common sense and urged by the common interest; every feeling of humanity and every consideration of religion enforces the belief that the time has come when a great onset is imperiously demanded to drive out intemperance from the land. . . . Here the question occurs — *What can be done? How can this woe be arrested?* The answer is plain. Nothing can be done but in one of the three following ways. You must either suffer people to drink *immoderately;* or you must endeavor to promote *moderation* in drinking; or you must try to persuade them to drink *none at all.* One of these plans must be adopted. Which shall we choose? The first is condemned already.

What say we to the second, *the moderate use* of intoxicating drinks? It has unquestionably the sanction of high and ancient ancestry. It is precisely the plan on which intemperance has been wrestled with ever since it was first discovered that "wine is a mocker" and that "strong drink is raging." But hence comes its condemnation. Its long use is its death witness. Were it new, we might hope something from its adoption. But it is old enough to have been tried to the uttermost. The wisdom, the energy, the benevolence of centuries have made the best of it. The attempt to keep down intemperance by endeavoring to persuade people to indulge only moderately in strong drink has been the world's favorite for ages; while every age has wondered that the vice increased so rapidly.

At last we have been awakened to a fair estimate of the success of the plan. And what is it? So far from its having shown the least tendency to exterminate the evil, it is the mother of all its abominations. All who have attained the stature of full-grown intemperance were once children in this nursery, sucking at the breasts of this parent. All the "men of strength to mingle strong drink," who are now full graduates in the vice and "masters in the arts" of drunkenness, began their education and served their apprenticeship under the discipline of moderate drinking. All that have learned to lie down in the streets and carry terror into their families, and whom intemperance has conducted to the penitentiary and the madhouse, may look back to this as the beginning of their course — the author of their destiny.

No man ever set out to use strong drink with the expectation of becoming eventually a drunkard. No man ever became a drunkard without having at first assured himself that he could keep a safe rein upon every disposition that might endanger his strict sobriety. "I am in no danger while I only take a little," is the first principle in the doctrine of intemperance. It is high time it were discarded. It has deluged the land with vice and sunk the population into debasement. The same results will ensue again, just in proportion as the moderate use of ardent spirits continues to be encouraged. Let the multitude continue to drink a little, and still our hundreds of thousands will annually drink to death.

It is settled, therefore, that to encourage moderate drinking is not the plan on which the temperance reformation can be successfully prosecuted. The faithful experiment of generation after generation decides that it must be abandoned. A cloud of witnesses, illustrating its consequences in all the tender mercies of a drunkard's portion, demand that it should be abandoned. Its full time is come. Long enough have we refused to open our eyes to the evident deceitfulness of its pretensions. At last the country is awaking and begins to realize the emptiness of this dream. Let it go as a dream and only be remembered that we may wonder how it deceived, and lament how it injured us.

But, if this be discarded, what plan of reformation remains? If nothing is to be expected from endeavoring to promote a *moderate* use of ardent spirits, and still less from an *immoderate* use, what can be done? There is but one possible answer. *Persuade people to use none at all. Total abstinence* is the only plan on which reformation can be hoped for. We are shut up to this. We have tried the consequences of encouraging people to venture but moderately into the atmosphere of infection; and we are now convinced that it was the very plan to feed its strength and extend its ravages. We are forced to the conclusion that to arrest the pestilence we must starve it. All the healthy must abstain from its neighborhood. All those who are now temperate must give up the use of the means of intemperance. The deliverance of this land from its present degradation and from the increasing woes attendant on this vice depends altogether upon the extent to which the principle of total abstinence shall be adopted by our citizens.

But suppose this principle universally adopted, would it clear the country of intemperance? Evidently it is the only, but is it the effectual remedy? Most certainly, if all temperate persons would disuse ardent spirits, they could not cease to be temperate. Many a drunkard, under the powerful check of their omnipresent reproof, would be sobered. His companions would totter, one after another, to their graves. A few years would see them buried and the land relinquished to the temperate. Then what would be the security against a new inroad of the exterminated vice? Why, public opinion would stand guard at every avenue by which it could come in.

Consider the operation of this influence. Why is it now so easy to entice a young man into the haunts of drunkenness? Because public opinion favors the use of the very means of his ruin. He may drink habitually and fasten upon himself the appetite of drink, till he becomes enchained and feels himself a slave; but if he has never fallen into manifest intoxication, he has forfeited no character in public opinion. All this is a direct result of the fact that those considered as temperate people set the example and patronize the snare of moderate drinking.

But suppose them to take the ground proposed and bear down with the whole force of their example and influence on the side of entire abstinence, would they not create an immense force of public opinion against the least use of ardent spirits? How then could a temperate man ever become a drunkard? He has not yet contracted the desire for ardent spirits; and how will he contract it? Will he risk his character; fly in the face of public feeling and opinion; despise all the warnings in the history of intemperance, to get at the use, and put himself under the torture of that for which, as yet, he has no disposition? Only post a wakeful public sentiment at the little opening of moderate drinking and the whole highway to the drunkard's ruin will be closed up. All its present travelers will soon pass away, while none will be entering to keep up the character of the road.

Most assuredly, then, the reformation of the land is in the power of public opinion. It is equally certain that public opinion will accomplish nothing but by setting its influence directly in opposition to *any* indulgence in strong drink. And it is just as plain that, in order to accomplish this, the temperate part of the population must create a power of example by setting out upon the firm and open ground of total abstinence. In proportion, then, as the temperate throughout the country shall come up to this ground will the redemption of our enslaved republic be accomplished. . . .

In order to exert ourselves with the best effect in the promotion of the several objects in this great cause to which young men should apply themselves, let us associate ourselves into *temperance societies*. We know the importance of associated exertions. We have often seen how a few instruments, severally weak, have become mighty when united. Every work, whether for evil or benevolent purposes, has felt the

life, and spur, and power of cooperation. The whole progress of the temperance reformation, thus far, is owing to the influence of *societies;* to the coming together of the temperate and the union of their resolutions, examples, and exertions under the articles of temperance societies.

Thus examples have been brought out, set upon a hill, and made secure. Thus the weak have been strengthened, the wavering confirmed, the irresolute emboldened. Thus public attention has been awakened, public feeling interested, and public sentiment turned and brought to bear. Thus works have been performed, information distributed, agencies employed, and a thousand instruments set in motion which no industry of individual unassociated action could have reached. Let temperance societies be multiplied. Every new association is a new battery against the stronghold of the enemy, and gives a new impulse to the hearts of those who have already joined the conflict. Let us arise, and be diligent, and be united; and may the God of mercy bless our work.

48.

ANONYMOUS: The Aims of the Philadelphia Trades' Union

The trades' unions were city-wide federations of individual trade societies that formed in the major cities between 1833 and 1836. Their principal objectives were increased wages and shorter hours; their main methods, boycotts and strikes. One of their most effective weapons was the closed shop. To maintain it, they blacklisted both the journeymen who were not union members and the employers who hired nonunion help. To forestall criticism from the press and division within their ranks they were avowedly nonpolitical. Their policies were formulated by delegates from each of the member unions and a newspaper was usually sponsored to keep the membership informed. The Philadelphia Trades' Union was perhaps the most successful of its kind. In June 1835, it supported seventeen trade associations striking for the ten-hour day. As a result of their quick success, the ten-hour day was secured by tradesmen throughout the country and the number of affiliated societies in the Philadelphia union greatly increased. The following communication appeared in the Philadelphia organ in February 1836 over the signature J. C.

Source: *Pennsylvanian*, February 9, 1836 [Commons, V, pp. 389-392].

THE TRADES' UNION of Philadelphia, is an association or confederation consisting of forty-eight trade societies or associations, sovereign and independent in themselves, but bound by ties of honor and interest to support and assist each other in cases of aggression or danger. Their purposes of formation are only to prevent themselves from being reduced to abject poverty and slavery through the avaricious graspings of capital and monopoly. In the month of March 1834, not two years since, they constituted themselves a body, at that time consisting only of thirteen societies, the largest one of which could not number 250 members. Now look at the contrast, with two societies numbering more than 900 each; four of more than 700; and a great proportion of from 200 to 300.

Our funds in our infancy were scarcely sufficient to bear the monthly expenses of the union's delegates, without affording any assistance to the represented societies. Now, our monthly receipts are generally from $400 to $500; and at the last monthly meeting the amount received reached the unexampled sum of $691.20. The number of delegates representing the societies will at the next elections probably amount to 400. The members in all may be calculated by the monthly collections. Each individual is bound to pay the sum of 6¼ cents into the hands of the delegates representing his society, and such other sum as the auxiliary may require for its own purposes; and for this trifling assessment, each man is protected from the rapacity of the greedy employer and sure of the support and the protection of nearly every mechanic in Philadelphia.

Within the last six months more than one-half of the societies in the union have struck, and no instance is known where a society has struck under the sanction of the union and failed in that strike. Neither has the union ever sanctioned any society without first appointing a committee to make diligent inquiry to prevent imposition on the part of the journeyman and, if possible, to avoid intolerance. They will grant assistance to no society who has not been represented six months.

The delegates to the union are removable semiannually; therefore, the danger of unjust and partisan influence has no groundwork, no foundation to build upon, as the individual who may be popular in the union this term may never sit in it again; and it is understood to be the best and most effectual plan to remove the delegates at least once a year.

The funds of the union are also secure against the powerful representation of the larger societies, each one of which selects one individual to transact the money matters of the institution, denominated the Finance Committee, and this alone is under their control, so that the society of 50 members has the same responsibility and interest in the funds that the society of 950 has. Auxiliary branches of the union have been frequently petitioned for in various parts of the state, and the union has at length determined to take that matter into consideration, and accordingly have appointed a committee to report on the petitions.

This, then, is the statistical account of the Philadelphia Trades' Union, which in the lapse of less than two years has more than trebled its original number. This is an institution that should be looked upon by every mechanic with gratitude and pride, presenting a beautiful specimen of mechanism in theory, and far more beautiful and beneficial in practice. This is the institution that has been designated as a nest of disorganizers, that has been assailed from the pulpit and the editorial throne. We preach no religion in the union. The followers of Christ acknowledge a time for all things; we do the same. The union was founded for other purposes, and, therefore, it is no place for discussion about theology.

We have laws in existence, that party, political, or religious sectarian questions shall not be discussed. Then how or why are we entitled to the abusive epithets bestowed on us; or still the more dangerous doctrines said to be inculcated by us? They are false, and the authors of such libels know them to be so. We believe that society, as it is now constituted, is calculated to produce increasing ruin on the great mass of the people; but we also know that the change must be gradual, as the evil has been; and we look for these changes, not through the subversion of the laws or the power of physical force but from the justice of our claims and the true administration of our fundamental laws. We wish to produce a moral change in society, by the appeals of reason, at the same time we expect to be stigmatized and cursed for our zeal and disregard of danger. . . .

As a proof of the employers' power over single societies, it would be well to know that, previous to the formation of the union, there were not more than six or eight trades in Philadelphia that had control over their own labor, whereas at this time there are more than fifty. This is a conclusive proof that the acknowledgment of trade societies and a protest against a general unity is produced by the power over the first and fears from the latter. The individuals in single societies, finding themselves, from want of funds or other circumstances, in danger, carried out the principle of self-defense further than the employers designed, therefore the opposition to it. If it was right in individuals of one trade to unite, it was equally just and proper for them to call in their brethren of other trades to assist them in establishing just rules and regulations for their trade, consequently upon their capital, the labor of their hands; but this objection, as well as the power of coercion we are said to exercise over the auxiliary members, should never be started in a republican government.

The Philadelphia Trades' Union is an exact prototype of the federal Union. Our principles are their principles; even the government is based on the same rules and laws on a miniature scale. For the truth of this assertion, for the defense of our principles and rights, we throw down the gauntlet of defiance and challenge any to oppose us in a fair field, conscious that he who knows the Trades' Union and is opposed to it is no friend to republican and federal America.

49.

Employer Opposition to Trade Unions

Masters' (or employers') associations to regulate the quality of goods dated back to colonial times, but in 1834 the employers began organizing to combat the growing strength of trade unions. Like the trade unions, employer associations were organized along trade lines. With the formation of centralized trades' unions, the individual employer associations became ineffective and some attempts were made to link them into city-wide federations. Although the employers were often able to act in concert, no formal federations materialized, and in the battles of this period the trades' unions generally had the upper hand. Only in combating the closed shop were the employers successful, for in 1835 the New York Supreme Court declared that any attempt on the part of a union to enforce a closed shop was a conspiracy injurious to trade, and hence illegal. The following preamble and resolutions were adopted at a meeting of the "Employers, Curriers and Leather Dealers, of the City of New York and Brooklyn," on March 24, 1836.

Source: *Morning Courier and New York Enquirer*, March 26, 1836 [Commons, V, pp. 309-311].

Whereas certain journeymen of the cities of New York, Brooklyn, and Newark have connected themselves with the society called "The Trades' Union Society," and have conspired together to raise their wages and to dictate to their employers what price they shall pay for the services of such journeymen curriers, on and after March 21, instant; and

Whereas we consider all such combinations dangerous because they threaten violence to those who do not and absolute pauperism to those who do comply with their rules and regulations; illegal because they are injurious to trade and prevent us from coming into successful competition with other manufactures of a similar kind in our neighboring towns and cities; unequal and unjust in their operations because they compel us to pay the same wages to the ordinary laborer as to the most skillful; unnecessary because labor, like every other commodity, will seek its own level and its true value in an open and unfettered market and in a country where individual rights, freedom of trade, of action, and employment are guaranteed to every citizen; and impolitic because they take from the honest and industrious mechanic every incentive to superior skill and renewed exertions by bringing down their services to a level with others of less merit and by taking from their hard-earned wages a portion to support the idle and unemployed members of the society, and because they give to the slothful and careless encouragement in their idleness and inattention by giving them relief when unemployed and full wages for their negligence when employed.

Therefore, *Resolved*, that while we acknowledge the right of every man, in his individual capacity, to demand whatever price he chooses for his labor; and while we are willing to give our journeymen such wages for their services as shall amply compensate them and enable them to prosper, and ourselves to compete successfully in open market with our neighbors; yet, we deny the rights and deprecate the policy of combining and conspiring to dictate terms on which journeymen shall be employed, or by which their labor shall be regulated.

Resolved, that we will not consent to give the bill of prices demanded on and after [the] 21st instant by the journeymen curriers, members of the Trades' Union Society, and that we will not be compelled to pay the same price to ordinary workmen as to the more skillful, merely because they are members of said society.

Resolved, that we will protect our own rights and interests of our fellow citizens against the destructive influence of the Trades' Union Society, and that we will not employ any man who is known to be a member of that or any other society which has for its object the dictation of terms or prices for which workmen shall engage themselves.

Resolved, that we will especially protect all journeymen curriers who are now or hereafter may be in our employ, who are not members of the Trades' Union or of any similar society.

50.

William Cullen Bryant: On the Right to Strike

In October 1835 a society of journeymen tailors demanded higher wages for its members. Fall was the busy season and the employers granted the wage increase, but the following January they combined to reduce them again. For three months thereafter the journeymen tailors went on strike. Meanwhile, a group of shoemakers in Geneva, New York, were convicted for conspiring to raise wages. When the decision in that case became known, the master tailors had the journeymen arrested on a similar charge. After the journeymen were convicted and fined, William Cullen Bryant, the renowned poet and editor of the liberal New York Evening Post, *wrote the following editorial. It was published in the* Post *on June 13, 1836.*

Source: *New York Evening Post*, June 13, 1836.

Sentence was passed on Saturday on the twenty "men who had determined not to work." The punishment selected on due consideration by the judge was that officers appointed for the purpose should immediately demand from each of the delinquents a sum of money which was named in the sentence of the court. The amount demanded would not have fallen short of the savings of many years. Either the offenders had not parted with these savings, or their brother workmen raised the ransom money for them on the spot. The fine was paid over as required.

All is now well; justice has been satisfied. But if the expenses of their families had anticipated the law and left nothing in their hands, or if friends had not been ready to buy the freedom of their comrades, they would have been sent to prison, and there they would have stayed until their wives and children, besides earning their own bread, had saved enough to redeem the captives from their cells.

Such has been their punishment. What was their offense? They had committed the crime of unanimously declining to go to work at the wages offered to them by their masters. They had said to one another, "Let us come out from the meanness and misery of our caste. Let us begin to do what every order more privileged and more honored is doing every day. By the means which we believe to be the best, let us raise ourselves and our families above the humbleness of our condition. We may be wrong, but we cannot help believing that we might do much if we were true brothers to each other, and would resolve not to sell the only thing which is our own, the cunning of our hands, for less than it is worth." What other things they may have done is nothing to the purpose; it was for this they were condemned; it is for this they are to endure the penalty of the law.

We call upon a candid and generous community to mark that the punishment inflicted upon these twenty "men who had determined not to work" is not directed against the offense of conspiring to prevent others by force from working at low wages, but expressly against the offense of settling by preconcert the compensation which they thought they were entitled to obtain. It is certainly superfluous to repeat that this journal would be the very last to oppose a law leveled at any attempt to molest the laborer who chooses to work for less than the prices settled by the union.

We have said, and to cut off cavil we say it now again, that a conspiracy to deter, by threats of violence, a fellow workman from arranging his own terms with his employers is a conspiracy to commit a felony: a conspiracy which, being a crime against liberty, we should be the first to condemn; a conspiracy which no strike should, for its own sake, countenance for a moment; a conspiracy already punishable by the statute, and far easier to reach than the one of which "the twenty" stood accused; but a conspiracy, we must add, that has not a single feature in common with the base and barbarous prohibition under which the offenders were indicted and condemned.

They were condemned because they had determined not to work for the wages that were offered them! Can anything be imagined more abhorrent to every sentiment of generosity or justice than the law which arms the rich with the legal right to fix, by assize, the wages of the poor? If this is not SLAVERY, we have forgotten its definition. Strike the right of associating for the sale of labor from the privileges of a freeman and you may as well at once bind him to a master or ascribe him to the soil. If it be not in the color of his skin and in the poor franchise of naming his own terms in a contract for his work, what advantage has the laborer of the North over the bondman of the South?

Punish by human laws a "determination not to work," make it penal by any other penalty than idleness inflicts, and it matters little whether the taskmasters be one or many, an individual or an order, the hateful scheme of slavery will have gained a foothold in the land. And then the meanness of this law, which visits with its malice those who cling to it for protection, and shelters with all its fences those who are raised above its threats. A late solicitation for its aid against employers is treated with derision and contempt, but the moment the "masters" invoked its intervention, it came down from its high place with most indecent haste and has now discharged its fury upon the naked heads of wretches so forlorn that their worst faults multiply their titles to a liberty which they must learn to win from livelier sensibilities than the barren benevolence of Wealth, or the tardy magnanimity of Power.

Since the above was written we have read the report of Judge Edwards' address on sentencing the journeymen. It will be found in another part of this paper. We see in this address an apparent disposition to mix up the question of *combination,* which is a lawful act, with that of *violence,* which is allowed on all hands to be unlawful. We repeat that it was for the simple act of combining not to work under a certain rate of wages, and not for a disturbance of the peace, that the twenty journeymen were indicted, tried, convicted, and punished. It was expressly so stated in Judge Edwards' charge to the jury which brought in the verdict of guilty; and whoever will look at the address made by him in pronouncing the sentence will find that he still maintains and repeats, in various forms of expression, the doctrine that combinations to demand a fixed rate of wages are unlawful and punishable.

This tyrannical doctrine we affirm to be a forced construction of the statute against conspiracies injurious to commerce — a construction which the makers of the law, we are sure, never contemplated. We are now told, however, that it will be insisted upon and enforced — let it be so — it is the very method by which either the courts of justice will be compelled to recede from their mistaken and arbitrary construction, or the legislature will interpose to declare that such is not the law. Carry it into effect impartially and without respect of persons and there will not be people enough left without the penitentiaries to furnish subsistence to those who are confined within them.

"Self-created societies," says Judge Edwards, "are unknown to the Constitution and laws, and will not be permitted to rear their crest and extend their baneful influence over any portion of the community." If there is any sense in this passage it means that self-created societies are unlawful and must be put down by the courts. Down, then, with every literary, every religious, and every charitable association not incorporated! What nonsense is this! Self-created societies *are* known to the Constitution and laws, for they are not prohibited, and the laws which allow them will, if justly administered, protect them.

But suppose, in charity, that the reporter has put this absurdity into the mouth of Judge Edwards, and that he meant only those self-created societies which have an effect upon trade and commerce. Gather up then and sweep to the penitentiary all those who are confederated to carry on any business or trade in concert, by fixed rules, and see how many men you would leave at large in this city. The members of every partnership in the place will come under the penalties of the law, and not only these but every person pursuing any occupation whatever who governs himself by a mutual understanding with others that follow the same occupation.

The judge observes that "combinations which operate to the injury of the employers or of the trade, will, in the regular course of events, be found injurious to journeymen." We heartily wish that all the doctrines of the address had been as sound as this. Combinations to the injury of trade necessarily injure workmen, and in this lies the remedy. Workmen will not, any more than employers, do what is to their own injury. If they combine without good grounds, their error carries its own penalty along with it, and may be safely left to be chastised by the suffering which is the natural consequence of such folly. The interposition of the law in that case is idle and presumptuous. You may as well make a law to prohibit people from going too thinly clad in cold weather.

"We have had in this country so little experience of these combinations," proceeds Judge Edwards, "that we are at a loss to know what degree of severity may be necessary to rid society of them." We wonder not at this embarrassment — the difficulties of which the judge speaks will be increased with every one of the penalties he threatens to impose. The severer the penalties, the more glaring will be the injustice of the law, the more it will be discussed, and the sooner will the legislature interfere.

England has had experience of these combinations, if we have not. England has had long, ample, and instructive experience, both of combinations and combination laws; and what is the lesson which this experience has taught her? She learned that "the attempts to enforce the provisions of the Combination Act," we quote the *Edinburgh Review*, "did infinitely more harm than good," and she accordingly, twelve years ago, blotted the combination laws from her statute book. She did this not with a Whig, or Radical, or reformed Parliament, but while the Tories were in power, and the realm was ruled by an aristocracy. Will not our own country be wise enough to profit by her experience without a taste of the evils by which it was acquired?

51.

Labor Unions and Conspiracy

On July 31, 1834, the Thompsonville Carpet Manufacturing Company of Connecticut brought suit for damages against certain labor leaders, charging that they had conspired to ruin the company's business by refusing to work and inducing others not to work following the company's refusal to grant a wage increase. Three trials resulted from this: the first suit for damages directed against labor in the United States. In the first (August 1834), the defendants were acquitted; in the second, before the state superior court, no verdict was reached; and in the third (January 1836), the defendants were acquitted after the jury was instructed that to combine to raise wages was, as such, legal. The verdict anticipated Commonwealth v. Hunt *(Massachusetts) by six years. The court reporter's account of the 1836 proceedings is reprinted here in part.*

Source: *Report of the Case of the Thompsonville Carpet Manufacturing Company, Versus William Taylor, etc., etc.,* Hartford, 1836, pp. 1-7, 57-62.

To the Sheriff of Hartford County, his Deputy, or any Constable of the Town of Simsbury within said County, Greeting:

By authority of the State of Connecticut, you are commanded to summon William Taylor, Edward Gorman, Wallace Baylie, and Thomas Norton of Simsbury in said county to appear before the County Court to be held at Hartford, within and for Hartford County, on the 2nd Tuesday of August, A.D. 1834, then and there to answer unto the Thompsonville Carpet Manufacturing Co., an incorporated company having its manufacturing establishment and office of business at Enfield, in said county, in a plea of the case, whereupon the plaintiffs declare and say that they are an incorporated company, incorporated by the name aforesaid by the laws of this state, with power to sue and be sued, to hold the real and personal estate, hereinafter mentioned, and to carry on the business of manufacturing carpets as hereinafter mentioned, and with the usual powers of corporation created for manufacturing purposes.

That on the 24th day of July, 1833, at said Enfield, the plaintiffs owned and possessed at a place called Thompsonville in said Enfield, land and buildings, and privileges of water of great value, to wit, $75,000, which the plaintiffs used and occupied for the purpose of manufacturing carpets, and also a great amount of machinery, implements of various kinds, and other personal estate of great value, to wit, $40,000, used by the plaintiffs for the same purpose; and had there and elsewhere a great amount of wool, yarn, and other stock of great value, to wit, of the value of $100,000, which they had for the sole and only purpose of manufacturing the same into carpets; and had then in their employ a great number, to wit, 100 persons, employed in the various processes of their said business of manufacturing carpets, and, among others, 60 ingrain carpet weavers and more, and had then many contracts of great value before that time entered into by them for the delivery of carpets then soon to be performed, and were prosecuting their said business successfully and profitably to the amount of $150,000 per annum, all which was then and there well known to the defendants.

And the defendants, well knowing the premises, and intending and contriving to injure the plaintiffs, then and there unlawfully, wantonly, wickedly, and maliciously did conspire, combine, confederate, and agree together to hinder, interrupt, and stop the plaintiffs' said business, and deprive the plaintiffs of the profits thereof, and subject them to the inconvenience, embarrassments and losses occasioned by its interruption, and then and there in pursuance of said unlawful, wicked, and malicious conspiracy, combination, confederacy, and agreement between them, the defendants as aforesaid had, did, at said Enfield on said 24th day of July, 1833, being themselves weavers in the plaintiffs' employ, unlawfully abandon the plaintiffs' employ, and falsely and deceitfully persuade and induce all the said ingrain carpet weavers in the plaintiffs' employ to abandon and quit the plaintiffs' employ and to refuse to work, and wrongfully and injuriously, by threats and falsehood, induce a great number of ingrain carpet weavers, to wit, 70, employed by the plaintiffs in their said business, to abandon the same, and did willfully, maliciously, and injuriously intimidate, dissuade, hinder, and prevent other carpet weavers from engaging in the plaintiffs' said business, although then and there ready and willing so to do.

By reason of which unlawful, wicked, and malicious conspiracy, combination, confederacy, and agreement between the defendants aforesaid and their said unlawful, injurious, willful and malicious acts and doings aforesaid in pursuance thereof, the plaintiffs' said business has been hindered, obstructed, and entirely stopped. And they, the plaintiffs, entirely deprived of all the profit and advantage thereof, and all use of their said real and personal estate employed therein, and of the labor and services of their said workmen, and their arrangements broken up for a long time, to wit, from said 24th day of July, 1833, to the 27th day of August, 1833, and they have been subjected to great loss and damage. . . .

The defendants . . . wrongfully contriving and devising to injure the plaintiffs in their said business, and unjustly to extort from the plaintiffs great sums of money for their, the defendants' labor and hire, in their, the defendants' art, mystery, and manual occupation of weavers, did at another and different time, to wit, at said Enfield on the 24th day of July, 1833, together with a great number of other weavers in the plaintiffs' employ, to wit, 60 and more, unlawfully assemble and meet together; and being so met did then and there corruptly and unjustly conspire, confederate, and agree among themselves that none of them would work thereafter at the usual and accustomed rates and prices at which they and others had been wont and accustomed to work, and to exact and demand from the plaintiffs the following prices: to wit, for plain grounds, 15 cents per yard; for fines, 11 cents per yard; for stripes above two shuttles and double whites, 15½ cents per yard; for double shot abouts, 16½ cents per yard; and for the three plies, 30 cents per yard.

And did then and there conspire, confederate, and agree that none of them would return to the plaintiffs' employ unless the plaintiffs would agree to pay the prices aforesaid, being more than the usual and accustomed prices, and did wrongfully and unlawfully conspire, confederate, and agree together to hinder and prevent all others from entering or continuing in the plaintiffs' employment in said business, and entirely to hinder and stop the plaintiffs' said business. And in pursuance of said conspiracy, confederacy, and agreement last aforesaid, the defendants at said Enfield, on said 24th day of July, 1833, and thence until the 27th day of August, 1833, together with their said other confederates, did remain and continue at said Enfield, united and combined in their said conspiracy, did refuse to return to their said work for the plaintiffs, did hinder and prevent all other workmen from entering into the plaintiffs' employ in said business, did by threats and intimidation, by persuasion and falsehood hinder and prevent from returning to their said work all of the plaintiffs' said workmen who were willing and desirous to do so, and did wantonly, injuriously, and unlawfully hinder, obstruct, and interrupt the plaintiffs' said business for a long time, to wit, from the 24th day of July, 1833, to the 27th day of August, 1833.

By reason of which unlawful, wicked, and malicious conspiracy, confederacy, and agreement of the defendants last aforesaid, and the wrongful and injurious acts and doings of the defendants in pursuance thereof, the plaintiffs lost all benefit of their said real and personal estate, last aforesaid, and of the labor of said workmen, and lost the profits of their said business, from the 24th day of July, 1833, for a long time, to wit, five weeks, and were subjected to great losses.

All which is to the damage of the plaintiffs $15,000, which to recover with first costs this suit is brought. Hereof fail not to make due service and return. Dated at Suffield this 31st day of July, A.D. 1834.

WILLIAM GAY,
Justice of the Peace

Defendants pleaded not guilty. . . .

DURING THE PROGRESS of the trial several questions were raised as to the admissibility of the testimony offered under the plaintiffs' declaration, but it is not thought necessary to insert them. The case was elaborately argued by the counsel for the respective parties. It was claimed by the counsel for the plaintiffs that if a man conspires for an end lawful, or unlawful, he conspires the means; that if a man conspires means, the natural effect of which is to produce a certain result, he conspires that result; that the defendants did conspire both the end and the means.

The end was the stoppage of the plaintiffs' works. The means by which this was to be effected was, first, by depriving the plaintiffs of the hands in their employment; and second, by throwing impediments in the way of their procuring other hands. That in tracing out a conspiracy it was necessary to look at all the circumstances of the case, the relative situation of the parties at the origin of their difficulties, and the manner in which each conducted until the company resumed their operations.

The testimony was thus completed, by which it was claimed that the various means set forth in the declaration as having been adopted by the defendants to accomplish their object had been fully made out.

The defendants' counsel claimed that the plaintiffs must prove: first, a combination; second, that the combination was unlawful, that the intent of the combination was effected, that to sustain a civil action, the intent must be acted on and the acts proved.

The defendants then claimed that a combination among workmen not to work below certain prices was not an indictable offense under our law, and laid no foundation for a civil action.

That this was the sole object of the defendants, and although a temporary suspension of the plaintiffs' work might result from the laborers leaving their employment, yet their object, and the means of obtaining it, were both lawful, and that no other means had by them been resorted to than the weapons of truth.

The counsel then examined the sources of evidence by which the plaintiffs attempted to prove their declaration: first, the parol; second, the written evidence. As to parol proof, it was said no evidence of any unlawful acts going to establish a conspiracy was adduced except from John Adams and John Ronald. That as to Adams, all his testimony relative to the course taken in the public meetings, the votes passed or acts done to interfere in any way with the company, or to prevent other hands from coming, in short, that all the principal facts testified to by him were sustained by no other solitary witness on the part of the plaintiffs, and were substantially contradicted by every witness whose attention was called to his evidence on the part of the defendants; and that as to Ronald, who testified but to one

or two facts of any importance, he was sustained by Adams only and contradicted by the united voice of the rest.

In addition to which, that he had testified twice before, and did not allude to the facts which the plaintiffs now attempted by his testimony to establish. They further claimed that although their own most important witnesses were now, and since the strike had continued in, the plaintiffs' employment, and liable at any moment to be discharged, that even by these witnesses, they had conclusively shown that no object was ever proposed or attempted, but to obtain a reasonable addition to their former wages.

That the written evidence consisted: first, of the petition; second, the resolutions; and third, the circular letter.

That the petition was admitted to be respectful and proper. That if laborers had a right to decline working except at specified prices, there was nothing in the resolves that were liable to objection. That as to the circular, it contained nothing but the truth, and that the defendants had an unquestionable right to send letters to other factories, or to individuals, containing the truth as to the differences that existed between them and the company.

The defendants claimed that it was not contended they had done any acts, except at public meetings, or by authority given them at the public meetings. That all the proof to implicate them was the acts of others.

They then contended that they could not be affected by the acts of others, unless it was shown that such acts were done in pursuance of an agreement to which they were parties. That the first meeting in the shop was held with the knowledge and approbation of the company, and to receive from them an answer to their petition; that no agreement was then entered into, except what is contained in the resolves sent to the company; that the shops, by order of the company, were immediately closed, and that all the combination which was ever entered into when the defendants were present, or in which they had any agency, was not to work, and to authorize the committee to write to other factories to tell the truth, and that if the jury found these facts to be true, then all the subsequent acts or declarations made or done by others, could not affect the defendants. . . .

The trial commenced on Monday, and the argument was concluded on Friday evening, when Chief Justice Williams proceeded to charge the jury in an able, lucid, and impartial manner. He explained to the jury the nature of the action, commented at large upon the testimony adduced by both parties, and as to the principles involved in the case he instructed the jury that the plaintiffs must prove a combination by the defendants to do an unlawful act, or to do a lawful act by unlawful means to the injury of the plaintiffs.

The charge in the plaintiffs' declaration was a combination to injure and destroy the plaintiffs' business, and it is alleged to have been entered into on the 24th day of July, 1833, and continued until the 27th of August following. The defendants claim that as the plaintiffs have given evidence tending to show a conspiracy on the 24th of July, they cannot prove one upon any other day. The law does not consider the day material. The plaintiffs are not confined to the day stated in the declaration, nor to the fact that they have attempted to prove the conspiracy upon that particular day. If they have succeeded in proving the conspiracy on any day between the 24th of July and the 27th of August, it is sufficient.

The testimony relative to the meetings after the first day is also proper as tending to show a conspiracy upon that day.

If a conspiracy is proved to have been entered into by the defendants and others, it has heretofore been held that it was not material that the others were not named in the declaration.

The act of conspiracy may be proved by direct evidence, or by circumstantial, and when proved, the acts or declarations of other persons who are not defendants, in pursuance of such concert, or conspiracy, is evidence against the defendants.

That such acts or declarations of others are not to be regarded as evidence of the combination or conspiracy itself so as in that respect to affect the defendants.

The act charged upon the defendants in this case is a conspiracy to interrupt and destroy the plaintiffs' business. The defendants claim that there was no agreement or concert on their part, except an agreement not to labor below certain prices. If that was the real nature of the agreement between the defendants, or the defendants and other workmen, it has been determined in this court that such agreement is not by our law an indictable offense, nor the subject of a civil action. But if the defendants conspired to interrupt and destroy the business of the plaintiffs, and thus compel them to pay the wages demanded, and have thus interrupted or destroyed the plaintiffs' business, and the plaintiffs have thus suffered damages, they are entitled to a verdict against the defendants.

On Saturday morning the jury returned a verdict of not guilty in the following form:

"In this case the jury find that the defendants are not guilty in manner and form, as the plaintiffs in their declaration have alleged, and therefore find for the defendants to recover their costs.

WILLIAM ALFORD,
Foreman

A true copy of verdict of jury in said case.

PHILO A. GOODWIN,
Clerk of Superior Court

The sum demanded in the declaration was $15,000. The defendants were in prison for a time upon the charge of conspiracy, at the suit of the plaintiffs. The defendants obtained a verdict in their favor in the

County Court from which the plaintiffs appealed. Another trial was had in the Superior Court, in which there was no verdict, and the trial here reported was the third which has been had in this case. The nature of the charge, together with the attendant circumstances and the importance of the principles involved, rendered this case one of unusual interest, and the result it is believed has met with public approbation.

Counsel for the plaintiffs, Wm. Hungerford and Wm. W. Ellsworth, Esqs. For the defendants, Calvin Goddard, Samuel H. Huntington, and Francis Parsons, Esqs.

As the reporter has been unable to obtain from either of the counsel who argued the cause even an epitome of their arguments, and as he took no minutes of them at the trial, he is unable to give any other than a very brief outline of the positions taken by them for their respective clients.

52.

The Evils of Female Labor

The growing concentrations of population and the new modes of doing business that accompanied the industrial expansion of the 1830s were factors that tended to intensify competition between employers. To cut costs, employers resorted to supplementing or replacing skilled craftsmen with partially trained laborers, women, children, and convicts. The trades' unions, of course, wanted to eliminate these alternative sources of labor. The following report on female labor was submitted to the National Trades' Union Convention held in Philadelphia on October 24-28, 1836, and was later reprinted in the union's newspaper.

Source: *National Laborer*, November 12, 1836 [Commons, VI, pp. 281-291].

THE COMMITTEE APPOINTED to report on the evils of female labor respectfully offer the following as the result of their opinions and conference on that subject, having in the discharge of their duty considered the subject in a moral, social, and pecuniary point of view; first, proceeding to explain and exhibit the errors of the system, and after to point out the only means of curtailing or arresting the evil.

The system of female labor, as practised in our cities and manufacturing towns, is surely the most disgraceful escutcheon on the character of American freemen, and one, if not checked by some superior cause, will entail ignorance, misery, and degradation on our children, to the end of time. "The physical organization, the natural responsibilities, and the moral sensibility of women prove conclusively that her labors should be only of a domestic nature." But if the character and attributes of any of God's creatures have been subverted, it has been woman, when forced by adventitious circumstances to become the abused hireling and drudge of the speculator and monopolist.

Let the workingmen of the United States

but consider what would become of the rising generation if the almost universal system of female labor should not be arrested. By reflecting one moment, everyone can see the consequences, and although it may promise and offer temporary gain to some, it should be passed and heeded as "the song of the siren" — everything at present or in future is destroyed by the illusion. The health of the young female, in the majority of cases, is injured by unnatural restraint and confinement, and deprived of the qualities essentially necessary in the culture and bearing of healthy children. Their morals frequently depart before their health, in consequence of being often crowded in such large numbers with all characters and all sexes; and what evil example this fails to do, necessity too often urges and palliates; and this one point of the subject, above all others, should arouse the jealous sensibilities of every moral man and more particularly of every parent.

These evils themselves are great and call loudly for a speedy cure; but still another objection to the system arises, which, if possible, is productive of the other evils: namely, the ruinous competition brought in active opposition to male labor, actually producing a reversion of the very good intended to do the guardian or parent, causing the destruction of the end which it aims to benefit; because, when the employer finds, as he surely will, that female assistance will compress his ends, of course the workman is discharged or reduced to a corresponding rate of wages with the female operative. By these means the parent, the husband, or the brother is deprived of a sufficient subsistence to support himself and family, when without the auxiliary aid of the female, by his own labor alone, he might have supported himself and family in decency and kept his wife or relative at home to perform the duties of the household.

Nor is the evil lessened in the case of females who work singly, or in reduced numbers. If possible, their competition is still more ruinous; because, in the first instance, when congregated in large numbers, they are generally the assistants of machinery, which destroys the necessity of manual labor. But in the latter case, all being done by the hand, the female in a short time becomes so expert as entirely to supersede the necessity of the male; and this fact is apparent to everyone: that, when the females are found capable of performing duty generally performed by the men, as a natural consequence, from the cheapness of their habits and dependent situation, they acquire complete control of that particular branch of labor. And if the evil stopped here, it might more readily be arrested; but the desire of gain is such that there are no limits that could confine it; and so long as employers are allowed to experiment on the labor of the sex, each trade, except it be of the most laborious character, is in danger of the innovation.

The committee will not attempt to conceal the fact that a serious question meets us in our opposition to the system. "If the mechanical labor, or the opposition labor of females are destroyed, can they employ their time usefully and profitably?" The committee will answer: not without a corresponding change in society, which must be produced by the extension of knowledge and education. In the early ages, we find that the women were usefully, healthily, and industriously employed, although differently engaged from their present occupations; and if in those early days a sufficiency of labor was found, as a matter of course, at the present day, with the increased demand, a sufficiency can be had in the family of everyone.

The evil, however, has been saddled upon us, and it is our duty, as well as interest, to propose such remedies as the case may require. Females themselves are very blind as to their real interest and imagine that each effort made to destroy the operation of the system is destructive to their interest, whereas it is virtually calculated to remove and destroy the very evils they now labor under; and it would be folly to urge a different course until they see the evil in all its colors. One thing, however, must be apparent to every reflecting female: that all her exertions are scarce sufficient to keep her alive; that the price of her labor each year is reduced; and that she in a measure stands in the way of the male when attempting to raise his prices or equalize his labor; and that there her efforts to sustain herself and family are actually the same as tying a stone around the neck of her natural protector, man, and destroying him with the weight she has brought to his assistance. This is the true and natural consequence of female labor when carried beyond the necessities of the family.

It is thus that the speculator can riot through his mines of gold, heedless of the tears and the degradation of his innocent victims. It is not enough that freemen have sunk below the level of humanity at the shrine of Mammon but their wives and daughters must be offered at the pyre. Is not avarice satisfied with a nation of fathers and sons, but our wives and daughters, the loved ones of our hearts and affections, shall be thrown into the spoilers' arms?

The committee acknowledge:

1. The system necessary in the present state of society;

2. That it is destructive in all its bearings;

3. That it must be destroyed by gradual means and by the active cooperation of the female operatives;

4. That the legislatures of the various states should be required to assist by the enactment of laws preventing females under a certain age from being employed in large factories, and then only under the care and superintendence of a parent.

It has already been shown an evil, but if anything more is required to prove it, it may be necessary to state that, in the New England states, printing, saddling, brushmaking, tailoring, whipmaking, and many other trades are in a certain measure governed by females; and as a matter of course the same system will spread over the country. It has been shown that the number of females employed in opposition to male labor, throughout the United States, exceeds 140,000, who labor on an average from twelve to fifteen hours per day, without that pure air and wholesome exercise which are necessary to health, and confinement with the consequent excess of toil, which checks the growth of the body, destroying in effect the natural powers of the mind and not unfrequently distorting the limbs. . . .

As an evidence of the injurious tendencies the introduction of the female system has upon the male operatives, we will take the societies composing the union of Philadelphia only. For example, of fifty-eight societies, twenty-four are seriously affected by female labor, to the impoverishing of whole families and benefit of none but the employers. It is presumed that this is a fair criterion to judge of the other sections of the union; and from all these calculations there is evident reason to believe that some of the different branches of operative mechanics will in time be superseded by female operatives to the entire exclusion of the males and the consequent introduction of dissipation, indolence, and crime.

We would not be understood by these suggestions to deprive the female portion of the community from earning by honest industry a livelihood, but to direct their attention to the other branches of female industry better calculated to promote health of body, and the still more noble attainments, the cultivation of the mind — believing that there are sufficient openings for female industry and invention much more profitable and not requiring that labor of body and constant incarceration required in factories.

That it must be destroyed by gradual means none can deny; a departure from which, if it were practicable, would reduce thousands to beggary, starvation, and crime.

That females themselves should arouse in this noble cause is again pressed by the committee, believing if the good and pure in all classes would but come out, much might be done to meliorate their condition. For instance, it is presumed there are twenty beneficial societies for females in the city of Philadelphia, composing in the aggregate 4,000 members. Now, if the humane in these societies could effect a reorganization in order to grant assistance to those imposed upon by employers, the good effects, no doubt, would be speedily felt.

In addition to their beneficial dues, let them assess each member 6¼ cents monthly, making the sum in addition 75 cents yearly, which could be felt by none, but which by the increased number of females who would subscribe from motives of charity, might be raised to an amount calculated to defeat the oppression of the heartless employer; because if the employer can but manage without their assistance two weeks, he is sure of defeating them. And on the other hand, if they could stand for three weeks, the pressing demand for their labor and the impracticability of foreign assistance would compel him to come to terms.

This simple plan itself would give confidence to the female, throws her in the company of those who were her friends, and by their united energies would do more to raise each other than all the Dorcas Societies in the world, who subscribe themselves "charitable ladies," for giving a woman 12½ cents for making a shirt, equaled as they are in "charity" only by the United States' Clothing Department in the city of Philadelphia, which has ground the seamstress down to the above sum, 12½ for the same article.

In the city of Philadelphia, a Society of Female Operatives exists, numbering near 400, governed on the same principles as the other trade societies, which, in time, no doubt, will effectuate much good; and two or three other societies are composed in part by females who have received a proportionate benefit with the males. Many means, no doubt, might be adopted to bring females in society; but until it is done, they have little hope of redress.

Another method might be resorted to. All those trades affected by female labor could regulate their laws in such way as to admit those females in their society, so that in case of difficulty they would be governed by their laws and receive their support, or raise the society of females and make one auxiliary to the other. Any of these measures might be tried without danger or loss, and there is no doubt one or the other with perseverance would succeed, but the committee would recommend the amalgamation of trade and beneficial societies.

While on this point of the subject, the committee cannot pass without a remark on the inconsistency of a certain class of females, and likewise to offer one more suggestion. The fact must be apparent to anyone that Sunday school societies and temperance societies have been mainly supported by females, as well also as foreign and domestic missions. Now, is it not a singular fact that females who would sacrifice their time and health to distribute tracts and collect moneys for the heathen could not devote a mite for their own oppressed countrywomen without the sacrifice of time or health? We do not object to these objects by any means; but while they are discharging the duties of humanity they should not overlook their own sex and kin. Let them endeavor to take away the provocation to crime by giving the poor female a sufficiency for her labor to support herself and orphans, and that act will be as acceptable in the eye of Heaven as any ever discharged by mortal. Besides, their efforts to distinguish themselves, if their motives be pure, which we do not question, are not always crowned with success, agents and impostors frequently reaping the fruit of their labors; whereas, did they but collect but half the sum to give to destitute females forced to abandon their labor, they themselves could divide the tribute without the least danger of imposition.

Of what avail has been all the sympathy expressed by some of the great men of this city? Have they ever proposed a single plan to benefit the female laborer? Much have they talked, but little have they done. We see among the fashionable ladies monthly contributions started, extending, as they do, through all classes of females, for one thing or the other thing, but we do not see them propose a penny or two-penny tax on the female portion of the community for their unfortunate sisters in adversity. This would be a noble thing; and the committee will propose to the charitable in those districts where females are oppressed, to form themselves in general societies for the benefit of female laborers; and if the donation be but two cents monthly, that sum will answer every purpose, provided it is subscribed to generally. The question will then soon be settled, whether those who have done so much have done so from the dictates of conscience or for the applause of the world.

The females employed in the Lowell Mills, by the adoption of such a suggestion, no doubt would have been able to starve their proprietors out instead of being defeated, as they probably will be. But to prevent a similar recurrence, they should immediately adopt energetic measures in the construction of societies to support each other in trouble; and by their failure, composed as they are of 7,000 in all, let others be cautioned. This is the only effectual remedy to be applied at this time. We must first curb the excess before we destroy the evil.

In relation to the right or propriety of legislatures interfering with the domestic arrangements of manufacturers or speculators, workingmen should not say one word. "The evil has arisen from partial legislation," and let legislation correct the evil. Take away from the wealthy the temptation held out by poverty and we will be more virtuous and more happy.

In concluding their report, the committee will observe [that] the suggestions thrown out are gratuitous, believing that nothing can be done without the cooperation of the females; they, however, have proposed the above remedies, hoping that the day is not far distant when some of them may be adopted to relieve this oppressed part of the community; they shall therefore close by offering the following:

Resolved, that in the opinion of this convention, the present system of female labor is highly injurious to the best interests of the working classes, to the great object of mental improvement, and consequent corruption of good morals.

Resolved, that this convention, from feelings of humanity, recommend to the different unions the propriety of assisting, with their advice and influence, the female operatives throughout the United States, in ameliorating their present unhappy situation under the female system of labor.

53.

On the Ruinous Competition of Convict Labor

To reduce labor costs, some employers in the 1830s resorted to the practice of letting out contracts to prisons. The reformers who favored this practice argued that it relieved the taxpayer by making the prison financially self-sustaining, and that it helped the prisoner to occupy his time while confined and to do useful work when released. The free laborer, however, viewed it as a threat to his status and wages. In 1834 the Trades' Union of New York induced the state legislature to investigate prison labor. The investigating commission, which included the union's president, Ely Moore, recommended that the practice be continued, but with limitations that would reduce it as a competitive threat. So sensitive were the union members on the subject that when Moore endorsed the report, many called him a traitor and demanded that he resign. The report printed below was submitted to the National Trades' Union Convention held in Philadelphia on October 24-28, 1836.

Source: *National Laborer*, November 26, 1836 [Commons, VI, pp. 297-298].

THE COMMITTEE TO WHICH WAS REFERRED the state prison question would respectfully report:

That at the last meeting of the National Convention there were several recommendations made in reference to this subject, which have not generally been acted upon; and they conceive that a renewal of those recommendations, with an earnest appeal to the energetic action of the different unions throughout the country, are sufficient grounds for the Committee to assume.

The Committee, not having sufficient data, cannot at this time enter into a detail of the system as acted upon in the different states. Suffice it to say that they are well aware that in almost all of them it appears to be the policy of our state legislators to tax, almost exclusively, the producers for the support of the convicts by teaching them mechanical occupations, that the result of their labor may be brought in ruinous competition with that of the honest artisan. Therefore, your Committee would recommend the adoption of the following resolutions, with a wish that the delegates would call the attention of their constituents to immediate action on this subject.

Resolved, that it be recommended to the operatives in the different sections of the country to use their strenuous exertions to effect a radical reform in their several penitentiary systems as far as regards the employment and teaching of convicts in those occupations which affect their moral and pecuniary interests; believing that the employment of convicts upon articles to compete with those manufactured by the honest portion of the community to be manifestly unjust, and the plan of teaching them mechanical branches to be a system which tends to make industry in productive labor a degraded occupation.

Resolved, that a committee of one from each union represented herein be appointed to report in writing, at the next annual convention . . . the various measures adopted to effect a reform, and the success attending such efforts since the action of this body.

54.

Robert Rantoul, Jr.: On the Barbarity of the Common Law

The struggle of Jacksonian reformers to replace the common law (that is, unwritten law or law by precedent) with statute or codified law met strong conservative opposition. A basic assumption of those who opposed the common law was enunciated by the dedicated reform lawyer, Robert Rantoul, when he wrote, in the selection that appears here, that "a law is a rule of action; but a rule which is unknown can govern no man's conduct." Those who opposed codification argued that it was impossible to provide unambiguously by prior enactment for all cases that might arise. As a result of Rantoul's agitation for codification in 1836, a committee was appointed by the Massachusetts state legislature to study the question. Its effectiveness was largely blocked, however, by Justice Story, a renowned proponent of the common law. The selection is taken from an oration at Scituate on July 4, 1836:

Source: *Memoirs, Speeches and Writings of Robert Rantoul, Jr.*,
Luther Hamilton, ed., Boston, 1854, pp. 277-282.

TRUE INDEPENDENCE requires us to forbear from longer aping foreign manners, when inconsistent with republican simplicity. It requires the corrupt portion of the population of our great cities to be kept in check by our sound, substantial yeomanry, our intelligent mechanics, and our hardy tars. These, we may safely trust, are uncontaminated.

Our legislation, also, should be of indigenous growth. The laws should be intelligible to all, equal in their operation, and should provide prompt and cheap remedies for their violation. The revision of the statutes of this commonwealth, just completed, has done something toward this great end — how much, the public are hardly yet aware. It would have been worth all the time, expense, and labor spent upon it, even though they had been ten times greater than they were. It is the most important act of our legislation since the Revolution. Not only is the whole mass systematized, condensed, simplified, modernized, and made consistent with itself but improvements, almost innumerable, have been introduced into every part, more in number and greater in value, than our General Court would have elaborated, in their ordinary mode of legislation, for many years.

But the revised statutes, excellent as they are, contrasted with the chaos for which they are substituted, still cover but a small part of the ground. We are governed, principally, by the common law; and this ought to be reduced, forthwith, to a uniform written code.

It is said by writers on the subject that there are numerous principles of the common law which are definitely settled and well known, and that the questionable utility of putting these into the form of a positive and unbending text is not sufficient to outweigh the advantages of leaving them to be applied by the courts, as principles of common law, whenever the occurrence of cases should require it.

How can that which is definitely settled and well known be applied otherwise than as a positive and unbending text? It is because judge-made law is indefinitely and vaguely settled and its exact limits unknown that it possesses the capacity of adapting itself to new cases, or, in other words, admits of *judicial legislation.*

Imperfect statutes are, therefore, commended because they leave the law, in the omitted cases, to be enacted by the judges. Why not carry the argument a little further and repeal the existing statutes, so that the judges may make all the laws? Is it because the Constitution forbids judges to legislate? Why, then, commend the legislation of judges?

The law *should be* a positive and unbending text, otherwise the judge has an arbitrary power, or *discretion;* and the discretion of a good man is often nothing better than caprice, as Lord Camden has very justly remarked, while the discretion of a bad man is an odious and irresponsible tyranny.

Why is an *ex post facto* law, passed by the legislature, unjust, unconstitutional, and void, while judge-made law, which from its nature must always be *ex post facto,* is not only to be obeyed but applauded? Is it because judge-made law is essentially aristocratical? It is said the judge only applies to the case the principles of common law which exist already; but the legislature applies to a whole class of cases the principles of common sense and justice which exist already and which have existed from a much more remote antiquity.

The common law sprang from the Dark Ages; the fountain of justice is the throne of the Deity. The common law is but the glimmering taper by which men groped their way through the palpable midnight in which learning, wit, and reason were almost extinguished; justice shines with the splendor of that fullness of light which beams from the Ineffable Presence. The common law had its beginning in time and in the time of ignorance; justice is eternal, even with the eternity of the all-wise and just Law-giver and Judge. The common law had its origin in folly, barbarism, and feudality;

justice is the irradiance of divine wisdom, divine truth, and the government of infinite benevolence. While the common law sheds no light but rather darkness visible that serves but to discover sights of woe, — justice rises, like the Sun of Righteousness, with healing on His wings, scatters the doubts that torture without end, dispels the mists of scholastic subtilty, and illuminates with the light that lights every man that comes into the world. Older, nobler, clearer, and more glorious, then, is everlasting justice than ambiguous, base-born, purblind, perishable common law. That which is older than the creation may indeed be extolled for its venerable age; but among created things, the argument from antiquity is a false criterion of worth. Sin and death are older than the common law; are they, therefore, to be preferred to it? The mortal transgression of Cain was anterior to the common law; does it therefore furnish a better precedent?

Judge-made law is *ex post facto* law and, therefore, unjust. An act is not forbidden by the statute law, but it becomes by judicial decision a crime. A contract is intended and supposed to be valid, but it becomes void by judicial construction. The legislature could not effect this, for the Constitution forbids it. The judiciary shall not usurp legislative power, says the Bill of Rights; yet it not only usurps but runs riot beyond the confines of legislative power.

Judge-made law is special legislation. The judge is human and feels the bias which the coloring of the particular case gives. If he wishes to decide the next case differently, he has only to *distinguish,* and thereby make a new law. The legislature must act on general views and prescribe at once for a whole class of cases.

No man can tell what the common law is, therefore, it is not law; for a law is a rule of action, but a rule which is unknown can govern no man's conduct. Notwithstanding this, it has been called the perfection of human reason.

Robert Rantoul, Jr.; engraving by T. Doney

The common law is the perfection of human reason, just as alcohol is the perfection of sugar. The subtle spirit of the common law is reason double distilled, till what was wholesome and nutritive becomes rank poison. Reason is sweet and pleasant to the unsophisticated intellect; but this sublimated perversion of reason bewilders, and perplexes, and plunges its victims into mazes of error.

The judge makes law by extorting from precedents something which they do not contain. He extends his precedents, which were themselves the extension of others, till, by this accommodating principle, a whole system of law is built up without the authority or interference of the legislator.

The judge labors to reconcile conflicting analogies and to derive from them a rule to decide future cases. No one knows what the law is *before* he lays it down; for it does not exist even in the breast of the judge. All the cases carried up to the tribunal of the last resort are capable of being argued, or they would not be carried there. Those which are not carried up are not law, for the Supreme Court might decide them differently. Those which are carried up, argued, and decided might have been decided differently,

as will appear from the arguments. It is, therefore, often optional with the judge to incline the balance as he pleases. In 40 percent of the cases carried up to a higher court, for a considerable term of years, terminating not long ago, the judgment was reversed. Almost any case, where there is any difference of opinion, may be decided either way, and plausible analogies found in the great storehouse of precedent to justify the decision. The law, then, is the final will or whim of the judge after counsel for both parties have done their utmost to sway it to the one side or the other.

No man knows what the law is *after* the judge has decided it. Because, as the judge is careful not to decide any point which is not brought before him, he restricts his decision within the narrowest possible limits; and though the very next case that may arise may seem, to a superficial observer and even upon a close inspection by an ordinary mind, to be precisely similar to the last, yet the ingenuity of a thoroughbred lawyer may detect some unsuspected shade of difference upon which an opposite decision may be founded. Great part of the skill of a judge consists in avoiding the direct consequences of a rule by ingenious expedients and distinctions, whenever the rule would operate absurdly; and as an ancient maxim may be evaded but must not be annulled, the whole system has been gradually rendered a labyrinth of apparent contradictions reconciled by legal adroitness.

Statutes, enacted by the legislature, speak the public voice. Legislators, with us, are not only chosen because they possess the public confidence but, after their election they are strongly influenced by public feeling. They must sympathize with the public and express its will; should they fail to do so, the next year witnesses their removal from office, and others are selected to be the organs of the popular sentiment.

The older portions of the common law are the work of judges who held their places during the good pleasure of the king, and, of course, decided the law so as to suit the pleasure of the king. In feudal times it was made up of feudal principles, warped, to be sure, according to the king's necessities. Judges now are appointed by the executive and hold their offices during good behavior — that is, for life — and are consequently out of the reach of popular influence. They are sworn to administer common law as it came down from the Dark Ages, excepting what has been repealed by the Constitution and the statutes, which exception they are always careful to reduce to the narrowest possible limits. With them, wrong is right if wrong has existed from time immemorial; precedents are everything; the spirit of the age is nothing. And suppose the judge prefers the common law to the constitutions of the state and of the Union or decides in defiance of the statute; what is the remedy? An astute argument is always at hand to reconcile the open violation of that instrument with the express letter of the Constitution, as in the case of the United States Bank, or to prove an obnoxious statute unconstitutional, as would have happened in the case of the Warren Bridge but for the firmness of Judge Morton. Impeachment is a bugbear which has lost its terrors. We must have democratic governors who will appoint democratic judges, and the whole body of the law must be codified.

It is said that where a chain of precedents is found running back to a remote antiquity, it may be presumed that they originated in a statute which, through lapse of time, has perished. Unparalleled presumption this! To suppose the legislation of a barbarous age richer and more comprehensive than our own. It was without doubt a thousand times more barren. But what if there were such statutes? The specimens which have survived do not impress us with a favorable opinion of those that may have been lost. Crudely conceived, savage in their spirit, vague, indeterminate, and unlimited in their terms, and incoherent when regard-

ed as parts of a system, the remains of ancient legislation are of little use at present, and what is lost was probably still more worthless. If such laws were now to be found in our statute book, they would be repealed at once; the innumerable judicial constructions which they might have received would not save them. Why then should supposed statutes, which probably never had any but an imaginary existence, which if they ever existed were the rude work of barbarians, which cannot now be ascertained, and if they could be, would be despised and rejected as bad in themselves and worse for our situation and circumstances — why should such supposed statutes govern, in the nineteenth century, the civilized and intelligent freemen of Massachusetts?

These objections to the common law have a peculiar force in America, because the rapidly advancing state of our country is continually presenting new cases for the decision of the judges; and by determining these as they arise, the bench takes for its share more than half of our legislation, notwithstanding the express provisions of the Constitution that the judiciary shall not usurp the functions of the legislature. If a common law system could be tolerable anywhere, it is only where everything is stationary. With us, it is subversive of the fundamental principles of a free government, because it deposits in the same hands the power of first making the general laws and then applying them to individual cases; powers distinct in their nature, and which ought to be jealously separated.

But even in England, common law is only a part of a system which, as a whole, would be incomplete without *equity*. We strive to make the part supply the place of the whole. Equity is the correction of that wherein the law by reason of its generality is deficient; yet we have taken the law, deficient as it confessedly is, without the correction, except in certain cases, where by degrees, and, almost without the knowledge of the people, equity powers have been given to the courts. A Court of Chancery would not be tolerated here for reasons which I have not time to enter upon; and without that adjunct, the common law system would not be tolerated in England. The remedy is to fuse both into one mass, adopting such principles of equity as are really necessary, simplifying the whole, enacting the result in the form of statutes, and, from time to time, supplying defects and omissions as they are discovered. It is hardly necessary to observe that, in doing this, opportunity should be taken to reform and remodel the great body of the law, which stands in need of such a revision more than any other science. Some immense advances, it is true, have been made within the last two years, of which the total abolition of special pleading is not the least remarkable. But instead of being satisfied with what has been gained, it should only encourage us to step forward more boldly in what remains to do. All American law must be statute law.

55.

Daniel Webster: Technical Progress and Prosperity

In a speech delivered to the Society for the Diffusion of Useful Knowledge in Boston in November 1836, Daniel Webster, Whig senator from Massachusetts, expressed the conservative view of progress and prosperity. Jacksonian Democrats denounced the corporation as a monopoly sanctioned by law; Webster extolled it as a means of financing progress under the control of law. Democrats were beginning to fear the effect of machines on labor; Webster looked forward to a reduction in prices that would make machine-made goods available to all. Democrats spoke of the conflict of classes; Webster spoke of the common interest and of a fluid society that obscured the lines between rich and poor.

Source: *The Writings and Speeches of Daniel Webster Hitherto Uncollected,* Boston, 1903, Vol. I, pp. 63-78.

ALL EDUCATION, HIGH OR LOW, is something beyond man's absolute physical necessities, and is an advance in the improvement of his intellectual nature. No men are born readers or writers, or with the knowledge which reading imparts. Is it not true, then, that the sudden extension of general knowledge and education which has been witnessed in our day is naturally to be ascribed to some sudden but vast improvement in the condition of the great mass of society? Is it not that that great mass, by the operation of some powerful cause or causes, has become suddenly to possess means, either in time, labor, or capital, beyond the mere necessities of life, and which it can apply to purposes of education? Is it not because shelter and food and clothing have become objects of easier attainment and, therefore, leave a greater degree of leisure and ability for improvement of the mind?

To me this appears to be the great cause of all. The progress of popular knowledge is, I think, mainly owing to the increased comforts and ability of the great mass of society. It is undoubtedly true, most true, that in this case the effect acts back, becomes itself a cause tending to the production of the same end. Popular knowledge, taking an impulse from an improved condition of the people, no doubt helps on that improvement. Cause and effect thus come to act reciprocally and to reproduce each other; but whether as original or as a concomitant and mutually acting agency, it is, I think, an improved condition of a great majority of the people, in regard to the means of living and of wealth, which is to be esteemed as the direct cause of the extraordinary diffusion of general knowledge.

But this result, if it be true, has conducted us but one step in the inquiry. The question only recurs under a new form. To what cause, or causes, is it that we are to refer this rapid improvement in the condition of society. If men and women are now better educated because they have more leisure and more means and more ability, how has it happened that in these respects any great improvement should be made suddenly? Wealth, or any considerable increase in the means of living, or the power of attaining higher degrees of comfort, is ordinarily a slow and painful attainment. Especially it would be wonderful, it might be said, if a whole society, or the greater part of it, should be hastening with rapid strides to this new degree of comfort, or of comparative wealth. But such undoubtedly is the truth in the most civilized states of Europe, and more emphatically is it true among ourselves.

There has been, in the course of half a century, an unprecedented augmentation of general wealth. Even within a shorter period, and under the actual observation of most of us, in our own country and our own circles, vastly increased comforts have come to be enjoyed by the industrious classes, and vastly more leisure and time are found for the cultivation of the mind. It would be easy to prove this by detailed comparisons between the present and the past, showing how far the present exceeds the past, in regard to the shelter, food, clothing, and fuel enjoyed by laboring families. But this is a truth so evident and so open to common observation as matter of fact, that proof by particular enumeration of circumstances becomes unnecessary. We may safely take the fact to be, as it certainly is, that there are certain causes which have acted with peculiar energy in our generation, and which have improved the condition of the mass of society with a degree of rapidity heretofore altogether unknown.

What, then, are these causes? This is an interesting question. It seems to me the main cause is the successful application of science to art; or, in other words, the progress of scientific art.

It is the general doctrine of writers on political economy, that labor is the source of wealth. This is undoubtedly true. The materials of wealth are in the earth, and in the seas, or in their productions; and it is labor only which obtains them, works upon them, and fashions them to the uses of man. The fertility of the soil is nothing, till labor cultivates it; the iron in the mountain rock is of no value, till the strong hand of labor has drawn it forth, separated it from the neighboring earths, and melted and forged it into a manufactured article.

The great agent, therefore, that procures shelter, and food, and raiment for man, is labor; that is to say, it is an active agency, it is some moving power, it is something which has action and effort, and is capable of taking hold of the materials with which the world supplies us, and of working them into shapes and forms such as shall administer to the wants and comforts of mankind.

The proposition of the philosophers, therefore, is true, that labor is the true source, and the only source of wealth; and it necessarily follows, that any augmentation of labor augments, to the same degree, the production of wealth. But when Adam Smith and his immediate followers laid down this maxim, it is evident that they had in view, chiefly, either the manual labors of agriculturists and artisans, or the active occupations of other productive classes.

It was the toil of the human arm that they principally regarded. It was labor, as distinct from capital. But it seems to me that the true philosophy of the thing is, that any labor, any active agency, which can be brought to act usefully on the earth, or its materials, is the source of wealth. The labor of the ox, and the horse, as well as that of man, produces wealth. That is to say, this labor, like man's labor, extracts from the earth the means of living, and these constitute wealth in its general political sense.

Now it has been the purpose, and a purpose most successfully and triumphantly obtained, of scientific art, to increase this active agency, which, in a philosophical point of view, is, I think, to be regarded as labor, by bringing the powers of the elements into active and more efficient operation, and creating millions of automatic laborers, all diligently employed for the benefit of man. The powers are principally steam, and the weight of water. The automatic machinery are mechanisms of infinitely various kinds.

[There are] two classes: first, when a series of operations is carried through by one power, till a perfect result is had, like factories; second, more [powers], single or united, steamboats, cars, and printing presses. We commonly speak of mechanic inventions as laborsaving machines; but it would be more philosophical to speak of them as labor-doing machines because they, in fact, are laborers. They are made to be active agents, to have motion and effect, and though without intelligence, they are guided by those laws of science which are exact and perfect, and they produce results, therefore, in general, more exact and accurate than the human hand is capable of producing.

When one sees Mr. Whittemore's carding machine in operation and looks at the complexity and accuracy of its operations, their rapidity, and yet their unbroken and undisturbed succession, he will see that in this machine (as well as in the little dog that turns it) man has a fellow laborer, and this fellow laborer is of immense power, of mathematical accuracy and precision, and of unwearied effort. And while he is thus a most skillful and productive laborer, he is, at the same time, a nonconsumer. His earnings all go to the use of man. It is over such engines, even with more propriety than on the apiary, that the motto might be written: *vos, non vobis, laborastis* [you work but not for yourself].

It is true that the machinery, in this and similar cases, is the purchase of capital. But human labor is the purchase of capital also, though the free purchase; and in communities less fortunate than ours, the human being himself, who performs the labor, is the purchase of capital. The work of machinery is certainly labor in all sense, as much as slave service, and in an enlarged sense, it is labor in [there is a blank space here in the manuscript] and regarding labor as a mere active power of production; whether that power be the hand of man, or the automatic movement of machinery, the general result is the same.

It is thus that the successful application of science to art increases the productive power and agency of the human race. It multiplies laborers without multiplying consumers, and the world is precisely as much benefited as if Providence had provided for our use millions of men, like ourselves in external appearance, who would work and labor and toil, and who yet required for their own subsistence neither shelter, nor food, nor clothing. These automata in the factories and the workshops are as much our fellow laborers, as if they were automata wrought by some Maelzel into the form of men, and made capable of walking, moving, and working, of felling the forest or cultivating the fields.

It is well known that the era of the successful application of science to arts, especially in the production of the great article of human subsistence, clothing, commenced about half a century ago. H. Arkwright predicted how productive human industry would become when no longer proportioned in its results to muscular strength. He had great sagacity, boldness, judgment, and power of arrangement. In 1770, England consumed 4 million pounds of cotton in manufactures; the United States none. The aggregate consumption of Europe and America is now 5 million. Arkwright deserves to be regarded as a benefactor of mankind. From the same period we may date the commencement in the general improvement in the condition of the mass of society, in regard to wealth and the means of living; and to the same period also we may assign the beginning of that spread of popular knowledge which now stamps such an imposing character on the times.

What is it, then, but this increased laboring power; what is it but these automatic allies and cooperators, who have come with such prodigious effect to man's aid in the great business of procuring the means of living, of comfort, and of wealth, out of the materials of the physical universe, which has so changed the face of society?

And this mighty agency, this automatic labor whose ability cannot be limited nor bounded, is the result of the successful application of science to art. Science has thus reached its greatest excellence, and achieved its highest attainment, in rendering itself emphatically, conspicuously, and in the highest degree useful to men of all classes and conditions. Its noblest attainment consists in conferring practical and substantial blessings on mankind.

"Practical mechanics," says a late ingenious and able writer, "is, in the preeminent sense, a scientific art." It is indeed true that the arts are growing everyday more and more perfect, from the prosecution of scientific researches. And it ought to put to the blush all those who decry any department of science, or any field of knowledge, as barren and unproductive; that man has, as yet, learned nothing that has not been, or may not be, capable of useful application. If we look to the unclouded skies, when the

moon is riding among the constellations, it might seem to us that the distance of that luminary from any particular star could be of no possible importance, or its knowledge of no practical use to man. Yet it is precisely the knowledge of that distance, wrought out and applied by science, that enables the navigator to decide, within a few miles, his precise place on the ocean, not having seen land in many months.

The high state of navigation, its safety and its dispatch, are memorials of the highest character in honor of science, and the application of science to the purposes of life. The knowledge of conic sections, in like manner, may appear quite remote from practical utility, yet there are mechanical operations of the highest importance, entirely dependent on an accurate knowledge, and a just application of the scientific rules pertaining to that subject. Therefore he who studies astronomy and explores the celestial system, a Laplace or Bowditch; or he who constructs tables for finding the longitude, or works out results and proportions applicable to machinery from conic sections, or other branches of mathematics; or he who fixes by precise rule the vibration of the pendulum, or applies to use the counterbalancing and mutually adjusting centripetal and centrifugal force of bodies, are laborers for the human race of the highest character and the greatest merit. . . .

It is false in morals to say that good principles do not tend to produce good practice; it is equally false in matters of science and of art to declare that knowledge produces no fruit.

Perhaps the most prominent instance of the application of science to art, in the production of things necessary to man's subsistence, is the use of the elastic power of steam, applied to the operations of spinning and weaving and dressing fabrics for human wear. All this mighty discovery bears directly on the means of human subsistence and human comfort. It has greatly altered commerce, agriculture, and even the habits of life among nations. It has affected commerce by creating new objects, or vastly increasing the importance of those before hardly known; it has affected agriculture by giving new value to its products; what would now be the comparative value of the soil of our Southern and Southwestern states if the spinning of cotton by machinery, the power loom, and the cotton gin, were struck out of existence? And it has affected habits by giving a new direction to labor and creating a multitude of new pursuits.

Bearing less on the production of the objects necessary to man's subsistence, but hardly inferior in its importance, is the application of the power of steam to transportation and conveyance by sea and by land. Who is so familiarized to the sight even now, as to look without wonder and amazement on the long train of cars, full of passengers and merchandise, drawn along our valleys, and the sides of our mountains themselves with a rapidity which holds competition [with] the winds?

This branch of the application of steam power is younger. It is not yet fully developed; but the older branch, its application to manufacturing machinery, is perhaps to be regarded as the more signal instance marking the great and glorious epoch of the application of science to the useful arts. From the time of Arkwright to our own days, and in our own country, from a period a little earlier than the commencement of the late war with England, we see the successive and astonishing effects of this principle, not newborn, indeed, in our time, but awakened, animated, and pushed forward to most stupendous results. It is difficult to estimate the amount of labor performed by machinery, compared with manual labor. It is computed that in England, on articles exported it is £30 million sterling per year. It would be useful if one with competent means should estimate the products of the annual labor of Massachusetts in manufactured articles carried from the state.

If these and other considerations may suffice to satisfy us that the application of science to art is the main cause of the sudden augmentation of wealth and comfort in modern times, a truth remains to be stated of the greatest magnitude, and the highest practical importance, and that is, that this augmentation of wealth and comfort is general and diffusive, reaching to all classes, embracing all interests, and benefiting, not a part of society, but the whole. There is no monopoly in science. There are no exclusive privileges in the workings of automatic machinery, or the powers of natural bodies. The poorest, as well as the richest man in society, has a direct interest, and generally the poor a far greater interest than the rich, in the successful operation of these arts, which make the means of living, clothing especially, abundant and cheap. The advantages conferred by knowledge in increasing our physical resources, from their very nature, cannot be enjoyed by a few only. They are all open to the many, and to be profitable, the many must enjoy it.

The products of science applied to art in mechanical inventions are made, not to be hoarded, but to be sold. Their successful operation requires a large market. It requires that the great mass of society should be able to buy and to consume. The improved condition of all classes, more ability to buy food and raiment, better modes of living, and increased comforts of every kind, are exactly what is necessary and indispensable in order that capital invested in automatic operations should be productive to the owners. Some establishments of this kind necessarily require large capital, such as the woolen and cotton factories. And in a country like ours, in which the spirit of our institutions, and all our laws, tend so much to the distribution and equalization of property, there are few individuals of sufficient wealth to build and carry on an establishment by their own means.

This renders a union of capitals necessary, and this among us is conveniently effected by corporations which are but partnerships regulated by law. And this union of many to form capital for the purpose of carrying on those operations by which science is applied to art, and comes in aid of man's labor in the production of things essential to man's existence, constitutes that aggregated wealth of which complaint is sometimes heard. It would seem that nothing could be plainer than that whatever reduces the price, whether of food or of clothing, must be in the end beneficial to the laboring classes. Yet it has not unfrequently happened that machinery has been broken and destroyed in England, by workmen, by open and lawless violence.

Most persons in our country see the folly as well as the injustice and barbarism of such proceedings; but the ideas in which these violences originated are no more unfounded and scarcely more disreputable, than those which would represent capital, collected, necessarily, in large sums, in order to carry on useful processes in which science is applied to art, in the production of articles useful to all, as being hostile to the common good, or having an interest separate from that of the majority of the community. All such representations, if not springing from sinister design, must be the result of great ignorance or great prejudice. It has been found by long experience in England that large capitalists can produce cheaper than small ones, especially in the article of cotton. Greater savings can be made and these savings enable the proprietor to go on, when he must otherwise stop. There is no doubt that it is to her abundant capital England is now indebted for whatever power of competition with the United States she now sustains, in producing cheap articles.

There are modes of applying wealth, useful principally to the owner, and not otherwise beneficial to the community than as they employ labor. Such are the erection of expensive houses, the embellishment of ornamental grounds, the purchase of costly furniture and equipages. These modes of expenditure, although entirely lawful and sometimes very proper, are yet not such as directly benefit the whole community. Not so with aggregate wealth employed in producing articles of general consumption. This mode of employment is, peculiarly and in an emphatic sense, an application of capital to the benefit of all. Anyone who complains of it, or decries it, acts against the greatest good of the greatest number. The factories, the steamboats, the railroads, and other similar establishments, although they require capital, and aggregate capital, are yet general and popular in all the good they produce.

The unquestionable operation of all these things has been not only to increase property, but to equalize it, to diffuse it, to scatter its advantages among the many, and to give content, cheerfulness, and animation to all classes of the social system. In New England, more particularly, has this been the result. What has enabled us to be rich and prosperous, notwithstanding the barrenness of our soil and the rigor of our climate? What has diffused so much comfort, wealth, and happiness among all classes, but the diligent employment of our citizens, in these processes and mechanical operations in which science comes in aid of handicraft?

Abolish the use of steam and the application of water power to machinery, and what would at this moment be the condition of New England? And yet steam and water power have been employed only, and can be employed only, by what is called aggregated wealth. Far distant be the day then when the people of New England shall be deceived by the specious fallacy that there are different and opposing interests in our community; that what is useful to one is hurtful to the rest; that there is one interest for the rich, and another interest for the poor; that capital is the enemy of labor, or labor the foe of capital. And let every laboring man, on whose understanding such a fallacy is attempted to be imposed, stop the mouth of the false reasoner at once, by stating the plain and evident fact, that while aggregated wealth has for years, in Massachusetts, been most skillfully and steadily employed in the productions which result from the application of science to art; thereby reducing the cost of many of the articles most essential to human life in all conditions; labor, meantime, has been constantly rising, and is at this very moment, notwithstanding the present scarcity of money, and the constant pressure on capital, higher than it ever was before in the history of the country. These are, indeed, facts which baffle all former dogmas of political economy.

In some of our most agricultural districts in the midst of our mountains, on whose tops the native forests still wave and where agricultural labor is high, in an unprecedented degree, even here automatic processes are carried on by water, and fabrics wrought out of materials which have been transported hundreds and thousands of miles, by sea and by land, and which fabrics go back again, some of them, for sale and consumption to the places where the raw material was produced. Carolina cotton is carried to the County of Berkshire, and Berkshire cotton goods are sold in Carolina. Meanwhile labor in Berkshire is not only in money price, but in comparison with the cost of the main articles of human subsistence, higher than it was ever known before. Writers on political economy may, perhaps, on facts like these see occasion to qualify their theories; meantime, it becomes every man to question and scrutinize severely, if not the motives, yet the reasoning and the logic of those who would persuade us that capital, employed in the most efficient modes of producing things useful, is hurtful to society. It would be quite as reasonable to insist that the weaving of paper, if that be the proper term, in consequence of recent most valuable mechanical inventions, should be [suppressed], and the power press, and the hydrostatic machine taken out of the printing houses, as being all hurt-

ful and injurious, although they may have reduced the price of books for general circulation one half.

The truth, in my opinion, rather is, that such is the enterprise of our people, such the astonishing amount of labor which they perform, and which they perform cheerfully because it is free and because it is profitable, and such the skill with which capital is used, that still more capital would be useful and that its introduction would be advantageous, and most of all to the busy and industrious classes. And let it never be forgotten, that with us labor is free, intelligent, respecting itself, and respected by other interests; that it accumulates; that it is provident; that it lays up for itself; and that these savings become capital, and their owners in time capitalists.

I cannot omit to notice, here, another fact peculiar to this country, and which should cause us to hesitate in applying to ourselves, and our condition, European maxims respecting capital and labor. In Europe, generally speaking, the laborer is always a laborer. He is destined to no better condition on earth, ordinarily he rises no higher. We see proofs, melancholy proofs, of this truth often in the multitudes who come to our own shores from foreign countries for employment. It is not so with the people of New England.

Capital and labor are much less distinctly divided with us. Few are they, on the one hand, who have need to perform no labor; few are they, on the other, who have no property or capital of their own. Or if there be those of the latter class among the industrious and the sober, they are young men who, though they are laborers today, will be capitalists tomorrow. A career of usefulness and enterprise is before them. If without moneyed capital, they have a capital in their intelligence, their knowledge, and their good habits. Around them are a thousand collections of automatic machinery, requiring the diligence of skillful and sober labor-

ers; before them is the ocean, always inviting to deeds of hardihood and enterprise;
behind them are the fertile prairies of the
West, soliciting cultivation; and over them
all is the broad banner of free institutions,
of mild laws, and parental government.
Would an American young man of good
health and good habits need say that he is
without capital? Or why should he discredit
his own understanding by listening to the
absurdity, that they who have earned property, and they who have not yet lived long
enough to earn it, must be enemies? The
proportion of those who have not capital,
such as to render them independent without
personal labor, and who are yet not without
some capital, is vastly larger in this community than any other. They form indeed the
great mass of our society. They are its life
and muscle; and long may they continue
free, moral, intelligent, and prosperous as
they now are.

56.

FRANKLIN PIERCE: The Military Academy

*Many Democrats followed Jackson's lead in condemning the Military Academy at
West Point, New York. The reasons for the attack are revealed in the following
speech delivered to the House of Representatives in 1836 by a young congressman
and future President, Franklin Pierce. As a result of the agitation by Pierce and
others, an investigation was undertaken by the House in 1837 substantiating Pierce's
objections. Although no sweeping reforms followed, a bill of 1838 extended from one
to four years a cadet's service obligation after completing his four-year course at
the Point. The Army, unwillingly, also instituted the practice (only haphazardly
resorted to in the past) of recruiting officers from among civilian applicants in 1838
and 1839; and the practice of elevating noncommissioned officers from the rank of
sergeant to lieutenant was begun in 1837 and later expanded.*

Source: Thomas Hart Benton, *Thirty Years View*, New York, 1886, Vol. I, pp. 641-645.

AN ATTEMPT WAS MADE during the last Congress to bring the subject of the reorganization of the Military Academy before the
country through a report of a committee.
The same thing has been done during the
present session, again and again, but all efforts have proved alike unsuccessful! Still,
you do not cease to call for appropriations;
you require the people's money for the support of the institution, while you refuse
them the light necessary to enable them to
judge of the propriety of your annual requi-
sitions.

Whether the amount proposed to be appropriated, by the bill upon your table, is
too great or too small or precisely sufficient
to cover the current expenses of the institution is a matter into which I will not at
present inquire; but I shall feel bound to
oppose the bill in every stage of its
progress. I cannot vote a single dollar until
the resolution of inquiry, presented by my
friend from Kentucky (Mr. Hawes) at an
early day in the session, shall be first taken
up and disposed of. . . .

Sir, why has this investigation been resisted? Is it not an institution which has already cost this country more than $3 million for which you propose, in this very bill, an appropriation of more than $130,000, and which, at the same time, in the estimation of a large portion of the citizens of this Union, has failed, eminently failed, to fulfill the objects for which it was established, of sufficient interest and importance to claim the consideration of a committee of this House and of the House itself? I should have expected the resolution of the gentleman from Kentucky (Mr. Hawes), merely proposing an inquiry, to pass without opposition had I not witnessed the strong sensation, nay, excitement, that was produced here, at the last session, by the presentation of his yet unpublished report. . . .

Sir, no man can feel more deeply interested in the Army, or entertain a higher regard for it, than myself. My earliest recollections connect themselves fondly and gratefully with the names of the brave men who, relinquishing the quiet and security of civil life, were staking their all upon the defense of their country's rights and honor. One of the most distinguished among that noble band now occupies and honors a seat upon this floor. It is not fit that I should indulge in expressions of personal respect and admiration, which I am sure would find a hearty response in the bosom of every member of this committee. I allude to him merely to express the hope that, on some occasion, we may have, upon this subject, the benefit of his experience and observation. And if his opinions shall differ from my own, I promise carefully to review every step by which I have been led to my present conclusions.

You cannot mistake me, sir; I refer to the hero of Erie. I have declared myself the friend of the Army. Satisfy me, then, what measures are best calculated to render it effective and what all desire it to be, and I go for the proposition with my whole heart.

But I cannot believe that the Military Academy, as at present organized, is calculated to accomplish this desirable end. It may, and undoubtedly does, send forth into the country much military knowledge; but the advantage which your Army, or that which will constitute your Army in time of need, derives from it, is by no means commensurate with the expense you incur.

Here, Mr. Chairman, permit me to say that I deny utterly the expediency and the right to educate, at the public expense, any number of young men who, on the completion of their education, are not to form a portion of your military force, but to return to the walks of private life. Such was never the operation of the Military Academy, until after the law of 1812; and the doctrine, so far as I have been able to ascertain, was first formally announced by a distinguished individual at this time sufficiently jealous of the exercise of executive patronage, and greatly alarmed by what he conceives to be the tendencies of this government to centralism and consolidation. It may be found in the report of the secretary of war communicated to Congress in 1819.

If it shall, upon due consideration, receive the sanction of Congress and the country, I can see no limit to the exercise of power and government patronage. Follow out the principle, and where will it lead you? You confer upon the national government the absolute guardianship of literature and science, military and civil; you need not stop at military science; anyone in the wide range of science becomes at once a legitimate and constitutional object of your patronage; you are confined by no limit but your discretion; you have no check but your own good pleasure. If you may afford instruction at the public expense in the languages, in philosophy, in chemistry, and in the exact sciences to young gentlemen who are under no obligation to enter the service of their country, but are, in fact, destined for civil life, why may you not, by parity of reasoning, provide the means of a legal, or theological, or medical education, on the ground that the recipients of your bounty will carry forth a fund of useful knowledge that may, at some time, under some circumstances, produce a beneficial influence, and promote "the general welfare." Sir, I fear that even some of us may live to see the day when this "general welfare" of your Constitution will leave us little ground to boast of a government of limited powers.

But I did not propose at this time to discuss the abstract question of constitutional right. I will regard the expediency alone; and, whether the power exist or not, its exercise, in an institution like this, is subversive of the only principle upon which a school conducted at the public expense can be made profitable to the public service — that of making an admission into your school, and an education there, secondary to an appointment in the Army. Sir, this distinctive feature characterized all your legislation and all executive recommendations down to 1810.

I may as well notice here, as at any time, an answer which has always been ready when objections have been raised to this institution; an answer which, if it has not proved quite satisfactory to minds that yield their assent more readily to strong reasons than to the authority of great names, has yet, unquestionably, exercised a powerful influence upon the public mind. It has not gone forth upon the authority of an individual merely, but has been published to the world with the approbation of a committee of a former Congress. It is this: that the institution has received, at different times, the sanction of such names as Washington, Adams, and Jefferson; and this has been claimed with such boldness, and in a form so imposing, as almost to forbid any question of its accuracy. If this were correct, in point of fact, it would be entitled to the most profound respect and consideration, and no change should be urged against the weight of such authority, without mature deliberation and thorough conviction of expediency. Unfortunately for the advocates of the institution, and fortunately for the in-

Museum of Fine Arts, Boston

Franklin Pierce; portrait by G. P. A. Healy

terests of the country, this claim cannot be sustained by reference to executive documents, from the first report of General Knox, in 1790, to the close of Mr. Jefferson's administration.

The error has undoubtedly innocently occurred by confounding the Military Academy at West Point as it was with the Military Academy at West Point as it is. The report of Secretary Knox just referred to is characterized by this distinctive feature: that the corps proposed to be organized were "to serve as an actual defense to the community," and to constitute a part of the active military force of the country, "to serve in the field, or on the frontier, or in the fortifications of the seacoast, as the commander in chief may direct." At a later period, the report of the secretary of war (Mr. McHenry), communicated to Congress in 1800, although it proposed a plan for military schools differing in many essential particulars from those which had preceded it, still retained the distinctive feature just named as characterizing the report of General Knox.

With regard to educating young men gratuitously, which, whatever may have been the design, I am prepared to show is the practical operation of the Academy as at present organized, I cannot, perhaps, exhibit more clearly the sentiments of the executive at that early day, urgent as was the occasion, and strong as must have been the desire, to give strength and efficiency to the military force, than by reading one or two paragraphs from a supplementary report of Secretary McHenry, addressed to the chairman of the Committee of Defense, January 31, 1800.

The secretary says:

Agreeably to the plan of the Military Academy, the directors thereof are to be officers taken from the Army; consequently, no expense will be incurred by such appointments. The plan also contemplates that officers of the Army, cadets, and noncommissioned officers shall receive instruction in the Academy. As the rations and fuel which they are entitled to in the Army will suffice for them in the Academy, no additional expense will be required for objects of maintenance while there. The expenses of servants and certain incidental expenses relative to the police and administration may be defrayed by those who shall be admitted, out of their pay and emoluments.

You will observe, Mr. Chairman, from the phraseology of the report that all were to constitute a part of your actual military force; and that whatever additional charges should be incurred were to be defrayed by those who might receive the advantages of instruction. These were provisions, just as they are important. Let me call your attention for a moment to a report of Colonel Williams which was made the subject of a special message communicated to Congress by Mr. Jefferson, March 18, 1808. The extract I propose to read, as sustaining fully the views of Mr. McHenry upon this point, is in the following words:

It might be well to make the plan upon such a scale as not only to take in the minor officers of the Navy, but also any youths from any of the states who might wish for such an education, whether designed for the Army or Navy, or neither, and let them be assessed to the value of their education, which might form a fund for extra or contingent expenses.

Sir, these are the true doctrines upon this subject; doctrines worthy of the administration under which they were promulgated, and in accordance with the views of statesmen in the earlier and purer days of the republic. Give to the officers of your Army the highest advantages for perfection in all the branches of military science, and let those advantages be open to all, in rotation, and under such terms and regulations as shall be at once impartial toward the officers and advantageous to the service; but let all young gentlemen who have a taste for military life and desire to adopt arms as a profession prepare themselves for subordinate situations at their own expense, or at the expense of their parents or guardians, in the same manner that the youth of the country are qualified for the professions of civil life. . . .

If the patience of the committee would warrant me, Mr. Chairman, I could show, by reference to executive communications and the concurrent legislation of Congress in 1794, 1796, 1802, and 1808, that prior to the last-mentioned date such an institution as we now have was neither recommended nor contemplated. Upon this point I will not detain you longer; but when hereafter confronted by the authority of great names, I trust we shall be told where the expressions of approbation are to be found. We may then judge of their applicability to the Military Academy as at present organized.

I am far from desiring to see this country destitute of a military academy; but I would have it a school of practice and instruction for officers actually in the service of the United States; not an institution for educating, gratuitously, young gentlemen who, on the completion of their term, or after a few months' leave of absence, resign their commissions and return to the pursuits of civil life. If anyone doubts that this is the practical operation of your present system, I refer him to the annual list of resignations to be found in the adjutant general's office.

Firmly as I am convinced of the necessity of a reorganization, I would take no step to create an unjust prejudice against the institution. All that I ask, and, so far as I know, all that any of the opponents of the institution ask is that, after a full and impartial investigation, it shall stand or fall upon its merits. I know there are graduates of the institution who are ornaments to the Army and an honor to their country; but they, and not the seminary, are entitled to the credit.

Here I would remark, once for all, that I do not reflect upon the officers or pupils of the Academy; it is to the principles of the institution itself, as at present organized, that I object. It is often said that the graduates leave the institution with sentiments that but ill accord with the feelings and opinions of the great mass of the people of that government from which they derive the means of education, and that many who take commissions possess few qualifications for the command of men, either in war or in peace. Most of the members of this House have had more or less intercourse with these young gentlemen, and I leave it for each individual to form his own opinion of the correctness of the charges. Thus much I will say for myself, that I believe that these and greater evils are the natural if not the inevitable result of the principles in which this institution is founded; and any system of education established upon similar principles, on government patronage alone, will produce like results, now and forever.

Sir, what are some of these results? By the report of the secretary of war, dated January 1831, we are informed that, "by an estimate of the last five years (preceding that date), it appears that the supply of the Army from the corps of graduated cadets has averaged about twenty-two annually, while those who graduated are about forty, making in each year an excess of eighteen. The number received annually into the Academy averages one hundred, of which only the number stated, to wit, forty, pass through the prescribed course of education at school, and become supernumerary lieutenants in the Army."

By the report of the secretary of war, December 1830, we are informed that the number of promotions to the Army from this corps for the last five years has averaged about twenty-two annually, while the number of graduates has been at an average of forty. This excess, which is annually increasing, has placed eighty-seven in waiting until vacancies shall take place, and show that in the next year, probably, and in the succeeding one, certainly, there will be an excess beyond what the existing law authorizes to be commissioned. There will then be 106 supernumerary brevet second lieutenants appurtenant to the Army, at an average annual expense of $80,000. Sir, that results here disclosed were not anticipated by Mr. Madison is apparent from a recurrence to his messages of 1810 and 1811.

In passing the law of 1812, both Congress and the President acted for the occasion, and they expected those who should succeed them to act in a similar manner. Their feelings of patriotism and resentment were aroused by beholding the privileges of freemen wantonly invaded, our glorious stars and stripes disregarded, and national and individual rights trampled in the dust. The war was pending. The necessity for increasing the military force of the country was obvious and pressing, and the urgent occasion for increased facilities for military instruction equally apparent. Sir, it was under circumstances like these, when we had not only enemies abroad but, I blush to say, enemies at home that the institution, as at present organized, had its origin. It will hardly be pretended that it was the original design of the law to augment the number of persons instructed beyond the wants of the public service.

Well, the report of the secretary shows that for five years prior to 1831 the Academy had furnished eighteen supernumeraries annually. A practical operation of this character has no sanction in the recommendation of Mr. Madison. The report demonstrates, further, the *fruitfulness* and *utility* of this institution, by showing the fact that but two-fifths of those who enter the Academy graduate, and that but a fraction more than one-fifth enter the public service.

This is not the fault of the administration of the Academy; it is not the fault of the young gentlemen who are *sent* there; on your present peace establishment there can be but little to stimulate them, particularly in the acquisition of military science. There can hardly be but one object in the mind of the student, and that would be to obtain an education for the purposes of civil life. The difficulty is that the institution has outlived both the occasion that called it into existence and its original design.

I have before remarked that the Academy was manifestly enlarged to correspond with the Army and militia actually to be called into service. Look, then for a moment at facts, and observe with how much wisdom, justice, and sound policy you retain the provisions of the law of 1812. The total authorized force of 1813, after the declaration of war, was 58,254; and, in October 1814, the military establishment amounted to 62,428. By the act of March 1815, the peace establishment was limited to 10,000, and now hardly exceeds that number. Thus you make a reduction of more than 50,000 in your actual military force to accommodate the expenses of the government to its wants. And why do you refuse to do the same with your grand system of public education? Why does that remain unchanged?

Why not reduce it at once, at least to the actual wants of the service, and dispense with your corps of supernumerary lieutenants?

Sir, there is, there can be, but one answer to the question, and that may be found in the war report of 1819, to which I have before had occasion to allude. The secretary says, "The cadets who cannot be provided for in the Army will return to private life, but in the event of a war their knowledge will not be lost to the country." Indeed, sir, these young gentlemen, if they could be *induced* to take the field, would, after a lapse of ten or fifteen years, come up from the bar, or it may be the pulpit, fresh in military science and admirably qualified for command in the face of an enemy.

The magazine of facts to prove at the same glance the extravagance and unfruitfulness of this institution is not easily exhausted; but I am admonished by the lateness of the hour to omit many considerations which I regard as both interesting and important. I will only detain the committee to make a single statement, placing side by side some aggregate results. There has already been expended upon the institution more than $3,300,000. Between 1815 and 1821, 1,318 students were admitted into the Academy; and of all the cadets who were ever there, only 265 remained in the service at the end of 1830. Here are the expenses you have incurred and the products you have realized.

I leave them to be balanced by the people. But for myself, believing as I do that the Academy stands forth as an anomaly among the institutions of this country; that it is at variance with the spirit if not the letter of the Constitution under which we live; so long as this House shall deny investigation into its principles and practical operation, I, as an individual member, will refuse to appropriate the first dollar for its support.

57.

JOHN SAVAGE: Slums as a Common Nuisance

Slums were a blight in every large Eastern city in the 1830s. With the growth of industry, wealthy city dwellers moved to more remote and quieter parts of town. The houses that they vacated were at first rented, story by story, to more prosperous workers, but in time, whole blocks of houses were profitably fragmented into minute apartments and rented to the very poor. It was cheaper for the landlord or agent to let the buildings decay and rebuild on the premises than to try and keep them in repair. Only gradually were laws enacted to cope with slums and with other problems that attended the growth of cities. The case of Meeker v. *Van Rensselaer (May 1836), reprinted below, confirmed a lower court verdict that upheld a landlord's right to tear down his property if it became a common nuisance.*

Source: 15 Wendell 397.

A dwelling house, cut up into small apartments, inhabited by a crowd of poor people, in a filthy condition, and calculated to breed disease is a *public nuisance*, and may be abated by individuals residing in the neighborhood by tearing it down, especially during the prevalence of a disease like the Asiatic cholera.

Parol evidence of the acts of a board of health of a city in directing the abatement of *nuisances* is not admissible; it should consist of *written minutes* of the proceedings or *written orders* of the board.

THIS WAS AN ACTION on the case tried at the Albany circuit in March 1833, before the Hon. James Vanderpoel, one of the circuit judges.

The declaration charged the defendant with pulling down five dwelling houses. On the trial it appeared that the dwelling houses consisted of one building, originally erected as a tanhouse, 70 feet long, 12 feet high, which was divided into five apartments.

These apartments, during the summer of 1832, while the Asiatic cholera prevailed in Albany, were inhabited, as one witness stated, by between forty and fifty, and as another stated, by between sixty and eighty Irish emigrants, each apartment containing two or three families. The premises were extremely filthy; under the floors were twenty tan vats, most of which were filled with putrid stagnant water, which oozed through the floors on walking over them. Some of the inmates were sick, and two, a woman and a child, lying dead in the house.

The premises were situated in the Fifth Ward of the city, in which ward the defendant, being at the time an alderman, resided. The inmates of the dwelling were requested to remove to temporary buildings erected by the corporation in a healthy part of the city, and were told that their luggage would be taken there free of expense. They refused, and the defendant directed the buildings to be torn down, which was done accordingly. Several witnesses testified that the premises were a nuisance which could be abated in no other way than that resorted to.

The defendant proved that the Board of Health of the city had directed the nuisance to be abated. To this proof the plaintiff objected, insisting that the minutes of the board or written evidence of their orders should be produced. The objection was overruled, and parol evidence was received. The plaintiff also objected to the proof given of the request to the inmates of the building to remove; which objection was overruled.

The plaintiff inquired of a witness whether there were not many other buildings in the city, similarly situated with those destroyed, in which the cellars had been drained and other measures resorted to for their purification, and whether any other buildings had been torn down. To this inquiry the defendant objected, and the objection was sustained.

The judge charged the jury, if they should find that the building torn down was a nuisance, and that the defendant resided in the neighborhood and had done no more than what was necessary to abate it, that they ought to find a verdict in his favor; but if they should find that the building was not a nuisance, then the defendant was liable to damages. The jury found a verdict for the defendant. The plaintiff asked for a new trial.

By the Court, Savage, C. J. It was not denied upon the trial that the building torn down was a common nuisance, nor was it upon the argument. It may not be improper, however, to refer to the cases collected in *Bacon's Abr. tit. Nuisance* to see what has been adjudged a nuisance. It may be proper to remark that a nuisance is an annoyance; anything that worketh hurt, inconvenience or damage. . . .

It is a common nuisance indictable to di-

vide a house in a town for poor people to inhabit in, by reason whereof it will be more dangerous in the time of sickness and infection of the plague. . . . So manufactures, lawful in themselves, may become nuisances, if erected in parts of towns where they cannot but greatly incommode the inhabitants and destroy their health. Whether the houses of the plaintiff were of that description, was fairly left to the jury by the judge in his charge. A more offensive nuisance cannot be imagined than the buildings described by the witnesses in this case.

The first exception taken on the trial was that the witness should not have been asked whether the inhabitants were not requested to leave the buildings before they were pulled down. The object of the inquiry no doubt was to show that the conduct of the defendant was not wanton, but that he was influenced by considerations of the public good and not of private injury to the plaintiff. The question was proper and unexceptionable.

It was objected that parol evidence should not have been received of the orders of the Board of Health. This objection was well taken. The Board of Health is a tribunal created by statute, clothed with large discretionary powers; and, being a public body, its acts should be proved by the highest and best evidence which the nature of the case admits of.

Every proceeding of a judicial character must be in writing. It is not to be presumed that minutes of their proceedings are not kept by such a body, and that determinations which seriously affect the property of individuals were not reduced to writing, but rest in parol. In the case of *Wormer* v. *The City of Albany* . . . the minutes of the proceedings of the Board were incorporated with the proceedings of the corporation, of which the Board of Health were members, and were proved by a witness a member of both boards. Here the proof was defective; but in my judgment it is not material, because the defendant did not need any authority from the Board of Health. As a citizen of the Fifth Ward, who desired to preserve the public health, and especially as an alderman, he was fully justified in every act done by him.

It was also objected that proof should have been received of other modes of abating nuisances than by pulling down houses. Such proof would have been wholly irrelevant. The proof in this case, from the plaintiff's own witness, was that there was no other way to correct the evil but by pulling down the building. Had it been proved that in the case of other nuisances draining or filling up had been resorted to, such proof would not have contradicted the testimony in this cause. In my opinion a new trial should be refused.

New trial denied.

58.

ABRAHAM LINCOLN: A Candidate Shows His Hand

Abraham Lincoln entered politics as an independent, running for the Illinois legislature from Sangamon County in 1832. He was defeated, but two years later he ran again as a Whig, and won. By 1836 he was a popular figure in the county, and of the seventeen candidates in the election of that year, he polled the highest vote. In a letter to the editor of the Sangamo Journal, *written and dated June 13, 1836, Lincoln confidently announced his candidacy for reelection. Hugh L. White, whom he pledged to support, was an independent candidate for President in 1836; White received the twenty-six electoral votes of Tennessee and Georgia.*

Source: *Sangamo Journal*, June 18, 1836.

To the Editor of the *Journal:*

In your paper of last Saturday, I see a communication over the signature of "Many Voters," in which the candidates who are announced in the *Journal* are called upon to "show their hands." Agreed. Here's mine!

I go for all sharing the privileges of the government who assist in bearing its burdens. Consequently, I go for admitting all whites to the right of suffrage who pay taxes or bear arms (by no means excluding females).

If elected, I shall consider the whole people of Sangamon my constituents, as well those that oppose as those that support me.

While acting as their representative, I shall be governed by their will, on all subjects upon which I have the means of knowing what their will is; and upon all others, I shall do what my own judgment teaches me will best advance their interests. Whether elected or not, I go for distributing the proceeds of the sales of the public lands to the several states, to enable our state, in common with others, to dig canals and construct railroads without borrowing money and paying interest on it.

If alive on the 1st Monday in November, I shall vote for Hugh L. White for President. Very respectfully,

A. LINCOLN

59.

William B. Travis: Message from the Alamo

After American settlers in Texas appealed in 1833 to the Mexican dictator, General Santa Anna, to grant Texas statehood within the Mexican federation, Santa Anna not only refused the request but abolished the federal system altogether. Texans, under Sam Houston, then drew up an ambiguous declaration of independence that brought Santa Anna with close to 4,000 troops across the Rio Grande. A small group of Texas volunteers under the command of Colonels William B. Travis and James Bowie and including the renowned Davy Crockett had occupied the ancient Alamo Mission in December 1835 — against the advice of Houston who said it could not be defended — and they were attacked by Santa Anna's army on February 23, 1836. The siege lasted twelve days, during which the 187 Texans killed from 1,000 to 1,600 Mexicans; but Travis and his men were finally overcome, and on March 6 were massacred to the last man. The independence of Texas was assured six weeks later when Houston defeated Santa Anna at the San Jacinto, his men shouting "Remember the Alamo!" as they went into battle. Travis sent the following appeal for help a few days before he died.

Source: Henderson Yoakum, *History of Texas*, New York, 1856, Vol. II, pp. 76-77.

Fellow Citizens and Compatriots:

I am besieged by a thousand or more of the Mexicans under Santa Anna. I have sustained a continued bombardment for twenty-four hours and have not lost a man. The enemy have demanded a surrender at discretion; otherwise the garrison is to be put to the sword if the place is taken. I have answered the summons with a cannon shot, and our flag still waves proudly from the walls.

I shall never surrender or retreat.

Then, I call on you in the name of liberty, of patriotism, and of everything dear to the American character to come to our aid with all dispatch. The enemy are receiving reinforcements daily and will no doubt increase to three or four thousand in four or five days. Though this call may be neglected, I am determined to sustain myself as long as possible and die like a soldier who never forgets what is due to his own honor and that of his country. *Victory or death!*

W. Barret Travis
Lieutenant Colonel Commanding

P.S. The Lord is on our side. When the enemy appeared in sight, we had not three bushels of corn. We have since found, in deserted houses, eighty or ninety bushels and got into the walls twenty or thirty head of beeves.

———◆———

Thermopylae had its messenger of defeat. The Alamo had none.

Message found written on the walls of the Alamo (in blood or candle smoke) when U.S. troops recaptured it from Santa Anna, after the massacre of March 6, 1836

View of the confluence of the Yellowstone and Missouri rivers; engraving of a Bodmer watercolor

PROBING THE FAR WEST

The Rocky Mountains in the 1820s and '30s were pictured in romantic images of unconquered natural grandeur and solitude. This was the era of the "mountain men," trappers who preferred freedom and loneliness to the pressures of civilization. But their heyday lasted less than ten years. In 1823 William H. Ashley sent a small party, led by Jedediah Smith, to trap in the Rockies. When the group returned with a huge catch of beaver, organized trapping had begun. Smith pioneered the route later followed by thousands of westward migrants. The trapping was so successful that Ashley, selling his interest to Smith in 1826, returned East a wealthy man. In the next three years Smith and his partners roamed the Rockies in search of beaver. Smith's two expeditions were feats of endurance and added greatly to general knowledge of the West. The first took him south to the Colorado River Valley, up the interior valleys of California, and eastward across the Sierras. The second described a great circle from Wyoming to southern California, northward to Oregon, and back to Wyoming. Smith sold out in 1829, when the immense profits of the early years were attracting competition from Astor's American Fur Company and the Hudson's Bay Company. Large trapping "brigades" poured into the mountains, often hiring away the older trappers or trailing them from place to place. Soon there were too few furs to go around, and by the end of the 1830s the mountains had been trapped out.

"Trapping Beaver" by Miller; (below) Jim Beckwourth and Antoine Clement, leading mountain men

"Bourgouis" Joe Walker and his squaw by Miller. Walker led an expedition to California in 1833-34 that was the first to cross the Sierra Nevada from the east. Walker Pass bears his name

Trappers' log cabin; painting by Miller

The paintings of Alfred Jacob Miller preserve the romantic image of the mountain
men. What is missing from Miller's record is
the brutalizing effect of the mountain man's
way of life. Divorced from civilization for
years, living alone or in small groups, generally with adopted squaws, the men were
warped by their struggle for survival. Their
savagery matched that of the Indians, into
whose hunting grounds they were intruding.
Mountain men were filthy, ate nothing but
meat — sometimes raw — and scalped
their victims as a matter of course. They
were inured to danger from constant exposure to it and of necessity placed small value on human life. But they knew the mountains and the Indians and were indispensable to the later immigrants as guides.

"Shooting Elk Among the Black Hills"

"Old Bill Burrows, a Free Trapper"; painting by Miller

"Caravan En Route"; painting by A. J. Miller of the supply wagons sent annually from St. Louis

The annual rendezvous, introduced by Ashley in 1825, was the major event of the season and was important to the success of the early trapping companies. Each year the trappers congregated at a designated time and place, usually in the Wind River Mountains or at Jackson's Hole, in Wyoming, to meet the supply train from the East. Furs were traded for goods and whiskey amidst a general scene of debauchery and hard bargaining. The appearance of men from the large fur companies at the 1832 rendezvous signaled the end of the "mountain man" era, as the independents and small companies were bought out.

(Left) Kennett McKenzie, head of the American Fur Company, called "The King of the Missouri"; (below) Indian procession in honor of Capt. W. D. Stewart during rendezvous in Wind River Mts.

Dr. John McLoughlin, head of Hudson's Bay Co. in the Oregon territory

(Above) Raid staged by Assiniboin Indians on a Blackfoot encampment outside Fort McKenzie, 1833; (below) interior of Ft. Laramie, a major fur trading post until 1849

Large Indian encampment near the Cut Rocks; painting by A. J. Miller

Miller's West

"Sioux Indians in the Mountains"; oil by A. J. Miller

Alfred J. Miller's paintings of the West were done from sketches made on a trip to the 1837 rendezvous, one of the last great gatherings. Miller was hired for the trip by a Scots nobleman, William Stewart, who was possessed by the excitement of the American West and wanted it recreated for his castle walls. Miller recorded in his notebooks many scenes of the Indians among whom he passed. He never became deeply involved with his subject, as had George Catlin, and the paintings Miller produced from his sketches are overly romantic. However, his glossy images of Indian life were popular and he continually recopied the scenes during the rest of his life.

"Indian Lodges"; painting by Miller

(Top) "Prairie on Fire"; (left)
"Medicine Circles"; (bottom)
"Approaching Buffalo"; all
watercolors by A. J. Miller

View of a Mandan village on the Missouri River. Women in the foreground are using "bull boats"

Bodmer sketches of (left) Mato-tope, Mandan chief, and (right) warrior in costume for dog dance

Bodmer and Maximilian meet members of the Minnetaree tribe

Bodmer's West

Books about America inevitably found an audience in Europe. Various "Travels" had been appearing for centuries and generally consisted of random observations by curious travelers. However, like Tocqueville, Maximilian, Prince of Wied-Neuwied, had more serious interests. He was an amateur scientist who devoted considerable attention to the details of Indian life. He brought a skilled Swiss artist, Karl Bodmer, with him on his trip west in 1832-34 and his "Travels" contain numerous illustrations of Indian artifacts and detailed descriptions of Indian social customs.

Bodmer's facsimile of an Indian painting from "Travels in the Interior of North America"

Interior of the hut of a Mandan chief; engraving made from a watercolor by Bodmer

"March of the Caravan" from "Commerce of the Prairie" by Josiah Gregg, trader on the Santa Fe

Santa Fe Trail

Mexican arrieros with an atajo of pack mules

The achievement of independence by Mexico in 1821 opened that country to American merchants excluded under Spanish rule. The Mexicans of the northern provinces possessed much wealth in gold, silver, and furs and were ready buyers of the goods brought in by Missouri traders. Enormous profits in this trade made the trek from Independence to Santa Fe feasible, in spite of Indian attacks, deserts, and mountains. The wagons traveled in large caravans as a protection against the Pawnees and Cherokees who continually resisted the intrusions. It was here that circling wagons was devised as a defense.

Camp Comanche; engraving from Gregg's book first published in 1844

60.

ANDREW JACKSON: The Independence of Texas

President Jackson privately favored recognizing and annexing the Lone Star State, and he did not discourage the voluntary assistance rendered by Americans to Texans in their fight for independence in 1836, but he did nothing in public. He wanted no war with Mexico; he feared that Congress would try to block an aggressive policy; and he desired to lessen rather than increase the sectional conflict that was being stirred up by the antislavery petitions flooding Congress. On March 3, 1837, Jackson reversed his policy and appointed a chargé d'affaires *to Texas, thereby recognizing it as an independent nation. By this time, Congress had voted funds for a diplomatic mission; Mexico clearly had no plans to reinvade; and, most important, the English were building commercial ties with Texas that were unfavorable to the United States. However, in his message to Congress of December 21, 1836, which is reprinted below, Jackson was still advocating a "wait and see" policy.*

Source: *A Digest of International Law,* John B. Moore, ed., Washington, 1906, Vol. I , pp. 98-101.

NO STEPS HAVE BEEN TAKEN by the executive toward the acknowledgment of the independence of Texas, and the whole subject would have been left without further remark on the information now given to Congress were it not that the two Houses at their last session, acting separately, passed resolutions "that the independence of Texas ought to be acknowledged by the United States whenever satisfactory information should be received that it had in successful operation a civil government capable of performing the duties and fulfilling the obligations of an independent power." This mark of interest in the question of the independence of Texas, and indication of the views of Congress, make it proper that I should somewhat in detail present the considerations that have governed the Executive in continuing to occupy the ground previously taken in the contest between Mexico and Texas.

The acknowledgment of a new state as independent and entitled to a place in the family of nations is at all times an act of great delicacy and responsibility, but more especially so when such state has forcibly separated itself from another of which it had formed an integral part and which still claims dominion over it. A premature recognition under these circumstances, if not looked upon as justifiable cause of war, is always liable to be regarded as a proof of an unfriendly spirit to one of the contending parties. All questions relative to the government of foreign nations, whether of the Old or New World, have been treated by the United States as questions of fact only, and our predecessors have cautiously abstained from deciding upon them until the clearest evidence was in their possession to enable them not only to decide correctly but to shield their decisions from every unworthy imputation.

In all the contests that have arisen out of the revolutions of France, out of the disputes relating to the Crowns of Portugal and Spain, out of the separation of the American possessions of both from the European governments, and out of the numerous and constantly occurring struggles for dominion in Spanish America, so wisely consistent with our just principles has been the action of our government that we have, under the most critical circumstances, avoided all censure, and encountered no other evil than that produced by a transient estrangement of goodwill in those against whom we have been by force of evidence compelled to decide.

It has thus made known to the world that the uniform policy and practice of the United States is to avoid all interference in disputes which merely relate to the internal government of other nations, and eventually to recognize the authority of the prevailing party without reference to our particular interests and views or to the merits of the original controversy. Public opinion here is so firmly established and well understood in favor of this policy that no serious disagreement has ever risen among ourselves in relation to it, although brought under view in a variety of forms, and at periods when the minds of the people were greatly excited by the agitation of topics purely domestic in their character.

Nor has any deliberate inquiry ever been instituted in Congress, or in any of our legislative bodies, as to whom belonged the power of originally recognizing a new state: a power the exercise of which is equivalent, under some circumstances, to a declaration of war; a power nowhere especially delegated, and only granted in the Constitution as it is necessarily involved in some of the great powers given to Congress — in that given to the President and Senate to form treaties with foreign powers, and to appoint ambassadors and other public ministers, and in that conferred upon the President to receive ministers from foreign nations.

In the preamble to the resolution of the House of Representatives, it is distinctly intimated that the expediency of recognizing the independence of Texas should be left to the decision of Congress. In this view, on the ground of expediency, I am disposed to concur; and do not, therefore, consider it necessary to express any opinion as to the strict constitutional right of the Executive, either apart from or in conjunction with the Senate, over the subject. It is to be presumed that on no future occasion will a dispute arise, as none has heretofore occurred, between the Executive and the legislature in the exercise of the power of recognition.

It will always be considered consistent with the spirit of the Constitution, and most safe, that it should be exercised, when probably leading to war, with a previous understanding with that body by whom war can alone be declared, and by whom all the provisions for sustaining its perils must be furnished. Its submission to Congress, which represents in one of its branches the states of the Union and in the other the people of the United States, where there may be reasonable ground to apprehend so grave a consequence, would certainly afford the fullest satisfaction to our own country, and a perfect guarantee to all other nations of the justice and prudence of the measures which might be adopted.

In making these suggestions, it is not my purpose to relieve myself from the responsibility of expressing my own opinions of the course the interests of our country prescribe and its honor permits us to follow.

It is scarcely to be imagined that a question of this character could be presented in relation to which it would be more difficult for the United States to avoid exciting the suspicion and jealousy of other powers, and maintain their established character for fair and impartial dealing. But on this, as on every other trying occasion, safety is to be found in a rigid adherence to principle.

In the contest between Spain and the revolted colonies, we stood aloof and waited not only until the ability of the new states to protect themselves was fully established but until the danger of their being again subjugated had entirely passed away. Then, and not until then, were they recognized. Such was our course in regard to Mexico herself. The same policy was observed in all the disputes growing out of the separation into distinct governments of those Spanish-American states who began or carried on the contest with the parent country, united under one form of government. We acknowledged the separate independence of New Grenada, of Venezuela, and of Ecuador only after their independent existence was no longer a subject of dispute, or was actually acquiesced in by those with whom they had been previously united.

It is true that with regard to Texas the civil authority of Mexico has been expelled, its invading army defeated, the chief of the republic himself captured, and all present power to control the newly organized government of Texas annihilated within its confines. But, on the other hand, there is, in appearance at least, an immense disparity of physical force on the side of Texas. The Mexican republic, under another executive, is rallying its forces under a new leader, and menacing a fresh invasion to recover its lost dominion.

Upon the issue of this threatened invasion, the independence of Texas may be considered as suspended; and were there nothing peculiar in the relative situation of the United States and Texas, our acknowledgment of its independence at such a crisis could scarcely be regarded as consistent with that prudent reserve with which we have hitherto held ourselves bound to treat all similar questions. But there are circumstances in the relations of the two countries which require us to act on this occasion with even more than our wonted caution.

Texas was once claimed as a part of our property, and there are those among our citizens who, always reluctant to abandon that claim, cannot but regard with solicitude the prospects of the reunion of the territory to this country. A large portion of its civilized inhabitants are emigrants from the United States, speak the same language with ourselves, cherish the same principles — political and religious — and are bound to many of our citizens by ties of friendship and kindred blood; and, more than all, it is known that the people of that country have instituted the same form of government with our own, and have, since the close of your last session, openly resolved, on the acknowledgment by us of their independence, to seek admission into the Union as one of the federal states.

This last circumstance is a matter of peculiar delicacy, and forces upon us considerations of the gravest character. The title of Texas to the territory she claims is identified with her independence; she asks us to acknowledge that title to the territory, with an avowed design to treat immediately of its transfer to the United States. It becomes us to beware of a too early movement as it might subject us, however unjustly, to the imputation of seeking to establish the claim of our neighbors to a territory, with a view to its subsequent acquisition by ourselves.

Prudence, therefore, seems to dictate that we should still stand aloof and maintain our present attitude, if not until Mexico itself, or one of the great foreign powers, shall recognize the independence of the new government, at least until the lapse of time or the course of events shall have proved beyond cavil or dispute the ability of the people of that country to maintain their separate sovereignty and to uphold the government constituted by them. Neither of the contending parties can justly complain of this course. By pursuing it, we are but carrying out the long-established policy of our government, a policy which has secured to us respect and influence abroad and inspired confidence at home.

1837

61.

Guns and Ballots

Election procedures on the frontier were often highly irregular, especially in campaigns for local offices. Voters were usually few, and the secrecy of the ballot was seldom attained. In some areas of the South, the military was assigned to patrol the election districts (or "beats"), as the only safeguard of free elections. Where troops were not available, citizen groups took matters into their own hands; then the voting became a mere formality, and the most powerful groups decided the results. The following news item dealing with the Murray County (Georgia) elections appeared in a Milledgeville paper in January 1837.

Source: *Federal Union*, January 24, 1837 [Commons, II, pp. 296-298].

IT IS A MATTER of painful regret with us, at all times, to be called upon by a sense of duty we owe ourselves, as a faithful journalist, to expose the lawless and outrageous conduct of anyone, however obscure that individual may be. But, upon the present occasion, we should consider ourselves highly culpable were we to withhold from a scrutinizing public the information we have recently received from the highest authority, in relation to the civil condition of that ill-fated county.

It has been reported to us, the truth of which we have not the least doubt, that the redoubtable Colonel William N. Bishop, on the day previous to the recent election, collected his "friends" to Spring Place, and armed each man with a musket for the sole purpose of conducting the pending election in his own way. That on Sunday evening some fifteen or twenty country people, unarmed and unprotected — known, however, to be opposed to the Bishop party — came into town intending to remain until the election was over. But before they had procured a shelter for the night, the Colonel, at the head of his company, charged upon them and informed them that they could not, nor should not, remain there, and at the same moment ordered his men to fire upon them, which was no sooner said than done, wounding four of them, one, it is said, mortally. The Colonel and his right-hand man, that pink of purity and truth, George W. Wacaser, next attacked two gentlemen riding in a carriage, and with the butts of their muskets, in a most shocking manner, bruised and mangled their heads and bodies.

On the day of the election, several travelers were peremptorily refused and actually prohibited from voting at that place, for no other reason, as it is supposed, than that the name of Colonel Alford was on their tickets. When the election was over, the returns from the several precincts of the county were excluded from the Spring Place election, and that one, made out and certified to the executive department alone, by which it, of course, appeared that the "friends" of Bishop were elected justices of the inferior court. This was the great object to be attained by him, cost what it might. The judiciary, as far as Murray County is concerned, as everybody knows who knows anything of the situation of affairs in that county, is a perfect dead letter. The law makes it the duty of the justices of the inferior court, the sheriff, and the clerk of the superior court to revise the jury box, and draw a jury.

The county of Murray has been in existence for three years and upward, but from the fact that Bishop has heretofore exercised an entire control over the inferior court, a jury has never been drawn for that county; consequently, the superior court there has never transacted any of its business except that of calling the appearance docket and disposing of bar motions. There are, as we are informed, fifteen or twenty debt cases returnable to that court against Bishop, and as many indictments for high offenses against the laws of the state; and hence it is, if he can again elect a court subservient to his will, a jury will not be drawn for the next four years, or if drawn, it will be a packed one.

We also understand that the opponents of Bishop, for several days after the election, were engaged in collecting a force, arms, etc., for the purpose of reducing that lawless bully to submission. How the affair has, or will, terminate we are unable to conjecture; but trust, for the honor and reputation of our state, such a state of things will no longer be suffered to exist.

62.

ANDREW JACKSON: Farewell Address

In his Farewell Address, written with the help of Chief Justice Roger B. Taney and delivered March 4, 1837, Andrew Jackson reviewed the accomplishments of his administration and explained the motivation of some of his policies. He looked back with satisfaction and prophesied the continuation of his program under his hand-picked successor, Martin Van Buren. Nineteenth-century historians did not view Jackson's eight years in office so complacently. An early biographer, James Parton, pointed to some of the contradictions in his character and in his achievements. Jackson "was a patriot and a traitor. He was one of the greatest generals and wholly ignorant of the art of war. . . . The first of statesmen, he never devised, he never framed a measure. . . . A most law-defying, law-obeying citizen. . . . A democrat autocrat. An urban savage. An atrocious saint." Modern writers, however, have tended to be more adulatory, and it is now generally agreed that Jackson, if he does not absolutely belong in the company of Washington, Jefferson, and Lincoln, occupies a place not far behind.

Source: *Farewell Address of Andrew Jackson to the People of the United States: and the Inaugural Address of Martin Van Buren, President of the United States,* Washington, 1837, pp. 3-16.

BEING ABOUT TO RETIRE finally from public life, I beg leave to offer you my grateful thanks for the many proofs of kindness and confidence which I have received at your hands. It has been my fortune, in the discharge of public duties, civil and military, frequently to have found myself in difficult and trying situations where prompt decision and energetic action were necessary and where the interest of the country required that high responsibilities should be fearlessly encountered; and it is with the deepest emotions of gratitude that I acknowledge the continued and unbroken confidence with which you have sustained me in every trial.

My public life has been a long one, and I cannot hope that it has, at all times, been free from errors. But I have the consolation of knowing that, if mistakes have been committed, they have not seriously injured the country I so anxiously endeavored to serve; and, at the moment when I surrender my last public trust, I leave this great people prosperous and happy, in the full enjoyment of liberty and peace, and honored and respected by every nation of the world.

If my humble efforts have, in any degree, contributed to preserve to you these blessings, I have been more than rewarded by the honors you have heaped upon me; and, above all, by the generous confidence with which you have supported me in every peril, and with which you have continued to animate and cheer my path to the closing hour of my political life. The time has now come when advanced age and a broken frame warn me to retire from public concerns; but the recollection of the many favors you have bestowed upon me is engraven upon my heart, and I have felt that I could not part from your service without making this public acknowledgment of the gratitude I owe you. And if I use the occasion to offer•to you the counsels of age and experience, you will, I trust, receive them with the same indulgent kindness which you have so often extended to me; and will, at least, see in them an earnest desire to perpetuate, in this favored land, the blessings of liberty and equal laws.

We have now lived almost fifty years under the Constitution framed by the sages and patriots of the Revolution. The conflicts in which the nations of Europe were engaged during a great part of this period, the spirit in which they waged war against each other, and our intimate commercial connections with every part of the civilized world rendered it a time of much difficulty for the government of the United States. We have had our seasons of peace and war, with all the evils which precede or follow a state of hostility with powerful nations. We encountered these trials with our Constitution yet in its infancy, and under the disadvantages which a new and untried government must always feel when it is called upon to put forth its whole strength, without the lights of experience to guide it or the weight of precedents to justify its measures. But we have passed triumphantly through all these difficulties. Our Constitution is no longer a doubtful experiment; and, at the end of nearly half a century, we find that it has preserved unimpaired the liberties of the people, secured the rights of property, and that our country has improved and is flourishing beyond any former example in the history of nations.

In our domestic concerns there is everything to encourage us; and if you are true to yourselves, nothing can impede your march to the highest point of national prosperity. The states which had so long been retarded in their improvement by the Indian tribes residing in the midst of them are at length relieved from the evil; and this unhappy race — the original dwellers in our land — are now placed in a situation where we may well hope that they will share in the blessings of civilization and be saved from that degradation and destruction to which they were rapidly hastening while they remained in the states. And while the safety and comfort of our own citizens have been greatly promoted by their removal, the philanthropist will rejoice that the remnant of that ill-fated race has been at length placed beyond the reach of injury or oppression, and that the paternal care of the general government will hereafter watch over them and protect them.

If we turn to our relations with foreign powers, we find our condition equally gratifying. Actuated by the sincere desire to do justice to every nation and to preserve the blessings of peace, our intercourse with them has been conducted on the part of this government in the spirit of frankness; and I take pleasure in saying that it has generally been met in a corresponding temper. Difficulties of old standing have been surmounted by friendly discussion and the mutual desire to be just; and the claims of our citizens, which had been long withheld, have at length been acknowledged and adjusted, and satisfactory arrangements made for their final payment. And with a limited and, I trust, a temporary exception, our relations with every foreign power are now of the most friendly character, our commerce continually expanding, and our flag respected in every quarter of the world.

These cheering and grateful prospects and these multiplied favors we owe, under Providence, to the adoption of the federal Constitution. It is no longer a question whether this great country can remain happily united and flourish under our present form of government. Experience, the unerring test of all human undertakings, has shown the wisdom and foresight of those who formed it; and has proved that in the union of these states there is a sure foundation for the brightest hopes of freedom and for the happiness of the people. At every hazard and by every sacrifice, this Union must be preserved.

The necessity of watching with jealous anxiety for the preservation of the Union was earnestly pressed upon his fellow citizens by the father of his country in his farewell address. He has there told us that "while experience shall not have demonstrated its impracticability, there will always be reason to distrust the patriotism of those who, in any quarter, may endeavor to weaken its bonds"; and he has cautioned us, in the strongest terms, against the formation of parties on geographical discriminations, as one of the means which might disturb our Union, and to which designing men would be likely to resort.

The lessons contained in this invaluable legacy of Washington to his countrymen should be cherished in the heart of every citizen to the latest generation; and, perhaps, at no period of time could they be more usefully remembered than at the present moment. For when we look upon the scenes that are passing around us and dwell upon the pages of his parting address, his paternal counsels would seem to be not merely the offspring of wisdom and foresight but the voice of prophecy foretelling events and warning us of the evil to come.

Forty years have passed since this imperishable document was given to his countrymen. The federal Constitution was then regarded by him as an experiment, and he so speaks of it in his address; but an experiment upon the success of which the best hopes of his country depended, and we all know that he was prepared to lay down his life, if necessary, to secure to it a full and a fair trial. The trial has been made. It has succeeded beyond the proudest hopes of those who framed it. Every quarter of this widely extended nation has felt its blessings and shared in the general prosperity produced by its adoption.

But amid this general prosperity and splendid success, the dangers of which he warned us are becoming every day more evident, and the signs of evil are sufficiently apparent to awaken the deepest anxiety in the bosom of the patriot. We behold systematic efforts publicly made to sow the seeds of discord between different parts of the United States and to place party divisions directly upon geographical distinctions; to excite the South against the North and the North against the South; and to force into the controversy the most delicate and exciting topics, topics upon which it is impossible that a large portion of the Union can ever speak without strong emotion.

Appeals, too, are constantly made to sectional interests in order to influence the election of the chief magistrate, as if it were desired that he should favor a particular quarter of the country instead of fulfilling the duties of his station with impartial justice to all; and the possible dissolution of the Union has at length become an ordinary and familiar subject of discussion. Has the warning voice of Washington been forgotten? Or have designs already been formed to sever the Union?

Let it not be supposed that I impute to all of those who have taken an active part in these unwise and unprofitable discussions a want of patriotism or of public virtue. The honorable feeling of state pride and local attachments find a place in the bosoms of the most enlightened and pure. But while such men are conscious of their own integrity and honesty of purpose, they ought never to forget that the citizens of other states are their political brethren; and that, however mistaken they may be in their views, the great body of them are equally honest and upright with themselves. Mutual suspicions and reproaches may in time create mutual hostility, and artful and designing men will always be found who are ready to foment these fatal divisions and to inflame the natural jealousies of different sections of the country. The history of the world is full of such examples and especially the history of republics.

What have you to gain by division and dissension? Delude not yourselves with the belief that a breach once made may be afterward repaired. If the Union is once severed, the line of separation will grow wider and wider, and the controversies which are now debated and settled in the halls of legislation will then be tried in fields of battle and determined by the sword. Neither should you deceive yourselves with the hope that the first line of separation would be the permanent one, and that nothing but harmony and concord would be found in the new associations formed upon the dissolution of this Union. Local interests would still be found there, and unchastened ambition. And if the recollection of common dangers in which the people of these United States stood side by side against the common foe; the memory of victories won by their united valor; the prosperity and happiness they have enjoyed under the present Constitution; the proud name they bear as citizens of this great republic; if all these recollections and proofs of common interest are not strong enough to bind us together as one people, what tie will hold united the new divisions of empire when these bonds have been broken and this Union dissevered?

The first line of separation would not last for a single generation; new fragments would be torn off; new leaders would spring up; and this great and glorious republic would soon be broken into a multitude of petty states, without commerce, without credit, jealous of one another, armed for mutual aggression, loaded with taxes to pay armies and leaders, seeking aid against each other from foreign powers, insulted and trampled upon by the nations of Europe, until, harassed with conflicts and humbled and debased in spirit, they would be ready to submit to the absolute dominion of any military adventurer and to surrender their liberty for the sake of repose. It is impossible to look on the consequences that would inevitably follow the destruction of this government and not feel indignant when we hear cold calculations about the value of the Union and have so constantly

before us a line of conduct so well calculated to weaken its ties.

There is too much at stake to allow pride or passion to influence your decision. Never for a moment believe that the great body of the citizens of any state or states can deliberately intend to do wrong. They may, under the influence of temporary excitement or misguided opinions, commit mistakes; they may be misled for a time by the suggestions of self-interest; but in a community so enlightened and patriotic as the people of the United States, argument will soon make them sensible of their errors, and, when convinced, they will be ready to repair them. If they have no higher or better motives to govern them, they will at least perceive that their own interest requires them to be just to others as they hope to receive justice at their hands.

But in order to maintain the Union unimpaired, it is absolutely necessary that the laws passed by the constituted authorities should be faithfully executed in every part of the country, and that every good citizen should, at all times, stand ready to put down, with the combined force of the nation, every attempt at unlawful resistance, under whatever pretext it may be made or whatever shape it may assume. Unconstitutional or oppressive laws may no doubt be passed by Congress, either from erroneous views or the want of due consideration. If they are within the reach of judicial authority, the remedy is easy and peaceful; and if, from the character of the law, it is an abuse of power not within the control of the judiciary, then free discussion and calm appeals to reason and to the justice of the people will not fail to redress the wrong. But until the law shall be declared void by the courts or repealed by Congress, no individual or combination of individuals can be justified in forcibly resisting its execution. It is impossible that any government can continue to exist upon any other principles. It would cease to be a government and be unworthy of the name if it had not the power to enforce the execution of its own laws within its own sphere of action.

It is true that cases may be imagined disclosing such a settled purpose of usurpation and oppression on the part of the government as would justify an appeal to arms. These, however, are extreme cases, which we have no reason to apprehend in a government where the power is in the hands of a patriotic people. And no citizen who loves his country would in any case whatever resort to forcible resistance, unless he clearly saw that the time had come when a freeman should prefer death to submission; for if such a struggle is once begun and the citizens of one section of the country arrayed in arms against those of another in doubtful conflict, let the battle result as it may, there will be an end of the Union and, with it, an end to the hopes of freedom. The victory of the injured would not secure to them the blessings of liberty; it would avenge their wrongs, but they would themselves share in the common ruin.

But the Constitution cannot be maintained nor the Union preserved in opposition to public feeling by the mere exertion of the coercive powers confided to the general government. The foundations must be laid in the affections of the people; in the security it gives to life, liberty, character, and property in every quarter of the country; and in the fraternal attachment which the citizens of the several states bear to one another as members of one political family, mutually contributing to promote the happiness of each other. Hence the citizens of every state should studiously avoid everything calculated to wound the sensibility or offend the just pride of the people of other states; and they should frown upon any proceedings within their own borders likely to disturb the tranquillity of their political brethren in other portions of the Union.

In a country so extensive as the United States and with pursuits so varied, the internal regulations of the several states must frequently differ from one another in important particulars; and this difference is unavoidably increased by the varying principles upon which the American colonies were originally planted; principles which had taken deep root in their social relations before the Revolution and, therefore, of necessity influencing their policy since they became free and independent states. But each state has the unquestionable right to regulate its own internal concerns according to its own pleasure; and while it does not interfere with the rights of the people of other states or the rights of the Union, every state must be the sole judge of the measures proper to secure the safety of its citizens and promote their happiness; and all efforts on the part of people of other states to cast odium upon their institutions, and all measures calculated to disturb their rights of property or to put in jeopardy their peace and internal tranquillity, are in direct opposition to the spirit in which the Union was formed and must endanger its safety.

Motives of philanthropy may be assigned for this unwarrantable interference; and weak men may persuade themselves for a moment that they are laboring in the cause of humanity and asserting the rights of the human race. But everyone, upon sober reflection, will see that nothing but mischief can come from these improper assaults upon the feelings and rights of others. Rest assured that the men found busy in this work of discord are not worthy of your confidence and deserve your strongest reprobation.

In the legislation of Congress, also, and in every measure of the general government, justice to every portion of the United States should be faithfully observed. No free government can stand without virtue in the people and a lofty spirit of patriotism; and if the sordid feelings of mere selfishness shall usurp the place which ought to be filled by public spirit, the legislation of Congress will soon be converted into a scramble for personal and sectional advantages. Under our free institutions, the citizens of every quarter of our country are capable of attaining a high degree of prosperity and happiness without seeking to profit themselves at the expense of others; and every such attempt must in the end fail to succeed, for the people in every part of the United States are too enlightened not to understand their own rights and interests and to detect and defeat every effort to gain undue advantages over them. And when such designs are discovered, it naturally provokes resentments which cannot always be easily allayed. Justice, full and ample justice, to every portion of the United States, should be the ruling principle of every freeman and should guide the deliberations of every public body, whether it be state or national.

It is well known that there have always been those among us who wish to enlarge the powers of the general government; and experience would seem to indicate that there is a tendency on the part of this government to overstep the boundaries marked out for it by the Constitution. Its legitimate authority is abundantly sufficient for all the purposes for which it was created; and its powers being expressly enumerated, there can be no justification for claiming anything beyond them. Every attempt to exercise power beyond these limits should be promptly and firmly opposed. For one evil example will lead to other measures still more mischievous; and if the principle of constructive powers, or supposed advantages, or temporary circumstances, shall ever be permitted to justify the assumption of a power not given by the Constitution, the general government will before long absorb all the powers of legislation, and you will have, in effect, but one consolidated government. From the extent of our country, its diversified interests, different pursuits, and different habits, it is too obvious for argument that a single consolidated government would be wholly inadequate to watch over and protect its interests; and every friend of our free institutions should be always prepared to maintain unimpaired and in full vigor the rights and sovereignty of the states and to confine the action of the general government strictly to the sphere of its appropriate duties.

There is, perhaps, no one of the powers conferred on the federal government so liable to abuse as the taxing power. The most productive and convenient sources of revenue were necessarily given to it, that it might be able to perform the important duties imposed upon it; and the taxes which it lays upon commerce being concealed from the real payer in the price of the article, they do not so readily attract the attention of the people as smaller sums demanded from them directly by the tax gatherer. But the tax imposed on goods enhances by so much the price of the commodity to the consumer; and, as many of these duties are imposed on articles of necessity which are daily used by the great body of the people, the money raised by these imposts is drawn from their pockets.

Congress has no right, under the Constitution, to take money from the people unless it is required to execute some one of the specific powers entrusted to the government; and if they raise more than is necessary for such purposes, it is an abuse of the power of taxation and unjust and oppressive. It may, indeed, happen that the revenue will sometimes exceed the amount anticipated when the taxes were laid. When, however, this is ascertained, it is easy to reduce them; and, in such a case, it is unquestionably the duty of the government to reduce them, for no circumstances can justify it in assuming a power not given to it by the Constitution nor in taking away the money of the people when it is not needed for the legitimate wants of the government.

Plain as these principles appear to be, you will yet find that there is a constant effort to induce the general government to go beyond the limits of its taxing power and to

Andrew Jackson; portrait by Asher B. Durand, 1835

impose unnecessary burdens upon the people. Many powerful interests are continually at work to procure heavy duties on commerce and to swell the revenue beyond the real necessities of the public service; and the country has already felt the injurious effects of their combined influence. They succeeded in obtaining a tariff of duties bearing most oppressively on the agricultural and laboring classes of society and producing a revenue that could not be usefully employed within the range of the powers conferred upon Congress; and, in order to fasten upon the people this unjust and unequal system of taxation, extravagant schemes of internal improvement were got up in various quarters to squander the money and to purchase support. Thus, one unconstitutional measure was intended to be upheld by another, and the abuse of the power of taxation was to be maintained by usurping the power of expending the money in internal improvements.

You cannot have forgotten the severe and doubtful struggle through which we passed when the Executive Department of the government, by its veto, endeavored to arrest this prodigal scheme of injustice and to bring back the legislation of Congress to the boundaries prescribed by the Constitution. The good sense and practical judgment of the people, when the subject was brought before them, sustained the course of the executive; and this plan of unconstitutional expenditure for the purpose of corrupt influence is, I trust, finally overthrown.

The result of this decision has been felt in the rapid extinguishment of the public debt and the large accumulation of a surplus in the treasury, notwithstanding the tariff was reduced and is now very far below the amount originally contemplated by its advocates. But, rely upon it, the design to collect an extravagant revenue and to burden you with taxes beyond the economical wants of the government is not yet abandoned. The various interests which have combined together to impose a heavy tariff and to produce an overflowing treasury are too strong and have too much at stake to surrender the contest. The corporations and wealthy individuals who are engaged in large manufacturing establishments desire a high tariff to increase their gains. Designing politicians will support it to conciliate their favor and to obtain the means of profuse expenditure for the purpose of purchasing influence in other quarters; and since the people have decided that the federal government cannot be permitted to employ its income in internal improvements, efforts will be made to seduce and mislead the citizens of the several states by holding out to them the deceitful prospect of benefits to be derived from a surplus revenue collected by the general government and annually divided among the states. And if, encouraged by these fallacious hopes, the states should disregard the principles of economy which ought to characterize every republican government and should indulge in lavish expenditures exceeding their resources, they will, before long, find themselves oppressed with debts which they are unable to pay, and the temptation will become irresistible to support a high tariff in order to obtain a surplus for distribution.

Do not allow yourselves, my fellow citizens, to be misled on this subject. The federal government cannot collect a surplus for such purposes without violating the principles of the Constitution and assuming powers which have not been granted. It is, moreover, a system of injustice, and, if persisted in, will inevitably lead to corruption and must end in ruin. The surplus revenue will be drawn from the pockets of the people, from the farmer, the mechanic, and the laboring classes of society; but who will receive it when distributed among the states, where it is to be disposed of by leading state politicians who have friends to favor and political partisans to gratify? It will certainly not be returned to those who paid it and who have most need of it and are honestly entitled to it. There is but one safe rule, and that is to confine the general government rigidly within the sphere of its appropriate duties. It has no power to raise a revenue or impose taxes except for the purposes enumerated in the Constitution; and if its income is found to exceed these wants, it should be forthwith reduced, and the burdens of the people so far lightened.

In reviewing the conflicts which have taken place between different interests in the United States and the policy pursued since the adoption of our present form of government, we find nothing that has produced such deep-seated evil as the course of legislation in relation to the currency. The Constitution of the United States unquestionably intended to secure to the people a circulating medium of gold and silver. But the establishment of a national bank by Congress with the privilege of issuing paper money receivable in the payment of the public dues, and the unfortunate course of legislation in the several states upon the same subject, drove from general circulation the constitutional currency and substituted one of paper in its place.

It was not easy for men engaged in the ordinary pursuits of business, whose attention had not been particularly drawn to the subject, to foresee all the consequences of a currency exclusively of paper; and we ought not, on that account, to be surprised at the facility with which laws were obtained to carry into effect the paper system. Honest and even enlightened men are sometimes misled by the specious and plausible statements of the designing. But experience has now proved the mischiefs and dangers of a paper currency, and it rests with you to determine whether the proper remedy shall be applied.

The paper system being founded on public confidence and having of itself no intrinsic value, it is liable to great and sudden fluctuations, thereby rendering property insecure and the wages of labor unsteady and uncertain. The corporations which create the paper money cannot be relied upon to keep the circulating medium uniform in amount. In times of prosperity, when confidence is high, they are tempted by the prospect of gain or by the influence of those who hope to profit by it to extend their issues of paper beyond the bounds of discretion and the reasonable demands of business. And when these issues have been pushed on from day to day until public confidence is at length shaken, then a reaction takes place, and they immediately withdraw the credits they have given; suddenly curtail their issues; and produce an unexpected and ruinous contraction of the circulating medium which is felt by the whole community.

The banks, by this means, save themselves, and the mischievous consequences of their imprudence or cupidity are visited upon the public. Nor does the evil stop here. These ebbs and flows in the currency and these indiscreet extensions of credit naturally engender a spirit of speculation injurious to the habits and character of the people. We have already seen its effects in the wild spirit of speculation in the public lands and various kinds of stock which, within the last year or two, seized upon such a multitude of our citizens and threatened to pervade all classes of society and to withdraw their attention from the sober pursuits of honest industry. It is not by encouraging this spirit that we shall best preserve public virtue and promote the true interests of our country.

But if your currency continues as exclusively paper as it now is, it will foster this eager desire to amass wealth without labor; it will multiply the number of dependents on bank accommodations and bank favors; the temptation to obtain money at any sacrifice will become stronger and stronger, and inevitably lead to corruption which will find its way into your public councils and destroy, at no distant day, the purity of your government. Some of the evils which arise from this system of paper press, with peculiar hardship, upon the class of society least able to bear it. A portion of this currency frequently becomes depreciated or worthless, and all of it is easily counterfeited in such a manner as to require peculiar skill and much experience to distinguish the counterfeit from the genuine note. These frauds are most generally perpetrated in the smaller notes, which are used in the daily transactions of ordinary business; and the losses occasioned by them are commonly thrown upon the laboring classes of society whose situation and pursuits put it out of their power to guard themselves from these impositions and whose daily wages are necessary for their subsistence.

It is the duty of every government so to regulate its currency as to protect this numerous class as far as practicable from the impositions of avarice and fraud. It is more especially the duty of the United States where the government is emphatically the government of the people, and where this respectable portion of our citizens are so proudly distinguished from the laboring classes of all other nations by their independent spirit, their love of liberty, their intelligence, and their high tone of moral character. Their industry in peace is the source of our wealth; and their bravery in war has

covered us with glory; and the government of the United States will but ill discharge its duties if it leaves them a prey to such dishonest impositions. Yet it is evident that their interests cannot be effectually protected unless silver and gold are restored to circulation.

These views alone of the paper currency are sufficient to call for immediate reform; but there is another consideration which should still more strongly press it upon your attention.

Recent events have proved that the paper money system of this country may be used as an engine to undermine your free institutions; and that those who desire to engross all power in the hands of the few and to govern by corruption or force are aware of its power and prepared to employ it. Your banks now furnish your only circulating medium, and money is plenty or scarce according to the quantity of notes issued by them. While they have capitals not greatly disproportioned to each other, they are competitors in business, and no one of them can exercise dominion over the rest. And although, in the present state of the currency, these banks may and do operate injuriously upon the habits of business, the pecuniary concerns, and the moral tone of society, yet, from their number and dispersed situation, they cannot combine for the purpose of political influence; and whatever may be the dispositions of some of them, their power of mischief must necessarily be confined to a narrow space and felt only in their immediate neighborhoods.

But when the charter for the Bank of the United States was obtained from Congress, it perfected the schemes of the paper system and gave to its advocates the position they have struggled to obtain from the commencement of the federal government down to the present hour. The immense capital and peculiar privileges bestowed upon it enabled it to exercise despotic sway over the other banks in every part of the country. From its superior strength it could seriously injure, if not destroy, the business of any one of them which might incur its resentment; and it openly claimed for itself the power of regulating the currency throughout the United States. In other words, it asserted (and it undoubtedly possessed) the power to make money plenty or scarce, at its pleasure, at any time, and in any quarter of the Union, by controlling the issues of other banks and permitting an expansion or compelling a general contraction of the circulating medium according to its own will.

The other banking institutions were sensible of its strength, and they soon generally became its obedient instruments, ready at all times to execute its mandates; and with the banks necessarily went, also, that numerous class of persons in our commercial cities who depend altogether on bank credits for their solvency and means of business; and who are, therefore, obliged for their own safety to propitiate the favor of the money power by distinguished zeal and devotion in its service.

The result of the ill-advised legislation which established this great monopoly was to concentrate the whole moneyed power of the Union, with its boundless means of corruption and its numerous dependents, under the direction and command of one acknowledged head; thus organizing this particular interest as one body and securing to it unity and concert of action throughout the United States and enabling it to bring forward, upon any occasion, its entire and undivided strength to support or defeat any measure of the government. In the hands of this formidable power, thus perfectly organized, was also placed unlimited dominion over the amount of the circulating medium, giving it the power to regulate the value of property and the fruits of labor in every quarter of the Union and to bestow prosperity or bring ruin upon any city or section of the country as might best comport with its own interest or policy.

We are not left to conjecture how the moneyed power, thus organized and with

such a weapon in its hands, would be likely to use it. The distress and alarm which pervaded and agitated the whole country when the Bank of the United States waged war upon the people in order to compel them to submit to its demands cannot yet be forgotten. The ruthless and unsparing temper with which whole cities and communities were oppressed, individuals impoverished and ruined, and a scene of cheerful prosperity suddenly changed into one of gloom and despondency ought to be indelibly impressed on the memory of the people of the United States.

If such was its power in a time of peace, what would it not have been in a season of war with an enemy at your doors? No nation but the freemen of the United States could have come out victorious from such a contest; yet, if you had not conquered, the government would have passed from the hands of the many to the hands of the few; and this organized money power, from its secret conclave, would have dictated the choice of your highest officers and compelled you to make peace or war as best suited their own wishes. The forms of your government might, for a time, have remained; but its living spirit would have departed from it.

The distress and sufferings inflicted on the people by the Bank are some of the fruits of that system of policy which is continually striving to enlarge the authority of the federal government beyond the limits fixed by the Constitution. The powers enumerated in that instrument do not confer on Congress the right to establish such a corporation as the Bank of the United States; and the evil consequences which followed may warn us of the danger of departing from the true rule of construction and of permitting temporary circumstances or the hope of better promoting the public welfare to influence, in any degree, our decisions upon the extent of the authority of the general government. Let us abide by the Constitution as it is written or amend it in the constitutional mode if it is found to be defective.

The severe lessons of experience will, I doubt not, be sufficient to prevent Congress from again chartering such a monopoly, even if the Constitution did not present an insuperable objection to it. But you must remember, my fellow citizens, that eternal vigilance by the people is the price of liberty; and that you must pay the price if you wish to secure the blessing. It behooves you, therefore, to be watchful in your states as well as in the federal government. The power which the moneyed interest can exercise, when concentrated under a single head, and with our present system of currency, was sufficiently demonstrated in the struggle made by the Bank of the United States. Defeated in the general government, the same class of intriguers and politicians will now resort to the states and endeavor to obtain there the same organization which they failed to perpetuate in the Union; and with specious and deceitful plans of public advantages and state interests and state pride they will endeavor to establish, in the different states, one moneyed institution with overgrown capital and exclusive privileges sufficient to enable it to control the operations of the other banks.

Such an institution will be pregnant with the same evils produced by the Bank of the United States, although its sphere of action is more confined; and in the state in which it is chartered the money power will be able to embody its whole strength and to move together with undivided force to accomplish any object it may wish to attain. You have already had abundant evidence of its power to inflict injury upon the agricultural, mechanical, and laboring classes of society, and over those whose engagements in trade or speculation render them dependent on bank facilities, the dominion of the state monopoly will be absolute, and their obedience unlimited. With such a bank and a paper currency, the money power would, in a few years, govern the state and control its

measures; and if a sufficient number of states can be induced to create such establishments, the time will soon come when it will again take the field against the United States and succeed in perfecting and perpetuating its organization by a charter from Congress.

It is one of the serious evils of our present system of banking that it enables one class of society, and that by no means a numerous one, by its control over the currency to act injuriously upon the interests of all the others and to exercise more than its just proportion of influence in political affairs. The agricultural, the mechanical, and the laboring classes have little or no share in the direction of the great moneyed corporations; and from their habits and the nature of their pursuits, they are incapable of forming extensive combinations to act together with united force. Such concert of action may sometimes be produced in a single city or in a small district of country by means of personal communications with each other; but they have no regular or active correspondence with those who are engaged in similar pursuits in distant places. They have but little patronage to give to the press and exercise but a small share of influence over it; they have no crowd of dependents above them who hope to grow rich without labor by their countenance and favor and who are, therefore, always ready to exercise their wishes.

The planter, the farmer, the mechanic, and the laborer all know that their success depends upon their own industry and economy and that they must not expect to become suddenly rich by the fruits of their toil. Yet these classes of society form the great body of the people of the United States; they are the bone and sinew of the country; men who love liberty and desire nothing but equal rights and equal laws and who, moreover, hold the great mass of our national wealth, although it is distributed in moderate amounts among the millions of freemen who possess it. But, with overwhelming numbers and wealth on their side, they are in constant danger of losing their fair influence in the government, and with difficulty maintain their just rights against the incessant efforts daily made to encroach upon them.

The mischief springs from the power which the moneyed interest derives from a paper currency which they are able to control; from the multitude of corporations with exclusive privileges which they have succeeded in obtaining in the different states and which are employed altogether for their benefit; and unless you become more watchful in your states and check this spirit of monopoly and thirst for exclusive privileges, you will, in the end, find that the most important powers of government have been given or bartered away, and the control over your dearest interests has passed into the hands of these corporations.

The paper money system and its natural associates, monopoly and exclusive privileges, have already struck their roots deep in the soil; and it will require all your efforts to check its further growth and to eradicate the evil. The men who profit by the abuses and desire to perpetuate them will continue to besiege the halls of legislation in the general government as well as in the states and will seek, by every artifice, to mislead and deceive the public servants. It is to yourselves that you must look for safety and the means of guarding and perpetuating your free institutions. In your hands is rightfully placed the sovereignty of the country and to you everyone placed in authority is ultimately responsible. It is always in your power to see that the wishes of the people are carried into faithful execution, and their will, when once made known, must sooner or later be obeyed. And while the people remain, as I trust they ever will, uncorrupted and incorruptible and continue watchful and jealous of their rights, the government is safe, and the cause of freedom will continue to triumph over all its enemies.

But it will require steady and persevering exertions on your part to rid yourselves of the iniquities and mischiefs of the paper system and to check the spirit of monopoly and other abuses which have sprung up with it and of which it is the main support. So many interests are united to resist all reform on this subject that you must not hope the conflict will be a short one nor success easy. My humble efforts have not been spared during my administration of the government to restore the constitutional currency of gold and silver; and something, I trust, has been done toward the accomplishment of this most desirable object. But enough yet remains to require all your energy and perseverance. The power, however, is in your hands, and the remedy must and will be applied if you determine upon it.

While I am thus endeavoring to press upon your attention the principles which I deem of vital importance in the domestic concerns of the country, I ought not to pass over, without notice, the important considerations which should govern your policy toward foreign powers. It is unquestionably our true interest to cultivate the most friendly understanding with every nation and to avoid by every honorable means the calamities of war; and we shall best attain this object by frankness and sincerity in our foreign intercourse, by the prompt and faithful execution of treaties, and by justice and impartiality in our conduct to all. But no nation, however desirous of peace, can hope to escape occasional collisions with other powers; and the soundest dictates of policy require that we should place ourselves in a condition to assert our rights if a resort to force should ever become necessary.

Our local situation, our long line of seacoast, indented by numerous bays, with deep rivers opening into the interior, as well as our extended and still increasing commerce, point to the navy as our natural means of defense. It will, in the end, be found to be the cheapest and most effectual; and now is the time, in a season of peace and with an overflowing revenue, that we can, year after year, add to its strength without increasing the burdens of the people. It is your true policy. For your navy will not only protect your rich and flourishing commerce in distant seas, but will enable you to reach and annoy the enemy and will give to defense its greatest efficiency by meeting danger at a distance from home.

It is impossible by any line of fortifications to guard every point from attack against a hostile force advancing from the ocean and selecting its object; but they are indispensable to protect cities from bombardment, dockyards, and naval arsenals from destruction; to give shelter to merchant vessels in time of war, and to single ships or weaker squadrons when pressed by superior force. Fortifications of this description cannot be too soon completed and armed and placed in a condition of the most perfect preparation. The abundant means we now possess cannot be applied in any manner more useful to the country; and when this is done and our naval force sufficiently strengthened and our militia armed, we need not fear that any nation will wantonly insult us or needlessly provoke hostilities. We shall more certainly preserve peace when it is well understood that we are prepared for war.

In presenting to you, my fellow citizens, these parting counsels, I have brought before you the leading principles upon which I endeavored to administer the government in the high office with which you twice honored me. Knowing that the path of freedom is continually beset by enemies who often assume the disguise of friends, I have devoted the last hours of my public life to warn you of the danger.

The progress of the United States under our free and happy institutions has sur-passed the most sanguine hopes of the founders of the republic. Our growth has been rapid beyond all former example — in numbers, in wealth, in knowledge, and all the useful arts which contribute to the comforts and convenience of man; and from the earliest ages of history to the present day, there never have been 13 million people associated together in one political body who enjoyed so much freedom and happiness as the people of these United States. You have no longer any cause to fear danger from abroad; your strength and power are well known throughout the civilized world, as well as the high and gallant bearing of your sons.

It is from within, among yourselves, from cupidity, from corruption, from disappointed ambition and inordinate thirst for power, that factions will be formed and liberty endangered. It is against such designs, whatever disguise the actors may assume, that you have especially to guard yourselves. You have the highest of human trusts committed to your care. Providence has showered on this favored land blessings without number and has chosen you as the guardians of freedom to preserve it for the benefit of the human race. May He who holds in His hands the destinies of nations make you worthy of the favors He has bestowed and enable you, with pure hearts and pure hands and sleepless vigilance, to guard and defend to the end of time the great charge He has committed to your keeping.

My own race is nearly run; advanced age and failing health warn me that before long I must pass beyond the reach of human events and cease to feel the vicissitudes of human affairs. I thank God that my life has been spent in a land of liberty and that He has given me a heart to love my country with the affection of a son. And, filled with gratitude for your constant and unwavering kindness, I bid you a last and affectionate farewell.

63.

GEORGE TEMPLETON STRONG: The Panic of 1837

The Panic of 1837, which engulfed England and the Continent as well as the United States, has been attributed to many factors. Following the collapse of the Bank of the United States, the number of state banks in the country multiplied and the amount of credit issued rose sharply. Land speculation, the extension of transportation facilities, and the purchase of stocks were all financed by credit, much of it ultimately dependent on European capital. The optimism that underlay the boom was dissipated by two factors: Gold flowed West as a result of Jackson's Specie Circular, which stipulated that specie alone was acceptable in the purchase of public land; and at the same time gold fled the country when English creditors called loans under pressure from the Continent. When a decline in cotton exports to England created an additional burden on specie payments, the Southern economy collapsed, precipitating a general panic. George Strong, a lawyer's son and a student at Columbia University, recorded the impact of the panic on the financial community of New York City during April and May 1837. The New York City banks suspended specie payments on May 10, 1837.

Source: *The Diary of George Templeton Strong,* Allan Nevins and
    Milton H. Thomas, eds., New York, 1952, pp. 60-65.

April 19. . . . State of things in Wall Street worse than ever. The whole city going to the devil in a pecuniary point of view.

April 21. . . . Afternoon. Wall Street. The blackness of darkness still hangs over it. Failure on failure. . . .

April 22, Saturday. . . . Philip Hone has gone to the d——l, figuratively speaking, having lost pretty much everything by his son, by Schenck & Co. (of Matteawan factory), and by some speculation moreover, all of which have eased him out of not much below $200,000. What will become of his sons now? For they have nothing to prop their conceit but their father's cash, and now that that is gone, what will become of them? . . .

April 27. . . . Matters very bad out-of-doors. Confidence annihilated; the whole community, big and little, traveling to ruin in a body. Strong fears entertained for the banks, and, if they go, God only knows what the consequences will be. Ruin here and on the other side of the Atlantic, and not only private ruin but political convulsion and revolution, I think, would follow such an event. My father looks and talks and evidently feels very gloomily on the subject. For myself, I feel very philosophic, on my own account. I firmly believe that in a moral point of view it would be all for my good to have to push my own way, entirely unsupported, and I think I am competent to do it. I have no very extravagant tastes that I know of, unless perhaps in the way of books, but I can't accuse myself of wasting money on dress or billiards or horses or on sprees or any other follies of that nature. . . .

As for the banks, they are losing from $5,000 to $50,000 daily in the way of specie, and everyone seems to have the same fears, though almost everyone is afraid (and I'm glad to see it) to give them utterance. Where in the name of wonder is this all to end?

May 1, Monday. . . . Arthur Tappan [abolitionist and philanthropist] has failed! Help him, ye niggers!

May 2. . . . Matters worse and worse in Wall Street as far as I can learn; everyone discouraged; prospect of universal ruin and general insolvency of the banks, which will be terrible indeed if it takes place. Workmen thrown out of employ by the hundred daily. Business at a stand; the coal mines in Pennsylvania stopped, and no fuel in prospect for next winter — delightful prospects, these.

May 3. . . . Went up to the office at six. Fresh failures, Talbot Olyphant & Co., among them. So they go — smash, crash. Where in the name of wonder is there to be an end of it? Near 250 failures thus far! Bush & Hillyer have stopped, but Giles [Hillyer] is as extensive as ever. . . .

May 4. . . . Terrible news in Wall Street. [John] Fleming, late president of the Mechanics Bank, found dead in his bed this morning. Some say prussic acid; others (and the coroner's jury) say "mental excitement" and apoplexy. Anyhow, there's a run on the bank — street crowded — more feeling of alarm and despondency in Wall Street than has appeared yet. The bank is to be kept open till five o'clock; politic move, that. Fears entertained that tomorrow the attack will be general on all the banks; if so, they'll go down and then all the banks from Maine to Louisiana must follow — universal ruin. People talk ominously about rebellions and revolutions on this side of the At-

lantic, and, if they come on this side, political disturbances will soon break out on the other.

There are matters of no little weight depending on the doings of Wall Street for the next four or five days. I wish I were ten or fifteen years older.

Afternoon. Studied till five. Went to the office. Things look no better. If my father would only bear up a little under this state of things, it would be better for him. But he's not calculated for such times. They oppress his spirits and weaken his nerves.

May 5. . . . Something like twenty failures yesterday! . . .

May 6. . . . There's a run on the Dry Dock Bank and the other banks have refused to sustain it! At least they are to have a meeting this night to decide definitely on the subject and there's scarcely a chance of their decision being favorable. Uncle Benjamin [Strong], the president, is almost dead with excitement and misery. He is personally involved to his utter ruin, so at least my father fears. He called this evening and had a kind of private consultation with my father. There's scarce a chance of the bank's going on.

May 7, Sunday. St. Paul's this morning and afternoon. Regular tirade against the ladies from [the Rev. John Frederic] Schroeder this morning, very tremendous indeed, how their extravagance was ruinous and their frivolity detestable, and so forth. My father was at Uncle Benjamin's all the afternoon and evening. The bank will not open tomorrow morning. It is very hard for him, in his old age, and he feels it deeply.

May 8. Not feeling very thorough on Anthon's stuff, I got leave of absence from the president and went down to Wall Street. There was a crowd round the bank ready to recommence the run on it, eagerly waiting for ten o'clock to begin it. But the only notice the bank took of ten o'clock was to close its windows also, much to the consternation of the multitude. The crowd increased rapidly, and I expected a fight, but they were at last dispersed by the Mayor [Aaron Clark], who made them a speech and told them that the other banks would redeem the Dry Dock bills. The mob dispersed incontinently for their cash; it was the best means that could have been thought of for scattering them. . . .

This affair of the Dry Dock Bank has gone better than I expected, but I fear it will prove the entering wedge to split up all Wall Street. The other banks are generally blamed for not sustaining it, and justly so.

Only imagine that [Uncle Benjamin] should actually have come to such a situation as to be afraid of personal insult if he go into the street! Yet so it is. What can be more dreadful? I can scarcely realize it — as kind and goodhearted and benevolent a man as ever breathed, his character unimpeached and unimpeachable, yet obliged to secure his house from attack and afraid of showing himself. These wretched banks and credit systems and paper wealth; they have done all this.

May 9. . . . As I expected, there's a run on all the banks, the depositors drawing out the specie as fast as the tellers can count it. They are in a dangerous situation most certainly, and, if they break, we shall have a revolution here. I don't see how they can help breaking; this run must increase every day, and they can't possibly stand it more than three or four days longer.

Studied hard all afternoon. George Anthon called at seven, and then I went up to Gurley's where those books are to be sold. Never saw books go so low. Bought about $25 worth of them for which I paid between $9 and $10. They sold for nothing, in fact.

Let me see what were my purchases. Browne's *Vulgar Errors,* a very fine folio edition; Hobbes, *Leviathan,* ditto, and moreover the *editio princeps;* and Camden's *Annals,* also folio and all three in the very

best of strong solid old binding I bought for $4 and one or two shillings. I have been asked $6 for a very inferior copy of the first alone! *Quevedo,* translated by L'Estrange, I got for twenty-five cents, a little collection of Greek epigrams for six cents! Prior's *Poems,* the earliest edition, a very magnificent folio, I got for $1.50! I had not the remotest idea of getting it, for I took it for granted it would bring $6 or $7, and even then very cheap. A very handsome quarto Catullus in fine binding and excellent type and paper I got for 95 cents, and, lastly, a folio Philostratus, Greek and Latin, for $3. Many other books that I would have given a good deal to have went in the same style, and I could have laid out $50 easily and got ten times the worth of my money, but I was afraid that in these hard times I should find it difficult to raise the wind for what I did get.

I understand that the banks are now in session to devise means of support. It will be of no use.

May 10. Extensive news in this morning's paper. The banks (except three) have concluded to stop specie payment!!! Glory to the Old General! Glory to little Matty, second fiddler to the great Magician! Glory— ay, and double patent glory — to the experiment, the specie currency, and all the glorious humbugs who have inflicted them on us.

Commerce and speculation here have been spreading of late like a card house, story after story and ramification after ramification, till the building towered up to the sky and people rolled up their eyes in amazement, but at last one corner gave way and every card that dropped brought down a dozen with it, and *sic transit gloria mundi!* How people have grown rich of late! I often wondered when I heard how Messrs. A.,B.,C., and D. were worth a million apiece and how people were now worth half a million, at least, before they could be called more than paupers. I often wondered where all the money had come from and how such a quantity of wealth had found its way into the country. But here's the result of it. No matter.

Went to college. The military out, in Park Place and in front of the City Hall. Wise precaution, that. McVickar losing terribly. Saw him this morning coming up from Wall Street. He looked ha[l] dead. . . .

Afternoon. The Bank of America, Mer[chants], and Manhattan, which has resolve[d] to try and hold out a little longer, hav[e] closed. Immense crowd and excitement i[n] Wall Street, but the military prevent an[y] disturbance.

64.

Martin Van Buren: Against Government Aid for Business Losses

Many of the "pet banks" in which federal funds had been deposited defaulted during the Panic of 1837. As a consequence of the bank failures and the inability to raise public funds in an economy beset by a severe depression, it appeared that the current expenses of the federal government could not be covered. To deal with this situation, Martin Van Buren, the newly elected President, called a special session of Congress that assembled in Washington on September 4, 1837. To solve the fiscal problems of the government, Van Buren proposed a further extension of the hard-money policy and backed an independent treasury. The proposal, which in effect meant that the government would handle its own funds and require payment in legal tender, was the final step in the divorce of bank and state that Jackson had initiated. The business community, which had been hoping for a revival of the National Bank, smoldered in silence. A portion of Van Buren's message is reprinted below.

Source: Richardson, III, pp. 324-346.

Two NATIONS, the most commercial in the world, enjoying but recently the highest degree of apparent prosperity and maintaining with each other the closest relations, are suddenly, in a time of profound peace and without any great national disaster, arrested in their career and plunged into a state of embarrassment and distress. In both countries we have witnessed the same redundancy of paper money and other facilities of credit; the same spirit of speculation; the same partial successes; the same difficulties and reverses; and, at length, nearly the same overwhelming catastrophe. The most material difference between the results in the two countries has only been that with us there has also occurred an extensive derangement in the fiscal affairs of the federal and state governments, occasioned by the suspension of specie payments by the banks.

The history of these causes and effects in Great Britain and the United States is substantially the history of the revulsion in all other commercial countries.

The present and visible effects of these circumstances on the operations of the government and on the industry of the people point out the objects which call for your immediate attention.

They are: to regulate by law the safekeeping, transfer, and disbursement of the public moneys; to designate the funds to be received and paid by the government; to enable the Treasury to meet promptly every demand upon it; to prescribe the terms of indulgence and the mode of settlement to be adopted, as well in collecting from individuals the revenue that has accrued as in withdrawing it from former depositories; and to devise and adopt such further measures, within the constitutional competency of Congress, as will be best calculated to revive the enterprise and to promote the prosperity of the country. . . .

The plan proposed will be adequate to all our fiscal operations during the remainder of the year. Should it be adopted, the Treasury, aided by the ample resources of the country, will be able to discharge punctually every pecuniary obligation. For the future all that is needed will be that caution and forbearance in appropriations which the diminution of the revenue requires and which the complete accomplishment or great forwardness of many expensive national undertakings renders equally consistent with prudence and patriotic liberality.

The preceding suggestions and recommendations are submitted in the belief that their adoption by Congress will enable the Executive Department to conduct our fiscal concerns with success so far as their management has been committed to it. While the objects and the means proposed to attain them are within its constitutional powers and appropriate duties, they will, at the same time, it is hoped, by their necessary

operation, afford essential aid in the transaction of individual concerns, and thus yield relief to the people at large in a form adapted to the nature of our government. Those who look to the action of this government for specific aid to the citizen to relieve embarrassments arising from losses by revulsions in commerce and credit lose sight of the ends for which it was created and the powers with which it is clothed.

It was established to give security to us all in our lawful and honorable pursuits, under the lasting safeguard of republican institutions. It was not intended to confer special favors on individuals or on any classes of them, to create systems of agriculture, manufactures, or trade, or to engage in them either separately or in connection with individual citizens or organized associations. If its operations were to be directed for the benefit of any one class, equivalent favors must in justice be extended to the rest; and the attempt to bestow such favors with an equal hand, or even to select those who should most deserve them, would never be successful.

All communities are apt to look to government for too much. Even in our own country, where its powers and duties are so strictly limited, we are prone to do so, especially at periods of sudden embarrassment and distress. But this ought not to be. The framers of our excellent Constitution and the people who approved it with calm and sagacious deliberation acted at the time on a sounder principle. They wisely judged that the less government interferes with private pursuits the better for the general prosperity. It is not its legitimate object to make men rich or to repair by direct grants of money or legislation in favor of particular pursuits, losses not incurred in the public service. This would be substantially to use the property of some for the benefit of others. But its real duty— that duty the performance of which makes a good government the most precious of human blessings

Metropolitan Museum of Art; gift of Mrs. Jacob H. Lazarus
Martin Van Buren; portrait by Henry Inman

— is to enact and enforce a system of general laws commensurate with, but not exceeding, the objects of its establishment, and to leave every citizen and every interest to reap under its benign protection the rewards of virtue, industry, and prudence.

I cannot doubt that on this as on all similar occasions the federal government will find its agency most conducive to the security and happiness of the people when limited to the exercise of its conceded powers. In never assuming, even for a well-meant object, such powers as were not designed to be conferred upon it, we shall in reality do most for the general welfare. To avoid every unnecessary interference with the pursuits of the citizen will result in more benefit than to adopt measures which could only assist limited interests, and are eagerly, but perhaps naturally, sought for under the pressure of temporary circumstances. If, therefore, I refrain from suggesting to Congress any specific plan for regulating the exchanges of the country, relieving mercantile embarrassments, or interfering with the ordinary operations of foreign or domestic commerce, it is from a conviction that such measures are not within the constitutional province of the general government, and that their adoption would not promote the real and permanent welfare of those they might be designed to aid.

The difficulties and distresses of the times, though unquestionably great, are limited in their extent, and cannot be regarded as affecting the permanent prosperity of the nation. Arising in a great degree from the transactions of foreign and domestic commerce, it is upon them that they have chiefly fallen. The great agricultural interest has in many parts of the country suffered comparatively little, and, as if Providence intended to display the munificence of its goodness at the moment of our greatest need, and in direct contrast to the evils occasioned by the waywardness of man, we have been blessed throughout our extended territory with a season of general health and of uncommon fruitfulness.

The proceeds of our great staples will soon furnish the means of liquidating debts at home and abroad, and contribute equally to the revival of commercial activity and the restoration of commercial credit. The banks, established avowedly for its support, deriving their profits from it, and resting under obligations to it which cannot be overlooked, will feel at once the necessity and justice of uniting their energies with those of the mercantile interest.

Four precepts: to break off customs; to shake off spirits ill-disposed; to meditate on youth; to do nothing against one's genius.

NATHANIEL HAWTHORNE, *American Notebooks*, Oct. 25, 1836

65.

DAVID HENSHAW: The Rights and Powers of Corporations

David Henshaw was a wealthy and conservative Democrat from Massachusetts. In return for supporting Jackson in 1827, he became the collector of the Port of Boston. The post gave him control over the local distribution of federal patronage, and consequently of the party of his state. In 1835 the Massachusetts Democrats split into radical and conservative wings, differing mainly over fiscal policy. While the conservatives wanted to limit the power of corporations, the radicals wanted to abolish them. During the Panic of 1837 the radicals gained control of the state party. To restrain radical sentiment, Henshaw published the tract, excerpts from which are reprinted below. But Henshaw's position did not prevail.

Source: *Remarks Upon the Rights and Powers of Corporations, etc., etc.,* by a Citizen of Boston, Boston, 1837.

BUSINESS CORPORATIONS, excluding banks and all large corporations for trading in money, when judiciously granted and suitably regulated, seem to me generally beneficial and the natural offspring of our social condition. But if they are to be placed beyond legislative control and are thus to become monopolies and perpetuities, they assume an aspect the reverse of this and become alarming excrescences upon the body politic. We may assume this axiom as perfectly sound: *that corporations can hold their rights upon no firmer basis nor different tenure than individuals hold theirs.*

The legislature exercises the undisputed right to regulate the business of individuals and to define their rights to property. It has first prohibited, then licensed, and then made penal, the selling of lottery tickets. It prohibits the selling of certain articles without a license therefor from designated officers. It forbids the selling of goods at auction without a license and the payment of a tax. It forbids the selling of other articles, except in certain quantities, and with certain brands put upon them by public officers —

unwise and vexatious regulations, I grant, but, still, who disputes the legality of the inspection laws?

It requires, in other cases, that the name of the vendor or packer be branded on the article sold. It prohibits people from doing business on certain days and on particular hours, as in the case of the laws respecting the observance of the Lord's Day, and selling goods by auction after sunset. It prohibits certain amusements, and has even affixed a fine to a particular exercise of the liberty of speech, as may be seen in the laws against gaming and profane swearing. It regulates the rights of inheritance, prescribes the rules for the transfer of property from individuals to individuals, and their rights and remedies in matters of private contract. And all these rules are changed at the will of the legislature.

What particular quality, then, is there in a law, in the form of a charter, or limited copartnership to a number of individuals, that places it beyond the power that created it, the legislative power, and gives to it the character of a contract in perpetuity? From the very nature of the case, the legislature must have the same right to repeal as to grant a charter. It has the same right, inherently, to repeal a special law or charter creating a bank, insurance company, manufactory, or any other business corporation that it has to repeal the general law of limited copartnerships. But this right to repeal the charters gives it no right to the private property of the corporation, any more than the right to repeal the general law of limited copartnerships gives it the right to the property of the partners.

In this state, the legislature transcends its constitutional power if it attempts to farm out the rights of the community and of succeeding generations by means of corporate perpetuities to individual or associated grantees. Our institutions abhor private perpetuities and monopolies as much as nature abhors a vacuum. The constitution of Massachusetts says: "No man, nor corporation, or association of men, have any other title to obtain advantages or particular or exclusive privileges, distinct from those of the community, than what arises from considerations of services rendered to the public."

It also says, "that government is instituted for the *common good;* for the protection, safety, prosperity, and happiness of the *people,* and *not* for the profit, honor, or private interest of any one man, family, or class of men: Therefore, the people alone have an incontestable, unalienable, and indefeasible right to institute government, to reform, alter, or totally change the same, when their protection, safety, prosperity, and happiness require it." Again it says, "that the legislature ought frequently to assemble for the redress of grievances, for *correcting,* strengthening, and confirming the laws, and for making new laws, as the *common good* requires."

The constitution of this state, though it allows and supposes that "particular and exclusive privileges, distinct from those of the community" may be granted by the legislature "to individuals, corporations, and associations of men," allows them to be granted only for services rendered. They must be considered by the legislature to be generally beneficial; they must conduce to the common good, or it has no constitutional power to grant them.

The framers of the constitution well knew that corporations and associations of men possessing "particular" privileges adapted to the nature and purposes of their pursuits were necessary in this community; that the charter for a college would not answer for the business of a church; that a charter to a glass manufactory would not answer for a bank; and they hence clothed the legislature with power to make these grants, limited, however, by the consideration that they are in consequence of the benefit they will confer on the public, that they will conduce to the *common good.*

They were, from their constitutional origin, to be considered public laws, for public purposes; and whenever they should cease to minister to the purposes of their creation, the common good, the legislature, for the time being, not only has a right but is in duty bound by the same constitution to "correct" them, either by making new laws respecting them or amending the old ones. There is no more propriety in saying that these institutions can only be controlled by general laws than in assuming that they can only be created by general laws; or than there would be in saying that the legislature cannot regulate the affairs of a single town or city by a particular or special law. Indeed, if these acts of incorporation or charters are not to be considered laws of the land, great wrong has been committed under them in so considering them for some purposes.

The legislature has no constitutional right, by a special act, to permit my neighbor to take my land for his own use against my consent. But it has a right to take my land or other property for public purposes, paying me therefor a just equivalent. If railroad, turnpike, canal, and the like corporations are mere private associations, existing for the benefit of the corporations and not for the common good, I would ask — What right have they to occupy my land against my consent?

All these corporations, then, exist by the law of the land and, like all other laws, are liable to modification at the legislative will. Such, in effect, has been the decision of the Supreme Court of the United States in regard to the Bank of the United States, in the cases of Maryland and Ohio, which states taxed that bank. The court decided that the Bank of the United States was a *public institution.* Such, too, was the opinion of the legislature of Massachusetts in revising the laws of the state. In the 3rd Section of the 2nd Chapter of the revised code, it is declared that "all acts of incorporation shall be deemed public acts."

There is more sound than substance in the term "vested rights," as applied to acts of incorporation. Every right any citizen holds is a vested right until he is divested of it; and the remark applies with equal truth to corporations as to individuals. But it by no means follows that, because they have a "vested right," they may not be legally divested of it. Last year, our farmers had a vested right to screw their hay into bundles and sell it as they pleased; this year the legislature has divested them of that right, unless they put the name of the packer on the bundle. This year, a bank has a vested right, vested for the common good, to loan its credit; next year, the legislature may, if it choose, divest it of that right if it will more conduce to the common good to divest it. And this, too, inherently, and without any special reservation in the charter to that effect. Numerous instances, in this and other states, might be cited where this power has been exercised upon banks and other charters of incorporation; but I omit them, preferring the question should be decided in the mind of the reader upon its own merits to relying upon precedents. Mere precedents have little binding force upon my mind.

The safety of the public and of corporations themselves depends on the establishing of these principles. Corporate charters would not be repealed, admitting this right to exist, as all experience teaches us, unless they had become a public grievance in the opinion of the legislature; in which case their "particular" privileges ought to be taken from them. They were originally granted to promote the common good; and whenever they cease to accomplish the purposes of their creation, an end should be put to their existence.

It being conceded by all that municipal corporations are public institutions, always controllable by the legislative will, there is no need now to examine their rights. I will therefore proceed to examine the remaining great class of American corporations, eleemosynary corporations. It is admitted in the previous remarks that the legislature, in changing or abrogating the charters of business corporations, acquired thereby no right to the property of the corporation. The franchises of such corporations, only, and not the property, belong to the public. It is not, however, certain that such are the rights of eleemosynary corporations.

It is the prevalent opinion and sanctioned, it is believed, by judicial decision — which, by the way, is not always good authority — that the property held by such institutions is private property, as much so as the property held by business corporations; that donations made to them must be always applied to the purposes prescribed by the donors; that if the trustees or directors are unfaithful to their trusts, their duties can be enforced by a court of chancery; that money thus given cannot be diverted from the original object of the donation by any legislative enactment; that if money be so diverted or the corporation cease to exist, it reverts, of right, to the donor or his heirs.

These principles, it is believed, are more in conformity with the English than the

American law. The powers, rights, and duties of these corporations, like those of every other social and political institution among us, depend upon our own and not upon the foreign law. And these powers, rights, and duties, like the laws of inheritance and dower, are subject to legislative changes and control. The right to give, receive, and, for the time being, to manage eleemosynary corporate funds, here, depends not upon the common law of Great Britain but upon our own statutes, and the particular charters of such institutions, which are themselves but special statutes, laws of the land, public acts, subject to the general principles that limit and control all statutes. The foundation of these rights is in the colonial law of 1641, as follows:

> Section 2. It is ordered by this court, and the authority thereof, that all gifts and legacies given and bequeathed to the college, schools of learning, or any *other public use* shall be truly and faithfully disposed of according to the true and declared intent of the donors. And all and every person or persons betrusted to receive or improve any such gifts or legacies shall be liable, from time to time, to give account of their disposal and management thereof to the county court of that shire where they dwell, and where such estate lie, who are hereby empowered to require the same when need be, and to appoint feoffees of trust to settle and manage the same according to the will of the donors.

This was a general law, not a contract; and, like the laws of inheritance, liable to subsequent modifications. It considers the college and schools as public institutions, and the property given to them as given to *public uses.* Harvard College, which was incorporated nine years later, in 1650, was empowered by that special act, also, to hold property to a limited amount, within the jurisdiction of Massachusetts. It was, nevertheless, during the colonial and provincial state, deemed a *public institution,* as much so as towns, and repeated acts passed respecting it.

The same power, under the state constitution, exists and is vested in the legislature to change the government of this college, that was possessed by the provincial legislature before the Revolution. The legislature has the power to direct the college and other like institutions, to report and give account, from time to time, to the General Court, instead of the county court of the shire, of the disposal and management of the funds entrusted to them, and, likewise, to make other laws directing the use and management of this *public property.* . . .

In this country we may say that all endowments are public, given under our laws, originally, for *public uses.*

Upon the principle before stated, and which applies as much to this class of corporations as to business corporations, that corporations can hold their rights on no different tenure, the laws of the land, than that on which individuals hold theirs, the legislature has a right to direct anew, by law, the application of these corporation funds. It constantly exercises a similar power over individual property. Until the act of the colony of 1641, no inhabitant had a right to give his property to a corporation to be applied to the uses he might designate, and no corporation had a right to receive it; that act gave him and them the right. He has also, under other laws of this state, the right to bequeath his property to his relatives or to others.

This is "a vested right," as much so as the right of a corporation to receive the bequest; but who would deny the power to the legislature to change the law in regard to wills and inheritances, to enact that no man shall give his property to these institutions; that it shall all, or any given portion of it, go to his kindred or his connections, or that a certain portion of it shall go to the public treasury? It is common, in some states, to take specified portions of the estates of deceased persons for public uses.

It has been objected that if a law were made to change the use of funds already given, it would be *ex post facto* and hence unconstitutional. Such, however, is not the case. The Supreme Court of the United States, in the case of Calder against Bull, . . . decided that the prohibition in the federal Constitution of *ex post facto* laws extends only to penal statutes and does not extend to cases affecting only the civil rights of individuals. The whole current of adjudicated cases has been in conformity to this view of the Constitution.

With respect to the rights of wives, a married woman now has a right, and of course a vested right, to the use of certain portions of her husband's real estate, if she survive him, of which her husband cannot divest her without her consent; but the legislature can change the law and divest her of this right, and this, too, though she has no voice in choosing the representatives.

Under existing laws the personal property of the wife becomes the property of the husband on marriage, but not her real estate. The legislature could change the law and vest in the husband the real as well as the personal estate. Can corporations, then, *the mere creatures of the law, created not for themselves, but for the common good,* claim rights superior to those of individuals, and above the reach of the legislative power? ! !

In maintaining the legislative authority to alter, amend, or totally to abolish all charters, I am far from advocating any general, indiscriminate, or wanton exercise of that power. The legislature, composed as it is of the representatives of the whole people, chosen annually, could have no motive to legislate upon this subject unless necessity and the common good required it, nor unless the people sanctioned it. When any institution of this kind, in any of its branches, from age or other causes, has ceased to answer the design of its creation, the common good, there should be a power in the legislature, and it ought to be exercised, to put an end to such institution.

Who shall judge of the wants of the existing generation: the living or the dead?

Who shall control the property of this world and prescribe its application: the dead, who once owned it in part, or the living, who own it entire? The conservatives cling to the dead; I am for the living. This right is inherent and exists in all communities, from the very nature of civil society; and, in this country, the principle is recognized in our written and fundamental law.

The Constitution gives to the legislature, for the time being, authority to pass laws creating and regulating these institutions for the common good; but one legislature has no constitutional competency to bind its successor, who is coequal in power, both holding their authority from the same constitution, and not the one from the other. Hence, happily, one legislature cannot bind another, and thus farm out, irrevocably, the rights of succeeding generations.

Where lies the difficulty in applying these principles to practice by amending or repealing all such acts of incorporation as may be found objectionable? The difficulty arises from the assumption of authority on the part of the Supreme Court of the United States, which, if submitted to, prostrates the power of the states to the footstool of that bench, that acts of incorporation are contracts between the state granting them and the corporators; and cannot be annulled except with the consent of the corporators, because the Constitution of the United States, the paramount law of the land, says that no state shall pass any laws impairing the obligation of contracts. This principle was maintained, if not established, in the case of the Dartmouth College, tried before the Supreme Court at Washington in 1819. . . .

Whatever was granted in the Constitution was meant to be a well-defined grant. It was never intended by those who framed and the people who adopted the Constitution that its powers should be enlarged by construction. So jealous and careful were the people upon this point that they adopted an amendment to guard against the apprehended evil. It is the 10th Article of amendment in the Constitution, as follows: "The powers not delegated to the United States by the Constitution, nor prohibited by it to the states, are reserved to the states respectively, or to the people." The framers intended a specific thing in the clause, inhibiting the states from passing laws impairing the obligations of contracts; they made use of the word "contracts" in its ordinary meaning, as it was then well understood.

It was to remedy the then well-known evil of tender laws, stop laws, and absolving laws. It was never designed to apply to the civil institutions of the states, but was confined in its application to contracts for the buying and selling of things. If there were any doubt as to this fact — but there appears to be none even on the mind of the chief justice — the testimony of Luther Martin, a member of the Convention from Maryland, in his letter or report to the legislature of his state, would remove it. It was meant, he says, only to secure the rights of debtor and creditor from the operations of state tender laws, stop laws, and bankrupt laws. Mr. Madison, another member of the Convention, in *The Federalist,* written about the period the Constitution was adopted, bears his testimony corroborative of the same fact.

The principle assumed by Judge Marshall and sanctioned by all the court except Judge Duval, in effect, annihilates the federal Constitution, or makes it a plastic mass in the hands of the Supreme Court to mean anything or nothing. It can mold the state institutions to suit the will of the Court.

The chief justice admits that this kind of contract was not in view when the Convention adopted and the people approved the inhibitory clause. But that, he says, is not enough; you must go further; you must show that if this case had been presented to them at the time, they would have rejected it; *and of this probability the court assume the sole right to judge.* The counsel for the state

show that the Convention had not this class of contracts in view when they framed the clause; their object and design were confined to property contracts and private rights; and all history bears testimony that the states never would have surrendered the very object for which they had contended before the Revolution and encountered its miseries and perils to attain — the right to regulate their own internal civil institutions. "Very true," say the Court, "but this particular class of cases did not occur to them at the time, and if it had, would they have excluded it? We decide that they would not; and consequently it is embraced within the meaning of the clause."

Thus the authority to regulate some of the most important civil institutions, and particularly that of education in the higher branches of literature and the sciences, the control over those seminaries where the citizens are educated who are destined to fill what are termed the liberal professions and, as ministers, lawyers, physicians, and men of letters, are to enter every city, town, hamlet, and family in the state and directly to influence the condition of society, is wrested from the states and confided to irresponsible perpetuities, thus made independent within the limits of the state. With such latitudinous and far-fetched constructions, the federal Constitution is whatever the federal judiciary may please to make it; and the states are in fact in possession of little more power than the bailiffs who officiate in the federal courts.

The case, from beginning to end, was tried and decided, in all its cardinal points, upon an assumption of facts and principles that have no real existence here. It is an English not an American decision made by a court who are English in all their legal learning and principles. The rights, powers, privileges, and duties of the corporation are gathered, not from the laws of New Hampshire, where alone we should look for them, but from British "authorities," that is, from the opinions of English judges, in what the court assume to be analogous cases, and English law writers, who have figured on the British bench, in British "reports," and British law books, for the last 500 or 1,000 years. The industrious research into the musty precedents of English judges and the misty opinions of English jurists so quaintly displayed by some members of the Court in deciding this cause might have been very praiseworthy and perhaps useful if they had been sitting on the King's Bench in Westminster; but they appear sadly grotesque from the supreme bench at Washington.

The Court assume that the grant was made by the king and is to be defined by the British law; when, upon the face of the charter, though, like the precepts of the courts, running in the name of the king, it appears to have been granted by the executive of New Hampshire, by the advice of the council of New Hampshire, attested by the seal of the province; and upon every principle of law and common sense, it is to be defined, limited, and controlled by the local laws of New Hampshire and by the nature of her political institutions.

The theory of colonial government maintained by the Americans before the Revolution and enforced by the Revolution was that the king is the supreme head, officiating as the executive personally in the realm of England, and by viceroys and governors in the colonies and his other dominions; that each branch thus constituted was a perfect state, having power to make laws binding within its jurisdiction.

No man in America was better acquainted with the rights of the colonies and the principles of the British constitution than Dr. Franklin. In 1769 he wrote as follows:

> Writers on this subject often confuse themselves with the idea that all the king's dominions make one state, which they do not, nor ever did since the Conquest. Our kings have ever had dominions not subject to the English Parliament. At first, the provinces of France, of which Jersey and Guernsey remain, always governed by their own laws, appealing to the king in council only, and not to our courts or the House of Lords. Scotland was in the same situation before the union. It had the same king, but a separate Parliament, and the Parliament of England had no jurisdiction over it; Ireland the same in truth, though the British parliament has *usurped* a dominion over it. *The colonies were originally settled in the idea of such extrinsic* dominions of the king, and the king only. Hanover is now such a dominion.

It was asserted by an English writer that the colonists "who first migrated from England to settle in America well knew they were still to continue the subjects of the same government." To which Dr. Franklin, in the piece before quoted from, replies,

> They well knew the contrary; they never would have gone if that had been the case. They fled from your government, which oppressed them. If they carried your government with them, and of course your laws, they had better have stayed and endured the oppression at home, and not have added to it all the hardships of making a new settlement. *They carried not your laws;* but had they carried your government and laws, they would now have been subject to spiritual courts, tithes, church acts of Parliament, game acts, etc., *which they were not, and never were, since their being out of the Realm.*

All our history from the landing of the Pilgrims at Plymouth to the time of the Declaration of Independence, bears testimony to the same point, the right of the colonies to be governed by laws passed by their local legislatures. . . .

New Hampshire, on her first organization as a separate province in 1680, asserted her right to exclusive legislation within her own limits by enacting in her first General Court that "no act, imposition, law, or ordinance should be made or imposed upon them, but such as should be made by the assembly and approved by the president and council."

New Hampshire, while a part of Massachusetts, was governed by her laws, among which was the act of 1641, respecting grants to colleges and schools, showing that they were deemed *public institutions;* and those laws continued to be the laws of New Hampshire until they were repealed; and this act never was repealed; and hence, when the charter of Dartmouth College was granted, it was under all the restrictions, limitations, and conditions to which this early and fundamental law subjected like institutions. It is to be judged by the colonial and not the English law; and by the colonial law it is a *public institution,* controllable by statute law, and *not* a private grant in the nature of a contract.

The charter of Dartmouth College, upon the face, also purports to be granted for public purposes, to enlighten the savage and to educate the citizen of New Hampshire. Though Dr. Wheelock was declared nominally to be the founder, it is well known that he gave comparatively little toward its funds. It was endowed with 44,000 acres of land; one whole township of which was given by the state; 500 acres in the town of Hanover, a public reservation, were bestowed upon it by Governor Wentworth; and besides these, about $1,700 were subscribed by citizens of New Hampshire, to be paid in labor, provisions, and building materials. From its very origin, it was deemed in New Hampshire to be a public institution, erected and endowed for public purposes. The legislature very early conferred upon it a civil jurisdiction of three miles square, and made the president of the college, *ex officio,* a magistrate to keep order. This is as much a franchise, in English law, as the charter itself; but who would deny the rights of the state legislature to repeal *this* law?

I have shown that all institutions of this nature, in Great Britain, are within the entire and absolute control of the Parliament. Judge Marshall says, "By the Revolution, the duties as well as the powers of government devolved on the people of New Hampshire. It is admitted that among the latter was comprehended the transcendent power of Parliament, as well as that of the Executive Department." I have shown that institutions of this kind, as early as 1641, were considered here as public institutions; that they depend upon local and not British law for their existence, their rights, powers, and duties; that, being public institutions, founded by virtue of colonial statute law, they were subject to the modifications which the local legislative authority chose to impose; and that it is admitted by the Supreme Court, even if they hold under the British law, [that] the people of New Hampshire, at the termination of the Revolution, had an unlimited control over the institution.

This control can have been abridged only in two ways; first, by the constitution of New Hampshire, and second, by the Constitution of the general government. The constitution of New Hampshire, which was adopted before the Constitution of the United States, and since twice, I believe, amended, says,

> Government being instituted for the common benefit, protection, and security of the whole community, and *not* for the private interest or emolument of any one man, family, or class of men, therefore . . . the people may, and of right ought to, reform the old or establish a new government.

It further says, "No subsidy, charge, tax, impost, or duty shall be established, fixed, laid, or levied, under any pretext whatsoever, without the consent of the people or their representatives in the legislature, or authority derived from that body." And in conformity with the first declaration of the province in 1680, the constitution of New Hampshire says, "Nor are the inhabitants of this state controllable by any other laws than those to which they or their representative body have given their assent."

It further says,

> Knowledge and learning, generally diffused through the community, being essential to the preservation of a free gov-

ernment; and spreading the opportunities and advantages of education through the various parts of the country, being highly conducive to promote this end; it shall be the duty of the legislators and magistrates, in all future periods of this government, to cherish the interests of literature and the sciences, and all seminaries and public schools, etc.

Allowing, for argument sake, that this college rested its rights originally upon English "authorities," and that, by the English law, the charter was a contract between the state and the grantees, irrepealable by the state, the state constitution, adopted previous to the Constitution of the United States, modified this grant and placed the institution within the legislative control. No institution could exist except those instituted for the general benefit, nor could any institution hold rights, whatever they might have previously acquired, after the adoption of the state constitution, which were adverse to the great principles established by that instrument. Whenever any institution had failed to promote the general benefit, the legislature had a right and were in duty bound to reform it.

Again, no tax could be raised or levied but by legislative authority. The income from the funds of the college and the rental of lands within the state are an indirect tax upon the people. The constitution enjoins upon the legislature to cherish seminaries of learning and public schools; this presupposes that it is to have a control over such institutions and that they are matters of great public interest. The people of New Hampshire are controllable by no other laws than those to which they have given their assent. They have never assented to the *independence* of Dartmouth College.

We repeat, if the charter were originally such a contract as to make it a perpetuity, the constitution of New Hampshire, made before the Constitution of the United States, destroyed that quality and placed the institution on the footing of all other public institutions, controllable by the legislative

will. The Constitution of the United States could not confer any new rights upon the college. It could at most only preserve what it then possessed; and as the charter, by the state constitution, if it ever possessed the character of a contract, had been deprived of that character, the inhibition of the United States Constitution, subsequently made, was inoperative upon it.

But, waiving all these considerations, and take the admission of Judge Marshall before quoted, and it is conclusive that the case was brought within the reach of that clause only by the boldest and most licentious construction, viz., "That it is more than possible the preservation of rights of this description was *not* particularly in the view of the framers of the Constitution when the clause under consideration was introduced into that instrument . . . nor of the American people when they adopted it." But as Judge Marshall did not know that this view would have been rejected if it had been presented, the Court *assume* that the clause does therefore embrace this class of civil institutions and give judgment accordingly.

I repeat, that admitting, for argument sake, the English definitions of corporations, as laid down by the Court, to apply to [the] Dartmouth College charter, and that it held its rights originally from the king in England and not from the provincial authority, then, from the foregoing admission of the chief justice, the case did not come within the inhibitory clause of the Constitution. The conclusions drawn by the Court are at war with their own premises. . . .

But this decision will be reversed; the erroneous doctrines of this Anglo-American bench will be overthrown; the true principles of our institutions will be reinstated in their pristine force and vigor; they will be recognized again in our courts of judicature; and we shall yet again reap the rich fruit of that precious and bloody sacrifice offered by our fathers upon the altar of patriotism — the right of being governed by our own written legislative law.

66.

Roger B. Taney and Joseph Story: *Charles River Bridge* v. *Warren Bridge*

In 1785 the Massachusetts legislature granted to the Charles River Bridge Company the right to build a toll bridge over the Charles River at Boston. This charter was extended for seventy years in 1792. But in 1828 a similar right was granted to another group, the Warren Bridge Company, which proposed to build a second and competing bridge beside the first. The older company then brought suit against the newer one, alleging an impairment of contract under the Constitution. The majority opinion of the U.S. Supreme Court, part of which is reprinted here, was written by Roger B. Taney, a Jackson appointee who had succeeded John Marshall as chief justice in 1836. The decision, handed down on February 14, 1837, favored Warren Bridge. Taney argued that in the absence of explicit provision — which in this case did not include a grant of monopoly — the interests of the community had precedence over the interests of a single corporation. Joseph Story, who had been Marshall's learned and devoted associate on the Supreme Court, was incensed at Taney's opinion. According to Daniel Webster, his dissent (also reprinted here in part) left the majority view "not a foot, nor an inch, of ground to stand on." Like other conservatives, Story thought property in danger with the appointment of Taney to the Court. "Now we feel with a pang the loss of Marshall," he lamented. "Now we sadly realize that we are to be under the reign of little men — a pigmy race, and that the sages of the last age are extinguished."

Source: 11 Peters 419.

Chief Justice Taney: The case most analogous to this, and in which the question came more directly before the Court, is the case of the *Providence Bank* v. *Billings* . . . which was decided in 1830. In that case, it appeared that the legislature of Rhode Island had chartered the bank in the usual form of such acts of incorporation. The charter contained no stipulation on the part of the state that it would not impose a tax on the bank, nor any reservation of the right to do so. It was silent on this point. Afterward, a law was passed imposing a tax on all banks in the state; and the right to impose this tax was resisted by the Providence Bank upon the ground that if the state could impose a tax, it might tax so heavily as to render the franchise of no value and destroy the institution; that the charter was a contract, and that a power which may in effect destroy the charter is inconsistent with it, and is impliedly renounced by granting it.

But the Court said that the taxing power was of vital importance and essential to the existence of government; and that the relinquishment of such a power is never to be assumed. And in delivering the opinion of the Court, the late chief justice states the principle, in the following clear and emphatic language. Speaking of the taxing power, he says, "as the whole community is interested in retaining it undiminished, that community has a right to insist that its abandonment ought not to be presumed, in a case in which the deliberate purpose of the state to abandon it does not appear."

The case now before the Court is, in principle, precisely the same. It is a charter from a state; the act of incorporation is silent in relation to the contested power. The argument in favor of the proprietors of the Charles River Bridge is the same, almost in words, with that used by the Providence Bank; that is, that the power claimed by the state, if it exists, may be so used as to destroy the value of the franchise they have granted to the corporation. The argument must receive the same answer; and the fact that the power has been already exercised, so as to destroy the value of the franchise, cannot in any degree affect the principle. The existence of the power does not, and cannot, depend upon the circumstance of its having been exercised or not.

It may, perhaps, be said, that in the case of the Providence Bank, this Court were speaking of the taxing power; which is of vital importance to the very existence of every government. But the object and end of all government is to promote the happiness and prosperity of the community by which it is established; and it can never be assumed that the government intended to diminish its power of accomplishing the end for which it was created. And in a country like ours, free, active, and enterprising, continually advancing in numbers and wealth, new channels of communication are daily found necessary, both for travel and trade, and are essential to the comfort, convenience, and prosperity of the people.

A state ought never to be presumed to surrender this power, because, like the taxing power, the whole community have an interest in preserving it undiminished. And when a corporation alleges that a state has surrendered, for seventy years, its power of improvement and public accommodation in a great and important line of travel, along which a vast number of its citizens must

daily pass, the community have a right to insist, in the language of this Court, above quoted, "that its abandonment ought not to be presumed, in a case, in which the deliberate purpose of the state to abandon it does not appear." The continued existence of a government would be of no great value, if, by implications and presumptions, it was disarmed of the powers necessary to accomplish the ends of its creation and the functions it was designed to perform transferred to the hands of privileged corporations.

The rule of construction announced by the Court was not confined to the taxing power, nor is it so limited in the opinion delivered. On the contrary, it was distinctly placed on the ground that the interests of the community were concerned in preserving, undiminished, the power then in question; and whenever any power of the state is said to be surrendered or diminished, whether it be the taxing power or any other affecting the public interest, the same principle applies, and the rule of construction must be the same. No one will question that the interests of the great body of the people of the state, would, in this instance, be affected by the surrender of this great line of travel to a single corporation, with the right to exact toll and exclude competition, for seventy years. While the rights of private property are sacredly guarded, we must not forget that the community also have rights, and that the happiness and well-being of every citizen depends on their faithful preservation.

Adopting the rule of construction above stated as the settled one, we proceed to apply it to the charter of 1785, to the proprietors of the Charles River Bridge. This act of incorporation is in the usual form and the privileges such as are commonly given to corporations of that kind. It confers on them the ordinary faculties of a corporation, for the purpose of building the bridge; and establishes certain rates of toll, which the company are authorized to take: this is the whole grant.

There is no exclusive privilege given to them over the waters of Charles River, above or below their bridge; no right to erect another bridge themselves, nor to prevent other persons from erecting one; no engagement from the state that another shall not be erected; and no undertaking not to sanction competition, nor to make improvements that may diminish the amount of its income. Upon all these subjects, the charter is silent; and nothing is said in it about a line of travel, so much insisted on in the argument, in which they are to have exclusive privileges. No words are used, from which an intention to grant any of these rights can be inferred; if the plaintiff is entitled to them, it must be implied, simply, from the nature of the grant, and cannot be inferred from the words by which the grant is made.

The relative position of the Warren Bridge has already been described. It does not interrupt the passage over the Charles River Bridge, nor make the way to it, or from it, less convenient. None of the faculties or franchises granted to that corporation have been revoked by the legislature; and its right to take the tolls granted by the charter remains unaltered. In short, all the franchises and rights of property enumerated in the charter, and there mentioned to have been granted to it, remain unimpaired.

But its income is destroyed by the Warren Bridge; which, being free, draws off the passengers and property which would have gone over it, and renders their franchise of no value. This is the gist of the complainant; for it is not pretended that the erection of the Warren Bridge would have done them any injury, or in any degree affected their right of property, if it had not diminished the amount of their tolls. In order, then, to entitle themselves to relief, it is necessary to show that the legislature contracted not to do the act of which they complain; and that they impaired, or in other words, violated, that contract by the erection of the Warren Bridge.

The inquiry, then, is, does the charter contain such a contract on the part of the state? Is there any such stipulation to be found in that instrument? It must be admitted on all hands that there is none; no words that even relate to another bridge, or to the diminution of their tolls, or to the line of travel. If a contract on that subject can be gathered from the charter, it must be by implication and cannot be found in the words used.

Can such an agreement be implied? The rule of construction before stated is an answer to the question: in charters of this description, no rights are taken from the public or given to the corporation beyond those which the words of the charter, by their natural and proper construction, purport to convey. There are no words which import such a contract as the plaintiffs in error contend for, and none can be implied; and the same answer must be given to them that was given by this Court to Providence Bank.

The whole community are interested in this inquiry, and they have a right to require that the power of promoting their comfort and convenience, and of advancing the public prosperity, by providing safe, convenient, and cheap ways for the transportation of produce and the purposes of travel shall not be construed to have been surrendered or diminished by the state; unless it shall appear by plain words that it was intended to be done.

But the case before the Court is even still stronger against any such implied contract, as the plaintiffs in error contend for. The Charles River Bridge was completed in 1786; the time limited for the duration of the corporation, by their original charter, expired in 1826. When, therefore, the law passed authorizing the erection of the Warren Bridge, the proprietors of Charles River

Bridge held their corporate existence under the law of 1792, which extended their charter for thirty years; and the rights, privileges, and franchises of the company must depend upon the construction of the last-mentioned law, taken in connection with the Act of 1785.

The Act of 1792, which extends the charter of this bridge, incorporates another company to build a bridge over Charles River; furnishing another communication with Boston, and distant only between one and two miles from the old bridge. The first six sections of this act incorporate the proprietors of the West Boston Bridge, and define the privileges, and describe the duties of that corporation. In the 7th Section, there is the following recital: "And whereas, the erection of Charles River Bridge was a work of hazard and public utility, and another bridge in the place of West Boston Bridge may diminish the emoluments of Charles River Bridge; therefore, for the encouragement of enterprise," they proceed to extend the charter of the Charles River Bridge, and to continue it for the term of seventy years from the day the bridge was completed; subject to the conditions prescribed in the original act, and to be entitled to the same tolls.

It appears, then, that by the same act that extended this charter, the legislature established another bridge, which they knew would lessen its profits; and this, too, before the expiration of the first charter, and only seven years after it was granted; thereby showing that the state did not suppose that, by the terms it had used in the first law, it had deprived itself of the power of making such public improvements as might impair the profits of the Charles River Bridge; and from the language used in the clauses of the law by which the charter is extended, it would seem that the legislature were especially careful to exclude any inference that the extension was made upon the ground of compromise with the bridge

Roger B. Taney; painting by Anderson

company, or as a compensation for rights impaired. On the contrary, words are cautiously employed to exclude that conclusion; and the extension is declared to be granted as a reward for the hazard they had run, and "for the encouragement of enterprise." The extension was given because the company had undertaken and executed a work of doubtful success; and the improvements which the legislature then contemplated might diminish the emoluments they had expected to receive from it.

It results from this statement that the legislature, in the very law extending the charter, asserts its rights to authorize improvements over Charles River which would take off a portion of the travel from this bridge and diminish its profits; and the bridge company accept the renewal thus given, and thus carefully connected with this assertion of the right on the part of the state. Can they, when holding their corporate existence under this law, and deriving their franchises altogether from it, add to the privileges expressed in their charter an implied agreement, which is in direct conflict with a portion of the law from which they derive their corporate existence? Can the legislature be presumed to have taken upon themselves an implied obligation contrary to its own acts and declarations contained in the same law?

It would be difficult to find a case justifying such an implication, even between individuals; still less will it be found where sovereign rights are concerned, and where the interests of a whole community would be deeply affected by such an implication. It would, indeed, be a strong exertion of judicial power, acting upon its own views of what justice required, and the parties ought to have done, to raise, by a sort of judicial coercion, an implied contract, and infer it from the nature of the very instrument in which the legislature appear to have taken pains to use words which disavow and repudiate any intention, on the part of the state, to make such a contract.

Indeed, the practice and usage of almost every state in the Union, old enough to have commenced the work of internal improvement, is opposed to the doctrine contended for on the part of the plaintiffs in error. Turnpike roads have been made in succession, on the same line of travel; the later ones interfering materially with the profits of the first. These corporations have, in some instances, been utterly ruined by the introduction of newer and better modes of transportation and traveling. In some cases, railroads have rendered the turnpike roads on the same line of travel so entirely useless that the franchise of the turnpike corporation is not worth preserving. Yet in none of these cases have the corporation supposed that their privileges were invaded or any contract violated on the part of the state.

Amid the multitude of cases which have occurred, and have been daily occurring, for the last forty or fifty years, this is the first

instance in which such an implied contract has been contended for and this Court called upon to infer it, from an ordinary act of incorporation, containing nothing more than the usual stipulations and provisions to be found in every such law. The absence of any such controversy, when there must have been so many occasions to give rise to it, proves that neither states, nor individuals, nor corporations ever imagined that such a contract could be implied from such charters. It shows that the men who voted for these laws never imagined that they were forming such a contract; and if we maintain that they have made it, we must create it by a legal fiction, in opposition to the truth of the fact and the obvious intention of the party. We cannot deal thus with the rights reserved to the states; and, by legal intendments and mere technical reasoning, take away from them any portion of that power over their own internal police and improvement which is so necessary to their well-being and prosperity.

And what would be the fruits of this doctrine of implied contracts on the part of the states, and of property in a line of travel by a corporation, if it would now be sanctioned by this Court? To what results would it lead us? If it is to be found in the charter to this bridge, the same process of reasoning must discover it in the various acts which have been passed, within the last forty years, for turnpike companies. And what is to be the extent of the privileges of exclusion on the different sides of the road? The counsel who have so ably argued this case have not attempted to define it by any certain boundaries. How far must the new improvement be distant from the old one? How near may you approach without invading its rights in the privileged line?

If this court should establish the principles now contended for, what is to become of the numerous railroads established on the same line of travel with turnpike companies, and which have rendered the franchises of the turnpike corporations of no value? Let it once be understood that such charters carry with them these implied contracts, and give this unknown and undefined property in a line of traveling, and you will soon find the old turnpike corporations awakening from their sleep and calling upon this Court to put down the improvements which have taken their place. The millions of property which have been invested in railroads and canals, upon lines of travel which had been before occupied by turnpike corporations will be put in jeopardy. We shall be thrown back to the improvements of the last century and obliged to stand still until the claims of the old turnpike corporations shall be satisfied; and they shall consent to permit these states to avail themselves of the lights of modern science, and to partake of the benefit of those improvements which are now adding to the wealth and prosperity, and the convenience and comfort, of every other part of the civilized world.

Nor is this all. This Court will find itself compelled to fix, by some arbitrary rule, the width of this new kind of property in a line of travel; for if such a right of property exists, we have no lights to guide us in marking out its extent, unless, indeed, we resort to the old feudal grants, and to the exclusive rights of ferries, by prescription, between towns; and are prepared to decide that when a turnpike road from one town to another had been made, no railroad or canal, between these two points, could afterward be established. This Court are not prepared to sanction principles which must lead to such results.

Justice Story: I maintain that, upon the principles of common reason and legal interpretation, the present grant carries with it a necessary implication that the legislature shall do no act to destroy or essentially to impair the franchise; that (as one of the learned judges of the state court expressed it) there is an implied agreement that the

Massachusetts Historical Society

Joseph Story; portrait by Chester Harding, 1828

state will not grant another bridge between Boston and Charlestown, so near as to draw away the custom from the old one; and (as another learned judge expressed it) that there is an implied agreement of the state to grant the undisturbed use of the bridge and its tolls, so far as respects any acts of its own or of any persons acting under its authority. In other words, the state, impliedly, contracts not to resume its grant, or to do any act to the prejudice or destruction of its grant.

I maintain that there is no authority or principle established in relation to the construction of crown grants or legislative grants which does not concede and justify this doctrine. Where the thing is given, the incidents, without which it cannot be enjoyed, are also given. . . . I maintain that a different doctrine is utterly repugnant to all the principles of the common law, applicable to all franchises of a like nature; and that we must overturn some of the best securities of the rights of property before it can be established.

I maintain that the common law is the birthright of every citizen of Massachusetts, and that he holds the title deeds of his property, corporeal and incorporeal, under it. I maintain that under the principles of the common law there exists no more right in the legislature of Massachusetts to erect the Warren Bridge, to the ruin of the franchise of the Charles River Bridge, than exists to transfer the latter to the former, or to authorize the former to demolish the latter. If the legislature does not mean in its grant to give any exclusive rights, let it say so, expressly, directly, and in terms admitting of no misconstruction. The grantees will then take at their peril, and must abide the results of their overweening confidence, indiscretion, and zeal.

My judgment is formed upon the terms of the grant, its nature and objects, its design and duties; and, in its interpretation, I seek for no new principles, but I apply such as are as old as the very rudiments of the common law.

But if I could persuade myself that this view of the case were not conclusive upon the only question before this Court, I should rely upon another ground, which, in my humble judgment, is equally decisive in favor of the plaintiffs. I hold that the plaintiffs are the equitable assignees (during the period of their ownership of the bridge) of the old ferry belonging to Harvard College, between Charlestown and Boston, for a valuable consideration; and, as such assignees, they are entitled to an exclusive right to the ferry, so as to exclude any new bridge from being erected between those places during that period. If Charles River Bridge did not exist, the erection of Warren Bridge would be a nuisance to that ferry, and would, in fact, ruin it. It would be exactly the case of *Chadwick* v. *The Proprietors of Haverhill Bridge;* which, notwithstanding all I have heard to the contrary, I deem of the very highest authority.

But, independently of that case, I should arrive at the same conclusion upon general principles. The general rights and duties of the owners of ferries, at the common law were not disputed by any of the learned judges in the state court to be precisely the same in Massachusetts as in England. I shall not, therefore, attempt to go over that ground with any further illustrations than what have already . . . been suggested. I cannot accede to the argument that the ferry was extinguished by operation of law by the grant of the bridge and the acceptance of the annuity. In my judgment, it was indispensable to the existence of the bridge, as to its termini, that the ferry should be deemed to be still a subsisting franchise; for, otherwise, the right of landing on each side would be gone.

I shall not attempt to go over the reasoning by which I shall maintain this opinion, as it is examined with great clearness and ability by Mr. Justice Putnam in his opinion in the state court, to which I gladly refer as expressing mainly all my own views on this topic. Indeed, there is in the whole of that opinion such a masculine vigor, such a soundness and depth of learning, such a forcible style of argumentation; such illustration, that in every step of my own progress I have sedulously availed myself of his enlightened labors. For myself, I can only say that I have as yet heard no answer to his reasoning; and my belief is that, in a judicial sense, it is unanswerable. . . .

Upon the whole, my judgment is that the act of the legislature of Massachusetts granting the charter of Warren Bridge is an act impairing the obligation of the prior contract and grant to the proprietors of Charles River Bridge; and, by the Constitution of the United States, it is, therefore, utterly void. I am for reversing the decree of the state court (dismissing the bill), and for remanding the cause to the state court for further proceedings, as to law and justice shall appertain.

67.

John L. O'Sullivan: The Greatest Good of the Greatest Number

The United States Magazine and Democratic Review *was founded in 1837 by John L. O'Sullivan, a free-lance journalist, and his brother-in-law, S. D. Langtree. Benjamin Butler, a radical Jacksonian, liked the idea of a literary magazine tied to the Democratic Party, and he agreed to underwrite the publication and prevailed on other Democrats to help finance it. Andrew Jackson was its first subscriber. The first issue appeared in October and included among its contributors Bryant, Hawthorne, and Whittier. O'Sullivan, who had been named editor, wrote a salutatory, "The Democratic Principle," part of which appears below; he argued, in good Jacksonian fashion, that "the greatest good of the greatest number" is best secured by majority rule.*

Source: *United State Magazine and Democratic Review,* October 1837, pp. 1-15.

THE CHARACTER AND DESIGN of the work of which the first number is here offered to the public are intended to be shadowed forth in its name, the *United States Magazine and Democratic Review.* It has had its origin in a deep conviction of the necessity of such a work, at the present critical stage of our national progress, for the advocacy of that high and holy *democratic principle* which was designed to be the fundamental element of the new social and political system created by the "American experiment"; for the vindication of that principle from the charges daily brought against it, of responsibility for every evil result growing out, in truth, of adventitious circumstances, and the adverse elements unhappily combined with it in our institutions; for its purification from those corruptions and those hostile influences by which we see its beneficent and glorious tendencies, to no slight extent, perverted and paralyzed; for the illustration of truth, which we see perpetually darkened and confused by the arts of wily error; for the protection of those great interests, not alone of our country but of humanity, looking forward through countless ages of the future, which we believe to be vitally committed with the cause of American democracy. This is, in broad terms, the main motive in which this undertaking has had its origin; this is the object toward which, in all its departments, more or less directly, its efforts will tend.

There is a great deal of mutual misunderstanding between our parties; but in truth, there does not exist in the people, with reference to its great masses, that irreconcilable hostility of opinions and leading principles which would be the natural inference from the violence of the party warfare in which we are perpetually engaged. There does exist, it is true, an essential opposition of principles, proceeding from opposite points of departure, between the respective political creeds or systems of our two great parties, the Democratic and the Whig, but we feel assured that the great body of the latter party, those who supply their leaders and leading interests with their votes, do not rightly understand the questions at issue in their true popular bearings; and that, if these could but be exhibited in their proper lights, to their sound minds and honest hearts, they would soon be found ranged, by the hundreds of thousands, under the broad and bright folds of our democratic banner.

So many false ideas have insensibly attached themselves to the term "democracy," as connected with our party politics, that we deem it necessary here, at the outset, to make a full and free profession of the cardinal principles of political faith on which we take our stand; principles to which we are devoted with an unwavering force of conviction and earnestness of enthusiasm which, ever since they were first presented to our minds, have constantly grown and strengthened by contemplation of them, and of the incalculable capabilities of social improvement of which they contain the germs.

We believe, then, in the principle of *democratic republicanism*, in its strongest and purest sense. We have an abiding confidence in the virtue, intelligence, and full capacity for self-government of the great mass of our people — our industrious, honest, manly, intelligent millions of freemen.

We are opposed to all self-styled "wholesome restraints" on the free action of the popular opinion and will, other than those which have for their sole object the prevention of precipitate legislation. This latter object is to be attained by the expedient of the division of power, and by causing all legislation to pass through the ordeal of successive forms; to be sifted through the discussions of coordinate legislative branches, with mutual suspensive veto powers. Yet all should be dependent with equal directness and promptness on the influence of public opinion; the popular will should be equally the animating and moving spirit of them all, and ought never to find in any of its own creatures a self-imposed power, capable

(when misused either by corrupt ambition or honest error) of resisting itself and defeating its own determined object. We cannot, therefore, look with an eye of favor on any such forms of representation as, by length of tenure of delegated power, tend to weaken that universal and unrelaxing responsibility to the vigilance of public opinion, which is the true conservative principle of our institutions.

The great question here occurs, which is of vast importance to this country (was it not once near dissolving the Union and plunging it into the abyss of civil war?), of the relative rights of majorities and minorities. Though we go for the republican principle of the supremacy of the will of the majority, we acknowledge, in general, a strong sympathy with minorities, and consider that their rights have a high moral claim on the respect and justice of majorities; a claim not always fairly recognized in practice by the latter, in the full sway of power, when flushed with triumph, and impelled by strong interests. This has ever been the point of the democratic cause most open to assault, and most difficult to defend.

This difficulty does not arise from any intrinsic weakness. The democratic theory is perfect and harmonious in all its parts; and if this point is not so self-evidently clear as the rest is generally, in all candid discussion, conceded to be, it is because of certain false principles of government which have, in all practical experiments of the theory, been interwoven with the democratic portions of the system, being borrowed from the example of anti-democratic systems of government. We shall always be willing to meet this question frankly and fairly. The great argument against pure democracy, drawn from this source, is this: Though the main object with reference to which all social institutions ought to be modeled is undeniably, as stated by the democrat, "the greatest good of the greatest number," yet it by no means follows that the greatest number always rightly understands its own greatest good.

Highly pernicious error has often possessed the minds of nearly a whole nation; while the philosopher in his closet, and an enlightened few about him, powerless against the overwhelming current of popular prejudice and excitement, have alone possessed the truth, which the next generation may perhaps recognize and practise, though its author, now sainted, has probably, in his own time, been its martyr. The original adoption of the truth would have saved perhaps oceans of blood and mountains of misery and crime. How much stronger, then, the case against the absolute supremacy of the opinion and will of the majority, when its numerical preponderance is, as often happens, comparatively small. And if the larger proportion of the more wealthy and cultivated classes of the society are found on the side of the minority, the disinterested observer may well be excused if he hesitate long before he awards the judgment, in a difficult and complicated question, in favor of the mere numerical argument. Majorities are often as liable to error of opinion, and not always free from a similar proneness to selfish abuse of power, as minorities; and a vast amount of injustice may often be perpetrated, and consequent general social injury be done, before the evil reaches that extreme at which it rights itself by revolution, moral or physical.

We have here, we believe, correctly stated the anti-democratic side of the argument on this point. It is not to be denied that it possesses something more than plausibility. It has certainly been the instrument of more injury to the cause of the democratic principle than all the bayonets and cannon that have ever been arrayed in support of it against that principle. The inference from it is that the popular opinion and will must not be trusted with the supreme and absolute direction of the general interests; that it must be subjected to the "conservative checks" of minority interests, and to the

regulation of the "more enlightened wisdom" of the "better classes," and those to whom the possession of a property "test of merit" gives what they term "a stake in the community." And here we find ourselves in the face of the great stronghold of the anti-democratic, or *aristocratic*, principle.

It is not our purpose, in this place, to carry out the discussion of this question. The general scope and tendency of the present work are designed to be directed toward the refutation of this sophistical reasoning and inference. It will be sufficient here to allude to the leading ideas by which they are met by the advocate of the pure democratic cause.

In the first place, the greatest number are *more likely*, at least as a general rule, to understand and follow their own greatest good than is the minority.

In the second, a minority is much more likely to abuse power for the promotion of its own selfish interests, at the expense of the majority of numbers — the substantial and producing mass of the nation — than the latter is to oppress unjustly the former. The social evil is also, in that case, proportionately greater. This is abundantly proved by the history of all aristocratic interests that have existed, in various degrees and modifications, in the world. A majority cannot subsist upon a minority; while the natural, and in fact uniform, tendency of a minority entrusted with governmental authority is to surround itself with wealth, splendor, and power, at the expense of the producing mass, creating and perpetuating those artificial social distinctions which violate the natural equality of rights of the human race, and at the same time offend and degrade the true dignity of human nature.

In the third place, there does not naturally exist any such original superiority of a minority class above the great mass of a community in intelligence and competence for the duties of government — even putting out of view its constant tendency to abuse from selfish motives and the safer honesty of the mass. The general diffusion of education; the facility of access to every species of knowledge important to the great interests of the community; the freedom of the press, whose very licentiousness cannot materially impair its permanent value, in this country at least, make the pretensions of those self-styled "better classes" to the sole possession of the requisite intelligence for the management of public affairs, too absurd to be entitled to any other treatment than an honest, manly contempt.

As far as superior knowledge and talent confer on their possessor a natural charter of privilege to control his associates, and exert an influence on the direction of the general affairs of the community, the free and natural action of that privilege is best secured by a perfectly free democratic system, which will abolish all artificial distinctions, and preventing the accumulation of any social obstacles to advancement, will permit the free development of every germ of talent, wherever it may chance to exist, whether on the proud mountain summit, in the humble valley, or by the wayside of common life.

But the question is not yet satisfactorily answered, how the relation between majorities and minorities, in the frequent case of a collision of sentiments and particular interests, is to be so adjusted as to secure a mutual respect of rights, to preserve harmony and goodwill, and save society from the *malum extremum discordia* — from being as a house divided against itself — and thus to afford free scope to that competition, discussion, and mutual moral influence which cannot but result, in the end, in the ascendancy of the truth and in "the greatest good of the greatest number."

On the one side, it has only been shown that the absolute government of the majority does not always afford a perfect guarantee against the misuse of its numerical power over the weakness of the minority. On the other, it has been shown that this chance of misuse is, as a general rule, far less than in the opposite relation of the ascendency of a minority; and that the evils attendant upon it are infinitely less, in every point of view, in the one case than the other. But this is not yet a complete or satisfactory solution of the problem. Have we but a choice of evils? Is there, then, such a radical deficiency in the moral elements implanted by its Creator in human society that no other alternative can be devised by which both evils shall be avoided, and a result attained more analogous to the beautiful and glorious harmony of the rest of his creation?

It were scarcely consistent with a true and living faith in the existence and attributes of that Creator so to believe; and such is not the democratic belief. The reason of the plausibility with which appeal may be made to the experience of so many republics, to sustain this argument against democratic institutions, is that the true theory of national self-government has been hitherto but imperfectly understood; bad principles have been mixed up with the good; and the republican government has been administered on ideas and in a spirit borrowed from the strong governments of the other forms; and to the corruptions and manifold evils which have never failed, in the course of time, to evolve themselves out of these seeds of destruction, is ascribable the eventual failure of those experiments, and the consequent doubt and discredit which have attached themselves to the democratic principles on which they were, in the outset, mainly based.

It is under the word "government" that the subtle danger lurks. Understood as a central consolidated power, managing and directing the various general interests of the society, all government is evil, and the parent of evil. A strong and active democratic *government*, in the common sense of the term, is an evil, differing only in degree and mode of operation, and not in nature, from a strong despotism. This difference is certainly vast, yet, inasmuch as these strong governmental powers must be wielded by human agents, even as the powers of the despotism, it is, after all, only a difference in degree; and the tendency to demoralization and tyranny is the same, though the development of the evil results is much more gradual and slow in the one case than in the other.

Hence the demagogue; hence the faction; hence the mob; hence the violence, licentiousness, and instability; hence the ambitious struggles of parties and their leaders for power; hence the abuses of that power by majorities and their leaders; hence the indirect oppressions of the general by partial interests; hence (fearful symptom) the demoralization of the great men of the nation, and of the nation itself, proceeding (unless checked in time by the more healthy and patriotic portion of the mind of the nation rallying itself to reform the principles and sources of the evil) gradually to that point of maturity at which relief from the tumult of moral and physical confusion is to be found only under the shelter of an energetic armed despotism.

The best government is that which governs least. No human depositories can, with safety, be trusted with the power of legislation upon the general interests of society so as to operate directly or indirectly on the industry and property of the community. Such power must be perpetually liable to the most pernicious abuse, from the natural imperfection, both in wisdom of judgment and purity of purpose, of all human legislation, exposed constantly to the pressure of partial interests; interests which, at the same time that they are essentially selfish and tyrannical, are ever vigilant, persevering, and subtle in all the arts of deception and corruption. In fact, the whole history of human society and government may be safely appealed to, in evidence that the abuse of such power a thousandfold more than overbalances its beneficial use.

Legislation has been the fruitful parent of nine-tenths of all the evil, moral and physical, by which mankind has been afflicted since the creation of the world, and by which human nature has been self-degraded, fettered, and oppressed. Government should have as little as possible to do with the general business and interests of the people. If it once undertakes these functions as its rightful province of action, it is impossible to say to it, "Thus far shalt thou go, and no farther." It will be impossible to confine it to the public interests of the *commonwealth*. It will be perpetually tampering with private interests and sending forth seeds of corruption which will result in the demoralization of the society. Its domestic action should be confined to the administration of justice, for the protection of the natural equal rights of the citizen, and the preservation of social order.

In all other respects, the *voluntary principle*, the principle of freedom, suggested to us by the analogy of the divine government of the Creator, and already recognized by us with perfect success in the great social interest of religion, affords the true "golden rule" which is alone abundantly competent to work out the best possible general result of order and happiness from that chaos of characters, ideas, motives, and interests — human society. Afford but the single nucleus of a system of administration of justice between man and man, and under the sure operation of this principle, the floating atoms will distribute and combine themselves, as we see in the beautiful natural process of crystallization, into a far more perfect and harmonious result than if government, with its "fostering hand," undertakes to disturb, under the plea of directing, the process. The natural laws which will establish themselves and find their own level are the best laws. The same hand was the author of the moral as of the physical world; and we feel clear and strong in the assurance that we cannot err in trusting, in the former, to the same fundamental principles of spontaneous action and self-regulation which produce the beautiful order of the latter.

This is then, we consider, the true theory of government, the one simple result toward which the political science of the world is gradually tending, after all the long and varied experience by which it will have dearly earned the great secret — the elixir of political life. This is the fundamental principle of the philosophy of democracy, to furnish a system of administration of justice, and then leave all the business and interests of society to themselves, to free competition and association — in a word, to the *voluntary principle* —

Let man be fettered by no duty, save
His brother's right — like his, inviolable.

It is borrowed from the example of the perfect self-government of the physical universe, being written in letters of light on every page of the great bible of nature. It contains the idea of full and fearless faith in the providence of the Creator. It is essentially involved in Christianity, of which it has been well said that its pervading spirit of democratic equality among men is its highest fact, and one of its most radiant internal evidences of the divinity of its origin. It is the essence and the one general result of the science of political economy. And this principle alone, we will add, affords a satisfactory and perfect solution of the great problem, otherwise unsolved, of the relative rights of majorities and minorities.

This principle, therefore, constitutes our "point of departure." It has never yet received any other than a very partial and imperfect application to practise among men, all human society having been hitherto perpetually chained down to the ground by myriads of Lilliputian fetters of artificial government and prescription. Nor are we yet prepared for its full adoption in this country. Far, very far indeed, from it; yet is our gradual tendency toward it clear and sure. How many generations may yet be required before our theory and practice of government shall be sifted and analyzed down to the lowest point of simplicity consistent with the preservation of some degree of national organization, no one can presume to prophesy. But that we are on the path toward that great result to which mankind is to be guided down the long vista of future years by the democratic principle — walking hand in hand with the sister spirit of Christianity — we feel a faith as implicit as that with which we believe in any other great moral truth.

This is all generalization, and therefore, though necessary, probably dull. We have endeavored to state the theory of the Jeffersonian democracy, to which we profess allegiance, in its abstract essence, however unpopular it appears to be, in these latter days, to "theorize." These are the original ideas of American democracy; and we would not give much for that "practical knowledge" which is ignorant of, and affects to disregard, the essential and abstract principles which really constitute the animating soul of what were else lifeless and naught. The application of these ideas to practice, in our political affairs, is obvious and simple. Penetrated with a perfect faith in their eternal truth, we can never hesitate as to the direction to which, in every practical case arising, they must point with the certainty of the magnetized needle; and we have no desire to shrink from the responsibility, at the outset, of a frank avowal of them in the broadest general language.

But having done so, we will not be further misunderstood, and we hope not misrepresented, as to immediate practical views. We deem it scarcely necessary to say that we are opposed to all precipitate radical changes in social institutions. Adopting "nature as the best guide," we cannot disregard the lesson which she teaches, when she accomplishes her most mighty results of the good and beautiful by the silent and slow operation of great principles, without the convulsions of too rapid action. *Festina lente* [make haste slowly] is an invaluable precept, if it be not abused. On the other hand, that specious sophistry ought to be no less watchfully guarded against, by which old evils always struggle to perpetuate themselves by appealing to our veneration for "the wisdom of our fathers," to our inert love of present tranquillity, and our natural apprehension of possible danger from the untried and unknown —

> Better to bear the present ills we know,
> Than fly to others that we know not of.

We are not afraid of that much dreaded phrase, "untried experiment," which looms so fearfully before the eyes of some of our most worthy and valued friends. The whole history of the progress hitherto made by humanity, in every respect of social amelioration, records but a series of "experiments." The American Revolution was the greatest of "experiments," and one of which it is not easy at this day to appreciate the gigantic boldness. Every step in the onward march of improvement by the human race is an "experiment"; and the present is most emphatically an age of "experiments." The eye of man looks naturally *forward;* and as he is carried onward by the progress of time and truth, he is far more likely to stumble and stray if he turn his face backward, and keep his looks fixed on the thoughts and things of the past. We feel safe under the banner of the democratic principle, which is borne onward by an unseen hand of Providence, to lead our race toward the high destinies of which every human soul contains the God-implanted germ; and of the advent of which — certain, however distant — a dim prophetic presentiment has existed, in one form or another, among all nations in all ages.

We are willing to make every reform in our institutions that may be commanded by the test of the democratic principle — to *democratize* them — but only so rapidly as shall appear, to the most cautious wisdom, consistent with a due regard to the existing development of public opinion and to the permanence of the progress made. Every instance in which the action of *government* can be simplified, and one of the hundred giant arms curtailed, with which it now stretches around its fatal protecting grasp over almost all the various interests of society, to substitute the truly healthful action of the free voluntary principle — every instance in which the operation of the public opinion and will, fairly signified, can be brought to bear more directly upon the action of delegated powers — we would regard as so much gained for the true interest of the society and of mankind at large. In this path we cannot go wrong; it is only necessary to be cautious not to go too fast. Such is, then, our democracy. . . .

The democratic cause is one which not only ought to engage the whole mind of the American nation — without any serious division of its energies, to carry forward the noble mission entrusted to her, of going before the nations of the world as the representative of the democratic principle and as the constant living exemplar of its results — but which ought peculiarly to commend itself to the generosity of youth its ardent aspirations after the good and beautiful, its liberal and unselfish freedom from narrow prejudices of interest.

For democracy is the cause of humanity. It has faith in human nature. It believes in its essential equality and fundamental goodness. It respects, with a solemn reverence to which the proudest artificial institutions and distinctions of society have no claim, the human soul. It is the cause of philanthropy. Its object is to emancipate the mind of the mass of men from the degrading and disheartening fetters of social distinctions and advantages; to bid it walk abroad through the free creation "in its own majesty"; to war against all fraud, oppression, and violence; by striking at their root, to reform all the infinitely varied human misery which has grown out of the old and false ideas by which the world has been so long misgoverned; to dismiss the hireling soldier; to spike the cannon and bury the bayonet; to burn the gibbet and open the debtor's dungeon; to substitute harmony and mutual respect for the jealousies and discord now subsisting between different classes of society as the consequence of their artificial classification. It is the cause of Christianity. . . .

And that portion of the peculiar friends and ministers of religion who now, we regret to say, cast the weight of their social influence against the cause of democracy, under the false prejudice of an affinity between it and infidelity (no longer, in this century, the case, and which, in the last, was but a consequence of the overgrown abuses of religion found, by the reforming spirit that then awakened in Europe, in league with despotism) understand but little either its true spirit or that of their own faith. It is, moreover, a cheerful creed, a creed of high hope and universal love, noble and ennobling; while all others, which imply a distrust of mankind, and of the natural moral principles infused into it by its Creator, for its own self-development and self-regulation, are as gloomy and selfish, in the tone of moral sentiment which pervades them, as they are degrading in their practical tendency, and absurd in theory, when examined by the light of original principles.

68.

WILLIAM HARPER: The Inequality of Men

William Harper's Memoir on Slavery, *part of which is reprinted here, is regarded as one of the most important pro-slavery statements in the history of the great controversy that led up to the Civil War. Harper, also the author of the South Carolina Nullification Ordinance of 1832, converted the earlier argument of Thomas R. Dew, that slavery is a positive good for master and slave alike, into a theory of human nature and human equality that in effect reduced the second paragraph of the Declaration of Independence to a nullity. Harper's arguments were taken up by John C. Calhoun in his speeches and writings; they thus gained national fame.*

Source: *Cotton Is King, and Pro-Slavery Arguments,* E. N. Elliot, ed., Augusta, Ga., 1860, pp. 549-563.

THE INSTITUTION OF DOMESTIC SLAVERY exists over far the greater portion of the inhabited earth. Until within a very few centuries, it may be said to have existed over the whole earth — at least in all those portions of it which had made any advances toward civilization. We might safely conclude, then, that it is deeply founded in the nature of man and the exigencies of human society. Yet, in the few countries in which it has been abolished — claiming, perhaps justly, to be farthest advanced in civilization and intelligence, but which have had the smallest opportunity of observing its true character and effects — it is denounced as the most intolerable of social and political evils. Its existence, and every hour of its continuance, is regarded as the crime of the communities in which it is found. Even by those in the countries alluded to, who regard it with the most indulgence or the least abhorrence, who attribute no criminality to the present generation, who found it in existence and have not yet been able to devise the means of abolishing it — it is pronounced a misfortune and a curse injurious and dangerous always, and which must be finally fatal to the societies which admit it. This is no longer regarded as a subject of argument and investigation. The opinions referred to are assumed as settled, or the truth of them as self-evident. If any voice is raised among ourselves to extenuate or to vindicate, it is unheard. The judgment is made up. We can have no hearing before the tribunal of the civilized world. . . .

President [Thomas] Dew [of the College of William and Mary] has shown that the institution of slavery is a principal cause of civilization. Perhaps nothing can be more evident than that it is the sole cause. If anything can be predicated as universally true of uncultivated man, it is that he will not labor beyond what is absolutely necessary to maintain his existence. Labor is pain to those who are unaccustomed to it, and the nature of man is averse to pain. Even with all the training, the helps, and motives of civilization, we find that this aversion cannot be overcome in many individuals of the most cultivated societies. The coercion of slavery alone is adequate to form man to habits of labor. Without it, there can be no accumulation of property, no providence for the future, no tastes for comfort or elegancies, which are the characteristics and essentials of civilization. He who has obtained the command of another's labor first begins to accumulate and provide for the future, and the foundations of civilization are laid. We find confirmed by experience that which is so evident in theory. Since the existence of man upon the earth, with no exception whatever, either of ancient or modern times, every society which has attained civilization has advanced to it through this process.

Will those who regard slavery as immoral, or crime in itself, tell us that man was not intended for civilization, but to roam the earth as a biped brute? . . . Or will they say that the Judge of all the earth has done wrong in ordaining the means by which alone that end can be obtained? . . . The act itself is good if it promotes the good purposes of God, and would be approved by Him, if that result only were intended. Do they not blaspheme the Providence of God who denounce as wickedness and outrage that which is rendered indispensable to His purposes in the government of the world? Or at what stage of the progress of society will they say that slavery ceases to be necessary, and its very existence becomes sin and crime? . . .

There seems to be something in this subject which blunts the preceptions and darkens and confuses the understandings and moral feelings of men. Tell them that, of necessity, in every civilized society, there must be an infinite variety of conditions and employments, from the most eminent and intellectual to the most servile and laborious; that the Negro race, from their temperament and capacity, are peculiarly suited to the situation which they occupy, and not less happy in it than any corresponding class to be found in the world; prove incontestably that no scheme of emancipation could be carried into effect without the most intolerable mischiefs and calamities to both master and slave, or without probably throwing a large and fertile portion of the earth's surface out of the pale of civilization — and you have done nothing. They reply that whatever may be the consequence, you are bound to do *right;* that man has a right to himself, and man cannot have property in man; that if the Negro race be naturally inferior in mind and character, they are not less entitled to the rights of humanity; that if they are happy in their condition, it affords but the stronger evidence of their degradation, and renders them still more objects of commiseration. They repeat, as the fundamental maxim of our civil policy, that all men are born free and equal, and quote from our Declaration of Independence, "that men are endowed by their Creator with certain inalienable *rights,* among which

SLAVERY AS IT EXISTS IN AMERICA.

SLAVERY AS IT   EXISTS IN ENGLAND

This anti-Abolitionist cartoon was one of many
contrasting the two forms of "slavery"

are life, liberty, and the pursuit of happiness." . . .

Notwithstanding our respect for the important document which declared our independence, yet if anything be found in it,
and especially in what may be regarded
rather as its ornament than its substance —
false, sophistical or unmeaning — that respect should not screen it from the freest
examination.

All men are born free and equal. Is it not
palpably nearer the truth to say that no
man was ever born free, and that no two
men were ever born equal? Man is born in
a state of the most helpless dependence on
others. He continues subject to the absolute
control of others, and remains without
many of the civil and all of the political
privileges of his society until the period
which the laws have fixed as that at which
he is supposed to have attained the maturity
of his faculties. Then inequality is further
developed, and becomes infinite in every society, and under whatever form of government. Wealth and poverty, fame or obscuri-

ty, strength or weakness, knowledge or ignorance, ease or labor, power or subjection,
mark the endless diversity in the condition
of men.

But we have not arrived at the profundity
of the maxim. This inequality is, in a great
measure, the result of abuses in the institutions of society. They do not speak of what
exists but of what ought to exist. Everyone
should be left at liberty to obtain all the
advantages of society which he can compass, by the free exertion of his faculties,
unimpeded by civil restraints. It may be
said that this would not remedy the evils of
society which are complained of. The inequalities to which I have referred, with the
misery resulting from them, would exist in
fact under the freest and most popular form
of government that man could devise.

But what is the foundation of the bold
dogma so confidently announced? Females
are human and rational beings. They may
be found of better faculties and better qualified to exercise political privileges, and to
attain the distinctions of society, than many
men; yet who complains of the order of society by which they are excluded from
them? For I do not speak of the few who
would desecrate them; do violence to the
nature which their Creator has impressed
upon them; drag them from the position
which they necessarily occupy for the existence of civilized society, and in which they
constitute its blessing and ornament — the
only position which they have ever occupied in any human society — to place them
in a situation in which they would be alike
miserable and degraded. Low as we descend
in combating the theories of presumptuous
dogmatists, it cannot be necessary to stoop
to this. . . .

We admit the existence of a moral law,
binding on societies as on individuals. Society must act in good faith. No man, or
body of men, has a right to inflict pain or
privation on others, unless with a view, after full and impartial deliberation, to prevent a greater evil. If this deliberation be

had, and the decision made in good faith, there can be no imputation of moral guilt. Has any politician contended that the very existence of governments in which there are orders privileged by law constitutes a violation of morality; that their continuance is a crime, which men are bound to put an end to, without any consideration of the good or evil to result from the change? Yet this is the natural inference from the dogma of the natural equality of men as applied to our institution of slavery — an equality not to be invaded without injustice and wrong, and requiring to be restored instantly, unqualifiedly, and without reference to consequences.

This is sufficiently commonplace, but we are sometimes driven to [the] commonplace. It is no less a false and shallow than a presumptuous philosophy which theorizes on the affairs of men as a problem to be solved by some unerring rule of human reason, without reference to the designs of a superior intelligence, so far as he has been placed to indicate them in their creation and destiny. Man is born to subjection. Not only during infancy is he dependent, and under the control of others; at all ages, it is the very bias of his nature that the strong and the wise should control the weak and the ignorant. So it has been since the days of Nimrod. The existence of some form of slavery in all ages and countries is proof enough of this. He is born to subjection as he is born in sin and ignorance.

To make any considerable progress in knowledge, the continued efforts of successive generations and the diligent training and unwearied exertions of the individual are requisite. To make progress in moral virtue, not less time and effort, aided by superior help, are necessary; and it is only by the matured exercise of his knowledge and his virtue that he can attain to civil freedom. Of all things, the existence of civil liberty is most the result of artificial institution. The proclivity of the natural man is to domineer or to be subservient. A noble re-sult, indeed, but in the attaining of which, as in the instances of knowledge and virtue, the Creator, for His own purposes, has set a limit beyond which we cannot go.

But he who is most advanced in knowledge is most sensible of his own ignorance, and how much must forever be unknown to man in his present condition. As I have heard it expressed, the farther you extend the circle of light, the wider is the horizon of darkness. He who has made the greatest progress in moral purity is most sensible of the depravity, not only of the world around him but of his own heart, and the imperfection of his best motives; and this he knows that men must feel and lament so long as they continue men. So, when the greatest progress in civil liberty has been made, the enlightened lover of liberty will know that there must remain much inequality, much injustice, much *slavery*, which no human wisdom or virtue will ever be able wholly to prevent or redress. . . . The condition of our whole existence is but to struggle with evils; to compare them, to choose between them, and, so far as we can, to mitigate them. To say that there is evil in any institution is only to say that it is human.

And can we doubt but that this long discipline and laborious process, by which men are required to work out the elevation and improvement of their individual nature and their social condition, is imposed for a great and benevolent end? Our faculties are not adequate to the solution of the mystery why it should be so; but the truth is clear that the world was not intended for the seat of universal knowledge, or goodness, or happiness, or freedom.

Man has been endowed by his Creator with certain inalienable rights, among which are life, liberty, and the pursuit of happiness. What is meant by the *inalienable* right of liberty? Has anyone who has used the words ever asked himself this question? Does it mean that a man has no right to alienate his own liberty; to sell himself and his posterity for slaves? This would seem to be the more obvious meaning. When the word "right" is used, it has reference to some law which sanctions it and would be violated by its invasion. It must refer either to the general law of morality or the law of the country — the law of God or the law of man. If the law of any country permitted it, it would of course be absurd to say that the law of that country was violated by such alienation. If it have any meaning in this respect, it would mean that, though the law of the country permitted it, the man would be guilty of an immoral act who should thus alienate his liberty. A fit question for schoolmen to discuss, and the consequences resulting from its decision as important as from any of theirs. Yet who will say that the man pressed by famine, and in prospect of death, would be criminal for such an act? Self-preservation, as is truly said, is the first law of nature. High and peculiar characters, by elaborate cultivation, may be taught to prefer death to slavery, but it would be folly to prescribe this as a duty to the mass of mankind.

If any rational meaning can be attributed to the sentence I have quoted, it is this: That the society or the individuals who exercise the powers of government are guilty of a violation of the law of God or of morality, when, by any law or public act, they deprive men of life or liberty, or restrain them in the pursuit of happiness. Yet every government does, and of necessity must, deprive men of life and liberty for offenses against society. Restrain them in the pursuit of happiness! Why, all the laws of society are intended for nothing else but to restrain men from the pursuit of happiness, according to their own ideas of happiness or advantage — which the phrase must mean if it means anything. And by what right does society punish by the loss of life or liberty? Not on account of the moral guilt of the criminal — not by impiously and arrogantly assuming the prerogative of the Almighty to dispense justice or suffering, according to moral desert. It is for its own protection; it

is the right of self-defense. . . . Society inflicts these forfeitures for the security of the lives of its members; it inflicts them for the security of their property, the great essential of civilization; it inflicts them also for the protection of its political institutions, the forcible attempt to overturn which has always been justly regarded as the greatest crime. . . .

And is it by this . . . well-sounding but unmeaning verbiage of natural equality and inalienable rights that our lives are to be put in jeopardy, our property destroyed, and our political institutions overturned or endangered? If a people had on its borders a tribe of barbarians, whom no treaties or faith could bind, and by whose attacks they were constantly endangered, against whom they could devise no security but that they should be exterminated or enslaved, would they not have the right to enslave them and keep them in slavery so long as the same danger would be incurred by their manumission? . . .

By what right is it that man exercises dominion over the beasts of the field; subdues them to painful labor, or deprives them of life for his sustenance or enjoyment? They are not rational beings. No, but they are the creatures of God, sentient beings, capable of suffering and enjoyment, and entitled to enjoy according to the measure of their capacities. Does not the voice of nature inform everyone that he is guilty of wrong when he inflicts on them pain without necessity or object? If their existence be limited to the present life, it affords the stronger argument for affording them the brief enjoyment of which it is capable. It is because the greater good is effected, not only to man but to the inferior animals themselves.

The care of man gives the boon of existence to myriads who would never otherwise have enjoyed it, and the enjoyment of their existence is better provided for while it lasts. It belongs to the being of superior faculties to judge of the relations which shall subsist between himself and inferior animals, and the use he shall make of them; and he may justly consider himself, who has the greater capacity of enjoyment, in the first instance. Yet he must do this conscientiously, and no doubt, moral guilt has been incurred by the infliction of pain on these animals, with no adequate benefit to be expected.

I do no disparagement to the dignity of human nature, even in its humblest form, when I say that on the very same foundation, with the difference only of circumstance and degree, rests the right of the civilized and cultivated man over the savage and ignorant. It is the order of nature and of God that the being of superior faculties and knowledge, and therefore of superior power, should control and dispose of those who are inferior. It is as much in the order of nature that men should enslave each other as that other animals should prey upon each other. I admit that he does this under the highest moral responsibility, and is most guilty if he wantonly inflicts misery or privation on beings more capable of enjoyment or suffering than brutes, without necessity or any view to the greater good which is to result. If we conceive of society existing without government, and that one man by his superior strength, courage, or wisdom could obtain the mastery of his fellows, he would have a perfect right to do so. He would be morally responsible for the use of his power, and guilty if he failed to direct them so as to promote their happiness as well as his own.

Moralists have denounced the injustice and cruelty which have been practised toward our aboriginal Indians, by which they have been driven from their native seats and exterminated, and no doubt with much justice. No doubt, much fraud and injustice has been practised in the circumstances and the manner of their removal. Yet who has contended that civilized man had no moral right to possess himself of the country? That he was bound to leave this wide and fertile continent, which is capable of sustaining uncounted myriads of a civilized race, to a few roving and ignorant barbarians? Yet if anything is certain, it is certain that there were no means by which he could possess the country without exterminating or enslaving them. Savage and civilized man cannot live together, and the savage can be tamed only by being enslaved or by having slaves. By enslaving alone could he have preserved them. And who shall take upon himself to decide that the more benevolent course, and more pleasing to God, was pursued toward them, or that it would not have been better that they had been enslaved generally, as they were in particular instances?

It is a refined philosophy, and utterly false in its application to general nature or the mass of humankind, which teaches that existence is not the greatest of all boons, and worthy of being preserved even under the most adverse circumstances. The strongest instinct of all animated beings sufficiently proclaims this. When the last red man shall have vanished from our forests, the sole remaining traces of his blood will be found among our enslaved population. The African slave trade has given, and will give, the boon of existence to millions and millions in our country who would otherwise never have enjoyed it, and the enjoyment of their existence is better provided for while it lasts. Or if, for the rights of man over inferior animals, we are referred to Revelation, which pronounces — "ye shall have dominion over the beasts of the field, and over the fowls of air," we refer to the same, which declares not the less explicitly — "Both the bondmen and bondmaids which thou shalt have shall be of the heathen that are among you. Of them shall you buy bondmen and bondmaids." . . .

Man, as I have said, is not born to civilization. He is born rude and ignorant. But it will be, I suppose, admitted that it is the design of his Creator that he should attain to civilization; that religion should be known; that the comforts and elegancies of life should be enjoyed; that letters and arts should be cultivated; in short, that there should be the greatest possible development of moral and intellectual excellence. It can hardly be necessary to say anything of those who have extolled the superior virtues and enjoyments of savage life — a life of physical wants and sufferings, of continual insecurity, of furious passions and depraved vices. Those who have praised savage life are those who have known nothing of it, or who have become savages themselves. But as I have said, so far as reason or universal experience instructs us, the institution of slavery is an essential process in emerging from savage life. It must then produce good and promote the designs of the Creator.

69.

John C. Calhoun: The Danger of Abolitionist Petitions

In 1835 the militant Abolitionists mounted a campaign to abolish slavery and the slave trade in the District of Columbia, where, they argued, in contradistinction to the Southern states, Congress had a right to legislate concerning the subject. By 1836 thousands of petitions (over 400,000 by 1839) had been received by Congress. In the House, Northern Conservatives and Southern Democrats combined to institute the so-called Gag Rule, according to which all such petitions were laid on the table but not read. Opposition to the Gag Rule, which had to be renewed at each session of Congress, was led by John Quincy Adams, former President and now a representative from Massachusetts. At the beginning of each Congress he took the opportunity to debate on the imposition of the rule to read a number of the petitions, and thus earned the sobriquet "Old Man Eloquent." This procedure enraged the slaveholders, who tried to silence him by every means short of violence. The Senate adopted a different procedure. There, it became traditional for the petitions to be read, whereupon a motion barring the petitioners' prayer would be proposed and passed. One of numerous speeches against the petitions by John C. Calhoun, who wanted the Senate to adopt a Gag Rule similar to that of the House, is reprinted here. Delivered in February 1837, it expresses the Southern position that the very existence of the Union was endangered by abolitionism.

Source: *Speeches of John C. Calhoun*, New York, 1843, pp. 222-226.

If the time of the Senate permitted, I should feel it to be my duty to call for the reading of the mass of petitions on the table, in order that we might know what language they hold toward the slaveholding states and their institutions; but as it will not, I have selected indiscriminately from the pile, two: one from those in manuscript and the other from the printed; and, without knowing their contents, will call for the reading of them so that we may judge, by them, of the character of the whole.

(Here the secretary, on the call of Mr. Calhoun, read the two petitions.)

Such . . . is the language held toward us and ours; the peculiar institutions of the

South, that on the maintenance of which the very existence of the slaveholding states depends, is pronounced to be sinful and odious, in the sight of God and man; and this with a systematic design of rendering us hateful in the eyes of the world, with a view to a general crusade against us and our institutions. This, too, in the legislative halls of the Union, created by these confederated states for the better protection of their peace, their safety, and their respective institutions. And yet we, the representatives of twelve of these sovereign states against whom this deadly war is waged, are expected to sit here in silence, hearing ourselves and our constituents day after day denounced, without uttering a word; if we but open our lips, the charge of agitation is resounded on all sides, and we are held up as seeking to aggravate the evil which we resist. Every reflecting mind must see in all this a state of things deeply and dangerously diseased.

I do not belong . . . to the school which holds that aggression is to be met by concession. Mine is the opposite creed, which teaches that encroachments must be met at the beginning and that those who act on the opposite principle are prepared to become slaves. In this case, in particular, I hold concession or compromise to be fatal. If we concede an inch, concession would follow concession — compromise would follow compromise — until our ranks would be so broken that effectual resistance would be impossible. We must meet the enemy on the frontier, with a fixed determination of maintaining our position at every hazard. Consent to receive these insulting petitions, and the next demand will be that they be referred to a committee in order that they may be deliberated and acted upon.

At the last session, we were modestly asked to receive them simply to lay them on the table, without any view of ulterior action. I then told the senator from Pennsylvania (Mr. Buchanan), who strongly urged that course in the Senate, that it was a position that could not be maintained, as the argument in favor of acting on the petitions, if we were bound to receive, could not be resisted. I then said that the next step would be to refer the petition to a committee, and I already see indications that such is now the intention. If we yield, that will be followed by another, and we would thus proceed, step by step, to the final consummation of the object of these petitions.

We are now told that the most effectual mode of arresting the progress of Abolition is to reason it down; and, with this view, it is urged that the petitions ought to be referred to a committee. That is the very ground which was taken at the last session in the other house; but, instead of arresting its progress, it has since advanced more rapidly than ever. The most unquestionable right may be rendered doubtful if once admitted to be a subject of controversy, and that would be the case in the present instance. The subject is beyond the jurisdiction of Congress; they have no right to touch it in any shape or form or to make it the subject of deliberation or discussion.

In opposition to this view, it is urged that Congress is bound by the Constitution to receive petitions in every case and on every subject, whether within its constitutional competency or not. I hold the doctrine to be absurd and do solemnly believe that it would be as easy to prove that it has the right to abolish slavery as that it is bound to receive petitions for that purpose. The very existence of the rule that requires a question to be put on the reception of petitions is conclusive to show that there is no such obligation. It has been a standing rule from the commencement of the government and clearly shows the sense of those who formed the Constitution on this point. The question on the reception would be absurd, if, as it contended, we are bound to receive; but I do not intend to argue the question. I discussed it fully at the last session, and the arguments then advanced neither have nor can be answered.

As widely as this incendiary spirit has spread, it has not yet infected this body, or the great mass of the intelligent and business portion of the North; but unless it be speedily stopped, it will spread and work upward till it brings the two great sections of the Union into deadly conflict. This is not a new impression with me. Several years since, in a discussion with one of the senators from Massachusetts (Mr. Webster), before this fell spirit had showed itself, I then predicted that the doctrine of the proclamation and the force bill — that this government had a right, in the last resort, to determine the extent of its own powers and enforce it at the point of the bayonet, which was so warmly maintained by that senator — would at no distant day arouse the dormant spirit of Abolitionism. I told him that the doctrine was tantamount to the assumption of unlimited power on the part of the government, and that such would be the impression on the public mind in a large portion of the Union.

The consequence would be inevitable — a large portion of the Northern states believed slavery to be a sin and would believe it to be an obligation of conscience to abolish it, if they should feel themselves in any degree responsible for its continuance, and that his doctrine would necessarily lead to the belief of such responsibility. I then predicted that it would commence, as it has, with this fanatical portion of society; and that they would begin their operation on the ignorant, the weak, the young, and the thoughtless, and would gradually extend upward till they became strong enough to obtain political control, when he, and others holding the highest stations in society, would, however reluctant, be compelled to yield to their doctrine or be driven into obscurity. But four years have since elapsed, and all this is already in a course of regular fulfillment.

Standing at the point of time at which we have now arrived, it will not be more difficult to trace the course of future events now than it was then. Those who imagine that the spirit now abroad in the North will die away of itself without a shock or convulsion have formed a very inadequate conception of its real character; it will continue to rise and spread, unless prompt and efficient measures to stay its progress be adopted. Already it has taken possession of the pulpit, of the schools, and, to a considerable extent, of the press — those great instruments by which the mind of the rising generation will be formed.

However sound the great body of the nonslaveholding states are at present, in the course of a few years they will be succeeded by those who will have been taught to hate the people and institutions of nearly one-half of this Union, with a hatred more deadly than one hostile nation ever entertained toward another. It is easy to see the end. By the necessary course of events, if left to themselves, we must become, finally, two people. It is impossible, under the deadly hatred which must spring up between the two great sections, if the present causes are permitted to operate unchecked, that we should continue under the same political system. The conflicting elements would burst the Union asunder, as powerful as are the links which hold it together. Abolition and the Union cannot coexist. As the friend of the Union, I openly proclaim it, and the sooner it is known the better. The former may now be controlled, but in a short time it will be beyond the power of man to arrest the course of events.

We of the South will not, cannot surrender our institutions. To maintain the existing relations between the two races inhabiting that section of the Union is indispensable to the peace and happiness of both. It cannot be subverted without drenching the country in blood and extirpating one or the other of the races. Be it good or bad, it has grown up with our society and institutions and is so interwoven with them that to destroy it would be to destroy us as a people. But let me not be understood as admitting, even by implication, that the existing relations between the two races, in the slaveholding states, is an evil. Far otherwise; I hold it to be a good, as it has thus far proved itself to be, to both, and will continue to prove so, if not disturbed by the fell spirit of Abolition.

I appeal to facts. Never before has the black race of Central Africa, from the dawn of history to the present day, attained a condition so civilized and so improved, not only physically but morally and intellectually. It came among us in a low, degraded, and savage condition, and, in the course of a few generations, it has grown up under the fostering care of our institutions, as reviled as they have been, to its present comparative civilized condition. This, with the rapid increase of numbers, is conclusive proof of the general happiness of the race, in spite of all the exaggerated tales to the contrary.

In the meantime, the white or European race has not degenerated. It has kept pace with its brethren in other sections of the Union where slavery does not exist. It is odious to make comparison; but I appeal to all sides whether the South is not equal in virtue, intelligence, patriotism, courage, disinterestedness, and all the high qualities which adorn our nature. I ask whether we have not contributed our full share of talents and political wisdom in forming and sustaining this political fabric; and whether we have not constantly inclined most strongly to the side of liberty and been the first to see and first to resist the encroachments of power. In one thing only are we inferior — the arts of gain. We acknowledge that we are less wealthy than the Northern section of this Union, but I trace this mainly to the fiscal action of this government, which has extracted much from and spent little among us. Had it been the reverse — if the exaction had been from the other section and the expenditure with us

— this point of superiority would not be against us now, as it was not at the formation of this government.

But I take higher ground. I hold that, in the present state of civilization, where two races of different origin and distinguished by color and other physical differences, as well as intellectual, are brought together, the relation now existing in the slaveholding states between the two is, instead of an evil, a good — a positive good. I feel myself called upon to speak freely upon the subject, where the honor and interests of those I represent are involved. I hold, then, that there never has yet existed a wealthy and civilized society in which one portion of the community did not, in point of fact, live on the labor of the other. Broad and general as is this assertion, it is fully borne out by history.

This is not the proper occasion, but, if it were, it would not be difficult to trace the various devices by which the wealth of all civilized communities has been so unequally divided and to show by what means so small a share has been allotted to those by whose labor it was produced, and so large a share given to the nonproducing class. The devices are almost innumerable, from the brute force and gross superstition of ancient times to the subtle and artful fiscal contrivances of modern. I might well challenge a comparison between them and the more direct, simple, and patriarchal mode by which the labor of the African race is among us commanded by the European. I may say, with truth, that in few countries so much is left to the share of the laborer and so little exacted from him or where there is more kind attention to him in sickness or infirmities of age. Compare his condition with the tenants of the poorhouses in the most civilized portions of Europe — look at the sick and the old and infirm slave, on one hand, in the midst of his family and friends, under the kind superintending care of his master and mistress, and compare it with the forlorn and wretched condition of the pauper in the poorhouse.

But I will not dwell on this aspect of the question. I turn to the political; and here I fearlessly assert that the existing relation between the two races in the South, against which these blind fanatics are waging war, forms the most solid and durable foundation on which to rear free and stable political institutions. It is useless to disguise the fact. There is, and always has been, in an advanced stage of wealth and civilization, a conflict between labor and capital. The condition of society in the South exempts us from the disorders and dangers resulting from this conflict; and which explains why it is that the political condition of the slaveholding states has been so much more stable and quiet than those of the North. The advantages of the former, in this respect, will become more and more manifest if left undisturbed by interference from without, as the country advances in wealth and numbers. We have, in fact, but just entered that condition of society where the strength and durability of our political institutions are to be tested; and I venture nothing in predicting that the experience of the next generation will fully test how vastly more favorable our condition of society is to that of other sections for free and stable institutions, provided we are not disturbed by the interference of others or shall have sufficient intelligence and spirit to resist promptly and successfully such interference.

It rests with ourselves to meet and repel them. I look not for aid to this government or to the other states; not but there are kind feelings toward us on the part of the great body of the nonslaveholding states; but, as kind as their feelings may be, we may rest assured that no political party in those states will risk their ascendency for our safety. If we do not defend ourselves, none will defend us; if we yield, we will be more and more pressed as we recede; and, if we submit, we will be trampled under-

foot. Be assured that emancipation itself would not satisfy these fanatics; that gained, the next step would be to raise the Negroes to a social and political equality with the whites; and, that being effected, we would soon find the present condition of the two races reversed. They, and their Northern allies, would be the masters, and we the slaves; the condition of the white race in the British West India Islands, as bad as it is, would be happiness to ours; there the mother country is interested in sustaining the supremacy of the European race. It is true that the authority of the former master is destroyed, but the African will there still be a slave, not to individuals, but to the community — forced to labor, not by the authority of the overseer but by the bayonet of the soldiery and the rod of the civil magistrate.

Surrounded as the slaveholding states are with such imminent perils, I rejoice to think that our means of defense are ample if we shall prove to have the intelligence and spirit to see and apply them before it is too late. All we want is concert, to lay aside all party differences, and unite with zeal and energy in repelling approaching dangers. Let there be concert of action, and we shall find ample means of security without resorting to secession or disunion. I speak with full knowledge and a thorough examination of the subject, and, for one, see my way clearly.

One thing alarms me — the eager pursuit of gain which overspreads the land and which absorbs every faculty of the mind and every feeling of the heart. Of all passions, avarice is the most blind and compromising — the last to see and the first to yield to danger. I dare not hope that anything I can say will arouse the South to a due sense of danger. I fear it is beyond the power of mortal voice to awaken it in time from the fatal security into which it has fallen.

70.

Aaron Clark: Immigrants in a Crowded City

During the worst depression the country had ever known, the mayor of New York,
Aaron Clark, was informed that 773 paupers were scheduled to arrive in British ships
at Amboy, New Jersey, and were to proceed from there to New York City. He submitted
the following letter to the Common Council on June 5, 1837. The Committee of Laws
reviewed the letter, endorsed the mayor's sentiments, and recommended that the mayor
be empowered to enforce the existing health laws and the Passenger Act, and to increase
the amount of commutation money paid by foreign passengers.

Source: John P. Sanderson, *Republican Landmarks: The Views and Opinions of*
American Statesmen on Foreign Immigration, Philadelphia, 1856, pp. 52-54.

THE LAWS OF THIS STATE require that the captain of every ship or vessel landing passengers in this city from a foreign country or from another state shall report the name, last legal settlement, place of birth, age, or occupation of such passenger to the mayor of the city, within twenty-four hours after arrival, under a penalty of $75 for each passenger so neglected to be reported; and that every person not being a citizen of the United States coming to this city with the intention to reside shall report himself to the mayor within twenty-four hours after arrival, under a penalty of $100 for neglecting to do so. . . .

The opinion is entertained that there is a settled arrangement in some parts of Europe to send their famishing hordes to our city. The operations of certain companies have been noticed. But contractors are becoming so covetous that they afflict this country with a pauper population in consideration of receiving from steerage passengers more than $2 per head extra for agreeing to land them in New York; instead of which these traders in foreign paupers secretly clear their vessels for Amboy, in New Jersey, there to land the said passengers, and

thereafter send them to New York by other conveyance or leave them to provide for themselves. Our city is generally the place to which they contract to be carried on leaving Liverpool.

This business is likely to be fiercely driven throughout the ensuing year. Hundreds of thousands of the population of portions of Europe are in a state of poverty, excitement, and wretchedness — the prospect before them very discouraging. The Old Country has more people than it is convenient to support. And although many of them feel no particular anxiety to leave their native land, they see others depart; they read the mixture of truth and fiction published by those employed to obtain passengers; they are assured they can easily return if they are not suited with the country; that certain employment, enormously high wages, and almost sure wealth await them. The times being more unpromising in other countries than in our own, they imagine they cannot change for the worse, and hither they come. They cannot fail to be an intolerable burden to us.

As soon as they arrive within our limits, many of them begin to suffer and to beg.

Some of those by the "Lockwoods" commenced as mendicants on the first day they saw our city, and some of them on the first night thereafter sought the watchhouse for a shelter; others solicited aid at the commissioners' office, and not a few at the mayor's residence. Nearly 2,000 arrive each week, and it is not likely that many months will elapse before the number per week will be 3,000. In the *Boreas,* which came in on Saturday, there were about 150 steerage passengers. They were landed from a lighter, near the foot of Rector Street, at 10 A.M., on Sunday. Some of them declared they had not means to obtain one day's storage for a chest.

Our streets are filled with the wandering crowds of these passengers, clustering in our city, unacquainted with our climate, without money, without employment, without friends, many not speaking our language, and without any dependence for food or raiment or fireside — certain of nothing but hardship and a grave; and to be viewed, of course, with no very ardent sympathy by those native citizens whose immediate ancestors were the saviors of the country in its greatest peril. Besides, many of them scorn to hold opinions in harmony with the true spirit of our government. They drive our native workmen into exile, where they must war again with the savage of the wilderness, encounter again the tomahawk and scalping knife, and meet death beyond the regions of civilization and of home. It is apprehended they will bring disease among us; and if they have it not with them on arrival, they may generate a plague by collecting in crowds within small tenements and foul hovels.

What is to become of them is a question of serious import. Our whole almshouse department is so full that no more can be received there without manifest hazard to the health of every inmate. Petitions signed by hundreds asking for work are presented in vain. Private associations for relief are al-most wholly without funds. Thousands must therefore wander to and fro on the face of the earth, filling every part of our once-happy land with squalid poverty and with profligacy. . . .

By Chapter 56, Section 16 of the laws and ordinances of the city of New York, it is enacted, that in all cases where the mayor shall deem it expedient to commute for alien passengers arriving at this port, instead of requiring indemnity bonds, he is authorized to receive such sum in lieu of such bonds, as he shall deem adequate, not less than $1 and not more than $10 for each passenger. I deem it my duty to inform the Common Council that it is my intention, hereafter, in all cases where it would not be unreasonable, to require and demand $10 for such commutation from each alien passenger. And on advising with the commissioners of the almshouse as to this intention, I am authorized to say that they approve and unite with me in it; and I am bound to believe that it will receive the sanction of the public. Our city should not, whenever it can be avoided, receive more persons likely to become chargeable. It will be a herculean task to employ and take care of those who are already within our jurisdiction. Our funds appropriated for charitable purposes promise no overplus. Provisions, fuel, and clothing for the almshouse are still very expensive.

Laborers are not sought after, and while we pity the griefs and sorrows of all our fellow creatures, we cannot deny that a preference, in the distribution of charities as well as place and employment, is due to the descendants of the soldiers of the Revolution, and to the heroes and sufferers of the second war of independence. It was asked by the fathers of American liberty. It has been promised to their sons. It cannot be conceded to aliens without great indignity to our native and adopted citizens; and if foreign paupers and vagrants come here for political purposes, it is proof irresistible "that our naturalization laws ought to be immediately revised," and the term of residence greatly extended to qualify them to vote or hold office. Many are, I admit, orderly, well-disposed men; but many of them are of the opposite character.

It is believed the action of the Common Council in the premises is particularly desirable. Our citizens had no serious turnouts, no riotous parades, no conspiracies against the business and families of quiet, industrious, and honest American operatives until after officious interference by mischievous strangers; and it is melancholy to observe that, in the mad career of some of these foreigners to destroy our happy system, they have lately recommended to a large meeting of our citizens that they should carry with them deadly weapons, of various kinds, to all our future public assemblages. These wild strangers should learn that to do so is not "peaceably" to assemble as provided by the Constitution. Indeed, a reason for taking proper measures to diminish the number of arrivals is drawn from the fact that, in addition to the great and grievous expense they would add to the city should they continue to be numerously thrown upon us, the Common Council will be called upon to provide an armed and a mounted police for both day- and night-time. Peace cannot be otherwise expected. Many of them come from places where nothing less secures tranquillity.

71.

Daniel D. Barnard: The American Experiment in Government

Daniel Barnard was a Whig member of the New York state senate and a United States congressman, but it is as a political theoretician and historian that he is best remembered. On the political spectrum of his day he occupied a position to the far right. He felt that the success of the American experiment in government was jeopardized by the so-called leveling principles — the common scramble for wealth and power — that he thought characterized the Jacksonian Era. His views were expressed in an address at Rutgers College on July 18, 1837, part of which appears here.

Source: *An Address Delivered Before the Philoclean and Peithessophian Societies of Rutgers College*, Albany, 1837.

The only rational theory of civil society with us is that it is based on human nature — on the discovered, true, and essential principles of humanity. In this view, it is sometimes called an experiment, and as such it is a first experiment. It had never been tried before. Neither Athens, nor Sparta, nor Rome, at any period, furnished a precedent for it. All experience in the business of government was rejected as affording anything fit to build upon. An entire new foundation was laid. It was found that all men are endowed with certain natural rights; that these rights are indefeasible and inalienable; that in this respect men stand toward each other on a footing of perfect equality, and owe to each other a perfect obligation to be forbearing and just.

And hence it followed of necessity that, in arranging the social system with a view to produce the result of government, for the purposes of protection, and control, and mutual benefit — since the invasion of these individual rights is always to be apprehended — the only true method was to let men keep watch and ward over their own rights; holding in their own hands the ultimate and absolute power of protection and defense. And this is democracy in principle, and this is the democracy which was intended to be embodied in our plan of government and carried out in practice; and it is a very different thing from what some men are pleased to teach, and from what many are made to understand as being democracy.

That we have found the true theory of government in these United States, I do not entertain a doubt. And if our attempt is to be regarded as an experiment, and I think it is, it is not because this theory requires to be proved. That is established already, and is properly the result of reasoning from principles which cannot be disputed. Still our attempt is an experiment. It is an experiment to prove, not that our theory of government is the true one, nor yet that God has endowed mankind with faculties which, properly cultivated, render them capable of self-government; for this is now proved, and has passed into a settled truth by what we have already done, if it was never established before — but our experiment is to prove whether or not, even here, where it is claimed that there is more hope of complete success for the trial than there could be anywhere else on earth; whether or not, even here, human nature and the general mind have actually yet made such an advance in knowledge, morals, wisdom, and true dignity as amounts to a settled, ascertained, and established fitness for the control and direction of the common government, in spite of all the sinister and evil

influences to which they are and are likely to be subjected. This, it seems to me, is the great question to be solved, and it is because of the important part which you, gentlemen, will certainly be called on to take in its solution that I am thus particular in stating it. . . .

What a considerate and wise man wishes to know at this day is — and it is a curiosity prompted by reasonable hopes and by a generous and large benevolence — it is, whether this new and happier form of civil society which we have found is likely to be enduring, outlasting convulsions and revolutions if they shall come — not merely whether the American people shall form one nation or be broken into a hundred, which is itself a question of no mean interest; but whether, come what may, the substance of our new and admirable methods in civil government shall be preserved; whether the green spot we have reached is an oasis in the desert or a fertile country beyond it; whether the shore we have touched, we who are the true discoverers of a new world and entitled, at least, to that honor, let events turn out as they will, whether this strand be really that of the great main, of a vast and habitable continent, or only that of a respectable island in its neighborhood, which, however, all political geography will forever set down as properly belonging to it, though it cannot be called a part of it — this is the sort of inquiry to which the philosophic and benevolent mind turns and bends. And since there are things about it which cannot now be known beyond vague conjecture, and which time and trial and examination can alone reveal, I hold such a mind to be quite as wise in its doubts and apprehensions as that of another man in his boast of an unreasoned and unreasonable confidence which he must be a happy man, if he feel, and a weak one or worse, to say so, if he do not. . . .

There are two principal modes by which individuals attempt to escape from that general equality of conditions which is the law of society with us. Wealth is one, and the other is politics; and together they form the main object and cause of those strifes and contentions with which the bosom of society is continually rent. Of course, I shall not be understood to speak of the pursuit of wealth or politics as a thing in itself to be condemned. Much less, I hope, shall I be suspected of that sort of radicalism which would refuse to accord to the possession of property, and to high public station, the considerations of respect and dignity which ought always belong to them.

In the pursuit of wealth, it is the means that are too commonly resorted to to acquire it, and the wretched notions which are entertained of its value and uses that are the objects of my abhorrence and contempt. And in the fevered and exhausting race for office and power, it is the free, voluntary, and almost universal sacrifice of independence, honesty, honor, and principle which is made to gain the advantage and to keep it, that is the occasion at once of the disgust and the alarm which I profess to feel. It is this latter evil, so monstrous and so full of peril, that I am chiefly concerned to exhibit and expose at the present time.

Since the people are the source of political power, since it is to be received at their hands, and only retained at their pleasure, the question instantly springs up in the mind of the dullest aspirant, how, and by what means, can this many headed but generally singlehearted being be best propitiated. It needs no precept from classic Greece, and her "Old Man eloquent," to make a politician see how useful and important it is to understand the people; and a little consideration shows him that, for the mere purpose of success, there is no intrinsic difficulty in the subject which need deter the weakest from the attempt. The people are men, with the dispositions, passions, and habits of men. . . .

To know that, naturally, men are jealous of superiors; that they envy the fortunate; that they hate distinctions, however essential or deserved, unless shared or created by themselves; and that in their plan of leveling, which they call equality, it is almost wholly a process of depression with scarcely an attempt at elevation; and to know that, in general, they are at the same time credulous, easily imposed on, apt to be deceived, susceptible of flattery, vain, trusting to appearances where there is no reality, and dazzled and captivated with any shows got up to astonish or amuse — here is a brief and imperfect summary, yet containing enough for the manual of any shrewd politician who might choose to take the field with a *vade mecum* of such comprehensive and excellent morality.

We see, at least, that the temptation to push forward to the experiment, when no other guide or authority than this, and only a moderate share of prudence and sagacity are demanded, must be nearly if not quite irresistible — too much so to make it at all wonderful that we find it in fact often unresisted. This political being who is so coveted and caressed by public men and by parties is no better or wiser than themselves, whatever solemn asseverations they may make to the contrary; and that they know too as well as we can tell them.

This being may be fairly represented by any average individual among themselves — anyone whose knowledge and acquaintance with principles, with public affairs and the world, whose judgment and opinions, prejudices and passions, temper and manners, sense, sentiments, and feelings, do not rise above or fall below the humble measure and standard to which the majority attain — only to make such a one a just and worthy representative of what the people are, we must give him, in our conceptions and estimate, a strength, a power, a torrent and tempest of energy both in his opinions and passions, and a physical potency also, such as never belong to persons, and can only be exhibited by numbers.

We the people are such, let politicians tell us what they will; and as for our wisdom and our morals, why the best that can be said with truth is that we are wise when we are wise, and moral when we are good; and it is as easy to judge both of our wisdom and our goodness as it is to judge of the wisdom and goodness of any individual whose acts and principles are known and understood. And we are insulted, therefore, with a gross attempt at base and degrading adulation, if we had sense enough to see it, when we are told that we are always wise and good; always right and correct in our principles, our opinions, and our measures; right in the objects we have in view, in the means we use, and in the sentiments we entertain; right in our views of public policy and the common good; right in our estimate of men as well as of things; right when we condemn and denounce, and when we acquit and applaud; right in theory and right in practice; right in our philosophy and right in our morality; right always and right in all things, and so right in everything that we cannot be wrong in anything. Oh, if this be so, what a convenient and admirable standard of right and wrong, and of wisdom and folly, the world has at last in us, the people! . . .

I am afraid we are fast losing, if we have not already lost, the original purity and brightness with which we set out; that our manners, our sentiments, and our virtue are falling into easy, consenting, and accommodating habits; that our patriotism is becoming narrow and selfish, degenerating into blind, vulgar, and corrupt attachments; that vicious and degrading sentiments do not shock us as they once did; that we are getting familiar with the taint that is in the air, which therefore no longer offends the sense, and now gives us no warning of the pollution in the midst of which we dwell and the poison we inhale. . . .

I look to the educated and literary class in the country to save it. No matter who commands for the voyage, if we cannot find pilots who understand the channels we must pass, with their windings and their soundings, who know where hidden dangers lurk and how only we may avoid them, and who will aid us with their skill and their counsel to bring us into port, still I would hope on; but I should think the odds most fearfully against us, and not much to choose between going down in the deep sea and waiting a little to be stranded in shoal water where we may perish no less miserably and certainly, though close upon the land. But there is more to be done than merely to conduct the business of navigation — to set the canvass, and hold the helm, and study the chart. We must take care that the ship be well found and well provided for the adventure, and especially that we be not caught in the midocean with unsound timbers in her. . . .

Now it is here, in the matter of principles and morals, and chiefly in what may well enough be called the morals of politics, that the services of the educated and literary class in the country are demanded. Gentlemen, I would not have you politicians; that is, I would not have you make a trade of politics or look solicitously for political elevation. You can serve your country better, with surer success, and with vastly more honor. And there is no profession or occupation, to which your tastes and inclinations may assign you which would not consist perfectly with such a duty, or which would be materially interrupted by it. Give your hearts, warm and honest, to your country and your fellowmen. Cast about you, each for himself, for the best mode of serving them. You have treasures of learning, and if you are wise you will have greater — offer these.

You have been trained to public speaking and to the use of that mighty instrument, the pen, and practice will give energy and strength and polish. Here is the possession of tremendous power over human thought and action — offer this. Cultivate habits of association and union among yourselves and with all who follow similar pursuits, and whose learning, tastes, temper, and elevation of character make them congenial spirits. There is strength and encouragement in association. There is power in combination and union. Let educated and literary men everywhere band themselves together, and together labor for the public welfare. There is no danger from this sort of class spirit and this kind of aristocracy. The more we can have of it the better. When mind leads in a community — mind trained in the ways of virtue and devoted to the cause of virtue — liberty is safe, and human happiness is secured as far as it is attainable on earth.

72.

WILLIAM ELLERY CHANNING: Against the Annexation of Texas

Immediately after the independence of Texas was formally recognized by the United States, on March 3, 1837, plans to annex Texas got under way. During 1837 and 1838 eight Northern state legislatures announced their opposition to annexation, and thousands of individual Northern protests against it were received by Congress. Among them was a letter, reprinted here in part, by William Ellery Channing, addressed to Henry Clay. Channing, a prominent pacifist and Abolitionist, derived his concept of Texans ("adventurers . . . . outcasts") from a pamphlet widely circulated in the North, The War in Texas, *by William Lundy. On August 4, 1837, three days after Channing's letter was written, the minister from Texas formally proposed that Texas be annexed. Partly as a result of the agitation against annexation, President Van Buren rejected the proposal.*

Source: *The Works of William E. Channing,* 8th edition, Boston, 1848, Vol. II, pp. 204-217.

HAVING UNFOLDED THE ARGUMENT against the annexation of Texas from the criminality of the revolt, I proceed to a second very solemn consideration, namely, that by this act our country will enter on a career of encroachment, war, and crime, and will merit and incur the punishment and woe of aggravated wrongdoing. The seizure of Texas will not stand alone. It will darken our future history. It will be linked by an iron necessity to long continued deeds of rapine and blood. Ages may not see the catastrophe of the tragedy, the first scene of which we are so ready to enact. It is strange that nations should be so much more rash than individuals; and this, in the face of experience which has been teaching from the beginning of society, that, of all precipitate and criminal deeds, those perpetrated by nations are the most fruitful of misery.

Did this country know itself, or were it disposed to profit by self-knowledge, it would feel the necessity of laying an immediate curb on its passion for extended territory. It would not trust itself to new acquisitions. It would shrink from the temptation to conquest. We are a restless people, prone to encroachment, impatient of the ordinary laws of progress, less anxious to consolidate and perfect than to extend our institutions, more ambitious of spreading ourselves over a wide space than of diffusing beauty and fruitfulness over a narrower field.

We boast of our rapid growth, forgetting that, throughout nature, noble growths are slow. Our people throw themselves beyond the bounds of civilization, and expose themselves to relapses into a semi-barbarous state, under the impulse of wild imagination, and for the name of great possessions. Perhaps there is no people on earth on whom the ties of local attachment sit so loosely. Even the wandering tribes of Scythia are bound to one spot, the graves of their fathers; but the homes and graves of our fathers detain us feebly. The known and familiar is often abandoned for the distant and untrodden; and sometimes the untrodden is not the less eagerly desired because belonging to others. We owe this spirit, in a measure, to our descent from men who left the Old World for the New, the seats of ancient cultivation for a wilderness, and who advanced by driving before them the old occupants of the soil. To this spirit we have sacrificed justice and humanity; and, through its ascendancy, the records of this young nation are stained with atrocities, at which communities grown gray in corruption might blush.

It is full time that we should lay on ourselves serious, resolute restraint. Possessed of a domain, vast enough for the growth of ages, it is time for us to stop in the career of acquisition and conquest. Already endangered by our greatness, we cannot advance without imminent peril to our institutions, union, prosperity, virtue, and peace. Our former additions of territory have been justified by the necessity of obtaining outlets for the population of the South and the West. No such pretext exists for the occupation of Texas. We cannot seize upon or join to ourselves that territory without manifesting and strengthening the purpose of setting no limits to our empire. We give ourselves an impulse, which will and must precipitate us into new invasions of our neighbors' soil. Is it by pressing forward in this course that we are to learn self-restraint? Is cupidity to be appeased by gratification? Is it by unrighteous grasping that an impatient people will be instructed how to hem themselves within the rigid bounds of justice?

Texas is a country conquered by our citizens; and the annexation of it to our Union will be the beginning of conquests, which, unless arrested and beaten back by a just and kind Providence, will stop only at the Isthmus of Darien. Henceforth, we must cease to cry, "Peace, peace." Our Eagle will whet not gorge its appetite on its first victim; and will snuff a more tempting quarry, more alluring blood in every new region which opens southward. To annex Texas is to declare perpetual war with Mexico. That word, "Mexico," associated in men's minds with boundless wealth, has already awakened rapacity. Already it has been proclaimed that the Anglo-Saxon race is destined to the sway of this magnificent realm; that the rude form of society which Spain established there is to yield and vanish before a higher civilization. Without this exposure of plans of rapine and subjugation, the result, as far as our will can determine it, is plain.

Texas is the first step to Mexico. The moment we plant our authority on Texas, the boundaries of those two countries will become nominal, will be little more than lines on the sand of the seashore. In the fact that portions of the Southern and Western states are already threatened with devastation through the impatience of multitudes to precipitate themselves into the Texan land of promise, we have a pledge and earnest of the flood which will pour itself still farther south, when Texas shall be but partially overrun.

Can Mexico look without alarm on the

approaches of this ever growing tide? Is she prepared to be a passive prey, to shrink and surrender without a struggle? Is she not strong in her hatred, if not in her fortresses or skill; strong enough to make war a dear and bloody game? Can she not bring to bear on us a force more formidable than fleets, the force of privateers, that is, of legalized pirates, which, issuing from her ports, will scour the seas, prey on our commerce, and add to spoliation, cruelty, and murder?

Even were the dispositions of our government most pacific and opposed to encroachment, the annexation of Texas would almost certainly embroil us with Mexico. This territory would be overrun by adventurers; and the most unprincipled of these, the proscribed, the disgraced, the outcasts of society, would, of course, keep always in advance of the better population. These would represent our republic on the borders of the Mexican states.

The history of the connection of such men with the Indians forewarns us of the outrages which would attend their contact with the border inhabitants of our southern neighbor. Texas, from its remoteness from the seat of government, would be feebly restrained by the authorities of the nation to which it would belong. Its whole early history would be a lesson of scorn for Mexico, an education for invasion of her soil. Its legislature would find in its position some color for stretching to the utmost the doctrine of state-sovereignty. It would not hear unmoved the cries for protection and vengeance which would break from the frontier, from the very men whose lawlessness would provoke the cruelties so indignantly denounced; nor would it sift very anxiously the question on which side the wrong began. To the wisdom, moderation, and tender mercies of the back settlers and lawgivers of Texas, the peace of this country would be committed.

Have we counted the cost of establishing and making perpetual these hostile relations with Mexico? Will wars, begun in rapacity, carried on so far from the center of the Confederation, and, of consequence, little checked or controlled by Congress, add strength to our institutions, or cement our Union, or exert a healthy moral influence on rulers or people? What limits can be set to the atrocities of such conflicts? What limits to the treasures which must be lavished on such distant borders? What limits to the patronage and power which such distant expeditions must accumulate in the hands of the executive? Are the blood and hard-earned wealth of the older states to be poured out like water to protect and revenge a new people, whose character and condition will plunge them into perpetual wrongs?

Is the time never to come when the neighborhood of a more powerful and civilized people will prove a blessing instead of a curse to an inferior community? It was my hope, when the Spanish colonies of this continent separated themselves from the mother country, and, in admiration of the United States, adopted republican institutions, that they were to find in us friends to their freedom, helpers to their civilization. If ever a people were placed by Providence in a condition to do good to a neighboring state, we of this country sustained such a relation to Mexico.

That nation, inferior in science, arts, agriculture, and legislation, looked to us with a generous trust. She opened her ports and territories to our farmers, mechanics, and merchants. We might have conquered her by the only honorable arms, by the force of superior intelligence, industry, and morality. We might silently have poured in upon her our improvements, and by the infusion of our population have assimilated her to ourselves. Justice, goodwill, and profitable intercourse might have cemented a lasting friendship.

And what is now the case? A deadly hatred burns in Mexico toward this country. No stronger national sentiment now binds her scattered provinces together than dread and detestation of republican America. She is ready to attach herself to Europe for defense from the United States. All the moral power which we might have gained over Mexico, we have thrown away; and suspicion, dread, and abhorrence have supplanted respect and trust.

I am aware that these remarks are met by a vicious reasoning, which discredits a people among whom it finds favor. It is sometimes said that nations are swayed by laws as unfailing as those which govern matter; that they have their destinies; that their character and position carry them forward irresistibly to their goal; that the stationary Turk must sink under the progressive civilization of Russia as inevitably as the crumbling edifice falls to the earth; that, by a like necessity, the Indians have melted before the white man, and the mixed, degraded race of Mexico must melt before the Anglo-Saxon. Away with this vile sophistry! There is no necessity for crime. There is no fate to justify rapacious nations any more than to justify gamblers and robbers in plunder.

We boast of the progress of society, and this progress consists in the substitution of reason and moral principle for the sway of brute force. It is true that more civilized must always exert a great power over less civilized communities in their neighborhood. But it may and should be a power to enlighten and improve, not to crush and destroy. We talk of accomplishing our destiny. So did the late conqueror of Europe; and destiny consigned him to a lonely rock in the ocean, the prey of an ambition which destroyed no peace but his own.

Hitherto I have spoken of the annexation of Texas as embroiling us with Mexico; but it will not stop here. It will bring us into collision with other states. It will, almost of necessity, involve us in hostility with European powers. Such are now the connections of nations that Europe must look with jealousy on a country whose ambition, sec-

onded by vast resources, will seem to place within her grasp the empire of the New World. And not only general considerations of this nature but the particular relation of certain foreign states to this continent must tend to destroy the peace now happily subsisting between us and the kingdoms of Europe. England, in particular, must watch us with suspicion, and cannot but resist our appropriation of Texas to ourselves. She has at once a moral and political interest in this question, which demands and will justify interference.

First, England has a moral interest in this question. The annexation of Texas is sought by us for the very purpose of extending slavery, and thus will necessarily give new life and extension to the slave trade. A new and vast market for slaves cannot, of course, be opened without inviting and obtaining a supply from abroad, as well as from this country. The most solemn treaties and ships of war lining the African coast do not and cannot suppress this infernal traffic, as long as the slaver, freighted with stolen, chained, and wretched captives, can obtain a price proportioned to the peril of the undertaking. Now, England has long made it a part of her foreign policy to suppress the slave trade; and, of late, a strong public feeling impels the government to resist, as far as may be, the extension of slavery. Can we expect her to be a passive spectator of a measure by which her struggles for years in the cause of humanity, and some of her strongest national feelings, are to be withstood? . . .

But England has a political as well as a moral interest in this question. By the annexation of Texas we shall approach her liberated colonies; we shall build up a power in her neighborhood to which no limits can be prescribed. By adding Texas to our acquisition of Florida, we shall do much toward girdling the Gulf of Mexico; and I doubt not that some of our politicians will feel as if our mastery in that sea were sure.

The West Indian Archipelago, in which

the European is regarded as an intruder, will, of course, be embraced in our ever-growing scheme of empire. In truth, collision with the West Indies will be the most certain effect of the extension of our power in that quarter. The example which they exhibit of African freedom, of the elevation of the colored race to the rights of men, is, of all influences, most menacing to slavery at the South. It must grow continually more perilous. These islands, unless interfered with from abroad, seem destined to be nurseries of civilization and freedom to the African race. The white race must melt more and more before the colored, if both are left to free competition. The Europeans, unnerved by the climate, and forming but a handful of the population, cannot stand before the African, who revels in the heat of the tropics, and is to develop under it all his energies.

Will a slaveholding people, spreading along the shores of the Mexican Gulf, cultivate friendly sentiments toward communities whose whole history will be a bitter reproach to their institutions, a witness against their wrongs, and whose ardent sympathies will be enlisted in the cause of the slave? Cruel, ferocious conflicts must grow from this neighborhood of hostile principles, of communities regarding one another with unextinguishable hatred. All the islands of the Archipelago will have cause to dread our power, but none so much as the emancipated. Is it not more than possible that wars, having for an object the subjugation of the colored race, the destruction of this tempting example of freedom, should spring from the proposed extension of our dominion along the Mexican Gulf? Can England view our encroachments without alarm? I know it is thought that, staggering as she does under her enormous debt, she will be slow to engage in war.

But other nations of Europe have islands in the same neighborhood to induce them to make common cause with her. Other nations look with jealousy on our peculiar institutions and our growing maritime power. Other nations are unwilling that we should engross or control the whole commerce of the Mexican Gulf. We ought to remember that this jealousy is sanctioned by our example. It is understood that at one period of the internal disorders of Spain which rendered all her foreign possessions insecure, we sought from France and Great Britain assurances that they would not possess themselves of Cuba. Still more, after the revolt of her colonies from Spain, and after our recognition of their independence, it was announced to the nations of Europe, in the message of the President, that we should regard as hostile any interference on their part with these new governments, "for the purpose of oppressing them, or controlling their destiny in any other way." I, of course, have no communication with foreign cabinets; but I cannot doubt that Great Britain has remonstrated against the annexation of Texas to this country. An English minister would be unworthy of his office who should see another state greedily swallowing up territories in the neighborhood of British colonies and not strive, by all just means, to avert the danger.

I have just referred to the warning given by us to the powers of Europe to abstain from appropriating to themselves the colonies torn from Spain. How will Europe interpret our act if we now seize Texas and take this stride toward Mexico? Will she not suspect that we purposed to drive away the older vultures in order to keep the victim to ourselves; that, conscious of growing power, we foresaw, in the exclusion of foreign states, the sure extension of our own dominion over the New World? Can we expect those powers, with such an example before them, to heed our warning? Will they look patiently on and see the young vulture feasting on the nearest prey, and fleshing itself for the spoils which their own possessions will next present? Will it be strange if hunger for a share of the plunder, as well as the principle of self-defense, should make this continent the object of their policy to an extent we have never dreamed?

It is of great and manifest importance that we should use every just means to separate this continent from the politics of Europe; that we should prevent, as far as possible, all connection, except commercial, between the Old and the New World; that we should give to foreign states no occasion or pretext for insinuating themselves into our affairs. For this end, we should maintain toward our sister republics a more liberal policy than was ever adopted by nation toward nation. We should strive to appease their internal divisions and to reconcile them to each other. We should even make sacrifices to build up their strength. Weak and divided, they cannot but lean upon foreign support. No pains should be spared to prevent or allay the jealousies which the great superiority of this country is suited to awaken.

By an opposite policy, we shall favor foreign interference. By encroaching on Mexico, we shall throw her into the arms of European states, shall compel her to seek defense in transatlantic alliance. How plain is it that alliance with Mexico will be hostility to the United States; that her defenders will repay themselves by making her subservient to their views; that they will thus strike root in her soil, monopolize her trade, and control her resources? And with what face can we resist the aggressions of others on our neighbor if we give an example of aggression? Still more, if by our advances we put the colonies of England in new peril, with what face can we oppose her occupation of Cuba? Suppose her, with that magnificent island in her hands, to command the Mexican Gulf and the mouths of the Mississippi; will the Western states find compensation for this formidable neighborhood in the privilege of flooding Texas with slaves?

Thus, wars with Europe and Mexico are to be entailed on us by the annexation of Texas. And is war the policy by which this country is to flourish? Was it for interminable conflicts that we formed our Union? Is it blood, shed for plunder, which is to consolidate our institutions? Is it by collision with the greatest maritime power that our commerce is to gain strength? Is it by arming against ourselves the moral sentiments of the world that we are to build up national honor? Must we of the North buckle on our armor to fight the battles of slavery; to fight for a possession which our moral principles and just jealousy forbid us to incorporate with our Confederacy?

In attaching Texas to ourselves, we provoke hostilities, and at the same time expose new points of attack to our foes. Vulnerable at so many points, we shall need a vast military force. Great armies will require great revenues and raise up great chieftains. Are we tired of freedom that we are prepared to place it under such guardians? Is the republic bent on dying by its own hands? Does not every man feel that, with war for our habit, our institutions cannot be preserved? If ever a country were bound to peace, it is this. Peace is our great interest. In peace our resources are to be developed, the true interpretation of the Constitution to be established, and the interfering claims of liberty and order to be adjusted. In peace we are to discharge our great debt to the human race, and to diffuse freedom by manifesting its fruits.

A country has no right to adopt a policy, however gainful, which, as it may foresee, will determine it to a career of war. A nation, like an individual, is bound to seek, even by sacrifices, a position which will favor peace, justice, and the exercise of a beneficent influence on the world. A nation provoking war by cupidity, by encroachment, and, above all, by efforts to propagate the curse of slavery, is alike false to itself, to God, and to the human race.

73.

Charles Hodge: The Education of Ministers

In 1837 a split occurred in the Presbyterian Church between the so-called Old and New Schools. Partisans of the New School, who advocated a more decentralized church government, favored relegating the education and appointment of evangelical ministers to the American Home Missionary Society, founded in 1826. The operation of this group was the last vestige of the Plan of Union of 1801 between Presbyterians and Congregationalists. The partisans of the Old School insisted that if Presbyterianism was to retain its characteristic theology, then ecclesiastical matters, including the education and appointment of ministers, must be controlled by the church board. The review from which the following selection is taken was published in the year of the division by Charles Hodge, a professor at the Princeton Seminary and a proponent of the Old School. It was directed against Nathaniel W. Taylor's A Plea for Voluntary Societies, *which work was gaining currency in New School quarters.*

Source: *Biblical Repertory and Princeton Review*, (Philadelphia), January 1837, pp. 112-118.

We have always readily admitted that there are purposes for which voluntary societies, embracing members of different religious denominations, are greatly to be preferred to separate ecclesiastical organizations. . . . Wherever the field of operation is common to different denominations, and the proper means for its cultivation are also the same for all, there is an obvious reason why all should unite. These conditions meet with regard to the Bible and tract societies, and in many important respects in regard to Sunday school unions. There are other cases in which voluntary societies of a denominational character may be either indispensable or highly desirable.

On the other hand, there are cases for which ecclesiastical organizations appear to us to be entitled to decided preference. To this class belong the work of educating ministers of the gospel and that of missions.

We shall proceed to state very briefly some of the grounds of this opinion.

In the first place, the object of these societies is strictly ecclesiastical as well as denominational. Every church has its peculiar system of opinions and form of government, which it is bound to preserve and extend. And in order to effect this object it is necessary that it should have under its own direction the means employed for its accomplishment. Of these means, beyond all comparison, the most important are the education of ministers, and the organization and support of churches. The men who decide where and how the rising ministry are to be educated, and who determine where they are to go when their education is completed, have the destiny of the church in their hands.

This being the case, is it wonderful that each denomination should wish not only to have this matter under their own control but confided to persons of its own selection? Is it wonderful that Presbyterians and Episcopalians should decline committing their candidates to the care of Congregationalists or Baptists? Or that they should be uneasy at seeing their churches supplied with ministers by a society in which some other denomination than their own has an equal or controlling influence? On the contrary, would not indifference on these points argue a strange and criminal unconcern about what they profess to regard as the truth and order of God? We consider, therefore, the extension of the principle of united action by voluntary societies to cases affecting the vital interests of separate denominations as fraught with evil. Even if these sects ought to be indifferent to their respective peculiarities, they are not, and the attempt to deal with them as though they were, must excite ill will and strife.

The answer to this objection, that the education and missionary societies do nothing but provide and sustain men to be examined and installed by the judicatories of the several denominations, is very far from being satisfactory. The mere right to examine before presbytery the candidates for ordination is not the only security which the church needs for the fidelity of her ministers. She wishes that by their previous training they should be made acquainted with her doctrines and become attached to her order. Reason and experience alike demonstrate that the perfunctory examination before an ecclesiastical body is altogether an inadequate barrier to the admission of improper men into the ministry, and that by far the most important security lies in the education and selection of the ministers themselves. If these matters are committed to other hands, everything is given up.

Again, the office assumed by these societies involves an encroachment on the rights and duties of ecclesiastical courts. This may

be inferred from what has already been said. One of the most important duties of the church in her organized capacity is the preservation of the truth. It is her business to see that faithful men are introduced into the ministry and set over her congregations. To discharge this duty properly, she must do more than merely examine men prepared and sent forth by other hands. She must herself see to their education and mission. These are in a great measure strictly ecclesiastical functions, which, to say the least, it is incongruous for societies composed for the most part of laymen and without any ecclesiastical appointment or supervision to perform. Indeed, it is one of the anomalies of the times that laymen should be the great directors and controllers of theological education and domestic missions.

We have already remarked that there are in the work of missions two distinct functions, the one ecclesiastical, the other secular. The one *must* be performed by church courts; the other *may* be performed by others. To the former belong the ordination, mission, direction, and supervision of evangelists; to the latter, the mere provision of the ways and means, and the administration of them.

There is a great difference between theory and practice on this subject. According to theory the committee of the Home Missionary Society may be the mere almoners of the churches' bounty. They may profess simply to stand at the door of the treasury to receive applications from feeble congregations and presbyteries. This is all very well. But if in practice they go much further than this and assume the direction of ecclesiastical persons, deciding where they are to labor, instructing them as to the discharge of their official duties, and requiring their missionaries to report to them on all these points, then do they assume the rights and privileges of an ecclesiastical court; they usurp an authority and power which do not belong to them and which they have no right to exercise.

People may cry out against all this as high churchism. It is Presbyterianism. And if they dislike it, let them renounce it and the name; but do not let them under the guise of Presbyterians undermine the whole fabric. There can be no doubt that, according to the system of our church, the control of ecclesiastical persons rests with ecclesiastical courts. Every licentiate and minister is under the direction of his own presbytery, and is bound to go where they send him and to stay where they place him. It is to them he is responsible for the right discharge of his official duties, and to them he is bound to report. For any set of men to assume this direction, supervision, and control of such licentiates and ministers is a direct interference with the rights of presbyteries.

If then, the Home Missionary Society practically assumes the direction and supervision of its 400 or 600 missionaries, if it regards them as its missionaries, sent by it, determined directly or indirectly as to the place or character of their labors by its authority or influence, and demanding accountability to that society or its committee, whatever be the theory of the matter, it is a practical subversion of the whole system of our church. . . .

It has already been intimated that one great objection to voluntary societies for the purpose of domestic missions and the education of candidates for the ministry is the power which they possess. We are aware that the use of this argument is apt to excite suspicion against those who employ it. But the truth ought to be looked at dispassionately and allowed its proper influence as estimated by reason, and not by an excited imagination or distempered feeling.

We say, then, that the power possessed by these societies is inordinate and danger-

Library of Congress

Charles Hodge

ous. It is a power, in the first place, to control the theological opinions of candidates by the direction of their whole professional education; and, in the second place, by means of these candidates thus prepared, extensively and materially to influence the character and action of the church. It is in the power of the Home Missionary Society, or of its Executive Committee, to determine what character, as to doctrine and policy, a large portion of our presbyteries shall assume. This cannot always be done at once, but by a steady purpose and a gradual progress it may be more or less rapidly accomplished. And this progress will not be slow, if three, six, or ten ministers are ordained at one time, by one presbytery, and then sent to one neighborhood. It would require little skill or talent for management in this manner to decide the complexion of any presbytery where there are many new and feeble congregations.

But further, this power enters our judicatories, and is there brought to bear on questions of doctrine, of order, and of discipline. This results not merely indirectly from the ascendancy obtained in congregations and presbyteries but from the influence which the prominent friends and officers of these societies possess over those connected with them. In assuming the existence of such influence, we make no disparaging reflection on those who are the subjects of it, beyond the assumption that they are men of like passions and infirmities with others. It is no reflection to assume that a set of men who owe their support to the kindness or agency of another set, and who have the natural feeling of obligation which arises from this fact, and who are open to the usual innocent and even amiable sentiments which arise from association and cooperation, should be led to act with their benefactors and to follow them as their natural leaders.

We say this is a dangerous power because it is apt to be unobserved. It is not the acknowledged authority of a prelatical bishop ascertained and limited by law, of an officer who has been elected for the very purpose of being the depository of this power. But it is an incident, a perquisite, a matter not taken into the account, without being, for that reason, the less real or the less extensive. It is dangerous, moreover, because it arises out of the church, and yet is made to bear upon all its internal operations. It is not the influence which superiority of wisdom, experience, piety, or talent bestows on one member of a judicatory above his fellows; but it is an influence which cannot be met and counteracted within the sphere of its operation.

Again, it is dangerous, because preeminently irresponsible. This irresponsibility arises from various sources, from the fact that it is not an official influence conferred by law, that it is intangible and secret, that those who wield it are independent of those on whom it operates. It is lodged in the hands of those who are not appointed by the church or responsible to it; of men who owe their station to votes of a society composed of persons of various denominations, who may be decidedly hostile to what the majority of our church considers its best interests.

All that we have already said to show that a society, composed as the Home Missionary Society is, is far less safe and efficient as an appointing and controlling body than the General Assembly, goes to prove the peculiar irresponsibility of the influence of which we are now speaking. Can it be doubted that if the secretary of that society had formed the purpose of doing all he could to influence the theological character of particular presbyteries and to control their course of policy, he might prosecute this purpose long and effectually without exciting the notice or animadversion of the society itself? This is not a purpose to be announced to his unsophisticated and pious lay-associates. Their cooperation might be secured without their ever conceiving of any other bearing of their measures than on the wants and wishes of the destitute.

———————◆———————

History shows you prospects by starlight, or, at best, by the waning moon.
Rufus Choate, "New England History"

74.

Ralph Waldo Emerson: The American Scholar

"In the four quarters of the globe," asked the caustic English wit Sydney Smith in 1820, "who reads an American book?" His review of Seybert's Annals of the United States went on to ask other contemptuous rhetorical questions. "What does the world yet owe to American physicians or surgeons? What new substances have their chemists discovered? . . . What new constellations have been discovered by the telescopes of Americans? What have they done in mathematics? Who drinks out of American glasses? or eats from American plates? or wears American coats or gowns? or sleeps in American blankets?" Of course these questions make little sense nowadays — the simple answer to all of them is, who doesn't? — but they troubled many Americans exceedingly in the generation after Smith's remarks. The implication of the first question — that no American had written a book worth reading — was invalidated very soon after it was expressed. The fifteen years from 1840 to 1855 have been called the golden age of American literature, and indeed they saw the publication of an astounding array of notable and lasting works that include Thoreau's Walden, *Hawthorne's* The Scarlet Letter, *Melville's* Moby Dick, *Whitman's* Leaves of Grass, *Dana's* Two Years Before the Mast, *the stories and poems of Poe, and some of the most important essays and poems of Emerson. The last named may have been the key to the whole movement. His* American Scholar, *an address delivered before the Phi Beta Kappa Society at Harvard in 1837, stirred the imagination of the undergraduates and sold widely on publication. Its effect was summed up in Oliver Wendell Holmes's remark that it was "our intellectual Declaration of Independence." As such, we follow in a long editorial tradition and anthologize it here.*

Source: *Orations, Lectures and Essays,* London, 1866, pp. 78-112.

Mr. President and Gentlemen:

I greet you on the recommencement of our literary year. Our anniversary is one of hope and, perhaps, not enough of labor. We do not meet for games of strength or skill, for the recitation of histories, tragedies, and odes, like the ancient Greeks; for parliaments of love and poesy, like the troubadours; nor for the advancement of science, like our contemporaries in the British and European capitals. Thus far, our holiday has been simply a friendly sign of the survival of the love of letters among a people too busy to give to letters any more. As such, it is precious as the sign of an indestructible instinct. Perhaps the time is already come when it ought to be, and will be, something else; when the sluggard intellect of this continent will look from under its iron lids and fill the postponed expectation of the world with something better than the exertions of mechanical skill.

Our day of dependence, our long apprenticeship to the learning of other lands, draws to a close. The millions that around us are rushing into life cannot always be fed on the sere remains of foreign harvests. Events, actions arise that must be sung, that will sing themselves. Who can doubt that poetry will revive and lead in a new age, as the star in the constellation Harp, which now flames in our zenith, astronomers announce, shall one day be the polestar for a thousand years?

In the light of this hope, I accept the topic which not only usage but the nature of our association seem to prescribe to this day — THE AMERICAN SCHOLAR. Year by year we come up hither to read one more chapter of his biography. Let us inquire what new lights, new events, and more days have thrown on his character, his duties, and his hopes.

It is one of those fables which, out of an unknown antiquity, convey an unlooked-for wisdom; that the gods, in the beginning, divided Man into men, that he might be more helpful to himself; just as the hand was divided into fingers the better to answer its end.

The old fable covers a doctrine ever new and sublime; that there is One Man, present to all particular men only partially, or through one faculty; and that you must take the whole society to find the whole man. Man is not a farmer, or a professor, or an engineer, but he is all. Man is priest, and scholar, and statesman, and producer, and soldier. In the *divided* or social state, these functions are parceled out to individuals, each of whom aims to do his stint of the joint work, while each other performs his. The fable implies that the individual, to possess himself, must sometimes return from his own labor to embrace all the other laborers. But, unfortunately, this original unit, this fountain of power, has been so distributed to multitudes, has been so minutely subdivided and peddled out, that it is spilled into drops and cannot be gathered. The state of society is one in which the members have suffered amputation from the trunk, and strut about so many walking monsters — a good finger, a neck, a stomach, an elbow, but never a man.

Man is thus metamorphosed into a thing, into many things. The planter, who is Man sent out into the field to gather food, is seldom cheered by any idea of the true dignity of his ministry. He sees his bushel and his cart, and nothing beyond, and sinks into the farmer, instead of Man on the farm. The tradesman scarcely ever gives an ideal worth to his work, but is ridden by the routine of his craft, and the soul is subject to dollars. The priest becomes a form; the attorney, a statute book; the mechanic, a machine; the sailor, a rope of the ship.

In this distribution of functions, the scholar is the delegated intellect. In the right state, he is *Man Thinking*. In the degenerate state, when the victim of society, he tends to become a mere thinker, or, still worse, the parrot of other men's thinking.

In this view of him, as Man Thinking, the whole theory of his office is contained. Him nature solicits with all her placid, all her monitory pictures; him the past instructs; him the future invites. Is not indeed every man a student, and do not all things exist for the student's behoof? And, finally, is not the true scholar the only true master? But the old oracle said, "All things have two handles: beware of the wrong one." In life, too often, the scholar errs with mankind and forfeits his privilege. Let us see him in his school, and consider him in reference to the main influences he receives.

I. The first in time and the first in importance of the influences upon the mind is that of nature. Every day, the sun; and, after the sunset, night and her stars. Ever the winds blow; ever the grass grows. Every day, men and women, conversing, beholding and beholden. The scholar must needs stand wistful and admiring before this great spectacle. He must settle its value in his mind. What is nature to him? There is never a beginning, there is never an end to the inexplicable continuity of this web of God, but always circular power returning into itself. Therein it resembles his own spirit, whose beginning, whose ending, he never can find — so entire, so boundless. Far too as her splendors shine, system on system, shooting like rays, upward, downward, without center, without circumference; in the mass and in the particle, nature hastens to render account of herself to the mind.

Classification begins. To the young mind, everything is individual, stands by itself. By and by, it finds how to join two things, and see in them one nature; then three, then three thousand; and so, tyrannized over by its own unifying instinct, it goes on tying things together, diminishing anomalies, discovering roots running underground, whereby contrary and remote things cohere and flower out from one stem. It presently learns that since the dawn of history there has been a constant accumulation and classifying of facts. But what is classification but the perceiving that these objects are not chaotic and are not foreign, but have a law which is also a law of the human mind?

The astronomer discovers that geometry, a pure abstraction of the human mind, is the measure of planetary motion. The chemist finds proportions and intelligible method throughout matter; and science is nothing but the finding of analogy, identity in the most remote parts. The ambitious soul sits down before each refractory fact: one after another, reduces all strange constitutions, all new powers, to their class and their law, and goes on forever to animate the last fiber of organization, the outskirts of nature, by insight.

Thus to him, to this schoolboy under the bending dome of day, is suggested that he and it proceed from one root; one is leaf and one is flower; relation, sympathy, stirring in every vein. And what is that root? Is not that the soul of his soul? A thought too bold; a dream too wild. Yet, when this spiritual light shall have revealed the law of more earthly natures; when he has learned

to worship the soul and to see that the natural philosophy that now is, is only the first gropings of its gigantic hand, he shall look forward to an ever expanding knowledge as to a becoming creator. He shall see that nature is the opposite of the soul, answering to it part for part. One is seal, and one is print. Its beauty is the beauty of his own mind. Its laws are the laws of his own mind. Nature then becomes to him the measure of his attainments. So much of nature as he is ignorant of, so much of his own mind does he not yet possess. And, in fine, the ancient precept, "Know thyself," and the modern precept, "Study nature," become at last one maxim.

II. The next great influence into the spirit of the scholar is the mind of the past — in whatever form, whether of literature, of art, of institutions, that mind is inscribed. Books are the best type of the influence of the past, and perhaps we shall get at the truth — learn the amount of this influence more conveniently — by considering their value alone.

The theory of books is noble. The scholar of the first age received into him the world around; brooded thereon; gave it the new arrangement of his own mind; and uttered it again. It came into him life; it went out from him truth. It came to him short-lived actions; it went out from him immortal thoughts. It came to him business; it went from him poetry. It was dead fact; now, it is quick thought. It can stand, and it can go. It now endures; it now flies; it now inspires. Precisely in proportion to the depth of mind from which it issued, so high does it soar, so long does it sing.

Or, I might say, it depends on how far the process had gone of transmuting life into truth. In proportion to the completeness of the distillation, so will the purity and imperishableness of the product be. But none is quite perfect. As no air pump can by any means make a perfect vacuum, so neither can any artist entirely exclude the conventional, the local, the perishable from his book, or write a book of pure thought, that shall be as efficient, in all respects, to a remote posterity as to contemporaries, or rather to the second age. Each age, it is found, must write its own books; or rather, each generation for the next succeeding. The books of an older period will not fit this.

Yet hence arises a grave mischief. The sacredness which attaches to the act of creation, the act of thought, is transferred to the record. The poet chanting was felt to be a divine man; henceforth, the chant is divine also. The writer was a just and wise spirit: henceforward, it is settled, the book is perfect; as love of the hero corrupts into worship of his statue. Instantly, the book becomes noxious: the guide is a tyrant. The sluggish and perverted mind of the multitude, slow to open to the incursions of Reason, having once so opened, having once received this book, stands upon it and makes an outcry if it is disparaged. Colleges are built on it. Books are written on it by thinkers, not by Man Thinking; by men of talent, that is, who start wrong, who set out from accepted dogmas, not from their own sight of principles. Meek young men grow up in libraries, believing it their duty to accept the views which Cicero, which Locke, which Bacon have given; forgetful that Cicero, Locke, and Bacon were only young men in libraries when they wrote these books.

Hence, instead of Man Thinking, we have the bookworm. Hence the book-learned class, who value books as such; not as related to nature and the human constitution but as making a sort of Third Estate with the world and the soul. Hence, the restorers of readings, the emendators, the bibliomaniacs of all degrees.

Books are the best of things, well used; abused, among the worst. What is the right use? What is the one end which all means

go to effect? They are for nothing but to inspire. I had better never see a book than to be warped by its attraction clean out of my own orbit, and made a satellite instead of a system. The one thing in the world of value is the active soul — the soul, free, sovereign, active. This every man is entitled to; this every man contains within him, although in almost all men obstructed and as yet unborn. The soul active sees absolute truth; and utters truth, or creates. In this action it is genius; not the privilege of here and there a favorite, but the sound estate of every man. In its essence it is progressive.

The book, the college, the school of art, the institution of any kind, stop with some past utterance of genius. This is good, say they; let us hold by this. They pin me down. They look backward and not forward. But genius always looks forward; the eyes of man are set in his forehead, not in his hindhead; man hopes; genius creates. To create — to create — is the proof of a divine presence. Whatever talents may be, if the man create not, the pure efflux of the Deity is not his; cinders and smoke there may be, but not yet flame. There are creative manners, there are creative actions and creative words; manners, actions, words, that is, indicative of no custom or authority, but springing spontaneous from the mind's own sense of good and fair.

On the other part, instead of being its own seer, let it receive from another mind its truth, though it were in torrents of light, without periods of solitude, inquest, and self-recovery, and a fatal disservice is done. Genius is always sufficiently the enemy of genius by overinfluence. The literature of every nation bears me witness. The English dramatic poets have Shakespearized now for two hundred years.

Undoubtedly there is a right way of reading, so it be sternly subordinated. Man Thinking must not be subdued by his instruments. Books are for the scholar's idle times. When he can read God directly, the hour is too precious to be wasted in other men's transcripts of their readings. But when the intervals of darkness come, as come they must, when the sun is hid and the stars withdraw their shining, we repair to the lamps which were kindled by their ray to guide our steps to the East again, where the dawn is. We hear that we may speak. The Arabian proverb says, "A fig tree, looking on a fig tree, becometh fruitful."

It is remarkable the character of the pleasure we derive from the best books. They impress us with the conviction that one nature wrote and the same reads. We read the verses of one of the great English poets, of Chaucer, of Marvell, of Dryden, with the most modern joy; with a pleasure, I mean, which is in great part caused by the abstraction of all *time* from their verses. There is some awe mixed with the joy of our surprise when this poet, who lived in some past world, two or three hundred years ago, says that which lies close to my own soul, that which I also had well-nigh thought and said. But for the evidence thence afforded to the philosophical doctrine of the identity of all minds, we should suppose some preestablished harmony, some foresight of souls that were to be, and some preparation of stores for their future wants, like the fact observed in insects who lay up food before death for the young grub they shall never see.

I would not be hurried by any love of system, by any exaggeration of instincts to underrate the book. We all know that as the human body can be nourished on any food, though it were boiled grass and the broth of shoes, so the human mind can be fed by any knowledge. And great and heroic men have existed who had almost no other information than by the printed page. I only would say that it needs a strong head to bear that diet. One must be an inventor to read well. As the proverb says, "He that would bring home the wealth of the Indies must carry out the wealth of the Indies."

There is then creative reading as well as creative writing. When the mind is braced by labor and invention, the page of whatever book we read becomes luminous with manifold allusion. Every sentence is doubly significant, and the sense of our author is as broad as the world. We then see what is always true: that as the seer's hour of vision is short and rare among heavy days and months, so is its record, perchance, the least part of his volume. The discerning will read, in his Plato or Shakespeare, only that least part, only the authentic utterances of the oracle; all the rest he rejects, were it never so many times Plato's and Shakespeare's.

Of course there is a portion of reading quite indispensable to a wise man. History and exact science he must learn by laborious reading. Colleges, in like manner, have their indispensable office — to teach elements. But they can only highly serve us when they aim not to drill but to create; when they gather from far every ray of various genius to their hospitable halls, and, by the concentrated fires, set the hearts of their youth on flame. Thought and knowledge are natures in which apparatus and pretension avail nothing. Gowns and pecuniary foundations, though of towns of gold, can never countervail the least sentence or syllable of wit. Forget this, and our American colleges will recede in their public importance while they grow richer every year.

III. There goes in the world a notion that the scholar should be a recluse, a valetudinarian, as unfit for any handiwork or public labor as a penknife for an axe. The so-called practical men sneer at speculative men, as if, because they speculate or *see*, they could do nothing. I have heard it said that the clergy, who are always, more universally than any other class, the scholars of their day, are addressed as women; that the rough, spontaneous conversation of men they do not hear, but only a mincing and diluted speech. They are often virtually disfranchised; and, indeed, there are advocates for their celibacy. As far as this is true of the studious classes, it is not just and wise.

Action is with the scholar subordinate, but it is essential. Without it, he is not yet man. Without it, thought can never ripen into truth. While the world hangs before the eye as a cloud of beauty, we cannot even see its beauty. Inaction is cowardice, but there can be no scholar without the heroic mind. The preamble of thought, the transition through which it passes from the unconscious to the conscious, is action. Only so much do I know, as I have lived. Instantly we know whose words are loaded with life and whose not.

The world — this shadow of the soul, or *other me* — lies wide around. Its attractions are the keys which unlock my thoughts and make me acquainted with myself. I run eagerly into this resounding tumult. I grasp the hands of those next me, and take my place in the ring to suffer and to work, taught by an instinct that so shall the dumb abyss be vocal with speech. I pierce its order; I dissipate its fear; I dispose of it within the circuit of my expanding life. So much only of life as I know by experience, so much of the wilderness have I vanquished and planted, or so far have I extended my being, my dominion. I do not see how any man can afford, for the sake of his nerves and his nap, to spare any action in which he can partake. It is pearls and rubies to his discourse. Drudgery, calamity, exasperation, want are instructors in eloquence and wisdom. The true scholar grudges every opportunity of action passed by as a loss of power. It is the raw material out of which the intellect molds her splendid products. A strange process, too, this, by which experience is converted into thought as a mulberry leaf is converted into satin. The manufacture goes forward at all hours.

The actions and events of our childhood and youth are now matters of calmest observation. They lie like fair pictures in the air. Not so with our recent actions, with the business which we now have in hand. On this we are quite unable to speculate. Our affections as yet circulate through it. We no more feel or know it than we feel the feet, or the hand, or the brain of our body. The new deed is yet a part of life, remains for a time immersed in our unconscious life. In some contemplative hour it detaches itself from the life like a ripe fruit, to become a thought of the mind. Instantly it is raised, transfigured; the corruptible has put on incorruption. Henceforth it is an object of beauty, however base its origin and neighborhood. Observe too the impossibility of antedating this act. In its grub state, it cannot fly, it cannot shine, it is a dull grub. But suddenly, without observation, the selfsame thing unfurls beautiful wings and is an angel of wisdom.

So is there no fact, no event in our private history which shall not, sooner or later, lose its adhesive, inert form and astonish us by soaring from our body into the empyrean. Cradle and infancy, school and playground, the fear of boys, and dogs, and ferules, the love of little maids and berries, and many another fact that once filled the whole sky, are gone already; friend and relative, profession and party, town and country, nation and world must also soar and sing.

Of course, he who has put forth his total strength in fit actions has the richest return of wisdom. I will not shut myself out of this globe of action and transplant an oak into a flowerpot, there to hunger and pine; nor trust the revenue of some single faculty and exhaust one vein of thought, much like those Savoyards who, getting their livelihood by carving shepherds, shepherdesses, and smoking Dutchmen for all Europe, went out one day to the mountain to find stock and discovered that they had whittled up the last of their pine trees. Authors we have, in numbers, who have written out their vein, and who, moved by a commendable prudence, sail for Greece or Palestine, follow the trapper into the prairie, or ramble round Algiers to replenish their merchantable stock.

If it were only for a vocabulary, the scholar would be covetous of action. Life is our dictionary. Years are well spent in country labors; in town; in the insight into trades and manufactures; in frank intercourse with many men and women; in science; in art; to the one end of mastering in all their facts a language by which to illustrate and embody our perceptions. I learn immediately from any speaker how much he has already lived through the poverty or the splendor of his speech. Life lies behind us as the quarry from whence we get tiles and copestones for the masonry of today. This is the way to learn grammar. Colleges and books only copy the language which the field and the work yard made.

But the final value of action, like that of books, and better than books, is that it is a resource. That great principle of undulation in nature that shows itself in the inspiring and expiring of the breath; in desire and satiety; in the ebb and flow of the sea; in day and night; in heat and cold; and, as yet more deeply ingrained in every atom and every fluid, is known to us under the name of Polarity: these "fits of easy transmission and reflection," as Newton called them, are the law of nature because they are the law of spirit.

The mind now thinks, now acts; and each fit reproduces the other. When the artist has exhausted his materials, when the fancy no longer paints, when thoughts are no longer apprehended, and books are a weariness, he has always the resource *to live*. Character is higher than intellect. Thinking is the function; living is the functionary. The stream retreats to its source. A great soul will be strong to live, as well as strong to think. Does he lack organ or medium to impart his truths? He can still fall back on this elemental force of living them. This is a total act. Thinking is a partial act. Let the grandeur of justice shine in his affairs. Let the beauty of affection cheer his lowly roof.

Those "far from fame," who dwell and act with him, will feel the force of his constitution in the doings and passages of the day better than it can be measured by any public and designed display. Time shall teach him that the scholar loses no hour which the man lives. Herein he unfolds the sacred germ of his instinct, screened from influence. What is lost in seemliness is gained in strength. Not out of those on whom systems of education have exhausted their culture comes the helpful giant to destroy the old or to build the new, but out of unhandselled savage nature; out of terrible Druids and Berserkers come at last Alfred and Shakespeare.

I hear therefore with joy whatever is beginning to be said of the dignity and necessity of labor to every citizen. There is virtue yet in the hoe and the spade, for learned as well as for unlearned hands. And labor is everywhere welcome; always we are invited to work; only be this limitation observed, that a man shall not for the sake of wider activity sacrifice any opinion to the popular judgments and modes of action.

I HAVE NOW SPOKEN of the education of the scholar by nature, by books, and by action. It remains to say somewhat of his duties.

They are such as become Man Thinking. They may all be comprised in self-trust. The office of the scholar is to cheer, to raise, and to guide men by showing them facts amid appearances. He plies the slow, unhonored, and unpaid task of observation. Flamsteed and Herschel, in their glazed observatories, may catalog the stars with the praise of all men, and, the results being splendid and useful, honor is sure. But he, in his private observatory, cataloging obscure and nebulous stars of the human mind, which as yet no man has thought of as such — watching, days and months sometimes for a few facts, correcting still his old records — must relinquish display and immediate fame. In the long period of his preparation, he must betray often an ignorance and shiftlessness in popular arts, incurring the disdain of the able who shoulder him aside. Long he must stammer in his speech; often forgo the living for the dead. Worse yet, he must accept — how often! — poverty and solitude. For the ease and pleasure of treading the old road, accepting the fashions, the education, the religion of society, he takes the cross of making his own, and, of course, the self-accusation, the faint heart, the frequent uncertainty and loss of time, which are the nettles and tangling vines in the way of the self-relying and self-directed; and the state of virtual hostility in which he seems to stand to society, and especially to educated society.

For all this loss and scorn, what offset? He is to find consolation in exercising the highest functions of human nature. He is one who raises himself from private considerations, and breathes and lives on public and illustrious thoughts. He is the world's eye. He is the world's heart. He is to resist the vulgar prosperity that retrogrades ever to barbarism by preserving and communicating heroic sentiments, noble biographies, melodious verse, and the conclusions of history. Whatsoever oracles the human heart, in all emergencies, in all solemn hours has uttered as its commentary on the world of actions, these he shall receive and impart. And whatsoever new verdict Reason from her inviolable seat pronounces on the passing men and events of today, this he shall hear and promulgate.

These being his functions, it becomes him to feel all confidence in himself and to defer never to the popular cry. He and he only knows the world. The world of any moment is the merest appearance. Some great decorum, some fetish of a government, some ephemeral trade, or war, or man, is cried up by half mankind and cried down by the other half, as if all depended on this particular up or down. The odds are that the whole question is not worth the poorest thought which the scholar has lost in listening to the controversy. Let him not quit his belief that a popgun is a popgun, though the ancient and honorable of the earth affirm it to be the crack of doom. In silence, in steadiness, in severe abstraction, let him hold by himself; add observation to observation, patient of neglect, patient of reproach, and bide his own time — happy enough if he can satisfy himself alone that this day he has seen something truly.

Success treads on every right step. For the instinct is sure that prompts him to tell his brother what he thinks. He then learns that in going down into the secrets of his own mind he has descended into the secrets of all minds. He learns that he who has mastered any law in his private thoughts is master to that extent of all men whose language he speaks, and of all into whose language his own can be translated.

The poet, in utter solitude remembering his spontaneous thoughts and recording them, is found to have recorded that which men in crowded cities find true for them also. The orator distrusts at first the fitness of his frank confessions, his want of knowledge of the person he addresses, until he finds that he is the complement of his hearers; that they drink his words because he fulfills for them their own nature; the deeper he dives into his privatest, secretest presentiment, to his wonder he finds this is the most acceptable, most public, and universally true. The people delight in it; the better part of every man feels: this is my music; this is myself.

In self-trust all the virtues are comprehended. Free should the scholar be — free and brave. Free even to the definition of freedom, "without any hindrance that does not arise out of his own constitution." Brave; for fear is a thing which a scholar by his very function puts behind him. Fear always springs from ignorance. It is a shame to him if his tranquillity, amid dangerous times, arise from the presumption that, like children and women, his is a protected class; or if he seek a temporary peace by the diversion of his thoughts from politics or vexed questions, hiding his head like an ostrich in the flowering bushes, peeping into microscopes, and turning rhymes, as a boy whistles to keep his courage up. So is the danger a danger still; so is the fear worse.

Manlike, let him turn and face it. Let him look into its eye and search its nature, inspect its origin, see the whelping of this lion, which lies no great way back; he will then find in himself a perfect comprehension of its nature and extent; he will have made his hands meet on the other side, and can henceforth defy it, and pass on superior. The world is his who can see through its pretension. What deafness, what stone-blind custom, what overgrown error you behold is there only by sufferance — by your sufferance. See it to be a lie, and you have already dealt it its mortal blow.

Yes, we are the cowed, we, the trustless. It is a mischievous notion that we are come late into nature; that the world was finished a long time ago. As the world was plastic and fluid in the hands of God, so it is ever to so much of His attributes as we bring to it. To ignorance and sin, it is flint. They adapt themselves to it as they may; but in proportion as a man has anything in him divine, the firmament flows before him and takes his signet and form. Not he is great who can alter matter, but he who can alter my state of mind. They are the kings of the world who give the color of their present thought to all nature and all art, and per-

suade men by the cheerful serenity of their carrying the matter, that this thing which they do is the apple which the ages have desired to pluck, now at last ripe, and inviting nations to the harvest.

The great man makes the great thing. Wherever Macdonald sits, there is the head of the table. Linnaeus makes botany the most alluring of studies, and wins it from the farmer and the herb woman; Davy, chemistry; and Cuvier, fossils. The day is always his who works in it with serenity and great aims. The unstable estimates of men crowd to him whose mind is filled with a truth, as the heaped waves of the Atlantic follow the moon.

For this self-trust, the reason is deeper than can be fathomed, darker than can be enlightened. I might not carry with me the feeling of my audience in stating my own belief. But I have already shown the ground of my hope, in adverting to the doctrine that man is one. I believe man has been wronged; he has wronged himself. He has almost lost the light that can lead him back to his prerogatives. Men are become of no account. Men in history, men in the world of today are bugs, are spawn, and are called "the mass" and "the herd." In a century, in a millennium, one or two men; that is to say, one or two approximations to the right state of every man. All the rest behold in the hero or the poet their own green and crude being; ripened, yes; and are content to be less, so *that* may attain to its full stature.

What a testimony, full of grandeur, full of pity, is borne to the demands of his own nature by the poor clansman, the poor partisan, who rejoices in the glory of his chief. The poor and the low find some amends to their immense moral capacity for their acquiescence in a political and social inferiority. They are content to be brushed like flies from the path of a great person, so that justice shall be done by him to that common nature which it is the dearest desire of all to see enlarged and glorified. They sun themselves in the great man's light and feel it to be their own element. They cast the dignity of man from their downtrod selves upon the shoulders of a hero, and will perish to add one drop of blood to make that great heart beat, those giant sinews combat and conquer. He lives for us, and we live in him.

Men, such as they are, very naturally seek money or power; and power because it is as good as money — the "spoils," so called, "of office." And why not? For they aspire to the highest, and this, in their sleepwalking, they dream is highest. Wake them, and they shall quit the false good and leap to the true, and leave governments to clerks and desks. This revolution is to be wrought by the gradual domestication of the idea of culture. The main enterprise of the world for splendor, for extent, is the upbuilding of a man. Here are the materials strewn along the ground. The private life of one man shall be a more illustrious monarchy, more formidable to its enemy, more sweet and serene in its influence to its friend than any kingdom in history. For a man, rightly viewed, comprehends the particular natures of all men. Each philosopher, each bard, each actor has only done for me, as by a delegate, what one day I can do for myself. The books which once we valued more than the apple of the eye, we have quite exhausted.

What is that but saying that we have come up with the point of view which the universal mind took through the eyes of one scribe; we have been that man and have passed on. First, one; then, another; we drain all cisterns, and, waxing greater by all these supplies, we crave a better and more abundant food. The man has never lived that can feed us ever. The human mind cannot be enshrined in a person who shall set a barrier on any one side to this unbounded, unboundable empire. It is one central fire, which, flaming now out of the lips of Etna, lightens the capes of Sicily, and now out of the throat of Vesuvius illuminates the towers and vineyards of Naples. It is one light which beams out of a thousand stars. It is one soul which animates all men.

BUT I HAVE DWELT perhaps tediously upon this abstraction of the scholar. I ought not to delay longer to add what I have to say of nearer reference to the time and to this country.

Historically, there is thought to be a difference in the ideas which predominate over successive epochs, and there are data for marking the genius of the Classic, of the Romantic, and now of the Reflective or Philosophical age. With the views I have intimated of the oneness or the identity of the mind through all individuals, I do not much dwell on these differences. In fact, I believe each individual passes through all three. The boy is a Greek; the youth, romantic; the adult, reflective. I deny not, however, that a revolution in the leading idea may be distinctly enough traced.

Our age is bewailed as the age of Introversion. Must that needs be evil? We, it seems, are critical; we are embarrassed with second thoughts; we cannot enjoy anything for hankering to know whereof the pleasure consists; we are lined with eyes; we see with our feet; the time is infected with Hamlet's unhappiness

Sicklied o'er with the pale cast of thought.

It is so bad then? Sight is the last thing to be pitied. Would we be blind? Do we fear lest we should outsee nature and God, and drink truth dry?

I look upon the discontent of the literary class as a mere announcement of the fact that they find themselves not in the state of mind of their fathers and regret the coming state as untried; as a boy dreads the water before he has learned that he can swim. If there is any period one would desire to be born in, is it not the age of Revolution; when the old and the new stand side by side and admit of being compared; when the energies of all men are searched by fear and by hope; when the historic glories of the old can be compensated by the rich possibilities of the new era? This time, like all times, is a very good one, if we but know what to do with it.

I read with some joy of the auspicious signs of the coming days, as they glimmer already through poetry and art, through philosophy and science, through church and state.

One of these signs is the fact that the same movement which effected the elevation of what was called the lowest class in the state, assumed in literature a very marked and as benign an aspect. Instead of the sublime and beautiful, the near, the low, the common was explored and poetized. That which had been negligently trodden under foot by those who were harnessing and provisioning themselves for long journeys into far countries is suddenly found to be richer than all foreign parts. The literature of the poor, the feelings of the child, the philosophy of the street, the meaning of household life are the topics of the time. It is a great stride. It is a sign, is it not, of new vigor when the extremities are made active; when currents of warm life run into the hands and the feet.

I ask not for the great, the remote, the romantic; what is doing in Italy or Arabia; what is Greek art, or Provençal minstrelsy; I embrace the common, I explore and sit at the feet of the familiar, the low. Give me insight into today, and you may have the antique and future worlds. What would we really know the meaning of? The meal in the firkin; the milk in the pan; the ballad in the street; the news of the boat; the glance of the eye; the form and the gait of the body — show me the ultimate reason of these matters; show me the sublime presence of the highest spiritual cause lurking, as always it does lurk, in these suburbs and extremities of nature; let me see every trifle bristling with the polarity that ranges it instantly on an eternal law; and the shop, the plough, and the ledger referred to the like cause by which light undulates and poets sing; and the world lies no longer a dull miscellany and lumber room, but has form and order. There is no trifle, there is no puzzle, but one design unites and animates the farthest pinnacle and the lowest trench.

This idea has inspired the genius of Goldsmith, Burns, Cowper, and, in a newer time, of Goethe, Wordsworth, and Carlyle. This idea they have differently followed and with various success. In contrast with their writing, the style of Pope, of Johnson, of Gibbon looks cold and pedantic. This writing is blood-warm. Man is surprised to find that things near are not less beautiful and wondrous than things remote. The near explains the far. The drop is a small ocean. A man is related to all nature. This perception of the worth of the vulgar is fruitful in discoveries. Goethe, in this very thing the most modern of the moderns, has shown us, as none ever did, the genius of the ancients.

There is one man of genius who has done much for this philosophy of life, whose literary value has never yet been rightly estimated; I mean Emanuel Swedenborg. The most imaginative of men, yet writing with the precision of a mathematician, he endeavored to engraft a purely philosophical ethics on the popular Christianity of his time. Such an attempt, of course, must have difficulty which no genius could surmount. But he saw and showed the connection between nature and the affections of the soul. He pierced the emblematic or spiritual character of the visible, audible, tangible world. Especially did his shade-loving muse hover over and interpret the lower parts of nature; he showed the mysterious bond that allies moral evil to the foul material forms, and has given in epical parables a theory of insanity, of beasts, of unclean and fearful things.

Another sign of our times, also marked by an analogous political movement, is the new importance given to the single person. Everything that tends to insulate the individual, to surround him with barriers of natural respect, so that each man shall feel the world is his, and man shall treat with man as a sovereign state with a sovereign state, tends to true union as well as greatness. "I learned," said the melancholy Pestalozzi, "that no man in God's wide earth is either willing or able to help any other man." Help must come from the bosom alone. The scholar is that man who must take up into himself all the ability of the time, all the contributions of the past, all the hopes of the future. He must be a university of knowledges. If there be one lesson more than another which should pierce his ear, it is: The world is nothing, the man is all; in yourself is the law of all nature, and you know not yet how a globule of sap ascends; in yourself slumbers the whole of Reason; it is for you to know all; it is for you to dare all.

Mr. President and Gentlemen, this confidence in the unsearched might of man belongs, by all motives, by all prophecy, by all preparation, to the American scholar. We have listened too long to the courtly muses of Europe. The spirit of the American freeman is already suspected to be timid, imitative, tame. Public and private avarice make the air we breathe thick and fat. The scholar is decent, indolent, complacent. See already the tragic consequence. The mind of this country, taught to aim at low objects, eats upon itself. There is no work for any

but the decorous and the complacent. Young men of the fairest promise, who begin life upon our shores, inflated by the mountain winds, shined upon by all the stars of God, find the earth below not in unison with these, but are hindered from action by the disgust which the principles on which business is managed inspire, and turn drudges, or die of disgust, some of them suicides.

What is the remedy? They did not yet see, and thousands of young men as hopeful now crowding to the barriers for the career do not yet see, that if the single man plant himself indomitably on his instincts and there abide, the huge world will come round to him. Patience, patience; with the shades of all the good and great for company; and for solace the perspective of your own infinite life; and for work the study and the communication of principles, the making those instincts prevalent, the conversion of the world. Is it not the chief disgrace in the world, not to be a unit, not to be reckoned one character, not to yield that peculiar fruit which each man was created to bear; but to be reckoned in the gross, in the hundred or the thousand, of the party, the section, to which we belong; and our opinion predicted geographically, as the north or the south?

Not so, brothers and friends; please God, ours shall not be so. We will walk on our own feet; we will work with our own hands; we will speak our own minds. The study of letters shall be no longer a name for pity, for doubt, and for sensual indulgence. The dread of man and the love of man shall be a wall of defense and a wreath of joy around all. A nation of men will for the first time exist, because each believes himself inspired by the Divine Soul which also inspires all men.

75.

Harriet Martineau: Mechanics and Working Girls

Harriet Martineau, an English writer who traveled extensively in the United States between 1834 and 1836, made contact with many of America's most influential men. Her experiences in the United States furnished material for two books, Society in America *(1837) and* A Retrospect of Western Travel *(1838), both of which were severely criticized for misrepresenting American life. Her blunders were often attributed to a hearing defect, but one contemporary, Frances Anne Kemble, records that she was the victim of persons who purposefully and shamefully imposed upon her "credulity and anxiety to obtain information." Despite her many errors, Miss Martineau made available to future generations a view of Jacksonian America that only a foreigner, who did not take any features of the native scene for granted, could provide.*

Source: *Society in America*, New York, 1837, Vol. II, Pt. 2, Ch. 3, Sec. 2: "Manufacturing Labor."

So MUCH IS SAID IN EUROPE of the scarcity of agricultural labor in the United States that it is a matter of surprise that manufactures should have succeeded as they have done. It is even supposed by some that the tariff was rendered necessary by a deficiency of labor; that by offering a premium on manufacturing industry, the requisite amount was sought to be drawn away from other employments and concentrated upon this. This is a mistake. There is every reason to suppose that the requisite amount of labor would have been forthcoming if affairs had been left to take their natural course.

It has been shown that domestic manufactures were carried on to a great extent so far back as 1790. From that time to this, they have never altogether ceased in the farmhouses, as the homespun, still so frequently to be seen all over the country, and the agricultural meetings of New England (where there is usually a display of domestic manufactures) will testify. The hands by which these products are wrought come to the factories when the demand for labor renders it worthwhile; and drop back into the farmhouses when the demand slackens.

It is not the custom in America for women (except slaves) to work out-of-doors. It has been mentioned that the young men of New England migrate in large numbers to the West, leaving an overproportion of female population, the amount of which I could never learn. Statements were made to me, but so incredible that I withhold them. Suffice it that there are many more women than men in from six to nine states of the Union. There is reason to believe that there was much silent suffering from poverty before the institution of factories; that they afford a most welcome resource to some thousands of young women, unwilling to give themselves to domestic service, and precluded, by the customs of the country, from rural labor. We have seen how large a

Harriet Martineau, portrait by Charles Osgood

proportion of the labor in the Lowell factories is supplied by women.

Much of the rest is furnished by immigrants. I saw English, Irish, and Scotch operatives. I heard but a poor character of the English operatives; and the Scotch were pronounced "ten times better." The English are jealous of their "bargain," and on the watch lest they should be asked to do more than they stipulated for. Their habits are not so sober as those of the Scotch, and they are incapable of going beyond the single operation they profess. Such is the testimony of their employers.

The demand for labor is, however, sufficiently imperious in all the mechanical departments to make it surprising that prison labor is regarded with such jealousy as I have witnessed. When it is considered how small a class the convicts of the United States are and are likely to remain, how essential labor is to their reformation, how few are the kinds of manufacture which

they can practise, and that it is of some importance that prison establishments should maintain themselves, it seems wholly unworthy of the intelligent mechanics of America that they should be so afraid of convict labor as actually to obtain pledges from some candidates for office to propose the abolition of prison manufactures.

I believe that the Sing Sing and Auburn prisons, in the state of New York, turn out a greater variety and amount of products than any others; and they have yet done very little more than maintain themselves. The Sing Sing convicts quarry and dress granite; the Auburn prisoners make clocks, combs, shoes, carpets, and machinery. They are cabinet- and chairmakers, weavers, and tailors. There were 650 prisoners when I was there; and of these, many were inexperienced workmen, and all were not employed in manufactures. Jealousy of such a set of craftsmen is absurd, in the present state of the American labor market.

I saw specimens of each of these kinds of labor. A few days after I entered the country, I was taken to an agricultural meeting, held annually at Pittsfield, Massachusetts. We were too late to see the best part of it — the dispensing of prizes for the best agricultural skill and for the choicest domestic manufactures. But there were specimens left which surprised me by the excellence of their quality — table and bed linen, diapers, blankets, and knitted wares. There was an ingenious model of a bed for invalids, combining many sorts of facilities for change of posture. There were nearly as many women as men at this meeting; all were well-dressed and going to and fro in the household vehicle, the country wagon, with the invariable bearskin covering the seat and peeping out on all sides. A comfortable display, from the remains of the dinner, was set out for us by smart mulatto girls, with snowberries in their hair. The mechanics' houses in this beautiful village would be enough, if they could be exhibited in England, to tempt over half her operatives to the New World.

The first cotton mill that I saw was at Paterson, New Jersey. It was set up at first with 900 spindles, which were afterward increased to 1,500; then to 6,000. Building was still going on when I was there. The girls were all well-dressed. Their hair was arranged according to the latest fashions which had arrived, via New York, and they wore calashes [hoods] in going to and fro between their dwellings and the mill. I saw some of the children barefooted, but carrying umbrellas, under a slight sprinkling of rain. I asked whether those who could afford umbrellas went barefoot for coolness or other convenience. The proprietor told me that there had probably been an economical calculation in the case. Stockings and shoes would defend only the feet, while the umbrella would preserve the gloss of the whole of the rest of the costume. . . .

I visited the corporate factory establishment at Waltham, within a few miles of Boston. The Waltham Mills were at work before those of Lowell were set up. The establishment is for the spinning and weaving of cotton alone and the construction of the requisite machinery. Five hundred persons were employed at the time of my visit. The girls earn $2, and some $3, a week, besides their board. The little children earn $1 a week. Most of the girls live in the houses provided by the corporation, which accommodate from six to eight each. When sisters come to the mill, it is a common practice for them to bring their mother to keep house for them and some of their companions, in a dwelling built by their own earnings. In this case, they save enough out of their board to clothe themselves and have their $2 or $3 a week to spare. Some have thus cleared off mortgages from their fathers' farms, others have educated the hope

of the family at college, and many are rapidly accumulating an independence. I saw a whole street of houses built with the earnings of the girls; some with piazzas and green venetian blinds, and all neat and sufficiently spacious.

The factory people built the church, which stands conspicuous on the green in the midst of the place. The minister's salary ($800 last year) is raised by a tax on the pews. The corporation gave them a building for a lyceum, which they have furnished with a good library and where they have lectures every winter — the best that money can procure. The girls have, in many instances, private libraries of some merit and value.

The managers of the various factory establishments keep the wages as nearly equal as possible and then let the girls freely shift about from one to another. When a girl comes to the overseer to inform him of her intention of working at the mill, he welcomes her and asks how long she means to stay. It may be six months or a year or five years or for life. She declares what she considers herself fit for and sets to work accordingly. If she finds that she cannot work so as to keep up with the companion appointed to her or to please her employer or herself, she comes to the overseer and volunteers to pick cotton or sweep the rooms or undertake some other service that she can perform.

The people work about seventy hours per week, on the average. The time of work varies with the length of the days, the wages continuing the same. All look like well-dressed young ladies. The health is good; or rather (as this is too much to be said about health anywhere in the United States) it is no worse than it is elsewhere.

These facts speak for themselves. There is no need to enlarge on the pleasure of an acquaintance with the operative classes of the United States.

The shoemaking at Lynn is carried on almost entirely in private dwellings, from the circumstance that the people who do it are almost all farmers or fishermen likewise. A stranger who has not been enlightened upon the ways of the place would be astonished at the number of small square erections, like miniature schoolhouses, standing each as an appendage to a dwelling house. These are the "shoe shops," where the father of the family and his boys work, while the women within are employed in binding and trimming. Thirty or more of these shoe shops may be counted in a walk of half a mile. When a Lynn shoe manufacturer receives an order, he issues the tidings. The leather is cut out by men on his premises; and then the work is given to those who apply for it, if possible, in small quantities, for the sake of dispatch. The shoes are brought home on Friday night, packed off on Saturday, and in a fortnight or three weeks are on the feet of dwellers in all parts of the Union. The whole family works upon shoes during the winter; and in the summer, the father and sons turn out into the fields or go fishing. I knew of an instance where a little boy and girl maintained the whole family, while the earnings of the rest went to build a house. I saw very few shabby houses.

Quakers are numerous in Lynn. The place is undoubtedly prosperous, through the temperance and industry of the people. The deposits in the Lynn Savings' Bank in 1834 were about $34,000, the population of the town being then 4,000. Since that time, both the population and the prosperity have much increased. It must be remembered, too, that the mechanics of America have more uses for their money than are open to the operatives of England. They build houses, buy land, and educate their sons and daughters.

It is probably true that the pleasures and pains of life are pretty equally distributed among its various vocations and positions; but it is difficult to keep clear of the impression which outward circumstances occasion, that some are eminently desirable. The mechanics of these Northern states appear to me the most favored class I have ever known. In England, I believe the highest order of mechanics to be, as a class, the wisest and best men of the community. They have the fewest base and narrow interests; they are brought into sufficient contact with the realities of existence without being hardened by excess of toil and care; and the knowledge they have the opportunity of gaining is of the best kind for the health of the mind. To them, if to any, we may look for public and private virtue.

The mechanics of America have nearly all the same advantages and some others. They have better means of living; their labors are perhaps more honored; and they are republicans, enjoying the powers and prospects of perfectly equal citizenship. The only respect in which their condition falls below that of English artisans of the highest order is that the knowledge which they have commonly the means of obtaining is not of equal value. The facilities are great — schools, lyceums, libraries, are open to them — but the instruction imparted there is not so good as they deserve. Whenever they have this, it will be difficult to imagine a mode of life more favorable to virtue and happiness than theirs.

There seems to be no doubt among those who know both England and America that the mechanics of the New World work harder than those of the Old. They have much to do besides their daily handicraft business. They are up and at work early about this; and when it is done, they read till late or attend lectures; or perhaps have their houses to build or repair or other care to take of their property. They live in a state and period of society where every man is answerable for his own fortunes and where there is, therefore, stimulus to the exercise of every power.

What a state of society it is when a dozen artisans of one town — Salem — are seen rearing each a comfortable one-story (or, as the Americans would say, two-story) house, in the place with which they have grown up! when a man who began with laying bricks criticizes, and sometimes corrects, his lawyer's composition; when a poor errand boy becomes the proprietor of a flourishing store before he is thirty; pays off the capital advanced by his friends at the rate of $2,000 per month; and bids fair to be one of the most substantial citizens of the place!

Such are the outward fortunes of the mechanics of America. Of their welfare in more important respects, to which these are but a part of the means, I shall have to speak in another connection.

There are troubles between employers and their workmen in the United States, as elsewhere; but the case of the men is so much more in their own hands there than where labor superabounds that strikes are of a very short duration. The only remedy the employers have, the only safeguard against encroachments from their men, is their power of obtaining the services of foreigners, for a short time. The difficulty of stopping business there is very great, the injury of delay very heavy; but the wages of labor are so good that there is less cause for discontent on the part of the workmen than elsewhere. All the strikes I heard of were on the question of hours, not of wages.

The employers are, of course, casting about to see how they can help themselves; and, as all are not wise and experienced, it is natural that some should talk of laws to prohibit trades unions. There is no harm in their talking of such; for the matter will never get beyond talk, unless, indeed, the combinations of operatives should assume any forms or comprehend any principles inconsistent with the republican spirit. The majority will not vote for any law which shall restrain any number of artisans from agreeing for what price they will sell their labor; though I heard several learned gentlemen agreeing, at dinner one day, that there ought to be such laws. On my objecting that the interest of the parties concerned would, especially in a free and rising country, settle all questions between labor and capital with more precision, fairness, and peace than any law, it was pleaded that intimidation and outrage were practised by those who combined against those who would not join them.

I found, on inquiry, that there is an ample provision of laws against intimidation and outrage, but that it is difficult to get them executed. If so, it would be also difficult to execute laws against combinations of workmen, supposing them obtained; and the grievance does not lie in the combination complained of but somewhere else. The remedy is (if there be indeed intimidation and outrage) not in passing more laws, to be in like manner defied, while sufficient already exist, but in enlightening the parties on the subjects of law and social obligation.

One day, in going down Broadway, New York, the carriage in which I was stopped for some time in consequence of an immense procession on the sidewalk having attracted the attention of all the drivers within sight. The marching gentlemen proceeded on their way, with an easy air of gentility. Banners were interposed at intervals; and, on examining these, I could scarcely believe my eyes. They told me that this was a procession of the journeymen mechanics of New York. Surely never were such dandy mechanics seen — with sleek coats, glossy hats, gay watch guards, and doeskin gloves!

I rejoice to have seen this sight. I had other opportunities of witnessing the prosperity of their employers, so that I could be fairly pleased at theirs. There need be no fear for the interests of either while the natural laws of demand and supply must protect each from any serious encroachment by the other. If they will only respect the law, their temporary disagreement and apparent opposition of interests will end in being mere readjustments of the terms on which they are to pursue their common welfare.

76.

Francis J. Grund: Reflections on America

Francis Grund grew up in Austria and came to America, as near as one can tell, in 1827. His career here went from teaching to journalism to politics; and his support of Jackson brought him diplomatic appointments in Europe. In writing The Americans, in Their Moral, Social, and Political Relations, *from which the selections below are taken, it was Grund's intent "to delineate those characteristic features which distinguish the Americans from the different nations of Europe" and to correct false impressions of Americans that had stemmed from "omitting all mention of those [qualities] which entitle them to honor and respect." The book was published in both England and America in 1837. It was one of many that fed the insatiable English appetite for information about the new land and the curiosity of Americans about foreign opinion.*

Source: *The Americans, in Their Moral, Social, and Political Relations,* Boston, 1837, pp. 37-41, 206-211, 223-224, 323-324.

THE HOUSES OF THE WEALTHIER CLASSES resemble those of the gentry in England, and are wanting in nothing which can materially contribute to comfort. Some of the higher elegancies of life, are, indeed, confined to a few imitators of European fashions; but there is a sufficiency of all that is essential and needful. No ostentatious attempt is ever made to display either fortune or riches; but, on the contrary, everything avoided which, being contrary to republican plainness, might offend or unnecessarily attract the attention of the people. Furniture, dress, carriages, etc., are all of the simplest construction; and the oldest and most aristocratic families set, in this respect, the example to the more recently promoted fashionables.

Whatever political reason there may exist for the prevalence of this taste, it is, nevertheless, a good one, and being shared by the great majority of the nation, impresses a peculiar character of simplicity on the domestic life of Americans. It is impossible for a European to live for any length of time in the United States, without being constantly reminded, in town or in the country, at home or abroad, that he is living in a republic, and that the sovereign power of that republic is solely vested in the majority; for, whatever is capable of exciting envy or jealousy by too glaring a distinction from the inferior classes, is condemned by public opinion and, on that account, studiously avoided by persons of all ranks of society. But then the great prosperity of the country enables even the laboring classes to enjoy comforts much beyond the reach of superior orders in Europe, and prevents the scale from becoming too low.

On entering the house of a respectable mechanic, in any of the large cities of the United States, one cannot but be astonished at the apparent neatness and comfort of the apartments; the large airy parlors, the nice carpets and mahogany furniture, and the tolerable good library showing the inmates' acquaintance with the standard works of English literature. These are advantages which but few individuals of the same class enjoy, by way of distinction, in Europe; but which, in America, are within the reasonable hopes and expectations of almost all the inferior classes.

What powerful stimulus is not this to industry? What premium on sobriety and unexceptionable conduct? A certain degree of respectability is, in all countries, attached to property, and is, perhaps, one of the principal reasons why riches are coveted. A poor man has certainly more temptations and requires more virtue to withstand them than one who is in tolerable circumstances. The motives of the rich are hardly ever questioned, while the poor are but too often objects of distrust and suspicion. . . .

The laboring classes in America are really less removed from the wealthy merchants and professional men than they are in any part of Europe; and the term "mob," with which the lower classes in England are honored, does not apply to any portion of the American community. With greater ease and comfort in his domestic arrangements, the laboring American acquires also the necessary leisure and disposition for reading; his circle of ideas becomes enlarged; and he is rendered more capable of appreciating the advantages of the political institutions of his country. Both thought and reflection may be crushed by excessive labor and the lofty aspirings of the mind enslaved by the cravings of the body.

Liberty, without promoting the material interests of man, is a thing altogether beyond the comprehension of the multitude; and there are many who, had they attained it, would, like the Israelites of old, wish themselves back to their fleshpots. I know not whether it is quest of liberty or property which causes Europeans to emigrate to America, but I am satisfied that there is an intimate connection between the two, and a constant reaction of one upon the other.

An excellent habit of the Americans, which is an incalculable promoter of domestic happiness, consists in their passing all the time which is not required for active business at home or in the circle of their acquaintance. To this custom must be ascribed the unusual number of happy marriages in the United States, which is the cornerstone of the high morality of the country. Public houses in America are almost wholly frequented by travelers; and the practice has recently been introduced into many of them not to sell wine or liquor of any description except to boarders.

But there is one deficiency in the general routine of pleasure in the United States which is particularly oppressive to the laboring classes, and consists in the almost total absence of public gardens or pleasure grounds in the large cities. There is nothing more favorable to a community of feeling, and a certain momentary oblivion of all ranks and distinctions, which attaches us more warmly to our kind than public places of rendezvous, frequented by all classes of society and enjoyed alike by all. In Europe, nearly every large city is adorned with them; and in Germany, every hamlet; but in America, they seem to be opposed to the domestic habits of the people. New York has something in the shape of a public garden in the establishment of Niblo's, and the

Battery. But there is, generally, an admission fee to both; and neither one nor the other is large enough to contain a considerable portion of the whole population of the city. The Battery, especially, can only be frequented in the evening, there being neither trees nor shrubs to afford the least shelter against the sun, though the place itself, from its elevation, commands a most beautiful view of the harbor.

Boston, alone, of all the cities in the United States, has a large public mall; but even this (the munificent gift of an individual) is but little frequented, though the scenery around it is highly picturesque, and the walks themselves shaded by a most superb double row of chestnuts. There seems to be no want of disposition on the part of the Bostonians generally to profit by these advantages; but unfortunately the taste of the fashionable society has pronounced a verdict against it, and avoids most carefully being mixed and confounded with the multitude.

This morbid sensitiveness on the part of the higher classes arises, unquestionably, from the total absence of any exterior distinction between themselves and the lower orders, which could point them out as objects of particular respect and reverence; but I must greatly mistake the general character of Americans if I am not right in the conjecture that a greater degree of condescension in the learned and wealthy could hardly fail of meeting with a proper acknowledgment on the part of the people; while, on the contrary, too great a reserve in the former must necessarily deprive them of a portion of that power and influence which they would, otherwise, be sure to possess. If the American people are guilty of any fault, it is certainly not ingratitude. Whoever has observed their conduct at public meetings, in presence of their favorite speakers and representatives, can testify to the unfeigned respect and uncommon propriety of manner with which they are wont to meet those whose stations and acquirements are really superior to their own. Nothing can be more pusillanimous than the fear of being confounded with the vulgar; and it is certainly the worst argument, in favor of real or assumed superiority, to dread the contact of those whom we affect to despise. May a more Christian and charitable feeling soon take the place of this mawkish resuscitation of aristocratic pride, which would befit certain orders in Europe infinitely better than the even-born citizens of a republic.

The style of buildings in America is chiefly English, with some slight variation in New York and Philadelphia; but, to the south, the houses are adapted to the climate, and of an architecture somewhat resembling the Spanish. The parlors are usually on the ground floor (in all the new houses they are on the first floor) and communicate with each other by folding doors. The story immediately above contains the chambers and the nursery, and the third and fourth floors are occupied by the remainder of the family and the servants. Nearly all the houses of the wealthier citizens contain a number of spare rooms reserved for the accommodation of guests from the country; and the same kind hospitality is frequently tendered to strangers. Most of the modern houses are of brick or stone, and generally from three to four stories high; the Americans showing great fondness for large and spacious dwellings, and the ground in the cities being already too dear to allow them to expatiate much in area.

The exterior of the buildings is less marked by style or elegance than the interior is clean and comfortable; and the custom prevails, as in England, for each family to occupy a house of its own. The principal ornament consists in a sort of portico of various dimensions and orders, and a flight of steps leading up to the entrance. In Boston and New York, these steps are commonly of sandstone or granite (a species of sienite); but in Philadelphia they are of beautiful white marble, which, by daily ablution, is kept as clean as the floor of the parlors, and contributes much to the neat appearance of the streets. . . .

It appears . . . that the universal disposition of Americans to emigrate to the Western wilderness, in order to enlarge their dominion over inanimate nature, is the actual result of an expansive power which is inherent in them, and which, by continually agitating all classes of society, is constantly throwing a large portion of the whole population on the extreme confines of the state in order to gain space for its development. Hardly is a new state or territory formed before the same principle manifests itself again, and gives rise to a further emigration; and so is it destined to go on until a physical barrier must finally obstruct its progress.

The Americans, who do not pretend to account for this principle at all, are nevertheless aware of its existence, and act and legislate on all occasions as if they were to enjoy the benefits of the next century. Money and property is accumulated for no other visible purpose than being left to the next generation, which is brought up in the same industrious habits, in order to leave *their* children a still greater inheritance. The laboring classes of Europe, the merchants, and even professional men, are striving to obtain a certain competency with which they are always willing to retire; the Americans pursue business with unabated vigor till the very hour of death, with no other benefits for themselves than the satisfaction of having enriched their country and their children. Fortunes, which, on the continent of Europe, and even in England, would be amply sufficient for an independent existence, are in America increased with an assiduity which is hardly equaled by the industrious zeal of a poor beginner, and the term of *"rentier"* is entirely unknown. The luxurious enjoyments which riches alone can procure are neither known nor coveted in the United States; and the possession of property, far from rendering them indolent, seems to be only an additional stimulus to unremitting exertion.

In this disposition of Americans, the attentive peruser of history must evidently behold a wise dispensation of Providence, though it may, for a time, impede the progress of refinement and the arts. Without the spirit of enterprise and the taste for active labor, the immense resources of the country, and the facility with which riches are acquired would become the means of individual and national corruption and the introduction of expensive habits, which would not only undermine the private morals of the people but eventually subvert their republican government.

The sudden introduction of European refinements, if it were possible to make them universal, would, at this period, be the ruin of the American Constitution. The framers of that noble work, perhaps the proudest achievement of the human mind, did not contemplate a state of society as it exists in Europe, and could, therefore, with safety, repose the highest power and trust in the virtue and integrity of the people. America was then but thinly settled and her population spread over a wide surface; her inhabitants were distinguished for the simplicity of their manners and the high moral rectitude of their character; they were a highly *civilized* people, though they could not have been called *refined* in the sense in which the term is applied in the fashionable circles of London and Paris. It was of the utmost importance for the safety of the government, which, at that time, was only an *experiment,* that the people should retain their simple habits, until age should give strength to the Constitution, and accustomed the people readily to submit to the newly instituted authorities. It was necessary for the rulers, as well as the governed, to acquire a *routine* of business, and to establish that mutual confidence in one another, without which every free government must soon be converted into despotism. . . .

Every new colony of settlers contains within itself a nucleus of republican institutions, and revives, in a measure, the history of the first settlers. Its relation to the Atlantic states is similar to the situation of the early colonies with regard to the mother country and contains the elements of freedom. Every society which is thus formed must weaken the fury of parties by diminishing the points of contact — while the growing power of the Western states becomes a salutary check on the spreading of certain doctrines, which are continually importing from Europe, and to the evil influence of which the Atlantic states are more particularly exposed.

The Western states, from their peculiar position, are supposed to develop all the resources and peculiarities of democratic governments, without being driven to excesses by the opposition of contrary principles. Their number, too, augments the intensity of republican life by increasing the number of rallying points, without which the principle of liberty would be too much weakened by expansion. It is a peculiarly happy feature of the Constitution of the United States that every state has itself an independent government and becomes thus the repository of its own liberties.

The inhabitant of Arkansas, Illinois, or Indiana, living on the confines of the state and the very skirts of civilization, would, in all probability, be less of a patriot if his attachment to the country were only to be measured by his adherence to the general government. He would be too remote from the center of action to feel its immediate influence, and not sufficiently affected by the political proceedings of the state to consider them paramount to the local interests of his neighborhood. Political life would grow fainter in proportion to its remoteness from the seat of legislation, and the energies of the people, instead of being roused by the necessity of action, would degenerate into a passive acknowledgement of the protection offered by the government. This is more or less the case in every country, except England and America, and perhaps the principal reason of their little progress in freedom. Hence the feverish excitement in their capitals and large towns, and the comparative inertness and palsy of the country.

Every town and village in America has its peculiar republican government, based on the principle of election, and is, within its own sphere, as free and independent as a sovereign state. On this broad basis rests the whole edifice of American liberty. Freedom takes its root at home, in the native village or town of an American. The county, representing the aggregate of the towns and villages, is but an enlargement of the same principle: the state itself represents the different counties; and the Congress of the United States represents the different states. In every place, in every walk of life, an American finds some rallying point or center of political attachment. His sympathies are first enlisted by the government of his native village; then, by that of the county; then, by the state itself; and finally, by that of the Union. If he is ambitious, he is obliged to make a humble beginning at home and figure in his native town or county; thence he is promoted to the dignity of representative or senator of his state; and it is only after he has held these preparatory stations that he can hope to enjoy the honor of representative or senator in the Congress of the nation. Thus the county is the preparatory school for the politician of the state, and the state furnishes him with a proper introduction to national politics.

The advantages of this system are manifold. It creates political action where otherwise all would be passiveness and stupor; it begets attachment to the institutions of the country by multiplying the objects of their political affection and bringing them within the sphere of every individual; it cools the passions of political parties by offering them frequent opportunities of spending themselves on various subjects and in various directions; it establishes a stronghold of liberty in every village and town, and accustoms all classes of society to a republican government; it enforces submission to laws and institutions which are the type of those of the nation; and it furnishes numerous schools for young politicians, obliging them to remain sufficiently long in each not to enter the university of Congress without age and proper experience. This system, while it lasts — and there are no symptoms of its being speedily abolished — will prevent novices in politics from entering the Senate or House of Representatives of the United States, and reserve the dignity of President for the wisdom of sexagenarians. . . .

The Western states of America are each a nursery of freedom; every new settlement is already a republic *in embryo.* They extend political life in every direction and establish so many new fortified points that the principle of liberty has nothing to dread from a partial invasion of its territory.

Every new state, therefore, is a fresh guarantee for the continuance of the American Constitution, and directs the attention of the people to new sources of happiness and wealth. It increases the interest of all in upholding the general government, and makes individual success dependent on national prosperity. But every year which is added to its existence increases its strength and cohesion by reducing obedience to a habit, and adding to the respect which is due to age. If it be true that the life of nations and political institutions resembles that of individuals, it is equally true that the different periods of their development are exposed to the same dangers. One-third of all that are born die in childhood; the greater number of them are healthy during the period of their manhood; and all must eventually die of old age. Climate and soil breed particular diseases, which must be cured according to their peculiar constitutions; but, of these, fevers and consumptions are the most dreaded. Violent cures are apt to weaken the system, but are often rendered unavoidable by a criminal delay of the proper remedies; and a total neglect of them is sure to produce an incurable distemper.

A child is exposed to more diseases than a man; and so is it with a young country. America is fast approaching her period of pupillarity, and the Constitution of a century will be established on a firmer basis than that of a dozen years. The people will have experienced its blessings and cherish it as the venerable inheritance of their fathers. Each succeeding generation will be born with an increased respect for it, and will be taught at school to consider it as the basis of their happiness. . . .

In the settlements of new districts it is seldom that Europeans are found to be actively engaged. This honor belongs almost exclusively to emigrants from New England, who may most emphatically be called the pioneers of the United States, and to whose enterprising spirit and recklessness of danger may be ascribed most of the valuable improvements of the country. They are, however, satisfied with tracing the road which the others are to follow and occupying the most important stations; the intervals are afterward filled up with settlers from other states and from Europe.

The character of the New England emigrants has been too well described by Washington Irving for me to attempt to add to it more than is necessary to understand a certain political type which may be observed in all states to which they have emigrated in large numbers. The talent of a New Englander is universal. He is a good farmer, an excellent schoolmaster, a very respectable preacher, a capital lawyer, a sagacious physician, an able editor, a thriving merchant, a shrewd peddler, and a most industrious tradesman. Being thus able to fill all the important posts of society, only a few emigrants from New England are required to imprint a lasting character on a new state, even if their number should be much inferior to that of the other settlers. The states of Ohio and Michigan, and even a large part of the state of New York, offer striking instances of this moral superiority acquired by the people of New England; but it would be wrong thence to conclude that their own habits do not undergo an important metamorphosis, or that, in their new relations in the Western states, they merely act as reformers, without being, in turn, influenced by the character of their fellow settlers.

The change, however, is altogether for the better. Their patriotism, instead of being confined to the narrow limits of New England — a fault with which they have been reproached as early as the commencement of the Revolutionary War — partakes there more of a *national* character. The continued intercourse with strangers from all parts of the world, but more particularly from the different states of the Union, serve in no small degree to eradicate from their minds certain prejudices and illiberalities with which they have but too commonly been reproached by their brethren of the South. Tolerance, the last and most humane offspring of civilization, is, perhaps, the only virtue of which the New Englander is usually parsimonious; but even this seems to improve and to thrive in the Western states; and I have no hesitation to say, that, in this respect, the inhabitants of those districts are by far more emancipated than those of the Atlantic states, whatever advantages the latter may possess with regard to refinement of manners. I know of no better specimen of human character than a New Englander transferred to the Western states. . . .

The increased facilities of intercourse, and especially the use of steam, are yet productive of another happy result, scarcely less deserving attention. The reduced expenses of traveling enable thousands of persons who would otherwise be obliged to remain stationary to try their fortunes abroad or to journey for information. Life consists in motion; and, as far as that goes, the United States present certainly the most animated picture of universal bustle and activity of any country in the world. Such a thing as rest or quiescence does not even enter the mind of an American, and its presence would to him be actually insupportable. The rates of fares and passages are so low and so well adapted to the means of the great bulk of the population that there is scarcely an individual so reduced in circumstances as to be unable to afford his "dollar or so" to travel a couple of hundred miles from home "in order to see the country and the improvements which are going on." On board the steamboats, meals are generally included in the price of passage, which, during a certain part of the season, is so reduced by opposition as hardly to pay for the board alone; in which case it is almost as cheap, or cheaper, to travel than to stay at home.

The influence of these proceedings on the minds of the laboring classes is incredible. Instead of being confined to the narrow circle of their own acquaintances, and occupied chiefly with the contemplation of the steeple of their own native village, they have the same opportunity of widening the sphere of their knowledge by traveling and personal observation of the manners of different people, which in other countries is enjoyed by gentlemen of moderate fortune, and from which the same order in Europe is almost entirely excluded. The absence of post chaises or any other vehicles exclusively for the conveyance of wealthy travelers compels the latter to accomplish their journeys in company with such men as they may chance to meet on the road; and if these happen to be mechanics or traders, an exchange of thought and sentiment takes place, which is often profitable to both parties. The laboring classes, which, in this manner, are brought in contact with the more polite orders of society, can hardly fail to improve in manners; and the higher and wealthier classes, who in most countries are totally ignorant of the sentiments and wants of the lower orders, receive, in turn, much valuable instruction, which, as it passes from one individual to another, is sure of finally reaching the halls of Congress. A mutual loss and compensation takes place, and the facilities of traveling are, again, employed in equalizing conditions.

77.

EDWARD BEECHER: The Riots at Alton

On November 7, 1837, the Reverend Elijah P. Lovejoy, editor of an Abolitionist paper founded in St. Louis, Missouri, and moved to free soil territory at Alton, Illinois, in 1836, was murdered while attempting to defend his press from a mob. The press had been destroyed by the citizens of Alton on three prior occasions. The final attempt occurred shortly after the charter convention of a state antislavery society that met at Upper Alton on October 26-28, 1837. Lovejoy's close associate, the Reverend Edward Beecher, described the events leading up to Lovejoy's death in Part One of the Narrative of Riots at Alton, *and in Part Two, from which the selection below is taken, discussed the principles involved.*

Source: *Narrative of Riots at Alton: in Connection with the Death of Rev. Elijah P. Lovejoy*, Alton, 1838, pp. 121-141.

THE FIRST DEVELOPMENTS of mob violence have not even a plausible pretext for their justification: and to palliate, connive at, or attempt to justify them is treason against God and against man.

Let us look at the facts of the case. A religious paper is established at St. Louis. Does its editor advocate the odious doctrines of the Abolitionists? No. Yet still he encounters the vengeance of the mob. Why? Because he dared to remonstrate against the profanation of the Sabbath and of his nation's flag for purposes of religious bigotry. Because he dared to remonstrate against the lawless proceedings of a mob, who burned alive a fellow man, without trial, judge, or jury. Because he indignantly re-buked the anarchical doctrines of a lawless judge who declared the power of the mob to be above the power of the law. And because, though no Abolitionist, he dared even to maintain that slavery was a great moral evil and ought as soon as possible to be removed.

He came to this state, his paper was reestablished, and he at first supposed that he would not be called on to oppose slavery as he had, and so said, but made no pledge to be silent; nay, expressly stated that he would not be bound.

At length, by the progress of his own mind and of events, he is convinced that it is his duty to speak; and he does it. Again, many in the state wish to organize themselves into a society for discussion and for moral influence, and consult him. He for a time puts them off; and, at last, in compliance with their wishes, proposes the inquiry — Is it best so to organize? — and asks for the opinions of friends.

And here violence begins. He is first falsely accused of violating a pledge, and then told that it is the will of a majority that he forbear to print. An editor of a neighboring city in a slave state applauds the spirit of the meeting, tells them that Mr. Lovejoy "has forfeited all claims on that or any other community," exhorts them "to eject from among them that minister of mischief, the *Observer*, or to correct its course"; and threatens them with the loss of trade unless they "put a stop to the efforts of these fanatics, or expel them from their community."

In the meeting no charges are made of an imprudent use of language or of a bad spirit. The simple head and front of his offending is that he holds certain opinions which the majority of the community do not like; and which they proclaim to be subversive of the interests of the place!

And is a freeman to submit to such atrocious tyranny as this? Are the rights of conscience nothing? Is duty to God nothing? Are sacred chartered privileges nothing? Is a foreign editor, without trial, judge, or jury, to proclaim a citizen of our state an outlaw, to say that all the bonds which once bound him to civil society are dissolved, and to point him out to the mob as deserving of nothing but wrath, unless he will at their dictation resign the dearest rights of the human soul? Is there no God? Are there no immutable principles of right? Is there no law, no justice, no fear of God? Have we no ruler but the demon of anarchy; and no Lord but that bloody, thousand-headed, murderous tyrant, the mob?

Had it been under Nero, Mr. Lovejoy might reasonably have fled. That bloody tyrant made no pretensions to reason or to the fear of God. But has a Christian nation sunk so low that, in the midst of laws, charters, and most sacred guarantees made for the express purpose of defending the rights of speech, and to be maintained and administered by Christian men, they will require a citizen, at the bidding of an infuriate mob, to sacrifice conscience, abandon every right, and seek for safety in inglorious flight? And yet, because Mr. Lovejoy refused to do this, he is stigmatized as stubborn, dogmatical, rash, and imprudent; and we are gravely told that he deserves no sympathy; and that on him the guilt of those atrocious deeds must rest which have infixed so indelible a stain on the American name!

If indeed it is so, it is time for us to know it, and cease our boastings of freedom and equal rights. Even the Inquisition itself was never guilty of deeds so atrocious. It gave to its miserable victims at least the forms of justice and a trial. Nor did it ever claim the power of rising superior to law. But in a Christian land even the show of justice is laid aside; and an innocent man, a man guilty of no crime or misdemeanor, a man who had done nothing to justify even the least excitement, is stripped at a blow of every right; all ties that bind him to the community are cut — and that solely because he will not bow the knee to the irresponsible censorship of a profligate mob.

Had Mr. Lovejoy been intemperate in his use of language it would not have furnished the slightest excuse for such proceedings. But he was not. Even this poor pretext is wanting. At the time of the meeting it was not even claimed. I know it has since been got up by some Eastern editors, who in all probability never read his paper. But it will not do. His exposition of views put forth to meet this crisis is marked by nothing so much as a calm, temperate, kind, and dignified style. It indicates the spirit of a man unwilling to provoke and anxious only to convince. And he even watched over his language on this subject with solicitous care.

And I fearlessly say that, from one article on slavery in the journal of the Colonization Society, which I have now in my eye, I can select more severity of language on the subject of slavery than from all Mr. Lovejoy ever wrote.

AGAIN, WHEN WE SAW THE EVIL coming on, we did all in our power to unite good men, allay excitement, and restore law.

It was my deep sense of the need of such an effort which induced me to give my name to the call. It was then my plan not to press the formation of a state society at the expense of division and mobs, but as this was the original cause of the excitement — for no man who has noticed facts can doubt it — to concede this point, and demand only a kind, friendly, uncommitted discussion; and a society of inquiry, if any organization was thought best. I urged on Brother Lovejoy and his friends that from a regard to the public peace they would yield their private feelings and plans. And what was Brother Lovejoy's reply? "You will not find me obstinate. For union and peace, I will give up anything but duty." And so said his friends. What more could they do?

I then explained to a number of the leading citizens of Alton the dangers of division among good men; and entreated them to unite, not in forming an antislavery society but in a friendly discussion; and pointed out a way in which, without any committal, they might modify the course of their brethren and avoid a mob. And when they approved these views, I made the result public, and invited the friends of unity among the good and of free inquiry to attend the approaching meeting. And what more could be done?

Now in this very critical aspect of affairs, after one mob had taken place and when another was threatened, it did seem to me that it would be cruel in the extreme, directly or indirectly, to add fuel to the fire which I was striving to quench. Public odium was already burning fearfully against a small and hated minority; and how could anyone take this very hour to add fresh intensity to the flame? Why not at least let the trial be made unimpeded by new accessions of odium and hostility?

And now, although I am willing to acquit the leaders of the Colonization Society of all deliberate malignity of purpose; and though the majority of those who joined it, I am sure, did not anticipate its results, yet no charity requires me to forbear to narrate what was actually done, or to delineate its effects.

In the first place, it seemed to be got up expressly to defeat the convention.

In the second place, it held out fully and prominently the idea that no plan of proceeding was rational or safe but the one proposed by itself.

Again, it passed a resolution designed to operate directly against the convention about to be held, and adapted to render it odious, by insinuations and innuendoes; as if it were to be composed of men who were accustomed to use un-Christian and abusive epithets against the slaveholding community, and to assume that they were the only friends of the slave or of his emancipation.

Again, the same clergyman and editor by whom this resolution was introduced, in his account of the meeting, takes it for granted that the meeting of the Colonization Society has rendered abortive all the plans of the friends of the convention, and remarks concerning them, "Doubtless a very few restless spirits will be disappointed, vexed, mortified, and may struggle for a time to enjoy notoriety." Now all this as individuals we could easily bear. It is little to be called restless spirits — disappointed, vexed, mortified, and striving for a brief notoriety. Though even if we had been such, and had been defeated, too, it is worthy neither of a man nor a Christian, much less of a minister of Christ, thus to exult over our anticipated fall.

Elijah P. Lovejoy

But in this light I do not view it. I regard not at all its influence on personal feeling; but its manifest tendencies at once to defeat all plans of conciliation or union, and all efforts to allay excitement, or to tranquilize the public mind; and to arouse to new intensity the fury of the mob.

Of whom was such language used? Of men obstinate and perverse, despising union and intent solely on arousing and inflaming the public mind? No; but of men who had gone to the uttermost limit of concession, and whose only demand was that they should not be compelled to give up every plan without deliberation or discussion at the bidding of a mob. Could not the editor of a religious paper, a professed minister of Christ, find any kinder language than this for such men? And could he calmly devise measures and plans, the only tendency of which was to shut them out from the sympathy of the good and expose them to the fury of the mob? And if such language ought ever to be used, was this the time and the place?

Well do I remember the emotions which filled my heart as first this language met my eye. It came at that very crisis when first I felt that it was fearfully probable that we were soon to be called to wrestle with the fury of a mob. And he who has never been called to pass through such a scene can never know what it is to be thus assailed in such an hour by a professed minister of his Savior and his God.

I am willing to make all possible allowances. Nor will I say that these good men wished to excite a mob. But I must say that if they had wished it they could not have used means more adapted to produce the result. And if they did not see the direct tendency of measures like these, some strange delusion had blinded their eyes. At all events the results were sure. The majority of good men stood aloof and left the convention a mark for its foes. . . .

THE TRUE SPIRIT OF INTOLERANCE now stood exposed. Events were so ordered by the Providence of God as to strip off every disguise. It now became plain that all attempts to conciliate and to discuss were vain; and nothing remained but to resist or to submit.

I am aware that even pride or resentment might dictate resistance to such demands as were made on us; and had these been our motives the act had deserved no praise. But though sinful passions might prompt to such a course, their entire absence would not lead to the reverse. Indeed, the more we reflected on our duties to God and the truth, and the more we considered the principles involved, the more did we feel that we could not retreat. We felt that a crisis had come, and in Mr. Lovejoy's view there was but the alternative — to conquer or to die. He had deliberately looked the matter through; and was willing either to triumph, should God permit, or to die, that the real nature of the malignant influences now at work might be fully disclosed and the nation at last be aroused. And, after solemn deliberation and much consultation and prayer, he took his ground to remain.

But it was of no use to remain without a press, and ruin to import presses and not defend them; for there was a moral certainty that presses to any number would be destroyed if no effort was made to protect them. And how could this be done? Was it not by endeavoring to arouse the citizens to sustain the laws? Had all been aroused to the effort, our end would have been at once secured. But all were not; a part were willing to act and a part were not. Still the law and civil power were not turned against us: under them we could act.

And the question was twofold: (1) Can we with this force maintain our ground? (2) If we fail, what will be the result? As to the first, they thought they could. If not, it would arouse the nation and test the principles of the case. Now all that was done was the carrying out of this plan; and if you find fault with the execution, you find fault with the plan.

It is objected to on these grounds:

1. That all defense of law by arms is wrong.

2. That the defense was part of a system of efforts to propagate the truth and was therefore propagating the truth by carnal weapons.

3. That a clergyman aided to make it.

As to the first, I can only say that so long as man is in the body, physical force must be used to secure moral results. God always has used it and always will. And all physical laws causing death, if they are violated, are laws made by God and sanctioned by the penalty of death to secure their observance. And it is the fear of this penalty that deters men from their violation. That in the Gospel He has authorized the maintenance of law by the sword, an instrument of death; and that no laws not sustained by this ultimate resort can have any binding power.

Nor is it rendering "evil for evil" in the sense forbidden by Christ to punish with death the man who aims to prostrate human law, any more than it is rendering "evil for evil" for God to punish a sinner for violating the laws of the universe. Nor is it true that no punishments are right but those which seek the sinner's good. Does God punish sinners forever for their own good; or to "set them forth as an example, suffering the vengeance of eternal fire," as He affirms.

The main design of punishment obviously is to deter from transgression. The certainty of an ultimate appeal to force is all that gives law any terrors to the wicked. The good may be a law unto themselves; but, as we are told by Paul, the law is not made for such, but for murderers and thieves and all who can be restrained by no higher motive than fear. In Alton all such fear had been nearly taken away. Had it been restored, had the conviction been deeply fixed that the large mass of the community would sustain the law by force, a small band of wicked men would never have dared to make the attack. It was the report of the committee and the resolutions of the meeting of citizens which took this fear away and emboldened the wicked in their deeds of violence and blood.

As to the fact that the defense was of a press — a part of a system of means for diffusing truth — it may be replied that in all well-organized Christian communities this principle is involved; and all arguments against it are deduced from a consideration of expediency or duty under an entirely different state of society. For example: An itinerant missionary, like the apostles under the persecuting Roman power, might be under obligations not to use force, but to flee from city to city when persecuted. Force could do no good: it was hopeless against the power of an empire. But for a man so situated it was best to have no wife, nor house, nor printing press, nor any other ties to fasten him to any spot. Again: An itinerant in a nominally Christian community, yet a community thoroughly degraded and corrupt, and refusing to enforce law, might be under obligation to pursue the same course; because force would be useless; and he could do nothing but flee from place to place and preach as he went.

But suppose, now, a minister is settled in a regular, well-organized Christian community, the vast majority of which are decided friends of Christianity and supporters of law. Now, if fifty or a hundred men out of thousands, excited to rage by some unwholesome truth, attempt to tear down his meetinghouse, is no resistance to be made? Or, if his person is assailed, shall he seek no defense from law, but flee? Or allow himself to be abused or slain?

Now suppose a body of men unite to disseminate the truth by means of missionaries or Bibles or tracts, and erect buildings and buy presses. If these are assailed, shall they not apply to the magistrate and seek the protection of the law? And, if needed, shall not force be used? And yet these are parts of a system the direct end of which is to disseminate the truth. The fact is that in the best states of society investments of capital in means of moral influence increase solely because they are protected by law; and when the law ceases to protect, or opposes them, they cease to exist. And if we lay down the principle that the means of exerting moral influence are not to be defended by force of arms because they are devoted to the high purposes of disseminating the truth, where shall we land? Stores and ships if used for making money may be protected; but if used for higher and nobler ends, not. And all presses, houses, churches, academies, or schools which are used for high moral and religious ends must be given up to the fury of a mob.

The fact is, the idea that defending the means of exerting moral influence, or the persons of those who use them is making use of carnal weapons to propagate the truth is an entire delusion. If it were so then every minister in the land is propagating the truth by carnal weapons. Are not all ministers defended by the law? And does not this rest ultimately on an appeal to force or arms if it is invaded? What matters it whether the necessity of using them occurs every day or not if it is known that they will be used whenever needed? The fact is that protecting a man when he is preaching is not propagating truth by carnal weapons; it only enables him to state the truth in safety. It compels no one to believe him. So, defending a press or an editor only enables him to print in safety; it compels no one to read or to believe. Did we attempt to compel men to believe at the point of the bayonet, that would be using carnal weapons to propagate truth. But who has done this?

Now, that all printing presses are under the protection of law has been heretofore considered the settled order of things in this state. Hence it was not a duty to leave Alton until it was settled that this is not the fact there. And we resolved to do all in our power to prevent this result from being established. But, if we failed, we intended so to fail that the atrocity of such a state of things should be clearly seen. We did not mean to give room to the inhabitants of Alton thereafter, when writhing under the lashings of public sentiment for having driven away a free press and smothered free discussion, to say to us, "You have stained the character of the city by your premature flight; the threats of an insignificant band of ruffians frighted you; if you had stayed we would have protected you." We did not mean to slip off and go to another spot, and have the same scenes acted over. This would but have extended the sphere of corruption and enlisted more and more on the side of anarchy. The only true policy was to test the question there and see if the law would give way; and if so, then to see if there is in our land moral energy enough to react. We looked upon it as a test question for our whole land; and so indeed it was. Deadly influences were at work; anarchical principles were eating out the very life of the body politic; and yet the nation was asleep; and nothing but an earthquake shock could arouse her to life.

Now, granting the soundness of these views — and that they are sound who can deny? — what was, in few words, the great end of our enterprise? It was either by victory to restore law to its power, or by death to disclose the astounding fact that in one portion of our land the reign of law was over and that of anarchy had begun. In full faith that God would use this event to arouse and to save the nation, slumbering on the brink of ruin, and thus produce the effect of which the *National Intelligencer* justly says: "It would be some consolation to humanity if we could safely count upon the effects thus anticipated, that the time had now come when the majesty of the laws is to be asserted; and when men may travel, speak, and write in the United States without coming under other surveillance than that legally provided," we took our stand.

Now, if the result is, through the blessing of God, the final restoration of a sound public sentiment on the great scale, law will reign again, even in Alton; and no more force will be needed. According to these views a sound public sentiment in the majority is essential to make the exercise of force useful in restraining a vicious and disorderly minority. But when the majority is unsound, law can no longer be sustained; and to use force on the small scale is vain, if in the body politic, as a whole, there is no restorative power. In such a case I would make no effort at defense; but, after the example of the apostles, flee before the storm.

It was not, then, a contest for abolition but for law and human society against anarchy and misrule. Now, if Brother Lovejoy was willing in such a contest to die; if with enlarged and far-reaching views he had calculated all these results — and that he had I well know — was it recklessness, was it obstinacy that urged him on, or a noble devotedness to the cause of God and man?

But he was a clergyman, it is said. So indeed he was. But he was a citizen nonetheless for that; and as a citizen he had rights and duties too. And is it, at this late day, to be laid down as a rule that for doing his duty in defending his rights as a citizen he is to forfeit his character as a minister of Christ?

But it is said he died with murderous weapons in his hands, and with the blood of a fellow being on them. The whole is false. He died in defense of justice, and of the law, and of right, and with the instrument of justice in his hands. Is it so, indeed? When the ruler, by the command of God, bears the sword, has he a murderous weapon in his hand? And if he executes a criminal, is the blood of a fellow creature on his hands? Who are they that use such language as this? The men who are in favor of chaplains on board of our ships of war and in our armies. The men who eulogize Ashmun, a clergyman, too, who, under the auspices of a benevolent society, gave orders to fire charge after charge of grapeshot among dense masses of his fellowmen. The men who eulogize with never ending paeans of praise the heroes of Bunker Hill, of Yorktown, of New Orleans. And is it said that these men acted in self-defense and in defense of inalienable rights? And did not Lovejoy, too? Is it said perhaps Ashmun did not fire the cannon himself? How much better is it to plan a battle and inspirit his soldiers to the contest than to fire himself? Do not all lawyers know that *qui facit per alium, facit per se* [who acts through another, acts for himself]? And how much better was it for clergymen in sermons and prayers, and by their presence, to urge our fathers on than to fight themselves? In point of morality there is not a shade of difference, and all know there is none in law.

There are men among us who are consistent; men at whose heresies the very persons who use this cant have been sorely alarmed; men who are stigmatized as "peace men" and "no human government men." At the heresies of such they have filled the land with clamor. And what now? Have they come over to their opinions, after all this outcry? Then why not strike their colors? Why keep on fighting? At one hour they stigmatize their views as false and pernicious; and the very next, what do we see? There are men who discard all these heresies and maintain that human governments ought to exist and to be defended by the sword; and maintain the rights of self-defense; and they actually go so far as to reduce their principles to practice. And all at once, smit with pious horror, they start back at the tragedy and talk of murderous weapons and the blood of a fellowman! Consistent men! Well may we say of such, "whereunto shall I liken the men of this generation?"

The fact is that the prejudices of some against certain opinions are so inveterate as to blind them even to the simplest truths. And such is their zeal to censure the defenders of a hated cause that they pour upon them volley after volley, as if utterly unconscious that to reach them they must first batter down every entrenchment of their own.

BUT IT IS SAID the majority of the citizens of Alton did not wish the press located there. What then? Have a majority a right to drive out a minority if they happen in the exercise of inalienable rights to do what they do not like; and if they will not go, murder them? And is it every editor's duty

to give up all his civil rights at the voice of the majority, and flee?

But this is not all. It is not a mere question of an editor's rights. All parties in the state have a right to the advantages of prominent commercial points. If any place is in a center of communication, like Alton, it is the best location for a paper; and any set of men in the state have a right, if they wish, to establish a paper there. Had it been a political paper in which citizens all over the state were interested, what would have been said of an effort to drive it away because the majority of Alton were opposed to its views?

But it is said "that it was injurious to the interests of the place to have it there." This allegation is both false and absurd. If its views were false, it was easy to answer them; but if true, can it be injurious to know the truth? It is said it would injure the character and trade of the place. Is it then injurious to any place to be known as the decided friend of free inquiry and the fearless protector of the rights of speech? Even if it had caused a loss of dollars and cents, is money the chief good and the loss of it the greatest of all evils? Is not an elevated character for morality, intelligence, good order, and religion worth more than untold sums of silver and gold? But how delusive the idea that such a character could injure the commercial interests of Alton. No! It was because I loved Alton and could not bear to see her fair fame blasted that I exerted myself to secure the restoration of law to the last. To have left Alton at the bidding of a mob could never have restored her lost character. This nothing but the entire restoration and inflexible maintenance of the law could do.

But it is said, your efforts only made the matter worse. So, too, the efforts of Christ did but make the last state of the Jews worse than the first; but general principles and a regard to the great whole urged him on. So, too, we felt that it was a question of principles; and the voice of the nation was with us, and a regard to the general good urged us on. Besides, who could know that our efforts would be vain? We believed, and on what seemed to us satisfactory grounds, that they would not be vain. Moreover, such a thing had never happened in our nation, as an entire prostration of the right of free discussion by a mob; and we did not and could not believe that it would take place there. We acted according to the evidence we had; and who could demand anything more? Duties are ours; results belong to God.

On whom, then, does the guilt of these transactions fall? First, on the guilty agents; and next, on all who excited, instigated, or countenanced them in their deeds. All who have aided to stigmatize with unjust reproach an innocent, meritorious, and suffering portion of their fellow citizens. Profligate editors, at the East and at the West, have a large account to render to God for these bloody deeds. All professedly religious men who have by rendering their fellow citizens odious in the eyes of an infuriated mob stimulated their hatred and urged them on. All who have refused to fear God more than man, and who, through fear of popular odium, have failed to oppose and rebuke the workers of iniquity. All who have allowed their prejudices against unpopular sentiments to render them traitorous to the great principles of human society and to the holy cause of God.

Who these are I shall not now particularize. I refer to the simple record of the past and leave it to a candid public to judge.

78.

ASA GREEN: Mob Violence

Asa Green, physician, journalist, and bookseller by turns, started writing satires
when he was about forty years old. His fifth book, A Glance At New York, *was*
published anonymously in 1837. It parodied the many literary works of the time that
pretended to be travel books but were really moral homilies. A Glance At
New York *contained short essays on such subjects as "Dandies" and "Water and*
Other Liquids." The selection reprinted here deals with "Mobs."

Source: *A Glance At New York*, New York, 1837, pp. 96-107.

ALL THE PRINCIPAL CITIES of the United States have had their mobs. The most famous of these, and the most worthy of the dignity of history — both on account of the cause, the character of the persons engaged, and the consequences that ensued — was the celebrated *tea mob* of Boston, in the year 1773, commonly called the "Boston Tea Party." Three years before that, the British soldiers were mobbed and assailed with stones and brickbats when they fired upon the Bostonians and killed five on the spot. In later times, the Boston mobs have been comparatively trivial affairs. But it must be confessed that the citizens of that sober metropolis, when once sufficiently wrought up to enact the mob, do the business in the most effectual manner of any people of the United States.

Baltimore has been emphatically called the "Mob City"; and, in the year 1812, certain of her people did her best, or their worst, to win for her that appellation. On that occasion fell several persons, among whom was General Lingan, a Revolutionary officer, who was murdered in the jail where he had been placed for security against the violence of the mob, whose animosity he had excited by his efforts in defending the house of Mr. Hanson, the editor of the *Federal Republican.* Hanson was opposed to the war, then recently declared, which was a favorite with the mob.

In 1835 — a year, as was likewise that of '34, infamous for mobs — Baltimore renewed her claim to be called the "mob city" by pulling down, or suffering to be pulled down, in a riot, the houses of some of her most distinguished citizens.

Philadelphia — the "city of brotherly love" — had her mobs in 1834, when some blood was spilt. In fact, the spirit of violence and misrule prevailed throughout the United States in the years '34 and '35; and it would have been strange indeed if Philadelphia had entirely escaped the epidemic.

The first mob of any great notoriety in New York, was called the "Doctors' Mob" — not because it was got up *by* the doctors but *against* them. This happened in the winter of 1787. Some medical students were imprudent enough to let it be known that they were engaged in the offices of dissection — actually dismembering the bodies of men who had not died the death of felons. And as it is ever considered by the populace a greater crime to exhume and dissect a dead man than to kill a live one,

so the populace of this city determined to make an example of these sons of Aesculapius. They rushed to the hospital and destroyed a number of anatomical preparations; and would have done the same by the students if they had not been rescued by the interference of the mayor, the sheriff, and some of the most intelligent citizens, who lodged them in jail for safekeeping. The mob then attacked the jail, and, in attempting to disperse them, John Jay was severely wounded in the head. Hamilton and others used their exertions in defense of the jail. The militia were at length called out; and the mob were finally dispersed by killing five and wounding seven or eight of their number.

The year '34 was famous, in New York, for the *anti-abolition mob.* Commencing on the Fourth of July, at an antislavery meeting in Chatham Street Chapel, it was not completely suppressed for several days. The Abolitionists, relying upon the Constitution, thought they had a right to express their opinions freely on all subjects, and among the rest on the subject of slavery. Relying on the Declaration of Independence, they deemed that all men were born free and equal; and that the blacks not only had a right to their liberty but that they were also entitled to an equal seat in public with their white brethren.

In the practical enjoyment of this idea, they were not molested either by the philosopher or the Christian, neither of whom attempted to disturb a union in which they were not compelled to join, and which was left equally free to all, either to choose or to reject.

But others were not so inclined to peace. In spite of the Declaration of Independence and the U.S. Constitution, they determined that all men were not born equal, and that there was one subject, at least, on which, in a free country, no man should publicly open his mouth. They resolved, therefore,

. . . that the Abolitionists should be routed. Wherefore, attacking them from the boxes, they hurled down upon their heads, in the pit, the benches, and whatever they could conveniently lay their hands on; and at last succeeded in driving them, with their colored friends, from the house.

The next exploit of the mob was the attack on the house of Lewis Tappan, the leader of the Abolitionists. Having broken in the doors and windows, they contented themselves with making a bonfire of all his furniture — valued at about $1,500 — and then, with great moderation, dispersed, to assemble again the next evening for further mischief. Their next achievement was the demolition of the windows and pews of the churches of the Rev. Dr. Cox and the Rev. Mr. Ludlow, both of which gentlemen were accused of being favorable to immediate abolition. The mob also attacked the church of the Rev. Peter Williams, a respectable colored clergyman, who happened to be of opinion that slavery was not the best possible condition for his African brethren.

Such were the principal proceedings of the anti-abolition mob of '34. How much longer they would have continued their outrages had they not been wearied with the business — or had they not begun, after about three days, to meet with some decided symptoms of opposition from the police — we know not.

To do justice to our worthy mayor and corporation, it must be acknowledged that, in almost all cases of outbreaks against the peace, they begin to bestir themselves very lustily after the mischief is fairly done. When the city is threatened with a riot, they strenuously keep their own peace until the mob is completely organized, the work of destruction commenced, and, in general, pretty well finished. It has been so in all the riots that have happened here within our recollection.

The last of these was the *flour riot*, which happened in the month of February of the present year. In consequence of the high price of bread growing out of the monopoly of flour by a few speculators in that article, the papers for several weeks had spoken in terms of indignation of the base avarice — the grinding cruelty — of those merchants who were said to be coining money, as it were, out of the very heart's blood of the people.

At length a great meeting was assembled in the Park to devise means for the cure of so great a grievance. Warm harangues were pronounced and spirited resolutions were passed. Whether these roused the feelings of the half-starved auditors, and first suggested to their minds the idea of taking vengeance on the flour monopolists, or whether the mob had been previously organized, as the conservators of the peace had been some hours before, informed; certain it is that immediately after the dismission of the meeting in the Park, a band of rioters proceeded to the store of Eli Hart & Co., the most obnoxious of all the flour monopolists; and, demolishing their windows and doors, threw out and destroyed two or three hundred barrels of flour, and nearly the like quantity of wheat. Whether they expected to make the remainder of those articles cheaper by destroying a part is not specified; but so rapidly did they work for two or three hours, in rolling out and staving in the casks of flour and wheat, that their contents lay mingled together, from one side of the street to the other, to the depth of two or three feet.

The worthy mayor was, by this time, on the ground before the mob had more than half completed the work in hand. The constables were also there, with their long pine sticks. The mayor — like a man of peace, as he is known to be — first began to make a speech. But the rioters, who had just been hearing a much finer oration in the Park, refused to listen, and even proceeded so far as to stop the flow of His Honor's eloquence with a handful of flour. They treated the constables and their staves of office with quite as little respect; for they broke the staves over the constables' backs.

The mayor and his posse were driven from the ground; but returning, after a while, with a larger force, they finally proved victorious. Another flour store was broken open by this mob, but nothing worthy of note achieved.

Theatrical rows occasionally grace New York, as well as other cities; but history can scarcely raise these to the dignity of mobs — at least such as we have seen in this city. The principal of these were the anti-Anderson and the anti-Wood rows at the Park Theater; the first, we think, was in 1831; the last was in 1836. They were each occasioned by imported singers. The first, while on board the ship crossing the Atlantic, was so imprudent as to "damn the Yankees" — meaning thereby Americans in general. And as the Americans, though they may abuse one another pretty heartily, will not allow foreigners to take the same liberty, so they determined, at least in New York, that Mr. Anderson should never raise a note on their boards; and they effectually executed their determination; besides smashing the windows and lamps in front of the theater.

The anti-Wood row originated chiefly in a private quarrel between the *Courier* and *Enquirer* and Wood, the singer. The *Courier* had made a statement respecting the rather uncourteous refusal of Mr. Wood to play at Mrs. Conduit's benefit; which statement, happening to be true, was taken in very high dudgeon by Mr. Wood. He insisted upon its being contradicted; and as the *Courier* did not choose, upon that occasion, to eat its own words, he brought the matter publicly upon the stage, accusing the editor of falsehood and ungentlemenly conduct.

This roused the ire of the editor, who invited the sovereign people to attend at the Park, at Wood's next appearance, and put him down; at the same time warning the police not to interfere. The police — alias the mob — did more than they were invited to. They burst in the doors of the theater and filled the house more perfectly than it was ever filled before. They, however, did little or no mischief; and only insisted, when High Constable Hays attempted to interfere, that that grave functionary should make them a speech from the stage. Wood challenged Webb, the editor of the *Courier*, who refused to meet him on the ground that he was not a gentleman. The former shortly after sailed for England.

Much has been said in the newspapers of the prevalence of the mob in this city; and we have thought it necessary, in taking a glance at things in general, to give also a chapter on mobs. But, on a careful review of the subject, we cannot find that New York is entitled to any great preeminence in the mob line; especially when the vast number and various character of her population is considered; and still more especially when the kindly forbearance of the city authorities allows such remarkable scope for the free exercise of the spirit of mobocracy.

By the rude bridge that arched the flood,
Their flag to April's breeze unfurled,
Here once the embattled farmers stood,
And fired the shot heard 'round the world.

R. W. EMERSON, "Concord Hymn," July 4, 1837

View of Manhattan from Brooklyn Heights, 1836

NEW YORK CITY

By the end of the 1830s New York was the center of an international commerce second only to that of London. New York firms had long handled the shipping between Europe and the South, and to this was added transatlantic packet runs and an increasing number of ocean steamers. Foreign trade and the lucrative business with the Midwest afforded by the Erie Canal also kept the New York wharves busy.

This trade and Jackson's war on the Bank of the United States caused Wall Street to replace Philadelphia's Chestnut Street as the financial center of the country. Mercantile houses, banks, and insurance companies were created to serve the interests of the city, two-thirds of whose population was engaged in trade or manufacture.

But the city found itself unable to deal with the growth that attended its new economic eminence. Streets were inadequate to carry the enormous traffic. Most were unpaved: dusty in good weather, mired after rain or snowfall. Broadway was paved, but holes and loose stones jolted the passing vehicles. Residents complained of the difficulty in reaching any part of the city and of the danger to pedestrians. The precipitous rise in population — from about 200,000 in 1830 to some 312,000 in 1840 — created more problems. The new industrial age had distributed its wealth inequitably, dictating poverty to a great proportion of urban population. To their number was added the wave of Irish immigrants who arrived without education, money, or skills. The Irish, indignant at the prejudices directed against them and unable to pay for good housing, crowded into such notorious areas as the Five Points (modern Chinatown) where the primitive police force could do little to prevent the formation of gangs — the Plug Uglies, Bowery B'hoys, Dead Rabbits, Hookers — who controlled the area and committed crimes in all sections of the city. Charles Dickens visited the Five Points in 1842 and found it as bad as England's worst industrial slums.

Novelty Iron Works, on the East River at 12th Street, manufactured mainly steam engines

The city, in its northward expansion, had reached 14th Street by 1840. Beyond that point were scattered residential areas and farms. Visitors at the time remarked that little remained of the 18th century architecture. Frequent fires and commercial expansion had destroyed most traces of the earlier time.

The fire of 1835, one of New York's worst, gutted 17 blocks of lower Manhattan. It started the evening of December 16, 1835, at the corner of Merchant and Pearl streets. Zero temperatures and gale force winds inhibited effective fire fighting, and $20 million worth of property was destroyed before the flames could be brought under control. The fire affected the city's commercial growth very little and the entire area was rebuilt in a matter of years.

(Above) The Merchants' Exchange; (below) arrival of the Great Western, 1838

Broadway, looking north from Canal Street. From a drawing made in 1835

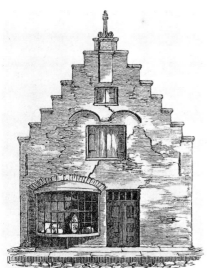

(Left) An old Dutch house, built in 1648. By 1830 it had been converted into a store and was one of the few remaining Dutch buildings in New York; (above) a view of the fire of 1835 from the bay

Design for the U.S. Customs House in New York by A. J. Davis in the pure Greek Revival style

Fall and winter fashions for 1837 and 1838 as advertised by a New York company

(Above and below) Elysian Fields, Hoboken, a favorite recreation spot for New Yorkers

Their new prosperity brought New Yorkers more leisure than they had ever known. Censuring of idleness and strict observance of the Sabbath became old-fashioned. The Sunday outing in the country was the favorite respite from the 6-day working week. Writers like Emerson chided city dwellers for their unhealthy pallor and urged them into the out-of-doors to enjoy the beauty of the countryside. There were cabs and omnibuses for trips beyond the city limits, and ferries to reach amusement parks such as the Elysian Fields in Hoboken, New Jersey. But some thought the Germans were taking liberties when they spent the entire Sunday merrily drinking in their beerhalls.

La Grange Terrace, La Fayette Place, an elegant apartment house in the Greek Revival mode

(Above) The elegant brougham carriage; (right) Mercantile Library reading room; (below) street auction, a common practice

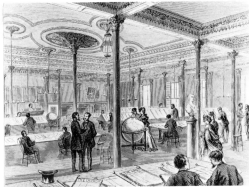

Food of all sorts was sold on the narrow dirty streets, mostly from horse-drawn wagons, but also from little stands. There was one huge market, the old Fulton Street Market, which provided opportunities for farmers to sell fresh produce and fishermen to sell their daily catch. Rotting vegetables and decayed meat were thrown on the street to be eaten by scavenging hogs. Cattle were driven through the streets, and all the refuse drained into the city's water supply. Few sanitary provisions were made; disease was rampant in the city, especially in the slum areas. After many minor outbreaks, a cholera epidemic swept the metropolis in the summer of 1832. The officials were roused, too late, to concern for cleanliness.

(Top) Fulton Street Market, 1834; (center) Street vendor's oyster stand; (bottom) interior of a butcher shop

The Hot Corn Seller

The Baker Cart

It is estimated that half the inhabitants fled New York to escape the danger: roads leading from Manhattan were jammed with refugees carrying their few portable possessions in panic flight; steamship companies made emergency trips to haul New Yorkers to eastern Long Island and to Connecticut havens on Long Island Sound. When the epidemic had ended, at least 4,000 New Yorkers were dead. Malaria, smallpox, and yellow fever were other common enemies, and the city officials at last began serious steps toward sanitation, especially by assuring a reasonably good water supply.

The Milk Man

The Charcoal Cart

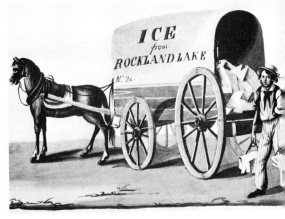

Watercolor sketches of New York street vendors by Nicolino Calyo

(Above) Typical fire fighting company of the time; (right) George Cousin, the "patent chimney sweep cleaner"

Patent drawing for a street sweeper

Public services in New York were not keeping up with the city's growth. Water was still primarily supplied by public wells, rain-water cisterns, and horse-drawn carts. Public sanitation measures were few. Fires were still fought by volunteer fire fighting companies, and in many areas private watchmen were hired to supplement the inadequate police protection against fire and robbery. The special problems of a large and diverse population were still met largely by private institutions that only extended their services to those able to pay.

A New York City watchman patrols the street

Southern view of the Halls of Justice, Centre-street.

New York African Free School, No. 2

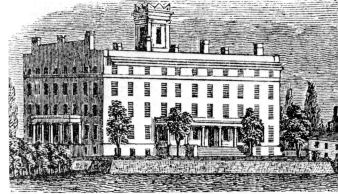

New York Institution for the Deaf and Dumb

View of New York Lunatic Asylum, 1832

City Hall

The Albany Regency controlled by Martin Van Buren and his allies was matched in New York City by the Tammany Hall organization. Machine politics as perfected by this Democratic organization formed a chain of influence and patronage extending from Washington to the ward and precinct levels. Tammany power derived from the immigrant blocs for whom the machine seemed to offer aid in a hostile environment. Hostility toward Catholics, and, therefore, toward German and Irish immigrants resulted in violent outbreaks in New York and elsewhere. By 1838 Aaron Clark, a Whig, was elected mayor of New York on an anti-Irish, anti-Catholic platform.

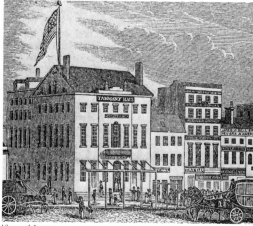

Tammany Hall, principal Democratic arm in New York

Aaron Clark (right), 1st Whig mayor of New York, won with an anti-immigrant campaign

HOW TO MAKE THE MARE GO.

1837 - 1838

79.

John Greenleaf Whittier: "The Farewell"

Many Abolitionists wrote stories and poems replete with sentimental and horrifying episodes in order to stir indignation against slavery. This tactic was criticized, even within their own ranks, because it was felt that the passion aroused in readers precluded a peaceful solution to the slavery question. However, the practice continued, reaching its apex, perhaps, in Harriet Beecher Stowe's Uncle Tom's Cabin *(1852). Whittier wrote stories and poems of this sort for thirty years. He had been drawn into the crusade against slavery by William Lloyd Garrison, the founder of the militant Abolitionist movement and the first editor to publish Whittier's verse. "The Farewell" is probably more effective as propaganda than as poetry.*

Source: *Complete Poetical Works*, Cambridge Edition, Boston, 1894.

❦ THE FAREWELL

Of a Virginia slave mother
to her daughters
sold into Southern bondage

Gone, gone,— sold and gone,
　To the rice swamp dank and lone.
There no mother's eye is near them,
There no mother's ear can hear them;
Never, when the torturing lash
Seams their back with many a gash,
Shall a mother's kindness bless them,
Or a mother's arms caress them.
　Gone, gone, — sold and gone,
　To the rice swamp dank and lone,
　From Virginia's hills and waters;
　Woe is me, my stolen daughters!

Gone, gone, — sold and gone,
　To the rice swamp dank and lone.
Where the slave whip ceaseless swings,
Where the noisome insect stings,
Where the fever demon strews
Poison with the falling dews,
Where the sickly sunbeams glare
Through the hot and misty air;
　Gone, gone,— sold and gone,
　To the rice swamp dank and lone,
　From Virginia's hills and waters;
　Woe is me, my stolen daughters!

Gone, gone, — sold and gone,
  To the rice swamp dank and lone.
Oh, when weary, sad, and slow,
From the fields at night they go,
Faint with toil, and racked with pain,
To their cheerless homes again,
There no brother's voice shall greet them,
There no father's welcome meet them.
  Gone, gone, — sold and gone,
    To the rice swamp dank and lone,
    From Virginia's hills and waters;
    Woe is me, my stolen daughters!

Gone, gone, — sold and gone,
  To the rice swamp dank and lone.
From the tree whose shadow lay
On their childhood's place of play;
From the cool spring where they drank;
Rock, and hill, and rivulet bank;
From the solemn house of prayer,
And the holy counsels there;
  Gone, gone, — sold and gone,
    To the rice swamp dank and lone,
    From Virginia's hills and waters;
    Woe is me, my stolen daughters!

Gone, gone, — sold and gone,
  To the rice swamp dank and lone;
Toiling through the weary day,
And at night the spoiler's prey.
Oh, that they had earlier died,
Sleeping calmly, side by side,
Where the tyrant's power is o'er,
And the fetter galls no more!
  Gone, gone, — sold and gone,
    To the rice swamp dank and lone,
    From Virginia's hills and waters;
    Woe is me, my stolen daughters!

Gone, gone, — sold and gone,
  To the rice swamp dank and lone.
By the holy love He beareth;
By the bruisèd reed He spareth;
Oh, may He, to whom alone
All their cruel wrongs are known,
Still their hope and refuge prove,
With a more than mother's love.
  Gone, gone, — sold and gone,
    To the rice swamp dank and lone,
    From Virginia's hills and waters;
    Woe is me, my stolen daughters!

1838

80.

J. J. FLOURNOY: Black Workers and White Labor

Southern slaveholders frequently trained their slaves in a trade and then hired them out to city employers by the month or the year. The rates paid for such labor were considerably less than the wages that white laborers, who had to support themselves, could afford to accept. By the time of the Civil War, skilled black labor had almost entirely replaced skilled white labor in many Southern cities. The following protest, addressed to the contractors for mason's and carpenter's work of Athens, Georgia, appeared in the local paper in January 1838.

Source: *Southern Banner*, January 13, 1838 [Commons, II, pp. 360-361].

I DESIRE YOUR CANDID CONSIDERATION of the views I shall here express. I ask no reply to them except at your own volition. I am aware that most of you have too strong antipathy to encourage the masonry and carpentry trades of your poor white brothers, that your predilections for giving employment in your line of business to ebony workers have either so cheapened the white man's labor, or expatriated hence, with but a few solitary exceptions, all the white masons and carpenters of this town.

The white man is the only real, legal, moral, and civil proprietor of this country and state. The right of his proprietorship reaches from the date of the studies of those white men Copernicus and Galileo, who indicated from the seclusion of their closets the sphericity of the earth; which sphericity hinted to another white man, Columbus, the possibility, by a westerly course of sailing, of finding land. Hence, by white man alone was this continent discovered; by the prowess of white men alone (though not always properly or humanely exercised) were the fierce and active Indians driven occidentally. And if swarms and hordes of infuriated red men pour down now from the Northwest, like the wintry blast thereof, the white men alone, aye, those to whom you decline to give money for bread and clothes for their famishing families, in the logic matter of withholding work from them, or employing Negroes, in the sequel, to cheapen their wages to a rate that amounts to a moral and physical impossibility for them, either to live here and support their families — would bare their breasts to the keen and whizzing shafts of the savage crusaders — defending Negroes too in the bargain, for if left to themselves without our aid, the Indians would or can sweep the Negroes hence, "as dewdrops are shaken from the lion's mane."

The right, then, gentlemen, you will no doubt candidly admit, of the white man to employment in preference to Negroes, who *must* defer to us since they live well enough on plantations, cannot be considered impeachable by contractors. It is a right more virtual and indisputable than that of agrarianism. As masters of the polls in a majority, carrying all before them, I am surprised the poor do not elect faithful members to the legislature, who will make it penal to prefer Negro mechanic labor to white men's. But of the premises as I have now laid them down, you will candidly judge for yourselves, and draw a conclusion with me, that white bricklayers and house joiners must henceforward have ample work and remuneration; and yourselves and other contractors will set the example and pursue it for the future without deviation.

81.

Mass Appeal of African Americans, Threatened with Disfranchisement

The original constitutions of most of the states were silent on the question of African American franchise. But, beginning in the 1820s, black voting rights were abrogated or severely curtailed, even in the Northern states, and most notably in New York, Ohio, New Jersey, and Pennsylvania. The action of the Pennsylvania Reform Convention of 1837 restricting the suffrage to white men was based on a decision by the state's Supreme Court (Fogg v. Hobbs, 1837) that African Americans were not freemen and therefore could not vote. Neither the many petitions against the change nor a mass protest meeting held in Philadelphia on March 14, 1838 (which produced the pamphlet reprinted below), could prevent disfranchisement.

Source: *Appeal of Forty Thousand Citizens, Threatened with Disfranchisement to the People of Pennsylvania,* Philadelphia, 1838.

WE APPEAL TO YOU from the decision of the "Reform Convention," which has stripped us of a right peaceably enjoyed during forty-seven years under the constitution of this commonwealth. We honor Pennsylvania and her noble institutions too much to part with our birthright, as her free citizens, without a struggle. To all her citizens the right of suffrage is valuable in proportion as she is free; but surely there are none who can so ill afford to spare it as ourselves.

Was it the intention of the people of this commonwealth that the convention to which the constitution was committed for revision and amendment should tear up and cast away its first principles? Was it made the business of the convention to deny "that all men are born equally free," by making political rights depend upon the skin in which a man is born or to divide what our fathers bled to unite, to wit, TAXATION and REPRESENTATION?

We will not allow ourselves for one moment to suppose that the majority of the people of Pennsylvania are not too respectful of the rights and too liberal toward the feelings of others, as well as too much enlightened to their own interests, to deprive of the right of suffrage a single individual who may safely be trusted with it. And we cannot believe that you have found among those who bear the burdens of taxation any who have proved, by their abuse of the right, that it is not safe in their hands. This is a question, fellow citizens, in which we plead *your* cause as well as our own. It is the safeguard of the strongest that he lives under a government which is obliged to respect the voice of the weakest.

When you have taken from an individual his right to vote, you have made the government, in regard to him, a mere despotism; and you have taken a step toward making it a despotism to all. To your women and children, their inability to vote at the polls may be no evil, because they are united by consanguinity and affection with those who can do it. To foreigners and paupers, the want of the right may be tolerable, because a little time or labor will make it theirs. They are candidates for the privilege, and hence substantially enjoy its benefits.

But when a distinct class of the community, already sufficiently the objects of prejudice, are wholly and forever disfranchised and excluded, to the remotest posterity, from the possibility of a voice in regard to the laws under which they are to live, it is the same thing as if their abode were transferred to the dominions of the Russian autocrat or of the Grand Turk. They have lost

their check upon oppression, their wherewith to buy friends, their panoply of manhood; in short, they are thrown upon the mercy of a despotic majority. Like every other despot, this despot majority will believe in the mildness of its own sway; but who will the more willingly submit to it for that?

To us, our right under the constitution has been more precious and our deprivation of it will be the more grievous, because our expatriation has come to be a darling project with many of our fellow citizens. Our abhorrence of a scheme which comes to us in the guise of Christian benevolence, and asks us to suffer ourselves to be transplanted to a distant and barbarous land, *because we are a "nuisance" in this,* is not more deep and thorough than it is reasonable. We love our native country, much as it has wronged us; and in the peaceable exercise of our inalienable rights, we will cling to it.

The immortal Franklin and his fellow laborers in the cause of humanity have bound us to our homes here with chains of gratitude. We are PENNSYLVANIANS, and we hope to see the day when Pennsylvania will have reason to be proud of us, as we believe she has now none to be ashamed! Will you starve our patriotism? Will you cast our hearts out of the treasury of the commonwealth? Do you count our enmity better than our friendship?

Fellow citizens, we entreat you, in the name of fair dealing, to look again at the just and noble charter of Pennsylvania freedom, which you are asked to narrow down to the lines of caste and color. The constitution reads as follows:

Article 3, paragraph 1. In elections by the citizens, every freeman of the age of twenty-one years, having resided in the state two years next before the election, and within that time paid a state or county tax, which shall have been assessed at least six months before the election, shall enjoy the rights of an elector, etc.

This clause guarantees the right of suffrage to us as fully as to any of our fellow citizens whatsoever, for:

1. Such was the intention of the framers. In the original draft, reported by a committee of nine, the word "WHITE"stood before "FREEMAN." On motion of Albert Gallatin it was stricken out, for the express purpose of including colored citizens within the pale of the elective franchise. . . .

2. We are CITIZENS. This, we believe, would never have been denied had it not been for the scheme of expatriation to which we have already referred. But as our citizenship has been doubted by some who are not altogether unfriendly to us, we beg leave to submit some proof, which we think you will not hastily set aside.

We were regarded as *citizens* by those who drew up the Articles of Confederation between the states in 1778. The fourth of the said articles contains the following language: "The free inhabitants of each of these states, paupers, vagabonds, and fugitives from justice excepted, shall be entitled to all privileges and immunities of free *citizens* in the several states." That we were not excluded under the phrase "paupers, vagabonds, and fugitives from justice" any more than our white countrymen is plain from the debates that preceded the adoption of the article. For, on the 25th of June, 1778, "the delegates from South Carolina moved the following amendment *in behalf of their state*. In Article 4, between the words *free* inhabitants, insert *white*. Decided in the negative; ayes, two states; nays, eight states; one state divided." Such was the solemn decision of the revolutionary Congress, concurred in by the entire delegation from our own commonwealth.

On the adoption of the present Constitution of the United States, no change was made as to the rights of citizenship. This is explicitly proved by the *Journal* of Congress. Take, for example, the following resolution passed in the House of Representatives, December 21, 1803: "On motion; *Resolved*, that the Committee appointed to inquire and report whether any further provisions are necessary for the more effectual protection of American seamen do inquire into the expediency of granting protections to such American seamen, *citizens of the United States*, as *are free persons of color*, and that they report by bill, or otherwise." —— *Journ. H. Rep.* 1st Sess., 8th Cong., p. 224.

Proofs might be multiplied. In almost every state we have been spoken of, either expressly or by implication, as *citizens*. In the very year before the adoption of the present constitution, 1789, the Pennsylvania Society for Promoting the Abolition of Slavery, etc., put forth an address, signed by Benjamin Franklin, President, in which they stated one of their objects to be, "to *qualify* those who have been restored to freedom, for the exercise and enjoyment of CIVIL LIBERTY." The Convention of 1790, by striking out the word "WHITE," fixed the same standard of *qualification* for all; and, in fact, granted and guaranteed "civil liberty" to all who possessed that qualification. Are we now to be told that the convention did not intend to include colored men, and that Benjamin Franklin did not know what he was about, forasmuch as it was impossible for a colored man to become a citizen of the commonwealth?

It may here be objected to us, that in point of fact we have lost by the recent decision of the [Pennsylvania] Supreme Court, in the case of *Fogg* v. *Hobbs*, whatever claim to the right of suffrage we may have had under the constitution of 1790; and hence have no reason to oppose the amended constitution. Not so. We hold our rights under the present constitution none the cheaper for that decision. The section already cited gives us all that we ask, all that we can conceive it in the power of language to convey.

Reject, fellow citizens, the partial, disfranchising constitution offered you by the Reform Convention, and we shall confidently expect that the Supreme Court will do us the justice and itself the honor to retract its decision. Should it not, our appeal will still be open to the conscience and common sense of the people, who through their chief magistrate and a majority of two-thirds of both branches of the legislature may make way to the bench of the Supreme Court for expounders of the constitution who will not do violence to its most sacred and fundamental principles.

We cannot forbear here to refer you to some points in the published opinion of the court as delivered by Chief Justice Gibson, which we believe will go far to strip it of the weight and authority ordinarily conceded to the decision of the highest tribunal (save the elections) of this commonwealth.

1. The court relies much on a decision *said to have been had* "ABOUT" forty-three years ago, the claim of which to a place in the repository of Pennsylvania law is thus set forth by the court itself:

> About the year 1795, as I have it from James Gibson, Esq., of the Philadelphia bar, the very point before us was ruled by the High Court of Errors and Appeals against the right of Negro suffrage. Mr. Gibson declined an invitation to be concerned in the argument, and therefore has no memorandum of the cause to direct us to the record. I have had the office searched for it; but the papers had fallen into such disorder as to preclude a hope of its recovery. Most of them were imperfect, and many were lost or misplaced. *But Mr. Gibson's remembrance of the decision is perfect and entitled to full confidence.*

Now, suppressing doubt, and supposing such a decision actually to have emanated from the then highest tribunal of the commonwealth, does not the fact that it was so utterly forgotten as not to have regulated the polls within the memory of the present generation, nor to have been brought up

against us in the Reform Convention, prove that it was virtually retracted? And if retracted, is it now to be revived to the overthrow of rights enjoyed without contradiction during the average life of man?

2. The court argues that colored men are not *freemen*, and hence not entitled by the present constitution to vote, because under laws prior to the constitution there *might be* individuals who were not slaves, and yet were not *freemen!* The deduction is that as the word "freeman" was, *before* the present constitution, used in a restricted sense, it must have been used in the same sense *in* it. The correctness of this interpretation will be tested by substituting, in Article 3, Section 1, for the word "freeman" the meaning which the court chooses to have attached to it. This meaning appears from the passages cited by the court to be *an elector*. Making the substitution, the article reads, "In elections by the citizens, every *elector*, of the age of twenty-one years, etc., shall enjoy the right of an *elector*, etc." — a proposition which sheds a very faint light upon the question of the extent of the elective franchise, and from which it would appear that there may be electors who are *not* to enjoy the rights of electors.

But taking the less restricted term "citizen," which the court also seems to think of the same force with "freeman," the article will read more sensibly, that "In elections by the citizens, every *citizen* of the age of twenty-one," who has paid taxes, etc., "shall enjoy the right of an elector." To what evidence does the court refer to show that a *colored* man may not be a *citizen?* To none whatever. We have too much respect for old Pennsylvania to believe that such puerile absurdity can become her fixed and irreversible law.

3. Since the argument above referred to, such as it is, does not rest upon color, it is not less applicable to the descendants of Irish and German ancestors than to ourselves. If there ever have been within the

commonwealth men, or sets of men, who though personally free were not technically *freemen,* it is unconstitutional, according to the doctrine of the court, for their descendants to exercise the right of suffrage, pay what taxes they may, till in "the discretion of the judges" their blood has "become so diluted in successive descents as to lose its distinctive character." Is this the doctrine of Pennsylvania freedom?

4. Lastly, the court openly rests its decision on the authority of a wrong which this commonwealth so long ago as 1780 solemnly acknowledged, and, to the extent of its power, forever repealed. To support the same *wrong* in *other states,* the constitution of *this,* when it uses the words "every freeman," must be understood to exclude every freeman of a certain color! The court is of opinion that the people of this commonwealth had no power to confer the rights of citizenship upon one who, were he in another state, *might be* loaded by its laws with "countless disabilities." Now, since in some of the states, men may be found in slavery who have not the slightest trace of African blood, it is difficult to see, on the doctrine of the court, how the constitution of Pennsylvania could confer the right of citizenship upon any person; and, indeed, how it could have allowed the emancipation of slaves of any color. To such vile dependence on its own ancient *wrongs,* and on the present *wrongs* of other states, is Pennsylvania reduced by this decision!

Are we then presumptuous in the hope that this grave sentence will be as incapable of resurrection fifty years hence as is that which the chief justice assures us was pronounced "*about* the year 1795"? No. The blessings of the broad and impartial charter of Pennsylvania rights can no more be wrested from us by legal subtlety than the beams of our common sun or the breathing of our common air.

What have we done to forfeit the inestimable benefits of this charter? Why should taxpaying colored men, any more than other taxpayers, be deprived of the right of voting for their representatives? It was said in the convention that this government belongs to the *whites.* We have already shown this to be false as to the past. Those who established our present government designed it equally for all. It is for you to decide whether it shall be confined to the European complexion in future.

Why should you exclude us from a fair participation in the benefits of the republic? Have we oppressed the whites? Have we used our rights to the injury of any class? Have we disgraced it by receiving bribes? Where are the charges written down, and who will swear to them? We challenge investigation. We put it to the conscience of every Pennsylvanian, whether there is, or ever has been, in the commonwealth, either a political party or religious sect which has less deserved than ourselves to be thus disfranchised. As to the charge of idleness, we fling it back indignantly. Whose brows have sweat for our livelihood but our own? As to vice, if it disqualifies us for civil liberty, why not apply the same rule to the whites, so far as they are vicious? Will you punish the innocent for the crimes of the guilty?

The execution of the laws is in the hands of the whites. If we are bad citizens let them apply the proper remedies. We do not ask the right of suffrage for the inmates of our jails and penitentiaries, but for those who honestly and industriously contribute to bear the burdens of the state. As to inferiority to the whites, if indeed we are guilty of it, either by nature or education, we trust our enjoyment of the rights of freemen will on that account be considered the less dangerous. If we are incompetent to fill the offices of state, it will be the fault of the whites only if we are suffered to disgrace them. We are in too feeble a minority to cherish a mischievous ambition. Fair protection is all that we aspire to.

We ask your attention, fellow citizens, to

facts and testimonies which go to show that, considering the circumstances in which we have been placed, our country has no reason to be ashamed of us, and that those have the most occasion to blush to whom nature has given the power.

By the careful inquiry of a committee appointed by the Pennsylvania Society for Promoting the Abolition of Slavery, it has been ascertained that the colored population of Philadelphia and its suburbs, numbering 18,768 souls, possess at the present time, of real and personal estate, not less than $1,350,000. They have paid for taxes during the last year $3,252.83; for house, water, and ground rent, $166,963.50. This committee estimate the income of the holders of real estate occupied by the colored people to be 7½ percent on a capital of about $2 million. Here is an addition to the wealth of their white brethren.

But the rents and taxes are not all; to pay them, the colored people must be employed in labor, and here is another profit to the whites, for no man employs another unless he can make his labor profitable to himself. For a similar reason, a profit is made by all the whites who sell to colored people the necessaries or luxuries of life. Though the aggregate amount of the wealth derived by the whites from our people can only be conjectured, its importance is worthy of consideration by those who would make it less by lessening our motive to accumulate for ourselves.

Nor is the profit derived from us counterbalanced by the sums which we in any way draw from the public treasures. From a statement published by order of the Guardians of the Poor of Philadelphia, in 1830, it appears that out of 549 outdoor poor relieved during the year, only 22 were persons of color, being about 4 percent of the whole number, while the ratio of our population to that of the city and suburbs exceeds 8¼ percent. By a note appended to the printed report above referred to, it ap-

pears that the colored *paupers* admitted into the almshouse for the same period did not exceed 4 percent of the whole. Thus it has been ascertained that they pay more than they receive in the support of their own poor. The various "mutual relief" societies of Philadelphia expend upward of $7,000 annually for the relief of their members when sick or disabled.

That we are not neglectful of our religious interests nor of the education of our children is shown by the fact that there are among us in Philadelphia, Pittsburgh, York, West Chester, and Columbia, 22 churches, 48 clergymen, 26 day schools, 20 Sabbath schools, 125 Sabbath school teachers, 4 literary societies, 2 public libraries, consisting of about 800 volumes, besides 8,333 volumes in private libraries, 2 tract societies, 2 Bible societies, and 7 temperance societies.

In other parts of the state we are confident our condition will compare very favorably with that in Philadelphia, although we are not furnished with accurate statistics.

Our fathers shared with yours the trials and perils of the wilderness. Among the facts which illustrate this, it is well known that the founder of your capital, from whom it bears the name of Harrisburg, was rescued by a *colored* man from a party of Indians who had captured and bound him to the stake for execution. In gratitude for this act, he *invited colored persons* to settle in his town, and offered them land on favorable terms. When our common country has been invaded by a foreign foe, colored men have hazarded their lives in its defense. Our fathers fought by the side of yours in the struggle which made us an independent republic.

Are we to be thus looked to for help in the "hour of danger," but trampled under foot in the time of peace? In which of the battles of the Revolution did not our fathers fight as bravely as yours for American liberty? Was it that their children might be disfranchised and loaded with insult that they endured the famine of Valley Forge and the horrors of the Jersey prison ship? Nay, among those from whom you are asked to wrench the birthright of CIVIL LIBERTY are those who themselves shed their blood on the snows of Jersey and faced British bayonets in the most desperate hour of the Revolution. . . .

Be it remembered, fellow citizens, that it is only for the *"industrious, peaceable, and useful"* part of the colored people that we plead. We would have the right of suffrage only as the reward of industry and worth. We care not how high the qualification be placed. All we ask is, that no man shall be excluded on account of his *color;* that the same rule shall be applied to all.

82.

WILLIAM ELLERY CHANNING AND ELLIS GRAY LORING: Petition on Behalf of Abner Kneeland

Abner Kneeland, a Jacksonian Democrat, was the founder of the First Society of Free Enquiry and publisher of the Boston Investigator. *In 1834 he was indicted for blasphemy. Three articles from the* Investigator *were cited in the charge, but only the one written by Kneeland was entered as evidence. Kneeland appealed his conviction and was tried three times by the Superior Court before being convicted again. (The verdict had political overtones for it appeared to support the Whig claim that the Democrats were atheists.) Finally, the case came before the state Supreme Court and in April 1838, Chief Justice Lemuel Shaw sentenced Kneeland to sixty days in jail. The petition reprinted here, requesting a pardon for Kneeland, was drawn up by William Ellery Channing and Ellis Gray Loring, and was signed by many others including Ralph Waldo Emerson, William Lloyd Garrison, Theodore Parker, and George Ripley. Kneeland finally served his sixty days.*

Source: William H. Channing, *The Life of William Ellery Channing*, 6th edition, Boston, 1899, pp. 504-505.

To His Excellency, the Governor of the Commonwealth of Massachusetts:

The undersigned respectfully represent that they are informed that Abner Kneeland, of the city of Boston, has been found guilty of the crime of blasphemy for having published in a certain newspaper called the *Boston Investigator*, his disbelief in the existence of God, in the following words: "Universalists believe in a god which I do not; but believe that their god, with all his

moral attributes (aside from nature itself) is nothing more than a chimera of their own imagination."

Your petitioners have learned, by an examination of the record and documents in the case made by one of their number, that the conviction of said Kneeland proceeded on the ground above stated. For though the indictment originally included two other publications, one of a highly irreverent, and the other of a grossly indecent, character, yet it appears by the report that, at the trial, the prosecuting officer mainly relied on the sentence above quoted, and that the judge who tried the case confined his charge wholly to stating the legal construction of its terms and the law applicable to it.

In these circumstances, the undersigned respectfully pray that Your Excellency will grant to the said Kneeland an unconditional pardon for the offense of which he has been adjudged guilty. And they ask this not from any sympathy with the convicted individual, who is personally unknown to most or all of them, nor from any approbation of the doctrines professed by him, which are believed by your petitioners to be as pernicious and degrading as they are false; but,

Because the punishment proposed to be inflicted is believed to be at variance with the spirit of our institutions and our age, and with the soundest expositions of those civil and religious rights which are at once founded in our nature and guaranteed by the constitutions of the United States and this Commonwealth;

Because the freedom of speech and the press is the chief instrument of the progress of truth and of social improvements, and is never to be restrained by legislation, except when it invades the rights of others or instigates to specific crimes;

Because, if opinion is to be subjected to penalties, it is impossible to determine where punishment shall stop, there being few or no opinions in which an adverse party may not see threatenings of ruin to the state;

Because truths essential to the existence of society must be so palpable as to need no protection from the magistrate;

Because the assumption by government of a right to prescribe or repress opinions has been the ground of the grossest depravations of religion and of the most grinding despotisms;

Because religion needs no support from penal law, and is grossly dishonored by interpositions for its defense, which imply that it cannot be trusted to its own strength and to the weapons of reason and persuasion in the hands of its friends;

Because, by punishing infidel opinions, we shake one of the strongest foundations of faith, namely, the evidence which arises to religion from the fact that it stands firm and gathers strength amid the severest and most unfettered investigations of its claims;

Because error of opinion is never so dangerous as when goaded into fanaticism by persecution, or driven by threatenings to the use of secret arts;

Because it is well known that the most licentious opinions have, by a natural reaction, sprung up in countries where the laws have imposed severest restraint on thought and discussion;

Because the influence of hurtful doctrines is often propagated by the sympathy which legal severities awaken toward their supporters;

Because we are unwilling that a man whose unhappy course has drawn on him general disapprobation should, by a sentence of the law, be exalted into a martyr or become identified with the sacred cause of freedom; and, lastly,

Because we regard with filial jealousy the honor of this Commonwealth and are unwilling that it should be exposed to reproach, as clinging obstinately to illiberal principles, which the most enlightened minds have exploded.

83.

ABRAHAM LINCOLN: The Danger to Our Liberty

On January 27, 1838, Lincoln, then twenty-eight, addressed the Young Men's Lyceum of Springfield, Illinois, on "The Perpetuation of Our Political Institutions." The speech was partially inspired by the mob-killing of the Abolitionist, Elijah P. Lovejoy, at nearby Alton, Illinois, not quite three months before. Much in the style and spirit of the speech anticipates Lincoln's later writings.

Source: Nicolay-Hay, I, pp. 35-50.

AS A SUBJECT FOR THE REMARKS of the evening, the perpetuation of our political institutions is selected.

In the great journal of things happening under the sun, we, the American people, find our account running, under date of the nineteenth century of the Christian era. We find ourselves in the peaceful possession of the fairest portion of the earth, as regards extent of territory, fertility of soil, and salubrity of climate. We find ourselves under the government of a system of political institutions, conducing more essentially to the ends of civil and religious liberty, than any of which the history of former times tells us. We, when mounting the stage of existence, found ourselves the legal inheritors of these fundamental blessings. We toiled not in the acquirement or establishment of them; they are a legacy bequeathed us, by a once hardy, brave, and patriotic, but now lamented and departed race of ancestors. Theirs was the task (and nobly they performed it) to possess themselves, and through themselves, us, of this goodly land; and to uprear upon its hills and its valleys a political edifice of liberty and equal rights; 'tis ours only to transmit these, the former, unprofaned by the foot of an invader; the latter, undecayed by the lapse of time and untorn by usurpation, to the latest generation that fate shall permit the world to know. This task of gratitude to our fathers, justice to ourselves, duty to posterity, and love for our species in general, all imperatively require us faithfully to perform.

How, then, shall we perform it? At what point shall we expect the approach of danger? By what means shall we fortify against it? Shall we expect some transatlantic military giant to step the ocean and crush us at a blow? Never! All the armies of Europe, Asia, and Africa combined, with all the treasure of the earth (our own excepted) in their military chest, with a Bonaparte for a commander, could not by force take a drink from the Ohio, or make a track on the Blue Ridge, in a trial of a thousand years.

At what point then is the approach of danger to be expected? I answer, if it ever reach us, it must spring up among us. It cannot come from abroad. If destruction be our lot, we must ourselves be its author and finisher. As a nation of freemen, we must live through all time or die by suicide.

I hope I am overwary; but if I am not,

there is, even now, something of ill omen among us. I mean the increasing disregard for law which pervades the country; the growing disposition to substitute the wild and furious passions, in lieu of the sober judgment of courts; and the worse than savage mobs, for the executive ministers of justice. This disposition is awfully fearful in any community; and that it now exists in ours, though grating to our feelings to admit, it would be a violation of truth and an insult to our intelligence to deny. Accounts of outrages committed by mobs form the everyday news of the times. They have pervaded the country, from New England to Louisiana; they are neither peculiar to the eternal snows of the former nor the burning suns of the latter; they are not the creature of climate, neither are they confined to the slaveholding or the nonslaveholding states. Alike, they spring up among the pleasure hunting masters of Southern slaves, and the order-loving citizens of the land of steady habits. Whatever, then, their cause may be, it is common to the whole country.

It would be tedious as well as useless to recount the horrors of all of them. Those happening in the state of Mississippi and at St. Louis are, perhaps, the most dangerous in example, and revolting to humanity. In the Mississippi case, they first commenced by hanging the regular gamblers — a set of men certainly not following for a livelihood a very useful or very honest occupation; but one which, so far from being forbidden by the laws, was actually licensed by an act of the legislature, passed but a single year before. Next, Negroes, suspected of conspiring to raise an insurrection, were caught up and hanged in all parts of the state; then, white men, supposed to be leagued with the Negroes; and finally, strangers, from neighboring states, going thither on business, were, in many instances, subjected to the same fate. Thus went on this process of hanging, from gamblers to Negroes, from Negroes to white citizens, and from these to strangers; till dead men were seen literally dangling from the boughs of trees upon every roadside; and in numbers almost sufficient to rival the native Spanish moss of the country, as a drapery of the forest.

Turn, then, to that horror-striking scene at St. Louis. A single victim was only sacrificed there. His story is very short, and is, perhaps, the most highly tragic of anything of its length that has ever been witnessed in real life. A mulatto man, by the name of McIntosh, was seized in the street, dragged to the suburbs of the city, chained to a tree, and actually burned to death; and all within a single hour from the time he had been a freeman, attending to his own business, and at peace with the world.

Such are the effects of mob law; and such are the scenes becoming more and more frequent in this land so lately famed for love of law and order; and the stories of which have even now grown too familiar to attract anything more than an idle remark.

But you are, perhaps, ready to ask, "What has this to do with the perpetuation of our political institutions?" I answer, it has much to do with it. Its direct consequences are, comparatively speaking, but a small evil; and much of its danger consists in the proneness of our minds to regard its direct as its only consequences. Abstractly considered, the hanging of the gamblers at Vicksburg was of but little consequence. They constitute a portion of population that is worse than useless in any community; and their death, if no pernicious example be set by it, is never matter of reasonable regret with anyone. If they were annually swept from the stage of existence by the plague or smallpox, honest men would, perhaps, be much profited by the operation.

Similar, too, is the correct reasoning in regard to the burning of the Negro at St. Louis. He had forfeited his life by the perpetration of an outrageous murder upon one of the most worthy and respectable citizens of the city; and had he not died as he did, he must have died by the sentence of the law in a very short time afterward. As to him alone, it was as well the way it was, as it could otherwise have been. But the example in either case was fearful.

When men take it in their heads today to hang gamblers, or burn murderers, they should recollect that, in the confusion usually attending such transactions, they will be as likely to hang or burn someone who is neither a gambler nor a murderer as one who is; and that, acting upon the example they set, the mob of tomorrow may, and probably will, hang or burn some of them by the very same mistake. And not only so; the innocent, those who have ever set their faces against violations of law in every shape, alike with the guilty, fall victims to the ravages of mob law; and thus it goes on, step by step, till all the walls erected for the defense of the persons and property of individuals are trodden down and disregarded. But all this even is not the full extent of the evil. By such examples, by instances of the perpetrators of such acts going unpunished, the lawless in spirit are encouraged to become lawless in practice; and having been used to no restraint but dread of punishment, they thus become absolutely unrestrained. Having ever regarded government as their deadliest bane, they make a jubilee of the suspension of its operations; and pray for nothing so much as its total annihilation.

While, on the other hand, good men, men who love tranquillity, who desire to abide by the laws and enjoy their benefits, who would gladly spill their blood in the defense of their country, seeing their property destroyed; their families insulted and their lives endangered; their persons injured; and seeing nothing in prospect that forebodes a change for the better, become tired of, and disgusted with, a government that offers them no protection; and are not much averse to a change in which they imagine they have nothing to lose. Thus, then, by the operation of this mobocratic spirit, which all must admit is now abroad in the land, the strongest bulwark of any government, and particularly of those constituted like ours, may effectually be broken down and destroyed — I mean the attachment of the people.

Whenever this effect shall be produced among us; whenever the vicious portion of population shall be permitted to gather in bands of hundreds and thousands, and burn churches, ravage and rob provision stores, throw printing presses into rivers, shoot editors, and hang and burn obnoxious persons at pleasure, and with impunity — depend on it, this government cannot last. By such things, the feelings of the best citizens will become more or less alienated from it; and thus it will be left without friends, or with too few, and those few too weak to make their friendship effectual. At such a time and under such circumstances, men of sufficient talent and ambition will not be wanting to seize the opportunity, strike the blow, and overturn that fair fabric which for the last half century has been the fondest hope of the lovers of freedom throughout the world.

I know the American people are much attached to their government; I know they would suffer much for its sake; I know they would endure evils long and patiently before they would ever think of exchanging it for another. Yet, notwithstanding all this, if the laws be continually despised and disregarded, if their rights to be secure in their persons and property are held by no better tenure than the caprice of a mob, the alienation of their affections from the government is the natural consequence; and to that, sooner or later, it must come.

Here then, is one point at which danger may be expected.

The question recurs: "How shall we fortify against it?" The answer is simple. Let every American, every lover of liberty, every well-wisher to his posterity, swear by the blood of the Revolution never to violate in the least particular the laws of the country; and never to tolerate their violation by others. As the patriots of '76 did to the support of the Declaration of Independence, so to the support of the Constitution and laws, let every American pledge his life, his property, and his sacred honor; let every man remember that to violate the law is to trample on the blood of his father and to tear the character of his own and of his children's liberty. Let reverence for the laws be breathed by every American mother to the lisping babe that prattles on her lap; let it be taught in schools, in seminaries, and in colleges; let it be written in primers, spelling books, and in almanacs; let it be preached from the pulpit, proclaimed in legislative halls, and enforced in courts of justice. And, in short, let it become the *political religion* of the nation; and let the old and the young, the rich and the poor, the grave and the gay, of all sexes and tongues, and colors and conditions, sacrifice unceasingly upon its altars.

While ever a state of feeling such as this shall universally, or even very generally, prevail throughout the nation, vain will be every effort and fruitless every attempt to subvert our national freedom.

When I so pressingly urge a strict observance of all the laws, let me not be understood as saying there are no bad laws, or that grievances may not arise for the redress of which no legal provisions have been made. I mean to say no such thing. But I do mean to say that, although bad laws, if they exist, should be repealed as soon as possible, still while they continue in force, for the sake of example, they should be religiously observed. So also in unprovided cases. If such arise, let proper legal provisions be made for them with the least possible delay; but, till then, let them, if not too intolerable, be borne with.

There is no grievance that is a fit object of redress by mob law. In any case that may arise, as for instance, the promulgation of abolitionism, one of two positions is necessarily true; that is, the thing is right within itself, and therefore deserves the protection of all law and all good citizens; or, it is wrong, and therefore proper to be prohibited by legal enactments; and in neither case is the interposition of mob law either necessary, justifiable, or excusable.

But, it may be asked, why suppose danger to our political institutions? Have we not preserved them for more than fifty years? And why may we not for fifty times as long?

We hope there is no sufficient reason. We hope all dangers may be overcome; but to conclude that no danger may ever arise would itself be extremely dangerous. There are now, and will hereafter be, many causes, dangerous in their tendency, which have not existed heretofore, and which are not too insignificant to merit attention. That our government should have been maintained in its original form from its establishment until now is not much to be wondered at. It had many props to support it through that period, which now are decayed and crumbled away. Through that period it was felt by all to be an undecided experiment; now, it is understood to be a successful one. Then, all that sought celebrity and fame, and distinction, expected to find them in the success of that experiment. Their *all* was staked upon it: their destiny was inseparably linked with it. Their ambition aspired to display before an admiring world a practical demonstration of the truth of a proposition which had hitherto been considered, at best, no better than problematical; namely, the capability of a people to govern themselves. If they succeeded, they were to be immortalized; their names were to be transferred to counties and cities and rivers and mountains; and to be revered and sung, and toasted through all time. If they failed, they were to be called knaves and fools and fanatics for a fleeting hour; then to sink and be forgotten.

They succeeded. The experiment is successful; and thousands have won their deathless names in making it so. But the game is caught; and I believe it is true that with the catching end the pleasures of the chase. This field of glory is harvested, and the crop is already appropriated. But new reapers will arise, and they, too, will seek a field. It is to deny what the history of the world tells us is true, to suppose that men of ambition and talents will not continue to spring up among us. And when they do, they will as naturally seek the gratification of their ruling passion as others have done before them. The question, then, is, can that gratification be found in supporting and maintaining an edifice that has been erected by others? Most certainly it cannot. Many great and good men sufficiently qualified for any task they should undertake may ever be found, whose ambition would aspire to nothing beyond a seat in Congress, a gubernatorial or a presidential chair; but such belong not to the family of the lion or the tribe of the eagle.

What! Think you these places would satisfy an Alexander, a Caesar, or a Napoleon? Never! Towering genius disdains a beaten path. It seeks regions hitherto unexplored. It sees no distinction in adding story to story upon the monuments of fame erected to the memory of others. It denies that it is glory enough to serve under any chief. It scorns to tread in the footsteps of any predecessor, however illustrious. It thirsts and burns for distinction; and, if possible, it will have it, whether at the expense of emancipating slaves or enslaving freemen. Is it unreasonable, then, to expect that some man possessed of the loftiest genius, coupled with ambition sufficient to push it to its utmost stretch, will at some time spring up among us? And when such a one does, it will require the people to be united with each other, attached to the government and laws, and generally intelligent to successfully frustrate his designs.

Distinction will be his paramount object; and although he would as willingly, perhaps more so, acquire it by doing good as harm, yet, that opportunity being past, and nothing left to be done in the way of building up, he would set boldly to the task of pulling down.

Here, then, is a probable case, highly dangerous, and such a one as could not have well existed heretofore.

Another reason which once was, but which, to the same extent, is now no more, has done much in maintaining our institutions thus far. I mean the powerful influence which the interesting scenes of the Revolution had upon the passions of the people as distinguished from their judgment. By this influence, the jealousy, envy, and avarice, incident to our nature and so common to a state of peace, prosperity, and conscious strength, were, for the time, in a great measure smothered and rendered inactive; while the deep-rooted principles of hate and the powerful motive of revenge, instead of being turned against each other, were directed exclusively against the British nation. And thus, from the force of circumstances, the basest principles of our nature were either made to lie dormant or to become the active agents in the advancement of the noblest of causes — that of establishing and maintaining civil and religious liberty.

But this state of feeling must fade, is fading, had faded, with the circumstances that produced it.

I do not mean to say that the scenes of the Revolution are now or ever will be entirely forgotten, but that, like everything else, they must fade upon the memory of the world and grow more and more dim by the lapse of time. In history, we hope, they will be read of and recounted so long as the Bible shall be read; but even granting that they will, their influence cannot be what it heretofore has been. Even then, they cannot be so universally known, nor so vividly felt, as they were by the generation just gone to rest. At the close of that struggle, nearly every adult male had been a participator in some of its scenes. The consequence was that of those scenes, in the form of a husband, a father, a son or a brother, a living history was to be found in every family; a history bearing the indubitable testimonies of its own authenticity, in the limbs mangled, in the scars of wounds received, in the midst of the very scenes related; a history, too, that could be read and understood alike by all, the wise and the ignorant, the learned and the unlearned.

But those histories are gone. They can be read no more forever. They were a fortress of strength; but, what invading foemen could never do the silent artillery of time has done; the leveling of its walls. They are gone. They were a forest of giant oaks; but the all-resistless hurricane has swept over them and left only, here and there, a lonely trunk, despoiled of its verdure, shorn of its foliage; unshading and unshaded, to murmur in a few more gentle breezes, and to combat with its mutilated limbs a few more ruder storms, then to sink and be no more.

They were the pillars of the temple of liberty; and now that they have crumbled away, that temple must fall, unless we, their descendants, supply their places with other pillars, hewn from the solid quarry of sober reason. Passion has helped us but can do so no more. It will in future be our enemy. Reason — cold, calculating, unimpassioned reason — must furnish all the materials for our future support and defense. Let those materials be molded into general intelligence, sound morality, and, in particular, a reverence for the Constitution and laws; and, that we improved to the last; that we remained free to the last; that we revered his name to the last; that, during his long sleep, we permitted no hostile foot to pass over or desecrate his resting place, shall be that which to learn the last trump shall awaken our Washington.

Upon these let the proud fabric of freedom rest as the rock of its basis; and as truly as has been said of the only greater institution, "The gates of hell shall not prevail against it."

84.

WILLIAM LLOYD GARRISON: Declarations of a Peace Convention

Societies dedicated to the avoidance of war were formed in New York and Massachusetts in 1815 and, shortly thereafter, in a number of other states. The local societies coalesced in 1828 into the American Peace Society which cooperated with peace societies throughout Europe. Within the American Peace Society a split developed between those who sanctioned defensive wars and those who would tolerate no war at all. When the society refused to condemn war without qualification, the dissidents walked out. William Lloyd Garrison led the splinter group that in 1838 formed the New England Non-Resistance Society. Its charter convention, held September 18-20, adopted Garrison's Declaration of Sentiments, which follows. Although the society declined after ten years, the sentence "Our country is the world, our countrymen are all mankind" was used as the slogan for the School Peace League that formed in the second decade of the twentieth century.

Source: *William Lloyd Garrison, The Story of His Life Told by His Children,* New York, 1885-1889, Vol. II, pp. 230-232.

ASSEMBLED IN CONVENTION from various sections of the American Union for the promotion of peace on earth and goodwill among men, we, the undersigned, regard it as due to ourselves, to the cause which we love, to the country in which we live, and to the world to publish a *declaration,* expressive of the principles we cherish, the purposes we aim to accomplish, and the measures we shall adopt to carry forward the work of peaceful, universal reformation.

We cannot acknowledge allegiance to any human government; neither can we oppose any such government by a resort to physical force. We recognize but one King and Lawgiver, one Judge and Ruler of mankind. We are bound by the laws of a kingdom which is not of this world; the subjects of which are forbidden to fight; in which *mercy* and *truth* are met together, and *righteousness* and *peace* have kissed each other; which has no state lines, no national partitions, no geographical boundaries; in which there is no distinction of rank, or division of caste, or inequality of sex; the officers of which are *peace,* its exactors *righteousness,* its walls *salvation,* and its gates *praise;* and which is destined to break in pieces and consume all other kingdoms.

Our country is the world, our countrymen are all mankind. We love the land of our nativity only as we love all other lands. The interests, rights, liberties of American citizens are no more dear to us than are those of the whole human race. Hence, we can allow no appeal to patriotism to revenge any national insult or injury. The Prince of Peace, under whose stainless banner we rally, came not to destroy but to save even the worst of enemies. He has left us an example that we should follow his steps. *God commendeth His love toward us, in that while we were yet sinners, Christ died for us.*

We conceive that if a nation has no right to defend itself against foreign enemies, or to punish its invaders, no individual possesses that right in his own case. The unit cannot be of greater importance than the aggregate. If one man may take life to obtain or defend his rights, the same license must necessarily be granted to communities, states, and nations. If *he* may use a dagger or a pistol, *they* may employ cannon, bombshells, land and naval forces. The means of self-preservation must be in proportion to the magnitude of interests at stake and the number of lives exposed to destruction. But if a rapacious and bloodthirsty soldiery, thronging these shores from abroad with intent to commit rapine and destroy life, may not be resisted by the people or magistracy, then ought no resistance to be offered to domestic troublers of the public peace or of private security. No obligation can rest upon Americans to regard foreigners as more sacred in their persons than themselves, or to give them a monopoly of wrongdoing with impunity.

The dogma that all the governments of the world are approvingly ordained of God, and that *the powers that be* in the United States, in Russia, in Turkey are in accordance with His will, is not less absurd than impious. It makes the impartial Author of human freedom and equality unequal and tyrannical. It cannot be affirmed that *the powers that be*, in any nation, are actuated by the spirit or guided by the example of Christ in the treatment of enemies; therefore, they cannot be agreeable to the will of God; and therefore, their overthrow, by a spiritual regeneration of their subjects, is inevitable.

We register our testimony, not only against all wars, whether offensive or defensive, but all preparations for war; against every naval ship, every arsenal, every fortification; against the militia system and a standing army; against all military chieftains and soldiers; against all monuments commemorative of victory over a fallen foe, all trophies won in battle, all celebrations in honor of military or naval exploits; against all appropriations for the defense of a nation by force and arms on the part of any legislative body; against every edict of government requiring of its subjects military service. Hence, we deem it unlawful to bear arms or to hold a military office.

As every human government is upheld by physical strength and its laws are enforced virtually at the point of the bayonet, we cannot hold any office which imposes upon its incumbent the obligation to compel men to do right on pain of imprisonment or death. We, therefore, voluntarily exclude ourselves from every legislative and judicial body, and repudiate all human politics, worldly honors, and stations of authority. If *we* cannot occupy a seat in the legislature or on the bench, neither can we elect *others* to act as our substitutes in any such capacity.

It follows that we cannot sue any man at law to compel him by force to restore anything which he may have wrongfully taken from us or others; but if he has seized our coat, we shall surrender up our cloak rather than subject him to punishment.

We believe that the penal code of the old covenant, *an eye for an eye, and a tooth for a tooth*, has been abrogated by Jesus Christ; and that, under the new covenant, the forgiveness instead of the punishment of enemies has been enjoined upon all His disciples, in all cases whatsoever. To extort money from enemies, or set them upon a pillory, or cast them into prison, or hang them upon a gallows is obviously not to forgive, but to take retribution. VENGEANCE IS MINE — I WILL REPAY, SAITH THE LORD.

The history of mankind is crowded with evidences proving that physical coercion is not adapted to moral regeneration; that the sinful dispositions of men can be subdued only by love; that evil can be exterminated from the earth only by goodness; that it is not safe to rely upon an arm of flesh, upon man whose breath is in his nostrils, to preserve us from harm; that there is great security in being gentle, harmless, long-suffering, and abundant in mercy; that it is only the meek who shall inherit the earth, for the violent who resort to the sword are destined to perish with the sword.

Hence, as a measure of sound policy; of safety to property, life, and liberty; of public quietude and private enjoyment, as well as on the ground of allegiance to Him who is King of kings and Lord of lords, we cordially adopt the nonresistance principle; being confident that it provides for all possible consequences, will ensure all things needful to us, is armed with omnipotent power, and must ultimately triumph over every assailing force.

85.

Joseph Smith: A Pillar of Light

Joseph Smith founded the Church of Jesus Christ of the Latter-day Saints (also known as the Mormon Church) in New York in 1830. The following year he led a small band of followers on the first of several migrations and established a theocracy in Kirtland, Ohio. In the selection reprinted below, Smith reveals his impatience with the conflicting sectarian claims that had prompted him ten years before to seek out a strong source of authority. He describes his revelations and the subsequent search for and surrender of the Golden Plates. Smith published his translation of the Plates as The Book of Mormon *in 1830. The passage quoted here is taken from a book of Smith's early revelations and writings,* The Pearl of Great Price. The Pearl *and* The Book of Mormon, *together with the* Doctrine and Covenants *(1835) describing Smith's later revelations, and the Bible, constitute the authoritative works of Mormonism. Smith began work on* The Pearl *around 1838.*

Source: *The Pearl of Great Price*, Salt Lake City, 1907, pp. 83-96.

In process of time my mind became somewhat partial to the Methodist sect, and I felt some desire to be united with them; but so great were the confusion and strife among the different denominations, that it was impossible for a person young as I was, and so unacquainted with men and things, to come to any certain conclusion who was right and who was wrong.

My mind at times was greatly excited, the cry and tumult were so great and incessant. The Presbyterians were most decided against the Baptists and Methodists, and used all the powers of either reason or sophistry to prove their errors, or, at least, to make the people think they were in error. On the other hand, the Baptists and Methodists in their turn were equally zealous in endeavoring to establish their own tenets and disprove all others.

In the midst of this war of words and tumult of opinions, I often said to myself, What is to be done? Who of all these parties are right; or, are they all wrong together? If any one of them be right, which is it, and how shall I know it?

While I was laboring under the extreme difficulties caused by the contests of these parties of religionists, I was one day reading the Epistle of James, First Chapter and Fifth Verse, which reads: "If any of you lack wisdom, let him ask of God, that giveth to all men liberally, and upbraideth not; and it shall be given him."

Never did any passage of Scripture come with more power to the heart of man than this did at this time to mine. It seemed to enter with great force into every feeling of my heart. I reflected on it again and again, knowing that if any person needed wisdom from God, I did; for how to act I did not know, and unless I could get more wisdom than I then had, I would never know; for the teachers of religion of the different sects understood the same passages of Scripture so differently as to destroy all confidence in settling the question by an appeal to the Bible.

At length I came to the conclusion that I must either remain in darkness and confusion or else I must do as James directs, that is, ask of God. I at length came to the determination to "ask of God," concluding that if He gave wisdom to them that lacked wisdom, and would give liberally and not upbraid, I might venture.

So, in accordance with this, my determination to ask of God, I retired to the woods to make the attempt. It was on the morning of a beautiful, clear day, early in the spring of 1820. It was the first time in my life that I had made such an attempt, for, amidst all my anxieties, I had never as yet made the attempt to pray vocally.

After I had retired to the place where I had previously designed to go, having looked around me and finding myself alone, I kneeled down and began to offer up the desires of my heart to God. I had scarcely done so, when immediately I was seized upon by some power which entirely overcame me, and had such an astonishing influence over me as to bind my tongue so that I could not speak. Thick darkness gathered around me, and it seemed to me for a time as if I were doomed to sudden destruction.

But, exerting all my powers to call upon God to deliver me out of the power of this enemy which had seized upon me, and at the very moment when I was ready to sink into despair and abandon myself to destruction — not to an imaginary ruin, but to the power of some actual being from the unseen world who had such marvelous power as I had never before felt in any being — just at this moment of great alarm, I saw a pillar of light exactly over my head, above the brightness of the sun, which descended gradually, until it fell upon me.

It no sooner appeared than I found myself delivered from the enemy which held me bound. When the light rested upon me, I saw two personages, whose brightness and glory defy all description, standing above me in the air. One of them spake unto me, calling me by name, and said, pointing to the other — "This is my beloved Son, hear him!"

My object in going to inquire of the Lord was to know which of all the sects was right, that I might know which to join. No sooner, therefore, did I get possession of myself, so as to be able to speak, than I asked the personages who stood above me in the light which of all the sects was right, and which I should join.

I was answered that I must join none of them, for they were all wrong; and the personage who addressed me said that all their creeds were an abomination to his sight; that those professors were all corrupt; that "they draw near to me with their lips, but their hearts are far from me; they teach for doctrines the commandments of men, having a form of godliness, but they deny the power thereof."

He again forbade me to join with any of them; and many other things did he say

Joseph Smith

and fifteen years of age, and my circumstances in life such as to make a boy of no consequence in the world, yet men of high standing would take notice sufficient to excite the public mind against me, and create a bitter persecution; and this was common among all the sects — all united to persecute me. . . .

I had . . . got my mind satisfied so far as the sectarian world was concerned; that it was not my duty to join with any of them, but to continue as I was until further directed. I had found the testimony of James to be true, that a man who lacked wisdom might ask of God, and obtain, and not be upbraided.

I continued to pursue my common vocations in life until the 21st of September, 1823, all the time suffering severe persecution at the hands of all classes of men, both religious and irreligious, because I continued to affirm that I had seen a vision.

During the space of time which intervened between the time I had the vision and the year 1823 — having been forbidden to join any of the religious sects of the day, and being of very tender years, and persecuted by those who ought to have been my friends and to have treated me kindly, and if they supposed me to be deluded to have endeavored in a proper and affectionate manner to have reclaimed me — I was left to all kinds of temptations. And, mingling with all kinds of society, I frequently fell into many foolish errors and displayed the weakness of youth and the foibles of human nature; which, I am sorry to say, led me into diverse temptations, offensive in the sight of God.

In consequence of these things, I often felt condemned for my weakness and imperfections; when, on the evening of the above-mentioned 21st of September, after I had retired to my bed for the night, I betook myself to prayer and supplication to

unto me, which I cannot write at this time. When I came to myself again, I found myself lying on my back, looking up into Heaven.

Some few days after I had this vision, I happened to be in company with one of the Methodist preachers . . . and, conversing with him on the subject of religion, I took occasion to give him an account of the vision which I had had. I was greatly surprised at his behavior; he treated my communication not only lightly but with great contempt, saying it was all of the devil; that there were no such things as visions or revelations in these days; that all such things had ceased with the apostles; and that there would never be any more of them.

I soon found, however, that my telling the story had excited a great deal of prejudice against me among professors of religion and was the cause of great persecution, which continued to increase; and though I was an obscure boy, only between fourteen

Almighty God for forgiveness of all my sins and follies, and also for a manifestation to me, that I might know of my state and standing before Him; for I had full confidence in obtaining a divine manifestation, as I previously had one.

While I was thus in the act of calling upon God, I discovered a light appearing in my room, which continued to increase until the room was lighter than at noonday, when immediately a personage appeared at my bedside, standing in the air, for his feet did not touch the floor.

He had on a loose robe of most exquisite whiteness. It was a whiteness beyond anything earthly I had ever seen; nor do I believe that any earthly thing could be made to appear so exceedingly white and brilliant. His hands were naked, and his arms also, a little above the wrist; so, also, were his feet naked, as were his legs, a little above the ankles. His head and neck were also bare. I could discover that he had no other clothing on but this robe, as it was open, so that I could see into his bosom.

Not only was his robe exceedingly white but his whole person was glorious beyond description, and his countenance truly like lightning. The room was exceedingly light, but not so very bright as immediately around his person. When I first looked upon him, I was afraid; but the fear soon left me.

He called me by name and said unto me that he was a messenger sent from the presence of God to me, and that his name was Moroni; that God had a work for me to do; and that my name should be had for good and evil among all nations, kindreds, and tongues, or that it should be both good and evil spoken of among all people.

He said there was a book deposited, written upon gold plates, giving an account of the former inhabitants of this continent and the source from whence they sprang. He also said that the fullness of the everlasting gospel was contained in it, as delivered by the Savior to the ancient inhabitants. Also, that there were two stones in silver bows — and these stones, fastened to a breastplate, constituted what is called the Urim and Thummim — deposited with the plates; and the possession and use of these stones were what constituted "seers" in ancient or former times; and that God had prepared them for the purpose of translating the book. . . .

Again, he told me, that when I got those plates of which he had spoken — for the time that they should be obtained was not yet fulfilled — I should not show them to any person; neither the breastplate with the Urim and Thummim; only to those to whom I should be commanded to show them; if I did I should be destroyed. While he was conversing with me about the plates, the vision was opened to my mind that I could see the place where the plates were deposited, and that so clearly and distinctly that I knew the place again when I visited it.

After this communication, I saw the light in the room begin to gather immediately around the person of him who had been speaking to me, and it continued to do so, until the room was again left dark, except just around him; when instantly I saw, as it were, a conduit open right up into Heaven, and he ascended till he entirely disappeared; and the room was left as it had been before this heavenly light had made its appearance.

I lay musing on the singularity of the scene and marveling greatly at what had been told to me by this extraordinary messenger; when, in the midst of my meditation, I suddenly discovered that my room was again beginning to get lighted; and, in an instant, as it were, the same heavenly messenger was again by my bedside.

He commenced, and again related the very same things which he had done at his first visit, without the least variation; which having done, he informed me of great judgments which were coming upon the earth, with great desolations by famine, sword, and pestilence; and that these grievous judgments would come on the earth in this generation. Having related these things, he again ascended as he had done before.

By this time, so deep were the impressions made on my mind that sleep had fled from my eyes, and I lay overwhelmed in astonishment at what I had both seen and heard. But what was my surprise when again I beheld the same messenger at my bedside, and heard him rehearse or repeat over again to me the same things as before; and added a caution to me, telling me that Satan would try to tempt me (in consequence of the indigent circumstances of my father's family) to get the plates for the purpose of getting rich. This he forbade me, saying that I must have no other object in view in getting the plates but to glorify God, and must not be influenced by any other motive than that of building His kingdom; otherwise I could not get them.

After this third visit, he again ascended into Heaven as before, and I was again left to ponder on the strangeness of what I had just experienced; when almost immediately after the heavenly messenger had ascended from me for the third time, the cock crowed, and I found that day was approaching, so that our interviews must have occupied the whole of that night.

I shortly after arose from my bed, and, as usual, went to the necessary labors of the day; but, in attempting to work as at other times, I found my strength so exhausted as to render me entirely unable. My father, who was laboring along with me, discovered something to be wrong with me and told me to go home. I started with the intention of going to the house; but, in attempting to cross the fence out of the field where we were, my strength entirely failed me and I fell helpless on the ground, and

for a time was quite unconscious of anything.

The first thing that I can recollect was a voice speaking unto me, calling me by name. I looked up and beheld the same messenger standing over my head, surrounded by light as before. He then again related unto me all that he had related to me the previous night, and commanded me to go to my father and tell him of the vision and commandments which I had received.

I obeyed; I returned to my father in the field and rehearsed the whole matter to him. He replied to me that it was of God, and told me to go and do as commanded by the messenger. I left the field and went to the place where the messenger had told me the plates were deposited; and owing to the distinctness of the vision which I had had concerning it, I knew the place the instant that I arrived there.

Convenient to the village of Manchester, Ontario County, New York, stands a hill of considerable size, and the most elevated of any in the neighborhood. On the west side of this hill, not far from the top, under a stone of considerable size, lay the plates, deposited in a stone box. This stone was thick and rounding in the middle on the upper side and thinner toward the edges, so that the middle part of it was visible above the ground, but the edge all around was covered with earth.

Having removed the earth, I obtained a lever, which I got fixed under the edge of the stone, and with a little exertion raised it up. I looked in, and there indeed did I behold the plates, the Urim and Thummim, and the breastplate, as stated by the messenger. The box in which they lay was formed by laying stones together in some kind of cement. In the bottom of the box were laid two stones, crossways of the box, and on these stones lay the plates and the other things with them.

I made an attempt to take them out, but was forbidden by the messenger, and was again informed that the time for bringing them forth had not yet arrived, neither would it, until four years from that time. But he told me that I should come to that place precisely in one year from that time, and that he would there meet with me, and that I should continue to do so until the time should come for obtaining the plates. . . .

At length the time arrived for obtaining the plates, the Urim and Thummim, and the breastplate. On the 22nd day of September, 1827, having gone as usual at the end of another year to the place where they were deposited, the same heavenly messenger delivered them up to me with this charge: that I should be responsible for them; that if I should let them go carelessly, or through any neglect of mine, I should be cut off; but that if I would use all my endeavors to preserve them until he, the messenger, should call for them, they should be protected.

I soon found out the reason why I had received such strict charges to keep them safe, and why it was that the messenger had said that when I had done what was required at my hand, he would call for them. For no sooner was it known that I had them, than the most strenuous exertions were used to get them from me. Every stratagem that could be invented was resorted to for that purpose. The persecution became more bitter and severe than before, and multitudes were on the alert continually to get them from me if possible. But by

the wisdom of God, they remained safe in my hands, until I had accomplished by them what was required at my hand. When, according to arrangements, the messenger called for them, I delivered them up to him; and he has them in his charge until this day, being the 2nd day of May, 1838.

The excitement, however, still continued; and rumor, with her thousand tongues, was all the time employed in circulating falsehoods about my father's family and about myself. If I were to relate a thousandth part of them, it would fill up volumes. The persecution, however, became so intolerable that I was under the necessity of leaving Manchester and going with my wife to Susquehanna County, in the state of Pennsylvania. While preparing to start — being very poor, and the persecution so heavy upon us that there was no probability that we would ever be otherwise — in the midst of our afflictions we found a friend in a gentleman by the name of Martin Harris, who came to us and gave me $50 to assist us on our journey. Mr. Harris was a resident of Palmyra Township, Wayne County, in the state of New York, and a farmer of respectability.

By this timely aid was I enabled to reach the place of my destination in Pennsylvania; and immediately after my arrival there I commenced copying the characters off the plates. I copied a considerable number of them, and, by means of the Urim and Thummim, I translated some of them, which I did between the time I arrived at the house of my wife's father, in the month of December, and the February following.

86.

JAMES FENIMORE COOPER: The American Scene

Cooper ended his seven-year stay in Europe in 1833, returning to America four years after Jackson came to power. According to his own testimony, he was particularly struck by two elements of the Jacksonian "revolution": Political and social power had come, as he put it, into the hands of "the majority"; and the talented and propertied few were accepting the change without objection and in silence. The American Democrat *(1838), three chapters of which appear here, was Cooper's response to the situation as he saw it. Cooper was a confirmed and dedicated Democrat; but he found much in the new American Democracy to criticize, especially its failure to retain such traditional values as good taste, intellectual and artistic standards, and the moral excellence embodied in the concept "gentleman." Cooper was misunderstood by his contemporaries. as he has often been misunderstood since. He was attacked by both conservatives and radicals, and subjected to such public vituperation that he brought a number of libel suits. (He won most of them and in the process helped establish effective libel laws in American courts.)*

Source: *The American Democrat*, Cooperstown, N.Y., 1838, pp. 73-83, 94-98.

ON PREJUDICE

PREJUDICE IS THE CAUSE of most of the mistakes of bodies of men. It influences our conduct and warps our judgment in politics, religion, habits, tastes, and opinions. We confide in one statesman and oppose another as often from unfounded antipathies as from reason; religion is tainted with uncharitableness and hostilities, without examination; usages are contemned; tastes ridiculed; and we decide wrong from the practice of submitting to a preconceived and an unfounded prejudice, the most active and the most pernicious of all the hostile agents of the human mind.

The migratory propensities of the American people and the manner in which the country has been settled by immigrants from all parts of the Christian world have

an effect in diminishing prejudices of a particular kind, though, in other respects, few nations are more bigoted or provincial in their notions. Innovations on the usages connected with the arts of life are made here with less difficulty than common: reason, interest, and enterprise proving too strong for prejudice; but in morals, habits, and tastes few nations have less liberality to boast of than this.

America owes most of its social prejudices to the exaggerated religious opinions of the different sects which were so instrumental in establishing the colonies. The Quakers, or Friends, proscribed the delightful and elevated accomplishment of music, as, indeed, did the Puritans, with the exception of psalmody. The latter confined marriage ceremonies to the magistrates, lest religion should be brought into disrepute! Most of those innocent recreations which help the charities, and serve to meliorate manners, were also forbidden, until an unnatural and monastic austerity, with a caustic habit of censoriousness, got to be considered as the only outward signs of that religious hope which is so peculiarly adapted to render us joyous and benevolent.

False and extravagant notions on the subject of manners never fail to injure a sound morality by mistaking the shadow for the substance. Positive vice is known by all, for happily, conscience and revelation have made us acquainted with the laws of virtue, but it is as indiscreet unnecessarily to enlarge the circle of sins as it is to expose ourselves to temptations that experience has shown we are unable to resist.

The most obvious American prejudices connected with morality are the notions that prevail on the subject of misspending time. That time may be misspent is undeniable; and few are they who ought not to reproach themselves with this neglect, but the human mind needs relaxation and amusement, as well as the human body. These are to be sought in the different expedients of classes, each finding the most satisfaction in those indulgences that conform the nearest to their respective tastes. It is the proper duty of the legislator to endeavor to elevate these tastes and not to prevent their indulgence. Those nations in which the cord of moral discipline, according to the dogmas of fanatics, has been drawn the tightest usually exhibit the gravest scenes of depravity on the part of those who break loose from restraints so ill-judged and unnatural.

On the other hand, the lower classes of society, in nations where amusements are tolerated, are commonly remarkable for possessing some of the tastes that denote cultivation and refinement. Thus do we find in Catholic countries that the men who in Protestant nations would pass their leisure in the coarsest indulgences, frequent operas and theatrical representations, classes of amusements which, well-conducted, may be made powerful auxiliaries of virtue, and which generally have a tendency to improve the tastes. It is to be remarked that these exhibitions themselves are usually less gross and more intellectual in Catholic than in Protestant countries — a result of this improvement in manners.

The condition of this country is peculiar and requires greater exertions than common in extricating the mind from prejudices. The intimate connection between popular opinion and positive law is one reason, since under a union so close there is danger that the latter may be colored by motives that have no sufficient foundation in justice. It is vain to boast of liberty if the ordinances of society are to receive the impression of sectarianism, or of a provincial and narrow morality.

Another motive peculiar to the country, for freeing the mind from prejudice, is the mixed character of the population. Natives of different sections of the United States and of various parts of Europe are brought in close contact; and without a disposition to bear with each other's habits, association becomes unpleasant and enmities are engendered. The main result is to liberalize the mind, beyond a question. Yet we see neighborhoods in which oppressive intolerance is manifested by the greater number, for the time being, to the habits of the less. This is a sore grievance, more especially when, as is quite frequently the case, the minority happen to be in possession of usages that mark the highest stage of civilization.

It ought never to be forgotten, therefore, that every citizen is entitled to indulge, without comment or persecution, in all his customs and practices that are lawful and moral. Neither is morality to be regulated by the prejudices of sects or social classes, but it is to be left strictly to the control of the laws, Divine and human. To assume the contrary is to make prejudice, and prejudice of a local origin, too, more imperious than the institutions. The justice, not to say necessity, of these liberal concessions is rendered more apparent when we remember that the parties meet as emigrants on what may be termed neutral territory, for it would be the height of presumption for the native of New York, for instance, to insist on his own peculiar customs — customs that other portions of the country perhaps repudiate — within the territory of New England, in opposition not only to the wishes of many of their brother emigrants but to those of the natives themselves.

ON STATION

STATION MAY BE DIVIDED into that which is political, or public, and that which is social, or private. In monarchies and aristocracies the two are found united, since the higher classes, as a matter of course, monopolize all the offices of consideration; but in democracies, there is not, nor is it proper that there should be, any intimate connection between them.

Political, or public, station is that which is derived from office, and, in a democracy, must embrace men of very different degrees of leisure, refinement, habits, and knowledge. This is characteristic of the institutions which, under a popular government, confer on political station more power than rank, since the latter is expressly avoided in this system.

Social station is that which one possesses in the ordinary associations, and is dependent on birth, education, personal qualities, property, tastes, habits, and, in some instances, on caprice, or fashion. Although the latter undeniably is sometimes admitted to control social station, it generally depends, however, on the other considerations named.

Social station, in the main, is a consequence of property. So long as there is civilization there must be the rights of property, and so long as there are the rights of property, their obvious consequences must follow. All that democracies legitimately attempt is to prevent the advantages which accompany social station from accumulating rights that do not properly belong to the condition, which is effected by pronouncing that it shall have no factitious political aids.

They who have reasoned ignorantly, or who have aimed at effecting their personal ends by flattering the popular feeling, have boldly affirmed that "one man is as good as another"; a maxim that is true in neither nature, revealed morals, nor political theory.

That one man is not as good as another in natural qualities is proved on the testimony of our senses. One man is stronger than another; he is handsomer, taller, swifter, wiser, or braver than all his fellows. In short, the physical and moral qualities are unequally distributed, and, as a necessary consequence, in none of them can one man be justly said to be as good as another. Perhaps no two human beings can be found so precisely equal in everything that one shall not be pronounced the superior of the other; which, of course, establishes the fact that there is no natural equality.

The advocates of exclusive political privileges reason on this circumstance by assuming that, as nature has made differences between men, those institutions which create political orders are no more than carrying out the great designs of Providence. The error of their argument is in supposing it a confirmation of the designs of nature to attempt to supplant her; for, while the latter has rendered men unequal, it is not from male to male, according to the order of primogeniture, as is usually established by human ordinances. In order not to interfere with the inequality of nature, her laws must be left to their own operations, which is just what is done in democracies after a proper attention has been paid to the peace of society by protecting the weak against the strong.

That one man is not deemed as good as another in the grand moral system of Providence is revealed to us in Holy Writ, by the scheme of future rewards and punishments, as well as by the whole history of those whom God has favored in this world for their piety or punished for their rebellion. As compared with perfect holiness, all men are frail; but, as compared with each other, we are throughout the whole of sacred history made to see that, in a moral sense, one man is not as good as another. The evildoer is punished, while they who are distinguished for their qualities and acts are intended to be preferred.

The absolute moral and physical equality that is inferred by the maxim that "one man is as good as another" would at once do away with the elections, since a lottery would be both simpler, easier, and cheaper than the present mode of selecting representatives. Men, in such a case, would draw lots for office as they are now drawn for juries. Choice supposes a preference, and preference, inequality of merit or of fitness.

We are, then, to discard all visionary theories on this head and look at things as they are. All that the most popular institutions attempt is to prohibit that one *race* of men shall be made better than another by law, from father to son, which would be defeating the intentions of Providence, creating a superiority that exists in neither physical nor moral nature, and substituting a political scheme for the will of God and the force of things.

As a principle, one man is as good as another in rights. Such is the extent of the most liberal institutions of this country, and this provision is not general. The slave is not as good as his owner, even in rights. But in those states where slavery does not exist, all men have essentially the same rights, an equality which, so far from establishing that "one man is as good as another" in a social sense, is the very means of producing the inequality of condition that

actually exists. By possessing the same rights to exercise their respective faculties, the active and frugal become more wealthy than the idle and dissolute; the wise and gifted, more trusted than the silly and ignorant; the polished and refined, more respected and sought than the rude and vulgar.

In most countries, birth is a principal source of social distinction, society being divided into castes, the noble having a hereditary claim to be the superior of the plebeian. This is an unwise and an arbitrary distinction that has led to most of the social diseases of the Old World, and from which America is happily exempt. But great care must be had in construing the principles which have led to this great change, for America is the first important country of modern times in which such positive distinctions have been destroyed.

Still, some legal differences and more social advantages are produced by birth, even in America. The child inherits the property and a portion of the consideration of the parent. Without the first of these privileges, men would not exert themselves to acquire more property than would suffice for their own personal necessities, parental affection being one of the most powerful incentives to industry. Without such an inducement, then, it would follow that civilization would become stationary or it would recede — the incentives of individuality and of the affections being absolutely necessary to impel men to endure the labor and privations that alone can advance it.

The hereditary consideration of the child, so long as it is kept within due bounds by being confined to a natural sentiment, is also productive of good, since no more active inducement to great and glorious deeds can offer than the deeply seated interest that man takes in his posterity. All that reason and justice require is effected by setting bounds to such advantages in denying hereditary claims to trusts and power; but evil would be the day, and ominous the symptom, when a people shall deny that any portion of the consideration of the ancestor is due to the descendant.

It is as vain to think of altogether setting aside sentiment and the affections in regulating human affairs as to imagine it possible to raise a nature, known to be erring and weak, to the level of perfection.

The Deity, in that terrible warning delivered from the Mount, where He declares that He "will visit the sins of the fathers upon the children, unto the third and fourth generation," does no more than utter one of those sublime moral truths, which, in conformity with His Divine Providence, pervade nature. It is merely an announcement of a principle that cannot safely be separated from justice, and one that is closely connected with all the purest motives and highest aspirations of man.

There would be a manifest injustice in visiting the offense of the criminal on his nearest of kin, by making the innocent man participate in the disgrace of a guilty relative, as is notoriously done most by those most disposed to rail at reflected renown, and not to allow of the same participation in the glory. Both depend upon a sentiment deeper than human laws, and have been established for purposes so evidently useful as to require no explanation. All that is demanded of us is to have a care that this sentiment do not degenerate to a prejudice, and that, in the one case, we do not visit the innocent too severely, or, in the other, exalt the unworthy beyond the bounds of prudence.

It is a natural consequence of the rights of property and of the sentiment named that birth should produce some advantages, in a social sense, even in the most democratical of the American communities. The son imbibes a portion of the intelligence, refinement, and habits of the father; and he shares in his associations. These must be enumerated as the legitimate advantages of birth, and without invading the private arrangements of families and individuals, and establishing a perfect community of education, they are unavoidable. Men of the same habits, the same degree of cultivation and refinement, the same opinions, naturally associate together, in every class of life. The day laborer will not mingle with the slave; the skillful mechanic feels his superiority over the mere laborer, claims higher wages and has a pride in his craft; the man in trade justly fancies that his habits elevate him above the mechanic so far as social position is concerned; and the man of refinement, with his education, tastes, and sentiments, is superior to all. Idle declamation on these points does not impair the force of things, and life is a series of facts. These inequalities of condition, of manners, of mental cultivation must exist, unless it be intended to reduce all to a common level of ignorance and vulgarity, which would be virtually to return to a condition of barbarism.

The result of these undeniable facts is the inequalities of social station, in America as elsewhere, though it is an inequality that exists without any more arbitrary distinctions than are indispensably connected with the maintenance of civilization. In a social sense, there are orders here, as in all other countries, but the classes run into each other more easily, the lines of separation are less strongly drawn, and their shadows are more intimately blended.

This social inequality of America is an unavoidable result of the institutions, though nowhere proclaimed in them, the different constitutions maintaining a profound silence on the subject, they who framed them probably knowing that it is as much a consequence of civilized society as breathing is a vital function of animal life. . . .

AN ARISTOCRAT AND
A DEMOCRAT

WE LIVE IN AN AGE when the words "aristocrat" and "democrat" are much used without regard to the real significations. An aristocrat is one of a few who possess the political power of a country; a democrat, one of the many. The words are also properly applied to those who entertain notions favorable to aristocratical or democratical forms of government. Such persons are not necessarily either aristocrats or democrats in fact, but merely so in opinion. Thus, a member of a democratical government may have an aristocratical bias, and vice versa.

To call a man who has the habits and opinions of a gentleman an aristocrat, from that fact alone, is an abuse of terms and betrays ignorance of the true principles of government, as well as of the world. It must be an equivocal freedom, under which everyone is not the master of his own innocent acts and associations, and he is a sneaking democrat, indeed, who will submit to be dictated to in those habits over which neither law nor morality assumes a right of control.

Some men fancy that a democrat can only be one who seeks the level — social, mental, and moral — of the majority, a rule that would at once exclude all men of refinement, education, and taste from the class. These persons are enemies of democracy as they at once render it impracticable. They are usually great sticklers for their own associations and habits, too, though unable to comprehend any of a nature that are superior. They are, in truth, aristocrats in principle, though assuming a contrary pretension, the groundwork of all their feelings and arguments being self. Such is not the intention of liberty, whose aim is to leave every man to be the master of his own acts; denying hereditary honors, it is true, as unjust and unnecessary, but not denying the inevitable consequences of civilization.

The Law of God is the only rule of conduct in this, as in other matters. Each man should do as he would be done by. Were the question put to the greatest advocate of indiscriminate association, whether he would submit to have his company and habits dictated to him, he would be one of the first to resist the tyranny; for they who are the most rigid in maintaining their own claims in such matters are usually the loudest in decrying those whom they fancy to be better off than themselves. Indeed, it may be taken as a rule in social intercourse that he who is the most apt to question the pretensions of others is the most conscious of the doubtful position he himself occupies; thus establishing the very claims he affects to deny by letting his jealousy of it be seen.

Manners, education, and refinement are positive things, and they bring with them innocent tastes which are productive of high enjoyments; and it is as unjust to deny their possessors their indulgence as it would be to insist on the less fortunate's passing the time they would rather devote to athletic amusements, in listening to operas for which they have no relish, sung in a language they do not understand.

All that democracy means is as equal a participation in rights as is practicable; and to pretend that social equality is a condition of popular institutions is to assume that the latter are destructive of civilization; for, as nothing is more self-evident than the impossibility of raising all men to the highest standard of tastes and refinement, the alternative would be to reduce the entire community to the lowest. The whole embarrassment on this point exists in the difficulty of making men comprehend qualities they do not themselves possess. We can all perceive the difference between ourselves and our inferiors, but when it comes to a question of the difference between us and our superiors, we fail to appreciate merits of which we have no proper conceptions. In face of this obvious difficulty, there is the safe and just governing rule already mentioned, or that of permitting everyone to be the undisturbed judge of his own habits and associations, so long as they are innocent and do not impair the rights of others to be equally judges for themselves. It follows that social intercourse must regulate itself, independently of institutions, with the exception that the latter, while they withhold no natural, bestow no factitious, advantages beyond those which are inseparable from the rights of property and general civilization.

In a democracy, men are just as free to aim at the highest attainable places in society as to obtain the largest fortunes; and it would be clearly unworthy of all noble sentiment to say that the groveling competition for money shall alone be free, while that which enlists all the liberal acquirements and elevated sentiments of the race is denied the democrat. Such an avowal would be at once a declaration of the inferiority of the system, since nothing but ignorance and vulgarity could be its fruits.

The democratic gentleman must differ in many essential particulars from the aristocratical gentleman, though in their ordinary habits and tastes they are virtually identical.

Their principles vary, and, to a slight degree, their deportment accordingly. The democrat, recognizing the right of all to participate in power, will be more liberal in his general sentiments, a quality of superiority in itself; but, in conceding this much to his fellowman, he will proudly maintain his own independence of vulgar domination as indispensable to his personal habits. The same principles and manliness that would induce him to depose a royal despot would induce him to resist a vulgar tyrant.

There is no more capital, though more common error than to suppose him an aristocrat who maintains his independence of habits; for democracy asserts the control of the majority, only in matters of law and not in matters of custom. The very object of the institution is the utmost practicable personal liberty, and to affirm the contrary would be sacrificing the end to the means.

An aristocrat, therefore, is merely one who fortifies his exclusive privileges by positive institutions, and a democrat, one who is willing to admit of a free competition in all things. To say, however, that the last supposes this competition will lead to nothing is an assumption that means are employed without any reference to an end. He is the purest democrat who best maintains his rights, and no rights can be dearer to a man of cultivation than exemptions from unseasonable invasions on his time by the coarse-minded and ignorant.

The publick is to be watched . . . in this country, as in other countries kings and aristocrats are to be watched.

JAMES FENIMORE COOPER, *The American Democrat*

"The First State Election in Detroit, Michigan, 1837"; painting by Thomas Mickel Burnham

THE MIDWEST

The states of the old Northwest were booming. Steamboats and canal barges rushed immigrants to the fertile lands. Towns exploded into cities. Settlers penetrated the remote parts of Ohio, Indiana, and Illinois. Michigan gained sufficient population to be admitted as a state in 1837.

This rapid growth and inflationary prosperity created a situation in Illinois that was typical of the period. In 1837 the Illinois legislature, with high expectations, authorized a grandiose plan for railroad and canal building. Sectional rivalry prevented agreement on any one route, and construction began simultaneously on many projects.

The legislature soon realized it lacked sufficient capital to bring any of the projects to completion, but it failed to substitute a workable plan. By 1840 the state was virtually bankrupt. Its legislature and commissioners resorted to financial juggling to meet the interest payments on state bonds sold to finance the program of internal improvements. In 1841, Illinois defaulted on the interest. It remained to John Ford, governor from 1842 to 1846, to save the credit of the state. He reduced the principle on the debt of some 15 million dollars, met interest payments, and started work to complete the Illinois and Michigan Canal.

(Above) **View of Cincinnati from across the Ohio River** by John C. Wild, c. 1835

River Towns

By the end of the 1830s several large cities had grown up along the Ohio and Mississippi rivers. Among these were Cincinnati and St. Louis, both of which owed much of their growth and prosperity to the steamboat and to river trade in general. The completion of the Ohio and Erie Canal, connecting the Ohio with Lake Erie, enhanced Cincinnati's position in this trade. Steamboat construction became a major industry in the city, as well as the manufacture of the plows, wagon wheels, and farm implements that were the first need of immigrants to the Midwest.

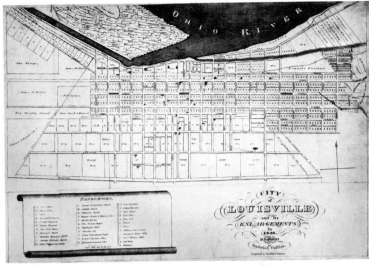

Plan of Louisville, Ky., in 1836. By this time a canal had been constructed bypassing the Falls of the Ohio and speeding river commerce

The Cincinnati waterfront at Front and Main streets in 1835 by Wild

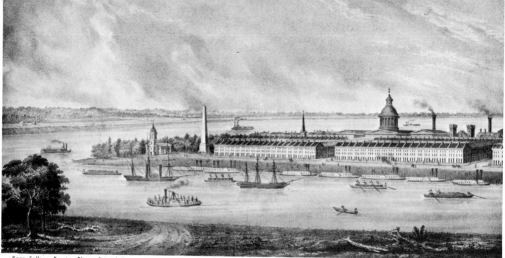

Plan for the design of Cairo, Ill., by William Strickland, 1838

(Above) View of Cairo, Ill., on the Mississippi by Antonio Mendelli; (below) "Snags on the Missouri"; painted by Carl Bodmer, indicates some of the difficulty of river navigation

View of St. Louis from the Mississippi River by George Catlin, 1839

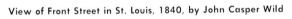

View of Front Street in St. Louis, 1840, by John Casper Wild

(Top) View of a farm on the prairies of Illinois; watercolor by Bodmer, 1833; (left) dwelling of a settler's farm in Indiana; also by Bodmer

(Left) Wood engraving relating to the financial setback experienced on the frontier following the Panic of 1837

(Above) Peter Cartwright, circuit rider; (right) clearing fallen trees

Illinois
Indiana
Ohio

The patterns of settlement in the Midwest brought settlers westward and then northward along the Ohio and Mississippi rivers before moving inland to the open farmlands.

In Indiana and Illinois, immigration increased the states' populations by about 200 percent in a decade and distributed homesteaders throughout the prairie lands of these states.

Chicago, with a population of 4,000 in 1837, was being transformed from a frontier outpost to a busy lake port.

Lithograph of Fort Dearborn, Chicago, in 1838, by Francis de Castelnau

Ohio, with more than a decade's head start in development, was turning to the business of providing for a settled population. Free public elementary education was well established by 1830. After 1836 the public education system was divided into elementary, grammar, and high schools. Ambitious canal building schemes were in progress. Cities like Cincinnati had long since passed the boom-town stage.

(Top and bottom) Views of Cincinnati, 1835; (left) meeting in African Methodist Church, Cincinnati

(Above) Philander Chase, first Episcopal bishop of Ohio and founder of Kenyon College (bottom) in 1824; (right) road scene near Thornville, Ohio, 1841; (center) Ohio University at Athens was first chartered in 1804

Partly influenced by the numerous sectarian colleges founded during the period, the Abolitionist movement was strong in Ohio. Oberlin College was notable for not restricting admissions on the basis of sex or race. In spite of some resistance because of the importance of trade with the South, there were 213 antislavery societies in Ohio by 1835. These Abolitionists formed a crucial link in the "Underground Railway."

View of Cleveland in 1834, looking east from the corner of Bank and St. Clair Streets

The completion of the Ohio and Erie Canal in 1832, connecting Lake Erie at Cleveland with the Ohio River at Portsmouth, changed Cleveland from an obscure settlement into a prosperous lake port. The city became a distribution point, dispatching manufactured goods to markets on the Ohio River, in the interior of Ohio, and in western Pennsylvania. Eastern shippers found they could reach these areas quickly and cheaply via the Erie Canal, Lake Erie, and the Ohio and Erie Canal.

Estimates of phenomenal population growth fell short after the financial crisis of 1837, but Cleveland increased from 1,900 in 1833 to more than 9,000 in 1837.

View of Cleveland looking east from Brooklyn Hill. Both engravings by Thomas Whelpley

1839

87.

Frances Anne Kemble: Life on a Georgia Plantation

The Abolitionist movement in England had a long history prior to its formation in the United States. Thus when Frances Anne Kemble, an English actress, came to the United States in 1832, she was already enlisted among slavery's foes. In 1834 she married a wealthy Philadelphian, Pierce Mease Butler, and two years after their marriage he inherited a plantation in Georgia. Fanny Kemble Butler thereby became the mistress of more than 700 slaves. The estate was comprised of two islands, one specializing in cotton and the other in rice, and the Butlers spent two months there in the winter of 1838-1839. Because her husband did not share her scruples about benefiting from the labor of slaves, Fanny confided her observations on plantation life to a diary. The Butlers were later divorced and Fanny returned to England. She published her diary in 1863 to discourage the British from supporting the Confederacy in the American Civil War and to promote sympathy for the North.

Source: *Journal of a Residence on a Georgian Plantation in 1838-1839*, New York, 1863, pp. 16-37.

Dear E———,

Minuteness of detail and fidelity in the account of my daily doings will hardly, I fear, render my letters very interesting to you now; but, cut off as I am here from all the usual resources and amusements of civilized existence, I shall find but little to communicate to you that is not furnished by my observations on the novel appearance of external nature, and the moral and physical condition of Mr. ———'s people. . . .

Is it not rather curious that Miss Martineau should have mentioned the erection of a steam mill for threshing rice somewhere in the vicinity of Charleston as a singular novelty, likely to form an era in Southern agriculture, and to produce the most desirable changes in the system of labor by which it is carried on? Now, on this estate alone there are three threshing mills — one worked by steam, one by the tide, and one by horses; there are two private steam mills on plantations adjacent to ours and a public one at Savannah, where the planters who have none on their own estates are in the habit of sending their rice to be threshed at a certain percentage. These have all been in operation for some years, and I, therefore, am at a loss to understand what made her hail the erection of the one at Charleston as likely to produce such immediate and happy results. . . .

I shall furnish you with no details but those which come under my own immediate observation.

To return to the rice mill. It is worked by a steam engine of 30 horsepower, and, besides threshing a great part of our own rice, is kept constantly employed by the neighboring planters, who send their grain to it in preference to the more distant mill at Savannah, paying, of course, the same percentage, which makes it a very profitable addition to the estate. Immediately opposite to this building is a small shed, which they call the cook's shop, and where the daily allowance of rice and corn grits of the people is boiled and distributed to them by an old woman, whose special business this is. There are four settlements or villages (or, as the Negroes call them, camps) on the island, consisting of from ten to twenty houses, and to each settlement is annexed a cook's shop with capacious caldrons, and the oldest wife of the settlement for officiating priestess.

Pursuing my walk along the river's bank, upon an artificial dike sufficiently high and broad to protect the fields from inundation by the ordinary rising of the tide — for the whole island is below high-water mark — I passed the blacksmith's and cooper's shops. At the first, all the common iron implements of husbandry or household use for the estate are made, and at the latter all the rice barrels necessary for the crop, besides tubs and buckets, large and small, for the use of the people, and cedar tubs, of noble dimensions and exceedingly neat workmanship, for our own household purposes. The fragrance of these when they are first made, as well as their ample size, renders them preferable as dressing-room furniture, in my opinion, to all the china foot tubs that ever came out of Staffordshire. . . .

I must inform you of a curious conversation which took place between my little girl and the woman who performs for us the offices of chambermaid here — of course, one of Mr. ———'s slaves. What suggested it to the child, or whence indeed she gathered her information, I know not; but children are made of eyes and ears, and nothing, however minute, escapes their microscopic observation. She suddenly began addressing this woman.

"Mary, some persons are free and some are not (the woman made no reply). I am a free person (of a little more than three years old). I say, I am a free person, Mary — do you know that?"

"Yes, missis."

"Some persons are free and some are not — do you know that, Mary?"

"Yes, missis, *here*," was the reply; "I know it is so here, in this world."

Here my child's white nurse, my dear Margery, who had hitherto been silent, interfered, saying: "Oh, then you think it will not always be so?"

"Me hope not, missis."

I am afraid, E———, this woman actually imagines that there will be no slaves in heaven; isn't that preposterous, now, when, by the account of most of the Southerners, slavery itself must be heaven, or something uncommonly like it? Oh, if you could imagine how this title "Missis," addressed to me and to my children, shocks all my feelings! Several times I have exclaimed: "For God's sake do not call me that!" and only been awakened by the stupid amazement of the poor creatures I was addressing to the perfect uselessness of my thus expostulating with them; once or twice, indeed, I have done more — I have explained to them, and they appeared to comprehend me well, that I had no ownership over them, for that I held such ownership sinful, and that, though I was the wife of the man who pretends to own them, I was, in truth, no more their mistress than they were mine.

Some of them, I know, understood me, more of them did not.

Our servants — those who have been selected to wait upon us in the house — consist of a man, who is quite a tolerable cook (I believe this is a natural gift with them, as with Frenchmen); a dairywoman, who churns for us; a laundrywoman; her daughter, our housemaid, the aforesaid Mary; and two young lads of from fifteen to twenty, who wait upon us in the capacity of footmen. As, however, the latter are perfectly filthy in their persons and clothes — their faces, hands, and naked feet being literally encrusted with dirt — their attendance at our meals is not, as you may suppose, particularly agreeable to me, and I dispense with it as often as possible. Mary, too, is so intolerably offensive in her person that it is impossible to endure her proximity, and the consequence is that, among Mr. ———'s slaves, I wait upon myself more than I have ever done in my life before. About this same personal offensiveness, the Southerners, you know, insist that it is inherent with the race, and it is one of their most cogent reasons for keeping them as slaves.

But, as this very disagreeable peculiarity does not prevent Southern women from hanging their infants at the breasts of Negresses, nor almost every planter's wife and daughter from having one or more little pet blacks sleeping like puppy dogs in their very bedchamber, nor almost every planter from admitting one or several of his female slaves to the still closer intimacy of his bed, it seems to me that this objection to doing them right is not very valid. I cannot imagine that they would smell much worse if they were free, or come in much closer contact with the delicate organs of their white fellow countrymen; indeed, inasmuch as good deeds are spoken of as having a sweet savor before God, it might be supposed that the freeing of the blacks might prove rather an odoriferous process than the contrary.

However this may be, I must tell you that this potent reason for enslaving a whole race of people is no more potent with me than most of the others adduced to support the system, inasmuch as, from observation and some experience, I am strongly inclined to believe that peculiar ignorance of the laws of health and the habits of decent cleanliness are the real and only causes of this disagreeable characteristic of the race, thorough ablutions and change of linen, when tried, have been perfectly successful in removing all such objections; and if ever you have come into anything like neighborly proximity with a low Irishman or woman, I think you will allow that the same causes produce very nearly the same effects. The stench in an Irish, Scotch, Italian, or French hovel is quite as intolerable as any I ever found in our Negro houses, and the filth and vermin which abound about the clothes and persons of the lower peasantry of any of those countries as abominable as the same conditions in the black population of the United States. A total absence of self-respect begets these hateful physical results, and in proportion as moral influences are remote, physical evils will abound. Well-being, freedom, and industry induce self-respect, self-respect induces cleanliness and personal attention, so that slavery is answerable for all the evils that exhibit themselves where it exists — from lying, thieving, and adultery to dirty houses, ragged clothes, and foul smells.

But to return to our Ganymedes. One of them — the eldest son of our laundrywoman and Mary's brother, a boy of the name of Aleck (Alexander) — is uncommonly bright and intelligent; he performs all the offices of a well-instructed waiter with great efficiency, and anywhere out of slaveland would be able to earn $14 or $15 a month for himself; he is remarkably good tempered and well disposed. The other poor boy is so stupid that he appears sullen from absolute darkness of intellect; instead of being a little lower than the angels, he is

Frances Anne Kemble; portrait by Thomas Sully

scarcely a little higher than the brutes, and to this condition are reduced the majority of his kind by the institutions under which they live. I should tell you that Aleck's parents and kindred have always been about the house of the overseer, and in daily habits of intercourse with him and his wife; and wherever this is the case the effect of involuntary education is evident in the improved intelligence of the degraded race. . . .

Now, E———, I have no intention of telling you a one-sided story, or concealing from you what are cited as the advantages which these poor people possess; you, who know that no indulgence is worth simple justice, either to him who gives or him who receives, will not thence conclude that their situation thus mitigated is, therefore, what it should be. On this matter of the $60 earned by Mr. ———'s two men much stress was laid by him and his overseer. I look at it thus: if these men were industrious enough, out of their scanty leisure, to earn $60, how much more of remuneration, of comfort, of improvement might they not have achieved were the price of their daily labor duly paid them instead of being unjustly withheld to support an idle young man and his idle family, i.e., myself and my children.

And here it may be well to inform you that the slaves on this plantation are divided into field hands and mechanics or artisans. The former, the great majority, are the more stupid and brutish of the tribe; the others, who are regularly taught their trades, are not only exceedingly expert at them but exhibit a greater general activity of intellect, which must necessarily result from even a partial degree of cultivation. There are here a gang (for that is the honorable term) of coopers, of blacksmiths, of bricklayers, of carpenters, all well acquainted with their peculiar trades. The latter constructed the wash-hand stands, clothes-presses, sofas, tables, etc., with which our house is furnished, and they are very neat pieces of workmanship — neither veneered or polished indeed, nor of very costly materials, but of the white pinewood planed as smooth as marble — a species of furniture not very luxurious perhaps, but all the better adapted, therefore, to the house itself, which is certainly rather more devoid of the conveniences and adornments of modern existence than anything I ever took up my abode in before.

It consists of three small rooms, and three still smaller, which would be more appropriately designated as closets, a wooden recess by way of pantry, and a kitchen detached from the dwelling — a mere wooden outhouse with no floor but the bare earth, and for furniture a congregation of filthy Negroes who lounge in and out of it like hungry hounds at all hours of the day and night, picking up such scraps of food as they can find about, which they discuss squatting down upon their hams, in which interesting position and occupation I generally find a number of them whenever I have sufficient hardihood to venture within those precincts, the sight of which and its tenants is enough to slacken the appetite of the hungriest hunter that ever lost all nice regards in the mere animal desire for food. Of our three apartments, one is our sitting, eating, and *living* room, and is sixteen feet by fifteen. The walls are plastered indeed, but neither painted nor papered. It is divided from our bedroom (a similarly elegant and comfortable chamber) by a dingy wooden partition covered all over with hooks, pegs, and nails, to which hats, caps, keys, etc., etc., are suspended in graceful irregularity. The doors open by wooden latches, raised by means of small bits of packthread — I imagine, the same primitive order of fastening celebrated in the touching chronicle of Red Riding Hood; how they shut I will not attempt to describe, as the shutting of a door is a process of extremely rare occurrence throughout the whole Southern country. The third room, a chamber with sloping ceiling, immediately over our sitting room and under the roof, is appropriated to the nurse and my two babies.

Of the closets, one is Mr. ———, the overseer's, bedroom, the other his office or place of business; and the third, adjoining our bedroom and opening immediately out-of-doors, is Mr. ———'s dressing room and *cabinet d'affaires*, where he gives audiences to the Negroes, redresses grievances, distributes red woolen caps (a singular gratification to a slave), shaves himself, and performs the other offices of his toilet. Such being our abode, I think you will allow there is little danger of my being dazzled by the luxurious splendors of a Southern slave residence. Our sole mode of summoning our attendants is by a packthread bell rope suspended in the sitting room. From the bedrooms we have to raise the windows and our voices, and bring them by power of lungs, or help ourselves — which, I thank God, was never yet a hardship to me. . . .

In the part of Georgia where this estate is situated, the custom of task labor is univer-

sal, and it prevails, I believe, throughout Georgia, South Carolina, and parts of North Carolina; in other parts of the latter state, however — as I was informed by our overseer who is a native of that state — the estates are small, rather deserving the name of farms, and the laborers are much upon the same footing as the laboring men at the North, working from sunrise to sunset in the fields with the farmer and his sons, and coming in with them to their meals, which they take immediately after the rest of the family.

In Louisiana and the new Southwestern slave states, I believe, task labor does not prevail; but it is in those that the condition of the poor human cattle is most deplorable. As you know, it was there that the humane calculation was not only made but openly and unhesitatingly avowed that the planters found it, upon the whole, their most profitable plan to work off (kill with labor) their whole number of slaves about once in seven years, and renew the whole stock. By-the-by, the Jewish institution of slavery is much insisted upon by the Southern upholders of the system; perhaps this is their notion of the Jewish jubilee, when the slaves were by Moses' strict enactment to be all set free.

Well, this task system is pursued on this estate; and thus it is that the two carpenters were enabled to make the boat they sold for $60. These tasks, of course, profess to be graduated according to the sex, age, and strength of the laborer; but in many instances this is not the case, as I think you will agree when I tell you that on Mr. ———'s first visit to his estates he found that the men and the women who labored in the fields had the same task to perform. This was a noble admission of female equality, was it not? And thus it had been on the estate for many years past. Mr. ———, of course, altered the distribution of the work, diminishing the quantity done by the women.

I had a most ludicrous visit this morning from the midwife of the estate — rather an important personage both to master and slave, as to her unassisted skill and science the ushering of all the young Negroes into their existence of bondage is entrusted. . . . Mr. ——— opened my room door, ushering in a dirty, fat, good-humored-looking old Negress, saying: "The midwife, Rose, wants to make your acquaintance."

"Oh massa!" shrieked out the old creature, in a paroxysm of admiration, "where you get this lilly alabaster baby?"

For a moment I looked round to see if she was speaking of my baby; but no, my dear, this superlative apostrophe was elicited by the fairness of *my skin:* so much for degrees of comparison. Now, I suppose that if I chose to walk arm in arm with the dingiest mulatto through the streets of Philadelphia nobody could possibly tell by my complexion that I was not his sister, so that the mere quality of mistress must have had a most miraculous effect upon my skin in the eyes of poor Rose. But this species of outrageous flattery is as usual with these people as with the low Irish, and arises from the ignorant desire, common to both the races, of propitiating at all costs the fellow creature who is to them as a Providence — or rather, I should say, a fate — for it is a heathen and no Christian relationship.

Soon after this visit, I was summoned into the wooden porch, or piazza, of the house to see a poor woman who desired to speak to me. This was none other than the tall, emaciated-looking Negress who, on the day of our arrival, had embraced me and my nurse with such irresistible zeal. She appeared very ill today, and presently unfolded to me a most distressing history of bodily afflictions. She was the mother of a very large family, and complained to me that, what with childbearing and hard field labor, her back was almost broken in two.

With an almost savage vehemence of gesticulation, she suddenly tore up her scanty clothing and exhibited a spectacle with which I was inconceivably shocked and sickened. The facts, without any of her corroborating statements, bore tolerable witness to the hardships of her existence. I promised to attend to her ailments and give her proper remedies; but these are natural results, inevitable and irremediable ones, of improper treatment of the female frame; and, though there may be alleviation, there cannot be any cure when once the beautiful and wonderful structure has been thus made the victim of ignorance, folly, and wickedness.

After the departure of this poor woman, I walked down the settlement toward the infirmary, or hospital, calling in at one or two of the houses along the row. These cabins consist of one room, about twelve feet by fifteen, with a couple of closets, smaller and closer than the staterooms of a ship, divided off from the main room and each other by rough wooden partitions, in which the inhabitants sleep. They have almost all of them a rude bedstead, with the gray moss of the forests for mattress, and filthy, pestilential-looking blankets for covering.

Two families (sometimes eight and ten in number) reside in one of these huts, which are mere wooden frames pinned, as it were, to the earth by a brick chimney outside, whose enormous aperture within pours down a flood of air, but little counteracted by the miserable spark of fire which hardly sends an attenuated thread of lingering smoke up its huge throat. A wide ditch runs immediately at the back of these dwellings, which is filled and emptied daily by the tide. Attached to each hovel is a small scrap of ground for a garden, which, however, is for the most part untended and uncultivated.

Such of these dwellings as I visited today were filthy and wretched in the extreme, and exhibited that most deplorable consequence of ignorance and an abject condition, the inability of the inhabitants to secure and improve even such pitiful comfort as might yet be achieved by them. Instead of the order, neatness, and ingenuity which might convert even these miserable hovels into tolerable residences, there was the careless, reckless, filthy indolence which even the brutes do not exhibit in their lairs and nests, and which seemed incapable of applying to the uses of existence the few miserable means of comfort yet within their reach. . . .

In the midst of the floor, or squatting round the cold hearth, would be four or five little children from four to ten years old, the latter all with babies in their arms, the care of the infants being taken from the mothers (who are driven afield as soon as they recover from child labor) and devolved upon these poor little nurses, as they are called, whose business it is to watch the infant, and carry it to its mother whenever it may require nourishment. To these hardly human little beings I addressed my remonstrances about the filth, cold, and unnecessary wretchedness of their room, bidding the older boys and girls kindle up the fire, sweep the floor, and expel the poultry.

For a long time my very words seemed unintelligible to them, till, when I began to sweep and make up the fire, etc., they first fell to laughing and then imitating me. The incrustations of dirt on their hands, feet, and faces were my next object of attack, and the stupid Negro practice (by-the-by, but a short time since nearly universal in enlightened Europe) of keeping the babies with their feet bare, and their heads, already well capped by nature with their wooly hair, wrapped in half a dozen hot, filthy coverings.

Thus I traveled down the "street," in every dwelling endeavoring to awaken a new perception, that of cleanliness, sighing, as I went, over the futility of my own exertions, for how can slaves be improved? Nevertheless, thought I, let what can be done; for it

may be that, the two being incompatible, improvement may yet expel slavery; and so it might, and surely would, if, instead of beginning at the end, I could but begin at the beginning of my task. If the mind and soul were awakened instead of mere physical good attempted, the physical good would result and the great curse vanish away; but my hands are tied fast, and this corner of the work is all that I may do. Yet it cannot be but, from my words and actions, some revelations should reach these poor people; and going in and out among them perpetually, I shall teach and they learn involuntarily a thousand things of deepest import. They must learn, and who can tell the fruit of that knowledge alone, that there are beings in the world, even with skins of a different color from their own, who have sympathy for their misfortunes, love for their virtues, and respect for their common nature — but oh! my heart is full almost to bursting as I walk among these most poor creatures.

The infirmary is a large two-story building, terminating the broad orange-planted space between the two rows of houses which form the first settlement; it is built of whitewashed wood, and contains four large-sized rooms. But how shall I describe to you the spectacle which was presented to me on entering the first of these? But half the casements, of which there were six, were glazed, and these were obscured with dirt, almost as much as the other windowless ones were darkened by the dingy shutters, which the shivering inmates had fastened to in order to protect themselves from the cold.

In the enormous chimney glimmered the powerless embers of a few sticks of wood, round which, however, as many of the sick women as could approach were cowering, some on wooden settles, most of them on the ground, excluding those who were too ill to rise; and these last poor wretches lay prostrate on the floor, without bed, mattress, or pillow, buried in tattered and filthy blankets, which, huddled round them as they lay strewn about, left hardly space to move upon the floor. And here, in their hour of sickness and suffering, lay those whose health and strength are spent in unrequited labor for us; those who, perhaps even yesterday, were being urged on to their unpaid task; those whose husbands, fathers, brothers, and sons were even at that hour sweating over the earth; whose produce was to buy for us all the luxuries which health can revel in, all the comforts which can alleviate sickness.

I stood in the midst of them, perfectly unable to speak, the tears pouring from my eyes at this sad spectacle of their misery, myself and my emotion alike strange and incomprehensible to them. Here lay women expecting every hour the terrors and agonies of childbirth; others who had just brought their doomed offspring into the world; others who were groaning over the anguish and bitter disappointment of miscarriages. Here lay some burning with fever; others chilled with cold and aching with rheumatism, upon the hard cold ground, the drafts and dampness of the atmosphere increasing their sufferings, and dirt, noise, and stench, and every aggravation of which sickness is capable, combined in their condition. Here they lay like brute beasts, absorbed in physical suffering; unvisited by any of those Divine influences which may ennoble the dispensations of pain and illness, forsaken, as it seemed to me, of all good; and yet, O God, Thou surely hadst not forsaken them! Now pray take notice that this is the hospital of an estate where the owners are supposed to be humane, the overseer efficient and kind, and the Negroes remarkably well-cared for and comfortable.

As soon as I recovered from my dismay, I addressed old Rose, the midwife, who had charge of this room, bidding her open the shutters of such windows as were glazed and let in the light. I next proceeded to make up the fire; but, upon my lifting a log for that purpose, there was one universal outcry of horror, and old Rose, attempting to snatch it from me, exclaimed: "Let alone, missis — let be; what for you lift wood? You have nigger enough, missis, to do it!" I hereupon had to explain to them my view of the purposes for which hands and arms were appended to our bodies, and forthwith began making Rose tidy up the miserable apartment, removing all the filth and rubbish from the floor that could be removed, folding up in piles the blankets of the patients who were not using them, and placing, in rather more sheltered and comfortable positions, those who were unable to rise. It was all that I could do, and having enforced upon them all my earnest desire that they should keep their room swept and as tidy as possible, I passed on to the other room on the ground floor, and to the two above, one of which is appropriated to the use of the men who are ill.

They were all in the same deplorable condition, the upper rooms being rather the more miserable inasmuch as none of the windows were glazed at all, and they had, therefore, only the alternative of utter darkness, or killing drafts of air from the unsheltered casements. In all, filth, disorder, and misery abounded; the floor was the only bed, and scanty begrimed rags of blankets the only covering. I left this refuge for Mr. ———'s sick dependents with my clothes covered with dust and full of vermin, and with a heart heavy enough, as you will well believe.

My morning's work had fatigued me not a little, and I was glad to return to the house, where I gave vent to my indignation and regret at the scene I had just witnessed to Mr. ——— and his overseer, who, here, is a member of our family. The latter told me that the condition of the hospital had appeared to him, from his first entering upon his situation (only within the last year), to require a reform, and that he had proposed it to the former manager Mr. K———, and Mr. ———'s brother, who is part proprietor of the estate, but, receiving no encouragement from them, had supposed that it was a matter of indifference to the owners, and had left it in the condition in which he had found it, in which condition it has been for the last nineteen years and upward.

This new overseer of ours has lived fourteen years with an old Scotch gentleman, who owns an estate adjoining Mr. ———'s, on the island of St. Simons, upon which estate, from everything I can gather and from what I know of the proprietor's character, the slaves are probably treated with as much humanity as is consistent with slavery at all, and where the management and comfort of the hospital, in particular, had been most carefully and judiciously attended to. With regard to the indifference of our former manager upon the subject of the accommodation for the sick, he was an excellent overseer, *videlicet* the estate returned a full income under his management, and such men have nothing to do with sick slaves: they are tools, to be mended only if they can be made available again; if not, to be flung by as useless, without further expense of money, time, or trouble. . . .

I forgot to tell you that in the hospital were several sick babies whose mothers were permitted to suspend their field labor in order to nurse them. Upon addressing some remonstrances to one of these, who, besides having a sick child was ill herself, about the horribly dirty condition of her baby, she assured me that it was impossible for them to keep their children clean; that they went out to work at daybreak and did not get their tasks done till evening, and that then they were too tired and worn out to do anything but throw themselves down and sleep. This statement of hers I mentioned on my return from the hospital, and the overseer appeared extremely annoyed by it, and assured me repeatedly that it was not true.

In the evening, Mr. ———, who had been over to Darien, mentioned that one of the storekeepers there had told him that, in the course of a few years, he had paid the Negroes of this estate several thousand dollars for moss, which is a very profitable article of traffic with them. They collect it from the trees, dry and pick it, and then sell it to the people in Darien for mattresses, sofas, and all sorts of stuffing purposes, which, in my opinion, it answers better than any other material whatever that I am acquainted with. . . .

There is a preliminary to my repose, however, in this agreeable residence, which I rather dread, namely, the hunting for, or discovering without hunting, in fine relief upon the whitewashed walls of my bedroom, a most hideous and detestable species of reptile called centipedes, which come out of the cracks and crevices of the walls, and fill my very heart with dismay. They are from an inch to two inches long, and appear to have not a hundred but a thousand legs. I cannot ascertain very certainly from the Negroes whether they sting or not, but they look exceedingly as if they might, and I visit my babies every night in fear and trembling lest I should find one or more of these hateful creatures mounting guard over them. Good night; you are well to be free from centipedes — better to be free from slaves.

88.

THEODORE WELD: Slavery As It Is

Theodore Weld was the most influential Abolitionist of his time, far more effective than Garrison. Both at Lane Theological Seminary in Cincinnati and at New York in the 1830s, he consolidated the antislavery movement in the North, converting many important persons. The following was the most widely read (100,000 copies were sold) of the many pamphlets he published. It served as the source for Uncle Tom's Cabin *and was compiled from thousands of Southern newspapers with the help of the Grimke sisters, noted Abolitionists from Charleston, one of whom Weld married. He afterwards (1841-1843) organized the antislavery bloc in Congress, led by John Quincy Adams. The book was published anonymously in 1839.*

Source: *American Slavery As It Is: Testimony of a Thousand Witnesses*, New York, 1839, pp. 7-9, 164-167.

READER, you are impaneled as a juror to try a plain case and bring in an honest verdict. The question at issue is not one of law but of fact — What is the actual condition of the slaves in the United States? A plainer case never went to a jury. Look at it. TWENTY-SEVEN HUNDRED THOUSAND PERSONS in this country, men, women, and children, are in SLAVERY. Is slavery, as a condition for human beings, good, bad, or indifferent? We submit the question without argument. You have common sense, and conscience, and a human heart — pronounce upon it. You have a wife, or a husband, a child, a father, a mother, a brother, or a sister — make the case your own, make it theirs, and bring in your verdict.

The case of Human Rights against Slavery has been adjudicated in the court of conscience times innumerable. The same verdict has always been rendered — "Guilty"; the same sentence has always been pronounced, "Let it be accursed"; and human nature, with her million echoes, has rung it round the world in every language under heaven, "Let it be accursed. Let it be accursed." His heart is false to human na-

ture who will not say "Amen." There is not a man on earth who does not believe that slavery is a curse. Human beings may be inconsistent, but human *nature* is true to herself. She has uttered her testimony against slavery with a shriek ever since the monster was begotten; and till it perishes amidst the execrations of the universe, she will traverse the world on its track, dealing her bolts upon its head, and dashing against it her condemning brand.

We repeat it, every man knows that slavery is a curse. Whoever denies this, his lips libel his heart. Try him; clank the chains in his ears and tell him they are for *him*. Give him an hour to prepare his wife and children for a life of slavery. Bid him make haste and get ready their necks for the yoke, and their wrists for the coffle chains, then look at his pale lips and trembling knees, and you have *nature's* testimony against slavery.

Two million seven hundred thousand persons in these states are in this condition. They were made slaves and are held such by force, and by being put in fear, and this for no crime! Reader, what have you to say of such treatment? Is it right, just, benevolent? Suppose I should seize you, rob you of your liberty, drive you into the field, and make you work without pay as long as you live — would that be justice and kindness, or monstrous injustice and cruelty?

Now, everybody knows that the slaveholders do these things to the slaves every day, and yet it is stoutly affirmed that they treat them well and kindly, and that their tender regard for their slaves restrains the masters from inflicting cruelties upon them. We shall go into no metaphysics to show the absurdity of this pretense. The man who *robs* you every day is, forsooth, quite too tenderhearted ever to cuff or kick you!

True, he can snatch your money, but he does it gently lest he should hurt you. He can empty your pockets without qualms, but if your *stomach* is empty, it cuts him to the quick. He can make you work a lifetime without pay, but loves you too well to let you go hungry. He fleeces you of your *rights* with a relish, but is shocked if you work bareheaded in summer or in winter without warm stockings. He can make you go without your *liberty,* but never without a shirt. He can crush, in you, all hope of bettering your condition by vowing that you shall die his slave, but, though he can coolly torture your feelings, he is too compassionate to lacerate your back; he can break your heart, but he is very tender of your skin. He can strip you of all protection and thus expose you to all outrages, but if you are exposed to the *weather,* half-clad and half-sheltered, how yearn his tender bowels!

What! Slaveholders talk of treating men well, and yet not only rob them of all they get, and as fast as they get it, but rob them of *themselves,* also; their very hands and feet, and all their muscles, and limbs, and senses, their bodies and minds, their time and liberty and earnings, their free speech and rights of conscience, their right to acquire knowledge and property and reputation; and yet they who plunder them of all these would fain make us believe that their soft hearts

ooze out so lovingly toward their slaves that they always keep them well-housed and well-clad, never push them too hard in the field, never make their dear backs smart, nor let their dear stomachs get empty.

But there is no end to these absurdities. Are slaveholders dunces, or do they take all the rest of the world to be, that they think to bandage our eyes with such thin gauzes? Protesting their kind regard for those whom they hourly plunder of all they have and all they get! What! When they have seized their victims and annihilated all their *rights,* still claim to be the special guardians of their *happiness!* Plunderers of their liberty, yet the careful suppliers of their wants? Robbers of their earnings, yet watchful sentinels round their interests, and kind providers of their comforts? Filching all their time, yet granting generous donations for rest and sleep? Stealing the use of their muscles, yet thoughtful of their ease? Putting them under drivers, yet careful that they are not hard-pushed? Too humane, forsooth, to stint the stomachs of their slaves, yet force their *minds* to starve, and brandish over them pains and penalties if they dare to reach forth for the smallest crumb of knowledge, even a letter of the alphabet!

It is no marvel that slaveholders are always talking of their *kind treatment* of their slaves. The only marvel is that men of sense can be gulled by such professions. Despots always insist that they are merciful. The greatest tyrants that ever dripped with blood have assumed the titles of "most gracious," "most clement," "most merciful," etc., and have ordered their crouching vassals to accost them thus. When did not vice lay claim to those virtues which are the opposites of its habitual crimes? The guilty, according to their own showing, are always innocent, and cowards brave, and drunkards sober, and harlots chaste, and pickpockets honest to a fault. . . .

As slaveholders and their apologists are volunteer witnesses in their own cause and are flooding the world with testimony that their slaves are kindly treated; that they are well-fed, well-clothed, well-housed, well-lodged, moderately worked, and bountifully provided with all things needful for their comfort, we propose, first, to disprove their assertions by the testimony of a multitude of impartial witnesses, and then to put slaveholders themselves through a course of cross-questioning which shall draw their condemnation out of their own mouths.

We will prove that the slaves in the United States are treated with barbarous inhumanity; that they are overworked, underfed, wretchedly clad and lodged, and have insufficient sleep; that they are often made to wear round their necks iron collars armed with prongs, to drag heavy chains and weights at their feet while working in the field, and to wear yokes, and bells, and iron horns; that they are often kept confined in the stocks day and night for weeks together, made to wear gags in their mouths for hours or days, have some of their front teeth torn out or broken off that they may be easily detected when they run away; that they are frequently flogged with terrible severity, have red pepper rubbed into their lacerated flesh, and hot brine, spirits of turpentine, etc., poured over the gashes to increase the torture; that they are often stripped naked, their backs and limbs cut with knives, bruised and mangled by scores and hundreds of blows with the paddle, and terribly torn by the claws of cats, drawn over them by their tormentors; that they are often hunted with bloodhounds and shot down like beasts, or torn in pieces by dogs; that they are often suspended by the arms and whipped and beaten till they faint, and, when revived by restoratives, beaten again till they faint, and sometimes till they die; that their ears are often cut off, their eyes knocked out, their bones broken, their flesh branded with red hot irons; that they are maimed, mutilated, and burned to death over slow fires. All these things, and more, and worse, we shall *prove*. Reader,

we know whereof we affirm, we have weighed it well; *more and worse* WE WILL PROVE.

Mark these words, and read on; we will establish all these facts by the testimony of scores and hundreds of eyewitnesses, by the testimony of *slaveholders* in all parts of the slave states, by slaveholding members of Congress and of state legislatures, by ambassadors to foreign courts, by judges, by doctors of divinity, and clergymen of all denominations, by merchants, mechanics, lawyers, and physicians, by presidents and professors in colleges and professional seminaries, by planters, overseers, and drivers. We shall show, not merely that such deeds are committed but that they are frequent; not done in corners but before the sun; not in one of the slave states but in all of them; not perpetrated by brutal overseers and drivers merely but by magistrates, by legislators, by professors of religion, by preachers of the gospel, by governors of states, by "gentlemen of property and standing," and by delicate females moving in the "highest circles of society."

We know, full well, the outcry that will be made by multitudes, at these declarations; the multiform cavils, the flat denials, the charges of "exaggeration" and "falsehood" so often bandied, the sneers of affected contempt at the credulity that can believe such things, and the rage and imprecations against those who give them currency. We know, too, the threadbare sophistries by which slaveholders and their apologists seek to evade such testimony. If they admit that such deeds are committed, they tell us that they are exceedingly rare, and therefore furnish no grounds for judging of the general treatment of slaves; that occasionally a brutal wretch in the *free* states barbarously butchers his wife, but that no one thinks of inferring from that the general treatment of wives at the North and West.

They tell us, also, that the slaveholders of the South are proverbially hospitable, kind, and generous, and it is incredible that they can perpetrate such enormities upon human beings; further, that it is absurd to suppose that they would thus injure their own property, that self-interest would prompt them to treat their slaves with kindness, as none but fools and madmen wantonly destroy their own property; further, that Northern visitors at the South come back testifying to the kind treatment of the slaves, and that the slaves themselves corroborate such representations. All these pleas, and scores of others, are bruited in every corner of the free states; and who that has eyes to see has not sickened at the blindness that saw not, at the palsy of heart that felt not, or at the cowardice and sycophancy that dared not expose such shallow fallacies. We are not to be turned from our purpose by such vapid babblings. . . .

The foregoing declarations touching the inflictions upon slaves are not haphazard assertions, nor the exaggerations of fiction conjured up to carry a point; nor are they the rhapsodies of enthusiasm, nor crude conclusions jumped at by hasty and imperfect investigation, nor the aimless outpourings either of sympathy or poetry; but they are proclamations of deliberate, well-weighed convictions, produced by accumulations of proof, by affirmations and affidavits, by written testimonies and statements of a cloud of witnesses who speak what they know and testify what they have seen; and all these impregnably fortified by proofs innumerable in the relation of the slaveholder to his slave, the nature of arbitrary power, and the nature and history of man. . . .

The barbarous indifference with which slaveholders regard the forcible sundering of husbands and wives, parents and children, brothers and sisters, and the unfeeling brutality indicated by the language in which they describe the efforts made by the slaves, in their yearnings after those from whom they have been torn away, reveals a "public opinion" toward them as dead to their ago-

ny as if they were cattle. It is well-nigh impossible to open a Southern paper without finding evidence of this. Though the truth of this assertion can hardly be called in question, we subjoin a few illustrations, and could easily give hundreds. . . .

From the *Southern Argus*, Oct. 31, 1837.
"Runaway — my negro man, Frederick, about 20 years of age. He is no doubt near the plantation of G. W. Corprew, Esq. of Noxubbee county, Mississippi, as *his wife belongs to that gentleman, and he followed her from my residence.* The above reward will be paid to any one who will confine him in jail and inform me of it at Athens, Ala.
"Athens, Alabama.
KERKMAN LEWIS."

From the *Savannah* (Ga.) *Republican*, May 24, 1838.
"$40 Reward. — Ran away from the subscriber in Savannah, his negro girl Patsey. She was purchased among the gang of negroes, known as the Hargreave's estate. She is no doubt lurking about Liberty county, at which place *she has relatives.*
EDWARD HOUSTOUN, of Florida."

From the *Charleston* (S.C.) *Courier*, June 29, 1837.
"$20 Reward will be paid for the apprehension and delivery, at the work-house in Charleston, of a mulatto woman, named Ida. It is probable she may have made her way into Georgia, where she has *connections.*
MATTHEW MUGGRIDGE."

From the *Norfolk* (Va.) *Beacon*, March 31, 1838.
"The subscriber will give $20 for the apprehension of his negro woman, Maria, who ran away about twelve months since. She is known to be lurking in or about Chuckatuch, in the county of Nansemond, where *she has a husband,* and *formerly belonged.*
PETER ONEILL."

From the *Macon* (Ga.) *Messenger*, Jan. 16, 1839.

"Ranaway from the subscriber, two negroes, Davis, a man about 45 years old; also Peggy, his wife, near the same age. Said negroes will probably make their way to Columbia county, as *they have children* living in that county. I will liberally reward any person who may deliver them to me.

NEHEMIAH KING."

From the *Petersburg* (Va.) *Constellation*, June 27, 1837.

"Ranaway, a negro man, named Peter. *He has a wife* at the plantation of Mr. C. Haws, near Suffolk, where it is supposed he is still lurking.

JOHN L. DUNN."

From the *Richmond* (Va.) *Whig*, Dec. 7, 1839.

"Ranaway from the subscriber, a negro man, named John Lewis. It is supposed that he is lurking about in New Kent county, where he professes to have *a wife*.

HILL JONES,
Agent for R. F. & P. Railroad Co."

From the *Richmond* (Va.) *Enquirer*, Feb. 20, 1838.

"$10 Reward for a negro woman, named Sally, 40 years old. We have just reason to believe the said negro to be now lurking on the James River Canal, or in the Green Spring neighborhood, where, we are informed, *her husband resides.* The above reward will be given to any person *securing* her.

POLLY C. SHIELDS.
Mount Elba, Feb. 19, 1838."

"$50 Reward. — Ran away from the subscriber, his negro man Pauladore, commonly called Paul. I understand GEN. R. Y.

HAYNE *has purchased his wife and children* from H. L. PINCKNEY, ESQ. and has them now on his plantation at Goosecreek, where, no doubt, the fellow is frequently *lurking.*

T. DAVIS."

"$25 Reward. — Ran away from the subscriber, a negro woman, named Matilda. It is thought she may be somewhere up James River, as she was claimed as *a wife* by some boatman in Goochland.

J. ALVIS."

"Stop the Runaway!!! — $25 Reward. Ranaway from the Eagle Tavern, a negro fellow, named Nat. He is no doubt attempting to *follow his wife, who was lately sold to a speculator* named Redmond. The above reward will be paid by Mrs. Lucy M. Downman, of Sussex county, Va."

Multitudes of advertisements like the above appear annually in the Southern papers. Reader, look at the preceding list — mark the unfeeling barbarity with which their masters and *mistresses* describe the struggles and perils of sundered husbands and wives, parents and children, in their weary midnight travels through forests and rivers, with torn limbs and breaking hearts, seeking the embraces of each other's love. In one instance, a mother, torn from all her children and taken to a remote part of another state, presses her way back through the wilderness, hundreds of miles, to clasp once more her children to her heart; but, when she has arrived within a few miles of them, in the same county, is discovered, seized, dragged to jail, and her purchaser told, through an advertisement, that she awaits his order. But we need not trace out the harrowing details already before the reader.

89.

A Protest Against Women Abolitionists

In 1839 some of the most influential members of the American Anti-Slavery Society submitted a document to the society protesting the assumption that the status of women within the Society was equal to the status of men. William Lloyd Garrison, who favored the integration of women within the Abolitionist movement, ridiculed the protest in the May 31, 1839, issue of the Liberator *by pointing out the similarity of its argument to that of the slaveholders. Then, in 1840, Garrison and his followers elected a woman to the Society's business committee. Garrison's opponents had in the past criticized his tactics — his language, his abuse of the clergy, and his aloofness from politics. With the election of a woman to the committee, a final break was precipitated, and Garrison's opponents withdrew from the organization in 1840. The protest of May 1839 — Garrison's comments appear at the end — is reprinted here.*

Source: *Liberator,* May 31, 1839.

PROTEST

WE, THE UNDERSIGNED, members and delegates of the American Anti-Slavery Society, as a duty and, therefore, a right, hereby protest against the principle assumed by a majority of persons representing said Society at its present meeting, that women have the right of originating, debating, and voting on questions which come before said Society, and are eligible to its various offices; and we protest against the assumption of said principle for the following, among other reasons, viz.:

1. Because it is contrary to the expectation, design, and spirit of the constitution of said Society, as clearly indicated by the proceedings of the framers of that instrument at the commencement, in the progress, and at the completion of the work. (1)

2. Because it is at variance with the construction of said instrument as made known by the constant usage of the Society from its first to its present meeting.

3. Because it is repugnant to the wishes, the wisdom, or the moral sense of many of the early and present members of said Society and devoted friends to the cause for which that Society was organized.

4. Because, though assumed by a majority of persons representing said Society in its present meeting, we believe it to be wide from the expression of the general sense of the Abolitionists of this country of either sex, and, if not objected to in this formal manner, might seem to be the unqualified and unlimited sanction of the friends of the slave and the asserters of his rights.

5. Because it is rather the expression of local and sectarian feelings, of recent origin, than of those broad sentiments which existed among the friends of our great enterprise at its beginning, and which led to the framing of the Society on a foundation where

all sects might stand and wield the potent weapon of our warfare against the oppression of our brethren.

6. Because, in conformity with these broad sentiments and in opposition to local and party peculiarity, the American Society, at its first meeting, so far from contemplating the principle which is now for the first time assumed by the aforesaid majority, recommended the organization of distinct societies of the female sex. (2)

7. Because, how much and how conscientiously soever we might differ in respect to the abstract question of the rights of women and the propriety of their action in large deliberative bodies, yet, waiving entirely any expression here of sentiment on this subject, we are persuaded that the principle which is, at this meeting, for the first time, assumed as aforesaid, is well fitted to bring *unnecessary* reproach and embarrassment to the cause of the enslaved, inasmuch as that principle is at variance with the general usage and sentiment of this and all other nations, under whatever form of government and of every age. And while we thus speak, we also declare that if the assumption of the aforesaid principle was, in our belief, demanded by the great law of right and by a divine constitution, necessary to rescue this nation from the great crime and curse of slavery, we would not hesitate to assume it in defiance of universal custom and sentiment, but would do so by openly and manfully changing either the constitution of our Society or our organization itself.

In offering this protest, we refrain from expressing any opinion respecting the propriety of those, whose right to the contemplated membership was contested, voting on the question of said right, as was done in the present case, preferring to leave such proceeding to the obvious conclusion of common sense. (3)

GARRISON'S NOTES

(1) The attentive reader can hardly fail to be struck with the resemblance which this "reason" bears to a very common argument of slaveholders against the construction which Abolitionists put upon the Declaration of Independence, the national and state constitutions, and the Bills of Rights. These documents (excepting some of the state constitutions) make no distinction of color or rank, but recognize the inalienable rights of *all* men. But, say the slaveholders, they were not intended to include Negroes, and therefore "it is contrary to the expectation, design, and spirit" of these instruments to insist that colored people should be admitted to the rights, privileges, and immunities of citizens on terms of equality with the whites!

There is no reason to suppose that the framers of the constitution of Massachusetts intended by that instrument to free the slaves. Was the decision of the supreme court, whereby liberty was proclaimed to all the inhabitants of Massachusetts, therefore null and void on that account? Nay, verily. Much is made of the fact that women were not signers of the Declaration of Sentiments, and that they have not heretofore been enrolled at our annual meetings. But this argument proves too much. There were no minors or Jews in the convention at Philadelphia in 1833. Does it therefore follow that all such persons are disqualified from being members of the American Anti-Slavery Society? We trow [think] not.

(2) So also it recommended the formation of young men's and juvenile societies. Are all minors, therefore, excluded from the privileges of membership?

(3) It should be remembered that several women voted in the negative on this question; *i.e., voted* that they *ought not to vote!*

90.

John Quincy Adams: The Declaration and the Constitution

To celebrate the fiftieth anniversary of Washington's inauguration, the New York Historical Society invited John Quincy Adams, ex-President and now a congressman from Massachusetts, to address it. Adams chose as his subject one that had been discussed and debated since the nation's inception: the nature of federal government. Against those who held that federalism meant a union of states, he argued that the Constitution had been intended to fulfill the philosophy of the Declaration of Independence by creating a union of the people. The speech, reprinted here in part, was delivered on April 30, 1839.

Source: *The Jubilee of the Constitution, A Discourse,* New York, 1839, pp. 13-118.

The motive for the Declaration of Independence was on its face avowed to be "a decent respect for the opinions of mankind"; its *purpose* to declare the *causes* which impelled the people of the English colonies on the continent of North America to separate themselves from the political community of the British nation. They declare *only* the *causes* of their separation, but they announce at the same time their assumption of the separate and equal station to which the laws of nature and of nature's God entitle them among the powers of the earth. Thus their first movement is to recognize and appeal to the laws of nature and to nature's God for their *right* to assume the attributes of sovereign power as an independent nation. . . .

It is not immaterial to remark that the signers of the Declaration, though qualifying themselves as the representatives of the United States of America, in general Congress assembled, yet issue the Declaration *in the name and by the authority of the good people of the colonies;* and that they declare, *not* each of the separate colonies but the *united colonies,* free and independent states. The whole people declared the colonies *in their united condition* of RIGHT, free, and independent states.

The dissolution of allegiance to the British Crown, the severance of the colonies from the British Empire, and their actual existence as independent states, thus declared of *right,* were definitely established *in fact* by war and peace. The independence of each separate state had never been declared of *right.* It never existed *in fact.* Upon the principles of the Declaration of Independence, the dissolution of the ties of allegiance, the assumption of sovereign power, and the institution of civil government are all acts of transcendent authority which the people *alone* are competent to perform; and, accordingly, it is in the name and by the authority of the people that two of these acts — the dissolution of allegiance, with the severance from the British Empire, and the declaration of the united colonies as free and independent states — were performed by that instrument.

But there still remained the last and crowning act, which the *people* of the Union alone were competent to perform — the institution of civil government for that compound nation, the United States of America.

At this day it cannot but strike us as extraordinary that it does not appear to have occurred to any one member of that assembly, which had laid down in terms so clear, so explicit, so unequivocal the foundation of all just government, in the imprescriptible rights of man, and the transcendent sovereignty of the people, and who, in those principles, had set forth their only personal vindication from the charges of rebellion against their king and of treason to their country, that their last crowning act was still to be performed upon the same principles — that is, the institution by the *people* of the United States, of a civil government, to guard and protect and defend them all. On the contrary, that same assembly which issued the Declaration of Independence, instead of continuing to act in the name and by the authority of the good people of the United States, had immediately, after the appointment of the committee to prepare the Declaration, appointed another committee of one member from each colony to prepare and digest the form of confederation to be entered into between the colonies.

That committee reported on the 12th of July, eight days after the Declaration of Independence had been issued, a draft of Articles of Confederation between the colonies. This draft was prepared by John Dickinson, then a delegate from Pennsylvania, who voted against the Declaration of Independence and never signed it — having been superseded by a new election of delegates from that state eight days after his draft was reported.

There was thus no congeniality of principle between the Declaration of Independence and the Articles of Confederation.

The foundation of the former were a superintending Providence — the rights of man and the constituent revolutionary power of the people. That of the latter was the sovereignty of organized power and the independence of the separate or disunited states. The fabric of the Declaration and that of the Confederation were each consistent with its own foundation, but they could not form one consistent, symmetrical edifice. They were the productions of different minds and of adverse passions — one, ascending for the foundation of human government to the laws of nature and of God, written upon the heart of man; the other, resting upon the basis of human institutions, and prescriptive law and colonial charters. The cornerstone of the one was *right;* that of the other was *power.*

The work of the founders of our independence was thus but half done. Absorbed in that more than herculean task of maintaining that independence and its principles, by one of the most cruel wars that ever glutted the furies with human woe, they marched undaunted and steadfast through that fiery ordeal, and consistent in their principles to the end, concluded, as an acknowledged sovereignty of the United States, proclaimed by their people in 1776, a peace with that same monarch whose sovereignty over them they had abjured in obedience to the laws of nature and of nature's God.

But for these United States, they had formed no constitution. Instead of resorting to the source of all constituted power, they had wasted their time, their talents, and their persevering, untiring toils in erecting and roofing and buttressing a frail and temporary shed to shelter the nation from the storm, or rather a mere baseless scaffolding on which to stand, when they should raise the marble palace of the people to stand the test of time.

Five years were consumed by Congress and the state legislatures in debating and altercating and adjusting these Articles of Confederation. The first of which was:

"Each state *retains* its sovereignty, freedom, and independence, and every power, jurisdiction, and right which is not by this Confederation expressly delegated to the United States, in Congress assembled."

Observe the departure from the language, and the consequent contrast of principles, with those of the Declaration of Independence. Each state RETAINS its sovereignty, etc. Where did each state get the sovereignty which it *retains?*

In the Declaration of Independence, the delegates of the colonies, in Congress assembled, *in the name and by the authority of the good people of the colonies,* declare, not each colony but the *united* colonies, in fact and of right, not *sovereign* but free and independent states. And why did they make this declaration in the name and by the authority of the one people of all the colonies? Because, by the principles before laid down in the Declaration, the people, and the people alone, as the rightful source of all legitimate government, were competent to dissolve the bands of subjection of all the colonies to the nation of Great Britain, and to constitute them free and independent states.

Now the people of the colonies, speaking by their delegates in Congress, had not declared *each* colony a sovereign, free, and independent state; nor had the people of each colony so declared the colony itself, nor could they so declare it, because each was already bound in union with all the rest — a union formed *de facto* by the spontaneous revolutionary movement of the whole people, and organized by the meeting of the first Congress, in 1774, a year and ten months before the Declaration of Independence.

Where, then, did *each* state get the sovereignty, freedom, and independence which the Articles of Confederation declare it *retains?* Not from the whole people of the whole Union; not from the Declaration of Independence; not from the people of the state itself. It was assumed by agreement between the legislatures of the several states and their delegates in Congress, without authority from or consultation of the people at all.

In the Declaration of Independence, the enacting and constituent party dispensing and delegating sovereign power is the whole *people* of the united colonies. The recipient party, invested with power, is the united colonies, declared United States.

In the Articles of Confederation, this order of agency is inverted. Each state is the constituent and enacting party, and the United States, in Congress assembled, the recipient of delegated power — and that power, delegated with such a penurious and carking hand, that it had more the aspect of a revocation of the Declaration of Independence than an instrument to carry it into effect. . . .

Washington, though in retirement, was brooding over the cruel injustice suffered by his associates in arms, the warriors of the Revolution; over the prostration of the public credit and the faith of the nation in the neglect to provide for the payment even of the interest upon the public debt; over the disappointed hopes of the friends of freedom; in the language of the address from Congress to the states of the 18th of April, 1783 — "the pride and boast of America, that the rights for which she contended were the rights of human nature."

At his residence of Mount Vernon, in March 1785, the first idea was started of a revisal of the Articles of Confederation by an organization of means differing from that of a compact between the state legislatures and their own delegates in Congress. A convention of delegates from the state legislatures, independent of the Congress itself, was the expedient which presented itself for effecting the purpose, and an augmentation of the powers of Congress for the regulation of commerce as the object for which this assembly was to be convened. In January 1786, the proposal was made and adopted in the legislature of Virginia and communicated to the other state legislatures.

The convention was held at Annapolis in September of that year. It was attended by delegates from only five of the central states, who, on comparing their restricted powers, with the glaring and universally acknowledged defects of the Confederation, reported only a recommendation for the assemblage of another convention of delegates to meet at Philadelphia, in May 1787, from all the states and with enlarged powers.

The Constitution of the United States was the work of this Convention. But in its construction the Convention immediately perceived that they must retrace their steps and fall back from a league of friendship between sovereign states to the constituent sovereignty of the *people*; from *power* to *right*; from the irresponsible despotism of state sovereignty to the self-evident truths of the Declaration of Independence. In that instrument, the right to institute and to alter governments among men was ascribed exclusively to the *people*; the ends of government were declared to be to *secure* the natural rights of man; and that *when* the government degenerates from the promotion to the destruction of that end, the right and the duty accrues to the people to dissolve this degenerate government and to institute another.

The signers of the Declaration further averred that the one people of the *united colonies* were then precisely in that situation — with a government degenerated into tyranny and called upon by the laws of nature and of nature's God to dissolve that government and to institute another. Then, in the name and by the authority of the good people of the colonies, they pronounced the dissolution of their allegiance to the King and their eternal separation from the nation of Great Britain, and declared the united colonies independent states. And here, as the representatives of the one people, they had stopped. They did not require the confirmation of this act, for the power to make the Declaration had already been conferred upon them by the people; delegating the power, indeed, separately in the separate colonies, not by colonial authority but by the spontaneous revolutionary movement of the people in them all.

From the day of that Declaration, the constituent power of the people had never been called into action. A confederacy had been substituted in the place of a government; and state sovereignty had usurped the constituent sovereignty of the people.

The Convention assembled at Philadelphia had themselves no direct authority from the people. Their authority was all derived from the state legislatures. But they had the Articles of Confederation before them, and they saw and felt the wretched condition into which they had brought the whole people, and that the Union itself was in the agonies of death. They soon perceived that the indispensably needed powers were such as no state government, no combination of them was, by the principles of the Declaration of Independence, competent to bestow. They could emanate only from the people. A highly respectable portion of the assembly, still clinging to the confederacy of states, proposed as a substitute for the Constitution a mere revival of the Articles of Confederation, with a grant of additional powers to the Congress. Their plan was respectfully and thoroughly discussed, but the want of a government and of the sanction of the people to the delegation of powers happily prevailed.

A constitution for the people and the distribution of legislative, executive, and judicial powers was prepared. It announced itself as the work of the people themselves; and as this was unquestionably a power assumed by the Convention not delegated to them by the people, they religiously confined it to a simple power to propose, and carefully provided that it should be no more than a proposal until sanctioned by the confederation Congress, by the state legislatures, and by the people of the several states, in conventions specially assembled by authority of their legislatures for the single purpose of examining and passing upon it.

And thus was consummated the work commenced by the Declaration of Independence — a work in which the people of the North American Union, acting under the deepest sense of responsibility to the Supreme Ruler of the universe, had achieved the most transcendent act of power that social man in his mortal condition can perform. Even that of dissolving the ties of allegiance which he is bound to his country, of renouncing that country itself, of demolishing its government, of instituting another government, and of making for himself another country in its stead.

And on that day, of which you now commemorate the fiftieth anniversary — on that 30th day of April, 1789 — was this mighty revolution, not only in the affairs of our own country but in the principles of government over civilized man, accomplished.

The Revolution itself was a work of thirteen years — and had never been completed until that day. The Declaration of Independence and the Constitution of the United States are parts of one consistent whole, founded upon one and the same theory of government, then new, not as a theory, for it had been working itself into the mind of man for many ages, and been especially expounded in the writings of Locke, but had never before been adopted by a great nation in practice.

There are yet, even at this day, many speculative objections to this theory. Even in our own country there are still philosophers who deny the principles asserted in the Declaration as self-evident truths; who deny the natural equality and inalienable

Library of Congress

John Quincy Adams; daguerreotype by Brady

rights of man; who deny that the people are the only legitimate source of power; who deny that all just powers of government are derived from the *consent* of the governed. Neither your time, nor perhaps the cheerful nature of this occasion, permit me here to enter upon the examination of this antirevolutionary theory which arrays state sovereignty against the constituent sovereignty of the people, and distorts the Constitution of the United States into a league of friendship between confederate corporations.

I speak to matters of fact. There is the Declaration of Independence and there is the Constitution of the United States — let them speak for themselves. The grossly immoral and dishonest doctrine of despotic state sovereignty, the exclusive judge of its own obligations, and responsible to no power on earth or in Heaven, for the violation of them, is not there. The Declaration says it is not in me. The Constitution says it is not in me. . . .

The signers of the Declaration of Independence themselves were the persons who had first fallen into the error of believing that a confederacy of independent states would serve as a substitute for the repudiated government of Great Britain. Experience had demonstrated their mistake, and the condition of the country was a shriek of terror at its awful magnitude. They did retrace their steps, not to extinguish the federative feature in which their union had been formed — nothing could be wider from their intention — but to restore the order of things conformably to the principles of the Declaration of Independence and as they had been arranged in the first plans for a confederation — to make the people of the Union the constituent body and the reservation of the rights of the states subordinate to the Constitution. Hence the delegation of power was not from each state retaining its sovereignty, and all rights not expressly delegated by the states, but from the people of each and of all the states to the United States, in Congress assembled, representing at once the whole people and all the states of the Union.

They retained the federative feature preeminently in the constitution of the Senate, and in the complication of its great powers — legislative, executive, and judicial — making that body a participant in all the great departments of constituted power. They preserved the federative principle and combined it with the constituent power of the people in the mode of electing the President of the United States, whether by the electoral colleges or by the House of Representatives voting by states. They preserved it even in the constitution of the House, the popular branch of the legislature, by giving separate delegations to the people of each state. But they expressly made the Constitution and constitutional laws of the United States paramount not only to the laws but to the constitutions of the separate states inconsistent with them.

I have traced step by step, in minute and tedious detail, the departure from the principles of the Declaration of Independence in the process of organizing the Confederation — the disastrous and lamentable consequences of that departure and the admirable temper and spirit with which the Convention at Philadelphia returned to those principles in the preparation and composition of the Constitution of the United States.

That this work was still imperfect, candor will compel us all to admit; though in specifying its imperfections, the purest minds and the most patriotic hearts differ widely from each other in their conclusions. Distrustful as it becomes me to be of my own judgment, but authorized by the experience of a full half century, during which I have been variously and almost uninterruptedly engaged in both branches of the legislature and in the executive departments of this government, and released, by my own rapid approach to the closing scene of life, from all possible influence of personal interest or ambition, I may perhaps be permitted to remark that the omission of a clear and explicit Declaration of Rights was a great defect in the Constitution as presented by the Convention to the people, and that it has been imperfectly remedied by the ten articles of amendment proposed by the first Congress under the Constitution, and now incorporated with it.

A Declaration of Rights would have marked in a more emphatic manner the return from the derivative sovereignty of the states to the constituent sovereignty of the people for the basis of the federal Union than was done by the words, "We the people of the United States," in the Preamble to the Constitution. A Declaration of Rights, also, systematically drawn up, as a part of the Constitution, and adapted to it with the consummate skill displayed in the consistent adjustment of its mighty powers, would have made it more complete in its unity and in its symmetry than it now appears, an elegant edifice, but encumbered with superadditions, not always in keeping with the general character of the building itself.

A Declaration of Rights, reserved by the constituent body, the people, might and probably would have prevented many delicate and dangerous questions of conflicting jurisdictions which have arisen and may yet arise between the general and the separate state governments. The rights reserved by the people would have been exclusively their own rights, and they would have been protected from the encroachments not only of the general government but of the disunited states. . . .

The first object of the people declared by the Constitution as their motive for its establishment, *to form a more perfect Union*, had been attained by the establishment of the Constitution itself; but this was yet to be demonstrated by its practical operation in the establishment of justice, in the insurance of domestic tranquillity, in the provision for the common defense, in the promotion of the general welfare, and in securing the blessings of liberty to the people themselves, the authors of the Constitution, and to their posterity.

These are the great and transcendental objects of all legitimate government; the primary purposes of all human association. For these purposes the Confederation had been instituted, and had signally failed for their attainment. How far have they been attained under this new national organization?

It has abided the trial of time. This day, fifty years have passed away since the first impulse was given to the wheels of this political machine. The generation by which it was constructed has passed away. Not one member of the Convention who gave this Constitution to their country survives. They have enjoyed its blessings so far as they were secured by their labors. They have been gathered to their fathers. That posterity for whom they toiled, not less anxiously than for themselves, has arisen to occupy their places and is rapidly passing away in its turn. A third generation, unborn upon the day which you commemorate, forms a vast majority of the assembly who now honor me with their attention.

Your city, which then numbered scarcely 30,000 inhabitants, now counts its numbers by hundreds of thousands. Your state, then numbering less than double the population of your city at this day, now tells its children by millions. The thirteen primitive states of the Revolution, painfully rallied by this Constitution to the fold from which the impotence and disuniting character of the Confederacy was already leading them astray, now reinforced by an equal number of younger sisters, and all swarming with an active, industrious, and hardy population, have penetrated from the Atlantic to the Rocky Mountains, and opened a paradise upon the wilds watered by the father of the floods. The Union, which at the first census, ordained by this Constitution, returned a people of less than 4 million of souls; at the next census, already commanded by law, the semi-central enumeration since that day, is about to exhibit a return of 17 million. Never, since the first assemblage of men in social union, has there been such a scene of continued prosperity recorded upon the annals of time.

How much of this prosperity is justly attributable to the Constitution, then first put upon its trial, may perhaps be differently estimated by speculative minds. Never was a form of government so obstinately, so pertinaciously contested before its establishment; and never was human foresight and sagacity more disconcerted and refuted by the event than those of the opposers of the Constitution. On the other hand, its results have surpassed the most sanguine anticipations of its friends. Neither Washington, nor Madison, nor Hamilton dared to hope that this new experiment of government would so triumphantly accomplish the purposes which the Confederation had so utterly failed to effect. . . .

The Constitution of the United States was republican and democratic; but the experience of all former ages had shown that, of all human governments, democracy was the most unstable, fluctuating, and short-lived; and it was obvious that if virtue — the virtue of the people — was the foundation of republican government, the stability and duration of the government must depend upon the stability and duration of the virtue by which it is sustained.

Now the *virtue* which had been infused into the Constitution of the United States, and was to give to its vital existence the stability and duration to which it was destined, was no other than the concretion of those abstract principles which had been first proclaimed in the Declaration of Independence; namely, the self-evident truths of the natural and unalienable rights of man, of the indefeasible constituent and dissolvent sovereignty of the people, always subordinate to a rule of right and wrong, and always responsible to the Supreme Ruler of the universe for the *rightful* exercise of that sovereign, constituent, and dissolvent power.

This was the platform upon which the Constitution of the United States had been erected. Its virtues, its republican character consisted in its conformity to the principles proclaimed in the Declaration of Independence, and as its administration must necessarily be always pliable to the fluctuating varieties of public opinion; its stability and duration by a like overruling and irresistible necessity was to depend upon the stability and duration in the hearts and minds of the people of that *virtue*, or, in other words, of those principles proclaimed in the Declaration of Independence and embodied in the Constitution of the United States. . . .

Every change of a President of the United States has exhibited some variety of policy from that of his predecessor. In more than one case, the change has extended to political and even to moral principle; but the policy of the country has been fashioned far more by the influences of public opinion and the prevailing humors in the two houses of Congress than by the judgment, the will, or the principles of the President of the United States. The President himself is no more than a representative of public opinion at the time of his election; and as public opinion is subject to great and frequent fluctuations, he *must* accommodate his policy to them; or the people will speedily give him a successor; or either house of Congress will effectually control his power.

It is thus, and in no other sense, that the Constitution of the United States is democratic; for the government of our country, instead of a democracy the most simple, is the most complicated government on the face of the globe. From the immense extent of our territory, the difference of manners, habits, opinions, and, above all, the clashing interests of the North, South, East, and West, public opinion formed by the combination of numerous aggregates becomes itself a problem of compound arithmetic, which nothing but the result of the popular elections can solve.

It has been my purpose, fellow citizens, in this discourse to show:

1. That this Union was formed by spontaneous movement of the *people* of thirteen English colonies, all subjects of the King of Great Britain, bound to him in allegiance and to the British Empire as their country; that the first object of this Union was united resistance against oppression, and to obtain from the government of their country redress of their wrongs.

2. That failing in this object, their petitions having been spurned and the oppressions of which they complained aggravated beyond endurance, their delegates in Congress, *in their name and by their authority,*

issued the Declaration of Independence —
proclaiming them to the world as *one people*,
absolving them from their ties and oaths of
allegiance to their king and country, renouncing that country; declaring the UNITED
colonies, independent states, and announc-
ing that this ONE PEOPLE of thirteen united,
independent states, by that act, assumed
among the powers of the earth that separate
and equal station to which the laws of nature and of nature's God entitled them.

3. That in justification of themselves for
this act of transcendent power, they proclaimed the principles upon which they held
all lawful government upon earth to be
founded; which principles were the natural,
unalienable, imprescriptible rights of man,
specifying among them, life, liberty, and the
pursuit of happiness; that the institution of
government is to *secure* to men in society
the possession of those rights; that the institution, dissolution, and reinstitution of government belong exclusively to THE PEOPLE
under a moral responsibility to the Supreme
Ruler of the universe; and that all the *just*
powers of government are derived from the
consent of the governed.

4. That under this proclamation of principles, the dissolution of allegiance to the
British King, and the compatriot connection
with the people of the British Empire, were
accomplished; and the *one people* of the
United States of America became one separate, sovereign, independent power, assuming an equal station among the nations of
the earth.

5. That this one people did not immediately institute a government for themselves. But instead of it, their delegates in
Congress, by authority from their separate
state legislatures, without voice or consultation of the people, instituted a mere Confederacy.

6. That this Confederacy totally departed from the principles of the Declaration of
Independence, and substituted, instead of
the constituent power of the people, an assumed sovereignty of each separate state as
the source of all its authority.

7. That as a primitive source of power,
this separate state sovereignty was not only
a departure from the principles of the Declaration of Independence but directly contrary to and utterly incompatible with
them.

8. That the tree was made known by its
fruits; that after five years wasted in its
preparation, the Confederacy dragged out a
miserable existence of eight years more, and
expired like a candle in the socket, having
brought the Union itself to the verge of dissolution.

9. That the Constitution of the United
States was a *return* to the principles of the
Declaration of Independence, and the exclu-
sive constituent power of the people; that it
was the work of the ONE PEOPLE of the
United States; and that those United
States, though doubled in numbers, still
constitute as a nation but ONE PEOPLE.

10. That this Constitution, making due
allowance for the imperfections and errors
incident to all human affairs, has under all
the vicissitudes and changes of war and
peace been administered upon those same
principles during a career of fifty years.

11. That its fruits have been, still making
allowance for human imperfection, a more
perfect Union, established justice, domestic
tranquillity, provision for the common defense, promotion of the general welfare, and
the enjoyment of the blessings of liberty by
the constituent *people* and their posterity to
the present day.

And now the future is all before us, and
Providence our guide.

91.

Hans Barlien: A People from All Nations of the World

Although the great influx of Scandinavians to America did not occur until after the Civil War, the Norwegians began coming in appreciable numbers in the 1840s. In Scandinavia land was scarce and relatively poor. Immigrants came primarily from small farming communities in search of larger and more fertile tracts of land. They were often attracted, in this early period, by the favorable reports of "American letters," such as the one reproduced below, that were circulated from hand to hand and printed in the local papers. The following letter, addressed to the Reverend Jens Rynning, was written from St. Francisville on the Des Moines River, Missouri, on April 23, 1839; it appeared in Morgenbladet (Christiania) in the same year.

Source: Blegen, pp. 52-54.

I ASSUME THAT NO ONE who knows the facts has wished to inform you about your son's fate, or has been in a position to do so. Since you probably should know the truth, I shall try to report it to you as well as I can.

Your son himself probably notified you that he had bought land and was living not very far from the city of Ottawa on the Fox River in the state of Illinois, 11.5° west of Washington and 41.5° latitude north, a swampy and unhealthful place which last autumn deprived him and most of the Norwegians there of their lives. The last to arrive there, a group of twenty who had been lured to the place by a Swede, likewise lost their lives along with the Swede.

This news was brought to us by a man who visited that part of the country last year. But neither he nor anyone else knew anything about Rynning's birthplace and parents.

I stayed in St. Louis for sixteen months to find out where the Norwegians were living and also to learn where land is available for those who want to come to America. I have found that all immigrants have let themselves be taken in by the land speculators who have bought up the land, and so settlers have been scattered over almost all of the states. But I have also found land in abundance that is fertile, healthful, and profitable in every respect. On my arrival I approached Congress and the Senate with a recommendation from the American minister in Copenhagen; I therefore expect to get from them a guarantee of the necessary land, so that no land speculator will bother the Norwegians who want to settle here.

This land is to the northeast of the Des Moines River and west of the Mississippi, that is, at 41° latitude north and 16° longitude west of Washington. You can claim the necessary land without buying it; and when in ten, twenty, or thirty years it comes up for sale, you can keep what you have claimed at $1.25 an acre, which will be very easy to do then even though you have to start out with nothing.

The most convenient way to get here is

to leave from Bergen, that is, when the group that wants to come over here is big enough either to charter or buy a ship, and sail north of Scotland direct to New Orleans, and from there take the big steamboats up the Mississippi 1,400 miles (234 Norwegian miles); then you land at Churchville opposite Warsaw at the mouth of the Des Moines River, from where it is 10 miles (1½ Norwegian miles) to this place. A man who is able to buy a cow and some tools may claim land at once and start on his own; but a man who has nothing can get a job at good daily wages, so that soon he will be able to claim his own land.

As the free land I have mentioned is part of the territory of Wisconsin and belongs, so to speak, to no one, it is the freest and is particularly suitable for the founding of a colony.

Our correspondence was interrupted by intervening circumstances, and my earlier letters, together with other papers and books of mine, are now in the hands of my son in Christiania. As a result, the matters mentioned above have not come to the attention of the public in the Old World.

All kinds of people from all nations of the world live together here like brothers and sisters; and in spite of the fact that there are no garrisons of soldiers, police, and the like, you never hear anything about theft, begging, or any noticeable ill will between neighbors. To me everybody is good, kind, and accommodating. Nobody here can take anything away from you by force; but he can do this by cunning, power of money, and forestallment. This I hope to prevent on our claims by the help of Congress

and so, in time, to succeed in uniting the Norwegians who are still here.

Speculators who have bought up vast stretches of land have usually got hold of some that is too swampy to be healthful. But since such land is generally very fertile, it is easy for them to lure on to it ignorant people, whose way to the grave is thereby considerably shortened.

Since Missouri is a slave state, there are a great many Negroes here. They are held in ignorance and have a superstitious kind of religion, for which they have their own ministers. If a theft is committed, people are sure that a colored person did it, much as a monkey would, so that it is not very difficult to get the stolen goods back; and the thief is given a number of lashes on his bare back, according to the circumstances.

The population of St. Louis is about 20,000. My smithy was in a basement facing the street and without a door; yet I never lost any tools, materials, or anything else in my shop, in spite of the fact that in the same house lived eight slaves who were often visited by other colored people passing my basement door. But then they bore me no malice as I was just pleasant and accommodating to them as to other people.

Since I now live 1,500 miles (about 250 Norwegian miles) from the coast, I know of no better way to get this letter delivered than to send it to New York, to one Miss Laumann from Christian County, requesting her to mail it to Norway.

Give my greetings to all those who are eager for information and tell them that I am as happy here as any person can be, and that those who want to come here may, with a little effort, live just as happily.

92.

MICHEL CHEVALIER: Work, Speculation, and Democracy

Michel Chevalier was sent to the United States by the French government in 1833 to study railroad and canal construction. Imbued with the teachings of Saint-Simon, Chevalier believed that the future course of civilization would be everywhere marked by the industrial development that was then discernible in America. He was an especially keen observer of American economic life. His observations were published in a series of letters that he sent to the Journal des Débats. *After Chevalier returned to France in 1835, these and other letters were published as a book,* Lettres sur l'Amérique du Nord *(1836). An expanded second edition was published in 1837, and a third in 1838. The first English edition,* Society, Manners, and Politics in the United States, *appeared in 1839.*

Source: *Society, Manners, and Politics in the United States,* John William Ward, ed., New York, 1961, pp. 261-272, 295-319.

IN GENERAL, THE AMERICAN is little disposed to be contented; his idea of equality is to be inferior to none, but he endeavors to rise in only one direction. His only means, like his only thought, is to subdue the material world; or, in other words, his means is industry in its various branches — business, speculation, work, action. To this sole object everything is subordinate — education, politics, private and public life. Everything in American society, from religion and morals to domestic usages and daily habits of life, is bent in the direction of this aim common to each and every one.

If there are some exceptions to this general rule, they are few and belong to two causes: first, American society, absorbed as it is in its work, is not destined to remain forever imprisoned in this narrow circle, and it already contains the germs of its future destiny, whatever it may be, in the centuries ahead; second, human nature, however finite, is not single and no force in the world

can stifle its eternal protest against exclusiveness in taste, institutions, and manners. Speculation and business, work and action, these, then, under various forms, are the special task which Americans have chosen with a zeal that amounts to fanaticism. This was marked out for them by the finger of Providence in order that a continent should be brought under the dominion of civilization with the least possible delay. . . .

With what zeal and devotion has the Anglo-American fulfilled his mission as a pioneer in a new continent! Behold how he makes his way over the rocks and precipices; see how he struggles face to face with the rivers, with the swamps, with the primeval forests; see how he slaughters the wolf and the bear, how he exterminates the Indian, who in his eyes is only another wild beast! In this conflict with the external world, with land and water, with mountains and the pestilential air, he appears full of that impetuosity with which Greece flung itself into Asia at the voice of Alexander; of that fanatical daring with which Mahomet inspired his Arabs for the conquest of the Eastern empire; of that delirious courage which animated our fathers forty years ago when they threw themselves upon Europe.

On the same rivers, therefore, where our colonists floated, carelessly singing in the bark canoe of the savage, they have launched fleets of superb steamers. Where we fraternized with the redskins, sleeping with them in the forests, living like them on the chase, traveling in their manner over rugged trails on foot, the persevering American has felled the aged trees, guided the plough, enclosed the fields, substituted the best breeds of English cattle for the wild deer, created farms, flourishing villages, and opulent cities, dug canals, and made roads. Those waterfalls which we admired as lovers of the picturesque and the height of which our officers measured at the risk of their lives, those he has shut up for the use of his mills and factories, regardless of the scenery.

If these countries had continued to belong to the French, the population would certainly have been more gay than the present American race; it would have enjoyed more highly whatever it might have possessed, but it would have had less comfort; and wealth and ages would have passed away before man had become master of those regions which have been reclaimed in less than fifty years by the Americans.

If we examine the acts passed by the local legislatures at each session, we shall find that at least three-fourths relate to the banks, which provide credit for the worker; to the establishment of new religious societies and churches, which are the citadels where the guardians of industry keep watch; to routes and means of communication — roads, canals, railways, bridges, and steamboats — which facilitate the access of the producer to the markets; to primary instruction for the use of the mechanic and the laborer; to various commercial regulations; or to the incorporation of towns and villages, the work of these hardy pioneers. There is no mention of an army; the fine arts are not so much as named; literary institutions and the higher scientific studies are rarely honored with notice.

The tendency of the laws is above all to promote industry, material labor, the task of the moment. In the states that are somewhat older, the laws are always marked by their respect for property, because the legislature feels that the greatest encouragement to industry is to respect its fruits. They are especially conservative of landed property, either from a lingering remembrance of the feudal laws of the mother country, or because they are anxious to preserve some element of stability in the midst of the general change; yet the laws generally pay less regard to the rights of property than is the case in Europe.

Woe to whatever is inactive and unproductive if it can be accused on however slight a foundation of resting upon monopoly and privilege! The rights of industry here have precedence over all others, efface all others, and it is on this account that, except in the affair of public credit in which the towns and states pique themselves on the most scrupulous exactness in fulfilling their engagements, in every dispute between the capitalists and the producer, the latter almost always has the better.

Everything is here arranged to facilitate industry; the towns are built on the English plan; men of business, instead of being scattered over the town, occupy a particular quarter, devoted exclusively to them, in which there is not a building used as a dwelling house and nothing but offices and warehouses to be seen. The brokers, bankers, and lawyers here have their cells, the merchants their counting-rooms; here the banks, insurance offices, and other companies have their chambers; and other buildings are filled from cellar to garret with articles of merchandise. At any hour, one merchant has but a few steps to go after any other, or after a broker or a lawyer.

This, it will be seen, is not according to the Paris fashion, by which a great deal of precious time is lost by men of business in running after one another; in this respect, Paris is the worst arranged commercial city in the world. New York is, however, inferior in this particular to London or Liverpool; it has nothing like the great docks and the Commercial House.

The manners and customs are those of a working, busy society. At fifteen, a man is engaged in business; at twenty-one, he is established, he has his farm, his workshop, his counting-room, or his office — in a word, his employment, whatever it may be. Twenty-one is also the age at which he gets married, and at twenty-two he is the father of a family and consequently has a powerful stimulus to excite him to industry. A man who has no profession and — which is nearly the same thing — who is not married, enjoys little consideration; he who is an active and useful member of society, who contributes his share to augment the national wealth and increase the numbers of the population, he only is looked upon with respect and favor.

The American is brought up with the idea that he will have some particular occupation, that he is to be a farmer, artisan, manufacturer, merchant, speculator, lawyer, physician, or minister, perhaps all in succession, and that if he is active and intelligent he will make his fortune. He has no conception of living without a profession, even when his family is rich, for he sees nobody about him not engaged in business. The man of leisure is a variety of the human species which the Yankee does not suppose to exist, and he knows that, though rich today, his father may be ruined tomorrow. Besides, the father himself is, as is customary, engaged in business and does not think of passing on his fortune; if the son wishes

to have one at present, let him make it himself!

The habits of life are those of an exclusively working people. From the moment he gets up, the American is at his work and he is absorbed in it till the hour of sleep. He never permits pleasure to distract him; public affairs alone have the right to take him for a few moments. Even mealtime is not for him a period of relaxation, when he might rest his weary brain in an intimate and restful environment. It is only a disagreeable interruption of business, an interruption which he accepts because it is inevitable, but which he cuts short as much as possible. In the evening, if no political meeting requires his attendance, if he does not go to discuss some question of public interest or to a religious meeting, he sits at home, thoughtful and absorbed in his meditations, whether on the transactions of the day or the projects of tomorrow.

He refrains from business on Sunday because his religion commands it, but it also requires him to abstain from all amusement and recreation — music, cards, dice, or billiards — under penalty of sacrilege. On Sunday an American would not dare to receive his friends. His servants would not consent to it, and on that day he can hardly secure their services for himself at an hour also convenient to them. A few days ago, the mayor of New York was accused by one of the newspapers of having entertained on Sunday some English noblemen who came from England in their own yacht to give the American democracy a strange idea of British tastes. The mayor hastened to declare publicly that he was too well acquainted with his duties as a Christian to entertain his friends on the Sabbath. Nothing is, therefore, more melancholy than the seventh day in this country; after such a Sunday, the labor of Monday is a delightful pastime. . . .

Tall, slender, and light of figure, the American seems built expressly for labor.

He has no equal for dispatch of business. No one else can conform so easily to new situations and circumstances; he is always ready to adopt new processes and implements, or to change his occupation. He is a mechanic by nature. Among us there is not a schoolboy who has not composed a ballad, written a novel, or drawn up a republican or monarchical constitution. In Massachusetts and Connecticut, there is not a laborer who has not invented a mchine or a tool. There is not a man of any importance who has not his scheme for a railroad, a project for a village or a town, or who has not some grand speculation in the drowned lands of the Red River, in the cotton lands of the Yazoo, or in the cornfields of Illinois.

Eminently a pioneer, the American type, he who is not more or less Europeanized, the pure Yankee, in a word, is not only a worker, he is a migratory worker. He has no root in the soil; he is a stranger to the worship of one's birthplace and family home; he is always in the mood to move on, always ready to start in the first steamer that comes along from the place where he had just now landed. He is devoured with a passion for movement, he cannot stay in one place; he must go and come, he must stretch his limbs and keep his muscles in play. When his feet are not in motion, his fingers must be in action; he must be whittling a piece of wood, cutting the back of his chair, or notching the edge of the table, or his jaws must be at work grinding tobacco. Whether it be that continual competition has given him the habit, or that he has an exaggerated estimate of the value of time, or that the unsettled state of everything around him keeps his nervous system in a state of perpetual agitation, or that he has come so from the hands of nature, he always has something to do, he is always in a terrible hurry.

He is fit for all sorts of work except those which require a careful slowness. Those fill

him with horror; it is his idea of hell. "We are born in haste," says an American writer,

we take our education on the run; we marry on the wing; we make a fortune at a stroke and lose it on the same manner, to make and lose it again ten times over in the twinkling of an eye. Our body is a locomotive going at the rate of twenty-five miles an hour; our soul, a high-pressure engine; our life is like a shooting star; and death overtakes us at last like a flash of lightning.

In the hotels and on board the steamboats, the door of the dining hall is crowded at the approach of a mealtime. As soon as the bell sounds, there is a general rush into the room and in less than ten minutes every place is occupied. In a quarter of an hour, out of 300 persons, 200 have left the table, and in ten minutes more not an individual is to be seen. On my passage from Baltimore to Norfolk, in the winter of 1834, I found that, despite the cold, three-fourths of the passengers had risen at 4 o'clock, and at 6, being almost the only person left abed and feeling sure that we must be near our port, I got up and went upon deck; but it was not until 8 o'clock that we came in sight of Norfolk.

On mentioning the fact afterward to an American, a man of sense who was on board at the same time and who, wiser than I, had lain abed till after sunrise: "Ah, sir," said he, "if you knew my countrymen better, you wouldn't be at all surprised at their getting up at 4 o'clock to arrive at 9. An American is always on the lookout lest any of his neighbors should get the start of him. If 100 Americans were going to be shot, they would contend for first place, so strong is their habit of competition."

"Work," says American society to the poor,

work, and at eighteen you shall get, you a simple worker, more than a captain in Europe. You shall live in plenty, be well-clothed, well-housed, and able to save. Be attentive to your work, be sober and religious, and you will find a devoted and submissive wife; you will have a more comfortable home than many of the higher classes in Europe. From a journeyman, you shall become a master; you shall have apprentices and dependents under you in turn; you will have credit without stint, become a manufacturer or agriculturist on a great scale; you will speculate and become rich, found a town and give it your own name; you will be a member of the legislature of your state or alderman of your city, and finally member of Congress; your son shall have as good a chance to be made President as the son of the President himself. Work, and if the fortune of business should be against you and you fall, you shall soon be able to rise again, for a failure is nothing but a wound in battle; it shall not deprive you of the esteem or confidence of anyone, if you have always been prudent and temperate, a good Christian and a faithful husband.

"Work," America says to the rich,

work and do not stop to think of enjoying your wealth. You shall increase your income without increasing your expenses; you shall enlarge your fortune, but it shall be only to increase the sources of labor for the poor and to extend your power over the material world. Be simple and severe in your exterior, but at home you may have the richest carpets, plate in abundance, the finest linens of Ireland and Saxony. Externally, your house will be on the same model with all others of the town; you will have neither livery nor equipage, you will not patronize the theater, which tends to relax morals; you will avoid play; you will sign the articles and pledges of the Temperance Society; you will not even indulge in good cheer; you shall set an example of constant attendance at your church; you shall always show the most profound respect for morals and religion, for the farmer and mechanic around you have their eyes fixed upon you; they take you for their model; they still acknowledge you to be the arbiter of manners and customs, although they have taken from you the political scepter. If you give yourself up to pleasure, to parade, to amusement, to dissipation and luxury, they also will give rein to their gross appetites and their violent passions. Your country will be ruined, and you will be ruined with it. . . .

I SAID THAT EVERYTHING has become an object of speculation; I was mistaken. The American, essentially practical in his views, will never speculate in tulips, even at New York, although the inhabitants of that city have Dutch blood in their veins. The principal objects of speculation are those subjects which chiefly occupy the calculating minds of the Americans, that is to say, cotton, land, city and town lots, banks, railroads.

The lovers of land in the North contest with each other for valuable timberlands; in the deep South, for Mississippi swamps and Alabama and Red River cotton lands; in the far West, for the cornfields and pastures of Illinois and Michigan. The unparalleled growth of some new towns has turned people's heads and there is a general rush to any location which is fortunately situated; as if, before ten years, three or four Londons, as many Parises, and a dozen Liverpools were about to display their streets, their monuments, their quays crowded with warehouses, and their harbors bristling with masts in the American wilderness. In New York enough building lots (a lot is generally from 22 to 25 feet front, and from 80 to 100 feet deep) have been sold for a population of 2 million; at New Orleans, for at least 1 million. Pestilential marshes and naked precipices of rock have been bought and sold as places to build. In Louisiana, the quagmires, the bottomless haunts of alligators, the lakes and cypress swamps, with 10 feet of water or slime, and in the North, the bed of the Hudson with 20, 30, or 50 feet of water, have found numerous purchasers.

Take the map of the United States; place yourself on the shore of Lake Erie, which twenty years ago was a solitary wilderness; ascend it to its head; pass thence to Lake St. Clair, and from that lake push on toward the north, across Lake Huron; go forward still, thread your way through Lake Michigan and advance southward till the water fails you; here you will find a little town by the name of Chicago, one of the outposts of our indefatigable countrymen when they had possession of America.

Chicago seems destined at some future period to enjoy an extensive trade; it will occupy the head of a canal which will connect the Mississippi with the lakes and the St. Lawrence; but at present it hardly numbers two or three thousand inhabitants. Chicago has behind it a country of amazing fertility; but this country is yet an uncultivated wilderness. Nevertheless the land for twenty-five miles around has been sold, resold, and sold again in small sections; not, however, at Chicago but at New York, which by the route actually traveled is 2,000 miles away. There you may find plans of enough Chicago lots for 300,000 inhabitants; this is more than any city of the New World at present contains. Surely, more than one buyer will count himself fortunate if, on examination, he finds no more than 6 feet of water on his purchase.

Speculations in railroads have been hardly less wild than those in land. The American has a perfect passion for railroads; he loves them, to use Camille Desmoulins' expression in reference to Mirabeau, as a lover loves his mistress. It is not merely because his supreme happiness consists in that speed which annihilates time and space; it is also because he sees, for the American always reasons, that this mode of communication is admirably adapted to the vast extent of his country, to its great maritime plain and to the level surface of the Mississippi Valley; and because he sees all around him in the native forest abundant materials for executing these works at a cheap rate. This is the reason why railroads are multiplied in such

Michel Chevalier

profusion, competing not only with each other but entering into a rivalry with the rivers and canals. If the works now in process of construction are completed (and I think that they will be), there will be within two years three distinct routes between Philadelphia and Baltimore, exclusive of the old post route; namely, two lines consisting wholly of railroads, and a third consisting in part of steamboats and in part of railroad. The line that has the advantage of half an hour over its rivals will be sure to crush them.

The manner of establishing banks, universally adopted here (it is the same for all enterprises which affect the public welfare, even when they are handed over to private enterprise), is this: A legislative act authorizes the opening of books for public subscription of stock and all persons have the right to subscribe on payment of a certain sum, say 5, 10, or 20 percent on the amount of stock taken by them. The day the books are opened is a matter of great moment.

In France, we queue up at the doors of the theaters; but in the United States, this year, lines of deeply anxious people form at the doors of those special places where the books for subscription to bank stocks are deposited. In Baltimore, the books were opened for a new bank, the Merchants' Bank, with a capital of $2 million; the amount subscribed was nearly $50 million. At Charleston, for a bank of the same capital, $90 million was subscribed, and, as the act in this instance required the advance of 25 percent, the sum actually paid in, in paper money to be sure, but yet in current bills at par, amounted to $22,500,000, or more than 11 times the capital required.

This rage for bank stock is easily explained. Most of the banks here are, in fact, irresponsible establishments which have the privilege of coining money from paper. The shareholders, by means of a series of ingenious contrivances, realize 8, 9, 10, and 12 percent interest on capital which they do not actually hold; and this in a country where the 5 percents of Pennsylvania and New York and the 6 percents of Ohio are at 110 to 115. The Ohio sixes! What would the heroes of Fort Duquesne think of that if they should come back?

Most of these speculations are imprudent; many of them are foolish. The boom today may and must be followed by a crisis tomorrow. Great fortunes, and many of them too, have sprung out of the earth since the spring; others will, perhaps, return to it before the fall. The American does not worry about that. Violent sensations are necessary to stir his vigorous nerves. Public opinion and the pulpit forbid sensual gratifications, wine, women, and the display of a princely luxury; cards and dice are equally prohibited; the American, therefore, has recourse to business for the strong emotions which he requires to make him feel life. He launches with delight into the ever moving sea of speculation. One day, the wave raises him to the clouds; he enjoys in haste the moment of triumph. The next day he disappears between the crests of the billows; he is little troubled by the reverse; he bides his time coolly and consoles himself with the hope of better fortune.

In the midst of all this speculation, while some enrich and some ruin themselves, banks spring up and diffuse credit; railroads and canals extend themselves over the country; steamboats are launched into the rivers, the lakes, and the sea; the career of the speculators is ever enlarging; the field for railroads, canals, steamers, and banks goes on expanding. Some individuals lose, but the country is a gainer; the country is peopled, cleared, cultivated; its resources are unfolded, its wealth increased. *Go ahead!*

If movement and the quick succession of sensations and ideas constitute life, here one lives a hundredfold more than elsewhere; here, all is circulation, motion, and boiling agitation. Experiment follows experiment; enterprise follows enterprise. Riches and poverty follow on each other's traces, and each in turn occupies the place of the other. While the great men of one day dethrone those of the past, they are already half overturned themselves by those of the morrow. Fortunes last for a season; reputations, for the twinkling of an eye. An irresistible current sweeps everything away, grinds everything to powder and deposits it again under new forms. Men change their houses, their climate, their trade, their condition, their party, their sect; the states change their laws, their officers, their constitutions. The soil itself, or at least the houses, partake in the universal instability.

The existence of social order in the bosom of this whirlpool seems a miracle, an inexplicable anomaly. One is tempted to think that such a society, formed of heterogeneous elements, brought together by chance, each following its own orbit according to the impulse of its own caprice or interest — one would think that after rising for one moment to the heavens, like a waterspout, such a society would inevitably fall flat in ruins the next; such is not, however, its destiny. Amid this general change there is one fixed point; it is the domestic fireside, or, to speak more clearly, the conjugal bed. An austere watchman, sometimes harsh even to fanaticism, wards off from this sacred spot everything that can disturb its stability; that guardian is religious sentiment. While that fixed point shall remain untouched, while that sentinel shall persist in his vigilant watch over it, the social system may make new somersaults and undergo new changes without serious risk; it may be pelted by the storm, but while it is made fast to that anchorage, it will neither split nor sink. It may even be broken up into different groups nearly independent of one another, but it will expand across the earth; it will still grow in energy, in resources, in extent.

The influence of the democracy is so universal in this country that it was quite natural for it to raise its head among speculators. There have, therefore, been strikes on the part of workmen who wish to share in the profits of speculation and who have demanded higher wages and less work. The demand for higher pay is just, since all provisions, all articles of consumption have risen in price. These coalitions are by no means timid in this country; the English practice of haranguing in public and getting up processions prevails here and the working class feels its strength, is conscious of its power, and knows how to make use of it. The different trades have held meetings in Philadelphia, New York, and other places, discussed their affairs publicly, and set forth their demands.

The women have had their meetings, as well as the men. That of the seamstresses of Philadelphia attracted notice; Matthew Carey, known as a political writer, presided, assisted by two clergymen. Among the various demands one might point out is that of the journeymen bakers, who, by virtue of the rights of man and the sanctity of the seventh day, would not make bread Sundays. The principal trades have decided that all work shall be suspended until the masters, if this name can be applied here except in derision, have acceded to their ultimatum. That everyone may know this, they have published their resolutions in the newspapers, signed by the president and secretaries of the meeting.

These resolutions declare that those workmen who shall refuse to conform to their provisions will have to abide the consequences of their refusal. The consequences have been that those refractory workmen who persisted in working have been driven with stones and clubs from their workshops without any interference on the part of the magistrates. The consequence is that, at this very moment, a handful of boatmen on the Schuylkill Canal prevent the coal boats from descending to the sea, lay an embargo upon them, and thus interrupt one of the most lucrative branches of the Pennsylvania trade, deprive the mariners and shipowners who transport the coal to all parts of the coast of wages and freights, and expose the miners to the danger of being dismissed from the mines. Meanwhile, the militia looks on; the sheriff stands with folded arms. If this minority of boatmen — for these acts of disorder are the work of a small minority — persists in their plans, a fight between them and the miners is conceivable.

In Philadelphia, the consequence has been that the carpenters, in order to reduce some contractors to terms, have set fire to several houses which were being built. This time the authorities at length interfered, the mayor issued a proclamation reciting that, whereas there is reason to believe these fires to be the work of some evil-minded persons, he offers $1,000 reward to whoever shall disclose the authors of the same. But it is' too late. The municipal authorities, for the purpose, it is said, of gaining a few votes on the side of the opposition, instead of interposing their power between the workmen and the masters, hastened from the first to comply with all the demands of the former, who were employed on the municipal works.

The philosopher, in whose eyes the present is but a point, may find reason to rejoice in considering these facts. Workmen and domestics in Europe live in a state of nearly absolute dependence which is favorable only to him who commands. Monarchists, republicans, the classes in between, all comport themselves toward the worker they employ or the domestic in their service as if he were a being of an inferior nature who owes his master all his zeal and all his efforts, but who has no claim on any return beyond a miserable pittance of wages. One may be permitted to wish for the establishment of a juster scale of rights and duties.

In the United States — the absolute principle of the popular sovereignty having been applied to the relations of master and servant, of employer and operative — the manufacturer, the contractor, and the entrepreneur, to whom the workmen give the law, endeavor to dispense with their aid as much as possible by substituting more and more machinery for human force; thus the most painful processes in the arts become less burdensome to the human race. The master, whose domestics obey him when they please and who pays dear for being badly and ungraciously served, favors, to the extent of his power, the introduction of mechanical contrivances for simplifying work in order to spare himself the inconveniences of such a dependence.

It would be worthwhile to study not only the great manufacturing machinery but the common hand tools and domestic utensils in this country. These utensils, tools, and machines exert a powerful influence upon the practical liberty of the greatest

number; it is by means of them that the most numerous class of society gradually frees itself from the yoke which tends to crush and abase it. In this point of view, what goes on here between employer and employee, between master and servant tends to hasten the coming of a future which every friend of humanity must hail with joy. But if philosophical satisfaction is amply present, physical comfort is almost absolutely wanting. Whoever is neither operative nor domestic, whoever, especially, has tasted and enjoyed the life of the cultivated classes in Europe will find the actual practical life in America, the mere bone and muscle, as it were, of life, to consist of a series of jars, disappointments, mortifications — I had almost said, of humiliations.

The independence of the workers is sometimes the ruin of the employers; the independence of servants involves the dependence of the women; condemns them to household labors little consonant with the finished education which many of them have received; and nails them to the kitchen and the nursery from the day of their marriage to the day of their death.

When the force of innovation, acting without check or balance, operates with an excess of energy, all classes suffer equally from the derangement. Not only what in Europe are called the higher classes (but which here must take another name) are deprived of a thousand little enjoyments which it is a matter of convention to despise in books and set speeches, although everyone sets a high value on them in practice but the whole social machine gets out of order, discomfort becomes general, and the extravagant claims of the lower classes, to speak as a European, recoil violently on themselves. At this very moment, for example, the Sybarites of Philadelphia whose hearts are set upon having fresh bread on Sunday are not the only persons who suffer or are threatened with suffering. If the exaggerated pretensions of the working classes are persisted in, the market will decline, there will be no demand for labor. Speculations, if not made solid by labor, will burst like soap bubbles, and, if a reaction comes, the operative, who is little used to economize, will feel it more forcibly than others. . . .

ALREADY, DEMOCRACY, especially in the Western states, is beginning to have its festivals which thrill its fibers and stir it with agreeable emotions. There are religious festivals, the Methodist camp meetings, where the people go with delight, despite the philosophical objections of other more middle-class sects who find fault with their heated zeal and noisy ranting, and despite, or rather in consequence of, the convulsive and hysterical scenes of the *anxious bench.* In the older states of the North there are political processions, pure party demonstrations for the most part, but which are interesting in that the democracy has a share in them; for it is the Democratic Party that gets up the most brilliant and animated.

Besides the camp meetings, the political processions are the only things in this country which bear any resemblance to festivals. The party dinners with their speeches and deluge of toasts are frigid, if not repulsive. For example, I have never seen a more miserable affair than the dinner given by the opposition, that is to say, by the middle class, at Powelton, in the neighborhood of Philadelphia. But I stopped involuntarily at the sight of the gigantic hickory poles which made their solemn entry on eight wheels for the purpose of being planted by the democracy on the eve of the election. I remember one of these poles, its top still crowned with green foliage, which came on to the sound of fifes and drums and was preceded by ranks of Democrats, bearing no other badge than a twig of the sacred tree in their hats. It was drawn by eight horses, decorated with ribands and mottoes. Astride the tree itself were a dozen Jackson men of

the first water, waving flags with an air of anticipated triumph and shouting, "Hurrah for Jackson!"

But this parade of the hickory tree was but a by-matter compared with the procession I witnessed in New York. It was the night after the closing of the polls when victory had gone to the Democratic Party. The procession was nearly a mile long; the Democrats marched in good order to the glare of torches; the banners were more numerous than I had ever seen in any religious festival; all were transparencies on account of the darkness. On some were inscribed the names of the Democratic societies or sections: *Democratic young men of the Ninth* or *Eleventh Ward;* others bore imprecations against the Bank of the United States; *Nick Biddle* and *Old Nick* were shown, more or less ingeniously, doing business together; it was their form of our banner with the prayer, "Deliver us from evil." Then came portraits of General Jackson, afoot and on horseback; there was one in the uniform of a general and another in the person of the Tennessee farmer with the famous hickory cane in his hand. Portraits of Washington and Jefferson, surrounded with Democratic mottoes, were mingled with emblems in all designs and colors. Among these figured an eagle — not a painting, but a real live eagle — tied by the legs, surrounded by a wreath of leaves, and hoisted upon a pole, after the manner of the Roman standards. The imperial bird was carried by a stout sailor, more pleased than was ever any city magistrate permitted to hold one of the cords of the canopy in a Catholic ceremony.

Farther than the eye could reach, the Democrats came marching on. I was struck with the resemblance of their air to the train that escorts the Eucharist in Mexico or Puebla. The American standard-bearers were as grave as the Mexican Indians who bore the sacred candles. The Democratic procession, also like the Catholic procession, had its halting places; it stopped before the houses of Jackson men to fill the air with cheers and before the doors of the leaders of the opposition to give three, six, or nine groans. If these scenes were to find a painter, they would be admired at some distant day no less than the triumphs and sacrificial pomps which the ancients have left us in marble and brass. For this is something more than the grotesque fashion of scenes immortalized by Rembrandt; this belongs to history, it belongs to the sublime; these are episodes of a wondrous epic which will bequeath a lasting memory to posterity, the memory of the coming of democracy.

Yet, as festivals and spectacles, these processions are much inferior to the revivals which take place in camp meetings. All festivals and ceremonies in which women do not take part are incomplete. Why is it that our constitutional ceremonies are so entirely devoid of interest? It is not because the actors are merely bourgeois citizens, respectable surely, but prosaic, and that the pomp of costumes and the fascination of the arts are banished from them; it is rather because women do not and cannot have a place in them. A wit has said that women are not poets but they are poetry itself. . . .

Take women from the tournaments and these become nothing more than fencing bouts; take away the *anxious bench* from camp meetings, remove those women who fall into convulsions, shriek, and roll on the ground, who, pale, disheveled, and haggard, cling to the minister from whom they inhale the Holy Spirit; or seize the hardened sinner at the door of the tent, or in the passageway, and strive to melt his stony heart; it will be in vain that a majestic forest overshadows the scene of a beautiful summer's night, under a sky that need not fear comparison with a Grecian heaven; in vain will you be surrounded with tents and numberless chariots that recall to mind the long train of Israel fleeing from Egypt; in vain the distant fires, gleaming among the trees,

will reveal the forms of the preachers gesticulating above the crowd; in vain will the echo of the woods fling back the tones of their voice; you will be weary of the spectacle in an hour. But camp meetings, as they are now conducted, have the power of holding the people of the West for whole weeks; some have lasted a month.

I allow that camp meetings and political processions are as yet only exceptions in America. A people has not a complete national character until it has its peculiar and appropriate amusements, national festivals, poetry. In this respect, it will not be easy to create an American nationality; the American has no past from which to draw inspiration. On quitting the old soil of Europe, on breaking off from England, his fathers left behind them the national chronicles, the traditions, the legends, all that constitutes country — that country which is not carried about on the soles of one's feet. The American, then, has become poor in ideality, in proportion as he has become rich in material wealth.

But a democracy always has some resource, so far as imagination is concerned. I cannot pretend to decide how the American democracy will supply the want of a past and of old recollections, any more than I can undertake to pronounce in what manner it will bridle itself and curb its own humors. But I am sure that America will have her festivals, her ceremonies, and her art, as I am sure that society in America will assume a regular organization; for I believe in the future of American society, or, to speak more correctly, of the beginnings of society, whose growth is visible on the east and still more on the west side of the Alleghenies. . . .

THERE IS SOMETHING in Richmond which offends me more than its bottomless mudholes, and shocks me more than the rudeness of the western Virginians whom I met here during the session of the legislature; it is slavery. Half of the population is black or mulatto. Physically, the Negroes are well-used in Virginia, partly from motives of humanity and partly because they are so much livestock raised for exportation to Louisiana; but, if there is no cause for complaint on the material level, morally they are treated as if they did not belong to the human race. Free or slave, the black is here denied all that can give him the dignity of man.

The law forbids the instruction of the slave or the free man of color in the simplest rudiments of learning, under the severest penalties. The slave has no family; he has no civil rights; he holds no property. The white man knows that the slave has opened his ear to the word which everything here proclaims aloud — liberty. He knows that in secret the Negro broods over schemes of vengeance and that the exploits and martyrdom of Gabriel, the leader of an old conspiracy, and of Turner, the hero of a more recent insurrection, are still related in the Negro cabins. The precautionary measures which this knowledge has induced the whites to adopt freeze the heart of a stranger with horror.

Richmond is noted for its tobacco and flour market. Richmond flour is prized at Rio de Janeiro as much as at New York, at Lima as well as at Havana. The largest flour mill in the world is at Richmond, running twenty pair of stones, containing a great variety of accessory machinery and capable of manufacturing 600 barrels of flour a day. The reputation of Richmond flour in foreign markets, like that of American flour in general, depends upon a system of inspection peculiar to the country which contravenes, indeed, the theory of absolute commercial freedom but is essential to the prosperity of American commerce and has never, that I have heard of, been a subject of complaint. The flour is inspected previous to export. The weight of each barrel and the quality of the flour are ascertained by the inspector and branded on the barrel-head. Superior qualities only can be exported; the inspection is real and thorough and is performed at the expense of the holder. The Havana, Brazilian, or Peruvian merchant is thus perfectly sure of the quality of the merchandise he buys; both the buyer and the seller find their advantage in it. Commerce can no more dispense with confidence in the market than with credit in the countinghouse.

Virginia tobacco is subjected to the same system of inspection. In general, all the coast states, all those from which produce is exported to foreign parts, have established this system and applied it to almost all articles in which frauds can be committed. Thus, in New York, wheat flour and Indian cornmeal, beef, pork, salt fish, potash, whale oil, lumber, staves, flaxseed, leather, tobacco, hops, spirits are all inspected.

In regard to flour, the law is more rigorous than in respect to other articles. The inspector brands with the word "light" those barrels which are not of the legal weight (the exportation of these barrels is also prohibited) and with the word "bad" those which are of poor quality. As for Indian corn, it is required that the grain shall have been kiln-dried before grinding. Flour from other states cannot be sold in the city of New York, even for local consumption, unless it has been inspected the same as if for exportation. Every inspector has the right to search vessels in which he suspects that there is flour that has not been inspected and to seize what has been loaded or what is ready for shipping. There are, besides, various other provisions and penalties to prevent fraud.

If the necessity of these inspections were not sufficiently proved by their good effects and by long experience, it would be by the abuses that prevail in those articles of commerce which are not subject to the system. Complaints have already been made in Liverpool that bales of cotton fraudulently consist of an inferior article concealed beneath an outer layer of good quality. From a report addressed to the American Chamber of Commerce from this center of the cotton trade by the principal cotton brokers, it appears that this is not a matter of just 2 or 3 bales in large shipments but of lots of 100 and 200 bales.

What! It will be said is there not, then, freedom of commerce in this classic land of liberty? No! Foreign commerce is not free in the United States, because Americans are not willing to expose the industry and commerce of a whole country to ruin by the first rogue that comes along. The people of this country is, above all else, a working people. Everyone is at liberty to work, to choose his profession, and to change it twenty times; everyone has the right to go and come on his business, at pleasure, and to transport his person and his occupation from the center to the circumference, and from the circumference to the center. If the country does not enjoy the political advantages of administrative unity, neither is it hampered in the most petty details of industry by excessive centralization. No man is obliged to go 600 miles to solicit the license and personal signature of a minister, overloaded with business and harassed by legislative oversight.

But American liberty is not a mystical, undefined liberty; it is a practical liberty, in harmony with the peculiar genius of the people and its peculiar destiny; it is a liberty of action and motion which the American uses to expand over the vast territory that Providence has given him and to subdue it to his uses. Liberty of movement is nearly absolute, with the exception of some restraints imposed by the observance of the Sabbath. Liberty, or rather independence, in matters of industry is also ample; but if it is abused by some individuals, the general tendency is to restrain them by law or by dictatorial measures, or by the influence of public opinion, sometimes expressed in mob rule.

The restraints on internal trade are few; there are, however, some restrictions upon hawkers and peddlers who impose on the credulity of country people. If no effective bankrupt law has yet been enacted, severe penalties are provided against false pretense. If stock-jobbing has not been prohibited, it is not from want of will on the part of the legislators, for they are fully alive to the evils of unproductive speculation which diverts needful capital from industry; it is because they do not see how it is to be effectually prevented. Besides, it is not easy to commit fraud in the United States in the domestic market. Here, everybody knows everybody else and everyone is on the watch against others, and it is not difficult to trace a fraud to its source.

For merchandise sent to a distant market, detection is not so easy. And, finally, there reigns here a sort of patriotism which is bolstered by self-interest, rightly understood, and by fear of public opinion, which maintains a certain degree of honesty in domestic affairs and a tone of morality which, if not wholly above reproach, is certainly far superior to what prevails among us; while, to many persons, all is fair in dealings with foreigners, whom they look upon as a kind of barbarian.

93.

FREDERICK MARRYAT: The English Language in America

The English sailor and popular novelist, Frederick Marryat, began an eighteen-month tour of the United States in the spring of 1837. His unconcealed distaste for what he saw in America earned him the hostility of the press, and the publication of his book, A Diary in America *(1839), did nothing to restore his reputation in the states. His declared intention in coming to America was to discover the effects of egalitarian democracy on a people still essentially English. He concluded that the effects were bad although well suited for the present to the New World, and that the English government should continue to be administered by the enlightened few.* A Diary in America *is divided into two parts: the first is a travelogue and the second is a series of essays or "remarks" from which the following chapter on "Language" is reprinted.*

Source: *A Diary in America*, London, 1839, Vol. II, pp. 217-247.

THE AMERICANS BOLDLY ASSERT that they speak better English than we do. . . . What I believe the Americans would imply by the above assertion is that you may travel through all the United States and find less difficulty in understanding, or in being understood, than in some of the counties of England, such as Cornwall, Devonshire, Lancashire, and Suffolk. So far they are correct; but it is remarkable how very debased the language has become in a short period in America. There are few provincial dialects in England much less intelligible than the following. A Yankee girl, who wished to hire herself out, was asked if she had any followers, or sweethearts? After a little hesitation, she replied, "Well, now, can't exactly say; I bees a sorter courted, and a sorter not; reckon more a sorter yes than a sorter no."

In many points the Americans have to a certain degree obtained that equality which they profess; and, as respects their language, it certainly is the case. If their lower classes are more intelligible than ours, it is equally true that the higher classes do not speak the language so purely or so classically as it is spoken among the well-educated English. The peculiar dialect of the English counties is kept up because we are a settled country; the people who are born in a county live in it, and die in it, transmitting their sites of labor or of amusement to their descendants, generation after generation, without change; consequently, the provincialisms of the language become equally hereditary.

Now, in America, they have a dictionary containing many thousands of words which, with us, are either obsolete or are provincialisms, or are words necessarily invented by the Americans. When the people of England emigrated to the States, they came from every county in England, and each county brought its provincialisms with it.

These were admitted into the general stock, and were since all collected and bound up by one Mr. Webster. With the exception of a few words coined for local uses (such as "snags" and "sawyers," on the Mississippi), I do not recollect a word which I have not traced to be either a provincialism of some English county, or else to be obsolete English. There are a few from the Dutch, such as *stoup,* for the porch of a door, etc. I was once talking with an American about Webster's dictionary, and he observed, "Well, now, sir, I understand it's the only one used in the Court of St. James, by the king, queen, and princesses, and that by royal order."

The upper classes of the Americans do not, however, speak or pronounce English according to our standard; they appear to have no exact rule to guide them, probably from a want of any intimate knowledge of Greek or Latin. You seldom hear a derivation from the Greek pronounced correctly, the accent being generally laid upon the wrong syllable. In fact, everyone appears to be independent, and pronounces just as he pleases.

But it is not for me to decide the very momentous question as to which nation speaks the best English. The Americans generally improve upon the inventions of others; probably they may have improved upon our language. . . .

Assuming this principle of improvement to be correct, it must be acknowledged that the Americans have added considerably to our dictionary; but, as I have before observed, this being a point of too much delicacy for me to decide upon, I shall just submit to the reader the occasional variations, or improvements, as they may be, which met my ears during my residence in America, as also the idiomatic peculiarities; and, having so done, I must leave him to decide for himself.

I recollect once talking with one of the first men in America, who was narrating to me the advantages which might have accrued to him if he had followed up a certain speculation, when he said, "Sir, if I had done so, I should not only have *doubled* and *trebled,* but I should have *fourbled* and *fivebled* my money."

One of the members of Congress once said, "What the honorable gentleman has just asserted I consider as *catamount* to a denial" (catamount is the term given to a panther or lynx).

"I presume," replied his opponent, "that the honorable gentleman means *tantamount*."

"No, sir, I do not mean *tantamount;* I am not so ignorant of our language not to be aware that *cata*mount and *tanta*mount are *an*onymous."

The Americans dwell upon their words when they speak — a custom arising, I presume, from their cautious, calculating habits; and they have always more or less of a nasal twang. I once said to a lady, "Why do you drawl out your words in that way?"

"Well," replied she, "I'd drawl all the way from Maine to Georgia rather than *clip* my words as you English people do."

Many English words are used in a very different sense from that which we attach to them. For instance: a *clever* person in America means an amiable, good-tempered person, and the Americans make the distinction by saying, "I mean English clever." Our *clever* is represented by the word "smart."

The verb "to admire" is also used in the East, instead of the verb "to like."

"Have you ever been at Paris?"

"No, but I should *admire* to go."

A Yankee description of a clever woman:

"Well, now, she'll walk right into you, and talk to you like a book"; or, as I have heard them say, "she'll talk you out of sight."

The word "ugly" is used for cross, ill-tempered. "I did feel so *ugly* when he said that."

Bad is used in an odd sense; it is employed for awkward, uncomfortable, sorry:

"I did feel so *bad* when I read that" — awkward.

"I have felt quite *bad* about it ever since" — uncomfortable.

"She was so *bad,* I thought she would cry" — sorry.

And as bad is tantamount to *not good,* I have heard a lady say, "I don't feel *at all good* this morning."

Mean is occasionally used for ashamed.

"I never felt so *mean* in my life."

The word "handsome" is oddly used.

"We reckon this very handsome scenery, sir," said an American to me, pointing to the landscape.

"I consider him very truthful," is another expression.

"He stimulates too much."

"He dissipates awfully."

And they are very fond of using the noun as a verb, as:

"I *suspicion* that's a fact."

"I *opinion* quite the contrary."

The word "considerable" is in considerable demand in the United States. In a work in which the letters of the party had been given to the public as specimens of good style and polite literature, it is used as follows:

"My dear sister, I have taken up the pen early this morning, as I intend to write *considerable.*"

The word "great" is oddly used for fine, splendid.

"She's the *greatest* gal in the whole Union."

But there is one word which we must surrender up to the Americans as their *very own,* as the children say. I will quote a passage from one of their papers:

"The editor of the *Philadelphia Gazette* is wrong in calling absquatiated a Kentucky *phrase* (he may well say phrase instead of *word*). It may prevail there, but its origin was in South Carolina, where it was a few years since regularly derived from the Latin,

as we can prove from undoubted authority. By the way, there is a little *corruption* in the word as the *Gazette* uses it, *absquatalized* is the true reading."

Certainly a word worth quarreling about!

"Are you cold, miss?" said I to a young lady, who pulled the shawl closer over her shoulders.

"Some," was the reply.

The English *what?* implying that you did not hear what was said to you, is changed in America to the word *how?*

"I reckon," "I calculate," "I guess," are all used as the common English phrase, "I suppose." Each term is said to be peculiar to different states, but I found them used everywhere, one as often as the other. I *opine* is not so common.

A specimen of Yankee dialect and conversation:

"Well, now, I'll tell you — you know Marble Head?"

"Guess I do."

"Well, then, you know Sally Hackett."

"No, indeed."

"Not know Sally Hackett? Why she lives at Marble Head."

"Guess I don't."

"You don't mean to say that?"

"Yes, indeed."

"And you really don't know Sally Hackett?"

"No, indeed."

"I guess you've heard talk of her?"

"No, indeed."

"Well, that's considerable odd. Now, I'll tell you — Ephrim Bagg, he that has the farm three miles from Marble Head — just as — but now, are you sure you don't know Sally Hackett?"

"No, indeed."

"Well, he's a pretty substantial man, and no mistake. He has got a heart as big as an ox, and everything else in proportion, I've a notion. He loves Sal the worst kind; and if she gets up there, she'll think she has got to Palestine (Paradise); arn't she a screamer? I were thinking of Sal mysel, for I feel lonesome, and when I am thrown into my store promiscuous alone, I can tell you I have the blues, the worst kind, no mistake — I can tell you that. I always feel a kind o' queer when I sees Sal, but when I meet any of the other gals I am as calm and cool as the Milky Way," etc.

The verb "to fix" is universal. It means to do anything.

"Shall I *fix* your coat or your breakfast first?" That is — "Shall I brush your coat, or *get ready* your breakfast first?"

Right away, for immediately or at once, is very general.

"Shall I fix it right away — *i.e.,* "Shall I do it immediately?"

In the West, when you stop at an inn, they say:

"What will you have? Brown meal and common doings, or white wheat and chicken *fixings*"— that is, "Will you have pork and brown bread, or white bread and fried chicken?"

Also, "Will you have a *feed* or a *check*?" — A dinner, or a luncheon?

In *full blast* — something in the extreme.

"When she came to meeting, with her yellow hat and feathers, was'n't she in *full blast?*"

But for more specimens of genuine Yankee, I must refer the reader to Sam Slick and Major Downing, and shall now proceed to some further peculiarities.

There are two syllables — "um," "hu" — which are very generally used by the Americans as a sort of reply, intimating that they are attentive, and that the party may proceed with his narrative; but, by inflection and intonation, these two syllables are made to express dissent or assent, surprise, disdain, and . . . a great deal more. The reason why these two syllables have been selected is that they can be pronounced without the trouble of opening your mouth, and you may be in a state of listlessness and repose while others talk. I myself found them very convenient at times, and gradually got into the habit of using them.

The Americans are very local in their phrases, and borrow their similes very much from the nature of their occupations and pursuits. If you ask a Virginian or Kentuckian where he was born, he will invariably tell you that he was *raised* in such a county — the term applied to horses, and, in breeding states, to men also.

When a man is tipsy (spirits being made from grain), they generally say he is *corned.*

In the West, where steam navigation is so abundant, when they ask you to drink they say, "Stranger, will you take in wood?" — the vessels taking in wood as fuel to keep the steam up, and the person taking in spirits to keep *his* steam up.

The roads in the country being cut through woods, and the stumps of the trees left standing, the carriages are often brought up by them. Hence the expression of, "Well, I am *stumped* this time."

I heard a young man, a farmer in Vermont, say, when talking about another having gained the heart of a pretty girl, "Well, how he contrived to *fork* into her young affections, I can't tell; but I've a mind to *put my whole team on* and see if I can't run him off the road."

The old phrase of "straining at a gnat, and swallowing a camel," is, in the Eastern states, rendered "straining at a *gate,* and swallowing a sawmill."

To *strike* means to attack. "The Indians have struck on the frontier"; "A rattlesnake *struck* at me."

To *make tracks* — to walk away. "Well, now, I shall *make tracks*"— from foot tracks in the snow.

Clear out, quit, and *put* all mean be off. "Captain, now, you *hush* or *put*"— that is, "Either hold your tongue, or be off." Also, "Will you shut, mister?" — *i.e.,* will you shut your mouth? *i.e.,* hold your tongue?

Curl up — to be angry — from the panther and other animals, when angry, raising their hair.

Rise my dandee up, from the human hair; and a nasty idea. "Wrathy" is another common expression. Also, "Savage as a meat axe."

Here are two real American words: *Sloping*, for slinking away; *Splunging*, like a porpoise.

The word "enthusiasm," in the South, is changed to "entuzzy-muzzy."

In the Western states, where the raccoon is plentiful, they use the abbreviation "'coon" when speaking of people. When at New York, I went into a hairdresser's shop to have my hair cut; there were two young men from the West — one under the barber's hands, the other standing by him.

"I say," said the one who was having his hair cut, "I hear Captain M——— is in the country."

"Yes," replied the other, "so they say; I should like to see the *'coon.*"

"I'm a *gone 'coon*" implies "I am distressed — or ruined — or lost." I once asked the origin of this expression, and was very gravely told as follows:

"There is a Captain Martin Scott in the United States Army who is a remarkable shot with a rifle. He was raised, I believe, in Vermont. His fame was so considerable through the state that even the animals were aware of it. He went out one morning with his rifle, and spying a raccoon upon the upper branches of a high tree, brought his gun up to his shoulder. When the raccoon, perceiving it, raised his paw up for a parley. 'I beg your pardon, mister,' said the raccoon, very politely, 'but may I ask you if your name is *Scott?*' — 'Yes,' replied the captain. — '*Martin* Scott?' continued the raccoon. — 'Yes,' replied the captain. — '*Captain* Martin Scott?' still continued the animal. — 'Yes,' replied the captain, 'Captain Martin Scott?' — 'Oh! then,' says the animal, 'I may just as well come down, for I'm a *gone 'coon.*'"

But one of the strangest perversions of the meaning of a word which I ever heard of is in Kentucky, where sometimes the word "nasty" is used for "nice." For instance, at a rustic dance in that state, a Kentuckian said to an acquaintance of mine, in reply to his asking the name of a very fine girl, "That's my sister, stranger; and I flatter myself that she shows the *nastiest* ankle in all Kentuck." *Unde derivatur*, from the constant rifle practice in that state, a good shot or a pretty shot is termed also a nasty shot, because it would make a *nasty* wound; *ergo*, a nice or pretty ankle becomes a *nasty* one.

The term for all baggage, especially in the South or West, is "plunder." This has been derived from the buccaneers, who for so long a time infested the bayous and creeks near the mouth of the Mississippi, and whose luggage was probably very correctly so designated.

I must not omit a specimen of American criticism.

"Well, Abel, what d'ye think of our native genus, Mister Forrest?"

"Well, I don't go much to theatricals, that's a fact; but I do think *he piled the agony up a little too high* in that last scene."

The gamblers on the Mississippi use a very refined phrase for "cheating" — "playing the advantages over him."

But, as may be supposed, the principal terms used are those which are borrowed from trade and commerce.

The "rest," or "remainder," is usually termed the "balance."

"Put some of those apples into a dish, and the *balance* into the storeroom."

When a person has made a mistake, or is out in his calculation, they say, "You missed a figure that time."

In a skirmish last war, the fire from the British was very severe, and the men in the

American ranks were falling fast, when one of the soldiers stepped up to the commanding officer and said, "Colonel, don't you think that we might compromise this affair?" "Well, I reckon I should have no objection to *submit it to arbitration* myself," replied the colonel.

Even the thieves must be commercial in their ideas. One rogue, meeting another, asked him what he had done that morning: "Not much," was the reply, "I've only *realized* this umbrella."

This reminds me of a conversation between a man and his wife, which was overheard by the party who repeated it to me. It appears that the lady was economically inclined, and, in cutting out some shirts for her husband, resolved that they should not descend much lower than his hips, as thereby so much linen would be saved. The husband expostulated, but in vain. She pointed out to him that it would improve his figure and make his nether garments set much better; in a word, that long shirttails were quite unnecessary. And she wound up her arguments by observing that linen was a very expensive article, and that she could not see what on earth was the reason that people should stuff so much *capital* into their pantaloons.

There is sometimes in the American metaphors an energy which is very remarkable.

"Well, I reckon, that from his teeth to his toenail, there's not a human of a more conquering nature than General Jackson."

One *gentleman* said to me, "I wish I had all hell boiled down to a pint, just to pour down your throat."

It is a great pity that the Americans have not adhered more to the Indian names, which are euphonious and very often musical; but, so far from it, they appear to have had a pleasure in dismissing them altogether. There is a river running into Lake Champlain, near Burlington, formerly called by the Indians the Winooski, but this name has been superseded by the settlers, who, by

way of improvement, have designated it the Onion River. The Americans have ransacked Scripture, and ancient and modern history, to supply themselves with names; yet, notwithstanding, there appears to be a strange lack of taste in their selection. On the route to Lake Ontario you pass towns with such names as Manlius, Sempronius, Titus, Cato, and then you come to *Butternuts.* Looking over the catalogue of cities, towns, villages, rivers, and creeks in the different states in the Union, I find the following repetitions:

Of towns, etc., named after distinguished individuals, there are: Washingtons, 43; Jacksons, 41; Jeffersons, 32; Franklins, 41; Madisons, 26; Monroes, 25; Perrys, 22; Fayettes, 14; Hamiltons, 13; Carrolls, 16; Adamses, 18; Bolívars, 8; Clintons, 19; Waynes, 14; Casses, 6; Clays, 4; Fultons, 17.

Of other towns, etc., there are: Columbias, 27; Centre Villes, 14; Fairfields, 17; Libertys, 14; Salems, 24; Onions, 28; Athenses, 10; Romes, 4; Crookeds, 22; Littles, 20; Longs, 18; Muds, 8; Little Muds, 1; Muddies, 11; Sandys, 39.

In colors they have: Clears, 13; Blacks, 33; Blues, 8; Vermillions, 14; Greens, 16; Whites, 15; Yellows, 10.

Named after trees: Cedars, 25; Cypresses, 12; Laurels, 14; Pines, 18.

After animals: Beavers, 23; Buffaloes, 21; Bulls, 9; Deers, 13; Dogs, 9; Elks, 11; Foxes, 12; Otters, 13; Raccoons, 11; Wolfs, 16; Bears, 12; Bear's Rump, 1.

After birds, etc.: Gooses, 10; Ducks, 8; Eagles, 8; Pigeons, 10; Fishes, 7; Turkeys, 12; Swans, 15; Pikes, 20.

The consequence of these repetitions is that if you do not put the name of the state, and often of the county in the state, in which the town you refer to may be, your letter may journey all over the Union, and, perhaps, after all, never arrive at its place of destination.

The states have already accommodated

each other with nicknames, as per example: Illinois people are termed Suckers; Missouri, Pukes; Michigan, Wolverines; Indiana, Hoosiers; Kentucky, Corn Crackers; Ohio, Buckeyes, etc.

The names of persons are also very strange; and some of [them] are, at all events, obsolete in England, even if they ever existed there. Many of them are said to be French or Dutch names Americanized. But they appear still more odd to us from the high-sounding Christian names prefixed to them, as, for instance, Philo Doolittle, Populorum Hightower, Preserved Fish, Asa Peabody, Alonzo Lilly, Alceus Wolf, etc. I was told by a gentleman that Doolittle was originally from the French De l'Hotel; Peabody from Pibaudiere; Bunker from Bon Coeur; that Mr. Ezekiel Bumpus is a descendant of Mons. Bon Pas, etc., all which is very possible. . . .

I cannot conclude . . . without adverting to one or two points peculiar to the Americans. They wish, in everything, to improve upon the Old Country, as they call us, and affect to be excessively refined in their language and ideas; but they forget that very often in the covering, and the covering only, consists the indecency, and that, to use the old aphorism — "Very nice people are people with very nasty ideas."

They object to everything nude in statuary. When I was at the house of Governor Everett, at Boston, I observed a fine cast of the Apollo Belvidere, but in compliance with general opinion it was hung with drapery, although Governor Everett himself is a gentleman of refined mind and high classical attainments, and quite above such ridiculous sensitiveness. In language it is the same thing; there are certain words which are never used in America, but an absurd substitute is employed. I cannot particularize them . . . lest I should be accused of indelicacy myself. I may, however, state one little circumstance which will fully prove the correctness of what I say.

When at Niagara Falls, I was escorting a young lady with whom I was on friendly terms. She had been standing on a piece of rock, the better to view the scene, when she slipped down, and was evidently hurt by the fall; she had, in fact, grazed her shin. As she limped a little in walking home, I said, "Did you hurt your leg much." She turned from me, evidently much shocked, or much offended; and not being aware I had committed any very heinous offense, I begged to know what was the reason of her displeasure. After some hesitation, she said that as she knew me well, she would tell me that the word "leg" was never mentioned before ladies.

I apologized for my want of refinement, which was attributable to my having been accustomed only to *English* society, and added that as such articles must occasionally be referred to, even in the most polite circles of America, perhaps she would inform me by what name I might mention them without shocking the company. Her reply was, that the word "limb" was used. "Nay," continued she, "I am not so particular as some people are, for I know those who always say limb of a table, or limb of a pianoforte."

There the conversation dropped; but a few months afterward I was obliged to acknowledge that the young lady was correct when she asserted that some people were more particular than even she was.

I was requested by a lady to escort her to a seminary for young ladies, and, on being ushered into the reception room, conceive my astonishment at beholding a square pianoforte with four *limbs*. However, that the ladies who visited their daughters, might feel in its full force the extreme delicacy of the mistress of the establishment, and her care to preserve in their utmost purity the ideas of the young ladies under her charge, she had dressed all these four limbs in modest little trousers, with frills at the bottom of them!

94.

John L. O'Sullivan: America and the Perfectibility of Man

The editorials below, which appeared in the Democratic Review *for September and November 1839, though unsigned, were almost certainly written by the editor, John L. O'Sullivan. Both reflect the exaggerated nationalism that marked this radical journal — especially the second, which anticipated the doctrine of "manifest destiny" that O'Sullivan was later to publicize (he coined the phrase in 1845). The* Review *began publication in 1837. O'Sullivan, passionately in search of native literary talent, engaged Hawthorne, Thoreau, Whitman, Poe, Longfellow, Bancroft, Whittier, Lowell, and many others as contributors. It quickly became the liveliest monthly of its day, gaining much of its vigor from its immersion in the ideals of the Jacksonian Democrats.*

Source: *United States Magazine and Democratic Review,* September, November 1839.

I.

The Course Of Civilization

NOT MANY YEARS AFTER the discovery of America, a learned academy of Paris offered a prize for the best disquisition that should be written on the probable influence of the New World. The wise men of the day were profuse in speculations suggested by the pregnant theme; they presented it in every form that reason or ingenuity could create; yet not one of them all, in the widest range of their musings, happened upon that means by which America was most deeply to affect the history and modify the condition of the Old World.

It may be supposed that they spoke profoundly of the vast stores of natural wealth her endless tracts disclosed, of their importance to the growing commerce of the age, of the impulse given to the awakening spirit of adventure, of the facility of access opened to the Indian seas, of the desirable outlet provided to the teeming population of the continent. But not a word was said, nor perhaps was it even imagined, that this land was destined to become the birthplace of a new society, constructed in a new spirit and on a new plan, attaining the highest reach of civilization, and ordained to work a thorough change in the structure of European government and social existence. But this was, in the designs of Providence, committed to the restless workings of that principle of progression which is man's chief distinction, awaiting the developments of the course of time. . . .

The history of humanity is the record of a grand march, more or less rapid, as it was now impeded by obstacles, and again facilitated by force, at all times tending to one point: the ultimate perfection of man. The course of civilization is the progress of man from a state of savage individualism to that of an individualism more elevated, moral, and refined. Personal separation and independence were the beginning, as they will be the end, of the great progressive movement, with this difference: that in its last and more perfectly developed condition, the sense of justice shall have supreme control over the individual will.

To the acceleration and extension of this progress, the various nations appearing upon the earth have contributed. As portions of humanity, they have taken part in the general onward movement. They have each had a mission to accomplish, special to themselves, though connected with the development of the entire human race. Step by step they have each removed from realms of thick darkness to regions of gradually increasing light. They have singly and collectively emerged from the abysses of ignorance and degradation to the pleasanter atmosphere of expanding intelligence.

We are enabled, by a large view of this career of nations, to group the successive stages of society in the orders of civilization, all tending to improve the social condition of man, to accomplish his destiny, though the latest has always been the purest, the most liberal, and the best. There is always in the latest civilization some element giving it superior worth and excellence.

The order of civilization first in point of time prevailed in the infancy of our race, before reason obtained the mastery of impulse, and the souls of men were filled with vast thoughts yet unsubmitted to severe discrimination and scrutiny. It may be called the *theocratic,* and, being the earliest departure of the race from barbarism, was born among the oldest people in the East, in Judea, Persia, and India. . . .

The second kind of civilization made its appearance in Rome and Greece, and the pervading idea of it was the indisputable supremacy of the state. Like the theological element in the East, the political element in these great nations gave form and color to all thoughts. A devotion to the public good was the chiefest of virtues; and all considerations of family, kindred, self-culture, and truth were obliged to give way to the aggrandizement of the state. The arts, science,

literature, wealth, education, and religion of society were matters of state concern, subordinate to its interests, and at all times directed to its elevation. . . . No rights, no ties, no retirement too sacred to be invaded by the public power. It was superior to all these; and, though less tyrannical than the blind superstitions which preceded it, was still unfavorable to any real refinement of social intercourse or the acquisition of personal virtue. Conquest and empire became the only glory, while the gentler arts of peace were despised.

The Middle Ages witnessed the rise of the third, or aristocratic, order of civilization, the leading feature of which was feudalism, or the spirit of exclusive rank and class. Power was then in the possession of the nobility, an order (assumed to be from birth better than all others) who wielded it for selfish purposes, exciting, through mutual envy and ambition, long and cruel wars. It was a sad time for the serfs and villains. Many and grievous were the burdens they were compelled to bear. Driven about like yoked cattle, forced to obey the nods of haughty barons, pouring out in the battlefields their life-blood for causes in which they had no interest, dying in hosts to gratify the rapacity or rage of some puppet of privilege, their condition could not have been other than miserable. Yet it was better than that of the ancient world.

All were not serfs. The predominant despotism was relieved and ameliorated by many circumstances of the age. It was not universal but divided and weakened by opposition and restraint, and often softened by the feelings of attachment springing up between the retainer and the lord. That relation gave room for the display of some of the finest traits of human character. It allowed of an intercourse and commerce among men that gradually liberalized the spirit of society, diffused the disposition to free inquiry and independent thought, which prostrated every mark of feudalism and set a glorious reformation in its place — a reformation enhancing art, literature, manners, and religion.

The last order of civilization, which is the democratic, received its first permanent existence in this country. Many events, it is true, in the remote history of the world prepared it for the reception of this principle, yet the peculiar duty of this country has been to exemplify and embody a civilization in which the rights, freedom, and mental and moral growth of individual man should be made the highest end of all social restrictions and laws. To this result the discipline of Providence has tended from the earliest history of the Anglo-American race.

The Old World was not the theater for the development of the new civilization, so different from all that had preceded it, so incompatible with the spirit and hostile to the prejudices of existing things. It needed a broader sphere than institutions founded in exclusiveness could afford, and in which so many elements of restriction and partiality mingled. A land separated from the influences of ancient arrangement; peculiar in its position, productions, and extent; wide enough to hold a numerous people; admitting, with facility, intercommunication and trade, vigorous and fresh from the hand of God, was requisite for the full and broad manifestation of the free spirit of the newborn democracy. Such a land was prepared in the solitudes of the Western Hemisphere.

And, then, the men sufficient to accomplish the work needed to be peculiar men. They were not to be striplings made effeminate by the luxuries of courts, or weak and artificial by corrupt refinement, but stern, resolute, enduring men, ardent worshipers of truth, profoundly penetrated by great thoughts, living by faith in eternal principles, and ready to face death in defense of conscience and right. Such men were the Pilgrim stock, the sires of the busy multitudes that now fill the land. Both the circumstances of their origin and early history,

and the relations of equality instituted among them as they set foot in the wilderness cooperated in the formation of the right character. They sprung from a nation whose bloody wars for years had nourished the manly spirit of courage and endurance. They lived at a time when unrelenting religious contests prepared all minds for desperate trials, and infused in them the sternest moral convictions. They brought with them none to reverence, none to assert an unjust domination. Kingly power they scarce recognized, aristocratic pretension they repelled, and priestly supremacy they had long resisted, even unto death. They came simply as men with the sacred rights and eternal interests of men.

The peculiar hazards of their position placed them upon grounds of equality. Mutual dangers strengthened mutual sympathy, while a common purpose fired them with a common zeal. Their first act, having reached this barren shore, was to frame a constitution whose object was the common good. A singular consistency pervaded the spirit of the early settlers, and the manifestations of it, in actual customs and laws. They asserted with remarkable directness and force the great doctrines of popular sovereignty, of political equality, of sacred individual rights. The supreme power they held to be derived not as a divine gift from God, not from the consent of monarchs, nor the concessions of nobility, but directly from the whole body of men. The perception of this truth distinguished them from the rest of the world. The same freedom from usurped authority which marked their religious career they carried into their political inquiries.

It is true, it is to be regretted it was only comparative freedom, not entire. Many errors were mingled in their conceptions of man's sacred inalienable rights. Their notions were strong but not comprehensive. They allowed truth with limitations. Without being grossly inaccurate, they were strangely confused. They respected private judgment, but confined it to certain subjects of thought. Conscience was sacred only within a circumscribed sphere. The full and ample discussion of certain topics was prohibited by painful penalties. The discipline and doctrine of a church themselves had organized was too high a theme for vulgar approach, too holy to be disturbed by profane touch. Religion, or the mysterious affinities of man to higher beings, they were unwilling to leave to his own soul. It was a thing to be controlled and regulated by the state, for which the arm of civil power was to be invoked, to compel outward conformity and force inward faith.

Here was their weakness. Here they departed from their own principles, and, submitting to the prejudices of the past, brought grievous tyranny on man. Here they were as intolerant and narrow-minded as the bigots of other nations, and a remoter age.

Yet it was impossible for a people of an origin like theirs, or of such convictions as they had, long to submit to oppression of any sort. Much as they were willing to concede to religious injustice at home, they were disposed to yield nothing to political usurpation abroad. The spirit of resistance awakened with the very first assertion of foreign control and arose as the arrogance of authority grew bold. The more formidable the danger, the more bold and unrelenting became their opposition. Purposes of freedom kept pace with despotic pretension. Every year gave them energy by augmenting the justice of their cause, and discovering new means and materials of strength; when, at last, after expostulation and remonstrance failed, a transcendent expression of popular will severed the chains of allegiance and made a whole nation free.

The Declaration of Independence was a tremendous act of revolution, founded upon the rights and sanctioned by the natural justice of mankind. The history of the world records nothing like it either for sublimity of purpose or importance of result. It was as peculiar in its design as it has been permanent and extensive in its influence. A nation, poising itself upon the rights of its people, solemnly absolved its political connection and instituted a government for itself; it did more, it instituted a government drawn from popular choice and confessing the equal rights of men. This was the origin of democratic liberty, the source of true civilization. It established the distinct existence of democracy as a social element, and began a reform destined to cease only when every man in the world should be finally and triumphantly redeemed.

What, then, is the nature of this democracy? What are its claims and objects as a social element? What its views of government; and what its means as well as hopes of success? Simply, it is the political ascendancy of the people. But let us attempt to state in what sense. It is not the government of a people permitted, in the plenitude of their power, to do as they please, regardless alike of the restraints of written law or individual right. A more terrible condition of society than this the wickedest despot could not readily conceive. Wild uproar would make room for fanatic excesses of passion or the alternate bloody triumph of miserable factions. Nor is it the government of the majority carried into the determination of all questions that concern the rights and duties of men. As a safe and wise arbiter of controversy, the will of the majority is to be respected.

Where thought and expression are free, it can seldom become oppressive. Adverse parties watch the movements of each other with sleepless vigilance, and, in cases of manifest violation of right, never fruitlessly invoke the correcting spirit of reform. Nothing is more certain to prostrate even the most triumphant party than the usurpation or unjust exercise of power. Still, to prevent the beginnings of evil, majorities must submit to restraint. There are some things over which they can rightly exert no control. There are personal feelings, domestic ties, social dependencies, commercial rights, too exalted or subtle to be meddled with by human legislation, and which legislation touches only to wither and destroy. They are to be set apart as sacred things, which the ruthless arm of power, though upheld by every letter of law and directed by the delegated will of overwhelming numbers, should never invade. Democracy, therefore, is the supremacy of the people, restrained by a just regard to individual rights — that condition of society which secures the full and inviolable use of every faculty.

Its foundation is the fact of perfect equality of rights among men. It recognizes the distinct existence of individual man in himself as an independent end and not barely as a means to be merged in a mass and controlled as a thing by public caprice or policy. His instinctive convictions, his irrepressible desires, his boundless capacity for improvement conspire with all the indications of Providence, with all the teachings of history, and all the designs of his internal condition and adjustment to make the doctrine of individual rights the greatest of political truths. Clearly to define and religiously to respect those rights is the highest, almost the only, duty of government. All its action beyond this tends to gross abuse and wrong. When it institutes partial laws, when it creates a superior class, when it erects artificial distinctions, when it grants monopoly, when it lays restraints upon free intercourse and trade, in short, when it establishes any law or custom of unequal operation, it departs from its true functions, it begins a course of injustice and fraud, it opens the way for any degree of oppression.

So severe is evenhanded justice that not even in the name of liberty can liberty be violated. Hence, governments perfect themselves in proportion as they allow a larger measure of freedom to remain with the people. Their first care should be to expand the sphere of individual action, to loosen the bonds of inequitable usages, to break the fetters of proscription, and to harmonize the interaction of mutually dependent wills by removing the distance and separation which is the source of jealousy and contest. It is true, a long time must elapse before the point of ultimate perfection is attained; though, meanwhile, the duty of democracy is to correct abuses, one after another, until the nature of individual man is thoroughly emancipated.

As an element of social progress, the recognition of these principles is of the utmost importance and weight. Until they are widely received and permanently adopted, there can be no complete civilization. If we apprehend it, civilization consists in the establishment of elevated social relations, upheld by lofty and refined personal character, or, in other words, the development among men of the best powers of the mind and heart. It suggests at once the idea of a high degree of advancement in social organization and in individual culture. It supposes a condition of prosperous trade, intellectual elevation, and moral development; but literature, science, politics, and morals must have reached a considerable progress, and physical comfort, commercial ease, and mental attainments be generally possessed by the people.

Now, one proposition is that the highest degree of civilization can only be reached by a rigid application of the democratic principle. Society can only find its true perfection by a broad recognition of the doctrine of individual and equal rights. As to its influence, in the first place, on outward prosperity merely, can anything be clearer than that industry will be productive in proportion to the freedom with which its energies are applied and its gains appropriated? To leave men free in the direction of their pursuits not only imparts immediate happiness but gives tenacity to their purposes and strength to their power of execution. They labor more effectively because they labor willingly.

What would be otherwise drudgery becomes pastime, attended by a pleasing conviction of usefulness and the calm assurance of ultimate competence. The stupid inertness of the man machine is exchanged for the cheerful vigor of the husbandman, and the depressing prospect of endless toil is brightened into a future of seductive ease. For acquisition would be secure from the exorbitant taxes of unrighteous government, while no pampered aristocratic class would hang or make weight upon society, or exclusive interest absorb and impede all the channels of commerce. Such a change introduced into all modes of enterprise would produce results of immeasurable magnitude and uniformly good.

It would tend to equalize the distribution of wealth. Without wholly removing poverty, it would lessen dependence. The strange contrasts created by overgrown affluence and wretched poverty would give place to apportionments of property more equitably adjusted to the degrees of personal capacity and merit; while the poor would be raised, the rich would be made better; restless heartburnings would cease to embitter the intercourse or provoke the deadly animosity of classes feeling themselves to be equals; arrogance on one side would engender no spleen on the other; and destitution, which is the fruitful parent of crime and misery, would occur only as the retributive consequence of ignorance and vice. All ranks of men would begin life on a fair field, "the world before them where to choose, and Providence their guide." Inclination and sagacity would select the sphere and dictate the mode and measure of exertion. Frugality and vigilance would compel success, and defeat and ruin be felt only as the requital of ill desert; or, if such things be, as vicissitudes inflicted by heaven among its inscrutable designs.

Library of Congress
John L. O'Sullivan

Every kind of labor being thus effectively applied, an abundance of products would compensate its toils. At the same time, means and leisure for nobler pursuits would be provided. Prosperity admits of various employments among men by augmenting the number and wants of a population, and at the same time commensurately multiplying its resources. As physical comforts increase, the taste for elevated and refined enjoyment springs up. The demand for artists, poets, and philosophers expands, science becomes a distinct pursuit, literature is made profitable, and all the more delicate and ennobling modes of exerting human faculties receive invigorating rewards.

Discovery and invention enlarge the scope, master strokes of genius stimulate the activity, lofty moral instructions refine the nature of thought. A humanizing influence spreads itself through public sentiment. High notions of justice soften while they give dignity to manners. Mind, warm in purposes of generosity, strong in adherence to virtue, takes the control of social movements; in short, we hold a people rich, powerful, enlightened, and no less happy in self-respect than in the universal regard of the world.

Nor less auspicious would be the adoption of the democratic idea to the elevation of individual character. In times past, the greater number of men have been nothing at all, because nothing was made of them. There was little in their circumstances to let them know that they were moral agents. All the influences around them were adapted to produce impressions directly the reverse. Living creatures they were, machines of curious workmanship, admirable as drudge horses, effective as self-moving engines of destruction — things wherewith superior classes might pamper themselves or ruin and destroy their adversaries — but more they were not. Neither the society of the past, or its governments, could teach men their true nature, or inspire them with self-reliance or cheer them with hope.

Were they not the unreasoning tools of power, were they not curs to be cuffed at will, chips to be hurled about at caprice? Well might they have said to their heartless oppressors — We have obeyed like cowering slaves, we have toiled until blood has stood upon our limbs as sweat, we have drained the dregs of life's bitterest cup, for your gratification, and what have you given us in return? Only curses and blows. And all this, because haughty man refused to confess his fellowman; because the lust of dominion expelled the sense of right; because the divine impress on each human soul was not read; or if read, despised.

Matters have since measurably advanced. The grinding foot of oppression has been raised, but not altogether removed. Better notions have grown up in the hearts of men, but, alas! how much is there to stifle and impede full growth. A hateful despotism still too often actuates human will; the spirit of exclusion, of scorn, of tyranny, of selfishness, still lingers about the high places and makes itself felt in the depths of society. Nothing short of the broadest reception of the principles of democracy can regenerate man. There must be something in his circumstances to remind him of his inherent worth; something that, amid withering and depressing care, will ever bring back the fresh consciousness of his manhood.

How can he whose life is perpetual toil, whose existence is lost in that of the many whose highest conception of excellence is fidelity to another's pleasure, whose only exercise of conscience and free will is in the stern struggle for subsistence — how can he attain a true insight of his immortal value? Some virtue, it is true, is found in the least favored conditions. There is room enough in the lowest walks for the sweet play of affection. There are everywhere friends to be esteemed, kindred to cherish, or a wife and children to love. There are endurance and energy imparted everywhere by the discipline of life, but how little is all this compared with the perfect stature of a man.

No, let it be understood that the same nature is common to all men, that they have equal and sacred claims, that they have high and holy faculties; that society respects and the whole force of government is pledged to protect their rights; and then will they acquire some adequate notion of who and what they are, of their divine origin, and their imperishable being. A feeling of exaltation and nobleness would pass into their souls, and the humblest person would expand with a sense of innate dignity — a sense that would raise him above the dusty, beaten paths of life, give a respite to depressing care, strengthen self-respect, infuse warm and liberal emotions, quicken the best sympathies, and lend animation and support to the noblest powers. He would feel at once that he was man, known and honored as such, of higher importance and more inestimable worth than the whole outward world.

In this ennobling influence, Christianity and democracy are one. What, indeed, is democracy but Christianity in its earthly aspect, Christianity made effective among the political relations of men. Christianity, in which it accords with every design of Providence, begins with individual man, addressing its lofty persuasions to him, and makes his full development its chief solicitude and care. The obstacles reared by artificial life it throws aside; the rubbish heaped by centuries of abuse upon the human spirit it removes, the better to unfold man's inward beauty and bring forth man's inward might. A single soul is worth more in its sight than suns or stars. It has a value more enduring than states. The proudest thrones may crumble, the broadest empires contract and become nothing, but the spirit of the meanest man can never perish; for it is the germ of an immortal, ever expanding, ever quickening existence.

II.

The Great Nation Of Futurity

THE AMERICAN PEOPLE, having derived their origin from many other nations, and the Declaration of National Independence being entirely based on the great principle of human equality, these facts demonstrate at once our disconnected position as regards any other nation; that we have, in reality, but little connection with the past history of any of them, and still less with all antiquity, its glories, or its crimes. On the contrary, our national birth was the beginning of a new history, the formation and progress of an untried political system, which separates us from the past and connects us with the future only; and so far as regards the entire development of the natural rights of man, in moral, political, and national life, we may confidently assume that our country is destined to be *the great nation* of futurity.

It is so destined because the principle upon which a nation is organized fixes its destiny, and that of equality is perfect, is universal. It presides in all the operations of the physical world, and it is also the conscious law of the soul — the self-evident dictate of morality which accurately defines the duty of man to man and consequently man's rights as man. Besides, the truthful annals of any nation furnish abundant evidence that its happiness, its greatness, its duration were always proportionate to the democratic equality in its system of government.

How many nations have had their decline and fall because the equal rights of the minority were trampled on by the despotism of the majority; or the interests of the many sacrificed to the aristocracy of the few; or the rights and interests of all given up to the monarchy of one? These three kinds of government have figured so frequently and so largely in the ages that have passed away that their history, through all time to come, can only furnish a resemblance. Like causes produce like effects, and the true philosopher of history will easily discern the principle of equality, or of privilege, working out its inevitable result. The first is regenerative because it is natural and right; the latter is destructive to society because it is unnatural and wrong.

What friend of human liberty, civilization, and refinement can cast his view over the past history of the monarchies and aristocracies of antiquity and not deplore that they ever existed? What philanthropist can contemplate the oppressions, the cruelties, and injustice inflicted by them on the masses of mankind and not turn with moral horror from the retrospect?

America is destined for better deeds. It is our unparalleled glory that we have no reminiscences of battlefields, but in defense of humanity, of the oppressed of all nations, of the rights of conscience, the rights of personal enfranchisement. Our annals describe no scenes of horrid carnage, where men were led on by hundreds of thousands to slay one another, dupes and victims to emperors, kings, nobles, demons in the human form called heroes. We have had patriots to defend our homes, our liberties, but no aspirants to crowns or thrones; nor have the American people ever suffered themselves to be led on by wicked ambition to depopulate the land, to spread desolation far and wide, that a human being might be placed on a seat of supremacy.

We have no interest in the scenes of antiquity, only as lessons of avoidance of nearly all their examples. The expansive future is our arena and for our history. We are entering on its untrodden space, with the truths of God in our minds, beneficent objects in our hearts, and with a clear conscience unsullied by the past. We are the nation of human progress; and who will, what can, set limits to our onward march? Providence is with us, and no earthly power can. We point to the everlasting truth on the first page of our national declaration, and we proclaim to the millions of other lands that "the gates of hell" — the powers of aristocracy and monarchy — "shall not prevail against it."

The far-reaching, the boundless future will be the era of American greatness. In its magnificent domain of space and time, the nation of many nations is destined to manifest to mankind the excellence of divine principles; to establish on earth the noblest temple ever dedicated to the worship of the Most High — the Sacred and the True. Its floor shall be a hemisphere; its roof the firmament of the star-studded heavens; and its congregation a union of many republics, comprising hundreds of happy millions, calling, owning no man master, but governed by God's natural and moral law of equality, the law of brotherhood — of "peace and goodwill among men."

But although the mighty constituent truth upon which our social and political system is founded will assuredly work out the glorious destiny herein shadowed forth, yet there are many untoward circumstances to retard our progress, to procrastinate the entire fruition of the greatest good to the human race. There is a tendency to imitativeness prevailing among our professional and literary men, subversive of originality of thought and wholly unfavorable to progress. Being in early life devoted to the study of the laws, institutions, and antiquities of other nations, they are far behind the mind and movement of the age in which they live. So much so that the spirit of improvement as well as of enfranchisement exists chiefly in the great masses — the agricultural and mechanical population.

This propensity to imitate foreign nations is absurd and injurious. It is absurd, for we have never yet drawn on our mental resources that we have not found them ample and of unsurpassed excellence; witness our constitutions of government, where we had no foreign ones to imitate. . . .

Our businessmen have also conned the lesson of example and devoted themselves body and mind to the promotion of foreign interests. If states can steep themselves in debt, with any propriety in times of peace, why may not merchants import merchandise on credit? If the one can bond the labor and property of generations yet unborn, why may not the other contract debts against the yearly crops and daily labor of their contemporary fellow citizens?

And our literature! — Oh, when will it breathe the spirit of our republican institutions? When will it be imbued with the Godlike aspiration of intellectual freedom — the elevating principle of equality? When will it assert *its* national independence and speak the soul — the heart of the American people? Why cannot our literati comprehend the matchless sublimity of our position among the nations of the world — our high destiny — and cease bending the knee to foreign idolatry, false tastes, false doctrines, false principles?

When will they be inspired by the magnificent scenery of our own world, imbibe the fresh enthusiasm of a new heaven and a new earth, and soar upon the expanded wings of truth and liberty? Is not nature as original; her truths as captivating; her aspects as various, as lovely, as grand; her Promethean fire as glowing in this, our Western Hemisphere, as in that of the East? And above all, is not our private life as morally beautiful and good, is not our public life as politically right, as indicative of the brightest prospects of humanity, and therefore as inspiring of the highest conceptions? Why, then, do our authors aim at no higher degree of merit than a successful imitation of English writers of celebrity? . . .

Hence it is that our professional, literary, or commercial aristocracy have no faith in the virtue, intelligence, or capability of the people. The latter have never responded to their exotic sentiments, nor promoted their views of a strong government irresponsible to the popular majority, to the will of the masses.

Yes, we are the nation of progress, of individual freedom, of universal enfranchisement. Equality of rights is the cynosure of our Union of states, the grand exemplar of the correlative equality of individuals; and while truth sheds its effulgence, we cannot retrograde without dissolving the one and subverting the other. We must onward to the fulfillment of our mission, to the entire development of the principle of our organization — freedom of conscience, freedom of person, freedom of trade and business pursuits, universality of freedom and equality. This is our high destiny, and in nature's eternal, inevitable decree of cause and effect we must accomplish it.

All this will be our future history, to establish on earth the moral dignity and salvation of man — the immutable truth and beneficence of God. For this blessed mission to the nations of the world which are shut out from the life-giving light of truth has America been chosen; and her high example shall smite unto death the tyranny of kings, hierarchs, and oligarchs, and carry the glad tidings of peace and goodwill where myriads now endure an existence scarcely more enviable than that of beasts of the field. Who, then, can doubt that our country is destined to be *the great nation* of futurity?

95.

"Life Is A Toil"

"Life Is A Toil" appeared in numerous nineteenth-century song collections and has been traced to the late 1830s. The verses express what is doubtless an ancient complaint, but the wide popularity of the song is particularly interesting, giving evidence as it does of the deep dissatisfaction of the supposedly happy and contented housewife of the early nineteenth century.

❧ LIFE IS A TOIL

One day as I wandered, I heard a complaining,
   And saw an old woman, the picture of gloom;
She gazed at the mud on her doorstep ('twas raining),
   And this was her song as she wielded her broom:
   Chorus:
   "Oh, life is a toil and love is a trouble,
      And beauty will fade and riches will flee;
   Oh, pleasures they dwindle and prices they double,
      And nothing is as I would wish it to be.

"It's sweeping at six and it's dusting at seven,
   It's victuals at eight and it's dishes at nine;
It's potting and panning from ten to eleven —
   We scarce break our fast till we plan how to dine.

"There's too much of worriment goes in a bonnet,
   There's too much of ironing goes in a shirt;
There's nothing that pays for the time you waste on it,
   There's nothing that lasts us but trouble and dirt.

"In March it is mud, it is snow in December,
   The mid-summer breezes are loaded with dust;
In fall the leaves litter; in rainy September
   The wallpaper rots and the candlesticks rust.

"Last night in my dreams I was stationed forever
   On a far little isle in the midst of the sea;
My one chance for life was a ceaseless endeavor
   To sweep off the waves ere they swept over me.

"Alas, 'twas no dream, for ahead I behold it;
   I know I am helpless my fate to avert."
She put down her broom and her apron she folded,
   Then lay down and died, and was buried in dirt.

MARITIME NEW ENGLAND

For all its textile mills and county fairs, the story of New England is the story of a maritime people. Yankee whalers and ships of the China trade ranged the oceans of the world, carrying their crews from the stern atmosphere of New England into exotic foreign ports, to the lush islands of the South Pacific for food and water and to Canton or Bombay for cargoes of tea, silk, and spices.

By 1830 American ships dominated world whaling markets. The profits in whale oil for lamps, whalebone for corsets, and spermaceti for candles amply repaid the labors of two- and three-year voyages to whaling grounds scattered from the Indian Ocean to the Bering Straits. For some, though, the adventure was payment enough. It was food for a lifetime of reminiscences and for growing legends of flinty ship captains, mythical monster whales, cannibals, and mutiny. The legends are rooted in fact. The

small whaleboats challenging animals twice their size and the oil-laden ships weathering a South Sea typhoon were enacting a drama universally understood. In the traditional saying, it was "a dead whale or a stove boat."

On the interminable whaling voyages and on the long haul across the Pacific to China, hard work, short rations, and close contact often brought problems of discipline and personality to the fore. Too often discipline was enforced with summary brutality from the masters. This was more of a problem on the merchant ships than on the whalers, where a successful voyage promised ample reward for everyone and the captain and many of the crew were fellow townsmen.

In the end, for a sailor drifting a thousand miles from land, the sea demanded humility: "Thy sea is so great, O Lord, and our boat is so small."

Whalers in New Bedford harbor, 1846, from Benjamin Russell's 700-foot panorama of a whaling trip

The Whaling Ports

Though the whaling industry covered all the seas, home ports were confined to the Atlantic Coast, from Long Island to northern Massachusetts. Nantucket and New Bedford were the most famous whaling towns, New Bedford particularly because it was also an important shipbuilding center. Sag Harbor, on Long Island, was also a major port.

The romantic aspects of whaling should not conceal the fact that it was a major business enterprise in the 19th century. Nearly 330 ships were registered out of the port of New Bedford in 1857, the peak year. Whale oil, candles, whalebone were raw materials, and substantial capital investment went into ships.

Southeastern view of New Bedford, from Barber's "Historical Collections," 1840

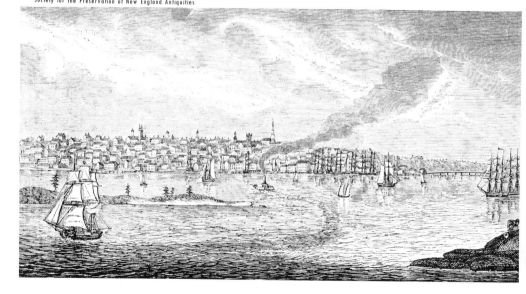

View of the town of Salem with the court-house in the center, from Barber's "Historical Collections"

(Left) Map of the harbors of Salem and surrounding towns drawn in the early 19th century by Nathaniel Bowditch; (below) stock certificate from Sag Harbor whaling company

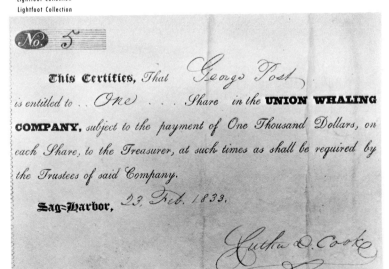

No. 5

This Certifies, That *George Post* is entitled to . . *One* . . . *Share* in the **UNION WHALING COMPANY,** *subject to the payment of One Thousand Dollars, on each Share, to the Treasurer, at such times as shall be required by the Trustees of said Company.*

Sag-Harbor, *23. Feb. 1833.*

Luther D. Cook

TREASURER.

Whaling ships from New Bedford in the harbor at Fayal in the Azores; from Russell's panorama

Whalers Roam the Seas

Other whales were hunted, too, but the great American whaling fleet primarily sought out the sperm whale, hunted off the Azores and in Brazilian waters even before the Revolution. A few years later the whaling fleets were rounding the South American coast and harpooning their prey throughout the Pacific Ocean and into the Indian Ocean. Profit sharing was the usual way of paying the crew on whalers: the hands received "lays" or shares in the proceeds of the voyage. This was one of the earliest forms of incentive payment. Each one, from master down to cabin boy, received a lay in proportion to the importance of his work.

Ships off the island of Pico in the Azores. Whalers stopped here for supplies

A shoal of sperm whales off the island of Hawaii; aquatint engraving dated 1838

Capt. John Howland, commander of a New Bedford whaling vessel in the mid-19th century

"In Memory of Robert Wentworth," watercolor of a seaman dated 1825

"South Sea Whale Fishing" by Robert Salmon, 1835

The recipe for whale oil, whalebone, and spermaceti began: "First you catch your whale." It was a grim and hazardous pursuit, with oar-propelled boats in the midst of a "pod" or herd of the ocean monsters. Harpooning the victim was only the beginning of what was often a wild chase. Success meant the backbreaking job of getting the whale to the ship, or the ship to the whale, and stripping tons of blubber, which was "tried out" (refined) into whale oil in vast kettles on deck. The oil was stored in barrels until port was reached.

Harpooning a whale; sketch by Robert Weir

Bringing dead whales back to the ship; painting by Salmon

Sketch from Weir's journal showing the crew in three whaleboats killing a whale

Cutting blubber into blocks called "horse pieces";
sketch by Weir when on the "Clara Bell"

"Horse pieces" further sliced into "Bible leaves"
being boiled in try-pots

Bailing highest grade sperm oil from a "case" in the whale's head

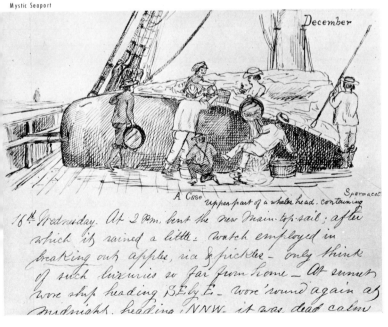

View of Honolulu in 1854 sketched by Paul Emmert

King Kamehameha

Island Paradise

Even before the heyday of the whaling ships, Hawaii was known to American mariners and traders who hunted seal in the Pacific and Antarctic and put in to the islands for repairs and supplies. American shipping to the Far East — the China ports and southeast Asia — dated from Capt. Robert Gray's voyage around the world late in the 18th century. Hawaii (the Sandwich Islands to early voyagers) was a favorite stopping place, and the first American missionaries arrived from New England in 1820, intent on protecting the morals of seamen as well as converting the heathen. Merchants followed in their wake and established Yankee businesses.

View of Honolulu in 1816 made by a Russian artist at the time Russia was trying to claim Hawaii

American Museum of Natural History

Titian Peale painted the volcano "Kileuea" (above) in 1840 while with a government scientific expedition in the Pacific. The expedition was led by Lt. Charles Wilkes

King Kamehameha I (1737-1819) unified the Hawaiian Islands under his rule by 1810 and successfully resisted encroachments by the Russians in 1816

The first inhabitants of the Hawaiian Islands came by sailing canoe from Tahiti and Samoa, 2,000 miles across the Pacific, in about 500 A.D. The islands quickly succumbed to the pressures of Western civilization in the 19th century. The trader's demands for sandalwood stripped the islands of that rare wood, while creating a taste for luxury among the nobles. The missionaries brought Christianity and an alphabet for the native language; a constitution and a legal code followed

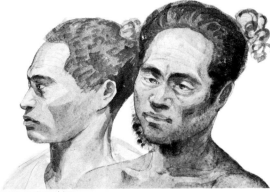

Honolulu Academy of Arts

Honolulu Academy of Arts

The flags of the nations trading there fly above the Canton trade center

The China Trade

Yankee trade with China began early and was largely conducted by Massachusetts merchants. Until 1842, Canton in south China was the only port at which foreign trade was permitted. Here, along the banks of the Pearl River, Chinese merchants built their hongs (monopolistic trading establish-ments). Vessels from around the world put in to load their cargoes of tea, silk, and spices — opium was also traded, though usually illegally. The Far East trade led to the design of the famed clippers ships that dominated the race to the eager markets in Europe and America.

Chinese workers in a Canton hong packing tea for shipment

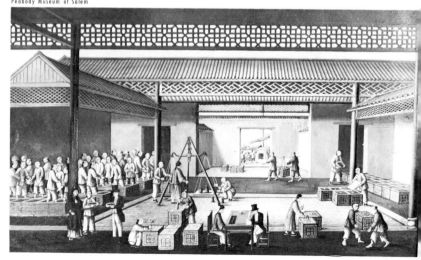

1840

96.

Martin Van Buren: Executive Order for a Ten-Hour Day

By 1836 a working day of ten hours was almost universal among organized laborers in most Eastern cities. Only in federal works was the twelve-hour day still maintained. When, in early 1835, the mechanics of the New York navy yards asked the secretary of the navy for a reduction of hours, their request was denied. The same appeal was made to Congress, but it refused to legislate working hours and wages. Then, in the summer of 1836, mechanics at the navy yard in Philadelphia struck for the ten-hour day and appealed directly to the President for support. He ordered that their demands be complied with. Thereafter other federal workers petitioned the President for like considerations and finally, on March 31, 1840, the ten-hour day was established in all government works by executive order.

Source: Richardson, III, p. 602.

The President of the United States, finding that different rules prevail at different places, as well in respect to the hours of labor by persons employed on the public works under the immediate authority of himself and the departments as also in relation to the different classes of workmen; and believing that much inconvenience and dissatisfaction would be removed by adopting a uniform course; hereby directs that all such persons, whether laborers or mechanics, be required to work only the number of hours prescribed by the ten-hour system.

97.

Richard Henry Dana: Despotism on the High Seas

R. H. Dana's literary fame rests on a single book, Two Years Before the Mast.
*Scion of a distinguished Boston family, Dana left Harvard after an attack of measles
weakened his eyesight and, to regain his health, shipped as a fo'c'sle hand or ordinary
seaman on the brig* Pilgrim, *out of Boston, in August 1834. After a two-year voyage
around the Horn and along the coast of California, Dana returned to Harvard, now
fully recovered, and graduated at the top of his class. His book, which appeared
in 1840, was an immediate and enduring success. It provided its Eastern readers
with their first accurate knowledge of California, and fascinated such persons as
President Polk with the promise of that faraway "paradise." Its sympathetic accounts
of the abuse to which sailors were subjected resulted in many reforms; and its
concluding chapter, reprinted here, was particularly effective in this regard. But it
was as a tale of high adventure that the work gained its reputation, and it remains one
of the great American books.*

Source: *Two Years Before the Mast,* New York, 1842, pp. 460-483.

THERE IS A WITCHERY IN THE SEA, its songs and stories, and in the mere sight of a ship, and the sailor's dress, especially to a young mind, which has done more to man navies and fill merchantmen than all the press gangs of Europe. I have known a young man with such a passion for the sea that the very creaking of a block stirred up his imagination so that he could hardly keep his feet on dry ground; and many are the boys, in every seaport, who are drawn away, as by an almost irresistible attraction, from their work and schools, and hang about the decks and yards of vessels with a fondness which, it is plain, will have its way.

No sooner, however, has the young sailor begun his new life in earnest than all this fine drapery falls off, and he learns that it is but work and hardship after all. This is the true light in which a sailor's life is to be viewed; and if in our books and anniversary speeches we would leave out much that is said about "blue water," "blue jackets," "open hearts," "seeing God's hand on the deep," and so forth, and take this up like any other practical subject, I am quite sure we should do full as much for those we wish to benefit.

The question is, what can be done for sailors as they are — men to be fed and clothed and lodged, for whom laws must be made and executed, and who are to be instructed in useful knowledge, and, above all, to be brought under religious influence and restraint? It is upon these topics that I wish to make a few observations.

In the first place, I have no fancies about equality on board ship. It is a thing out of the question, and certainly, in the present state of mankind, not to be desired. I never knew a sailor who found fault with the orders and ranks of the service; and if I expected to pass the rest of my life before the mast, I would not wish to have the power of the captain diminished an iota. It is absolutely necessary that there should be one head and one voice to control everything and be responsible for everything. There are emergencies which require the instant exercise of extreme power. These emergencies do not allow of consultation; and they who would be the captain's constituted advisers might be the very men over whom he would be called upon to exert his authority.

It has been found necessary to vest in every government, even the most democratic, some extraordinary and, at first sight, alarming powers; trusting in public opinion, and subsequent accountability, to modify the exercise of them. These are provided to meet exigencies, which all hope may never occur, but which yet by possibility may occur; and if they should, and there were no power to meet them instantly, there would be an end put to the government at once.

So it is with the authority of the shipmaster. It will not answer to say that he shall never do this and that thing, because it does not seem always necessary and advisable that it should be done. He has great cares and responsibilities; is answerable for everything and is subject to emergencies which perhaps no other man exercising authority among civilized people is subject to. Let him, then, have powers commensurate with his utmost possible need; only let him be held strictly responsible for the exercise of them. Any other course would be injustice as well as bad policy.

In the treatment of those under his authority, the captain is amenable to the common law, like any other person. He is liable at common law for murder, assault and battery, and other offenses; and, in addition to this, there is a special statute of the United States which makes a captain or other officer liable to imprisonment for a term not exceeding five years, and to a fine not exceeding $1,000, for inflicting any cruel punishment upon, withholding food from, or in any other way maltreating a seaman. This is the state of the law on the subject; while the relation in which the parties stand and the peculiar necessities, excuses, and provocations arising from that relation are merely circumstances to be considered in each case.

As to the restraints upon the master's exercise of power, the laws themselves seem, on the whole, to be sufficient. I do not see that we are in need, at present, of more legislation on the subject. The difficulty lies rather in the administration of the laws; and this is certainly a matter that deserves great consideration, and one of no little embarrassment.

In the first place, the courts have said that public policy requires that the power of the master and officers should be sustained. Many lives and a great amount of property are constantly in their hands, for which they are strictly responsible. To preserve these, and to deal justly by the captain and not lay upon him a really fearful responsibility and then tie up his hands, it is essential that discipline should be supported.

In the second place, there is always great allowance to be made for false swearing and exaggeration by seamen, and for combinations among them against their officers; and it is to be remembered that the latter have often no one to testify on their side. These are weighty and true statements, and should not be lost sight of by the friends of seamen. On the other hand, sailors make many complaints, some of which are well-founded.

On the subject of testimony, seamen labor under a difficulty full as great as that of the captain. It is a well-known fact that they are usually much better treated when there are passengers on board. The presence of passengers is a restraint upon the captain, not only from his regard to their feelings, and to the estimation in which they may hold him, but because he knows they will be influential witnesses against him if he is brought to trial.

Though officers may sometimes be inclined to show themselves off before passengers, by freaks of office and authority, yet cruelty they would hardly dare to be guilty of. It is on long and distant voyages, where there is no restraint upon the captain and none but the crew to testify against him, that sailors need most the protection of the law.

On such voyages as these, there are many cases of outrageous cruelty on record, enough to make one heartsick and almost disgusted with the sight of man; and many, many more which have never come to light and never will be known until the sea shall give up its dead. Many of these have led to mutiny and piracy — stripe for stripe, and blood for blood. If on voyages of this description the testimony of seamen is not to be received in favor of one another, or too great a deduction is made on account of their being seamen, their case is without remedy, and the captain, knowing this, will be strengthened in that disposition to tyrannize, which the possession of absolute power without the restraints of friends and public opinion is too apt to engender.

It is to be considered, also, that the sailor comes into court under very different circumstances from the master. He is thrown among landlords and sharks of all descriptions; is often led to drink freely; and comes upon the stand unaided and under a certain cloud of suspicion as to his character and veracity. The captain, on the other hand, is backed by the owners and insurers, and has an air of greater respectability; though, after all, he may have but a little better education than the sailor, and sometimes (especially among those engaged in certain voyages that I could mention), a very hackneyed conscience.

These are the considerations most commonly brought up on the subject of seamen's evidence; and I think it cannot but be obvious to everyone that here positive legislation would be of no manner of use. There can be no rule of law regulating the weight to be given to seamen's evidence. It must rest in the mind of the judge and jury;

and no enactment or positive rule of court could vary the result a hair in any one case. The effect of the sailor's testimony in deciding a case must depend altogether upon the reputation of the class to which he belongs, and upon the impression he himself produces in court by his deportment, and by those infallible marks of character which always tell upon a jury.

In fine, after all the well-meant and specious projects that have been brought forward, we seem driven back to the belief that the best means of securing a fair administration of the laws made for the protection of seamen, and certainly the only means which can create any important change for the better, is the gradual one of raising the intellectual and religious character of the sailor, so that, as an individual and as one of a class, he may, in the first instance, command the respect of his officers, and, if any difficulty should happen, may upon the stand carry that weight which an intelligent and respectable man of the lower class almost always does with a jury.

I know there are many men who, when a few cases of great hardship occur, it is evident that there is an evil somewhere, think that some arrangement must be made, some law passed, or some society got up, to set all right at once. On this subject there can be no call for any such movement; on the contrary, I fully believe that any public and strong action would do harm, and that we must be satisfied to labor in the less easy and less exciting task of gradual improvement, and abide the issue of things working slowly together for good.

Equally injudicious would be any interference with the economy of the ship. The lodging, food, hours of sleep, etc., are all matters which, though capable of many changes for the better, must yet be left to regulate themselves. And I am confident that there will be, and that there is now, a gradual improvement in all such particulars.

The forecastles of most of our ships are small, black, and wet holes, which few landsmen would believe held a crew of ten or twelve men on a voyage of months or years; and often, indeed, in most cases, the provisions are not good enough to make a meal anything more than a necessary part of a day's duty. And, on the score of sleep, I fully believe that the lives of merchant seamen are shortened by the want of it.

I do not refer to those occasions when it is necessarily broken in upon; but, for months, during fine weather, in many merchantmen, all hands are kept, throughout the day; and, then, there are eight hours on deck for one watch each night. Thus it is usually the case that at the end of a voyage, where there has been the finest weather and no disaster, the crew have a wearied and worn-out appearance. They never sleep longer than four hours at a time, and are seldom called without being really in need of more rest. There is no one thing that a sailor thinks more of as a luxury of life on shore than a whole night's sleep.

Still, all these things must be left to be gradually modified by circumstances. Whenever hard cases occur, they should be made known, and masters and owners should be held answerable, and will, no doubt, in time, be influenced in their arrangements and discipline by the increased consideration in which sailors are held by the public. It is perfectly proper that the men should live in a different part of the vessel from the officers; and if the forecastle is made large and comfortable, there is no reason why the crew should not live there as well as in any other part. In fact, sailors prefer the forecastle. It is their accustomed place, and in it they are out of the sight and hearing of their officers.

As to their food and sleep, there are laws, with heavy penalties, requiring a certain amount of stores to be on board and safely stowed; and, for depriving the crew unnecessarily of food or sleep, the captain is liable at common law, as well as under the statute before referred to. Further than this, it would not be safe to go. The captain must be the judge when it is necessary to keep his crew from their sleep; and sometimes a retrenching, not of the necessaries but of some of the little niceties of their meals, as for instance, *duff* on Sunday, may be a mode of punishment, though I think generally an injudicious one.

I could not do justice to this subject without noticing one part of the discipline of a ship which has been very much discussed of late and has brought out strong expressions of indignation from many — I mean the infliction of corporal punishment. . . . I can sincerely say that the simple mention of the word flogging brings up in me feelings which I can hardly control. Yet, when the proposition is made to abolish it entirely and at once; to prohibit the captain from ever, under any circumstances, inflicting corporal punishment, I am obliged to pause, and, I must say, to doubt exceedingly the expediency of making any positive enactment which shall have that effect.

If the design of those who are writing on this subject is merely to draw public attention to it, and to discourage the practice of flogging, and bring it into disrepute, it is well; and, indeed, whatever may be the end they have in view, the mere agitation of the question will have that effect, and, so far, must do good. Yet I should not wish to take the command of a ship tomorrow, running my chance of a crew, as most masters must, and know, and have my crew know, that I could not, under any circumstances, inflict even moderate chastisement. I should trust that I might never have to resort to it; and, indeed, I scarcely know what risk I would not run and to what inconvenience I would not subject myself rather than do so. Yet not to have the power of holding it up *in terrorem*, and indeed of protecting myself, and all under my charge, by it, if some extreme case should arise, would be a situation I should not wish to be placed in my-self, or to take the responsibility of placing another in.

Indeed, the difficulties into which masters and officers are liable to be thrown are not sufficiently considered by many whose sympathies are easily excited by stories, frequent enough and true enough, of outrageous abuse of this power. It is to be remembered that more than three-fourths of the seamen in our merchant vessels are foreigners. They are from all parts of the world. A great many from the north of Europe, and besides Frenchmen, Spaniards, Portuguese, Italians, men from all parts of the Mediterranean, together with Lascars, Negroes, and perhaps worst of all, the offcasts of British men-of-war, and men from our own country who have gone to sea because they could not be permitted to live on land.

As things now are, many masters are obliged to sail without knowing anything of their crews until they get out at sea. There may be pirates or mutineers among them; and one bad man will often infect all the rest; and it is almost certain that some of them will be ignorant foreigners, hardly understanding a word of our language, accustomed all their lives to no influence but force, and perhaps nearly as familiar with the use of the knife as with that of the marlinespike.

No prudent master, however peaceably inclined, would go to sea without his pistols and handcuffs. Even without such a crew as I have supposed, kindness and moderation would be the best policy and the duty of every conscientious man; and the administering of corporal punishment might be dangerous and of doubtful use. But the question is, not what a captain ought generally to do but whether it shall be put out of the power of every captain, under any circumstances, to make use of even moderate chastisement. As the law now stands, a parent may correct moderately his child, and the master his apprentice, and the case of the shipmaster has been placed upon the same principle.

The statutes and the common law as expounded in the decision of courts and in the books of commentators are express and unanimous to this point, that the captain may inflict moderate corporal chastisement for a reasonable cause. If the punishment is excessive or the cause not sufficient to justify it, he is answerable; and the jury are to determine, by their verdict in each case, whether, under all the circumstances, the punishment was moderate and for a justifiable cause.

This seemed to me to be as good a position as the whole subject can be left in. I mean to say that no positive enactment, going beyond this, is needed or would be a benefit either to masters or men in the present state of things. This again would seem to be a case which should be left to be the gradual working of its own cure.

As seamen improve, punishment will become less necessary; and as the character of officers is raised, they will be less ready to inflict it; and, still more, the infliction of it upon intelligent and respectable men will be an enormity which will not be tolerated by public opinion and by juries, who are the pulse of the body politic.

No one can have a greater abhorrence of the infliction of such punishment than I have, and a stronger conviction that severity is bad policy with a crew. Yet I would ask every reasonable man whether he had not better trust to the practice becoming unnecessary and disreputable; to the measure of moderate chastisement and a justifiable cause being better understood, and thus, the act becoming dangerous, and in course of time to be regarded as an unheard-of barbarity, than to take the responsibility of prohibiting it, at once, in all cases and in whatever degree by positive enactment?

There is, however, one point connected with the administration of justice to seamen to which I wish seriously to call the attention of those interested in their behalf, and, if possible, also of some of those concerned in that administration. This is the practice which prevails of making strong appeals to the jury in mitigation of damages, or to the judge, after a verdict has been rendered against a captain or an officer, for a lenient sentence, on the grounds of their previous good character, and of their being poor and having friends and families depending upon them for support.

These appeals have been allowed a weight which is almost incredible and which, I think, works a greater hardship upon seamen than any one other thing in the laws or the execution of them. Notwithstanding every advantage the captain has over the seamen in point of evidence, friends, money, and able counsel, it becomes apparent that he must fail in his defense. An appeal is then made to the jury, if it is a civil action, or to the judge for a mitigated sentence, if it is a criminal prosecution, on the two grounds I have mentioned.

The same form is usually gone through in every case. In the first place, as to the previous good character of the party. Witnesses are brought from the town in which he resides to testify to his good character and to his unexceptional conduct when on shore. They say that he is a good father, or husband, or son, or neighbor, and that they never saw in him any signs of cruel, tyrannical disposition. I have even known evidence admitted to show the character he bore when a boy at school. The owners of the vessel and other merchants, and perhaps the president of the insurance company, are then introduced; and they testify to his correct deportment, express their confidence in his honesty, and say that they have never seen anything in his conduct to justify a suspicion of his being capable of cruelty or tyranny.

This evidence is then put together, and great stress is laid upon the extreme respectability of those who give it. They are the companions and neighbors of the captain, it is said — men who know him in his business and domestic relations, and who knew him in his early youth. They are also men of the highest standing in the community, and who, as the captain's employers, must be supposed to know his character.

The testimony is then contrasted with that of some half dozen obscure sailors, who, the counselor will not forget to add, are exasperated against the captain because he has found it necessary to punish them moderately, and who have combined against him; and if they have not fabricated a story entirely, have at least so exaggerated it that little confidence can be placed in it.

The next thing to be done is to show to the court and jury that the captain is a poor man and has a wife and family, or other friends, depending upon him for support; that if he is fined, it will only be taking bread from the mouths of the innocent and helpless, and laying a burden upon them which their whole lives will not be able to work off; and that if he is imprisoned, the confinement, to be sure, he will have to bear, but the distress consequent upon the cutting him off from his labor and means of earning his wages will fall upon a poor wife and helpless children, or upon an infirm parent. These two topics, well put and urged home earnestly, seldom fail of their effect.

In deprecation of this mode of proceeding, and in behalf of men who I believe are every day wronged by it, I would urge a few considerations which seem to me to be conclusive.

First, as to the evidence of the good character the captain sustains on shore. It is to be remembered that masters of vessels have usually been brought up in a forecastle; and upon all men, and especially upon those taken from lower situations, conferring of absolute power is too apt to work a great change.

There are many captains whom I know to be cruel and tyrannical men at sea, who yet, among their friends and in their families, have never lost the reputation they bore in childhood. In fact, the sea captain is seldom at home, and when he is, his stay is short, and during the continuance of it he is surrounded by friends who treat him with kindness and consideration, and he has everything to please and at the same time to restrain him. He would be a brute, indeed, if, after an absence of months or years, during his short stay, so short that the novelty and excitement of it has hardly time to wear off, and the attentions he receives as a visitor and stranger hardly time to slacken — if, under such circumstances, a townsman or neighbor would be justified in testifying against his correct and peaceable deportment.

With the owners of the vessel, also, to which he is attached, and among merchants and insurers generally, he is a very different man from what he may be at sea, when his own master, and the master of everybody and everything about him. He knows that upon such men and their good opinion of him he depends for his bread. So far from their testimony being of any value in determining what his conduct would be at sea, one would expect that the master who would abuse and impose upon a man under his power would be the most compliant and deferential to his employers at home.

As to the appeal made in the captain's behalf on the ground of his being poor and having persons depending upon his labor for support, the main and fatal objection to it is that it will cover every case of the kind, and exempt nearly the whole body of masters and officers from punishment the law has provided for them. There are very few, if any, masters or other officers of merchantmen in our country who are not poor men, and having either parents, wives, children, or other relatives depending mainly or wholly upon their exertions for support in life. Few others follow the sea for subsistence.

Now if this appeal is to have weight with courts in diminishing the penalty the law would otherwise inflict, is not the whole class under a privilege which will, in a degree, protect it in wrongdoing? It is not a thing that happens now and then. It is the invariable appeal, the last resort of counsel when everything else has failed. I have known cases of the most flagrant nature, where, after every effort has been made for the captain, and yet a verdict rendered against him, and all other hope failed, this appeal has been urged, and with such success that the punishment has been reduced to something little more than nominal; the court not seeming to consider that it might be made in almost every such case that could come before them.

It is a little singular, too, that it seems to be confined to cases of shipmasters and officers. No one ever heard of a sentence for an offense committed on shore being reduced by the court on the grounds of the prisoner's poverty and the relation in which he may stand to third persons. On the contrary, it has been thought that the certainty that disgrace and suffering will be brought upon others as well as himself is one of the chief restraints of the criminally disposed. Besides, this course works a peculiar hardship in the case of a sailor; for if poverty is the point in question, the sailor is the poorer of the two; and if there is a man on earth who depends upon whole limbs and an unbroken spirit for support, it is the sailor. He, too, has friends to whom his hard earnings may be a relief and whose hearts will bleed at any cruelty or indignity practised upon him.

Yet I never knew this side of the case to be once adverted to in these arguments addressed to the leniency of the court which are now so much in vogue; and certainly they are never allowed a moment's consideration when a sailor is on trial for revolt or for an injury done to an officer. Notwithstanding the many difficulties which lie in a seaman's way in a court of justice, presuming that they will be modified in time, there would be little to complain of were it not for these two appeals.

It is no cause of complaint that the testimony of seamen against their officers is viewed with suspicion, and that great allowance is made for combinations and exaggeration. On the contrary, it is the judge's duty to charge the jury on these points, strongly. But there is reason for objection, when, after a strict cross-examination of witnesses, after the arguments of counsel and the judge's charge, a verdict is found against the master that the court should allow the practice of hearing appeals to its lenity, supported solely by evidence of the captain's conduct when on shore (especially where the case is one in which no evidence but that of sailors could have been brought against the accused), and then, on this ground, and on the invariable claims of the wife and family, be induced to cut down essentially the penalty imposed by a statute made expressly for masters and officers of merchantmen and for no one else. . . .

The manner of shipping men . . . it is well known, is usually left entirely to shipping masters, and is a cause of a great deal of difficulty which might be remedied by the captain, or owner, if he has any knowledge of seamen, attending to it personally. One of the members of the firm to which our ship belonged, Mr. S ———, had been himself a master of a vessel, and generally selected the crew from a number sent down to him from the shipping office. In this way he almost always had healthy, serviceable, and respectable men; for anyone who has seen much of sailors can tell pretty well at first sight by a man's dress, countenance, and deportment what he would be on board ship.

This same gentleman was also in the habit of seeing the crew together and speaking to them previously to their sailing. On the day before our ship sailed, while the crew were getting their chests and clothes on board, he went down into the forecastle and spoke to them about the voyage, the clothing they would need, the provision he had made for them, and saw that they had a lamp and a few other conveniences.

If owners or masters would more generally take the same pains, they would often save their crews a good deal of inconvenience, besides creating a sense of satisfaction and gratitude which makes a voyage begin under good auspices and goes far toward keeping up a better state of feeling throughout its continuance.

It only remains for me now to speak of the associated public efforts which have been making of late years for the good of seamen — a far more agreeable task than that of finding fault, even where fault there is. The exertions of the general association, called the American Seamen's Friend Society, and of the other smaller societies throughout the Union, have been a true blessing to the seaman, and bid fair, in course of time, to change the whole nature of the circumstances in which he is placed and give him a new name as well as a new character.

These associations have taken hold in the right way, and aimed both at making the sailor's life more comfortable and creditable, and at giving him spiritual instruction. Connected with these efforts, the spread of temperance among seamen by means of societies called, in their own nautical language, Windward-Anchor Societies, and the distribution of books; the establishment of Sailors' Homes where they can be comfortably and cheaply boarded, live quietly and decently, and be in the way of religious services, reading, and conversation; also the institution of Savings Banks for Seamen; the distribution of tracts and Bibles — are all means which are silently doing a great work for this class of men. These societies make the religious instruction of seamen their prominent object.

If this is gained, there is no fear but that all other things necessary will be added unto them. A sailor never becomes interested in religion without immediately learning to read, if he did not know how before; and regular habits, forehandedness (if I may use the word) in worldly affairs, and hours reclaimed from indolence and vice, which follow in the wake of the converted man, make it sure that he will instruct himself in the knowledge necessary and suitable to his calling. The religious change is the great object. If this is secured, there is no fear but that knowledge of things of the world will come in fast enough.

With the sailor, as with all other men, in fact, the cultivation of the intellect and the spread of what is commonly called useful knowledge while religious instruction is neglected is little else than changing an ignorant sinner into an intelligent and powerful one. That sailor upon whom, of all others, the preaching of the Cross is least likely to have effect is the one whose understanding has been cultivated while his heart has been left to its own devices.

I fully believe that those efforts which have their end in the intellectual cultivation of the sailor; in giving him scientific knowledge; putting it in his power to read everything, without securing first of all a right heart which shall guide him in judgment; in giving him political information and interesting him in newspapers — an end in the furtherance of which he is exhibited at ladies' fairs and public meetings and complimented for his gallantry and generosity — are all doing a harm which the labors of many faithful men cannot undo.

The establishment of Bethels in most of our own seaports and in many foreign ports frequented by our vessels, where the gospel is regularly preached; and the opening of "Sailors' Homes," which I have before mentioned, where there are usually religious services and other good influences, are doing a vast deal in this cause.

But it is to be remembered that the sailor's home is on the deep. Nearly all his life must be spent on board ship; and to secure a religious influence there should be the great object. The distribution of Bibles and tracts into cabins and forecastles will do much toward this. There is nothing which will gain a sailor's attention sooner and interest him more deeply than a tract, especially one which contains a story. It is difficult to engage their attention in mere essays and arguments, but the simplest and shortest story, in which home is spoken of, kind friends, a praying mother or sister, a sudden death, and the like, often touches the hearts of the roughest and most abandoned.

The Bible is to the sailor a sacred book. It may lie in the bottom of his chest voyage after voyage; but he never treats it with positive disrespect. I never knew but one sailor who doubted its being the inspired Word of God; and he was one who had received an uncommonly good education, except that he had been brought up without any early religious influence. The most abandoned man of our crew, one Sunday morning, asked one of the boys to lend him his Bible. The boy said he would, but was afraid he would make sport of it. "No!" said the man, "I don't make sport of God Almighty." This is a feeling general among sailors and is a good foundation for religious influence.

A still greater gain is made whenever, by means of a captain who is interested in the eternal welfare of those under his command, there can be secured the performance of regular religious exercises and the exertion on the side of religion of that mighty influence which a captain possesses for good or for evil.

There are occurrences at sea which he may turn to great account: a sudden death, the apprehension of danger or the escape from it, and the like; and all the calls for gratitude and faith. Besides, this state of things alters the whole current of feelings between the crew and their commander. His authority assumes more of the parental character; and kinder feelings exist.

Godwin, though an infidel, in one of his novels, describing the relation in which a tutor stood to his pupil, says that the conviction the tutor was under, that he and his ward were both alike awaiting a state of eternal happiness or misery, and they must appear together before the same judgment seat, operated so upon his naturally morose disposition as to produce a feeling of kindness and tenderness toward his ward, which nothing else could have caused. Such must be the effect upon the relation of masters and common seamen.

There are now many vessels sailing under such auspices, in which great good is done. Yet I never happened to fall in with one of them. I did not hear a prayer made, a chapter read in public, nor see anything approaching to a religious service for two years and a quarter. There were, in the course of the voyage, many incidents which made, for the time, serious impressions upon our minds, and which might have been turned to our good; but there being no one to use the opportunity and no services, the regular return of which might have kept something of the feeling alive in us, the advantage of them was lost to some, perhaps, forever.

The good which a single religious captain may do can hardly be calculated. In the first place, as I have said, a kinder state of feeling exists on board the ship. There is no profanity allowed; and the men are not called by any opprobrious names, which is a great thing with sailors. The Sabbath is observed. This gives the men a day of rest, even if they pass it in no other way.

Such a captain, too, will not allow a sailor on board his ship to remain unable to read his Bible and the books given to him, and will usually instruct those who need it in writing, arithmetic, and navigation; since he has a good deal of time on his hands which he can easily employ in such a manner. He will also have regular religious services; and, in fact, by the power of his example, and, where it can judiciously be done, by the exercise of his authority, will give a character to the ship and all on board.

In foreign ports, a ship is known by her captain; for there being no general rules in the merchant service, each master may adopt a plan of his own. It is to be remembered, too, that there are, in most ships, boys of a tender age whose characters for life are forming, as well as old men whose lives must be drawing toward a close.

The greater part of sailors die at sea; and when they find their end approaching, if it does not, as is often the case, come without warning, they cannot, as on shore, send for a clergyman or some religious friend to speak to them of that hope in a Savior, which they have neglected, if not despised, through life; but if the little hull does not contain such a one within its compass, they must be left without human aid in their great extremity.

When such commanders and such ships as I have just described shall become more numerous, the hope of the friends of seamen will be greatly strengthened, and it is encouraging to remember that the efforts among common sailors will soon raise up such a class; for those of them who are brought under these influences will inevitably be the ones to succeed to the places of trust and authority. If there is on earth an instance where a little leaven may leaven the whole lump, it is that of a religious shipmaster.

It is to the progress of this work among seamen that we must look with the greatest confidence for the remedying of those numerous minor evils and abuses that we so often hear of. It will raise the character of sailors, both as individuals and as a class. It will give weight to their testimony in courts of justice, secure better usage to them on board ship, and add comforts to their lives on shore and at sea.

There are some laws that can be passed to remove temptation from their way and to help them in their progress; and some changes in the jurisdiction of the lower courts, to prevent delays, may, and probably will, be made. But generally speaking, more especially in things which concern the discipline of ships, we had better labor in this great work, and view with caution the proposal of new laws and arbitrary regulations, remembering that most of those concerned in the making of them must necessarily be little qualified to judge of their operation.

Without any formal dedication of my narrative to that body of men of whose common life it is intended to be a picture, I have yet borne them constantly in mind during its preparation. I cannot but trust that those of them into whose hands it may chance to fall will find in it that which shall render any professions of sympathy and good wishes on my part unnecessary. And I will take the liberty, on parting with my reader, who has gone down with us to the ocean, and "laid his hand upon its mane," to commend to his kind wishes, and to the benefit of his efforts, that class of men with whom, for a time, my lot was cast. I wish the rather to do this, since I feel that whatever attention this book may gain, and whatever favor it may find, I shall owe almost entirely to that interest in the sea, and those who follow it, which is so easily excited in us all.

98.

Orestes A. Brownson: Labor and Social Democracy

Orestes Brownson's essay, "The Laboring Classes," part of which is reprinted here, was a review of Thomas Carlyle's Chartism. *In it, Brownson added a revolutionary note to what was otherwise fairly standard religious and political reformist thought of the time. He contended that the last step in elevating the laboring class to its rightful place in society would be the abolition of hereditary property. The piece was published during the election year of 1840 in the* Boston Quarterly Review, *which Brownson had founded. The journal was a favorite of Democratic Boston intellectuals, and the Whigs charged that Brownson's heterodoxy was ordinary Democratic doctrine. In fact the Boston Democrats were far from agreeing with Brownson's views, but they did continue to insist on his right to publish them and refused to denounce him.*

Source: *Boston Quarterly Review*, July 1840, pp. 366-395.

No one can observe the signs of the times with much care without perceiving that a crisis as to the relation of wealth and labor is approaching. It is useless to shut our eyes to the fact, and, like the ostrich, fancy ourselves secure because we have so concealed our heads that we see not the danger. We or our children will have to meet this crisis. The old war between the King and the Barons is well-nigh ended, and so is that between the Barons and the Merchants and Manufacturers — landed capital and commercial capital. The businessman has become the peer of My Lord. And now commences the new struggle between the operative and his employer, between wealth and labor. Everyday does this struggle extend further and wax stronger and fiercer; what or when the end will be, God only knows.

In this coming contest there is a deeper question at issue than is commonly imagined; a question which is but remotely touched in your controversies about United States Banks and subtreasuries, chartered banking and free banking, free trade and corporations, although these controversies may be paving the way for it to come up. We have discovered no presentiment of it in any king's or queen's speech, nor in any president's message. It is embraced in no popular political creed of the day, whether christened Whig or Tory, *juste-milieu* or Democratic. No popular senator, or deputy, or peer seems to have any glimpse of it; but it is working in the hearts of the million, is struggling to shape itself, and one day it will be uttered, and in thunder tones. Well will it be for him, who, on that day, shall be found ready to answer it.

What we would ask is, throughout the Christian world, the actual condition of the laboring classes, viewed simply and exclusively in their capacity of laborers? They constitute at least a moiety of the human race. We exclude the nobility, we exclude also the middle class, and include only actual laborers, who are laborers and not proprietors, owners of none of the funds of production, neither houses, shops, nor lands, nor implements of labor, being therefore solely dependent on their hands. We have no means of ascertaining their precise proportion to the whole number of the race; but we think we may estimate them at one-half. In any contest they will be as two to one, because the large class of proprietors who are not employers but laborers on their own lands or in their own shops will make common cause with them.

Now we will not so belie our acquaintance with political economy as to allege that these alone perform all that is necessary to the production of wealth. We are not ignorant of the fact that the merchant, who is literally the common carrier and exchange dealer, performs a useful service, and is, therefore, entitled to a portion of the proceeds of labor. But make all necessary deductions on his account, and then ask what portion of the remainder is retained, either in kind or in its equivalent, in the hands of the original producer, the workingman? All over the world this fact stares us in the face, the workingman is poor and depressed, while a large portion of the nonworkingmen, in the sense we now use the term, are wealthy.

It may be laid down as a general rule, with but few exceptions, that men are rewarded in an inverse ratio to the amount of actual service they perform. Under every government on earth the largest salaries are annexed to those offices which demand of their incumbents the least amount of actual labor, either mental or manual. And this is in perfect harmony with the whole system of repartition of the fruits of industry, which obtains in every department of society. Now here is the system which prevails, and here is its result. The whole class of simple laborers are poor, and in general unable to procure anything beyond the bare necessaries of life.

In regard to labor two systems obtain; one, that of slave labor; the other, that of free labor. Of the two, the first is, in our judgment, except so far as the feelings are concerned, decidedly the least oppressive. If the slave has never been a free man, we think, as a general rule, his sufferings are less than those of the free laborer at wages. As to actual freedom, one has just about as much as the other. The laborer at wages has all the disadvantages of freedom and none of its blessings, while the slave, if denied the blessings, is freed from the disadvantages. We are no advocates of slavery, we are as heartily opposed to it as any modern Abolitionist can be; but we say frankly that, if there must always be a la-

Orestes Brownson, 1843

boring population distinct from proprietors and employers, we regard the slave system as decidedly preferable to the system at wages.

It is no pleasant thing to go days without food, to lie idle for weeks, seeking work and finding none, to rise in the morning with a wife and children you love, and know not where to procure them a breakfast, and to see constantly before you no brighter prospect than the almshouse. Yet these are no infrequent incidents in the lives of our laboring population. Even in seasons of general prosperity, when there was only the ordinary cry of "hard times," we have seen hundreds of people in a not very populous village, in a wealthy portion of our common country, suffering for the want of the necessaries of life, willing to work and yet finding no work to do. Many and many is the application of a poor man for work, merely for his food, we have seen rejected. These things are little thought of, for the applicants are poor; they fill no conspicuous place in society, and they have no biographers. But their wrongs are chronicled in heaven.

It is said there is no want in this country. There may be less than in some other countries. But death by actual starvation in this country is, we apprehend, no uncommon occurrence. The sufferings of a quiet, unassuming but useful class of females in our cities, in general seamstresses, too proud to beg or to apply to the almshouse, are not easily told. They are industrious; they do all that they can find to do; but yet the little there is for them to do, and the miserable pittance they receive for it, is hardly sufficient to keep soul and body together. And yet there is a man who employs them to make shirts, trousers, etc., and grows rich on their labors.

He is one of our respectable citizens, perhaps is praised in the newspapers for his liberal donations to some charitable institution. He passes among us as a pattern of morality, and is honored as a worthy Christian. And why should he not be, since our *Christian* community is made up of such as he, and since our clergy would not dare question his piety, lest they should incur the reproach of infidelity, and lose their standing and their salaries? Nay, since our clergy are raised up, educated, fashioned, and sustained by such as he? Not a few of our churches rest on Mammon for their foundation. The basement is a trader's shop.

We pass through our manufacturing villages, most of them appear neat and flourishing. The operatives are well-dressed, and we are told, well-paid. They are said to be healthy, contented, and happy. This is the fair side of the picture; the side exhibited to distinguished visitors. There is a dark side, moral as well as physical. Of the common operatives, few, if any, by their wages, acquire a competence. A few of what Carlyle terms not inaptly the "body servants" are well-paid, and now and then an agent or an overseer rides in his coach. But the great mass wear out their health, spirits, and morals without becoming one whit better off than when they commenced labor.

The bills of mortality in these factory villages are not striking, we admit, for the poor girls, when they can toil no longer, go home to die. The average life, working life we mean, of the girls that come to Lowell, for instance, from Maine, New Hampshire, and Vermont, we have been assured, is only about three years. What becomes of them then? Few of them ever marry; fewer still ever return to their native places with reputations unimpaired. "She has worked in a Factory," is almost enough to damn to infamy the most worthy and virtuous girl. We know no sadder sight on earth than one of our factory villages presents, when the bell at break of day, or at the hour of breakfast, or dinner, calls out its hundreds or thousands of operatives. We stand and look at these hard-working men and women hurrying in all directions and ask ourselves — where go the proceeds of their labors?

The man who employs them, and for whom they are toiling as so many slaves, is one of our city nabobs, reveling in luxury; or he is a member of our legislature, enacting laws to put money in his own pocket; or he is a member of Congress, contending for a high tariff to tax the poor for the benefit of the rich; or in these times he is shedding crocodile tears over the deplorable condition of the poor laborer, while he docks his wages 25 percent; building miniature log cabins, shouting Harrison and "hard cider." And this man, too, would fain pass for a Christian and a republican. He shouts for liberty, stickles for equality, and is horrified at a Southern planter who keeps slaves.

One thing is certain, that of the amount actually produced by the operative, he retains a less proportion than it costs the master to feed, clothe, and lodge his slave. Wages is a cunning device of the devil, for the benefit of tender consciences, who would retain all the advantages of the slave system without the expense, trouble, and odium of being slaveholders.

Messrs. Thome and Kimball, in their account of emancipation in the West Indies, establish the fact that the employer may have the same amount of labor done, 25 percent cheaper than the master. What does this fact prove, if not that wages is a more successful method of taxing labor than slavery? We really believe our Northern system of labor is more oppressive, and even more mischievous to morals, than the Southern. We, however, war against both. We have no toleration for either system. We would see the slave a man, but a freeman, not a mere operative at wages. This he would not be were he now emancipated. Could the Abolitionists effect all they propose, they would do the slave no service. Should emancipation work as well as they say, still it would do the slave no good. He would be a slave still, although with the title and cares of a freeman. If, then, we had no constitutional objections to Abolitionism, we could not, for the reason here implied, be Abolitionists.

The slave system, however, in name and form, is gradually disappearing from Christendom. It will not subsist much longer. But its place is taken by the system of labor at wages, and this system, we hold, is no improvement upon the one it supplants. Nevertheless, the system of wages will triumph. It is the system which in name sounds honester than slavery, and in substance is more profitable to the master. It yields the wages of iniquity, without its opprobrium. It will, therefore, supplant slavery, and be sustained — for a time.

Now, what is the prospect of those who fall under the operation of this system? We ask, is there a reasonable chance that any considerable portion of the present generation of laborers shall ever become owners of a sufficient portion of the funds of production to be able to sustain themselves by laboring on their own capital, that is, as independent laborers? We need not ask this question, for everybody knows there is not.

Well, is the condition of a laborer at wages the best that the great mass of the working people ought to be able to aspire to? Is it a condition — nay, can it be made a condition — with which a man should be satisfied; in which he should be contented to live and die?

In our own country this condition has existed under its most favorable aspects, and has been made as good as it can be. It has reached all the excellence of which it is susceptible. It is now not improving but growing worse. The actual condition of the workingman today, viewed in all its bearings, is not so good as it was fifty years ago. If we have not been altogether misinformed, fifty years ago, health and industrious habits constituted no mean stock in trade; and, with them, almost any man might aspire to competence and independence. But it is so no longer. The wilderness has receded, and already the new lands are beyond the reach of the mere laborer, and the employer has him at his mercy. If the present relation subsist, we see nothing better for him in reserve than what he now possesses, but something altogether worse.

We are not ignorant of the fact that men born poor become wealthy, and that men born to wealth become poor; but this fact does not necessarily diminish the numbers of the poor, nor augment the numbers of the rich. The relative numbers of the two classes remain, or may remain, the same. But be this as it may; one fact is certain — no man born poor has ever, by his wages, as a simple operative, risen to the class of the wealthy. Rich he may have become, but it has not been by his own manual labor. He has in some way contrived to tax for his benefit the labor of others. He may have accumulated a few dollars which he has placed at usury, or invested in trade; or he may, as a master workman, obtain a premium on his journeymen; or he may have from a clerk passed to a partner, or from a workman to an overseer. The simple market wages for ordinary labor has never been ad-

equate to raise him from poverty to wealth. This fact is decisive of the whole controversy, and proves that the system of wages must be supplanted by some other system, or else one-half of the human race must forever be the virtual slaves of the other.

Now, the great work for this age and the coming is to raise up the laborer, and to realize in our own social arrangements and in the actual condition of all men that equality between man and man, which God has established between the rights of one and those of another. In other words, our business is to emancipate the proletaries as the past has emancipated the slaves. This is our work. There must be no class of our fellowmen doomed to toil through life as mere workmen at wages. If wages are tolerated it must be, in the case of the individual operative, only under such conditions that, by the time he is of a proper age to settle in life, he shall have accumulated enough to be an independent laborer on his own capital — on his own farm or in his own shop. Here is our work. How is it to be done?

Reformers in general answer this question, or what they deem its equivalent, in a manner which we cannot but regard as very unsatisfactory. They would have all men wise, good, and happy; but in order to make them so, they tell us that we want not external changes but internal; and, therefore, instead of declaiming against society and seeking to disturb existing social arrangements, we should confine ourselves to the individual reason and conscience; seek merely to lead the individual to repentance and to reformation of life; make the individual a practical, a truly religious man, and all evils will either disappear or be sanctified to the spiritual growth of the soul.

This is doubtless a capital theory, and has the advantage that kings, hierarchies, nobilities — in a word, all who fatten on the toil and blood of their fellows — will feel no difficulty in supporting it. Nicholas of Russia, the Grand Turk, his Holiness the Pope will hold us their especial friends for advocating a theory which secures to them the odor of sanctity even while they are sustaining by their anathemas or their armed legions a system of things of which the great mass are and must be the victims. If you will only allow me to keep thousands toiling for my pleasure or my profit, I will even aid you in your pious efforts to convert their souls. I am not cruel; I do not wish either to cause or to see suffering; I am, therefore, disposed to encourage your labors for the souls of the workingman, providing you will secure to me the products of his bodily toil. So far as the salvation of his soul will not interfere with my income, I hold it worthy of being sought; and if a few thousand dollars will aid you, Mr. Priest, in reconciling him to God, and making fair weather for him hereafter, they are at your service. I shall not want him to work for me in the world to come, and I can indemnify myself for what your salary costs me by paying him less wages. A capital theory this, which one may advocate without incurring the reproach of a disorganizer, a Jacobin, a leveler, and without losing the friendship of the rankest aristocrat in the land.

This theory, however, is exposed to one slight objection, that of being condemned by something like 6,000 years' experience. For 6,000 years its beauty has been extolled, its praises sung, and its blessings sought, under every advantage which learning, fashion, wealth, and power can secure; and, yet, under its practical operations, we are assured that mankind, though totally depraved at first, have been growing worse and worse ever since.

For our part, we yield to none in our reverence for science and religion; but we confess that we look not for the regeneration of the race from priests and pedagogues. They have had a fair trial. They cannot construct the temple of God. They cannot conceive its plan, and they know not how to build. They daub with untempered mortar, and the walls they erect tumble down if so much as a fox attempt to go up thereon. In a word, they always league with the people's masters, and seek to reform without disturbing the social arrangements which render reform necessary. They would change the consequences without changing the antecedents, secure to men the rewards of holiness, while they continue their allegiance to the devil. We have no faith in priests and pedagogues. They merely cry peace, peace, and that too when there is no peace, and can be none.

We admit the importance of what Dr. Channing in his lectures on the subject we are treating recommends as "self-culture." Self-culture is a good thing, but it cannot abolish inequality, nor restore men to their rights. As a means of quickening moral and intellectual energy, exalting the sentiments, and preparing the laborer to contend manfully for his rights, we admit its importance, and insist as strenuously as anyone on making it as universal as possible; but as constituting in itself a remedy for the vices of the social state, we have no faith in it. As a means it is well, as the end it is nothing.

The truth is, the evil we have pointed out is not merely individual in its character. It is not, in the case of any single individual, of any one man's procuring, nor can the efforts of any one man, directed solely to his own moral and religious perfection, do aught to remove it. What is purely individual in its nature, efforts of individuals to perfect themselves, may remove. But the evil we speak of is inherent in all our social arrangements and cannot be cured without a radical change of those arrangements. Could we convert all men to Christianity in both theory and practice, as held by the most enlightened sect of Christians among us, the evils of the social state would remain untouched. Continue our present system of trade, and all its present evil consequences will follow, whether it be carried on by your best men or your worst. Put your best men, your wisest, most moral, and most religious men at the head of your paper-money banks, and the evils of the present banking system will remain scarcely diminished.

The only way to get rid of its evils is to change the system, not its managers. The evils of slavery do not result from the personal characters of slave masters. They are inseparable from the system, let who will be masters. Make all your rich men good Christians, and you have lessened not the evils of existing inequality in wealth. The mischievous effects of this inequality do not result from the personal characters of either rich or poor but from itself, and they will continue just so long as there are rich men and poor men in the same community. You must abolish the system or accept its consequences. No man can serve both God and Mammon. If you will serve the devil, you must look to the devil for your wages; we know no other way.

Let us not be misinterpreted. We deny not the power of Christianity. Should all men become good Christians, we deny not that all social evils would be cured. But we deny in the outset that a man, who seeks merely to save his own soul, merely to perfect his own individual nature, can be a good Christian. The Christian forgets himself, buckles on his armor, and goes forth to war against principalities and powers, and against spiritual wickedness in high places. No man can be a Christian who does not begin his career by making war on the mischievous social arrangements from which his brethren suffer. He who thinks he can be a Christian and save his soul without seeking their radical change has no reason to applaud himself for his proficiency in Christian science, nor for his progress toward the kingdom of God. Understand Christianity, and we will admit that, should all men become good Christians, there would be nothing to complain of. But one might as well undertake to dip the ocean dry with a clamshell as to undertake to cure the evils of the social state by converting men to the Christianity of the Church.

The evil we have pointed out, we have said, is not of individual creation, and it is not to be removed by individual effort, saving so far as individual effort induces the combined effort of the mass. But whence has this evil originated? How comes it that all over the world the working classes are depressed, are the low and vulgar, and virtually the slaves of the nonworking classes? This is an inquiry which has not yet received the attention it deserves. It is not enough to answer that it has originated entirely in the inferiority by nature of the working classes; that they have less skill and foresight, and are less able than the upper classes to provide for themselves, or less susceptible of the highest moral and intellectual cultivation. Nor is it sufficient for our purpose to be told that Providence has decreed that some shall be poor and wretched, ignorant and vulgar; and that others shall be rich and vicious, learned and polite, oppressive and miserable. We do not choose to charge this matter to the will of God. "The foolishness of man perverteth his way, and his heart fretteth against the Lord."

God has made of one blood all the nations of men to dwell on all the face of the earth, and to dwell there as brothers, as members of one and the same family; and although He has made them with a diversity of powers, it would, perhaps, after all, be a bold assertion to say that He has made them with an inequality of powers. There is nothing in the actual difference of the powers of individuals which accounts for the striking inequalities we everywhere discover in their condition. The child of the plebeian, if placed early in the proper circumstances, grows up not less beautiful, active, intelligent, and refined than the child of the patrician; and the child of the patrician may become as coarse, as brutish as the child of any slave. So far as observation on the original capacities of individuals goes, nothing is discovered to throw much light on social inequalities.

The cause of the inequality we speak of must be sought in history, and be regarded as having its root in Providence, or in human nature, only in that sense in which all historical facts have their origin in these. We may perhaps trace it in the first instance to conquest, but not to conquest as the ultimate cause. . . . Conquest may undoubtedly increase the number of slaves; but in general it merely adds to the number and power of the middle class. It institutes a new nobility, and degrades the old to the rank of commoners. This is its general effect. We cannot, therefore, ascribe to conquest . . . the condition in which the working classes are universally found. They have been reduced to their condition by the priest, not by the military chieftain. . . .

The priest is universally a tyrant, universally the enslaver of his brethren, and therefore it is Christianity which condemns him. It could not prevent the reestablishment of a hierarchy, but it prepared for its ultimate destruction by denying the inequality of blood, by representing all men as equal before God, and by insisting on the celibacy of the clergy. The best feature of the Church was in its denial to the clergy of the right to marry. By this it prevented the new hierarchy from becoming hereditary, as were the old sacerdotal corporations of India and Judea. . . .

We may offend in what we say, but we cannot help that. We insist upon it, that the complete and final destruction of the priestly order, in every practical sense of the word "priest," is the first step to be taken toward elevating the laboring classes. Priests are, in their capacity of priests, necessarily enemies to freedom and equality. All reasoning demonstrates this, and all history proves it. There must be no class of men set apart and authorized, either by law or fashion, to speak to us in the name of God, or to be the interpreters of the word of God. . . .

The next step in this work of elevating the working classes will be to resuscitate the Christianity of Christ. The Christianity of the Church has done its work. We have had enough of that Christianity. It is powerless for good, but by no means powerless for evil. It now unmans us and hinders the growth of God's kingdom. . . .

According to the Christianity of Christ no man can enter the kingdom of God who does not labor with all zeal and diligence to establish the kingdom of God on the earth; who does not labor to bring down the high, and bring up the low; to break the fetters of the bound and set the captive free; to destroy all oppression, establish the reign of justice, which is the reign of equality, between man and man; to introduce new heavens and a new earth, wherein dwelleth righteousness, wherein all shall be as brothers, loving one another, and no one possessing what another lacketh. No man can be a Christian who does not labor to reform society, to mold it according to the will of God and the nature of man; so that free scope shall be given to every man to unfold himself in all beauty and power, and to grow up in the stature of a perfect man in Christ Jesus. No man can be a Christian who does not refrain from all practices by which the rich grow richer and the poor poorer, and who does not do all in his power to elevate the laboring classes, so that one man shall not be doomed to toil while another enjoys the fruits; so that each man shall be free and independent, sitting under "his own vine and fig tree with none to molest or to make afraid."

We grant the power of Christianity in working out the reform we demand; we agree that one of the most efficient means of elevating the workingmen is to Christianize the community. But you must Christianize it. It is the Gospel of Jesus you must preach, and not the gospel of the priests. Preach the Gospel of Jesus, and that will turn every man's attention to the crying evil we have designated, and will arm every Christian with power to effect those changes in social arrangements which shall secure to all men the equality of position and condition, which it is already acknowledged they possess in relation to their rights. But let it be the genuine gospel that you preach, and not that pseudo-gospel, which lulls the conscience asleep, and permits men to feel that they may be servants of God while they are slaves to the world, the flesh, and the devil; and while they ride roughshod over the hearts of their prostrate brethren. We must preach no gospel that permits men to feel that they are honorable men and good Christians, although rich and with eyes standing out with fatness, while the great mass of their brethren are suffering from iniquitous laws, from mischievous social arrangements, and pining away for the want of the refinements and even the necessaries of life.

We speak strongly and pointedly on this subject, because we are desirous of arresting attention. We would draw the public attention to the striking contrast which actually exists between the Christianity of Christ, and the Christianity of the Church. . . .

Now, the evils of which we have complained are of a social nature. That is, they have their root in the constitution of society as it is, and they have attained to their present growth by means of social influences, the action of government, of laws, and of systems and institutions upheld by society, and of which individuals are the slaves. This being the case, it is evident that they are to be removed only by the action of society, that is, by government, for the action of society is government.

But what shall government do? Its first doing must be an *undoing*. There has been thus far quite too much government, as well as government of the wrong kind. The first act of government we want is a still further limitation of itself. It must begin by circumscribing within narrower limits its powers. And then it must proceed to repeal all laws which bear against the laboring classes, and then to enact such laws as are necessary to enable them to maintain their equality. We have no faith in those systems of elevating the working classes which propose to elevate them without calling in the aid of the government. We must have government and legislation expressly directed to this end.

But, again, what legislation do we want so far as this country is concerned? We want first the legislation which shall free the government, whether state or federal, from the control of the Banks. The Banks represent the interest of the employer, and, therefore, of necessity, interests adverse to those of the employed; that is, they represent the interests of the business community in opposition to the laboring community. So long as the government remains under the control of the Banks, so long it must be in the hands of the natural enemies of the laboring classes, and may be made — nay, will be made — an instrument of depressing them yet lower. It is obvious, then, that if our object be the elevation of the laboring classes, we must destroy the power of the Banks over the government, and place the government in the hands of the laboring classes themselves, or in the hands of those, if such there be, who have an identity of interest with them.

But this cannot be done so long as the Banks exist. Such is the subtle influence of credit, and such the power of capital, that a banking system like ours, if sustained, necessarily and inevitably becomes the real and efficient government of the country. We have been struggling for ten years in this country against the power of the Banks, struggling to free merely the federal government from their grasp, but with humiliating success. At this moment, the contest is almost doubtful — not indeed in our mind but in the minds of no small portion of our countrymen. The partisans of the Banks count on certain victory. The Banks discount freely to build "log cabins," to purchase "hard cider," and to defray the expense of manufacturing enthusiasm for a cause which is at war with the interests of the people. That they will succeed we do not for one moment believe; but that they could maintain the struggle so long, and be as strong as they now are, at the end of ten years' constant hostility, proves but all too well the power of the Banks, and their fatal influence on the political action of the community. The present character, standing, and resources of the Bank party, prove to a demonstration that the Banks must be destroyed or the laborer not elevated.

Uncompromising hostility to the whole banking system should therefore be the motto of every working man, and of every friend of Humanity. The system must be destroyed. On this point there must be no misgiving, no subterfuge, no palliation. The system is at war with the rights and interest of labor, and it must go. Every friend of the system must be marked as an enemy to his race, to his country, and especially to the laborer. No matter who he is, in what party he is found, or what name he bears, he is, in our judgment, no true democrat, as he can be no true Christian.

Following the destruction of the Banks, must come that of all monopolies, of all *privilege*. There are many of these. We cannot specify them all; we therefore select only one, the greatest of them all, the privilege which some have of being born rich while others are born poor. It will be seen at once that we allude to the hereditary descent of property, an anomaly in our American system, which must be removed or the system itself will be destroyed. . . . [I] . . . say . . . that as we have abolished hereditary monarchy and hereditary nobility, we must complete the work by abolishing hereditary property. A man shall have all he honestly acquires, so long as he himself belongs to the world in which he acquires it. But his power over his property must cease with his life, and his property must then become the property of the state, to be disposed of by some equitable law for the use of the generation which takes his place. Here is the principle without any of its de-

tails, and this is the grand legislative measure to which we look forward. We see no means of elevating the laboring classes which can be effectual without this.

And is this a measure to be easily carried? Not at all. It will cost infinitely more than it cost to abolish either hereditary monarchy or hereditary nobility. It is a great measure, and a startling. The rich, the business community will never voluntarily consent to it, and we think we know too much of human nature to believe that it will ever be effected peaceably. It will be effected only by the strong arm of physical force. It will come, if it ever come at all, only at the conclusion of war, the like of which the world as yet has never witnessed, and from which, however inevitable it may seem to the eye of philosophy, the heart of Humanity recoils with horror.

We are not ready for this measure yet. There is much previous work to be done, and we should be the last to bring it before the legislature. The time, however, has come for its free and full discussion. It must be canvassed in the public mind, and society prepared for acting on it. No doubt they who broach it, and especially they who support it, will experience a due share of contumely and abuse. They will be regarded by the part of the community they oppose, or may be thought to oppose, as "graceless varlets," against whom every man of substance should set his face. But this is not, after all, a thing to disturb a wise man, nor to deter a true man from telling his whole thought. He who is worthy of the name of man speaks what he honestly believes the interests of his race demand, and seldom disquiets himself about what may be the consequences to himself. Men have, for what they believed the cause of God or man, endured the dungeon, the scaffold, the stake, the cross, and they can do it again, if need be. This subject must be freely, boldly, and fully discussed, whatever may be the fate of those who discuss it.

99.

Albert Brisbane: Social Waste and the Benefits of Association

In Social Destiny of Man: or, Association and Reorganization of Industry *(1840),*
from which the following selection is taken, Albert Brisbane adapted the doctrines of
the Frenchman Charles Fourier to the American milieu. Fourier, and Brisbane after
him, believed that the social destiny of man could be fulfilled by reorganizing society
into a series of communities, or phalanxes, in which the divisive passions could be
channeled into socially useful ends. By thus eliminating waste and poverty, complete
class harmony could be achieved. The most influential proponent of "Associationism,"
as Fourierism in America was called, was the journalist Horace Greeley; and its most
famous testing ground was the utopian community, Brook Farm.

Source: *Social Destiny of Man: or, Association and Reorganization of Industry,*
Philadelphia, 1840, Ch. 7.

Individual economy, both vexatious and contrary to nature, is the only economy known in civilization. Its practice — tantamount to individual privation — is zealously preached by moralists and sages; and what are the riches of civilization, with all its stinting and parsimony? Positive poverty for seven-eighths, and relative poverty for the remaining eighth.
DEAN

It is not surprising that the *Political* order has alone been the object of study, while the *Industrial* order, incomparably more essential to the happiness of mankind, has been almost entirely neglected.
A. TAMISIER

WASTE! WASTE!! WASTE!!!

THE OBSERVATIONS CONTAINED in the foregoing chapters will, we trust, be sufficient to convince the reader of the vast and foolish waste which results from our present social mechanism; and of the colossal economies and profits, which would arise from association and combination in industrial interests. These observations could be extended infinitely, but the reader, by observing atten-tively the effects of our incoherent system, examples of which he meets at every step around him, cannot fail to be convinced of the absence of everything like order, economy, and foresight in our present system of society.

If such characteristics marked the operations of an individual, it would be easy to foresee that, so far from attaining riches, he must inevitably sink into poverty and want. The same law is applicable to society; the absence of association and economy in our whole system of industry plunges the social world into indigence and want, the source of endless discord, depravity, and degradation. This great fact escapes the attention of men, because each individual, anxious only to escape from the common evil and to secure himself a sufficiency so as to enjoy tranquillity in the state of general privation and anxiety around him, sees nor cares not for the mass. In the confused efforts, however, which are made by each and all to attain the great desideratum, fortune, they only trample each other down; and after all we find in society, that the greater the conflict and strife of individuals, the greater the collective poverty and depravity. England illustrates this fact fully; no country has carried all branches of industry to the extent she has done, and nowhere is there such a hideous contrast of poverty and wealth.

The same efforts combined would have secured riches and happiness to all, but no one has time to stop to consider upon this fact; each individual flatters himself with the idea that if seven-eighths of those who were making the same efforts before him have failed, he may, nevertheless, with better management, succeed. He strives to secure his happiness isolatedly and separately from the race; if his fellows suffer and he does not, it is to him as if suffering did not exist. No collective action, so essential to the welfare of all, takes place. In the meantime, our planet rolls on in its course, carrying with it a restless, depraved, half-famished, discordant, and warring race!

If we wish to find the most perfect picture of waste and disorder, we must search for it in our large cities. It is there that we will find our *cut-up* system, in which everything is reduced to the measure and selfishness of the individual, producing an incoherence and complication which might properly be termed a combination for the production of evil; for it would seem as if things were so organized as to cause the greatest possible number of evils and ensure their most rapid propagation. Each house, for example, has its sink of filth, the miasmas of which the whole population must breathe. The poverty or neglect, or both combined, of a single family produce a contagious disease which extends to a thousand others, among which there will be indigent ones enough to keep it in existence.

The neglect of one person, of a child, or a servant, perhaps, in whom it is often necessary to confide, burns down not only the house of one family but a hundred others with it; or the misplaced economy of a stovepipe causes a loss of the same kind, which would be sufficient to construct all

the apparatus necessary for warming a town or the manor house of a phalanx. Where everything is left to the ignorance, cupidity, carelessness, or inability of individuals, no guarantees of a general nature can exist or be put in practice.

It is from the poverty of the mass in our large cities that the greatest abuses take place. If a capitalist builds damp cellars, garrets without ventilation, small and confined rooms, close courtyards without light and circulation, and with hardly the conveniences necessary to the wants of its inmates, he is sure to find droves of indigent families who will stow themselves away in these tenements, making of them hotbeds of disease and nurseries of demoralization. Moralists wonder that human nature can be as depraved as they find it in our societies, and they seek in the *heart* the source of all this depravity; it is only surprising that human nature should bear so much, and murmur so little, and that with its load of social evil and misery, so much goodwill and gaiety still remain.

If we cite examples of material waste, we should rank, next to that of fires, which we mentioned above, the loss occasioned by the tearing down of buildings, from being badly constructed or from speculation. This waste in many of our large cities must be enormous, and is due to want of combination and foresight. What absence of order, in an architectural point of view, on the part of society not to be able to plan its buildings so as to answer the wants of the community for twenty years in advance! The widening, straightening, and lengthening of streets form another gigantic item of waste. All these abuses arise from the fact that in planning our cities and towns, no system, no method exists.

There is no adaption of architecture to our wants and requirements; our houses are as little suited to our physical welfare as our social laws are to our attractions and passions. It is to be observed that this enormous waste and expenditure are *paid* by productive industry, upon which an immense indirect tax is laid, which is not perceived. The farmers, manufacturers, and mechanics must produce the means for paying in the end for everything: cities, ships, canals, railroads, etc.

Men become, however, so accustomed to the order of things in which they live that these facts do not strike them. Not conceiving the possibility of changing the social mechanism, it appears to them natural and permanent. If, however, they could be brought to doubt its efficacy, or rather its infallibility, and examine it with scrutinizing attention, a social skepticism would take the place of their present blindness. It is a result deeply to be desired. Vegetating as the world does in its present social condition, all improvements in science and industry are of no use to the great mass; their poverty does not diminish with these improvements; and the increased means of enjoyment, the refinement of luxury to which they give rise only excite that mass to every kind of fraud and falseness to obtain a share of and participate in them.

Riches are the leading wish of man, and in this country wealth has become the all-absorbing object of desire. In this strife after wealth in which millions are engaged, why has it not been perceived that not one-twentieth can succeed? If but one-third of the population are producers, if production is the only source of riches, and if our system of consumption in isolated households is so complicated that the small amount produced by the third does not go one-half as far as it would in a system of combination and association (or in other words, if one-half of the small product created by the producing third of society is wasted), how is it possible that even the common wants of the entire population, setting aside all superfluity, can be satisfied?

Let us draw a comparison which will explain this clearly. Suppose that, out of three persons living together, one alone was engaged in producing, while the other two were idle. It is very evident that the active laborer could not alone produce enough to maintain himself and the other two comfortably. But if we suppose, in addition, that each has a separate house, has his meals prepared separately in his own dwelling, the small product of the producer would not go near as far as if they lived together and economized their means; to the loss caused by the idleness of two inactive persons is to be added the waste of separate and complicated preparations. This is a perfect illustration of the present state of things. One-third of the population produce; two-thirds are nonproducers.

Instead of uniting and associating for the purpose of making the insufficient product of the labor of the active third go as far as possible, the most excessive complication and waste takes place, there being as many separate houses, kitchens, cooks, fires, etc., as there are families. The result is that the population of all countries, except this, are removed but one degree from starvation. . . .

Nearly 3 million Negro producers, whose labor pays for our imported luxuries, are merely supplied with their physical wants. We may as well say with Fourier:

> Can a more frightful disorder than that which exists upon this globe be conceived? One-half of the earth is invaded by wild beasts, or savages, which is about the same thing; as to the other half which is under cultivation, we see three-quarters of it occupied by barbarians who enslave the producers and women, and who in every respect violate justice and reason. There remains consequently an eighth of the globe in possession of the civilized, who boast of their improvements while giving to indigence and corruption their fullest development.

But to return to our subject. If we accept and approve of the system which allots to each family a separate house, we must approve of the effects which result from such a system. With 400 families and 400 separate dwellings, all the cares and duties attendant upon providing for a household must be gone through with 400 times, until the complication becomes frightful. Four hundred persons must be sent to market to make 400 separate purchases, who lose time enough in selecting articles wanted and in bargaining to produce them nearly. The 400 houses imply that there are 400 *dark holes*, called kitchens, in which 400 *poor creatures* must pass their time over a hot fire in the middle of summer. Four hundred monotonous meals are prepared, three-fourths of them badly so, which give rise to as many discords as there are dishes. As neither mistresses nor servants are satisfied in this system, the former scold, and the latter are indifferent or faithless.

If an ox is killed, it is cut up and disposed of in an infinite number of little lots; every hogshead of sugar, every box of tea has to be retailed out pound by pound; this excess of complication increases ten times the number of butchers and dealers necessary, whose intermediate profits are a heavy indirect tax upon the consumer. The more we go into these details, the more we shall be convinced that with this waste and want of system individual economies are illusive, and that the mass must suffer poverty and privation under the best of governments. . . .

But politicians scarcely dare put forth the hypothesis of a social reform and a change in the condition of mankind. The human race have so long been curbed under the yoke of misfortune that suffering is believed to be the law of their nature. The views and belief of politicians have so adapted themselves to this doctrine that it has become a dogmatical part of their creed; they have asserted it so often that they must stand by their declarations. Their personal and party interests have also become so entwined with the present state of things that they are even led to support the present social subversion. Add to this the apathy of the world, its disbelief in the possibility of a great change, and we have the explanation why *no social* principles are discussed, and why no efforts are made to ameliorate the condition of that vast mass of suffering, helpless, and degraded beings who form three-fourths of the population of the globe.

It is time this stupid policy, if all disbelief in a social reform can be called such, should be denounced; the mass, we trust, have become intelligent enough to demand some effective reforms at the hands of their political leaders, so active in administrative reforms, and so clamorous in their protestations of love for the people.

Nine permanent evils characterize the course of our societies; let the mass call upon those leaders to discover the principles of a society which will produce nine results directly opposed to them, will guarantee social happiness, and give us the standard of a true social organization.

Nine Permanent Scourges of Civilization

Indigence
Fraud
Oppression
War
Derangement of climate
Diseases artificially produced: plague, yellow fever, cholera, smallpox, etc.
Vicious circle, without any opening for improvement
UNIVERSAL SELFISHNESS
DUPLICITY OF SOCIAL ACTION

Nine Permanent Benefits to Be Attained

General riches
Practical truth in all relations of life
Effective liberty in the same
Constant peace
Equilibrium of temperature and climate
System of preventive medicine and extirpation of artificial diseases
Opening offered to all improvements and ameliorations

COLLECTIVE AND INDIVIDUAL PHILANTHROPY
UNITY OF SOCIAL ACTION

Such are the benefits association would realize; but can we look for cooperation from men whose interests, as we said, are concentrated in personal success? The circle of our civilized politics is very narrow, but it insures the successful individual, often without merit or great effort, applause for the day, and frequently pecuniary reward with it. Immediate and personal advantage only stimulates the great majority; the idea of a social reform which would change the destiny of mankind, although vast and sublime, is too far off, too severed from all personal advantages to find many adherents and enthusiasts. There must be, however, some characters so constituted as to feel the want of an object, high and lasting, with which to connect their efforts, so that something may remain to show that they lived upon this earth, and that their intellectual was not as fleeting as their material existence. It is among such temperaments that we must seek for the advocates of the great social reform which the present age may have the glory of achieving!

100.

A Catholic Petition for Common School Funds

In 1824 the Board of Aldermen of the City of New York were empowered by the state legislature to select those schools qualified to receive state funds. Beginning in 1825 the Board channeled practically all the city's school funds away from parochial schools, which had hitherto received common funds, to a nonsectarian private organization, the Public School Society. Despite having two Catholic members, the Society distributed almost all of the funds to Protestant schools. The Catholic Petition for Common School Funds was written on September 21, 1840, and was also endorsed by some of New York City's Jews. While the petition was denied, a nonsectarian public school system was created for New York City in 1842, and, in time, the Public School Society ceased to function.

Source: *Complete Works of the Most Rev. John Hughes, D.D., Archbishop of New York,* Lawrence Kehoe, ed., New York, 1866, Vol. I, pp. 102-107.

To the Honorable the Board of Aldermen of the City of New York, the Petition of the Catholics of New York Respectfully Represents:

That your petitioners yield to no class in their performance of, and disposition to perform, all the duties of citizens. They bear, and are willing to bear, their portion of every common burden; and feel themselves entitled to a participation in every common benefit.

This participation, they regret to say, has been denied them for years back in reference to common school education in the city of New York, except on conditions with which their conscience, and, as they believe, their duty to God did not and do not leave them at liberty to comply.

The rights of conscience in this country are held by the Constitution and universal consent to be sacred and inviolate. No stronger evidence of this need be adduced than the fact that one class of citizens are exempted from the duty or obligation of defending their country against an invading foe, out of delicacy and deference to the rights of conscience which forbids them to take up arms for any purpose.

Your petitioners only claim the benefit of this principle in regard to the public education of their children. They regard the public education which the state has provided as a common benefit in which they are most desirous and feel that they are entitled to participate; and therefore they pray your Honorable Body that they may be permitted to do so without violating their conscience. But your petitioners do not ask that this prayer be granted without assigning their reasons for preferring it.

In ordinary cases, men are not required to assign the motives of conscientious scruples in matters of this kind. But your petitioners are aware that a large, wealthy, and concentrated influence is directed against their claim by the corporation called the Public School Society. And that this influence, acting on a public opinion already but too much predisposed to judge unfavorably of the claims of your petitioners, requires to be met by facts which justify them in thus appealing to your Honorable Body, and which may, at the same time, convey a more correct impression to the public mind. Your petitioners adopt this course the more willingly because the justice and impartiality which distinguish the decisions of public men in this country inspire them with the confidence that your Honorable Body will maintain, in their regard, the principle of the rights of conscience, if it can be done

without violating the rights of others, and on no other condition is the claim solicited.

It is not deemed necessary to trouble your Honorable Body with a detail of the circumstances by which the monopoly of the public education of children in the city of New York, and of the funds provided for that purpose at the expense of the state, have passed into the hands of a private corporation, styled in its Act of Charter, "The Public School Society of the City of New York." It is composed of men of different sects or denominations. But that denomination, [The Society of] Friends, which is believed to have the controlling influence, both by its numbers and otherwise, holds as a peculiar *sectarian principle* that any formal or official teaching of religion is, at best, unprofitable.

And your petitioners have discovered that such of *their* children as have attended the public schools, are generally, and at an early age, imbued with the same principle: that they become intractable, disobedient, and even contemptuous toward their parents — unwilling to learn anything of religion — as if they had become illuminated and could receive all the knowledge of religion necessary for them by instinct or inspiration. Your petitioners do not pretend to assign the cause of this change in their children; they only attest the fact as resulting from their attendance at the public schools of the Public School Society.

This Society, however, is composed of gentlemen of various sects, including even one or two Catholics; but they profess to exclude all sectarianism from their schools. If they do not exclude sectarianism, they are avowedly no more entitled to the school funds than your petitioners or any other denomination of professing Christians. If they do, as they profess, exclude sectarianism, then your petitioners contend that they exclude Christianity, and leave to the advantage of infidelity the tendencies which are given to the minds of youth by the influence of this feature and pretension of their system.

If they could accomplish what they profess, other denominations would join your petitioners in remonstrating against their schools. But they do not accomplish it. Your petitioners will show your Honorable Body that they do admit what Catholics call sectarianism (although others may call it only religion) in a great variety of ways.

In their 22nd report, as far back as the year 1827, they tell us, page 14, that they "are aware of the importance of early religious instruction," and that none but what is "exclusively general and scriptural in its character should be introduced into the schools under their charge." Here, then, is their own testimony that they did introduce and authorize "religious instruction" in their schools. And that they solved, with the utmost composure, the difficult question on which the sects disagree, by determining *what kind* of "religious instruction" is "exclusively general and scriptural in its character." Neither could they impart this "early religious instruction" themselves. They must have left it to their teachers; and these, armed with official influence, could impress those "early religious instructions" on the susceptible minds of the children with the authority of dictators.

The Public School Society, in their report for the year 1832, page 10, describe the effect of these "early religious instructions" without, perhaps, intending to do so; but yet precisely as your petitioners have witnessed it, in such of their children as attended those schools. "The age at which children are usually sent to school affords a much better opportunity to mold their minds to peculiar and exclusive forms of faith than any subsequent period of life." In page 11 of the same report, they protest against the injustice of supporting "religion in any shape" by public money; as if the "early religious instruction" which they had

themselves authorized in their schools, five years before, was not "religion in some shape" and was not supported by public taxation. They tell us again, in more guarded language, "The Trustees are deeply impressed with the importance of imbuing the youthful mind with religious impressions, and they have endeavored to attain this object, as far as the nature of the institution will admit" (report of 1837).

In their annual report they tell us that "they would not be understood as regarding religious impressions in early youth as unimportant; on the contrary, they desire to do all which may with propriety be done to give a right direction to the minds of the children entrusted to their care. Their schools are uniformly opened with the reading of the Scriptures, and the class books are such as recognize and enforce the great and generally acknowledged principles of Christianity" (page 7).

In their 34th Annual Report, for the year 1839, they pay a high compliment to a deceased teacher for "the moral and religious influence exerted by her over the 300 girls daily attending her school," and tell us that it could not but have had a lasting effect on many of their "susceptible minds" (page 7). And, yet, in all these "early religious instructions, religious impressions, and religious influence," essentially anti-Catholic, your petitioners are to see nothing sectarian; but if in giving the education which the state requires they were to bring the same influences to bear on the "susceptible minds" of their *own* children in favor, and not against, their *own* religion, then this society contends that it would be sectarian!

Your petitioners regret that there is no means of ascertaining to what extent the teachers in the schools of this Society carried out the views of their principals on the importance of conveying "early religious instructions" to the "susceptible minds" of their children. But they believe it is in their power to prove that in some instances the

Scriptures have been explained as well as read to the pupils.

Even the reading of the Scriptures in those schools your petitioners cannot regard otherwise than as sectarian, because Protestants would certainly consider as such the introduction of the Catholic Scriptures, which are different from theirs, and the Catholics have the same ground of objection when the Protestant version is made use of.

Your petitioners have to state further, as grounds of their conscientious objections to those schools, that many of the selections in their elementary reading lessons contain matter prejudicial to the Catholic name and character. The term "popery" is repeatedly found in them. This term is known and employed as one of insult and contempt toward the Catholic religion, and it passes into the minds of children with the feeling of which it is the outward expression. Both the historical and religious portions of the reading lessons are selected from Protestant writers, whose prejudices against the Catholic religion render them unworthy of confidence in the mind of your petitioners, at least so far as their own children are concerned.

The Public School Society have heretofore denied that their books contained anything reasonably objectionable to Catholics. Proofs of the contrary could be multiplied, but it is unnecessary, as they have recently retracted their denial and discovered, after fifteen years' enjoyment of their monopoly, that their books do contain objectionable passages. But they allege that they have proffered repeatedly to make such corrections as the Catholic clergy might require.

Your petitioners conceive that such a proposal could not be carried into effect by the Public School Society without giving just ground for exception to other denominations. Neither can they see with what consistency that Society can insist, as it has done, on the perpetuation of its monopoly,

when the trustees thus avow their incompetency to present unexceptionable books without the aid of the Catholic or any other clergy. They allege, indeed, that with the best intentions they have been unable to ascertain the passages which might be offensive to Catholics. With their intentions, your petitioners cannot enter into any question. Nevertheless, they submit to your Honorable Body that this Society is eminently incompetent to the superintendence of public education if they could not see that the following passage was unfit for the public schools, and especially unfit to be placed in the hands of Catholic children.

They will quote the passage as one instance, taken from *Putnam's Sequel*, page 266:

> Huss, John, a zealous reformer from popery, who lived in Bohemia toward the close of the fourteenth and beginning of the fifteenth centuries. He was bold and persevering; but at length, trusting himself to the deceitful Catholics, he was by them brought to trial, condemned as a heretic, and burnt at the stake.

The Public School Society may be excused for not knowing the historical inaccuracies of this passage; but surely assistance of the Catholic clergy could not have been necessary to an understanding of the word "deceitful" as applied to all who profess the religion of your petitioners.

For these reasons, and others of the same kind, your petitioners cannot, in conscience, and consistently with their sense of duty to God and to their offspring, entrust the Public School Society with the office of giving "a right direction to the minds of their children." And yet this Society claims that office, and claims for the discharge of it the common school funds, to which your petitioners, in common with other citizens, are contributors. Insofar as they are contributors, they are not only deprived of any benefit in return, but their money is employed to the damage and detriment of their religion, in the minds of their own children and of the rising generation of the community at large. The contest is between the *guaranteed* rights, civil and religious, of the citizen, on the one hand, and the pretensions of the Public School Society, on the other; and while it has been silently going on for years, your petitioners would call the attention of your Honorable Body to its consequences on that class for whom the benefits of public education are most essential — the children of the poor.

This class (your petitioners speak only so far as relates to their own denomination), after a brief experience of the schools of the Public School Society, naturally and deservedly withdrew all confidence from it. Hence the establishment by your petitioners of schools for the education of the poor. The expense necessary for this was a second taxation, required not by the laws of the land but by the no less imperious demands of their conscience.

They were reduced to the alternative of seeing their children growing up in entire ignorance, or else taxing themselves anew for private schools, while the funds provided for education and contributed in part by themselves were given over to the Public School Society, and by them employed as has been stated above.

Now your petitioners respectfully submit that without this confidence, no body of men can discharge the duties of education as intended by the state and required by the people. The Public School Society are, and have been at all times, conscious that they had not the confidence of the poor. In their 28th report, they appeal to the ladies of New York to create or procure it, by the "persuasive eloquence of female kindness" (page 5). And from this they pass, on the next page, to the more efficient eloquence of coercion under penalties and privations to be visited on all persons, "whether emigrants or otherwise," who, being in the circumstances of poverty referred to, should not send their children to some "public or other daily school."

In their 27th report, pages 15 and 16, they plead for the doctrine, and recommend it to public favor by the circumstance that it will affect but "few natives." But why should it be necessary at all, if they possessed that confidence of the poor, without which they need never hope to succeed? So well are they convinced of this that no longer ago than last year they gave up all hope of inspiring it, and loudly call for coercion by "the strong arm of the civil power" to supply its deficiency.

Your petitioners will close this part of their statement with the expression of their surprise and regret that gentlemen who are themselves indebted much to the respect which is properly cherished for the rights of conscience should be so unmindful of the same rights in the case of your petitioners. Many of them are by religious principle so pacific that they would not take up arms in the defense of the liberties of their country, though she should call them to her aid; and, yet, they do not hesitate to invoke the "strong arm of the civil power" for the purpose of abridging the private liberties of their fellow citizens, who may feel equally conscientious.

Your petitioners have to deplore, as a consequence of this state of things, the ignorance and vice to which hundreds, nay, thousands of their children are exposed. They have to regret, also, that the education which they can provide, under the disadvantages to which they have been subjected, is not as efficient as it should be. But should your Honorable Body be pleased to designate their schools as entitled to receive a just proportion of the public funds which belong to your petitioners in common with other citizens, their schools could be improved for those who attend, others now growing up in ignorance could be received, and the ends of the legislature could be accomplished — a result which is manifestly hopeless under the present system.

Your petitioners will now invite the attention of your Honorable Body to the objections and misrepresentations that have been urged by the Public School Society to granting the claim of your petitioners. It is urged by them that it would be appropriating money raised by general taxation to the support of the Catholic religion. Your petitioners join issue with them and declare unhesitatingly that if this objection can be established the claim shall be forthwith abandoned. It is objected that though we are taxed as *citizens,* we apply for the benefits of education as *Catholics.* Your petitioners, to remove this difficulty, beg to be considered in their application in the identical capacity in which they are taxed — viz.: as citizens of the commonwealth.

It has been contended by the Public School Society that the law disqualifies schools which admit any profession of religion from receiving any encouragements from the school fund. Your petitioners have two solutions for this pretended difficulty.

1. Your petitioners are unable to discover any such disqualification in the law, which merely delegates to your Honorable Body the authority and discretion of determining what schools or societies shall be entitled to its bounty.

2. Your petitioners are willing to fulfill the conditions of the law so far as religious teaching is proscribed during school hours.

In fine, your petitioners, to remove all objections, are willing that the material organization of their schools and the disbursements of the funds allowed for them shall be conducted and made by persons unconnected with the religion of your petitioners, even the Public School Society, if it should

please your Honorable Body to appoint them for that purpose. The public may then be assured that the money will not be applied to the support of the Catholic religion.

It is deemed necessary by your petitioners to save the Public School Society the necessity of future misconception, thus to state the things which are *not* petitioned for. The members of that Society, who have shown themselves so impressed with the importance of conveying *their* notions of "early religious instruction" to the "susceptible minds" of Catholic children, can have no objection that the parents of the children, and teachers in whom the parents have confidence, should do the same, provided no law is violated thereby, and no disposition evinced to bring the children of other denominations within its influence.

Your petitioners, therefore, pray that your Honorable Body will be pleased to designate as among the schools entitled to participate in the common school fund, upon complying with the requirements of the law and the ordinances of the corporation of the city — or for such other relief as to your Honorable Body shall seem meet — St. Patrick's School, St. Peter's School, St. Mary's School, St. Joseph's School, St. James' School, St. Nicholas' School, Transfiguration Church School, and St. John's School.

And your petitioners further request, in the event of your Honorable Body's determining to hear your petitioners on the subject of their petition, that such time may be appointed as may be most agreeable to your Honorable Body, and that a full session of your Honorable Board be convened for that purpose.

101.

HORACE MANN: On the Art of Teaching

As president of the Massachusetts state senate, Horace Mann signed the Education Bill of 1837 that created the first state board of education. He thereupon gave up his senate seat as well as a promising political career and for twelve years presided over the board. Between 1837 and 1848 Mann wrote twelve annual reports in which he expounded a philosophy of public education that became the basis of the common school program in Massachusetts. The reports, which were disseminated throughout the country, his lecture tours, the popular Common School Journal, *which he founded, and the concrete examples of extensive educational reforms in his state, made Mann's the greatest name in the nineteenth-century common school movement. The portion of the* Fourth Annual Report (1840) *reprinted here treats of teacher qualifications.*

Source: *Annual Reports of the Secretary of the Board of Education of Massachusetts for the Years 1839-1844,* Boston, 1891, pp. 53-91.

A BRIEF CONSIDERATION of a few of the qualifications essential to those who undertake the momentous task of training the children of the state will help us to decide the question, whether the complaints of the committees, in regard to the incompetency of teachers, are captious and unfounded; or whether they proceed from enlightened conceptions of the nature of their duties and office, and therefore require measures to supply the deficiency.

1. One requisite is a knowledge of common-school studies. Teachers should have a perfect knowledge of the rudimental branches which are required by law to be taught in our schools. They should understand, not only the rules which have been prepared as guides for the unlearned but also the principles on which the rules are founded — those principles which lie beneath the rules and supersede them in practice, and from which, should the rules be lost, they could be framed anew. Teachers should be able to teach *subjects,* not manuals merely.

This knowledge should not only be thorough and critical but it should be always ready at command for every exigency; familiar like the alphabet, so that, as occasion requires, it will rise up in the mind instantaneously and not need to be studied out with labor and delay. For instance; it is not enough that the teacher be able to solve and elucidate an arithmetical question by expending half an hour of schooltime in trying various ways to bring out the answer; for that half hour is an important part of the school session, and the regular exercises of the school must be shortened or slurred over to repair the loss.

Again; in no school can a teacher devote his whole and undivided attention to the exercises as they successively recur. Numerous things will demand simultaneous attention. While a class is spelling or reading, he may have occasion to recall the roving attention of one scholar; to admonish another by word or look; to answer some question put by a third; or to require a fourth to execute some needed service. Now, if he is not so familiar with the true orthography of every word that his ear will instantaneously detect an error in the spelling, he will, on all such occasions, pass by mistakes without notice, and therefore without correction, and thus interweave wrong instruction with right through all the lessons of the school. If he is not so familiar, too, both with the rules of reading, and with the standard of pronunciation for each word, that a wrong emphasis or cadence, or a mispronounced word, will jar his nerves and recall even a wandering attention, then innumerable errors will glide by his own ear unnoticed, while they are stamped upon the minds of his pupils.

These remarks apply with equal force to recitations in grammar and geography. A critical knowledge respecting all these subjects should be so consciously present with him that his mind will gratefully respond to every right answer or sign made by the scholar, and shrink from every wrong one, with the quickness and certainty of electrical attraction and repulsion. . . .

However much other knowledge a teacher may possess, it is no equivalent for a mastership in the rudiments. It is not more true in architecture than in education that the value of the work in every upper layer depends upon the solidity of all beneath it. The leading, prevailing defect in the intellectual department of our schools is a want of thoroughness, a proneness to be satisfied with a verbal memory of rules instead of a comprehension of principles, with a knowledge of the names of things, instead of a knowledge of the things themselves; or, if some knowledge of the things is gained, it is too apt to be a knowledge of them as isolated facts and unaccompanied by a knowledge of the relations which subsist between them and bind them into a scientific whole. That knowledge is hardly worthy of the name which stops with things, as individuals, without understanding the relations existing between them. The latter constitutes indefinitely the greater part of all human knowledge.

For instance, all the problems of plane geometry, by which heights and distances are measured, and the contents of areas and cubes ascertained, are based upon a few simple definitions which can be committed to memory by any child in half a day. With the exception of the comets, whose number is not known, there are but thirty bodies in the whole solar system. Yet, on the relations which subsist between these thirty bodies is built the stupendous science of astronomy. How worthless is the astronomical knowledge which stops with committing to memory thirty names!

At the normal school at Barre during the last term the number of pupils was about fifty. This number might have been doubled if the visitors would have consented to carry the applicants forward at once into algebra and chemistry and geometry and astronomy, instead of subjecting them to a thorough review of common-school studies. One of the most cheering auguries in regard to our schools is the unanimity with which the committees have awarded sentence of condemnation against the practice of introducing into them the studies of the university to the exclusion or neglect of the rudimental branches. By such a practice a pupil foregoes all the stock of real knowledge he might otherwise acquire; and he receives, in its stead, only a show or counterfeit of knowledge, which, with all intelligent persons, only renders his ignorance more conspicuous.

A child's limbs are as well fitted in point of strength to play with the planets before he can toss a ball as his mind is to get any conception of the laws which govern their stupendous motions before he is master of common arithmetic. For these and similar considerations, it seems that the first intellectual qualification of a teacher is a critical thoroughness, both in rules and principles, in regard to all the branches required by law to be taught in the common schools; and a power of recalling them in any of their parts with a promptitude and certainty hardly inferior to that with which he could tell his own name.

2. The next principal qualification in a teacher is the *art of teaching*. This is happily expressed in the common phrase *aptness to teach*, which in a few words comprehends many particulars. The ability to acquire and the ability to impart are wholly different talents. The former may exist in the most liberal measure without the latter. It was a remark of Lord Bacon that "the art of well-delivering the knowledge we possess is among the secrets left to be discovered by future generations." Dr. Watts says, "There are some very learned men who know much themselves, but who have not the talent of communicating their knowledge." Indeed, this fact is not now questioned by any intelligent educationist. Hence we account for the frequent complaints of the committees that those teachers who had sustained an examination in an acceptable manner failed in the schoolroom through a want of facility in communicating what they knew.

The ability to acquire is the power of understanding the subject matter of investigation. Aptness to teach involves the power of perceiving how far a scholar understands the subject matter to be learned, and what, in the natural order, is the next step he is to take. It involves the power of discovering and of solving at the time the exact difficulty by which the learner is embarrassed. The removal of a slight impediment, the drawing aside of the thinnest veil which happens to divert his steps or obscure his vision is worth more to him than volumes of lore on collateral subjects.

How much does the pupil comprehend of the subject? What should his next step be? Is his mind looking toward a truth or an error? The answer to these questions must be intuitive in the person who is apt to teach. As a dramatic writer throws himself successively into the characters of the drama he is composing that he may express the ideas and emotions peculiar to each, so the mind of a teacher should migrate, as it were, into those of his pupils to discover what they know and feel and need; and then, supplying from his own stock what they require, he should reduce it to such a form and bring it within such a distance that they can reach out and seize and appropriate it.

He should never forget that intellectual truths are naturally adapted to give intellectual pleasure; and that, by leading the minds of his pupils onward to such a position in relation to these truths that they themselves can discover them, he secures to them the natural reward of a new pleasure with every new discovery, which is one of the strongest as well as most appropriate incitements to future exertion.

Aptness to teach includes the presentation of the different parts of a subject in a natural order. If a child is told that the globe is about 25,000 miles in circumference before he has any conception of the length of a mile or of the number of units in a thousand, the statement is not only utterly useless as an act of instruction but it will probably prevent him ever afterward from gaining an adequate idea of the subject. The novelty will be gone, and yet the fact unknown. Besides, a systematic acquisition of a subject knits all parts of it together, so that they will be longer retained and more easily recalled. To acquire a few of the facts gives us fragments only; and even to master all the facts, but to obtain them promiscuously, leaves what is acquired so unconnected and loose that any part of it may be jostled out of its place and lost, or remain only to mislead.

Aptness to teach, in fine, embraces a

knowledge of methods and processes. These are indefinitely various. Some are adapted to accomplish their object in an easy and natural manner; others, in a toilsome and circuitous one; others, again, may accomplish the object at which they aim with certainty and dispatch, but secure it by inflicting deep and lasting injuries upon the social and moral sentiments. We are struck with surprise on learning, that, but a few centuries since, the feudal barons of Scotland, in running out the lines around their extensive domains, used to take a party of boys and whip them at the different posts and landmarks in order to give them a retentive memory as witnesses in case of future litigation or dispute. Though this might give them a vivid recollection of localities, yet it would hardly improve their ideas of justice or propitiate them to bear true testimony in favor of the chastiser. But do not those who have no aptness to teach sometimes accomplish their objects by a kindred method?

He who is apt to teach is acquainted, not only with common methods for common minds but with peculiar methods for pupils of peculiar dispositions and temperaments; and he is acquainted with the principles of all methods whereby he can vary his plan according to any difference of circumstances.

The statement has been sometimes made that it is the object of normal schools to subject all teachers to one inflexible, immutable course of instruction. Nothing could be more erroneous; for one of the great objects is to give them a knowledge of modes as various as the diversity of cases that may arise, that, like a skillful pilot, they may not only see the haven for which they are to steer but know every bend in the channel that leads to it. No one is so poor in resources for difficult emergencies as they may arise as he whose knowledge of methods is limited to the one in which he happened to be instructed. It is this way that rude nations go on for indefinite periods, imitating what they have seen and teaching only as they were taught.

3. Experience has also proved that there is no necessary connection between literary competency, aptness to teach, and the power to manage and govern a school successfully. They are independent qualifications; yet a marked deficiency in any one of the three renders the other nearly valueless. In regard to the ordinary management or administration of a school, how much judgment is demanded in the organization of classes so that no scholar shall either be clogged and retarded, or hurried forward with injudicious speed, by being matched with an unequal yoke-fellow! Great discretion is necessary in the assignment of lessons in order to avoid, on the one hand, such shortness in the tasks as allows time to be idle; and, on the other, such overassignments as render thoroughness and accuracy impracticable, and thereby so habituate the pupil to mistakes and imperfections that he cares little or nothing about committing them.

Lessons, as far as it is possible, should be so adjusted to the capacity of the scholar that there should be no failure in a recitation not occasioned by culpable neglect. The sense of shame, or of regret for ignorance, can never be made exquisitely keen if the lessons given are so long or so difficult as to make failures frequent. When "bad marks," as they are called, against a scholar become common, they not only lose their salutary force but every addition to them debases his character, and carries him through a regular course of training which prepares him to follow in the footsteps of those convicts who are so often condemned, that, at length, they care nothing for the ignominy of the sentence. Yet all this may be the legitimate consequence of being unequally mated or injudiciously tasked. It is a sad sight, in any school, to see a pupil marked for a deficiency without any blush of shame or sign of guilt; and it is never done with impunity to his moral character.

The preservation of order, together with the proper dispatch of business, requires a mean between the too much and the too little in all the evolutions of the school, which it is difficult to hit. When classes leave their seats for the recitation stand and return to them again, or when the different sexes have a recess, or the hour of intermission arrives, if there be not some order and succession of movement, the school will be temporarily converted into a promiscuous rabble, giving both the temptation and the opportunity for committing every species of indecorum and aggression. In order to prevent confusion, on the other hand, the operations of the school may be conducted with such military formality and procrastination — the second scholar not being allowed to leave his seat until the first has reached the door or the place of recitation, and each being made to walk on tiptoe to secure silence — that a substantial part of every school session will be wasted in the wearisome pursuit of an object worth nothing when obtained.

When we reflect how many things are to be done each half day, and how short a time is allotted for their performance, the necessity of system in regard to all the operations of the school will be apparent. System compacts labor; and when the hand is to be turned to an almost endless variety of particulars, if system does not preside over the whole series of movements, the time allotted to each will be spent in getting ready to perform it. With lessons to set; with so many classes to hear; with difficulties to explain; with the studious to be assisted; the idle to be spurred; the transgressors to be admonished or corrected; with the goers and comers to observe; with all these things to be done, no considerable progress can be made if one part of the wheel is not coming up to the work while another is going down.

And if order do not pervade, the school as a whole, and in all its parts, all is lost.

And this is a very difficult thing; for it seems as though the school were only a point, rescued out of a chaos that still encompasses it, and is ready on the first opportunity to break in and reoccupy its ancient possession. As it is utterly impracticable for any committee to prepare a code of regulations coextensive with all the details which belong to the management of a school, it must be left with the teacher; and hence the necessity of skill in this item of the long list of his qualifications.

The government and discipline of a school demands qualities still more rare, because the consequences of error in these are still more disastrous. What caution, wisdom, uprightness, and sometimes even intrepidity are necessary in the administration of punishment! After all other means have been tried, and tried in vain, the chastisement of pupils found to be otherwise incorrigible is still upheld by law and sanctioned by public opinion. But it is the last resort, the ultimate resource, acknowledged on all hands to be a relic of barbarism, and yet authorized because the community, although they feel it to be a great evil, have not yet devised and applied an antidote.

Through an ignorance of the laws of health, a parent may so corrupt the constitution of his child as to render poison a necessary medicine; and, through an ignorance of the laws of mind, he may do the same thing in regard to punishment. When the arts of health and of education are understood, neither poison nor punishment will need to be used, unless in most extraordinary cases. The discipline of former times was inexorably stern and severe; and, even if it were wished, it is impossible now to return to it. The question is, what can be substituted, which, without its severity, shall have its efficiency? . . .

A school should be governed with a steady hand, not only during the same season but from year to year; substantially the same extent of indulgence being allowed and the same restrictions imposed. It is injurious to the children to alternate between the extremes of an easy and a sharp discipline. It is unjust also for one teacher to profit by letting down the discipline of a school, and thus throw upon his successor the labor of raising it up to its former level.

4. In two words the statute opens to all teachers an extensive field of duty by ordaining that all the youth in the schools shall be taught "good behavior." The framers of the law were aware how rapidly good or bad manners mature into good or bad morals; they saw that good manners have not only the negative virtue of restraining from vice but the positive one of leading, by imperceptible gradations, toward the practice of almost all the social virtues.

The effects of civility or discourtesy, of gentlemanly or ungentlemanly deportment, are not periodical or occasional, merely, but of constant recurrence; and all the members of society have a direct interest in the manners of each of its individuals, because each one is a radiating point, the center of a circle which he fills with pleasure or annoyance, not only for those who voluntarily enter it but for those, who, in the promiscuous movements of society, are caught within its circumference. Good behavior includes the elements of that equity, benevolence, conscience, which, in their great combinations, the moralist treats of in his books of ethics and the legislator enjoins in his codes of law.

The schoolroom and its playground, next to the family table, are the places where the selfish propensities come into most direct collision with social duties. Here, then, a right direction should be given to the growing mind. The surrounding influences which are incorporated into its new thoughts and feelings, and make part of their substance, are too minute and subtle to be received in masses like nourishment; they are rather imbibed into the system unconsciously by every act of respiration, and are constantly insinuating themselves into it through all the avenues of the senses. If, then, the manners of the teacher are to be imitated by his pupils, if he is the glass at which they "do dress themselves," how strong is the necessity that he should understand those nameless and innumerable practices in regard to deportment, dress, conversation, and all personal habits that constitute the difference between a gentleman and a clown!

We can fear some oddity or eccentricity in a friend whom we admire for his talents or revere for his virtues; but it becomes quite a different thing when the oddity or the eccentricity is to be a pattern or model from which fifty or a hundred children are to form their manners. It was well remarked by the ablest British traveler who has ever visited this country that, among us, "every male above twenty-one years of age claims to be a sovereign. He is, therefore, *bound to be a gentleman.*"

5. On the indispensable, all-controlling requisite of moral character, I have but a single suggestion to make in addition to those admirable views on this subject which are scattered up and down through the committees' reports. This suggestion relates to the responsibility resting on those individuals who give letters of recommendation or certificates of character to candidates for schools. Probably one-half, perhaps more, of all the teachers in the state are comparatively strangers in the respective place where they are employed. Hence the examining committee, in the absence of personal knowledge, must rely upon testimonials exhibited before them. These consist of credentials brought from abroad, which are sometimes obtained through the partialities of relationship, interest, or sect; or even given lest a refusal should be deemed an unneighborly act, and the applicant should be offended or alienated by a repulse.

But are interests of such vast moment as the moral influence of teachers upon the rising generation to be sacrificed to private considerations of relationship or predilection, or any other selfish or personal motive whatever? It may be very agreeable to a person to receive the salary of a teacher, but this fact has no tendency to prove his fitness for the station. If so, the poorhouse would be the place to inquire for teachers; and what claim to conscience or benevolence can that man have who jeopards the permanent welfare of fifty or a hundred children for the private accommodation of a friend?

In regard to pecuniary transactions, it is provided by the laws of the land that whoever recommends another as responsible and solvent becomes himself liable for the debts which may be contracted, under a faith in the recommendation, should it prove to have been falsely given. The recommendation is held to be a warranty; and it charges its author with all its losses incurred, within the scope of a fair construction. It is supposed that, without this responsibility, the expanded business of trade and commerce would be restricted to persons possessing a mutual knowledge of each other's trustworthiness or solvency.

But why should the precious and enduring interests of morality be accounted of minor importance and protected by feebler securities than common traffic? Why should the man who has been defrauded by an accredited peddler have his remedy against the guarantor, while he who is instrumental in inflicting upon a district, and upon all the children in a district, the curse of a dissolute, vicious teacher, escapes the condign punishment of general execration?

In the contemplation of the law, the school committee are sentinels stationed at the door of every schoolhouse in the state to see that no teacher ever crosses its threshold who is not clothed, from the crown of his head to the sole of his feet, in garments of virtue; and they are the enemies of the human race — not of contemporaries only but of posterity — who, from any private or sinsiter motive, strive to put these sentinels to sleep in order that one who is profane or intemperate, or addicted to low associations, or branded with the stigma of any vice may elude the vigilance of the watchmen, and be installed over the pure minds of the young as their guide and exemplar.

If none but teachers of pure tastes, of good manners, of exemplary morals had ever gained admission into our schools, neither the schoolrooms nor their appurtenances would have been polluted as some of them now are with such ribald inscriptions and with the carvings of such obscene emblems as would make a heathen blush. Every person, therefore, who indorses another's character, as one befitting a school teacher, stands before the public as his moral bondsman and sponsor, and should be held to a rigid accountability.

102.

Daniel Webster: For a Uniform Bankruptcy Law

It has been estimated that over 400,000 bankruptcies resulted from the depression that swept the country in the late 1830s and early 1840s. President Van Buren's proposal for bankruptcy legislation in 1837 came to nought but, as the number of business failures increased, pressure for federal legislation mounted. In April 1840, Daniel Webster, senator from Massachusetts, introduced a bill providing for a uniform bankruptcy law in an atmosphere of increased tolerance for the bankrupt. That same month two other bankruptcy bills were offered in the Senate, and on April 22 the chairman of the judiciary committee, Senator Wall of New Jersey, proposed an amendment to Webster's bill. Webster's argument against Wall's amendment was delivered on May 18, 1840, and is reprinted in part below. Webster's bill, without the amendment, was passed in 1841.

Source: *The Writings and Speeches of Daniel Webster,* Boston, 1903, Vol. IX, pp. 3-25.

THE POWER OF CONGRESS over the subject of bankruptcies, the most useful mode of exercising the power under the present circumstances of the country, and the duty of exercising it, are the points to which attention is naturally called by everyone who addresses the Senate.

In the first place, as to the power. It is fortunately not an inferred or constructive power but one of the express grants of the Constitution. "Congress shall have power to establish uniform laws on the subject of bankruptcies throughout the United States." These are the words of the grant; there may be questions about the extent of the power, but there can be none of its existence.

The bill which has been reported by the committee provides for voluntary bankruptcies only. It contains no provisions by which creditors, on an alleged act of bankruptcy, may proceed against their debtors, with a view to subject them and their property to the operation of the law. It looks to no coercion by a creditor to make his debtor a subject of the law against his will. This is the first characteristic of the bill, and in this respect it certainly differs from the former bankrupt laws of the United States, and from the English bankrupt laws.

The bill, too, extends its provisions, not only to those who, either in fact or in contemplation of law, are traders but to all persons who declare themselves insolvent or unable to pay their debts and meet their engagements, and who desire to assign their property for the benefit of their creditors. In this respect, also, it differs from the former law and from the law of England.

The questions, then, are two: (1) Can Congress constitutionally pass a bankrupt law which shall include other persons besides traders? (2) Can it pass a law providing for voluntary cases only; that is, cases in which the proceedings originate only with the debtor himself?

The consideration of both these questions is necessarily involved in the discussion of the present bill inasmuch as it has been denied that Congress has power to extend bankrupt laws farther than to merchants and traders, or to make them applicable to voluntary cases only. This limitation of the power of Congress is asserted on the idea that the framers of the Constitution, in conferring the power of establishing bankrupt laws, must be presumed to have had reference to the bankrupt laws of England, as then existing; and that the laws of England then existing embraced none but merchants and traders, and provided only for involuntary or coercive bankruptcies.

Now, sir, in the first place, allow me to remark that the power is granted to Congress in the most general and comprehensive terms. It has one limitation only, which is that laws on the subject of bankruptcies shall be uniform throughout the United States. With this qualification, the whole subject is placed within the discretion and under the legislation of Congress. The Constitution does not say that Congress shall have power to pass *a* bankrupt law, nor to introduce *the* system of bankruptcies. It declares that Congress shall have power to "establish uniform laws on the subject of bankruptcies throughout the United States." This is the whole clause; nor is there any limitation or restriction imposed by any other clause. . . .

Whenever a man's means are insufficient to meet his engagements and pay his debts, the fact of bankruptcy has taken place; a case of bankruptcy has arisen, whether there be a law providing for it or not.

There may be bankruptcies, or cases of bankruptcy, where there are no bankrupt laws existing. Or bankrupt laws may exist which shall extend to some bankruptcies, or some cases of bankruptcy, and not to others. We constantly speak of bankruptcies happening among individuals without reference to existing laws. Bankruptcies, as facts, or occurrences, or cases for which Congress is authorized to make provision, are failures. A learned judge has said that a law on the subject of bankruptcies, in the sense of the Constitution, is a law making provision for persons failing to pay their debts. Over the whole subject of these bankruptcies, or these failures, the power of Congress, as it stands on the face of the Constitution, is full and complete. . . .

I think, then, that Congress may pass a law which shall include persons not traders, and which shall include voluntary cases only. And I think, further, that the amendment proposed by the honorable member from New Jersey is, in effect, exactly against his own argument. I think it admits all that he contends against. In the first place, he admits voluntary bankruptcies, and there were none such in England in 1789. This is clear. And in the next place, he admits anyone who will say that he has been concerned in trade; and he maintains, and has asserted, that in this country anybody may say that. Anybody, then, may come in under the bill. The only difference is, unless he is bona fide a trader, he must come in under a disguise, or in an assumed character. Whatever be his employment, occupation, or pursuit, he must come in as a trader, or as one who has been concerned or engaged in trade. The honorable member attempts a distinction between the traders and those who can say that they have been engaged in trade. I cannot see the difference. It is too fine for me. . . .

The gentleman's real object is, not to confine the bill to traders but to embrace everybody; and yet he deems it necessary for every person applying to state, and to swear, that he has been engaged in trade. This seems to me to be both superfluous and objectionable; superfluous, because, if we have a right to bring in persons under one name, we may bring in the same persons under another name, or by a general description; objectionable, because it requires men to state what may very much resemble a falsehood, and to make oath to it.

Suppose a farmer or mechanic to fail, can he take an oath that he has been engaged in trade? If the objection to bring in others than traders is well founded in the Constitution, surely mere form cannot remove it. Words cannot alter things. The Constitution says nothing about traders. Yet the honorable gentleman's amendment requires all applicants to declare themselves traders; and if they will but say so, and swear so, it shall be so received, and nobody shall contradict it. In other words, a fiction, not very innocent, shall be allowed to overcome an unconstitutional objection. . . .

Leaving this very important part of the case, another question arises upon the proposed amendment. Shall the bankruptcy act, in its application to individuals, be voluntary only, or both voluntary and compulsory? It is well known that I prefer that it should be both. I think all insolvent and failing persons should have power to come in under its provisions and be voluntary bankrupts; and I think, too, that, as to those who are strictly merchants and traders, creditors ought to have a right to proceed against them, on the commission of the usual acts of bankruptcy, and subject them to the provisions of the act.

But the committee think otherwise. They find many objections to this from many parts of the country, and especially from the West. In a country so extensive, with a people so various, with such different ideas and habits in regard to punctuality in commercial dealings, great opposition is anticipated to any measure so strict and so penal as a coercive bankruptcy. I content myself, therefore, with what I can get. I content myself with the voluntary bankruptcy. I am free to confess my leading object to be to relieve those who are at present bankrupts, hopeless bankrupts, and who cannot be discharged or set free but by a bankrupt act passed by Congress.

I confess that their case forms the great motive of my conduct. It is their case which has created the general cry for the measure. Not that their interest is opposed to the interest of creditors; still less that it is op-posed to the general good of the country. On the contrary, I believe that the interest of creditors would be greatly benefited even by a system of voluntary bankruptcy alone, and I am quite confident that the public good would be eminently promoted. In my judgment, all interests concur; and it is the duty of providing for these unfortunate insolvents, in a manner thus favorable to all interests, which I feel urging me forward on this occasion.

And now, sir, whence does this duty arise which appears to me so pressing and imperative? How has it become so incumbent upon us? What are the considerations, what the reasons, which have so covered our tables with petitions from all classes and all quarters, and which have loaded the air with such loud and unanimous invocations to Congress to pass a bankrupt law?

Let me remind you, then, in the first place, sir, that, commercial as the country is, and having experienced as it has done, and experiencing as it now does, great vicissitudes of trade and business, it is almost forty years since any law has been in force by which any honest man, failing in business, could be effectually discharged from debt by surrendering his property. The former bankrupt law was repealed on the 19th of December, 1803. From that day to this, the condition of an insolvent, however honest and worthy, has been utterly hopeless, so far as he depended on any legal mode of relief. This state of things has arisen from the peculiar provisions of the Constitution of the United States, and from the omission by Congress to exercise this branch of its constitutional power.

By the Constitution, the states are prohibited from passing laws impairing the obligation of contracts. Bankrupt laws impair the obligation of contracts if they discharge the bankrupt from his debts without payment. The states, therefore, cannot pass such laws. The power, then, is taken from the states, and placed in our hands. It is true that it has been decided that, in regard to contracts entered into after the passage of any state bankrupt law, between the citizens of the state having such law, and sued in the state courts, a state discharge may prevail. So far, effect has been given to state laws.

I have great respect, habitually, for judicial decisions; but it has, nevertheless, I must say, always appeared to me that the distinctions on which these decisions are founded are slender, and that they evade, without answering, the objections founded on the great political and commercial objects intended to be secured by this part of the Constitution. But these decisions, whether right or wrong, afford no effectual relief. The qualifications and limitations which I have stated render them useless, as to the purpose of a general discharge. So much of the concerns of every man of business is with citizens of other states than his own, and with foreigners, that the partial extent to which the validity of state discharges reaches is of little benefit.

The states, then, cannot pass effectual bankrupt laws; that is, effectual for the discharge of the debtor. There is no doubt that most, if not all, the states would now pass such laws if they had the power, although their legislation would be various, interfering, and full of all the evils which the Constitution of the United States intended to provide against. But they have not the power; Congress, which has the power, does not exercise it. This is the peculiarity of our condition. The states would pass bankrupt laws, but they cannot; we can, but we will not. And between this want of power in the states and want of will in Congress, unfortunate insolvents are left to hopeless bondage. . . .

It is true they are not imprisoned; but there may be, and there are, restraint and bondage outside the walls of the jail, as well as in. Their power of earning is, in truth, taken away, their faculty of useful employment is paralyzed, and hope itself become extinguished. Creditors, generally, are not inhuman or unkind; but there will be found some who hold on, and the more a debtor struggles to free himself, the more they feel encouraged to hold on. The mode of reasoning is that the more honest the debtor may be, the more industrious, the more disposed to struggle and bear up against his misfortunes, the greater the chance is that, in the end, especially if the humanity of others shall have led them to release him, their own debts may be finally recovered. . . .

Sir, I verily believe that the power of perpetuating debts against debtors, for no substantial good to the creditor himself, and the power of imprisonment for debt, at least as it existed in this country ten years ago, have imposed more restraint on personal liberty than the law of debtor and creditor imposes in any other Christian and commercial country. If any public good were attained, any high political object answered by such laws, there might be some reason for counseling submission and sufferance to individuals. But the result is bad, every way. It is bad to the public and to the country, which loses the efforts and the industry of so many useful and capable citizens. It is bad to creditors, because there is no security against preferences, no principle of equality, and no encouragement for honest, fair, and seasonable assignments of effects.

As to the debtor, however good his intentions or earnest his endeavors, it subdues his spirit and degrades him in his own esteem; and if he attempts anything for the purpose of obtaining food and clothing for his family, he is driven to unworthy shifts and disguises, to the use of other persons' names, to the adoption of the character of agent and various other contrivances, to keep the little earnings of the day from the reach of his creditors. Fathers act in the name of their sons, sons act in the name of their fathers; all constantly exposed to the greatest temptation to misrepresent facts and to evade the law, if creditors should strike. All this is evil, unmixed evil. And what is it all for? Of what benefit to anybody? Who likes it? Who wishes it? What class of creditors desire it? What consideration of public good demands it? . . .

Mr. President, let us atone for the omissions of the past by a prompt and efficient discharge of present duty. The demand for this measure is not partial or local. It comes to us, earnest and loud, from all classes and all quarters. The time is come when we must answer it to our own consciences if we suffer longer delay or postponement.

High hopes, high duties, and high responsibilities concentrate themselves on this measure and this moment. With a power to pass a bankrupt law, which no other legislature in the country possesses, with a power of giving relief to many, doing injustice to none, I again ask every man who hears me, if he can content himself without an honest attempt to exercise that power? We may think it would be better to leave the power with the states; but it was not left with the states; they have it not, and we cannot give it to them. It is in our hands, to be exercised by us, or to be forever useless and lifeless.

103.

HENRY CLAY: Against the Growing Power of the Executive

In the election of 1840 the Whigs ran William Henry Harrison, a sixty-seven year old military hero of the War of 1812, against the incumbent, Martin Van Buren. Henry Clay had aspired to be the Whig candidate, but he stumped hard for Harrison nonetheless. In the following campaign speech, which Clay delivered in Hanover County, Virginia, June 27, 1840, he summarized the Whig platform. In order to promote their economic program, the Whigs, in the tradition of the Federalists, favored strengthening the role of the central government at the expense of the states; and by way of repudiating the policies of Jackson (whose successor Van Buren was), they advocated lessening the power of the executive branch of the government, and strengthening that of the legislature.

Source: Colton, VIII, pp. 197-214.

WHY IS THE PLOW DESERTED, the tools of the mechanic laid aside, and all are seen rushing to gatherings of the people? What occasions those vast and unusual assemblages, which we behold in every state and in almost every neighborhood? Why those conventions of the people, at a common center, from all the extremities of this vast Union, to consult together upon the sufferings of the community and to deliberate upon the means of deliverance? Why this rabid appetite for public discussions? What is the solution for the phenomenon which we observe of a great nation agitated upon its whole surface and at its lowest depths, like the ocean when convulsed by some terrible storm? There must be a cause, and no ordinary cause. . . .

In my deliberate opinion, the present distressed and distracted state of the country may be traced to the single cause of the action, the encroachments, and the usurpations of the executive branch of the government. . . .

The late President of the United States advanced certain new and alarming pretensions for the Executive Department of the government, the effect of which, if established and recognized by the people, must inevitably convert it into a monarchy. The first of these, and it was a favorite principle with him, was that the Executive Department should be regarded as a unit. By this principle of unity, he meant and intended that all the executive officers of government should be bound to obey the commands and execute the orders of the President of the United States, and that they should be amenable to him and he be responsible for them. Prior to his administration, it had been considered that they were bound to observe and obey the Constitution and laws, subject only to the general superintendence of the President, and responsible by impeachment, and to the tribunals of justice, for injuries inflicted on private citizens. . . .

But to construct the scheme of practical despotism while all the forms of free government remained, it was necessary to take one further step. By the Constitution, the President is enjoined to take care that the laws be executed. This injunction was merely intended to impose on him the duty of a general superintendence; to see that offices were filled; officers at their respective posts in the discharge of their official functions; and all obstructions to the enforcement of the laws were removed, and, when necessary for that purpose, to call out the militia. No one ever imagined, prior to the administration of President Jackson, that a President of the United States was to occupy himself with supervising and attending to the execution of all the minute details of every one of the hosts of offices in the United States.

Under the constitutional injunction just mentioned, the late President put forward that most extraordinary pretension that the Constitution and laws of the United States were to be executed *as he understood them;* and this pretension was attempted to be sustained by an argument equally extraordinary — that the President, being a sworn officer, must carry them into effect according to his sense of their meaning. The Constitution and laws were to be executed, not according to their import, as handed down to us by our ancestors, as interpreted by contemporaneous expositions, as expounded by concurrent judicial decisions, as fixed by an uninterrupted course of congressional legislation, but in that sense in which a President of the United States happened to understand them!

To complete this executive usurpation, one further object remained. By the Constitution, the command of the Army and the Navy is conferred on the President. If he could unite the purse with the sword, nothing would be left to gratify the insatiable thirst for power. In 1833 the President seized the Treasury of the United States, and from that day to this it has continued substantially under his control. The seizure was effected by the removal of one secretary of the treasury, understood to be opposed to the measure, and by the dismissal of another who refused to violate the law of the land upon the orders of the President. . . .

The sum of the whole is that there is but one power, one control, one will in the state. All is concentrated in the President. He directs, orders, commands the whole machinery of the state. . . .

General Jackson was a bold and fearless reaper, carrying a wide row, but he did not gather the whole harvest; he left some gleanings to his faithful successor; and he seems resolved to sweep clean the field of power. The duty of inculcating on the official corps the active exertion of their personal and official influence was left by him to be enforced by Mr. Van Buren, in all popular elections. It was not sufficient that the official corps was bound implicitly to obey the will of the President. It was not sufficient that this obedience was coerced by the tremendous power of dismission. It soon became apparent, that the corps might be beneficially employed to promote, in other matters than the business of their offices, the views and interests of the President and his party.

They are far more efficient than any standing army of equal numbers. A standing army would be separated and stand out from the people, would be an object of jealousy and suspicion; and, being always in corps or in detachments, could exert no influence on popular elections. But the official corps is dispersed throughout the country, in every town, village, and city, mixing with the people, attending their meetings and conventions, becoming chairmen and members of committees, and urging and stimulating partisans to active and vigorous exertion. Acting in concert and, throughout the whole Union, obeying orders issued from the center, their influence, aided by executive patronage, by the Post Office Department, and all the vast other means of the executive is almost irresistible. . . .

But the Army and Navy are too small and, in composition, are too patriotic to subserve all the purposes of this administration. Hence, the recent proposition of the secretary of war, strongly recommended by the President, under color of a new organization of the militia, to create a standing force of 200,000 men, an amount which no conceivable foreign exigency can ever make necessary. It is not my purpose now to enter upon an examination of that alarming and most dangerous plan of the Executive Department of the federal government. It has justly excited a burst of general indignation; and nowhere has the disapprobation of it been more emphatically expressed than in this ancient and venerable commonwealth.

The monstrous project may be described in a few words. It proposes to create the force by breaking down Mason and Dixon's Line, expunging the boundaries of states; melting them up in a confluent mass, to be subsequently cut up into ten military parts; alienates the militia from its natural association; withdraws it from the authority and command and sympathy of its constitutional officers appointed by the states; puts it under the command of the President; authorizes him to cause it to be trained, in palpable violation of the Constitution; and subjects it to be called out from remote and distant places, at his pleasure, and on occasions not warranted by the Constitution! . . .

Let Mr. Van Buren be reelected in November next and it will be claimed that the people have thereby approved of this plan of the secretary of war. . . .

I have thus, fellow citizens, exhibited to you a true and faithful picture of executive power as it has been enlarged and expanded within the last few years, and as it has been proposed further to extend it. It overshadows every other branch of the government. The source of legislative power is no longer to be found in the Capitol but in the palace of the President. In assuming to be a part of the legislative power, as the President recently did, contrary to the Constitution, he would have been nearer the actual fact if he had alleged that he was the sole legislative power of the Union. How is it possible for public liberty to be preserved, and the constitutional distributions of power, among the departments of government, to be maintained unless the executive career be checked and restrained? . . .

And yet the partisans of this tremendous

executive power arrogate to themselves the name of Democrats, and bestow upon us, who are opposed to it, the denomination of Federalists! . . .

What are the positions of the two great parties of the present day? Modern democracy has reduced the federal theory of a strong and energetic executive to practical operation. It has turned from the people, the natural ally of genuine democracy, to the executive; and, instead of vigilance, jealousy, and distrust, has given to that department all its confidence, and made to it a virtual surrender of all the powers of government. The recognized maxim of royal infallibility is transplanted from the British monarchy into modern American democracy; and the President can do no wrong!

This new school adopts, modifies, changes, renounces, renews opinions at the pleasure of the executive. Is the Bank of the United States a useful and valuable institution? Yes, unanimously pronounces the Democratic legislature of Pennsylvania. The President vetoes it as a pernicious and dangerous establishment. The Democratic majority in the same legislature pronounce it to be pernicious and dangerous. The Democratic majority of the House of Representatives of the United States declare the deposits of the public money in the Bank of the United States to be safe. The President says they are unsafe and removes them. The democracy say they are unsafe and approve the removal. The President says that a scheme of a subtreasury is revolutionary and disorganizing. The democracy say it is revolutionary and disorganizing. The President says it is wise and salutary. The Democracy say it is wise and salutary.

The Whigs of 1840 stand where the Republicans of 1798 stood, and where the Whigs of the Revolution were, battling for liberty, for the people, for free institutions, against power, against corruption, against executive encroachments, against monarchy.

We are reproached with struggling for offices and their emoluments. If we acted on the avowed and acknowledged principle of our opponents, "that the spoils belong to the victors," we should indeed be unworthy of the support of the people. No! fellow citizens; higher, nobler, more patriotic motives actuate the Whig Party. Their object is the restoration of the Constitution, the preservation of liberty, and rescue of the country. If they were governed by the sordid and selfish motives acted upon by their opponents, and unjustly imputed to them, to acquire office and emolument, they have only to change their names and enter the presidential palace. The gate is always wide open, and the path is no narrow one which leads through it. The last comer, too, often fares best.

On a resurvey of the few past years, we behold enough to sicken and sadden the hearts of true patriots. Executive encroachment has quickly followed upon executive encroachment; persons honored by public confidence, and from whom nothing but grateful and parental measures should have flowed, have inflicted stunning blow after blow, in such rapid succession that, before the people could recover from the reeling effects of one, another has fallen heavily upon them. Had either of various instances of executive misrule stood out separate and alone, so that its enormity might have been seen and dwelt upon with composure, the condemnation of the executive would have long since been pronounced; but it has hitherto found safety and impunity in the bewildering effects of the multitude of its misdeeds.

The nation has been in the condition of a man who, having gone to bed after his barn has been consumed by fire, is aroused in the morning to witness his dwelling house wrapped in flames. So bold and presumptuous had the executive become that, penetrating in its influence the hall of a coordinate branch of the government by means of a submissive or instructed majority of the

Senate, it has caused a record of the country to be effaced and expunged, the inviolability of which was guaranteed by a solemn injunction of the Constitution! And that memorable and scandalous scene was enacted only because the offensive record contained an expression of disapprobation of an executive proceeding.

If this state of things were to remain — if the progress of executive usurpation were to continue unchecked — hopeless despair would seize the public mind, or the people would be goaded to acts of open and violent resistance. But, thank God, the power of the President, fearful and rapid as its strides have been, is not yet too great for the power of the elective franchise; and a bright and glorious prospect in the election of William Henry Harrison has opened upon the country.

The necessity of a change of rulers has deeply penetrated the hearts of the people; and we everywhere behold cheering manifestations of that happy event. The fact of his election alone, without reference to the measures of his administration, will powerfully contribute to the security and happiness of the people. It will bring assurance of the cessation of that long series of disastrous experiments which have so greatly afflicted the people. Confidence will immediately revive, credit be restored, active business will return, prices of products will rise; and the people will feel and know that, instead of their servants being occupied in devising measures for their ruin and destruction, they will be assiduously employed in promoting their welfare and prosperity. . . .

The first, and, in my opinion, the most important object, which should engage the serious attention of a new administration is that of circumscribing the executive power, and throwing around it such limitations and safeguards as will render it no longer dangerous to the public liberties. . . . With the view, therefore, to the fundamental character of the government itself, and especially

of the executive branch, it seems to me that, either by amendments of the Constitution, when they are necessary, or by remedial legislation, when the object falls within the scope of the powers of Congress, there should be:

First, a provision to render a person ineligible to the office of President of the United States after a service of one term.

Much observation and deliberate reflection have satisfied me that too much of the time, the thoughts, and the exertions of the incumbent are occupied, during his first term, in securing his reelection. The public business, consequently, suffers; and measures are proposed or executed with less regard to the general prosperity than to their influence upon the approaching election. If the limitation to one term existed, the President would be exclusively devoted to the discharge of his public duties; and he would endeavor to signalize his administration by the beneficence and wisdom of its measures.

Second, the veto power should be more precisely defined and be subjected to further limitations and qualifications.

Although a large, perhaps the largest, proportion of all the acts of Congress passed at the short session of Congress since the commencement of the government were passed within the three last days of the session, and when, of course, the President for the time being had not the ten days for consideration, allowed by the Constitution, President Jackson, availing himself of that allowance, has failed to return important bills. When not returned by the President within the ten days, it is questionable whether they are laws or not. It is very certain that the next Congress cannot act upon them by deciding whether or not they shall become laws, the President's objections notwithstanding. All this ought to be provided for.

At present, a bill returned by the President can only become a law by the concurrence of two-thirds of the members of each house. I think if Congress passes a bill after discussion and consideration, and, after weighing the objections of the President, still believes it ought to pass, it should become a law provided a majority of *all* the members of each house concur in its passage. If the weight of his argument and the weight of his influence conjointly cannot prevail on a majority, against their previous convictions, in my opinion, the bill ought not to be arrested. Such is the provision of the constitutions of several of the states, and that of Kentucky among them.

Third, the power of dismission from office should be restricted, and the exercise of it be rendered responsible.

The constitutional concurrence of the Senate is necessary to the confirmation of all important appointments; but, without consulting the Senate, without any other motive than resentment or caprice, the President may dismiss, at his sole pleasure, an officer created by the joint action of himself and the Senate. The practical effect is to nullify the agency of the Senate. There may be, occasionally, cases in which the public interest requires an immediate dismission without waiting for the assembling of the Senate; but in all such cases the President should be bound to communicate fully the grounds and motives of the dismission. The power would be thus rendered responsible. Without it, the exercise of the power is utterly repugnant to free institutions, the basis of which is perfect responsibility, and dangerous to the public liberty. . . .

Fourth, the control over the Treasury of the United States should be confided and confined exclusively to Congress; and all authority of the President over it, by means of dismissing the secretary of the treasury or other persons having the immediate charge of it, be rigorously precluded.

You have heard much, fellow citizens, of the divorce of banks and government. After crippling them and impairing their utility, the executive and its partisans have systematically denounced them. The executive and the country were warned again and again of the fatal course that has been pursued; but the executive nevertheless persevered, commencing by praising and ending by decrying the state banks. Under cover of the smoke which has been raised, the real object all along has been, and yet is, to obtain the possession of the money power of the Union. That accomplished and sanctioned by the people — the union of the sword and the purse in the hands of the President effectually secured — and farewell to American liberty.

The subtreasury is the scheme for effecting that union; and, I am told, that of all the days in the year, that which gave birth to our national existence and freedom is the selected day to be disgraced by ushering into existence a measure imminently perilous to the liberty, which, on that anniversary, we commemorate in joyous festivals. Thus, in the spirit of destruction which animates our rulers, would they convert a day of gladness and of glory into a day of sadness and mourning. Fellow citizens, there is one divorce urgently demanded by the safety and the highest interests of the country — a divorce of the President from the Treasury of the United States.

And, fifth, the appointment of members of Congress to any office, or any but a few specific offices, during their continuance in office and for one year thereafter, should be prohibited.

This is a hackneyed theme, but it is not less deserving of serious consideration. The Constitution now interdicts the appointment of a member of Congress to any office created, or the emoluments of which have been increased while he was in office. In the purer days of the republic, that restriction might have been sufficient; but in these more degenerate times, it is necessary, by an amendment of the Constitution, to give the principle greater extent.

These are the subjects, in relation to the permanent character of the government itself, which, it seems to me, are worthy of the serious attention of the people and of a new administration. There are others of an administrative nature which require prompt and careful consideration.

First, the currency of the country, its stability and uniform value, and, as intimately and indissolubly connected with it, the insurance of the faithful performance of the fiscal services necessary to the government should be maintained and secured by exercising all the powers requisite to those objects with which Congress is constitutionally invested. These are the great ends to be aimed at; the means are of subordinate importance. Whether these ends, indispensable to the well-being of both the people and the government are to be attained by sound and safe state banks, carefully selected and properly distributed, or by a new Bank of the United States, with such limitations, conditions, and restrictions as have been indicated by experience, should be left to the arbitrament of enlightened public opinion.

Candor and truth require me to say that, in my judgment, while banks continue to exist in the country, the services of a Bank of the United States cannot be safely dispensed with. I think that the power to establish such a bank is a settled question; settled by Washington and by Madison, by the people, by forty years' acquiescence, by the judiciary, and by both of the great parties which so long held sway in this country. I know and I respect the contrary opinion which is entertained in this state.

But, in my deliberate view of the matter, the power to establish such a bank being settled, and being a necessary and proper power, the only question is as to the expediency of its exercise. And on questions of mere expediency, public opinion ought to have a controlling influence. Without banks, I believe we cannot have a sufficient currency; without a Bank of the United States, I fear we cannot have a sound currency. But it is the end, that of a sound and sufficient currency, and a faithful execution of the fiscal duties of government, that should engage the dispassionate and candid consideration of the whole community.

There is nothing in the name of the Bank of the United States which has any magical charm, or to which any one need be wedded. It is to secure certain great objects, without which society cannot prosper; and if, contrary to my apprehension, these objects can be accomplished by dispensing with the agency of a Bank of the United States and employing that of state banks, all ought to rejoice and heartily acquiesce, and none would more than I should.

Second, that the public lands, in conformity with the trusts created expressly or by just implication on their acquisition, be administered in a spirit of liberality toward the new states and territories, and a spirit of justice toward all the states.

The land bill, which was rejected by President Jackson, and acts of occasional legislation will accomplish both these objects. I regret that the time does not admit of my exposing here the nefarious plans and purposes of the administration as to this vast national resource. That, like every other great interest of the country, is administered with the sole view of the effect upon the interests of the party in power. A bill has passed the Senate and is now pending before the House, according to which, $40 million are stricken from the real value of a certain portion of the public lands by a short process; and a citizen of Virginia, residing on the southwest side of the Ohio, is not allowed to purchase lands as cheap, by half a dollar per acre, as a citizen living on the northwest side of that river. I have no hesitation in expressing my conviction that the whole public domain is gone if Mr. Van Buren be reelected.

Third, that the policy of protecting and encouraging the production of American industry, entering into competition with the rival productions of foreign industry, be adhered to and maintained on the basis of the principles and in the spirit of the compromise of March 1833.

Protection and national independence are, in my opinion, identical and synonymous. The principle of abandonment of the one cannot be surrendered without a forfeiture of the other. Who, with just pride and national sensibility, can think of subjecting the products of our industry to all the taxation and restraints of foreign powers, without effort on our part to counteract their prohibitions and burdens by suitable countervailing legislation? The question cannot be, ought not to be, one of principle but of measure and degree. I adopt that of the compromise act, not because that act is irrepealable, but because it met with the sanction of the nation. Stability, with moderate and certain protection, is far more important than instability, the necessary consequence of high protection. But the protection of the compromise act will be adequate, in most, if not as to all interests.

The 20 percent which it stipulates, cash duties, home valuations, and the list of free articles inserted in the act for the particular advantage of the manufacturer, will insure, I trust, sufficient protection. Altogether, they will amount probably to no less than 30 percent, a greater extent of protection than was secured prior to the act of 1828, which no one stands up to defend.

Now the valuation of foreign goods is made not by the American authority, except in suspected cases, but by foreigners and abroad. They assess the value and we the duty; but as the duty depends, in most cases, upon the value, it is manifest that those who assess the value fix the duty. The home valuation will give our government what it rightfully possesses, both the power to ascertain the true value of the thing which it taxes as well as the amount of that tax.

Fourth, that a strict and wise economy in the disbursement of the public money be steadily enforced; and that, to that end, all useless establishments, all unnecessary offices and places, foreign and domestic, and all extravagance, either in the collection or expenditure of the public revenue, be abolished and repressed.

I have not time to dwell on details in the application of this principle. I will say that a pruning knife, long, broad, and sharp, should be applied to every department of the government. There is abundant scope for honest and skillful surgery. The annual expenditure may, in reasonable time, be brought down from its present amount of about $40 million to nearly one-third of that sum.

Fifth, the several states have made such great and gratifying progress in their respective systems of internal improvement, and have been so aided by the distribution under the deposit act that, in future, the erection of new roads and canals should be left to them, with such further aid only from the general government as they would derive from the payment of the last installment under that act, from an absolute relinquishment of the right of Congress to call upon them to refund the previous installments, and from their equal and just quotas to be received by a future distribution of the net proceeds from the sales of the public lands.

And, sixth, that the right to slave property, being guaranteed by the Constitution, and recognized as one of the compromises incorporated in that instrument by our ancestors, should be left where the Constitution has placed it, undisturbed and unagitated by Congress.

104.

WILLIAM LADD: International Organizations to Keep the Peace

William Ladd of Maine founded the American Peace Society in 1828 and remained its leader until his death in 1841. Unlike William Lloyd Garrison, who led a splinter group advocating unmitigated pacifism out of the Society in 1838, Ladd devoted himself to advancing concrete proposals for bringing war to an end. Two such proposals — that a congress of nations be called to agree on the principles of international law, and that an international court be established to arbitrate disputes — were put forward by Ladd in an Essay on a Congress of Nations, *published in 1840. The essay, of which the introductory argument appears here, drew on material submitted by a number of contestants in a competition sponsored by the Society. Nevertheless, the two proposals, both of which were put into effect in the twentieth century, originated with Ladd.*

Source: *Prize Essays on a Congress of Nations*, Boston, 1840, pp. 631-634.

IT IS A GENERALLY ACKNOWLEDGED PRINCIPLE that nations have no moral right to go to war until they have tried to preserve peace by every lawful and honorable means. This the strongest advocate for war in these enlightened days will not deny, whatever might have been the opinion of mankind on the subject in darker ages. When a nation has received an injury, if it be of such a magnitude as in the opinion of the injured party ought not to be submitted to, the first thing to be done is to seek an explanation from the injuring nation; and it will be often found that the injury was unintentional, or that it originated in misapprehension and mistake, or that there is no real ground of offense. Even where the ground of offense is undeniable, and in the opinion of the world the injured nation has a *right* to declare war, it is now generally believed that they are not so likely to obtain redress and reparation by war as by forbearance and negotiation; and that it is their bounden duty, both to themselves and to the world at large, to exhaust every means of negotiation before they plunge themselves and other nations into the horrors and crimes of war.

The United States had much ground of complaint against Great Britain during Washington's administration. Instead of declaring war, Jay was sent to England, and full and complete satisfaction was obtained for all the injuries received, by the influence of moral power alone; for we had not then a single ship of war on the ocean. At a subsequent period, with twice the population and twenty times the means of offense, impatient of a protracted negotiation, we resorted to war, and got no reparation of injuries or satisfaction whatever except revenge, bought at an enormous expense of men and money, and made peace, leaving every cause of complaint in the *statu quo ante bellum.* Had we protracted the negotiation thirty days longer, the war and all its evils, physical and moral, would have been avoided.

Sometimes negotiations have failed altogether to obtain redress. Then, an offer of arbitration should follow. Now, what we are seeking for is a regular system of arbitration and the organization of a board of arbitrators, composed of the most able civilians in the world, acting on well-known principles established and promulgated by a congress of nations. If there were such a court, no civilized nation could refuse to leave a subject of international dispute to its adjudication. Nations have tried war long enough. It has never settled any principle and generally leaves dissensions worse than it found them. It is, therefore, high time for the Christian world to seek a more rational, cheap, and equitable mode of settling international difficulties.

When we consider the horrible calamities which war has caused, the millions of lives it has cost, and the unutterable anguish which it produces, not only on the battlefield and in the military hospital but in the social circle and the retired closet of the widow and orphan, we have reason to conclude that the Inquisition, the slave trade, slavery, and intemperance, all put together, have not caused half so much grief and anguish to mankind as war. . . .

When we consider that war is the hotbed of every crime, and that it is the principal obstacle to the conversion of the heathen, and that it sends millions unprepared suddenly into eternity, every *Christian* ought to do all he can to prevent the evil in every way in his power, not only by declaiming against war and showing its sin and folly by assisting to bring forward a plan which is calculated to lessen the horrors and frequency of war. Should all the endeavors of every philanthropist, statesman, and Christian in the world be successful in preventing only one war, it would be a rich reward for their labor. If only once in a century, two nations should be persuaded to leave their disputes to a court of nations, and thereby one war be avoided, all the expense of maintaining such a court would be repaid with interest.

We, therefore, conclude that every man, whether his station be public or private, who refuses to lend his aid in bringing forward this plan of a congress and court of nations neglects his duty to his country, to the world, and to God, and does not act consistently with the character of a statesman, philanthropist, or Christian.

105.

ANONYMOUS: Mike Fink and Davy Crockett

The following encounter between Mike Fink and Davy Crockett was reported in the Crockett Almanac *for 1840. The Almanacs were popular from the mid-1830s to the mid-1850s. In addition to the ordinary contents of an almanac, they included tall tales about, and ostensibly by, Davy Crockett. Both Crockett and Fink were popular Western heroes whose lives had become enveloped in myth. Crockett in real life was a backwoods congressman and Fink a keelboat man on the Mississippi River.*

Source: *Crockett Almanac*, Nashville, Vol. II, No. 2, 1840, p. 11.

I EXPECT, STRANGER, you think old Davy Crockett war never beat at the long rifle; but he war tho. I expect there's no man so strong but what he will find some one stronger. If you havent heerd tell of one Mike Fink, I'll tell you something about him, for he war a helliferocious fellow, and made an almighty fine shot.

Mike was a boatman on the Mississip, but he had a little cabbin on the head of the Cumberland, and a horrid handsome wife, that loved him the wickedest that ever you see. Mike only worked enough to find his wife in rags, and himself in powder, and lead, and whiskey, and the rest of the time he spent in nocking over bar and turkeys, and bouncing deer, and sometimes drawing a lead on an injun.

So one night I fell in with him in the woods, where him and his wife shook down a blanket for me in his wigwam. In the morning sez Mike to me, "I've got the handsomest wife, and the fastest horse, and the sharpest shooting iron in all Kentuck, and if any man dare doubt it, I'll be in his hair quicker than hell could scorch a feather."

This put my dander up, and sez I, "I've nothing to say agin your wife, Mike, for it cant be denied she's a shocking handsome woman, and Mrs. Crockett's in Tennessee, and I've got no horses. Now, Mike, I dont exactly like to tell you you lie about what you say about your rifle, but I'm d — d if you speak the truth, and I'll prove it. Do you see that are cat sitting on the top rail of your potato patch, about a hundred and fifty yards off? If she ever hears agin, I'll be shot if it shant be without ears." So I blazed away, and I'll bet you a horse, the ball cut off both the old tom cat's ears close to his head, and shaved the hair off clean across the skull, as slick as if I'd done it with a razor, and the critter never stirred nor knew he'd lost his ears till he tried to scratch 'em. "Talk about your rifle after that, Mike!" sez I.

"Do you see that are sow off furder than the eend of the world," sez Mike, "with a litter of pigs round her," and he lets fly. The old sow give a grunt, but never stirred in her tracks, and Mike falls to loading and firing for dear life, till he hadn't left one of them are pigs enough tail to make a toothpick on. "Now," sez he, "Col. Crockett, I'll be pretticularly obleedged to you if you'll put them are pig's tails on again," sez he.

"That's onpossible; Mike," sez I, "but you've left one of 'em about an inch to steer by, and if it had a-been my work, I wouldn't have done it so wasteful. I'll mend your shot." And so I lets fly and cuts off the apology he'd left the poor cretur for decency. I wish I may drink the whole of Old Mississip, without a drop of the rale stuff in it, if you wouldn't have thort the tail had been drove in with a hammer.

That made Mike a kinder sorter wrothy, and he sends a ball after his wife as she was going to the spring after a gourd full of water, and nocked half her coom [comb] out of her head, without stirring a hair, and calls out to her to stop for me to take a blizzard at what was left on it. The angeliferous critter stood still as a scarecrow in a cornfield, for she'd got used to Mike's tricks by long practiss.

"No, no Mike," sez I, "Davy Crockett's hand would be sure to shake, if his iron war pointed within a hundred mile of a shemale, and I give up beat, Mike, and as we've had our eye-openers a-ready, we'll now take a flem-cutter, by way of an anti-fogmatic, and then we'll disperse."

―――――◆―――――

Thar's a great rejoicin' among the bears of Kaintuck, and the alligators of the Mississippi rolls up thar shiny ribs to the sun, and has grown so fat and lazy that they will hardly move out of the way for a steamboat. The rattlesnakes come up out of thar holes and frolic within ten foot of the clearings, and the foxes goes to sleep in the goose-pens. It is bekase the rifle of Crockett is silent forever, and the print of his moccasins is found no more in our woods.

ANON., "The Death of Davy Crockett," *Crockett Almanac*

Index of Authors

*The numbers in brackets
indicate selection numbers
in this volume*

ADAMS, JOHN QUINCY (July 11, 1767-Feb. 23, 1848), diplomat and statesman. Sixth President of the United States (1825-29); U.S. senator from Massachusetts (1803-08); minister to St. Petersburg (1809-14); minister to Great Britain (1815); secretary of state under Monroe; U.S. representative (1831-48). **[90]** See also Author Index, Vols. 4, 5.

AUDUBON, JOHN JAMES (April 26, 1785-Jan. 27, 1851), artist and naturalist. Wrote and illustrated *The Birds of America* (1827-38) and *Ornithological Biography* (1831-39), with 435 color paintings of the birds of the Eastern and Southern United States. **[22]**

BANCROFT, GEORGE (Oct. 3, 1800-Jan. 17, 1891), historian, diplomat, politician, and educator. Secretary of the navy (1845-46) under Polk; founded the U.S. Naval Academy, Annapolis; minister to Great Britain (1846-49); author of Andrew Johnson's first annual message; minister to Germany (1867-74); wrote *History of the United States* (10 vols., 1834-74). **[28]** See also Author Index, Vol. 5.

BARLIEN, HANS (fl. 1839), Norwegian traveler and letter writer. **[91]**

BARNARD, DANIEL D. (Sept. 11, 1796-April 24, 1861), lawyer, public official, and historian. U.S. representative from New York (1827-29, 1839-45); minister to Prussia (1850-53). **[71]**

BEAUMONT, GUSTAVE DE (1802-1866), French traveler and author. Accompanied Alexis de Tocqueville to America; wrote *Marie; or, Slavery in the United States* (1835). **[32]**

BEECHER, EDWARD (Aug. 27, 1803-July 28, 1895), clergyman and educator. Pastor (1826-30) of Park Street Congregational Church, Boston; president (1830-44) of Illinois College; a founder of the first antislavery society in Illinois; Pastor (1844-54) of Salem Street Church, Boston, and (1855-71) of First Congregational Church, Galesburg, Ill.; founder and editor (1849-53) of *The Congregationalist*. **[77]**

BRISBANE, ALBERT (Aug. 22, 1809-May 1, 1890), social reformer. Wrote *Social Destiny of Man* (1840), *Association* (1843), and other works on Fourierism. **[99]**

BROWNSON, ORESTES A. (Sept. 16, 1803-April 17, 1876), clergyman and writer. Universalist minister (1826-29); Unitarian minister (1832-44); converted to Roman Catholicism (1844); published *Brownson's Quarterly* (1844-65, 1872-75) as a journal of personal opinion. **[98]** See also Author Index, Vol. 9.

BRYANT, WILLIAM CULLEN (Nov. 3, 1794-June 12, 1878), poet, editor, and lawyer. Co-editor and co-owner (1829-78) of the *New York Evening Post;* wrote "Thanatopsis" (1817), "To a Waterfowl" (1817), "The Flood of Years" (1876). **[50]** See also Author Index, Vol. 5.

CALHOUN, JOHN C. (March 18, 1782-March 31, 1850), political philosopher, lawyer, and statesman. U.S. representative from South Carolina (1811-17); secretary of war under Monroe; Vice-President of the United States (1825-32) under J. Q. Adams and Jackson; U.S. senator (1833-43, 1845-50); secretary of state (1844-45) under Tyler. [69] See also Author Index, Vols. 4, 5, 7, 8.

CAREY, MATHEW (1760-1839), journalist and publisher. Born Dublin, Ireland; worked for Benjamin Franklin in Paris; immigrated to U.S. (1784); his *American Museum* and *Addresses* for the Philadelphia Society for the Promotion of National Industry advocated U.S. national economic development. [6]

CHANNING, WILLIAM ELLERY (April 7, 1780-Oct. 2, 1842), clergyman and author. Pastor (1803-42) of Boston Federal Street Church; founded (1825) the American Unitarian Association; wrote *Negro Slavery* (1835) in behalf of the Abolitionist cause, *Remarks on National Literature* (1830), *Self Culture* (1838). [72, 82] See also Author Index, Vols. 4, 5.

CHEVALIER, MICHEL (1806-1879), French economist. Follower of Saint-Simon and advocate of free trade. [92]

CHILD, LYDIA M. (Feb. 11, 1802-Oct. 20, 1880), social reformer; author. Edited *Juvenile Miscellany*, the first children's periodical in U.S.; with her husband edited (1840-44) the *Anti-Slavery Standard;* wrote numerous books in behalf of the rights of women, slaves, freedmen, and Indians. [2] See also Author Index, Vol. 7.

CLARK, AARON (fl. 1837), mayor of New York City. [70]

CLAY, HENRY (April 12, 1777-June 29, 1852), lawyer and statesman. U.S. senator from Kentucky (1806-07, 1810-11, 1831-42, 1849-52); U.S. representative (1811-14, 1815-21, 1823-25) and House speaker in all years but 1821; secretary of state under J. Q. Adams. [11, 103] See also Author Index, Vols. 4, 5, 8.

COLE, THOMAS (Feb. 1, 1801-Feb. 11, 1848), painter. Founder of the Hudson River School of painters of romantic landscapes, typified by his series "The Voyage of Life" and "The Course of Empire." [46]

COOPER, JAMES FENIMORE (Sept. 15, 1789-Sept. 14, 1851), novelist. Wrote tales of the frontier, travel books, social and political criticism; authored Leatherstocking Tales (*The Pioneers*, 1823; *The Last of the Mohicans*, 1826; *The Prairie*, 1827; *The Pathfinder*, 1840; *The Deerslayer*, 1841) and of *The American Democrat* (1838). [86] See also Author Index, Vol. 5.

CROCKETT, DAVY (Aug. 17, 1786-March 6, 1836), frontiersman. U.S. representative from Tennessee (1827-31, 1833-35); became a legendary symbol of the tough frontiersman in numerous books and plays, and in his own *Autobiography* (1834); died in the sack of the Alamo. [19, 21]

DANA, RICHARD HENRY (Aug. 1, 1815-Jan. 6, 1882), lawyer and author. Wrote *Two Years Before the Mast* (1840). [97]

DAVIS, CHARLES A. (1795-1867), merchant and political satirist. Wrote the *Letters of Major Downing* (1834), a witty satire of the events of the Jackson administration. [10]

DWIGHT, THEODORE (March 3, 1796-Oct. 16, 1866), author and educator. Editor (1845-52) of *Dwight's American Magazine;* wrote a series of books describing his travels in America and Europe. [17]

EMERSON, RALPH WALDO (May 25, 1803-April 27, 1882), poet, essayist, and philosopher. Wrote *Nature* (1836) and *Essays* (1841, 1844) on his transcendentalist philosophy, and for many years kept his *Journals;* edited (1842-44) the *Dial;* lectured in England and in the U.S. on a variety of subjects, such as self-reliance, individual freedom, and abolition of slavery. [74] See also Author Index, Vols. 7, 8, 9.

EMMETT, DANIEL DECATUR (Oct. 29, 1815-June 28, 1904), minstrel singer and composer. Wrote both words and music for "Dixie" (1859), which became the unofficial national anthem of the South. [8] See also Author Index, Vol. 9.

EVERETT, EDWARD (April 11, 1794-Jan. 15, 1865), Unitarian clergyman, orator, educator, and statesman. Pastor of the Brattle Street Church, Boston; editor (1820-24) of the *North American Review;* U.S. representative from Massachusetts (1825-35); governor (1836-40); minister to Great Britain (1841-45); president (1846-49) of Harvard College; secretary of state (1852-53) under Fillmore; U.S. senator (1853-54). [7] See also Author Index, Vols. 5, 7.

FINNEY, CHARLES G. (Aug. 29, 1792-Aug. 16, 1875), evangelist, theologian, and educator. Pastor (1832-37) of Second Free Presbyterian Church, New York City; professor of theology (1835-66) and president (1851-66) of Oberlin College. [31]

FISK, THEOPHILUS (1801-1867), Universalist clergyman, editor, and lecturer. Edited (from 1835) *Priestcraft Unmasked,* the *New Haven Examiner,* the *Boston Reformer* and (from 1844) the Washington, D.C., *Kendall's Expositor.* [25]

FLOURNOY, J. J. (fl. 1838), letter writer. [80]

GARRISON, WILLIAM LLOYD (Dec. 12, 1805-May 24, 1879), Abolitionist leader and journalist. Founded (1831) the *Liberator;* helped establish (1833) the American Anti-Slavery Society; its president (1843-65); advocate of immediate emancipation and of woman suffrage; opposed the American Colonization Society; wrote *Thoughts on African Colonization* (1832). [84] See also Author Index, Vol. 5.

GOUGE, WILLIAM M. (Nov. 10, 1796-July 14, 1863), financial writer. Edited (1823-26) the *Philadelphia Gazette* and (1841-42) the *Journal of Banking;* wrote *A Short History of Paper Money and Banking* (1833). [9]

GREEN, ASA (Feb. 11, 1789-c. 1837), physician and author. Wrote *A Glance At New York* (1837). [78]

GRUND, FRANCIS J. (1798-Sept. 29, 1863), teacher, editor, and author. Born Austria; wrote *The Americans, in Their Moral, Social, and Political Relations* (1837). [76]

HARPER, WILLIAM (Jan. 17, 1790-Oct. 10, 1847), jurist and political writer. Wrote *Memoir on Slavery* (1837) as a refinement of the conservative Southern position on state's rights and slavery. [68]

HENSHAW, DAVID (April 2, 1791-Nov. 11, 1852), public official and political leader. Founded (1821) the *Boston Statesman;*

secretary of the navy (1843-44) under Tyler; Democratic Party leader in Massachusetts (1844-52). [65]

HODGE, CHARLES (Dec. 27, 1797-June 19, 1878), Presbyterian theologian. Founded (1825) the *Biblical Repertory and Princeton Review;* professor of biblical literature and of theology (1822-77) at Princeton Theological Seminary. [73]

HOVLAND, GJERT (fl. 1835), Norwegian traveler and letter writer. [24]

INGRAHAM, JOSEPH H. (Jan. 25-26, 1809-Dec. 18, 1860), clergyman and author. Protestant Episcopal missionary and priest in Mississippi, Alabama, and Tennessee (1852-60); wrote adventure novels and a collection of letters, *The Sunny South* (1860). [23]

JACKSON, ANDREW (March 15, 1767-June 8, 1845), lawyer, statesman, and soldier, known as "Old Hickory." Seventh President of the United States (1829-37); U.S. representative from Tennessee (1796-97); U.S. senator (1797-98, 1823-25); justice of the Tennessee Supreme Court (1798-1804); major general of the state militia (1802); major general of U.S. Army (1814); governor of the Florida Territory (1821). [12, 34, 60, 62] See also Author Index, Vols. 5, 7.

JOHNSON, WILLIAM (?-1851), Mississippi businessman; kept diary for 16 years. [45]

KEMBLE, FRANCES ANNE (Nov. 27, 1809-Jan. 15, 1893), English actress and author. Wrote *Journal of a Residence in America* (1835), *Journal of a Residence on a Georgian Plantation* (1863). [87]

LADD, WILLIAM (May 10, 1778-April 9, 1841), clergyman and pioneer in the theory of international organization. "Apostle of peace"; opponent of slavery; founded (1828) the American Peace Society; wrote *An Essay on a Congress of Nations* (1840). [104]

LEGGETT, WILLIAM (April 30, 1801-May 29, 1839), journalist. Assistant editor (1829-36) under William Cullen Bryant of the *New York Evening Post;* editor (1836-37) of the *Plaindealer* and the *Examiner.* [16]

LIEBER, FRANCIS (March 18, 1800-Oct. 2, 1872), political scientist and educator.

Born Germany; fled to U.S. (1827); planned and edited *Encyclopedia Americana* (1829-33); professor of history and political economy (1835-56) at South Carolina College, (1857-65) at Columbia University, and (1865-72) at Columbia Law School; wrote *Manual of Political Ethics* (1838-39), *On Civil Liberty and Self-Government* (1853). **[18]**

LINCOLN, ABRAHAM (Feb. 12, 1809-April 15, 1865), lawyer and statesman. Sixteenth President of the United States (1861-65); U.S. representative from Illinois (1847-49); defeated in senatorial campaign (1858) by Stephen A. Douglas; issued the Emancipation Proclamation (Jan. 1, 1863); delivered dedicatory address at Gettysburg National Cemetery (Nov. 19, 1863); assassinated by John Wilkes Booth, a fanatical actor, only five days after Lee's surrender to Grant at Appomattox Courthouse. **[58, 83]** See also Author Index, Vols. 8, 9.

LORING, ELLIS GRAY (April 14, 1803-May 24, 1858), lawyer and Abolitionist. Officer of the New England Anti-Slavery Society; financial supporter of the *Liberator*. **[82]**

McDUFFIE, GEORGE (Aug. 10, 1790-March 11, 1851) lawyer, orator, and public official. U.S. representative from South Carolina (1821-34); governor (1834-36); U.S. senator (1842-46). **[41]** See also Author Index, Vol. 5.

McILVAINE, CHARLES P. (Jan. 18, 1799-March 13, 1873), Protestant Episcopal bishop. Deacon (1820-24) of Christ Church, Georgetown, D.C.; chaplain (1821-22) of the U.S. Senate; chaplain (1825-27) of U.S. Military Academy at West Point; bishop of Ohio (1831-73). **[47]**

MADISON, JAMES (March 16, 1751-June 28, 1836), statesman. Fourth President of the United States (1809-17); member (1780-81) of the Continental Congress, (1781-83) of the Congress of the Confederation, and (1787) of the Constitutional Convention; author with John Jay and Alexander Hamilton of *The Federalist* (1787-88); U.S. representative from Virginia (1789-97); secretary of state under Jefferson; Rector (1826-36) of the University of Virginia. **[13]** See also Author Index, Vols. 3, 4, 5.

MANN, HORACE (May 4, 1796-Aug. 2, 1859), educator. First secretary (1837-48) of the Massachusetts Board of Education; revolutionized public school organization and teaching methods; established (1839) the first state teachers college; U.S. representative (1848-53); president (1853-59) of Antioch College. **[101]** See also Author Index, Vols. 7, 8.

MARRYAT, FREDERICK (July 10, 1792-Aug. 9, 1848), English naval officer and novelist. Traveled in U.S. and Canada (1837-39) and published his critical impressions in 1839. **[93]**

MARTINEAU, HARRIET (June 12, 1802-June 27, 1876), English novelist and writer on social, historical, and economic themes. Visited U.S. (1834-36) and gave support to the Abolitionist cause; wrote *Society in America* (1837). **[75]**

MOORE, ELY (July 4, 1798-Jan. 27, 1860), labor leader and public official. First president (1833) of the New York City General Trades' Union and editor of the *National Trades' Union*; first chairman (1834) of the National Trades' Union; U.S. representative from New York (1834-39). **[5]**

MORSE, SAMUEL F. B. (April 27, 1791-April 2, 1872), artist and inventor. Founder and first president (1826-45) of the National Academy of Design; developed the first working electromagnetic telegraph (*c.* 1835) and Morse code, an alphabet composed of dots and dashes (*c.* 1838); commissioned by Congress to build a telegraph line between Baltimore and Washington, and on May 24, 1844, sent the first message, "What hath God wrought!" **[33]**

O'SULLIVAN, JOHN L. (Nov. 1813-Feb. 24, 1895), journalist and diplomat. Founder and first editor (1837-46) of the *United States Magazine and Democratic Review*; editor (1844-46) of the *New York Morning News*; chargé d'affaires and minister to Portugal (1854-58). **[67, 94]** See also Author Index, Vol. 7.

PAULDING, JAMES KIRKE (Aug. 22, 1778-1860), public official and author. Secretary of the navy (1838-41) under Van Buren; satirized British conduct in *The Diverting History of John Bull* (1812), and employed typically American themes in *Westward Ho!* (1832) and *A Life of Washington* (1835). [35] See also Author Index, Vol. 4.

PIERCE, FRANKLIN (Nov. 23, 1804-Oct. 8, 1869); lawyer and public official. Fourteenth President of the United States (1853-57); U.S. representative from New Hampshire (1833-37); U.S. senator (1837-42); brigadier general in Mexican War (1847). [56]

RANTOUL, ROBERT, JR. (Aug. 13, 1805-Aug. 7, 1852), lawyer and political and social reformer. Member (1837-42) of the Massachusetts Board of Education and advocate of a tax-supported school system; U.S. district attorney (1846); U.S. senator (1851); U.S. representative (1851-52). [54]

ROBINSON, FREDERICK (1799-?), journalist and political leader. Massachusetts legislator (1834); advocate of the General Trades' Union; left the Democratic Party (*c.* 1850) because of his antislavery views. [15] See also Author Index, Vol. 5.

SAVAGE, JOHN (Feb. 22, 1779-Oct. 19, 1863), jurist and public official. U.S. representative from New York (1815-19); chief justice of the New York Supreme Court. [36, 57]

SEDGWICK, THEODORE (Dec. 1780-Nov. 7, 1839), lawyer and writer. Massachusetts legislator (1824-25, 1827); wrote *Public and Private Economy* (1836-39). [37]

SEWARD, WILLIAM H. (May 16, 1801-Oct. 10, 1872), lawyer and statesman. Governor of New York (1838-42); U.S. senator (1849-61); secretary of state under Lincoln and Johnson. Negotiated the purchase of Alaska from Russia (1867). [30] See also Author Index, Vols. 7, 8, 9, 10.

SMITH, JOSEPH (Dec. 23, 1805-June 27, 1844), founder of the Mormon religion. Published a "history of the true church in America," said to have been divinely revealed to him, as *The Book of Mormon* (1830); founded (April 6, 1830) the Church of Jesus Christ of the Latter-day Saints; moved his congregation from New York to Kirtland, Ohio (1831), then to Missouri (1838), and to Nauvoo, Ill., where he was jailed and shot to death by an anti-Mormon mob. [85]

STEVENS, THADDEUS (April 4, 1792-Aug. 11, 1868), lawyer and public official. U.S. representative from Pennsylvania (1849-53, 1859-68); leader of the Radical Republicans in Congress after the Civil War; proposed and managed the impeachment trial of Andrew Johnson. [29] See also Author Index, Vol. 9.

STORY, JOSEPH (Sept. 18, 1779-Sept. 10, 1845), educator, legal writer, and jurist. U.S. representative from Massachusetts (1808-09); professor of law (1829-45) at Harvard College and a principle organizer of and teacher in Harvard Law School; associate justice (1811-45) of the U.S. Supreme Court. [66]

STRONG, GEORGE TEMPLETON (1801-?), diarist. [63] See also Author Index, Vol. 9.

TANEY, ROGER B. (March 17, 1777-Oct. 12, 1864), jurist. U.S. attorney general (1831-33) and secretary of the treasury (1833-34) under Jackson; adviser to Jackson in the Bank War of 1832; chief justice (1836-64) of the U.S. Supreme Court, where he rendered the majority opinion in *Dred Scott* v. *Sandford* (1857). [66] See also Author Index, Vol. 8.

TOCQUEVILLE, ALEXIS DE (July 29, 1805-April 16, 1859), French historian and politician. Traveled in U.S. (1831-32) with Gustave de Beaumont to observe American prisons and published a report in 1832; wrote *Democracy in America* (1835-40), a classic study of the American political system. [44] See also Author Index, Vol. 5.

TRAVIS, WILLIAM B. (Aug. 9, 1809-March 6, 1836), lawyer and soldier. Leader of the Texas settlers eager to resist Mexican authority; commanded Texas force of 187 men at the Alamo, killed there in Santa Anna's siege. [59]

VAN BUREN, MARTIN (Dec. 5, 1782-July 24, 1862), lawyer, political leader, and public official. Eighth President of the United States (1837-41); attorney general of New York (1816-19); U.S. senator